A DICTIONARY OF
BRITISH FOLK-TALES

A DICTIONARY OF
BRITISH
FOLK-TALES

IN THE
ENGLISH LANGUAGE

INCORPORATING THE
F. J. NORTON COLLECTION

KATHARINE M. BRIGGS

PART A
FOLK NARRATIVES
VOLUME I

LONDON
ROUTLEDGE & KEGAN PAUL
1970

First published 1970
by Routledge & Kegan Paul Ltd
Broadway House, 68–74 Carter Lane
London, E.C. 4
Printed in Great Britain
at the University Printing House, Cambridge
(Brooke Crutchley, University Printer)
© K. M. Briggs 1970
SBN 7100 6363 6

CONTENTS

VOLUME 1

VOLUME 2

INTRODUCTION

The scope of the collection

The tales included in this Dictionary are not translated tales—except for a few translated from the medieval Latin, which must originally have been told in Middle English. A number of them were of Celtic origin, but only those are included that were told, by word of mouth, in English. It had been my original intention to include those Celtic stories from Eire, the Highlands of Scotland, Wales and the Isle of Man which had been translated or re-told in English. I decided, however, that the tales translated from the Celtic languages are by now so numerous as to need many volumes for their fair presentation, and to do justice even to these it would be better to be a Celtic scholar. I have therefore, with deep regret, abandoned this mass of beautiful material to be dealt with later, by a worthier scholar.

It may be that I have thereby abandoned tales which I could have used. It is possible that Crofton Croker's stories, for instance, were told by English-speaking Irishmen, and I might have used tales like "Jamie Freel and the Young Lady", published in *Irish Fairy and Folk Tales* and told in the Ulster dialect; but the determination between English and Gaelic tales raises many difficult problems, and I could get no definitive ruling from Celtic scholars; so I have regretfully abandoned many delightful tales.

The arrangement of the tales

This Dictionary falls into two main sections, FOLK NARRATIVES and FOLK LEGENDS. These are sometimes called "Folk-Tales" and "*Sagen*", but where possible I have preferred to use English names for the English kinds of stories. The main distinction between Folk Narratives and Folk Legends is clear enough: Folk Narrative is Folk Fiction, told for edification, delight or amusement, Folk Legend was once believed to be true. Even such modern folk legends as "The Stolen Corpse" are generally told by someone who knew the lawyer who dealt with the difficulty, or the cousin of the young people to whom it happened. Ghost stories, anecdotes of fairies and tales of the Devil were once related as matters of fact, often with the very name of the person who first had the experience.

A difficulty arises when these tales are handed on by people who no longer believe them, for entertainment or as curiosities. Then they begin to be embellished with picturesque touches, new circumstances, and the legend becomes a fiction. This is particularly true of the *Origin Legends* and of many of the *Local Legends* which are far separated from the time in which they were believed. The adorners of the tale who sprang up in the wake of the Gothic Revival distorted the original legend almost out of recognition. Some of Roby's legends, for instance, are so fantastically ornamented that we can hardly understand what is supposed to have happened in them, and yet most of them are probably founded upon real traditions.

Within the two main groups classification becomes even more difficult, and these subdivisions have been kept as wide and inclusive as possible. The Folk Narratives are divided into five groups—alphabetically arranged, as the tales are. These groups are *Fables and Exempla*, *Fairy Tales*, *Jocular Tales*, *Novelle*, and *Nursery Tales*. The *Fables* are those animal stories after the manner of Aesop that point a moral or satirize human frailties, to which are added *exempla*, tales used for moral illustration. The Fairy Tales are narratives containing or hinging upon supernatural happenings. We have in English no good substitute for the German "*Märchen*", but I have chosen the perhaps ambiguous *Fairy Tales* instead of "Wonder Tales" as being better rooted in English tradition. The word "faerie" was originally used to describe a state of enchantment rather than a fairy person, so I have chosen to retain it, though a section of anecdotes about Fairies is to be found among the Legends, and may cause a little confusion.

The *Jocular Tales* form a great body of drolls, noodle stories, bawdy tales, and so on, that are handed about for entertainment. They are better taken in small doses, for they soon cloy if they are gulped down. It is impossible to give anything like a complete collection of these stories. The most one can do is to give a representative selection of them, for they vary a good deal in type. It is hoped that specimens of every type except the really obscene are to be found here.

The *Novelle* are those narratives in which there is no explicitly supernatural element. In making this subdivision I followed the precedent set by the Aarne–Thompson Tale-Type Index, though it might well be argued that these tales are only other versions of the *Fairy Tales*. "Sugar and Salt", for instance (Type 923) is a naturalistic version of "Cap o' Rushes" (Type 510). Sometimes the magical element seems to be introduced or omitted almost by chance. Nevertheless, there is a difference in the general atmosphere of the tales which justifies a different category for them.

As for the *Nursery Tales*, such stories as "Henny-Penny" and "The Old Woman and the Pig" are obviously invented for small children and of a type to be appreciated by the very young. There are others, however, in this group which may strike the modern reader as unsuitable to be told to children. These are the tales of horror, which are meant to startle the hearers with a sudden shout at the end. Our ancestors were less sensitive about frightening children than we are, and regarded fear as an essential part of a child's education. The point of these tales, however, is not educational; they meet a demand from the majority of the listeners themselves. Most children have moods in which they love to be frightened, and it is this want that such tales as "Teeny-Tiny" and "The Strange Visitor" supply.

The subdividing of the Legends is a more complex matter, and in the Legends, as in the *Jocular Tales*, it is impossible to be all-inclusive. Anyone can quarrel with these subdivisions and say that there are too many or too few, that inessentials have been included and essentials omitted. Anyone may quarrel with them, and indeed most people will. They have been divided mainly under the subjects treated, and run as follows: *Black Dogs, Bogies, Devils, Dragons, Fairies, Ghosts, Giants, Historical Legends, Local Legends, Origin Myths, Saints, The Supernatural, Witches*, and a few unclassified *Miscellaneous Legends* at the end. It will be seen that a good many of these categories cross. Witches are closely allied with the Devil, and Ghost Stories may be absorbed into Local Legends, which again have a close relationship to history. Cross-references will sometimes help searchers for a tale, and where the tales fall into definite types the Index of Tale-Types and Migratory Legends at the beginning of the Dictionary will be found useful. A further difficulty is that these tales are alphabetically arranged, and many of them have no real titles, while the titles of others vary in different collections. Different tales have sometimes the same title too. There may be a long search before the reader who is looking for one particular tale, but in the course of it it is hoped that he will light upon a good many things that he can enjoy.

Sources of tales, and modern collectors

The sources of the tales in this collection are as various as the tales themselves. Some of them have been written down very early, and come from written sources earlier still, from the *Jatakas* and other Oriental collections, very often through the *Gesta Romanorum*. It is difficult to be sure of the date at which these stories passed into folk tradition. They sprang from it in the first place, received literary treatment, and then sank back into the stream of folk tradition. Most of these are International Tale-Types. The supernatural legends taken from the medieval chronicles are rather different. Such tales, for instance, as "The Green Children" are not literary in origin but recount real folk-beliefs of their day. If we move forward a century or two we have still, of course, to rely on written sources. In some of the Celtic areas oral transmission was very exact, for the Tale was formed and disciplined in the Bardic Schools, and even when the Bards disappeared the lesson of accurate transmission was not forgotten. Some Highland storytellers in the nineteenth century recited stories to be found in the early Irish manuscripts with almost verbal exactitude. This accuracy is not to be found in the English-speaking areas. From references scattered through plays, poems and prose writings of the sixteenth and seventeenth centuries it is clear that there was a great body of oral narrative extant at that period. Some of it is lost except for these references—we only know, for instance, of the existence of Type 426 (Snow-White and Rose-Red) from Peele's *Old Wives' Tale*—but some survives in chap-book form, produced before Grimms' *Household Tales* were collected. "Cap o' Rushes" and "The Princess of Canterbury" are examples of these. Unfortunately our early antiquaries were more interested in beliefs and customs than in old wives' tales. We have several folk legends from Aubrey, but no real folk narratives. It was not until the end of the eighteenth century that the collectors of "popular antiquities" began to turn their attention to narratives and legends. The interest grew, partly owing to the influence of Walter Scott and partly to the publication of the Grimms' *Household Tales*. Folk narrative was collected earlier in Ireland and Scotland than in England, though Ritson was already republishing printed material in the eighteenth century. Southey's interest in folklore led to the publication of Mrs Bray's Letters to Southey in 1838. (Scott's *Minstrelsy of the Scottish Border* had been published in 1801. The Grimms' *Kinder- und Haus-Märchen* was published in 1814–15, and its first translation in 1823. Crofton Croker was collecting from 1812 to 1815, and published his *Irish Fairy Legends* in 1825.)

After that time interest grew rapidly, and more accurate methods of recording began to be considered necessary. J. W. Thoms started a good folklore section in *Notes and Queries*, *The Gentleman's Magazine* had long recorded interesting oddments, and some valuable material appeared in *The Athenaeum*. After the founding of the Folk-Lore Society in 1878, many excellent tales were recorded in the Society's journals. The thirty years of 1880 to 1910 were the great years of folk-tale publication. Many of the books published, such as the County Folk-Lore books of the Folk-Lore Society, were collections of already printed matter, but orally collected stories were also published, such as Hunt's *Popular Romances of the West of England*, which followed the earlier and very interesting *Traditions and Hearthside Stories* by Bottrell. Since the Second World War there has been a fresh recrudescence of interest in folklore. International scholarship insists on more accurate methods of collection and checking, and this is reflected in England as well as in Scotland and Ireland, though England has no School of English Studies to compare with Eire's Commission of Folklore Studies or Scotland's School of Scottish Studies. The work in England is done by individuals and is quite unsupported by the state except for the Institute of Dialect and Folk Life Studies attached to the School of English at Leeds University. Even in Ulster folklore has more recognition. The collectors in Scotland owe a great deal to a knowledgeable use of tape-recorders, and the School of Scottish Studies houses a most remarkable collection of tapes. In Eire the method of collection is rather by an accurate transcription of folk material made by a number of field collectors, carefully trained. The amount of material gathered is staggering. In St Fagan's Museum in Wales the emphasis is perhaps rather on folk life than on folk narrative, yet a certain number of folk-tales have been recorded and preserved. In the Isle of Man the growing interest in the Manx language has resulted in the collection of a number of tales to supplement Waldron's early work. Mona Douglas and Walter Gill have been notable pioneers here, and a collection of excellent tales by Dora Broome came out in the Puffin Books, though it is unfortunately now out of print.

A number of oral folk-tale collections have lately become available in England, though many of the collectors had started their work in pre-war days, and it has only lately come to light because of the fresh interest taken in it. The Gypsy Lore Society pursued and published its researches in the rather sparse days of the early 1900s. John Sampson, Dora Yates and T. W. Thompson were the chief of these. Some of their tales were produced early enough to be published by Jacobs in his *English Fairy Tales*, but Dora Yates has only recently ceased collecting, and T. W. Thompson is happily still with us. During the early years of the First World War he collected twelve notebooks of stories and lore from the north-country gypsies, and he hopes to have them published shortly. In the meantime he has kindly allowed them to be summarized for inclusion in this book, and it will be seen that some of them are of special interest because they are versions of Aarne–Thompson tale-types not otherwise known in this country at the present day. "Mossy-coat" is one of them which I have been allowed to include in full. These gypsy tales, and those told by the "travelling people" of Scotland show the variation imposed on international types by the medium through which they have been transmitted. The two races of "travelling people" give a very different flavour to the tales they tell.

Professor E. M. Wilson collected a number of jocular tales from Westmorland, which were first published in *Folk-Lore* and afterwards in *The Folktales of England*; and recently Roy Palmer has started a collection on the same lines in the northern Midlands, which he has kindly made available for this book. In Devon Theo Brown and J. R. W. Cox-head have collected folk legends, and a fresh light has been thrown on the stark traditions of the Fen Country by W. H. Barrett in his two books of *Tales of the Fens*. We owe the discovery of this remarkable storyteller to the researches of Enid Porter of the Cambridge Folk Museum, who has also found other Fenmen and has edited their tales. Ruth Tongue's researches have laid open a wealth of tradition and narrative whose continued existence has hitherto been unsuspected. Ruth Tongue began her collection in Somerset in early childhood and has continued it until the present day. Though Somerset has been her chief collecting-ground she has roots in Lincolnshire and has met people from all over the country; in the course of her life she has gathered tales and legends from many of the counties of England.

Mr F. J. Norton of Cambridge has recorded a few tales at first hand, but his great work has been the collection and arrangement of tales from printed sources, both books and periodicals, chiefly those that can be fitted into the Aarne–Thompson Index. These have been copied in an elegant and legible hand into six large manuscript volumes, with a bibliography and notes. All this has been most generously handed over to me, and much of it is incorporated in the Dictionary. Anyone who glances even cursorily over the following pages will see how much the Dictionary owes to this gift. What cannot be seen is the beautiful accuracy of the transcription, in which hardly a correction needed to be made.

After the publication of this Dictionary the Norton Collection will be housed in the Library of the Folklore Society.

As for the format of these tales: some are given at full length, and most of these have been exactly transcribed. In some of the earlier tales, however, the punctuation has been modified to make them easier to follow, and I have felt at liberty to use what punctuation I think best in the transcribed tapes. Again, for the sake of ease, the dialect in some of the tales has been modified, though many specimens of real dialect are given. Many of the highly ornate nineteenth-century versions have been summarized or shortened so that they may be enjoyed by the ordinary reader. In all cases the sources have been given, and may be consulted by the curious student. The summaries vary from a bare skeleton to a short, readable tale. The published forms of some of the orally collected tales are occasionally given in reference, and may be found to differ slightly from those in the Dictionary, which were taken directly from the narrator. An example is "The Apple-Tree Man" (A. II).

ACKNOWLEDGEMENTS

There are so many people whom I have to thank for their help, contributions and advice that I fear that some may be omitted, and to these I make my apologies.

First, I must thank Mrs V. E. Nash-Williams for the wonderful work she has done. Every story in the book has been typed by her, often from my cramped handwriting, and besides this she has written a great number of the summaries, toiled with me over the proofs and bibliographies and given me a great deal of good advice.

Next I must thank Mr F. J. Norton for the magnificent gift of his great collection, touched on at more length in my Introduction.

Another great source of tales has been the splendidly hospitable School of Scottish Studies, which has allowed me free access to their tapes. I am specially indebted to Dr Hamish Henderson and Mr Maurice Fleming for their masterly recordings, to Mr John Elliot for the use of his Notebook, lodged in the School, and to Mrs Macdonald for much help. Mr Stewart Sanderson, of the Leeds University Folk-Life Survey, has given me access to the Thompson Collection, and other help.

Professor Ó. Duilearga, Mr Ó. Suilleabhain, Dr Thomas Wall and other members of the Irish Folk-Life Commission have given me valuable advice, and the hospitality of their immense collection, of which I have unfortunately only been able to avail myself for comparison. Ulster Folk Life Museum and Mr Paterson of the Armagh Museum have been most helpful, and I have to thank them for some stories which have been used in Part B. The Copenhagen Nordisk Institut for Folkedigtning has been equally hospitable, and I have to thank Professor Bødker for much information and for the gift of many offprints, used chiefly in Part B.

Of living collectors of Folktales I have chiefly to thank Ruth L. Tongue for making her wonderful collection of tales freely available to me, Mr W. H. Barrett for many borrowings from his two books of Fen stories, Mr Roy Palmer for his new collection of humorous tales from the Midlands, Mr Thompson for permission to summarize the tales from his Notebooks, soon we hope to be published in full, and numerous friends and correspondents who have sent me individual stories. I must also specially thank the Folklore Society for permission to use a quantity of invaluable material from its publications, ranging over ninety years.

Scholars from Europe and from the United States have been generous with their help and advice. Among many I must especially thank Professor Stith Thompson, whose Type and Motif Index Lists have been my constant *vade mecum*, Mr Ernest Baughman, who generously presented me with his *Type and Motif Index of the Folktales of England and North America* as soon as it was published, Professor R. D. Dorson, Professor F. L. Utley for gifts of offprints and Professor Archer Taylor for gifts of offprints and for much-valued advice and encouragement.

I should like to thank Miss Sprigg and Miss Third of Routledge for their patient help, and also the staff of Cambridge University Press, my typists, Mrs Sutherland and Mrs Upton, and a posse of volunteer typists who came to my aid when time was short.

The editor gratefully acknowledges the following copyright-owners and publishers for their kind permission to reprint tales: George Allen & Unwin Ltd for *In my Solitary Life* by Augustus Hare; Mr W. H. Barrett for *Tales from the Fens* and *More Tales from the Fens*; B. T. Batsford Ltd for *English Folklore* by Christina Hole; Blackie & Son Ltd for *Round the World Fairy Tales* by Amabel Williams-Ellis; Miss Theo Brown for "The Sow of Merripit" and "Salted Down"; Cambridge University Press for *Dialect of Hackness* by G. H. Cowling; Chapman & Hall Ltd for *Shepherd's Country* by H. J. Massingham; The Clarendon Press for *Celtic Folk-lore* by John Rhys; The Dalesman Publishing Co. Ltd for "The Strong Man of Cowling", "The Austwick Cuckoo", "Choosing a Worker", "The Mouse in the Ale-Cask", "Punctuality", "The Other Fellow's Side", "The Quickest Road", "The Best-tempered Woman", "The Missing Wife", "Bribery" and "The Greater Need"; J. M. Dent & Sons Ltd for *A Book of Gypsy Folk Tales* by Dora E. Yates; Gerald Duckworth & Co. Ltd. for *The Villages of the White Horse* and *Round about the Upper Thames* by Alfred Williams; David Higham Associates Ltd for *A Wiltshire Village* by H. Tanner; The Hogarth Press Ltd for *The Well at the World's End* by N. and W. Montgomerie; Miss Christina Hole and the Folk-Lore Society for permission to use the Society's publications; Hutchinson & Co. Ltd and Mrs Jennifer Ellis for *Thatched with Gold* by Mabell, Countess of Airlie; Mr Peter Leather for *Folk-lore of Herefordshire* by Helen E. Leather; Thomas Nelson & Sons Ltd for *Folk Tales of Yorkshire* edited by H. L. Gee and *Folk Tales of the North Country* edited by F. Grice; Oliver & Boyd Ltd for *More Highland Folk Tales* by Macdonald Robertson; Penguin Books Ltd for *The Puffin Book of Nursery Rhymes* by Walter Opie; Mr Paul Plumb and the B.B.C. for "Mother Shipton's House"; The Shetland Times Folk Society[1] for the *Shetland*

---

[1] I have been asked to append some notes on the Shetland dialect to the tales, and as they are scattered through the two parts of the book this seems the best place to do so.

After Shetland became part of Scotland in 1469 the Old Norse Language of the Islands began to die out, and by the middle of the eighteenth century had been replaced by the

Folk Book; Mr and Mrs Robin Tanner for a tale from *A Wiltshire Village*; Mr T. W. Thompson for *Journal of the Gypsy Lore Society*; Western Press for *Legends of Devon* by J. R. W. Coxhead.

In some cases, it has not been possible to trace the copyright owners.

Shetland Dialect, which in many ways resembles Lowland Scots, but contains a large number of Norse words, and altered forms of English words. For example, th is changed to t. or d. "Faider" for "father", etc., a familiar second person singular has been retained, "du, dine, dee". "the" is written and pronounced "da". Pronunciation through the Island is not uniform, but a uniform spelling has been decided on for the sake of clarity.

A LIST OF BOOKS QUOTED, CITED AND CONSULTED

TYPE AND MOTIF INDEX CATALOGUES

AARNE, A. *The Types of the Folktale.* A Classification and Bibliography, translated and enlarged by Stith Thompson. F.F. Communications, 74. 2nd revision. Helsinki, 1961.

BAUGHMAN, E. W. *Type and Motif Index of the Folk-Tales of England and North America.* F.L. Series, no. 20. Bloomington and The Hague, 1966.

BORDMAN, GERALD. *Motif-Index of the English Metrical Romances.* Helsinki, 1963.

BRUNVAND, J. H. "A Classification of Shaggy Dog Stories", *Journal of American Folk-Lore,* LXXVI, 1963, pp. 42–68.

CHRISTIANSEN, R. TH. *The Migratory Legends.* A Proposed List of Types, with a Systematic Catalogue of the Norwegian Variants. Helsinki, 1958.

KRISTENSEN, E. T. *Danske Sagn,* I–VI. 1892–1901. New edn., København, 1928–39.

O'SUILLEABHAIN, SEAN. *Handbook of Irish Folk-Lore.* Educational Society of Ireland, 1942.

O'SUILLEABHAIN, S. and CHRISTIANSEN, R. TH. *The Types of the Irish Folk-Tale.* Helsinki, 1963.

ROTUNDA, D. P. *Motif-Index of the Italian Novella.* Bloomington, U.S.A., 1942.

THOMPSON, STITH. *Motif-Index of Folk Literature.* 6 vols. F.F. Communications, 106–9, 116, 117. Helsinki, 1955.

SOURCES OF TALES

ADAM OF COBHAM. Early English Text Society, 1865. ('The Wright's Chaste Wife', 1462.)

ADAM DE LA HALLE. *Le Jeu Adam, Œuvres Complètes du Trouvière Adam de la Halle.* Paris, 1872.

ADAMS, H. G. *Our Feathered Families: The Birds of Prey.* London, 1863.

ADDY, SIDNEY OLDALL. "Derbyshire Folk-Lore", *Memorials of Old Derbyshire,* edited by J. C. Cox. London, 1907.

"Four Yorkshire Folktales", *Folk-Lore,* VIII, pp. 393–6.

A Glossary of Words used in the Neighbourhood of Sheffield. A Supplement to *The Sheffield Glossary.* London, 1888–91.

Household Tales, with other Traditional Remains. Collected in the Counties of York, Lincoln, Derby and Nottingham. London and Sheffield, 1895.

AIRLIE, MABELL, COUNTESS OF. *Thatched with Gold: The Memoirs of Mabell, Countess of Airlie.* London, 1962.

AKERMAN, J. Y. *Wiltshire Tales.* London, 1853.

ALLIES, JABEZ. *On the Ancient British, Roman and Saxon Antiquities and Folklore of Worcestershire.* London, 1840.

Ignis Fatuus, or Will o' the Wisp and the Fairies. Worcester, 1846.

ANDREWS, W. "The Lee Penny", *The Border Counties Magazine.*

(editor). *Ecclesiastical Curiosities.* Hull, 1899.

(editor). *Bygone Lincolnshire.* London, 1891.

Antiquary, The. A Magazine devoted to the Study of the Past, 51 vols. London (1880–1915).

Archaeological Review, 4 vols. London, 1888–90.

Archaeologist and Journal of Antiquarian Science, The. 2 vols. London, 1841–2.

ARMSTRONG, ARCHIBALD. *Archie Armstrong's Book of Jests. Banquet of Jests,* reprinted from the original Editions. Edinburgh, 1872.

ARNOLD, *Chronicle.* Antwerp, 1502.

ASSER. *Life of Alfred, Six Old English Chronicles,* edited by J. A. Giles. London, 1848.

ATKINSON, J. C. *Forty Years in a Moorland Parish.* London, 1891.

AUBREY, JOHN. *Brief Lives,* edited by Andrew Clark, 2 vols. Oxford, 1898.

    Hypomnemata Antiquaria, Bodleian MS. Aubrey III.

    Miscellanies, 5th. edn. London, 1890.

    Natural History and Antiquities of the County of Surrey, 5 vols. London, 1718–19.

AXON, W. E. A. *The Black Knight of Ashton.* Manchester, 1870.

    Bygone Sussex. London, 1897.

    Cheshire Gleanings. Manchester, 1884.

    Stray Chapters in Literature, Folklore and Archaeology. London, 1888.

BALDRY, G. *The Rabbit-skin Cap: A Tale of a Norfolk Countryman's Youth,* edited by L. R. Haggard. London, 1939.

BALES, E. G. "Folk-Lore from West Norfolk", *Folk-Lore,* L. London, 1939.

BALFOUR, MRS. *Examples of Printed Folk-Lore concerning Northumberland,* collected by Mrs Balfour. *County Folk-Lore IV.* Folk-Lore Society, 1903.

    "Coat o' Clay", *Folk-Lore,* I. London, 1890.

    "Legends of the Cars", *Folk-Lore,* II. London, 1891.

BARBER, J. G. *Unique Traditions, chiefly of the West and South of Scotland.* Glasgow, c. 1889.

BARING-GOULD, SABINE. *A Book of Dartmoor.* London and Plymouth, 1900.

    A Book of Folk-Lore. London, n.d.

    A Book of the West, 2 vols. London and Plymouth, 1899.

    Devonshire Characters and Strange Events. London and Plymouth, 1908.

    Household Tales. appendix to W. Henderson, *Notes on the Folklore of the Northern Counties of England and the Borders.* London, 1886.

    Lives of the Saints, 16 vols. Edinburgh, 1914.

    Songs and Ballads of the West. London, 1892.

    Strange Survivals. London, 1892.

    The Vicar of Morwenstow. London, 1876.

    Yorkshire Oddities, Anecdotes and Strange Events, 2 vols. London, 1874.

    "Yorkshire Riddles, collected at Horbury, etc., in 1864...", *Yorkshire County Magazine,* II, Bingley, 1892.

BARRETT, W. H. *Tales from the Fens.* London, 1963.

    More Tales from the Fens. London, 1964.

BASSET, FLETCHER S. *Legends and Superstitions of the Sea and Sailors.* London, 1885.

BATES, A. *Gossip about Old Grimsby.* Grimsby, 1893.

BEAUMONT, G. F. *A History of Coggeshall in Essex.* London, 1890.

BECKETT, A. "A Dissertation on Sussex Proverbs and Curious Sayings", *Sussex County Magazine,* I. Lewes, 1926.

BELL, J. Y. "The Pear-Drum", story in *Folk-Lore,* LXVI. London, 1955.

BETHUNE, ALEXANDER and JOHN. *Tales of the Scottish Peasantry.* Edinburgh, 1884.

A LIST OF BOOKS QUOTED, CITED AND CONSULTED

BETT, HENRY. *English Legends*. London, 1952.
English Myths and Traditions. London, 1956.

BILLSON, CHARLES JAMES. *Leicestershire and Rutland*, collected and edited by C. J. Billson. *County Folk-Lore I*, Printed Extracts, 3. Folk-Lore Society.

BLACK, G. F. (editor). *County Folk-Lore III. Orkney and Shetland Islands*. Folk-Lore Society, 1903.

BLAKEBOROUGH, R. *Wit, Character, Folklore and Customs of the North Riding of Yorkshire*, 1898. 2nd edn. 2 vols. Saltdown by Sea, 1911.

BLIND, K. "A Grimm's Story in a Shetland Folklore Version", *Archaeological Review*, I. London, 1888.

BLOOM, J. H. *Folk-Lore, Old Customs, and Superstitions in Shakespeareland*. London, 1930.

BOGER, E. *Somerset Worthies*. London, 1888.

BOGG, EDMUND. *A Thousand Miles in Wharfedale*. London, 1892.
A Thousand Miles of Wandering along the Roman Wall, the Old Border Region, Lakeland and Ribblesdale, 2 vols. Leeds, 1898.

Book of Scottish Story, The, edited by T. D. Morison. Glasgow, 1896.

BOTTRELL, WILLIAM. *Traditions and Hearthside Stories of West Cornwall*. Penzance, 1870.

BOVET, RICHARD. *Pandaemonium, or The Devil's Cloyster*. 1684.

BOWKER, JAMES. *Goblin Tales of Lancashire*. London, 1883.

BRAY, MRS A. E. *Traditions, Legends, Superstitions and Sketches of Devonshire, on the Borders of the Tamar and Tavy*, 3 vols. London, 1838.

BRERETON, H. L. *The History of Gordonstoun*. Published by *The Gordonstoun Record*.

BREWER, E. C. *A Dictionary of Phrase and Fable*. New edn. London, 1877–80.

BRIDGE, J. C. "Some Cheshire Customs, Proverbs and Folk-Lore", in *Memorials of Old Cheshire*, edited by E. Barber and P. H. Ditchfield. London, 1910.

BRIGGS, JOHN, *Remains*. Kirkby Lonsdale, 1825.
The Lonsdale Magazine, II. 1821.

BRIGGS, K. M. *The Personnel of Fairyland*. Oxford, 1953.

BRIGGS, K. M. and TONGUE, RUTH L. *The Folktales of England*. London and Chicago, 1965.

BRISCOE, J. P. *The Book of Nottinghamshire Anecdote*. Nottingham, 1879.
Nottingham Facts and Fancies. Nottingham, 1879.
Nottinghamshire Folk-Lore. Nottingham, 1873.

BROCKIE, J. *Legends and Superstitions of the County of Durham*. Sunderland, 1886.

BROWN, THEO. *Tales of a Dartmoor Village*. Reprinted from *Transactions of the Devonshire Association*, XCIII, 1961.

BUCHAN, P. *Ancient Ballads and Songs of the North of Scotland*, 2 vols. Edinburgh, 1875.
Ancient Scottish Tales: an Unpublished Collection made by P. Buchan, with an Introduction by J. A. Fairley. Reprinted from the *Transactions of the Buchan Field Club*, 9. 50 Copies printed. Peterhead, 1908.

BUCHANAN, GEORGE. *The Witty and Entertaining Exploits of George Buchanan, commonly called the King's Fool*. John Cheap the Chapman's Library, I. Glasgow, 1877. Reprint of a late eighteenth-century chapbook.

BURGESS, J. J. HALDANE, "Some Shetland Folklore", *Scottish Review*, XXV. Paisley, 1895.

BURNE, C. S. "Reminiscences of Lancashire and Cheshire when George IV was King", *Folk-Lore*, XX, pp. 203–7, 1909.

BURNE, C. S. "Staffordshire Folk and Their Lore", *Folk-Lore*, VII, pp. 366–86, 1896.

BURNE, C. S. and JACKSON, G. F. *Shropshire Folk-Lore: A Sheaf of Gleanings.* London, 1883.

BUTLER, CHARLES. *Feminine Monarchie.* 1634.

Bye-gones, 1888 and 1889. 2nd series, I–IX.

Bygone Lincolnshire, see Andrews, W.

CAIUS, T. *Vindiciae Antiquitatis Academiae Oxoniensis contra J. Caium, Cantabrigiensem. In lucem ex autographo emisit T. Hearnius.* 2 vols. Oxonii, 1730.

CAMIDGE, W. *County Folk-Lore II*, article, "From Ouse Bridge to Naburn Lock", York, 1890.

CAMPBELL, J. F. *Popular Tales of the West Highlands*, 4 vols. 1890–3. Paisley and London.

Canterbury Tales, Composed for the Entertainmen tof all Ingenious Young Men and Maidens. London, W. Dicey, Bow Churchyard, *c.* 1790, no. VIII.

CARTER, R. W. Article in *Folk-Lore*, VIII, "Choice Notes from *Notes and Queries*", on "Osmotherly".

CAXTON, W. *The Golden Legend*, translation from *Legenda Aurea* of Jacobus de Voragine [1422].

CHALMERS, A. *Biographical Dictionary of Eminent Persons*, XXIII, article on "William Noy, the Three Glaziers and the Alewife".

The General Biographical Dictionary, 31 vols. London, 1812–17.

CHAMBERS, R. *Book of Days*, 2 vols. London and Edinburgh, 1864.

Popular Rhymes of Scotland. Edinburgh, 1890.

Scottish Jests and Anecdotes, to which are added a Selection of Choice English and Irish Jests. 2nd edn. Edinburgh, 1838.

CHAPPELL, W. *Popular Music of the Olden Time*, 2 vols. London, n.d. [*c.* 1860].

CHATTO, W. A. *Facts and Speculations on the Origin and History of Playing Cards.* London, 1848.

CHETWYND-STAPYLTON, H. E. *The Stapletons of Yorkshire.* London, 1897.

CHILD, F. J. *The English and Scottish Popular Ballads*, 5 vols. New York, 1957.

Choice Notes from Notes and Queries, Folk-Lore. London, 1859.

CLARKE, THE REV. T. *Specimens of the Westmorland Dialect.* Kendal, 1872.

CLARKSON, C. *History and Antiquities of Richmond.* Richmond, Yorks, 1821.

CLOUSTON, W. A. *The Book of Noodles: Stories of Simpletons; or, Fools and their Follies.* London, 1888.

Popular Tales and Fictions; their Migrations and Transformations, 2 vols. Edinburgh, 1887.

Cobler of Caunterburie, The. Chapbook. 1590.

Collection of Jests, Epigrams, Epitaphs, etc. Edinburgh, 1753.

COLLIER, J. *The Works of Tim Bobbin Esq. in Prose and Verse:* with a Memoir of the Author, by J. Corry.... Manchester, 1862.

Colliery Guardian, The. 1865.

Conjuror, The, or The Turkey and the Ring. A Comic Tale. London, 1808[?].

Constitutional Monthly Advertiser and Review of General Literature and Current Events. London, 1853.

COOPER, ERNEST. *Mardles from Suffolk.* London, 1932.

COOPER, N. "The Hares' Parliament", article in *Ulster Folk-Life*, 1959.

COPE, SIR W. H. *A Glossary of Hampshire Words and Phrases*. English Dialect Society, London, 1883.

Cornhill Magazine, IX, 1864. Anonymous article, "Yorkshire".

COUCH, JONATHAN. *History of Polperro*. London, 1932.

COUCH, T. Q. "The Longstone", *Notes and Queries*, 6, vii, April 1883.

Countryman, The, XXIX, no. 2, 1944, "Pan-Mugs", contributed by A. L.

County Folk-Lore, I–VIII. Folk-Lore Society, London, 1895–1965.

COURTNEY, M. A. *Cornish Feasts and Folk-Lore*. Penzance, 1890.

"Cornish Folk-Lore", *Folk-Lore Journal*, v. London, 1887.

COWLING, G. H. *The Dialect of Hackness, North-East Yorkshire; with Original Specimens and a Word-list*. Cambridge Archaeological and Ethnographical Series, 1915.

COX, J. C. (editor). *Memorials of Old Derbyshire*. London, 1907.

COXHEAD, J. R. W. *The Devil in Devon*. West Country Handbooks, II, 1967.

Devon Traditions and Fairy Tales. Exmouth, 1959.

Legends of Devon, with introduction by C. Hole, Western Press, 1954.

CRAWFORD, P. *In England Still*. Bristol, 1938.

CROMEK, R. H. *Remains of Galloway and Nithsdale Song*. London, 1810.

CROSSING, W. *A Hundred Years on Dartmoor*. Plymouth, 1901.

Tales of the Dartmoor Pixies. London and Plymouth, 1890.

CROWE, CATHERINE. *The Night Side of Nature; or, Ghosts and Ghost Seers*. London, 1848.

CRUDEN, A. 'Stray Notes on the Folk-Lore of Aberdeenshire and the North-East of Scotland', *Folk-Lore*, XXV.

CUNDALL, J. *A Treasury of Pleasure Books for Young People*. S. Lowe & Son, 1856.

CUNNINGHAM, ALLAN. *Traditional Tales of the English and Scottish Peasantry*. 2 vols. London, 1874.

CUNNINGHAM, R. H. *Amusing Prose Chap-Books, Chiefly of the Last Century*. London, 1889.

Curious and Entertaining History of Valerio the Treacherous Innkeeper, The. Chapbook, c. 1600.

Dalesman, The, I, ii. 1939, Clapham, Yorks.

DAMANT, M. "Folk Tales", *Folk-Lore*, VI, 305–6.

DARTNELL, G. E. and GODDARD, THE REV. E. H. *Wiltshire Glossary*. The English Dialect Society, London, 1893.

DAVIDSON, J. *Axminster during the Civil War in the Seventeenth Century*. 1881.

DE LA MARE, WALTER. *Animal Stories; Chosen, Arranged and in Some Part Rewritten*. London, 1939.

Come Hither. London, 1923.

DE LA PRYME, ABRAHAM. *The Diary of Abraham de la Pryme*, edited by Charles Jackson. Published by the Surtees Society, 1870.

DENHAM, M. A. *The Denham Tracts*, a collection of Folk-Lore by M. A. Denham, and reprinted from the original Tracts and Pamphlets printed by him between 1846 and 1859. Edited by J. Hardy, 2 vols. (Publications of the Folk-Lore Society, Nos. 29, 35.) London, 1892–5.

DENNISON, W. TRAIL. "Orkney Folklore—Sea Myths", *Scottish Antiquary*, V.

Devonshire Association, Report and Transactions of the.

DICKENS, CHARLES. *The Uncommercial Traveller*. London, 1892.

DICKINSON, W. *Cumbriana*. London, 1876.

A Glossary of the Words and Phrases of Cumberland. Whitehaven, 1859.

Distressed Child in the Wood, The, or, The Cruel Unkle. Chapbook, 1706.

DIXON, J. *Ancient Poems, Ballads and Songs of the Peasantry of England*. 1857, reissue 1860.

DOBSON, W. *Rambles by the Ribble*. 1st series. Preston, 1864.

Dorset County Chronicle, The. November 1886.

DOUGLAS, SIR GEORGE. *Scottish Fairy and Folk Tales*. London, n.d.

East Anglian; or, Notes and Queries on subjects connected with the Counties of Suffolk, Cambridge, Essex and Norfolk. 4 vols. New series, 3 vols. Lowestoft, Ipswich, and Norwich, 1858–1910.

EDLESTON, ALICE. "The Bull, the Tup, the Cock and the Steg", "Canny Jack". *Folk-Lore*, XX, 1909.

EDMONSTON, ELIZA. *Sketches and Tales of the Shetland Islands*. Edinburgh, 1856.

EDMONSTON, THE REV. B. and SAXBY, JESSIE M. *The Home of a Naturalist*. London, 1888.

EGERTON, J. COKER. *Sussex Folk and Sussex Ways*, edited by H. Wace. New edn. London, 1892.

"The Essex Men's Well", *Essex Review*, XXXII.

ELDER, ABRAHAM. *Tales and Legends of the Isle of Wight*. London, 1839.

ELLIOTT, JOHN. *Notebooks*, I–IX. School of Scottish Studies.

EVANS, A. B. *Leicestershire Words, Phrases, and Proverbs*. 1881.

EYRE, MARGARET. "Folk-Lore of the Wye Valley", *Folk-Lore*, XVI. London, 1905.

Facetiae Cantabrigienses. London, 1825.

FAIRLEY, J. A. See Buchan, *Ancient Scottish Tales*.

FARMER, J. A. *A Wanderer's Gleanings, Round and About Gloucestershire*. Cheltenham, 1927.

FARRALL, T. *Betty Wilson's Cummerland Teals*. Carlisle, 1876, 2nd edn. 1886.

FIELD, J. E. *The Myth of the Pent Cuckoo. A Study in Folklore*. London, 1913.

FISON, LOIS A. *Merry Suffolk*, by L. A. Fison, with "Tom Tit Tot" and sequel, by Mrs W. Thomas. London, 1899.

FITZHUGH, *The Lord Fitzhugh and his Neighbour, Lord Baliol, or, the Parish Magazine, a Monthly Illustrated Periodical Localised for both Sides of the Tees*. Barnard Castle, n.d.

Folkestone Fiery Serpent, The, with notes by "A Wise Man of the East". 2nd edn. Dover, 1844.

Folk-Lore: A Quarterly Review of Myth, Tradition, Institution and Customs, I—. Folk-Lore Society. London, 1890.

Folk-Lore Journal, 7 vols. Folk-Lore Society. London, 1883–9.

Folk-Lore Record, 5 vols. Folk-Lore Society. London, 1878–82.

FORD, ROBERT. *Thistledown*. A Book of Scottish Humorous Characters, Folk-Lore, Stories and Anecdote. Paisley, 1913.

FRASER, JOHN. *The Humorous Chap-books of Scotland*, 2 vols. *c*. 1889.

Friar and the Boy, The. 1617.

Gammer Gurton's Garland. London, 1810. See Ritson, Joseph.

GEE, H. L. *Folk Tales of Yorkshire*. London, 1952.

Gentleman's Magazine, The, 306 vols. London, 1732–1922.

Gentleman's Magazine Library, The, edited by G. L. Gomme. London, 1885.

GEPP, E. *An Essex Dialect Dictionary.* 2nd edn. London, 1923.

GERRISH, W. B. "A Hertfordshire St George", *Folk-Lore,* XII, 1901.

GERVASE OF TILBURY. *Otia Imperialia,* III. Hanover, 1856.

GIBBINGS, W. W. (publishers). *Folk-Lore and Legends, Scotland.* London, 1889.

GLYDE, J. *The Norfolk Garland.* A Collection of the Superstitions, Beliefs and Prac-
tices, Proverbs, Curious Customs, Ballads and Songs of the People of Norfolk...,
compiled and edited by J. Glyde. London, 1872.

GOMME, A. B. "The Green Lady", *Folk-Lore,* VII, 1896.

GOMME, G. L. (editor). "Tom Hickathrift", Chapbook, *c.* 1660. For the Villon Society. Pepysian Library.

English Traditions and Foreign Customs. Gentleman's Magazine Library, 1885.

GOULD, R. T. *Oddities.* London, 1928.

GRAHAM, DOUGAL ("SHELLAB"). *The Collected Writings of.* Glasgow, *c.* 1889.

GREGOR, W. *Notes on the Folk-Lore of the North-East of Scotland,* Folk-Lore Society
Publications, 7. London, 1881.

"Some Folk-tales and Word-jingles from Aberdeen and Banffshires", *Folk-Lore
Journal,* III, 1885.

"Three Folk-tales from Old Meldrum, Aberdeenshire," *Folk-Lore Journal,* II. 1884.

"Water in a Sieve", *Folk-Lore Journal,* I, 1883.

GRICE, F. *Folk Tales of the North Country,* drawn from Northumberland and Durham.
Nelson, 1944.

*Grinning Made Easy, or, Funny Dick's unrivalled collection of jests, jokes, bulls, epigrams
etc. with many other Descriptions of Wit and Humour.* John Cheap the Chapman's
Library, I. Glasgow, 1877.

GROOME, FRANCIS HINDES. *Gypsy Folk-Tales.* London, 1899.

GROVES, MURIEL. *The History of Shipton-under-Wychwood.* London, 1934.

GURDON, LADY EVELINE CAMILLA. *Suffolk,* collected and edited by the Lady
Eveline Camilla Gurdon, with introduction by E. Clodd. *County Folk-Lore I,*
Printed Extracts, II. Folk-Lore Society, London, 1893.

"The Clock", *Folk-Lore,* III, 1892.

GUTCH, MRS (editor). *East Riding of Yorkshire. County Folk-Lore VI.* Folk-Lore
Society, London, 1912.

Examples of Printed Folk-Lore concerning Lincolnshire, collected by Mrs Gutch and
M. Peacock. *County Folk-Lore V; Printed Extracts,* 7. Folk-Lore Society, 1908.

*Examples of Printed Folk-Lore concerning the North Riding of Yorkshire, York and
the Ainsty,* collected and edited by Mrs Gutch. *County Folk-Lore II.* Printed
Extracts, 4. Folk-Lore Society, 1901.

HACKWOOD, F. W. *Staffordshire Stories, Historical and Legendary.* a miscellany of
County Lore and Anecdote. Stafford, 1906.

HALLIWELL[-PHILLIPPS], JAMES ORCHARD (editor). *The Merry Tales of the Wise
Men of Gotham.* London, 1840.

The Nursery Rhymes of England. 4th edn. London, 1842.

HALLIWELL[-PHILLIPS] J. O. *Nursery Rhymes and Nursery Tales.* London, n.d.
[*c.* 1843].

Illustrations of the Fairy Mythology of "A Midsummer Night's Dream". London, 1845.

Popular Rhymes and Nursery Tales. a Sequel to *The Nursery Rhymes of England.*
London, 1849.

HARDWICK, CHARLES. *Traditions, Superstitions and Folklore*. Manchester and London, 1872.

HARE, AUGUSTUS. *In My Solitary Life*. London, 1953. From *Memorials of a Quiet Life*, 1871.

The Years with Mother. London, 1952. From *Memorials of a Quiet Life*. 1871.

HARLAND, J. and WILKINSON, T. T. *Lancashire Legends, Traditions, Pageants, Sports, etc*. With a rare Tract of the Lancashire Witches. London, 1873.

HARTLAND, E. S. (editor). *English Fairy and Folk Tales*. London, n.d.

Gloucestershire, County Folk-Lore I. Printed Extracts, 1. Folk-Lore Society. London, 1892.

"The Treasure on the Drinn", *Folk-Lore Journal*, VI, 1888.

HAWKER, R. S. *Footprints of Former Men in Far Cornwall*. London, 1903.

HAYWARD, LILIAN. "The Two Hares", article in *Folk-Lore*, L, 1939.

HAZLITT, W. CAREW. *Fairy Tales, Legends and Romances illustrating Shakespeare*. London, 1875.

National Tales and Legends. London, 1899.

(editor) *The Sack-Full of News* (first published 1673).

Shakespeare's Jest-Books, 1864.

HEAD, THOMAS. *Legends, Tales and Songs in the Dialect of the Peasantry of Gloucestershire*. Cirencester, 1900.

HEANLEY, R. M. "The Vikings: Traces of their Folklore in Marshland". Paper read before the Viking Club, London, and printed in the *Saga Book*, III, Part I. January 1902.

HEARNE, T. See Caius, T. *Vindiciae Antiquitatis Academiae Oxoniensis*.

HENDERSON, GEORGE. *The Popular Rhymes, Sayings and Proverbs of the County of Berwick*. Newcastle-on-Tyne, 1856.

HENDERSON, HAMISH. *Scottish Studies*, II, i.

HENDERSON, WILLIAM. *Notes on the Folk-Lore of the Northern Counties of England and the Borders*. With an Appendix on *Household Tales* by S. Baring-Gould. London, 1866. New edn. 1879.

HEWETT, SARAH. *Nummits and Crummits*. London, 1900.

The Peasant Speech of Devon. 2nd edn. London, 1892.

HEYWOOD, THOMAS. *Hierarchie of the Blessed Angels*. 1635.

HIBBERT, SAMUEL. *A Description of the Shetland Islands*. Edinburgh, 1822.

HISLOP, ALEXANDER. *The Book of Scottish Anecdote*. c. 1889.

Historie of the Damnable Life and Deserved Death of Dr. J. Faustus. 1592. Reprinted in Thoms, *Early English Prose Romances*.

History of Jack and the Giants, The. Glasgow, 1807.

History, The, of the Four Kings of Canterbury, Colchester, Cornwall and Cumberland, their Queens and Daughters: being the merry tales of Tom Hodge and his Schoolfellows. Chapbook. Glasgow, 1799.

HODGE, G. "Remembered Wraiths and Tokens", *Old Cornwall*, III. 1937–42.

HODGSON, JOHN. *History of Northumberland*. 3 vols. Newcastle, 1827–40.

HOLE, CHRISTINA. *English Folk-Lore*. London, 1939.

English Folk-Heroes. London, 1948.

Traditions and Customs of Cheshire. London, 1937.

HOLLINGWORTH, *Chronicles of Manchester*.

HOLLINGWORTH, A. *History of Stowmarket*. Ipswich, 1844.

HONE, W. *The Table Book of Daily Recreation and Information, and Year Book*. New edn. in 2 pts. London, 1833.

HOSKINS, W. G. and FINBERG, H. P. R. *Devonshire Studies*. London, 1952.

HUDSON, J. A. and NEVINSON, J. L. "Sir John Schorne and his Boot". *Country Life*, 1962.

HUGHES, T. *The Scouring of the White Horse; or, The Long Vacation Ramble of a London Clerk*. Cambridge, 1859.

HÜLLEN, GEORG. *Von Prinzen, Trollen und Herrn Fro*. Schloss Bentlage bei Rheine, 1956.

HUNT, ROBERT. *Popular Romances of the West of England*. Reprinted London, 1930.

HYSLOP, J. *Echoes from the Border Hills*, edited by his son, R. Hyslop. Sunderland, 1912.

IGGLESDEN (SIR C.), *A Saunter through Kent with Pen and Pencil*. Ashford, Kent, 1900.

INGLEDEW, C. J. D. *The Ballads and Songs of Yorkshire*, transcribed by C. J. D. Ingledew. London, 1860.

Ipswich Journal, Suffolk Notes and Queries, 1878.

Jack and the Giants, see *History of*. Chapbook, n.d.

JACK, J. *The Key of the Forth; or, Historical Sketches of the Island of May*. Edinburgh, 1858.

Jacke of Dover. His Quest of Inquirie, or his privy search for the veriest fool in England. London, 1604.

JACKSON, C. See De la Pryme, A. *Diary*.

JACKSON, GEORGINA F. *Shropshire Folk-Lore: A Sheaf of Gleanings*, edited by C. S. Burne from the collections of G. F. Jackson. London, 1883. See Burne.

JACKSON, K. "The Barn is Burning" (by K. Jackson and E. M. Wilson), *Folk-Lore*, XLVII, pp. 190–202, 1936.

JACOBS, JOSEPH. *The Fables of Aesop*. New York, 1894.

    English Fairy Tales, collected by J. Jacobs. London, 1890.

    More English Fairy Tales, collected and edited by J. Jacobs. London, 1894.

JAMIESON, R. *Illustrations of Northern Antiquities*, from the Earlier Teutonic and Scandinavian Romances...with Notes and Dissertations. R. Jamieson, Sir W. Scott, and H. W. Weber. Edinburgh, 1814.

J.C. *The Scottish Journal of Topography, Antiquities, Traditions, etc.* September 1847–July 1848 ("Folklore of Clackmannanshire etc." by J. C.) Edinburgh, 1848.

JENNINGS, MYRA E. "A Lay Ghost-Layer", *Old Cornwall*, Summer Number, 1934.

JERROLD, WALTER. *Highways and Byways of Kent*. London, 1907.

JERVIS, ANDREW. *The Land of the Lindsays*, corrected and edited by James Gammock. 1882.

JEWETT, W. HENRY. "The Wild Hunstman", *Folk-Lore*, XVIII, 1907.

John Cheap the Chapman's Library: The Scottish Chap Literature of Last Century, Classified: With Life of D. Graham. 3 vols. Glasgow, 1877–8.

JOHNSON, RICHARD. *The History of the Seven Champions of Christendom* (abridged), c. 1770, from *The Most Famous History....*1590.

JONES, W. H. *The Folk-tales of the Magyars*, collected by Kriza, Erdélyi, Pap, and others, translated and edited with comparative notes by W. H. Jones and L. L. Kropf. Publications of the Folk-Lore Society, 13. London, 1889.

Journal of the English Folk Dance and Song Society. London, 1932–64.

Journal of the Folk-song Society. 8 vols. London, 1899–1931.

Journal of the Gypsy Lore Society. 3 vols. New Series, 9 vols. 3rd Series, 1—. Edinburgh, 1899—.

JOYCE, REV. W. W. *Moorside Tales and Talk.* 1915.

KEIGHTLEY, THOMAS. *The Fairy Mythology.* . . . New edn. London, 1850.

KELLY, W. K. *Curiosities of Indo-European Tradition and Folk-lore.* London, 1863.

KENT, E. G. *Lindum Lays and Legends.* London, 1861.

KINLOCH MSS. V, 103. In handwriting of James Beattie, "The Cruel Mother".

KIRKBY, B. *Granite Chips and Clints; or, Westmorland in Words.* Appleby, 1900.

Lakeland Words. Kendal, 1895.

LANG, ANDREW. "A Far-travelled Tale" ("Nicht Nought Nothing"), *Revue Celtique,* III, *Customs and Myth.*

The Green Fairy Book. London, 1892.

"English and Scotch Fairy Tales", *Folk-Lore,* I, pp. 289–312, 1890.

LATHAM, C. "West Sussex Superstitions", *Folk-Lore Record,* I, 1878.

LEATHER, E. M. *Folk-Lore of Herefordshire.* 1913.

Folk-Lore of the Shire, the Memorials of Old Herefordshire. 1904.

LEYDEN, J. *The Complaynt of Scotland,* written in 1548, with preliminary dissertation and glossary (by J. Leyden). Edinburgh, 1801.

LONG, W. H. *A Dictionary of the Isle of Wight Dialect.* 2nd edn. 1931.

LONGSTAFFE, W. HYLTON. *Richmondshire, its Ancient Lords and Edifices.* London, 1853.

LOWSLEY, B. *A Glossary of Berkshire Words and Phrases.* English Dialect Society. London, 1888.

MACQUOID, THOMAS and KATHARINE. *About Yorkshire.* London, 1883.

MALONE, E. *Merrie Tales of the Mad Men of Gotham.* n.d., reprinted, 1613.

MANNING, P. "Stray Notes on Oxfordshire Folklore, VI, Folk-tales" (partly from the collections of T. J. Carter, of Oxford), *Folk-Lore,* XIV. London, 1903.

MARTINEAU, HARRIET. *A Complete Guide to the English Lakes.* Windermere, 1855.

MASSINGHAM, H. J. *Country.* London, 1934.

Shepherd's Country. London, 1938.

Wold without End. London, 1932.

MATHEWS, F. W. *Tales of the Blackdown Borderland.* Somerset Folk Series, 13. London, 1923.

MATTHEW, PARIS, *English History from the Year 1235 to 1273,* translated by the Rev. J. A. Giles. London, 1902.

MATTHEWS, J. H. Article in *Notes and Queries,* X, 8.

Merry Suffolk. 1899.

MAYHEW, H. *London Labour and the London Poor,* 3 vols. London, 1861.

MILLER, HUGH. *Old Red Sandstone.* Edinburgh, 1841.

Scenes and Legends of the North of Scotland. Edinburgh, 1872.

My Schools and Schoolmasters. Edinburgh, 1852.

MILLER, JOE, *Joe Miller's Jest Book;* forming a rich Banquet of Wit and Humour. London, 1834.

Joe Miller's Jests: With Copious Additions. London, 1836.

Joe Miller's Complete Jest Book, II. 1841.

Miscellanea of the Rymour Club. Edinburgh, 1906–28.

MITCHELL and DICKIE. *Philosophy of Witchcraft*. Paisley, 1839.
MONTGOMERIE, N. and W. *The Well at the World's End*. Hogarth Press, 1956.
Monthly Chronicle of North-country Lore and Legend, 5 vols. Newcastle-on-Tyne, 1887–91.
MORRIS, M. C. F. *Yorkshire Folk-talk*. 2nd edn. London, 1911.
    Yorkshire Reminiscences. London, 1922.
Mother Goose's Book of Nursery Rhymes and Songs, edited by E. and G. Rhys. Everyman's Library, no. 473. London, 1931.
Mother Goose, Entertaining Tales of. 1817.
Mother Goose's Fairy Tales. London, 1878.
Mother Goose's Melody. 1796.
Mother Goose's Nursery Rhymes. 1877.
NEVINSON, J. L. See Hudson, J. A.
NEWBIGGING, THOMAS. *Lancashire Humour*. London, 1900.
NICHOLSON, J. *Folk Lore of East Yorkshire*. London, 1890.
NICHOLSON, WILLIAM. *Poetical Works*. Castle Douglas, 1781.
NIMMO, *History of Stirlingshire* (note in Denham Tracts, II).
NOAKE, JOHN. *The Rambler in Worcestershire*. 1848.
NORTHALL, G. F. *Folk Phrases of Four Counties*, English Dialect Society. London, 1894.
NORTHCOTE, ROSALIND, See *Report and Transactions of the Devonshire Association*, 32.
NORTON, F. J. *Collection*. MS. (6 vols.).
    Supplementary Collection. MS. (1 vol.).
Notes and Queries, series I–VIII.
Notes and Queries for Somerset and Dorset, I—. Sherborne, 1890—.
NUGENT, LORD. *Memorials of John Hampden*. 2 vols. London, 1832.
OESTERLY, DR H. *Shakespeare's Jest Book—A Hundred Merry Tales*.
Old Cornwall, II, 1931–6.
Old Friends with New Faces (A.L.O.E.). London, 1859.
Old Mother Goose's Rhymes and Tales, 1889.
OPIE, I. and P. *Oxford Dictionary of Nursery Rhymes*. London, 1951.
    The Puffin Book of Nursery Rhymes. London, 1963.
ORD, JOHN WALLER. *The History and Antiquities of Cleveland*. 1846.
Originals and Analogues of some of Chaucer's Canterbury Tales, edited by F. J. Furnivall, E. Brock and W. A. Clouston. London, 1888.
ORMEROD, FRANK. *Lancashire Life and Character*. Rochdale.
Our Meigle Book. See Scottish Women's Rural Institute compilations.
PALMER, ROY, *Anecdotes and Tales*, chiefly from the Black Country. MS. collected 27 December 1966.
    Stories from Ewan MacColl and Charles Parker. MS.
PARKINSON, T. *Yorkshire Legends and Traditions* as Told by her Ancient Chroniclers, her Poets, and Journalists. 2 vols. London, 1888–9.
Pasquil's Jests. 1604. See Hazlitt, *Shakespeare's Jest Books*.
PATERSON, T. G. F. Contributions to *Ulster Folk-Life*. I, 1938.
PAUL, WILLIAM. *Past and Present of Aberdeenshire, or, Reminiscences of Seventy Years*. 2nd edn. Aberdeen, 1881.

PEACOCK, M. See also Gutch (Mrs), *Examples of Printed Folk-Lore concerning Lincolnshire.*
"The Glass Mountain", *Folk-Lore*, IV, 1893.
"The Folklore of Lincolnshire", *Folk-Lore*, XII. 1901.
Tales and Rhymes in the Lindsey Folk-Speech. London, 1886.
Penny Budget of Wit and Package of Drollery, pp. 200–18 of *Amusing Prose Chap-Books,* Cunningham, R. H. (q.v.).
PERCY, T. *Reliques of Ancient English Poetry,* 4 vols. London, 1765.
POOLE, C. H. *Customs, Traditions and Superstitions of Somerset.* 1883.
RALPH OF COGGESHALL. *Chronicon Anglicanum.* Rolls Series, 66. 1857. Printed in *Rerum Britannicarum Medii Aevi Scriptores.*
REANEY, P. H. *A Grammar of the Dialect of Penrith* (Cumberland), descriptive and historical, with specimens and a glossary. Publications of the University of Manchester English Series, 15. Manchester, 1927.
REID, ALAN. *Kinghorn: a Short History and Description of a Notable Fifeshire Town and Parish.* Kirkcaldy, 1906.
Reliquary, The. A Depository for Precious Relics—Legendary, Biographical, and Historical. 34 vols. London, 1860–94.
Report and Transactions of the Devonshire Association, I—. Plymouth 18—.
Restless Ghost, or, Wonderful news from Northamptonshire and Southwark. Pamphlet. 1676.
RICHARDSON, M. A. *The Local Historian's Table Book* of Remarkable Occurrences, Historical Facts, Traditions . . . Connected with the Counties of Newcastle-upon-Tyne, Northumberland, and Durham. Legendary Division, 3 vols. London, 1843–6.
RITSON, JOSEPH. *Fairy Tales.* London, 1831.
Gammer Gurton's Garland; or, *The Nursery Parnassus,* collected by J. Ritson. London, 1810.
ROBERTSON, D. J. "Kate Crackernuts, Peerifool", *Longman's Magazine,* XIII and XIV.
ROBERTSON, MACDONALD. *More Highland Folktales.* Edinburgh and London, 1964.
ROBY, JOHN. *Traditions of Lancashire.* 2 vols. London, 1926. (First published 1829.)
ROGER OF WENDOVER, *Chronicle.* (Flowers of History.) London, 1849.
ROGERS, W. H. H. *Memorials of the West.* Exeter, 1889.
ROPER, WILLIAM. *The Mirour of Vertue in Worldly Greatness, or, The Life of Sir Thomas More, Knight.* London, 1903.
RORIE, D. "Stray Notes on the Folk-lore of Aberdeenshire and the North-East of Scotland", *Folk-Lore*, XXV, 1914.
ROSE, W. *Fifty Years Ago,* by a Native Resident (Walter Rose).
Little Booklets on Haddenham Village, 1. Haddenham, 1931.
Round about our Coal Fire. Chapbook, 1740. Reprinted, c. 1883.
RUDKIN, E. "Grim and his Man Böndel", *Folk-Lore,* December 1935.
"Tommy Lindum", *Folk-Lore,* December 1955.
RYE, W. *The Recreations of a Norfolk Antiquary.* Holt, 1920.
SALISBURY, J. *A Glossary of Words and Phrases used in S.E. Worcestershire.* English Dialect Society, London, 1893.
SALMON, L. "Folk-Lore in the Kennet Valley", *Folk-Lore,* XIII, 1902.

SAMPSON, JOHN. "Two Stories of Cornelius Price", *Journal of the Gypsy Lore Society*, 3rd series, IX, 1930.
"Tales in a Tent", *Journal of the Gypsy Lore Society*, III, 1892.

SANDYS, W. *Specimens of Cornish Provincial Dialect*, Collected and Arranged by Uncle Jan Treenoodle (i.e. W. Sandys). London, 1846.

SAUNDERS, BERNARD. *Legends and Traditions of Huntingdonshire*. London, 1883.

SAVORY, A. H. *Grain and Chaff from an English Manor*. Oxford, 1920.

SAXBY, JESSIE M. E. *Shetland Traditional Lore*. Edinburgh, 1932.

SCOT, REGINALD. *The Discoverie of Witchcraft*. London, 1584.

Scotch Haggis, The. A Selection of Choice *Bon Mots*. In *John Cheap the Chapman's Library*. Glasgow, 1877.

SCOTT, SIR WALTER, *Tales of a Grandfather*, 3 vols. London and Glasgow, 1923.
Minstrelsy of the Scottish Border, 4 vols. Edinburgh, 1932.

SCOTT, SIR W., R. JAMIESON AND H. W. WEBER. *Illustrations of Northern Antiquities*. Edinburgh, 1814.

Scottish Jests (English section). R. Chambers. London, 1838.

SCOTTISH WOMEN'S RURAL INSTITUTES. *The Largo Village Book* (S.W.R.I. Compilation). Cupar-Fife, 1932.
Our Meigle Book, Dundee, 1932.

Seven Champions of Christendom. Chapbook. See Johnson, Richard.

SHERRACOMBE, WILL. *Devonshire Folk*. London, 1937.

SHERREN, WILKINSON. *The Wessex of Romance*. New and revised edn. London, 1908.

Shetland Folk Book, The. II, edited by E. S. Reid Tait. Lerwick, 1951; III, edited by T. A. Robertson and John J. Graham. Lerwick, 1957.

Short Stories for School and Home Reading. London and Edinburgh, 1878.

SIMPKINS, JOHN EWART. *Examples of printed Folk-Lore concerning Fife*, with some Notes on Clackmannan and Kinross shires, collected by J. E. Simpkins. *County Folk-Lore*, VII. Printed Extracts, 9–11. Folk-Lore Society, London.

SIMPSON, E. B. *Folk Lore in Lowland Scotland*. London, 1908.

SMALL, A. *Interesting Roman Antiquities Recently Discovered in Fife*. Edinburgh, 1823.

SOUTHEY, ROBERT. *The Doctor*, IV. London, 1834–47.

SPENCE, JOHN. *Shetland Folk-Lore*. Lerwick, 1899.

STAPLETON, ALFRED. *All about the Merry Tales of Gotham*. 2nd edn. Nottingham, 1910.

STEEL, FLORA ANNIE. *English Fairy Tales*. London, 1918.

STEPHENS, G. "Two English Folk-tales', *Folk-Lore Record*, 3, II, 1881.
See also under Sternberg, below.

STERNBERG, T. *The Dialect and Folk-Lore of Northamptonshire*. London, 1851.
"Popular Stories of the English Peasantry", by T. Sternberg, H. B. C. and G. Stephens). 3 parts. *Notes and Queries*, I and V.

Stone Circles of Cornwall, The. Reprinted from the Transactions of the Penzance Natural History and Antiquarian Society. 1893–4.

Stories on Proverbs. London, 1854.

STUBBES, PHILIP. *The Anatomie of Abuses*, 1585. Reprinted London, 1836.

SUFFLING, E. R. *History and Legends of the Broad District*. London, 1891.

Sussex County Magazine, 1—. Lewes, 1926—.

SWAINSON, C. *Folk-Lore and Provincial Names of British Birds.* Folk-Lore Society, 1886.

TANNER, HEATHER and ROBIN. *Wiltshire Village.* London, 1939.

TAYLOR, *Wit and Mirth.* (Period of James I.)

TAYLOR, A. S. *"Billy Tyson's Coortin'",* and other Sketches in the Westmorland Dialect. 2nd edn. Kendal, 1886.

TAYLOR, E. S. *The History of Playing Cards....* London, 1865.

TAYLOR, MARK R. "Norfolk Folklore", *Folk-Lore,* XL, 1929.

THISTLETON DYER, T. F. *Folk-Lore of Shakespeare.* London, 1883.

The Ghost World. London, 1893.

THOMAS, N. W. "Christ and the Peas", *Folk-Lore,* VIII, 1897.

THOMAS, MRS W. See Fison, Lois A., *Merry Suffolk* ...

THOMPSON, T. W. "English Gypsy Folk-Tales and other Traditional Stories", *Journal of the Gypsy Lore Society,* n.s., 8. Grindleton, 1914–15.

Thompson Notebooks, MS. Twelve Notebooks of stories from Gypsies, lodged in the Institute of Dialect and Folk Life, the University of Leeds. Awaiting publication.

THOMS, W. J. *Anecdotes and Traditions.* London, 1839.

Four Transcripts, see Wright, Thomas.

Early English Prose Romances. London, 1889.

THOROTON, ROBERT. *History of Nottinghamshire;* republished with large additions by J. Throsby. 3 vols. London, 1797.

Times, The, London.

Times Literary Supplement, The, London.

Tom Thumb, The Little, J. O. Halliwell-Phillipps. London, 1860.

TONGUE, RUTH. L. *Forgotten Folk Tales.* MS.

"Somerset Folklore", *County Folk-Lore,* VIII. The Folk-Lore Society, 1965.

Contributions to *Von Prinzen, Trollen und Herrn Fro.* 1962, "The Man in the Wilderness". 1964, "That's Enough to go on with", "A Piece in my Pocket".

Contributions to *People's Meeting Place:* "Four Eggs a Penny", "Old Echo", "Room for a Little One", "Two Moons in May", "Chimbly Charlie", "The Spring of the Sixpence". (Awaiting publication.)

Transactions of the Second International Folk-Lore Congress. London, 1891.

Transactions of the Penzance Natural History and Antiquarian Society, New series, 4 vols. Plymouth, 1880–98.

Transactions of the Rymour Club. See *Miscellanea of the Rymour Club.*

TREGELLAS, I. T. *Peeps into the Haunts and Homes of the Rural Population of Cornwall.* Truro, 1868.

UDAL, J. S. "Dorsetshire Children's Games, etc." *Folk-Lore Journal,* VII, 1889.

Dorsetshire Folk-Lore, 1922.

Ulster Folk-life, 1959—.

URE, DAVID. *History of Rutherglen and East Kilbride.* Glasgow, 1793.

VARDEN, JOHN T. *Traditions, Superstitions and Folklore.* East Anglian Handbook, 1885.

VITRY, JACQUES DE. *Exempla,* edited by T. F. Crane. 1890.

VICKERS, REV. W. V. Letter in *The Times,* 15 November 1935, on "Old Parr".

WADDELL, HELEN. *Beasts and Saints.* London, 1934.

WALFORD, CORNELIUS. *Notes and Queries,* 6, II, 4 November 1882, p. 368, "Coggeshall Jobs".

WATKINS, W. J. H. "A Cycle of Stories current in Radnorshire", *Folk-Lore*.

WEEKS, W. *Devonshire Yarns*. New edn. greatly enlarged. Exeter, 1926.

WENDOVER, ROGER OF, *Chronicle*. 2 vols. London, 1849.

WHERRY, B. A. "Wizardry on the Welsh Border", *Folk-Lore*, XV, 1904.

Whetstone, A, for dull wits, or, A Posy of New and Ingenious Riddles. London, c. 1780.

WHITAKER, THOMAS DUNHAM. *A History of Richmondshire, in the North Riding of the County of York*. 2 vols. London, 1823.

Whitby Magazine, II, 1828 quoted in *County Folk-Lore*, II, 1899.

WHITCOMBE, MRS H. PENNELL. *Bygone Days in Devonshire and Cornwall*, with Notes of Existing Superstitions and Customs. London, 1874.

WHITE, JOHN PAGEN. *Lays and Legends of the English Lake Country*, with Copious Notes. London, 1873.

WHITE, WALTER. *All Round the Wrekin*. London, 1860.

A Month in Yorkshire. London, 1858.

Whittington, the History of Sir Richard. By T. H. Edited, with an introduction, by H. B. Wheatley. *Folk-Lore Tracts*, I, v. London, 1885.

WILKIE, J. *Bygone Fife, from Culross to St Andrews*. London, 1931.

WILKINSON, G. J. *Illustrated Guide to Lincolnshire*. Lincoln, 1900.

WILKINSON, T. T. See Harland, J. *Lancashire Legends* ....

WILLIAM OF NEWBURY. *Gulielmi Newbrigensis Historia sive Chronica Rerum Anglicarum*. Oxon. 1719.

WILLIAMS, ALFRED. *Folk-songs of the Upper Thames*. London, 1923.

Round about the Upper Thames. London, 1922.

The Villages of the White Horse. London, 1913.

WILLIAMS-ELLIS, A. *Fairy Tales from the British Isles, Retold*. London, 1966. *Round the World Fairy Tales, Retold*. London, 1966.

WILSON, E. M. "Some Humorous English Folk-tales", 3 parts, *Folk-Lore*, XLIX and LIV, 1938, 1943.

"The Tale of the Religious Card-Player", *Folk-Lore*, L, 1939.

See also Jackson, K. "The Barn is Burning".

WILSON, WILLIAM. *Folklore and Genealogies of Uppermost Nithsdale*. Dumfries, 1904.

Word-lore. The 'folk' magazine. 3 vols. London, 1926–8.

WRIGHT, ELIZABETH MARY. *Rustic Speech and Folk-Lore*. London, 1913.

WRIGHT, THOMAS. "Four Transcripts", edited by W. J. Thoms. *Folk-Lore Record*, II, 1879.

Wright's Chaste Wife, The. Early English Text Society, edited by Furnivall, 1865.

WYBARNE, J. *The New Age of Old Names*. London, 1609.

YATES, DORA E. *A Book of Gypsy Folk-Tales*. London, 1948.

YORKE, STEPHEN. *Tales of the North Riding*. 2 vols. London, 1871.

YOUNG, REV. GEORGE. *A History of Whitby and Streonshall Abbey*, 2 vols. Whitby, 1817.

ZALL, P. M. (editor). *A Hundred Merry Tales and Other English Jest Books of the Fifteenth and Sixteenth Centuries*. Lincoln, Nebraska, 1963.

A LIST OF BOOKS QUOTED, CITED AND CONSULTED

BOOKS REFERRED TO AND CITED

AARNE, ANTTI. *Schwänke über Schwerhörige Menschen,* Finnish Folklore Fellows, no. 20. Helsinki, 1914.

AELFRIC. *Lives of the Saints,* edited by W. W. Skeat. Early English Text Society, 1885.

AIKEN, RILEY. *A Packload of Mexican Tales.* Publications of the Texas Folklore Society, XII, 1935.

ANDERSEN, HANS CHRISTIAN. *Fairy Tales,* 4 vols. Edited by Svend Larsen. Translated by R. P. Keigwin. London, 1958.

ANDERSON, WALTER. *Kaiser und Abt: die Geschichte einer Schwanks.* F.F. Communications, 42. Helsinki, 1923.

ARCHAEOLOGICAL INSTITUTE. *Memoirs of the Archaeological Institute of Northumberland,* I.

Archivio per lo Studio delle Tradizioni Popolari, 28 vols. Palermo, 1890–1912.

ASHTON, JOHN. *Chap-Books of the Eighteenth Century.* London, 1882.

Athenaeum, The. 94 vols. London, 1828–1921.

AUBREY, JOHN. *Remaines of Gentilisme and Judaisme,* 1686–7. London, 1881.

AXON, W. E. A. Article in *The Antiquary,* XI, 1885, on "The Pedlar of Swaffham".

Lancashire Greetings. Manchester, 1883.

The Reliquary. January, 1868.

BACON, A. M. and PARSONS, E. C. "Folk-Lore from Elizabeth City County", *Journal of American Folk-lore,* XXXV.

BARING-GOULD, S. *Curious Myths of the Middle Ages.* London, 1889.

Little Guide to Devon. London and Edinburgh, 1907.

Songs and Ballads of the West, 1892. Later edition, *Songs of the West: Folksongs of Devon and Cornwall,* collected by S. Baring-Gould, H. F. Sheppard and F. W. Bussell. 7th edn. in one vol. London, 1928.

BASILE, GIOVANNI. *Il Pentamerone.* Naples, 1674. Translated and edited by Benedetto Croce and N. M. Penser. 2 vols. London, 1932.

BASSETT, RENÉ. *Contes Populaires Berbères,* 2 vols. Paris, 1887.

Nouveaux Contes Berbères. Paris, 1897.

BAUM, PAULL FRANKLIN. "The Three Dreams or 'Dream-bread' Story", *Journal of American Folk-Lore,* xxx. New York, 1917.

Béaloideas, I, article by R. Th. Christiansen, "A Gaelic Fairy Tale in Norway".

II, Eighty-three examples of "The Three Sons".

III, version of "The Wren and the Mouse", 1931.

XIV, Forty-one versions of "The Fisherman and his Wife".

XXI, A version of "Long Credit".

BEAUMONT and FLETCHER. *The Knight of the Burning Pestle.* London, 1613.

BEDE, THE VENERABLE. *Ecclesiastical History,* edited by C. Plummer. Cambridge, 1896.

BELLOC, H. *The Four Men: A Farrago.* London, 1902.

BLADÉ, JEAN FRANÇOIS. *Contes Populaires recueillis en Agenais...* suivis de notes comparatives par R. Köhler. Paris, 1874.

BLAIR, *Rambling Recollections* (Notes in Denham Tracts).

BLOMEFIELD, F. *History of Norfolk.* London, 1805–10.

BOCCACCIO. *Decameron,* IX, no. 6. First translated 1620. "The *Decameron,* containing an Hundred pleasant Novels. 2 vols. Isaac Jaggard".

BØDKER. *De Gamle Vijses Exempler oc Haffsprock*. København, 1951–3.

BOGGS, R. S. "North Carolina Folktales current in the 1820s", *Journal of American Folklore*, XLVII, 1934.

BOLTE, J. and POLIVKA, G. *Anmerkungen zu den Kinder- und Hausmärchen der Brüder Grimm*, 5 vols. Leipzig, 1913–31.

BRAND, JOHN. *Popular Antiquities*, 3 vols. edited by Ellis. London, 1849.

BRANDANE, JOHN. *Rory Aforesaid, One-Act Plays of To-day*, 3rd series. London, 1926.

BRANSTON, BRIAN. *The Lost Gods of England*. London, 1957.

BRAYBROOKE, RICHARD GRIFFIN NEVILLE (3rd Baron). *Diary and Correspondence of S. Pepys*, with a life and notes. 6th edn., 4 vols. London, 1858.

BRIDIE, JAMES. *A Sleeping Clergyman and other Plays*. London, 1934.

BRIGGS, K. M. *The Fairies in Tradition and Literature*. London and Chicago, 1967.
Pale Hecate's Team. London, 1962.

BROCKETT, J. T. *A Glossary of North-country Words in Use....* Newcastle-on-Tyne, 1829.

BROGDEN, J. E. *Provincial Words and Expressions Current in Lincolnshire*. London, 1866.

BROOME, DORA. *Fairy Tales from the Isle of Man*. London, 1951.

BROWN, A. L. "Camlaun and the Death of Arthur", *Folk-Lore*, LXIII.

BROWN, FRANK C. *The Frank C. Brown Collection of North Carolina Folklore*, 7 vols. Durham, N.C., 1952—.

BROWN, THEO. "The Black Dog", *Folk-Lore*, LXIX, September 1958.

BROWN, W. N. "The Silence-Wager Stories: Their Origin and Diffusion", *American Journal of Philology*, XLIII.

BURNE, COL. A. H. and YOUNG, LT.-COL. P. *The Great Civil War*. A Military History of the First Civil War, 1642–1646. London, 1959.

BURTON, SIR R. F. *Supplemental Nights to the Book of the Thousand Nights and a Night*, with notes anthropological and explanatory (partly by W. A. Clouston and W. F. Kirby). 6 vols. in 7. Printed for the Burton Club, U.S.A.

Bye-gones Relating to Wales and the Border Counties, Oswestry, 1871—.

CAMDEN, W. *Camden's "Britannia"...*enlarged...by Richard Gough. 2nd edn. II, 1806.

CAMPBELL, MARIE. *Tales of Cloud-Walking Country*. Bloomington, U.S.A., 1958.

CERF, BENNETT. *Laughing Stock*. New York, 1945.

CHAMBERS, E. K. *Early English Lyrics*. London, 1907.
The English Folk-Play. Oxford, 1933.

CHESTERTON, G. K. *Collected Poems*. London, 1927.

CHRISTIANSEN, R. TH. *Studies in Irish and Scandinavian Folk-Tales*. Copenhagen, 1959.
Norske Eventyr. En systematisk fortegneise efter trykte og utrykte kilder. (*Norske Folkeminder*, 2.) Kristiania, 1921.

C. J. T. *Folk-lore and Legends* (Ireland).

CLARK, GEORGE. *The Campden Wonder*. Oxford, 1959.

CLARKE, MARY. *Stories to Tell*. London.
More Stories to Tell. London.

CLODD, EDWARD. *Tom Tit Tot:* An Essay on Savage Philosophy in Folk-tale. London, 1898.

CLOUSTON, W. A. *Flowers from a Persian Garden* and other Papers. London, 1890.

CLOUSTON, W. A. and FURNIVALL, F. J. *Originals and Analogues of some of Chaucer's "Canterbury Tales"*.

COFFIN, T. P. "The Golden Ball and the Hangman's Tree", *Folklore International*, U.S.A., 1967.

COLLINSON, JOHN *History and Antiquities of the County of Somerset*, 3 vols. Bath, 1791.

COOMARASWAMY, "The Loathly Bride", *Speculum*, 1945.

COSTELLO, J. *The Bard of the Dales, or, Poems and Miscellaneous Pieces*, partly in the Yorkshire Dialect. London, 1850.

COULTON, G. G. *Social Life in Britain from the Conquest to the Reformation*. Cambridge, 1918.

COX, MARION ROALFE. *Cinderella. Publications of the Folk-Lore Society*, XXXI, 1892.

CROKER, J. CROFTON. *Fairy Legends and Traditions of the South of Ireland*. 3 parts. London, 1825–8.

CRUIKSHANK, GEORGE. *George Cruikshank's Fairy Library*, c. 1853.

DÄUMLING, *Studie über den Typus des Mädchen ohne Hände*. Munich, 1912.

DAWKINS, RICHARD M. *More Greek Folk-Tales*. Oxford, 1955.

DE LA MARE, WALTER. *Told Again*. Oxford, 1927.

DELEHAYE, HIPPOLYTE. *Legends of the Saints*, translated by D. Attwater, London, 1962.

DEL RIO. *Disquisitionum Magicarum Libri Sex*. First published in Louvain, 1599.

DESPÉRIERS, JEAN BONAVENTURE. *Cymbalum Mundi* (Ouvrages d'esprit), 1958.
  The Mirrour of Mirth and pleasant Conceits, translated by T. D.
  Sources and Analogues of the "Nouvelles Récréations et Joyeux Devis". J. W. Hassell, 1956.

DICKENS, CHARLES. *A Tale of Two Cities*. London, 1859.

Dictionary of National Biography, 22 vols.

DITCHFIELD, P. H. *Old English Customs Extant at the Present Time*. London, 1896.

Dr Lamb's Darling. Witchcraft Pamphlet. London, 1653.

DORSON, R. M. *American Folklore*. Chicago, 1964.
  Buying the Wind. Chicago, 1964.
  "Dialect Stories of the Upper Peninsula", *Journal of American Folklore*, LXI, 1948.
  Negro Folk-Tales from Michigan. Cambridge, Mass., 1956.

DRAYTON, M. *Polyolbion*, the Works of Michael Drayton, edited by J. W. Hebel, IV. Oxford, 1933.

Dublin University Magazine, January 1867 (article on "Chickie Birdie").

DUNHILL, SNOWDEN. *The Life of Snowden Dunhill written by Himself*, 5th edn. Yorks. August 1883.

EDWARDS, C. L. "Bahama Songs and Stories; a Contribution to Folk-Lore". *Memoirs of the American Folk-lore Society*, III. Boston, 1895.

EHLERS, J. *Schleswig-Holsteènsch Räthselbok* .... Kiel, 1865.

EVANS, A. J. "The Rollright Stones and their Folklore", *Folk-Lore*, VI, 1895.

Fabula, I. W. E. Roberts, article on "The Princess of Colchester", 1957; Duncan Macdonald, article on "Long Stories". See also Greverus.

FANSHAWE, LADY. *Memoirs of Lady Fanshawe, Wife of Sir Richard Fanshawe.* London, 1905.

FLORENCE OF WORCESTER. *Chronicon ex Chronicis.* 1st printed edn., London, 1592.

Folktales of Japan, edited by Keigo Seki, translated by Robert J. Adams. London and Chicago, 1963.

FORDOUN, JOHN (IOHANNES DE FORDUN). *Scotichronicon,* edited by Thomas Hearne. Oxford, 1722.

FOTHERGILL, J. *An Innkeeper's Diary.* London, 1939.

FOUNTAINHALL, LORD JOHN. *Decisions,* MSS. *The Decisions of Sir John Lauder of Fountainhall, 1666–1668.* Printed in full by the Bannatyne Club, 1840.

FRY, CHRISTOPHER. *A Phoenix too Frequent.* London, 1946.

FUNGERUS, JOHANNES FRISIUS. *Etymologion Latino-Graecum.* Franc. 1605.

GAIMAR, GEOFFREY, *Estorie de Engles,* Caxton Society. See Appendix to Wright's edition of Gaimar. *Gesta Herewardii Saxonis* in Michel, *Chroniques Anglo-Normandes,* II.

GASKELL, MRS. *Silvia's Lovers.* London, 1863.

GEROULD, GORDON H. *The Grateful Dead.* Folk-Lore Society, London, 1908.

Gesta Romanorum. Translated by C. Swan, revised and edited by Wyman Hooper. London, 1905.

GILL, W. W. *A Second Manx Scrapbook.* London, 1932.

GOLDSMITH, OLIVER. *Life of Beau Nash.* London, 1762.

GOMME, A. B. *Dictionary of British Folk-Lore,* part I, *The Traditional Games of England, Scotland and Ireland,* 2 vols. London, 1898.

GRAHAM, PATRICK. *Sketches Descriptive of Picturesque Scenery on the Southern Confines of Perthshire.* Edinburgh, 1806.

GREENE, ROBERT. *Friar Bacon and Friar Bungay,* 1594.

GREVERUS, INA-MARIA. "Die Geschenke des Kleinen Volkes", *Fabula,* I, 1957.

GRICE, F. *Folk-Tales of the West Midlands.* London, 1944.

GRIFFIN, G. *The Collegians,* Dublin, 1919.

GRIMM, *Fairy Tales.* London, 1948.

GRIMM, JACOB. *Teutonic Mythology,* III, translated by James Stallybrass. London, 1883.

GROSE, F. *A Classical Dictionary of the Vulgar Tongue.* 2nd edn. London, 1788.

HANS, MARCIA and BABCOCK, LYNNE. *There's an Elephant in my Sandwich.* New York, 1963.

HARDY, JAMES. "Popular History of the Cuckoo", *Folk-Lore Record,* II, 1879.

HARDY, THOMAS. *Far from the Madding Crowd.* Wessex Edition, London, 1925.

HARRIS, JOEL. *Nights with Uncle Remus.* Boston, 1883.

HARRISON, W. H. *Mother Shipton Investigated.* London, 1881.

HARTLAND, E. S. Article in *Folk-Lore,* I, on "Lady Godiva".
The Science of Fairy Tales. London, 1891.

HASTINGS, JAMES, *Encyclopaedia of Religion and Ethics,* 13 vols. Edinburgh, 1908–26.

HENNINGSEN, GUSTAV. *Kemsten at Lyne Lødret,* Nordisk Institut for Folkedigtning. Studien no. 1. København, 1961.

HENRY OF HUNTINGDON. *Historia Anglorum,* to 1154. First published in 1596, in Savile's *Scriptores post Bedam.*

HERRICK, ROBERT. *Poems.* Oxford, 1915.

HEYWOOD, JOHN. *The Play of the Weather.* 1533.

HEYWOOD, THOMAS. *The Rape of Lucrece.* 1608.

The Wise Woman of Hogsden. 1638.

HIBBARD, LAURA A. *Mediaeval Romance in England.* New York, 1924.

HOGG, JAMES. *The Ettrick Shepherd's Tales and Sketches,* 6 vols. Glasgow, 1837.

HOLE, CHRISTINA. *Haunted England.* London, 1950.

Saints in Folklore. New York, 1965.

Traditions and Customs of Cheshire. London, 1937.

HOLLAND, R. *A Glossary of Words used in the County of Chester.* English Dialect Society, London, 1884–6.

HOLME, CONSTANCE. *The Splendid Faring.* London, 1933.

HOPKINS, MATTHEW. *Discovery of Witches,* 1607.

HOTHAM, DURRANT. *The "Mysterium Magistrum" of Jacob Behmen.* London, 1654.

HOVEDEN (or HOWDEN), ROGER OF. *Chronicle,* to 1201. First printed in *Scriptores post Bedam,* 1596. Translated by H. T. Riley, 2 vols. London, 1853.

HULL, ELEANOR. *Folklore of the British Isles.* London, 1926.

HULME, F. E. *Natural History, Lore and Legend.* London, 1895.

HYDE, DOUGLAS. *Beside the Fire.* Dublin, 1890.

INGELEND, THOMAS. *The Disobedient Child.* 1560.

INGELOW, JEAN. *Poems by Jean Ingelow.* London, 1867.

JACOBS, JOSEPH. *Celtic Fairy Tales.* London, 1892.

JALALUDDIN, c. 1260. "Pedlar of Swaffham" story in *Nasnavi.*

JONES, MARY EIRWEN. *Folk-tales of Wales.* Oxford, 1949.

Journal of American Folklore, I—. American Folklore Society, Boston, 1888—.

KARKEEK, PAUL Q. *Transactions of the Devonshire Association,* XIV, 1882. Article on "The Witch of Ashreigney".

KEEN, MAURICE. *The Outlaws of Mediaeval Legend.* London, 1961.

KENNEDY, PATRICK. *Legendary Fictions of the Irish Celts.* London, 1886.

Old Fireside Tales of Wexford. Dublin University *Magazine,* January, 1867.

The Fireside Stories of Ireland. London, 1870.

The Key of Solomon, British Museum. Addit. MS. 36674.

KINLOCH, GEORGE R. *Ancient Scottish Ballads,* recovered from tradition and never before published. London and Edinburgh, 1827. MSS. 7 vols. 1826—. (See Child, V, p. 398.)

KIPLING, RUDYARD. *Rewards and Fairies.* London, 1910.

KIRK, ROBERT. *The Secret Commonwealth of Elves, Fauns, and Fairies.* Stirling, 1943. (Includes Andrew Lang's introduction to the earlier edition.)

LANG, ANDREW. *The Brown Fairy Book.* London, 1904.

The Crimson Fairy Book. new edn. London, 1935.

LARWOOD, J. and HOTTEN, J. C. *The History of Signboards from the Earliest Times to the Present Day.* London, 1966.

LAW, L. A. "Death and Burial Customs in Wiltshire", edited with notes by W. Crooke, *Folk-Lore,* XI, 1900.

Lay of Havelock the Dane, The, edited by W. Skeat. Oxford, 1902.

LAYARD, CECIL E. *Seasalter, Borough, Manor and Parish.* Whitstable, c. 1930.

LEAN, V. S. *Collectanea: Collections of Proverbs (English and Foreign), Folk-Lore and Superstitions,* 4 vols. Bristol, 1902–4.

LEE, LAURIE. *Cider with Rosie.* London, 1959.

LEGRAND, É. *Recueil de Contes Populaires Grecs.* (Coll. de Chansons et de Contes Populaires.) Paris, 1881.

LEISHMAN, JAMES FLEMING. *Linton Leaves.* London, 1937.

Leisure Hour, The. London, 1878.

LELAND, JOHN. *Itinerary, Rutter and Rutlandshire,* edited by Thomas Hearne. London, 1710–12.

LIEBRECHT, F. *Orient and Occident,* II, note on "Marking the Boat".

LLOYD, DAVID (CANON OF ST ASAPH). *State Worthies, or, The Statesmen and Favourites of England since the Reformation.* 2nd edn. with additions. London, 1670.

Lincolnshire Architectural Society and *Yorkshire Architectural Society,* Reports and papers read at meetings of the architectural societies of the counties of Lincoln and Nottingham, County of York, Archdeaconries of Northampton and Oakham, County of Bedford, Diocese of Worcester and County of Leicester, I–XVI. Lincoln, 1851–1902.

Lincolnshire Notes and Queries; a quarterly journal, 24 vols. Horncastle, 1889—.

LONES, T. E. "Darlaston Geese", *Folk-Lore,* XX.

LONG, W. H. *A Dictionary of the Isle of Wight Dialect.* 2nd edn. Portsmouth, 1931.

LONGFELLOW, H. W. *The Golden Legend.* London, 1893.

Longman's Magazine, XIV. D. J. Robertson, article on "Peerifool".

LOWER, M. A. *Chronicles of Pevensey,* with Notices Biographical, Topographical and Antiquarian. Lewes, 1846.

Old Speech and Manners in Sussex, Sussex Archaeological Collections, 13, 1861.

MACDONAGH, RICHARD, *Irish Life and Character.* London, 1898.

MACDOUGALL, J. and CALDER, G. *Folk Tales and Fairy Lore in Gaelic and English.* Edinburgh, 1910.

MACGREGOR, GEORGE. *The History of Burke and Hare.* Glasgow, c. 1889.

MCINNES, REV. D. *Waifs and Strays of Celtic Tradition,* I. London, 1889.

MACKENZIE, DONALD A. *Scottish Folk Lore and Folk Life.* London and Glasgow, 1935.

MACMANUS, S. *Donegal Fairy Stories.* London, 1900.

MACRITCHIE, DAVID. *Fians, Fairies and Picts.* London, 1893.

MACTAGGART, JOHN. *The Scottish Gallovidian Encyclopaedia,* c. 1889.

MASEFIELD, JOHN. *Collected Poems.* London, 1923.

MASSINGER, PHILIP. *The Picture.* London, 1630.

MEE, ARTHUR. *The Children's Encyclopaedia.* London, 1908–10.

MEGAS, G. A. *Greek Tales* (selected), 2 vols. Athens, 1962.

MOBERLY, MISS ANNE and JOURDAIN, MISS ELEANOR F. *An Adventure.* London, 1937.

MORISON, S. *Manx Fairy Tales.* 1911.

MUNSTER, COUNTESS OF. *My Memories and Miscellanies.* London, 1904.

MUSSET, ALFRED DE. *Comedies by Alfred de Musset,* translated and edited with an introduction by L. S. Gwynn. London, n.d.

NEWELL, W. W. "English Folk Tales in America", *Journal of American Folklore,* I and II, 1888.

NICHOLS, JOHN. *History of Leicestershire,* 4 vols. Leicester, 1795–1811.

Progresses of King James I, 4 vols. London, 1828.

NICHOLSON, JOHN. *Folk-Lore of East Yorkshire.* Driffield, 1890.

NORTH, T. J. *Sunken Cities*. Cardiff, 1957.

NORTHALL, G. F. *English Folk-rhymes*, a Collection of Traditional Verses relating to Places and Persons, Customs, Superstitions, etc. London, 1892.

Notes and Queries, Devon and Cornwall, XX.

NOTESTEIN, WALLACE. *A History of Witchcraft in England, from 1558 to 1718*. American Historical Association, 1911.

PARTRIDGE, ERIC. *The Shaggy Dog Story: Its Origin, Development and Nature*. London, 1953.

PAXTON, MATTHEW, "Crooked Crookham", in *Denham Tracts*, I.

PEELE, G. *Old Wives' Tale*. 1595.

Penny Histories, "A Strange and Wonderfull RELATION of an Old Woman ..." Seventeenth century. Bodleian MS. Wood, 704.

PENNY, JAMES ALPASS. *Folklore Round Horncastle*. 1915.

PERKINS, A. E. "Riddles from Negro Schoolchildren in New Orleans, La.", *Journal of American Folklore*, XV.

PILLET, DR ALFRED. *Das Fabliau von Les Trois Bossus Ménestrels*. 1901.

PITCAIRN, SIR ROBERT. *Ancient Criminal Trials in Scotland*. Edinburgh, 1833.

PLUNKETT, MISS ALICE. *Merry Games*.

Queen Elizabeth's Virginal Book, Morley, version of "The Untrue Wife's Song", arrangement in *First Book of Consort Lessons*, 1599.

RADFORD, E. and M. A. *Encyclopaedia of Superstitions*, edited and revised by C. Hole. London, 1961.

RAMSAY, E. B. *Reminiscences of Scottish Life and Character*. Edinburgh, 1858.

RANKE, KURT. "Die Zwei Brüder", Folk-Lore Fellows' Communications, CXIV. Helsinki.

RHYS, JOHN. *Celtic Folk-Lore, Welsh and Manx*, 2 vols. Oxford, 1901.

ROBERTS, CECIL E. *Gone Rustic*. London, 1934.

ROEDER, HELEN. *Saints and their Attributes*. London, 1955.

Romance of King Orfeo, The, in W. C. Hazlitt, *Fairy Tales, Legends and Romances illustrating Shakespeare and other Early English Writers*. London, 1875.

ROOTH, A. B. *The Cinderella Cycle*. Lund, 1951.

ROSENBERG, NEIL. MS. Unpublished thesis on "Talking Parrot Comic Stories", Indiana University, Bloomington, U.S.A.

SACHS, HANS. "The Wandering Scholar". *Seven Shrovetide Plays*. London, 1930.

SAXO GRAMMATICUS, *The Nine Books of the Danish History of Saxo Grammaticus*. Translated by Oliver Elton, 2 vols. The Norrœna Society.

SCOTT, SIR WALTER. *The Poetical Works*, author's edition, with Notes and Memoir. Edinburgh, n.d.

SEKI, KEIGO. *Folktales of Japan*. Chicago and London, 1963.

The Seven Sages, English metrical MS. text, composed in the late seventeenth century, edited by Wright. Percy Society's Publications, XVI.

SHARP, CECIL. *English Folk-Songs from the Southern Appalachians*, edited by Maud Karpeles. Oxford, 1932.

SHARP, CECIL, and BARING-GOULD, S. *English Folk-Songs for Schools*. London.

SIKES, WIRT. *British Goblins*. London, 1880.

SINCLAIR, CATHERINE. *Holiday House*. Edinburgh, 1839.

Sir Gawayne and the Green Knight, edited by Morris and Gollancz. London, 1920. (Recent edition by Neville Coghill.)

SPOONER, BARBARA C. *John Tregeagle of Trevorder: Man and Ghost*. Truro, 1935.

STEEL, FLORA ANNIE. *English Fairy Tales*, retold. London, 1918.

STRAPAROLA, GIOVANNI FRANCESCO. *The Nights of Straparola*, first translated into English by W. G. Waters. London, 1894.

STECKMESSER, KENT L. "Robin Hood and the American Outlaw", *Journal of American Folklore*, vol. 79. no. 312, pp. 348–55.

STRICKLAND, AGNES. *The Lives of the Queens of England, from the Norman Conquest.* 1864. 6 vols. Reprinted. London, 1915.

SUCHIER, *Der Schwanke von der Viermal Getöten Leiche*. 1922.

SWAHN, JAN-OJVIND. *The Tale of Cupid and Psyche*. Lund, 1955.

SWAYNE, REV. W. S. *History and Antiquities of Stalbridge*. 1889.

SYDOW, C. W. VON Article on Type 2142E ("Types of the Irish Folktales") in *Festschrift to Prof. E. A. Knock*. Lund, 1934.

Tales from The Dalesman 1939 to 1965. Clapham, Yorks.

TAYLOR, ARCHER. "The Merchant of Chichester", *Journal of American Folklore*, LX. "The Monk who was Four Times Slain", *Modern Philology*, XV, 1917. "The Predestined Wife", *Fabula*, II.

TAYLOR, RUPERT. *Political Prophecy in England*. New York, 1911.

THOMPSON, ERNEST SETON. *Two Little Savages*. London and New York, 1908.

THOMPSON, T. *The Life of Mother Shipton, a New Comedy*, n.d. [c. 1660].

THORPE, BENJAMIN. *Northern Mythology*, 3 vols. London, 1851.

TIDDT, R. J. E. *The Mummer's Play*. Oxford, 1923.

TREGELLAS, I. T. *Peeps into the Haunts and Homes of the Rural Population of Cornwall*. New edn. Truro, 1868.

WALKER, J. W. "The Historical Robin Hood", *Yorkshire Archaeological Journal*, 1944.

WALLER, JOHN. *The Shaggy Dog and other Surrealist Fables*. London, 1955.

WARD, H. L. D. *Catalogue of Romances in the Department of Manuscripts in the British Museum*, I and II. London, 1883 and 1893.

WATKINS, W. J. "A Cycle of Stories Current in Radnorshire", *Folk-Lore*, XLIII, 1932.

WATSON, W. G. W. *Somerset Life and Character*, Somerset Folk Series, 17. London, 1924.

WAUGH, A. and BENWELL, G. *Sea Enchantresses, the Tale of the Mermaid and her Kin*. London, 1961.

WEBSTER, JOHN. *The Displaying of Supposed Witchcraft, etc.*, by John Webster, Practitioner in Physick, London. Printed by J. M., 1677.

WEINBRANT, LENNIE, STEUR, LEONARD and SLOAN, HARRY. *The Elephant Book*. Los Angeles, 1963.

WELLS, J. E. *A Manual of Writings in Middle English*. New Haven, 1916.

WELSFORD, ENID. *The Fool, His Social and Literary History*. Gloucester, Mass., 1966.

WESSELSKI, A. *Heinrich Bebel's Schwänke*, II. Munich, 1907.

Der Hodscha Nasreddin, 2 vols. Weimar, 1911.

Die Schwänke und Schnurrer des Pfarrers Arlotts. 9 vols. Berlin, 1910.

West Sussex Gazette and South of England Advertiser.

WHISTLER, C. W. "Local Traditions of the Quantocks", *Folk-Lore*, XIX, 1908.

WHITE, W. *White's History, Gazetteer and Directory of Lincolnshire*. London, 1882.

WILLIAM OF MALMESBURY. *Chronicle*, translated and edited by J. A. Giles. London, 1897.

WILSON, BARBARA KER. *Scottish Folk-Tales and Legends*. London, 1954.

Wisdom of Dr. Dodypol. Anon. 1600.

WISE, J. R. *The New Forest, its History and its Scenery*. London, 1863.

WOOD, ANTHONY À. *Athenae Oxonienes.*, 2nd edn., 2 vols. London, 1721.

WRIGHT, JOSEPH. *The English Dialect Dictionary*, 6 vols. London, 1898–1905.

WYBARNE, J. *The New Age of Old Names*. London, 1609.

YARINGTON, ROBERT. *Two Lamentable Tragedies, or, Two Tragedies in One*. London, 1601.

YONGE, CHARLOTTE M. "The Cat of Cat Copse", *The Monthly Packet*, Christmas 1879.

The History of Sir Thomas Thumb. Edinburgh and London, 1855.

"The Prince and the Page", *The Monthly Packet*, January to December 1865.

ZŎNG-IN-ZŎB, *Folk Tales from Korea*. London, 1952.

INDEX OF TALE-TYPES AND
MIGRATORY LEGENDS

For particulars of these and other Type-Index Lists used see the first part of the List of Books Quoted, Cited and Consulted. It will be noticed that the numbers in the Migratory Legends are consecutive to those in the Aarne–Thompson Tale Type Index. They are numbered five, ten, fifteen, etc. The intermediate numbers, marked by a star, are my own suggested types. Ernest Baughman occasionally interpolates a type number in his book *Type and Motif Index of the Folktales of England and North America*. Where these have been used "Baughman" has been added to the type name.

A TALE-TYPES

TALE-TYPE	EXAMPLES
1* THE FOX STEALS THE BASKET	"The Fox and the Magpie" [A. I
34 THE WOLF DIVES INTO THE WATER FOR THE REFLECTED CHEESE	"The Wolf, the Laborer, the Fox and the Cheese" [A. I
56 FOX DESTROYS THE YOUNG OF THE MAGPIES, WHO AVENGE THEMSELVES	"The Fox and the Magpie" [A. I
100* THE PARROT ABUSES THE DOG	1 "The Hawk and the Parrot, Parrot VII" [A. III 2 "The Scotch Parrot, Parrot X" [A. III
110 BELLING THE CAT	"Belling the Cat" [A. I
111 THE CAT AND THE MOUSE CONVERSE	1 "The Cattie sits in the Kiln-Ring Spinning" [A. V 2 "Mouse and Mouser" [A. V
111A* THE DRUNKARD'S PROMISE	1 "The Mouse in the Ale-Cask" [A. III 2 "Dutch Courage" [A. III
113A THE KING OF THE CATS IS DEAD	"The King of the Cats" [B. V
113B (distant variant) THE CAT AS SHAM HOLY MAN	"The Harnit and the Bittle" [A. I
124 BLOWING THE HOUSE IN	1 "The Three Wee Pigs" [A. V 2 "The Three Little Pigs" [A. V 3 "The Three Little Pigs" [A. V 4 "The Deukie and the Tod" [A. V

	7 "The Lambton Worm"	[A. II
	8 "Saint George"	[B. XI
	9 "The Red Etin"	[A. II
	10 "Jack and the King's Daughter"	[A. II

301A THE THREE STOLEN PRINCESSES   1   "The Little Red Hairy Man"
[A. II

2   "The Little Redman"   [A. II

Norton also cites "Old Bluebeard", from Mrs Jane Gentry, Hot Springs, N. Carolina.

302   THE OGRE'S HEART IN THE EGG   "The Widow's Son and an Old Man"   [A. II

303   THE TWINS OR BLOOD BROTHERS   1   "Child Rowland"   [A. II
(or 312D)

(variant with element of 812)   2   "The Red Etin"   [A. II
  3   "The King of England"   [A. II
  4   "The Ticky Wee Man"   [A. II
  5   "The Three-Legged Hare"   [A. II
  6   "The Dräglin' Hogney"   [A. II
303, parts 3 and 5, distant variant   7   "Allison Gross"   [A. II
  8   "The Fish of Gold"   [A. II

Norton also cites "Tom Fisher and John Fisher", from *Some County Cork Folk Tales*, A. Ni Chróinin, 1930.

304   THE HUNTER   "The White-Milk Deer"   [A. II

311   THREE SISTERS RESCUED FROM THE MOUNTAIN (rescued by their sister)   "Peerifool"   [A. II

(variant)   "Captain Murderer"   [A. II

312D   BROTHER SAVES HIS   1   "Child Rowland"   [A. II
312B (var.) SISTER AND BROTHERS   2   "The Clever Little Tailor"   [A. II
327B   FROM THE DRAGON
1088

313   THE GIRL AS HELPER IN THE   1   "The Green Man of Knowledge"
HERO'S FLIGHT   [A. II
  2   "Green Sleeves"   [A. II
(variant)   3   "The Leaves that Hung but never Grew"   [A. II
  4   "Nicht Nought Nothing"   [A. II
  5   "Silly Jack and the Robin"   [A. II
  6   "The Black Cloak"   [A. II
  7   "Clever Pat"   [A. II
  8   "The Black Dog of the Wild Forest"   [A. II

313 *cont.*   9 "Daughter Greengown"   [A. II
                                                  10 "The White-Milk Deer"   [A. II

Norton also has "Lady Featherflight", from Cambridge, Mass.; "De Debble and Young
Prince had a Race", *JAFL* (1891), IV; "The Wren and the Mouse", from County Cork.

313 variants   "Young Bekie"   [A. II
                                                  "Becket's Parents"   [B VIII

325 THE MAGICIAN AND HIS PUPIL   1 "The Black King of Morocco"
                                                                            [A. II
                                     2 "The King of the Black Art"
                                                                            [A. II

325* APPRENTICE AND GHOST   1 "The Master and His Pupil"
                                                                            [A. II
                                     2 "Mass John Scott"   [B. VI
                                     3 "Auld Scairie and the Black
                                     Art"   [B. XIII

326 THE YOUTH WHO WANTED TO   1 "The Devil and the Hogshead"
     KNOW WHAT FEAR WAS   [B. III
                                     2 "Ashypelt"   [A. II
                                     3 "The Boy who feared Nothing"
                                                                            [A. II
                                     4 "A Wager won"   [A. III
                                     5 "The Dauntless Girl"   [A. II
(distant variant)   6 "The Death Bree"   [B. VI

326A SOUL RELEASED FROM TORMENT   1 "Lousy Jack and his Eleven
                                     Brothers"   [A. II
                                     2 "The Grey Castle"   [A. II
                                     3 "The Haunted Castle"   [A. II
                                     4 "The Golden Ball"   [A. II
                                     5 "The Three Golden Balls" [A. V
                                     6 "The Black Cat"   [A. II
                                     7 "The King of the Cats"   [A. II
                                     8 "Twopenny Priss"   [A. II
                                     9 "The Cutler and the Tinker"
                                                                            [A. II

Many other versions in Norton I, pp. 156–79, as follows: "The Girl and the Skull", *Joe
Miller's Jests*, p. 93; "Skeleton", Bacon-Parsons, p. 299; "The Wager", *Folk Lore*, XV,
p. 104; "The Gibbet", Jackson-Burne, pp. 592–3; "The Challenge", F. A. Law, *Death and
Burial Customs in Wiltshire*; "The Boy (or Girl) who died of Fear", and many other
American versions.

326B THE FEARLESS YOUTH   1 "Resurrection Men"   [A. III
                                     2 "The Man who didn't believe
                                     in Ghosts and 'Chantments'" [A. II
                                     3 "Down the Rotten Row"   [A. III

327 THE CHILDREN AND THE OGRE   1 "Black Brottie"   [A. II
                                     2 "Mally Whuppie"   [A. II
                                     3 "Mr Miacca"   [A. V

| 327B | THE DWARF AND THE GIANT (loose variant) | | "The Clever Little Tailor" | [A. II |

327C	THE DEVIL CARRIES THE CHILDREN HOME IN A SACK	1	"Jack the Buttermilk"	[A. II
		2	"The Enchanted Mountain"	[A. II
		3	"Fairy Jip and Witch One-Eye"	[A. II
		4	"Tib and the Old Witch"	[A. II

See "Two Lost Babes" (American), from R. Chase, *Grandfather Tales*; Norton also gives three Irish tales: "Jim, Jack and Perley", from T. Kavanagh, *Kilkenny Folk-Tales*, *Béaloideas*, II, pp. 10–12; "Hairy Rouchy", from Kennedy, *Old Fireside Stories of Wexford*, "Whittlegaire", from *Folk-Lore*, IV (1893), *Folk-Lore Gleanings from County Leitrim*, Leland L. Duncan. (These are type 327B.)

328	THE BOY STEALS THE GIANT'S TREASURE	1	Jack and the Beanstalk A	[A. II
		2	Jack and the Beanstalk B	[A. II
		3	Jack and the Beanstalk C	[A.II

Norton also gives two American versions, I, pp. 209–12.

| | | 4 | "Mally Whuppie" | [A. II |
| | | 5 | "Jack the Giant-Killer B" | [A. II |

See also types 1088, 507A.

| 328 and 1535 | | 6 | "Jack and the Giants" | [A. II |

330	THE SMITH OUTWITS THE DEVIL	1	"The Smith and the Devil"	[A. II
		2	"Dule upon Dun"	[A. II
		3	"The Man who wouldn't go out at Night"	[A. II
		4	"The Devil's Whetstone"	[B. III
		5	"The Blacksmith who sold himself to the Devil"	[A. II
		6	"Will the Smith"	[A. II
		7	"The Old Smith"	[A. II

| 331 | THE SPIRIT IN THE BOTTLE | | "The Ghost in the Bottle" | [B. VI |

See also Clouston, *Fictions*, and Sutherland Dempster, *Folk-Lore Journal* (1888), p. 153.

| 331 (variant) | | | "Yallery Brown" | [A. II |

| 333 | THE GLUTTON | | "Finn and the Dragon" | [A. II |

| 361 | BEARSKIN (The Task) | | "The Coat" | [A. II |

| 363 | THE VAMPIRE | | "Wanted, a Husband" | [A. II |

365	THE DEAD BRIDEGROOM CARRIES OFF HIS BRIDE	1	"The Lovers of Porthgwarra"	[B. VI
		2	"The Spectre Bridegroom"	[B. VI
		3	"The Tragedy of Sweet William and Fair Nancy"	[B. VI

365 (variant)	4 "Yorkshire Jack"	[B. VI
	5 "The Suffolk Miracle"	[B. VI
	6 "The Fair Maid of Clifton"	
		[B. VI
366 (variant) THE MAN FROM THE GALLOWS	1 "The Bone"	[A. V
	2 "The Gay Lady that went to Church"	[A. V
	3 "The Golden Arm"	[A. V
	4 "Ma Uncle Sandy"	[A. V
	5 "The Old Man at the White House"	[A. V
	6 "Peggy with the Wooden Leggy"	[A. V
	7 "The Liver"	[A. V
	8 "The Strange Visitor"	[A. V
	9 (a & b) "Teeny-Tiny"	[A. V

Variants: "The Bone" from Cheshire, R. Holland, *Cheshire Glossary*, p. 37; "The Silver Toe", Texas, *FLS* v, pp. 41–2, also from Arkansas, N. Carolina; "Chunk o' Meat", Chase, *Grandfather Tales*, p. 222.

400 THE MAN ON A QUEST FOR HIS LOST WIFE	1 "The Princess of the Blue Mountains"	[A. II
	2 "Wild Edric"	[A. II
401 THE PRINCESS TRANSFORMED INTO A DEER (distant variants)	1 "The Enchanted Man"	[A. II
	2 "The Singing Bride"	[A. II
402 THE MOUSE (CAT, FROG, ETC.) AS BRIDE	1 "The Three Feathers" or "Jack and the Puddock"	[A. II
	2 "The Three Feathers"	[A. II
402 A* PRINCESS TRANSFORMED TO TOAD IS DISENCHANTED BY HERO'S KISS	1 "Lady Isabel and the Elf-Knight"	[A. II
	2 "The Marriage of Sir Gawain"	[A. II
432 I THE PRINCE AS BIRD	"Earl Mar's Daughter"	[A. II
433 (variant) THE PRINCE AS SERPENT	"The Laidley Worm"	[A. II
440 THE FROG KING	1 "The Frog"	[A. II
	2 "The Frog Prince"	[A. II
	3 "The Frog Sweetheart"	[A. II
	4 "The Paddo"	[A. II
	5 "The Well of the World's End"	[A. II

Norton also gives the following versions: "The Maiden and the Frog" (verse) Halliwell, *Popular Rhymes*, pp. 43–7; "The Prince Paddock", from a letter of Sir Walter Scott, quoted by Edgar Taylor in *Gammer Grethel* (1839), p. 344.

425 THE SEARCH FOR THE LOST HUSBAND	1 "The Black Bull of Norroway"	[A. II

425A	THE MONSTER (ANIMAL) AS BRIDEGROOM	2	"The Glass Mountain"	[A. II
		3	"The Glass Mountains"	[A. II
		4	"The Red Bull of Norroway"	[A. II
425C	BEAUTY AND THE BEAST	5	"The Small-Tooth Dog"	[A. II
		6	"Sorrow and Love"	[A. II
		7	"The Stove"	[A. II
		8	"The Three Feathers"	[A. II

Cf. "Whiteberry Whittington", Chase, *Grandfather Tales*, p. 52; *JAFL*, XXXVIII, pp. 357–9.

450A			"Allison Gross"	[A. II
451	THE MAIDEN WHO SEEKS HER BROTHERS		"The Seven Brothers"	[A. II
470 I (variant)	FRIENDS IN LIFE AND DEATH		"Thomas the Rhymer"	[B. V
471A	THE MONK AND THE BIRD	1	"The Noontide Ghost"	[A II.
		2	"The Stone-Mason of the Charltons"	[A. II
480	THE SPINNING-WOMEN BY THE SPRING	1	"The Glass Ball"	[A. II
		2	"The Glass House"	[A. II
		3	"The Green Lady" (*a*)	[A. II
			"The Green Lady" (*b*)	
		4	"The Little Watercress Girl"	[A. II
		5	"The Three Heads in the Well"	[A. II
		6	"The Man with a Long Nose"	[A. II
		7	"The Bottle of Water from the World's End Well"	[A. II
		8	"The Old Witch"	[A. II
		9	"The Three Gold Heads"	[A. II
		10	"The Wal at the World's End"	[A. II

Norton also gives the following: "The Old Hag's Long Leather Bag", from S. MacManus, *Donegal Fairy Stories*, pp. 233–56 (London, 1900); Norton II, pp. 7–12; "The Two Girls", p. 16, from Henderson, pp. 349–50; "Old Gally Mander", from *JAFL*, XXXVIII, pp. 368–70; "The Three Brothers and the Bag", *JAFL*, VIII, pp. 143–4; "The Bad Gal and the Good Gal", *Texas Folk-Lore*, pp. 43–5; "The Maid in the Country Underground", Kennedy, pp. 33–7 (Irish).

500	THE NAME OF THE HELPER		"Duffy and the Devil"	[A. II
	Cf. 310 and 311	2	"Peerifool"	[A. II
		3	"Titty Tod"	[A. II
		4	"Tom Tit Tot"	[A. II

500 *cont.* 5 "The Gipsy Woman", sequel
to "Tom Tit Tot" [A. II
6 "Whuppity Stoorie" [A. II

501 THE THREE OLD WOMEN HELPERS I "Habetrot" [A. II
2 "A Various Whuppity Stoorie" [A. II

Norton gives also "The Lazy Beauty and her Aunts", from Kennedy, *Old Fireside Stories of Wexford. Dublin University Magazine*, 1867. pp. 18–20.

502 (variant) THE WILD MAN "Three for a Pot" [A. II

503 THE GIFTS OF THE LITTLE I "The Man with the Hump" [A. II
PEOPLE
2 "The Two Humps" [A. II

503 (variants) 3 "Food and Fire and Company" [A. II
4 "Goblin Combe" [A. II
5 "That's Enough to go on with" [A. II

503 III 6 "The Miser and the Fairies of the Gump" [A. II

505 THE DEAD MAN AS HELPER I "Jack and the Ghosts" [A. II
2 "Four Eggs a Penny" [A. II

507A THE MONSTER'S BRIDE I "Jack and the Giants" [A. II
2 "The Little Cinder Girl" [A. II
3 "The Red Etin" [A. II

510 CINDERELLA AND CAP O' RUSHES I "Ashpitel" [A. II
510 (variant) 2 "The Broken Pitcher" [A. II
510B 3 "Cap o' Rushes"
"The Princess and the Golden Cow" [A. II
4 "Catskin" [A. II

510 (variant) 5 "The Girl who went through Fire, Water and the Golden Gate" [A. II

510 (distant variant) 6 "The Grey Castle" [A. II
7 "The Little Cinder-Girl" [A. II
510B 8 "Mossycoat" [A. II
9 "Rashie Coat" [A. II
10 "Rashin Coatie" [A. II
11 "The Red Calf" [A. II
12 "Rushen Coatie" [A. II
13 "Tattercoats" [A. II
14 "Ashey Pelt" [A. II
15 "The Black Yow" [A. II
510 (variant) 16 "Finger Lock" [A. II

511A THE LITTLE RED OX	1 "De Little Bull-calf, de Three Giants and de Fiery Dragon" [A. II	
	2 "The Little Black Bull", or "The Little Bull-calf" [A. II	
513* (variant) THE EXTRAORDINARY COMPANIONS	"The Little Red Hairy Man" [A. II	

Norton II (pp. 97–9) gives, under 513B, THE LAND AND WATER SHIP, "Hardy Hardback", from N. Carolina, *JAFL*, XXXVIII, pp. 346–9, and I. G. Carter, *Tales from the Southern Blue Ridge*, 3.

531 FERDINAND THE TRUE AND FERDINAND THE FALSE	"The Giant and the Seven Heads" [A. II
533 THE SPEAKING HORSEHEAD	"Roswal and Lilian" [A. IV
550 (variant) or 554 THE BIRD, THE HORSE AND THE PRINCESS	"The King of the Herrings" [A. II
551 THE SONS ON A QUEST FOR A WONDERFUL REMEDY FOR THEIR FATHER	1 "The King of England and the Golden Apples" [A. II 2 "The Water of Life" [A. II
554 THE GRATEFUL ANIMALS	1 "The King of the Herrings" [A. II
554A* KING OF THE HERRINGS B	2 "King's Jack" [A. II 3 "The Red Lion of the Forest" [A. II
555 THE FISHER AND HIS WIFE	"The Old Woman who lived in a Vinegar Bottle" [A. II
559 DUNG BEETLE	"Jack and his Bargains" [A. II

Norton II, p. 24, quotes a version from Boggs, *N. Carolina*, p. 297, "The Girl Who Never Laughed".

560 THE MAGIC RING	1 "Jack and his Golden Snuff-Box" [A. II

Also in Norton (II, p. 126), "The Grateful Beasts", from Kennedy, *Fireside Stories of Ireland*, pp. 95–8.

563 THE ASS, THE TABLE AND THE STICK	1 "The Ass, the Table and the Stick." [A. II 2 "The Boy and his Wages" [A. II 3 "The Seven Mysteries of the Luck" [A. II

See also: "Jack and the North-West Wind", R. Chase, *Jack Tales* (variant of "Boots and the North Wind"), Norton II, p. 136 (two versions). Also in Norton (II, p. 145), "Tablecloth, Donkey and Club", from *JAFL*, XXX, pp. 210–12. "The Three Gifts", II, 142, from Kennedy (Wexford).

565 (cf. 325* Sorcerer's apprentice)   1   "The Master and his Pupil" [A. II
    THE MAGIC MILL   2   "The Old Handmill"   [A. II

Also in Norton (II, p. 150), "The Magic Storm".

566   THE THREE MAGIC OBJECTS AND   "Fortunatus"   [A. II
    THE WONDERFUL FRUIT

569   THE KNAPSACK, THE HAT AND   1   "Habie's Whistle"   [A. II
    THE HORN   2   "The King of the Cats"   [A. II
        3   "The Magic Knapsack"   [A. II

570   THE RABBIT HERD   1   "Jock and His Lulls"   [A. II

577   THE KING'S TASKS   "The Three Brothers and the
        Three Tasks"   [A. II

Also in Norton (II, p. 159), "The Enchanted Lady", *JAFL*, XXXIII (1945), from Isabel
Gordon-Carter, *Mountain White Folk-Lore*, no. 5, pp. 350–1. See also R. Chase, *Jack
Tales*.

571   ALL STICK TOGETHER   "Lazy Jack"   [A. II

585   THE SPINDLE, THE SHUTTLE   "Jack and the Ghosts"   [A. II
    AND THE NEEDLE

592   THE DANCE AMONG THORNS   "The Friar and the Boy"   [A. II

613 (?)   THE TWO TRAVELLERS   "The Lion, the Leper and the
        Tod"   [A. I

650   STRONG JOHN   1   "Strong Jack"   [A. II
        2   "The Twenty-one-Year Old
        Giant"   [A. II

650 (variant)   3   "Tom Hickathrift"   [A. II
        4   "Tom and the Giant Blunder-
        buss"   [A. II

653   THE FOUR SKILLFUL BROTHERS   1   "The Three Sons"   [A. II

673   THE WHITE SERPENT'S FLESH   1   "Sir James Ramsey of Banff"
        [B. XII
        2   "Michael Scott"   [B. III

700   TOM THUMB   1   "Dathera Dad"   [B. V
        2   "Tom Thumb"   [A. II

706   THE MAIDEN WITHOUT HANDS   1   "The Cruel Stepmother"   [A. II
        2   "Daughter Doris"   [A. II

708   THE WONDER-CHILD   1   "De Little Fox"   [A. II
        2   "The Little Squirrel"   [A. II

709   SNOW-WHITE   "Snow-White"   [A. II

711   THE BEAUTIFUL AND UGLY TWIN   "Kate Crackernuts"   [A. II

This type has been arbitrarily bestowed upon *"Kate Crackernuts"*, which has no special resemblance to it.

720   MY MOTHER SLEW ME, MY   1   "Applie and Orangie"   [A. II
      FATHER ATE ME   2   "The Little Bird"   [A. II
                                  3   "The Milk-White Doo"   [A. II
                                  4   "Orange and Lemon"   [A. II
                                  5   "Pippety-Pew"   [A. II
                                  6   "The Rose-Tree" ("The
                                      Wicked Stepmother")   [A. II
                                  7   "Rosy"   [A. II
                                  8   "The Satin Frock"   [A. II
variant   9   "Fair Ellen of Radcliffe"   [B. VIII

Norton also gives: "The Cruel Stepmother and her Little Daughter", from Blakeborough, *Wit etc. of the North Riding of Yorkshire*, 2nd edn pp. 263–5; *"Lemon, Apple and Orange"*, from *Journal of the Folk-Song Society*, II (1906); pp. 295–6; from F. Kidson, Liverpool; three other brief versions from Southport and Lincolnshire; and "The Murderous Mother", three very short versions from America.

726   THE OLDEST ON THE FARM   1   "The Oldest on the Farm" [A. III
                                  2   "The Key of Craigiehow" [A. II
                                  3   "The Painswick Ancients" [A. III
                                  4   "The Three Old Men of
                                      Painswick"   [A. III
                                  5   "Old Parr"   [B. VIII

736A   THE RING OF POLYCRATES   "Saint Egwin"   [B. XI
variant

Norton also gives *Old Jenkins* (II, p. 207), from Clouston, *Popular Tales*, II, p. 97; a version from the Cotswolds, in *JCRC*, 30 October 1937; and one from a Mr Ward, of Ashbourne, Derbyshire, told on 4 July 1937.

745A   THE PREDESTINED TREASURE   "The Miser of Winchelsea"   [B. IX

750   THE WISHES   1   "The Woodman and the Fairy"
                                      or "The Three Wishes"   [A. II
                                      "The Three Wishes"   [A. II
750AI   2   "Simmerwater"   [B. IX
                                  3   "Bomere Pool"   [B. IX
                                  4   "The Three Wishes"   [A. III

750B   HOSPITALITY REWARDED   5   "Christ and the Peas"   [A. I
                                  6   "A Loaf of Bread"   [B. IX
                                  7   "The Traveller's Corn-Sack"
                                                                    [B. IX

750*   HOSPITALITY BLESSED   "The Poor Widow and her Son"
                                                                    [A. II

Norton (II, pp. 221–4) also gives brief versions from Gutch and Peacock, pp. 163, 286; from L. Salmon, *Folk-Lore of the Kennet Valley*, p. 423 (Berkshire); Leather, *Herefordshire*, p. 79; Suffling, *Norfolk Broads*, pp. 161–2; Henderson, 2nd edn p. 82; from an old woman of the North Riding.

751   THE GREEDY PEASANT-WOMAN   1   "The Greedy Peasant-Woman"
    [A. I

751A   THE PEASANT-WOMAN IS   2   "The Owl was a Baker's
    CHANGED INTO A WOODPECKER   Daughter"   [A. II

752B   THE FORGOTTEN WIND   "Answer to Prayer"   [A. III

Norton (II, p. 231) also gives a similar story from L. Salmon, *Folk-Lore in the Kennet Valley*, *Folk-Lore*, XIII, p. 419.

753   CHRIST AND THE SMITH   1   "The Blacksmith from Ireland"
    [A. II
    2   "The Old Smith"   [A. II
753* (variant)   3   "St Aloys and the Lame Nag"
    [B. XI
753   4   "Will the Smith"   [A. II
    5   "The Smith and his Dame"   [A. II

Norton (II, pp. 233–4), gives a version from *Kilkenny Folk-Lore*, "Robin the Blacksmith", collected by T. Kavanagh, *Béaloideas*, II, pp. 346–8.

766   THE SEVEN SLEEPERS   1   "King Herla"   [A. II
    2   "The Noontide Ghost"   [A. II
    3   "The Piper of Glendevon"   [B. IX
    4   "The Stone-Mason of the
    Charltons"   [A. II
    5   "Potter Thompson"   [B. XI
    6   "The Key of Craigachow"   [A. II
    7   "Canobie Dick and Thomas
    of Ercildoun"   [B. IX
    8   "Sir Guy the Seeker"   [B. IX
    9   "The Wizard of Alderley Edge"
    [B. XII
variant   10   "The Fairies of Merlin's Craig"
    [B. V

777 (formerly 754***)   1   "The Wandering Jew"   [B. XII
    THE WANDERING JEW   2   "The Curse of the Shoemakers"
    [B. XII

779B*   DISRESPECTFUL CHILDREN   "The Pear Drum"   [A. V
    PUNISHED

780   THE SINGING BONE   1   "Binnorie"   [A. II
780 (variant)   2   "St Kenelm"   [B. XI

802   THE PEASANT IN HEAVEN   1   "Crowdy of Highworth"   [A. III
    2   "A Pitman's Dream" (heaven)
    [A. III
    3   "A Pitman's Dream" (hell)
    [A. III
    4   "St Antony's"   [A. III

810   THE SNARES OF THE EVIL ONE   1   "The Fisherman and his Wife"
    [A. II

(variant)

2 "The Man who wouldn't go out at Night" [A. II

3 "The Vicar and the Devil" [B. III

4 "Meg o' Meldon's Treasure" [B. VI

5 "Faust" [B. III

812 THE DEVIL'S RIDDLE

1 "The Devil's Riddle" [A. II

812* THE DEVIL'S RIDDLE OTHERWISE SOLVED

1 "Jack o' Kent's Funeral" [B. III

2 "The Man in the Wilderness" [A. II

813B THE ACCURSED GRANDSON

1 "The Man who wouldn't go out at Night" [A. II

2 "The Man who Sold his Soul to the Devil" [B. III

815* THE SHOEMAKER WHO MADE SHOES FOR THE DEVIL

1 "The Devil and the Tailor" [A. II

2 "The Cresswell Tailor" [B. III

3 "The Devil and the Blacksmith" [B. III

817* DEVIL LEAVES AT MENTION OF GOD'S NAME

1 "The Devil's Bolts" [B. III

2 "Diabolic Invitation to Supper" [B. III

3 "The Timber and the Devil" [B. III

819* THE DEVIL'S PORTRAIT

"The Little Boy and the Devil" [B. III

821B THE DEVIL AS ADVOCATE

1 "George Buchanan and the Eggs" [A. III

2 "The Treacherous Innkeeper" [B. III

Norton (II, p. 242), also gives a version from *JAFL*, IX, p. 278, from Pamela T. Smith, *Two Negro Stories from Jamaica*.

835A* HOW THE DRUNK MAN WAS CURED

1 "Not so easy Cured" [A. III

2 "The Clerk of Bartholmy" [A. III

836 and 751 PRIDE IS PUNISHED

"The First Cornish Mole" [A. I

851 THE PRINCESS WHO CANNOT SOLVE THE RIDDLE

"The Young Prince" [A. IV

852 THE HERO FORCES THE PRINCESS TO SAY "THAT IS A LIE"

1 "Jack and the King, or, 'You're a Liar'" [A. IV

2 "The King of the Liars" [A. IV

853	HERO CATCHES THE PRINCESS WITH HER OWN WORDS	1	"The Foolish Brother"	[A. IV
		2	"The Princess of Canterbury"	[A. II
		3	"Daft Jack and the Heiress"	[A. IV
		4	"The Three Questions"	[A. IV
870A	THE LITTLE GOOSE-GIRL		"Duncombe"	[B. IX
875 or 910	THE CLEVER PEASANT GIRL	1	"A Pottle o' Brains"	[A. III
		2	"Thomasina Bonaventure"	[B. IX
		3	"Gobborn Seer"	[A. IV
882A*	SUITORS AT THE SPINNING WHEEL		"The Wright's Chaste Wife"	[A. IV

Norton (II, pp. 256–7), gives an Irish version from Kennedy, *Fireside Stories*, pp. 91–4, "The Poor Girl that became a Queen".

882	WAGER ON THE WIFE'S CHASTITY	"The 'Pinated Englishman and Hellfire Jack"	[A. IV
885A	THE SEEMINGLY DEAD	"The Gay Goshawk"	[A. II
887	GRISELDA (variant)	"The Nut-Brown Maid"	[A. IV
888A	THE WIFE WHO WOULD NOT BE BEATEN	"Right Nought"	[A. III
893	THE UNRELIABLE FRIENDS	"True Friendship"	[A. IV
900 (variant)	KING THRUSHBEARD	"Ina the King"	[B. VIII
903A*	QUICK-TEMPERED MAIDEN FINDS A MAN EQUALLY QUICK-TEMPERED	"The Watchers by the Well"	[A. II

Norton (II, pp. 262–3), gives an Irish version, *The Haughty Princess*, from Kennedy, *Fireside Stories*, pp. 114–16.

910	PRECEPTS BOUGHT OR GIVEN PROVE CORRECT	1	"The Tale of Ivan"	[A. IV
		2	"The Three Good Advices"	[A. IV
910A	WISE THROUGH EXPERIENCE	3	"The Tinner of Chyannor"	[A. IV
variant		4	"Master Vavasour and Turpin His Man"	[A. III
910B	THE SERVANT'S GOOD COUNSELS	5	"Yalla Britches"	[A. IV
910D	THE TREASURE OF THE HANGING MAN	6	"The Heir of Linne"	[A. IV
910G or 875	MAN BUYS A PENNYWORTH OF WIT	7	"A Pottle o' Brains"	[A. III
920B	WHAT KIND OF BIRD?		"The Sons of the Conqueror"	[B. VIII
920C	TEST OF PATERNITY		"Friar Bacon V"	[B. XIII

921 THE KING AND THE PEASANT'S SON	1 "Farmer Gag's Clever Son"	[A. III
	2 "The Clever Boy"	[A. IV
	3 "Jack Hornby"	[A. III
	4 "The King and the Peasant's Son"	[A. III
	5 "Under the Earth I go"	[A. IV
	6 "Discreet Answers"	[A. III
	7 "Jack and the Vicar"	[A. III
	8 "Lord Craven"	[A. III
921 (distant variants)	1 "The King and the Hermit"	[A. IV
	2 "The King and the Northern Man"	[A. IV
	3 "The King and the Tanner"	[A. IV
921B* THIEF, BEGGAR, MURDERER	"The Friar who told the Five Children's Fortunes	[A. III

Norton (II, p. 272), gives a version from *JAFL*, "Tales from the South Blue Ridge", I. G. Carter, pp. 370–1, "The King and Old George Buchanan".

922 THE SHEPHERD SUBSTITUTING FOR THE PRIEST ANSWERS THE KING'S QUESTIONS	1 "The Independent Bishop"	[A. IV
	2 "King John and the Abbot of Canterbury"	[A. IV
	3 "The King and the Miller"	[A. IV
922 (or 853?)	4 "Silly Jack"	[A. IV
	5 "Three Questions"	[A. IV
922	6 "Two Little Scotch Boys"	[A. III
	7 "The Story of the Miller"	

Norton (II, pp. 277–9), also gives a version of "The Three Questions" from Ireland contributed to *Béaloideas* II, by S. Ó'Duilearga; and one from *JAFL*, XIX, pp. 58–9. See also "George Buchanan and the Bishop" (pt. 1, section 3), from *John Cheap the Chapman*, pp. 11–12.

923 LOVE LIKE SALT	1 "Cap o' Rushes"	[A. IV
	2 "Sugar and Salt"	[A. IV
924B THE LANGUAGE OF SIGNS MISUNDERSTOOD	1 "The Miller at the Professors' Examination"	[A. IV
	2 "The Professor of Signs"	[A. IV
	3 "The Professor of Signs"	[A. IV
927 OUT-RIDDLING THE JUDGE	1 "The Life-Saving Riddle"	[A. IV
	2 "The Condemned Man's Riddle"	[A. IV
	3 "A Riddle Story"	[A. IV
	4 "Under the Earth I Go"	[A. IV

Norton also has 52 pages (III, 1*a*–1*z*, 1 A–1 Z) of examples of the life-saving riddle from many countries, including America.

930 FATED BRIDE'S RING IN THE SEA   1   "The Bride who had never been Kissed"   [A. IV
   2   "The Stepney Lady"   [A. II
   3   "Fairest of All Others"   [A. II
   4   "The Fish and the Ring"   [A. II

Norton (III, p. 2) also gives a long ballad *The Yorkshire Knight, or the Fortunate Farmer's Daughter*, from *The Ballads and Songs of Yorkshire*, by C. J. D. Ingledew (London, 1860), pp. 193–202.

934 (changed from 932*)   "Osmotherly" or "Rosemary
   THE PRINCE AND THE STORM   Topping"   [B. IX

939A   KILLING THE RETURNED   1   "The Penryn Tragedy"   [B. VIII
    SOLDIER   2   "A Lay Ghost-Layer"   [B. VI

955   THE ROBBER BRIDEGROOM   1   "Mr Fox"   [A. IV
   2   "The Cellar of Blood"   [A. IV
   3   "Dr. Forster"   [A. II

955 (variant)   1   "Bobby Rag"   [A. IV
   2   "The Oxford Student"   [B. IX
   3   "The Lass 'at seed her own Grave dug"   [B. VIII
   4   "Mr. Fox's Courtship"   [A. IV
   5   "The Girl who got up a Tree"   [A. IV

956A   AT THE ROBBER'S HOUSE   1   "The Black and his Master"   [A. IV
   2   "A Burker Story"   [B. VIII
   3   "The Time I ran away with my Brothers"   [B. VIII

956B   THE CLEVER MAIDEN AT   1   "The Brave Maid-Servant" [A. IV
    HOME KILLS THE ROBBERS   2   "The Clever Maid and the Robber"   [A. IV
   3   "The Cook at Combewell" [B. IX
   4   "The Hand"   [A. II
   5   "The Robber and the Housekeeper"   [A. IV
   6   The Servant-Maid of the High Spital"   [B. IX
   7   "Mary the Maid of the Inn"   [B. IX

958E*   DEEP SLEEP BROUGHT ON   "The Hand of Glory"   [B. XII
    BY ROBBER

958D*   ROBBER AS BEGGAR   "The Long Pack"   [B. IX

960A   THE CRANES OF IBYCUS   "The Shepherd and the Crows"   [B. XII

964	THIEF DECEIVED INTO BETRAYING HIMSELF BY A GESTURE		"The Thief Detected" [A. III
967	MAN SAVED BY A SPIDER		"Bruce and the Spider" [B. VIII
973	PLACATING THE STORM		"Brown Robyn's Confession" [A. II
974	THE HOMECOMING HUSBAND	1	"Hind Horn", [A. IV
		2	"Two Irish Lads in Canada" [A. IV
		3	"Drake and his Lady" [B. VIII
		4	"Drake's Cannon Ball" [B. VII
982 (formerly 946) or 980A	SUPPOSED CHEST OF GOLD INDUCES CHILDREN TO CARE FOR AGED FATHER		"The Ungrateful Sons" [A. IV
990	THE SEEMINGLY DEAD REVIVES	1	"Mrs Killigrew" [B. VIII
		2	"Lady Restored to Life" [B. VIII
		3	"The Thievish Sexton" [B. VIII
		4	"The Thievish Sexton" [B. VIII
		5	"Lady Mount Edgcumbe" [B. VIII
		6	"Mrs. Erskine." [B. VIII
1006	CASTING EYES	1	"Casting Sheep's Eyes" [A. III
1006 and 113		2	"Pat and the five Pigeons" [A. II
1009	GUARDING THE STRONG-ROOM DOOR	1	"The French Man-Servant" [A. III
		2	"Pulling the Door" [A. III
		3	"Mr. Vinegar" [A. V
1030	THE CROP DIVISION	1	"The Tops and the Butts" [B. III
		2	"Jack o' Kent and the Devil" [B. III
		3	"The Farmer and the Boggart" [B. II
1030 (and 1090)		4	"The Bogie's Field" [B. II
		5	"The Devil's Whetstone" [B. III
		6	"Davies and his Friend in Partnership" [B. III
		7	"Davies and the Man in Black" [B. III

Norton (III, pp. 59, 60) also gives versions from Boggs, *N. Carolina*, p. 292, no. 3, from *JAFL*, xxx, p. 175, and from N. C. Parsons, *Tales from Guildford County*.

1036	HOGS WITH CURLY TAILS	1	"Jack o' Kent and the Pigs" [B. III
		2	"Dickey Kent, the Devil and the Pigs" [B. III

1074	CONTEST BETWEEN MAN AND OGRE: RACE	1 "The Fox and the Hedgehog" [A. I
		2 "The Hare and the Prickly-Backed Urchin" [A. I
		3 "How the Hedgehog ran the Devil to Death" [A. I
1088	EATING CONTEST	1 "The Big Wind" [A. II
		2 "Jack the Giant-Killer" (one episode) [A. II
		3 "The Clever Little Tailor" [A. II
1090	CONTEST BETWEEN MAN AND OGRE: MOWING CONTEST	1 "The Longstone" [B. III
	see also 1030	2 "The Farmer and the Boggart" [B. II
		3 "How Davies and the Devil had a mowing contest" [B. III
		4 "Sir Barney Brograve and the Devil" [B. III
1093	CONTEST IN WORDS	1 "The Fause Knight upon the Road" [A. II
		2 "Harpkin" [A. II
1096	THE TAILOR AND OGRE IN A SEWING CONTEST	"The Devil and the Tailor" [A. II
1117 (variant)	THE OGRE'S PITFALL	"Jack the Giant-Killer" (one episode) [A. II
1119	THE OGRE KILLS HIS OWN CHILDREN	"Mally Whuppie" [A. II
1137	THE OGRE BLINDED (Polyphemus)	1 "Maggie Moloch" [B. V
		2 "Jack and the Giant of Dalton Mill" [A. II
		3 "Burn Sel' Blame Sel'" [B. V
		4 "Ainsel" [B. V
		5 "Masell" [A. II

Other variants: "Me A'an Sell", "The Brownie of Bledroch". [B. V

1170	A MAN SELLS HIS SOUL TO THE DEVIL	1 "How Davies had the Muck Spread" [B. III
		2 "The Devil spreads Muck" [B. III
1174	MAKING A ROPE OF SAND	1 "The Devil and the Schoolmaster" [B. III
		2 "The Schoolmaster of Bury" [B. III

1174 (variant)   3 "Sir James Carnegie of Pitarro"
                                                                      [B. III
                                           4 "Michael Scott and the Devil"
                                                                      [B. III

Cf. Leather, *Herefordshire*, p. 40. Norton quotes "The Devil at Cockerham", Harland and
Wilkinson, *Lancashire Legends*, pp. 241–3.

1175 STRAIGHTENING THE CURLY   "The Devil and the Farmer"   [A. II
       HAIR

1178 UNRAVELLING A NET   "The Piece in my Pocket"   [A. II

1180 CATCHING WATER IN A SIEVE   1 "Water in a Sieve"   [A. II
                                     2 "How Davies Puzzled the
                                     Devil"   [B. III
                                     3 "The Girl who Fetched Water
                                     in a Riddle"   [A. II

1182 (variant)   THE LEVEL BUSHEL   1 "The Blacksmith who Sold
                                     himself to the Devil"   [A. II
                                     2 "The Man that Sold himself to
                                     the Devil"   [B. III

1185 THE FIRST CROP   "The First Crop   [B. XIII

1187 MELEAGER   1 "The Green Mist"   [B. III
                                     2 "Betty's Candle"   [B. III
                                     3 "The Demon Mason"   [B. III
                                     4 "The Candle"   [B. III
                                     5 "The Devil at Little Dunkeld
                                     Manse"   [B. III

1191 THE DOG ON THE BRIDGE   1 "The Curious Cat"   [B. III
                                     2 "The Bridge at Kentchurch"
                                                                   [B. III

1199(?) THE LORD'S PRAYER   "The Demon Mason"   [B. III

1200 NUMSKULL STORIES   1 "Borrowdale Follies"   [A. III
                                     2 "The Cannings Vawk"   [A. III
                                     3 "The Coggeshall Jobs"   [A. III
                                     4 "Darlaston Geese"   [A. III
                                     5 "The Essex Men's Well"   [A. III
                                     6 "Folkestone Fiery Serpent"
                                                                   [A. III
                                     7 "The Wise Men of Gotham"
                                                                   [A. III
                                     8 "Isle of Wight People"   [A. III
                                     9 "Lancashire Follies"   [A. III
                                     10 "Lorbottle Follies"   [A. III

1200 *cont.*

11 "Miscellaneous Gibes" [A. III

(*a*) "Nicobore and his Money"
[A. III

(*b*) "Newbiggin" [A. III

12 "Norfolk Follies" [A. III

13 "Pal Hall's Quiffs" [A. IIII

14 "Pevensey Follies" [A. III

15 "The Rope-Bound Cliff"
(Austwick Carles) [A. III

16 "Shropshire Follies" [A. III

17 "Staffordshire Follies" [A. III

18 "Wiltshire Follies" [A. III

19 "Educating Pigs" [A. III

20 "Growing the Church" [A. III

21 "The Moon in the Well" [A. III

1210 THE COW IS TAKEN TO THE
ROOF TO GRAZE

1 "The Three Sillies" [A. III

Norton also gives versions from 1. Gotham, A. Stapleton, *All about the Merry Tales of Gotham* (2nd edn, Nottingham, 1910), p. 64 (from a Mrs Stocker of Gotham, *c.* 1900); 2. Austwick Hall; T. Parkinson, *Yorkshire Legends and Traditions* II (1889), pp. 192–3; 3. Dobson, *Ribble*, I, p. 41; 4. Guildford, *JAFL*, XXX, p. 192.

1213 THE PENT CUCKOO

1 "The Borrowdale Cuckoo"
[A. III

2 "The Cuckoo-Penners" [A. III

3 "Folkestone Fiery Serpent"
[A. III

1221 SHUTTING OUT THE FEVER

4 "Coggeshall Jobs" [A. III

5 "Darlaston Geese" [A. III

1231 THE ATTACK ON THE CRAYFISH

"Wise Men of Gotham" [A. III

1241A (variant) PULLING THE TREE

"Austwick Carles C" [A. III

1242A CARRYING PART OF THE LOAD

1 "Pal Hall's Quiffs" [A. III

2 "Wise Men of Gotham" [A. III

1245 SUNLIGHT CARRIED IN A BAG
INTO THE WINDOWLESS HOUSE

1 "Austwick Carles D" [A. III

2 "Coggeshall Jobs" [A. III

1248 TREE-TRUNKS LAID CROSSWISE
OF THE SLEDGE

"Bolliton Jackdaws" [A. III

1250 BRINGING WATER FROM THE
WELL

"The Moon in the Bottom of the
Well" [A. III

1255 A HOLE TO THROW THE
EARTH IN

"The Essex Men's Well" [A. III

1260 THE PORRIDGE IN THE ICE-HOLE

1 "Austwick, Carles A" [A. III

		2 "Wise Men of Gotham"	[A. III
		"The Best's at the Bottom"	
		(Austwick Carles A)	[A. III
1270	THE DRYING OF THE CANDLE	"Yabberton Yawnies"	[A. III
1276*	PRAYER FOR CHANGE OF WIND	"Answer to Prayer"	[A. III
1278	THE BELL (OR THE LIKE) FALLS INTO THE SEA	1 "Marking the Boat	[A. III
		2 "The Captain's Shovel"	[A. III
1278*	UNDER THE CLOUD	"Whittle to the Tree"	[A. III
1282	HOUSE BURNED DOWN TO RID IT OF INSECTS	"Wise Men of Gotham"	[A. III
1284	PERSON DOES NOT KNOW HIMSELF	"The Wrong Man"	[A. III
1286	JUMPING INTO THE BREECHES	"The Three Sillies"	[A. III
1287	NUMSKULLS UNABLE TO COUNT THEIR OWN NUMBER	1 "The Wise Men of Gotham"	[A. III
		2 "Lorbottle Follies"	[A. III
1288	NUMSKULLS CANNOT FIND THEIR OWN LEGS	"Tangled Legs"	[A. III
1291	ONE CHEESE SENT OUT TO BRING BACK ANOTHER	"The Wise Men of Gotham"	[A. III
1291A	POT SENT TO WALK HOME	"The Table put out to walk"	[A. III
1295*	THE SEVENTH CAKE SATISFIES	"The Real Problem"	[A. III
1295B*	MAN ON CAMEL HAS DOOR BROKEN DOWN SO THAT HE CAN RIDE IN	"Austwick Carles: the Bull in the Field"	[A. III
1297*	JUMPING INTO THE RIVER AFTER THEIR COMRADE	"Austwick Carles A"	[A. III
1310*	THE CRAB IS THOUGHT TO BE THE DEVIL	1 "The Shapwick Monster"	[A. III
		2 "The Dabchick"	[A. III
		3 "Lincolnshire Yellowbreasts"	[A. III
		4 "The Folkestone Fiery Serpent"	[A. III
1316	RABBIT THOUGHT TO BE COW	1 "Droll: the hunted Hare"	[A. III
		2 "Palmer's Anecdotes"	[A. III
		3 "The Brownie and the Hare"	[B. VI

1319 PUMPKIN SOLD AS ASS'S EGG | 1 "Horse's Egg" [A. III
2 "Mare's Egg" [A. III

1319A* WATCH MISTAKEN FOR THE DEVIL'S EYE | 1 "The Austwick Carles and the Watch" [A. III
2 "Two Irish Tramps" [A. III
3 "We Killed Him" [A. III
4 "Three Irish Tramps" [A. III

1319J FOOL EATS BEETLES | "Has Plummocks Legs?" [A. III

1321 FOOLS FRIGHTENED | "A True Story about Henry S." [A. III

1322A* THE GRUNTING PIG | 1 "The Henpecked Husband" [A. III
2 "The Sheepstealers of the Blackdown Hills" [B. IX
3 "Take Two wi't" [A. III
4 "The Hangman's Stone" [B. IX
5 "Jacob Stone and the Owl" [A. III
6 "Farmer Tickle and the Owl" [A. III
7 "How Mr. Lenine gave up Courting" [A. III

1326 MOVING THE CHURCH | "Coggeshall Jobs: Moving the Church" [A. III

1327 EMPTYING THE MEAL-SACK | "The Wise Men of Gotham buying Sheep" [A. III

1332 WHICH IS THE GREATEST FOOL? | "Fimber Village Tales" [A. III

1334 THE LOCAL MOON | 1 "The Slibburn Müne" [A. III
2 "Cannings Vawk and the Comet" [A. III

1335 THE EATEN MOON | 1 "Drinking the Moon" [A. III
2 "How the Old Jack Donkey swallowed the Moon" [A. III
3 "The Eaten Moon" [A. III

1335A RESCUING THE MOON | 1 "Wiltshire Follies" [A. III
2 "Wise Men of Gotham" [A. III
3 "Coggeshall Jobs" [A. III

1336 and 1250 DIVING FOR CHEESE; BRINGING WATER FROM THE WELL | 1 "The Moon in the Horsepond" [A. III
2 "The Moon in the Well" [A. III

1336A	MAN DOES NOT RECOGNIZE HIS OWN REFLECTION IN THE WATER	"The Farmer and his Wife and the Mirror"	[A. III
1338*	NOODLES THINK THE OLD MOON IS BROKEN UP INTO STARS	"The Old Moon Broken up into Stars"	[A. III
1339B	FOOL IS UNACQUAINTED WITH BANANAS	"The First Banana"	[A. III
1340	THE CALF'S HEAD GETS STUCK IN THE GATE (POT)	"The Calf's Head"	[A. III

Norton also gives a version from the Isle of Wight; W. G. Watson, *Somerset Life and Character* (1924), p. 55; and one each from Essex and Surrey.

1345*	STORIES DEPENDING UPON PUNS	"Captain Silk"	[A. III
1350	THE LOVING WIFE	1 "The Loving Wife" 2 "Old John and Young John"	[A. III [A. III
1351	THE SILENCE WAGER	"The Jamming Pan"	[A. III
1358	TRICKSTER SURPRISES ADULTERESS AND LOVER	"Lorenzo Dow and the Devil"	[A. III
1359	THE HUSBAND OUTWITS THE PARAMOUR	"Thomas of Reading"	[B. IX
1360C	OLD HILDEBRAND	"Little Dicky Milburn"	[A. III

Norton also gives versions as follows: J.C.G. in *NQ*, I, XII, p. 498. Sung by his "Old Father" (Liverpool); *NQ*, I, VI, p. 227, from "C." (1952). Heard some 65 years earlier, from his (?) nurse: *NQ*, I, VI, p. 75 (?), anon.; Buchan, *Ancient Ballads*, II, song, pp. 210–11, explanation, pp. 27–8; and one from Boggs, pp. 394–5, no. 24A.

1363	TALE OF THE CRADLE	"The Miller of Abingdon"	[A. III
1365A	WIFE FALLS INTO A STREAM	"The Contrary Wife"	[A. III
1365	THE OBSTINATE WIFE	1 "Knife or Scissors" 2 "How Madde Coomes, when his Wife was drowned, sought her against the Streame"	[A. III [A. III

Norton also gives two versions from Boggs, *N. Carolina*, p. 306, no. 26, p. 171.

1375 (formerly 1375*) WHO CAN RULE HIS WIFE?		1 "The Grey Mare is the Better Horse" 2 "The Grey Mare" 3 "The Henpecked Husband"	[A. III [A. III [A. III
1380	THE FAITHLESS WIFE	"The False Old Mawkin"	[A. III

1381	THE SAUSAGE RAIN	1	"Silly Jack and the Factor"	
				[A. III
		2	"Adventures of a Parrot"	[A. III
1381E	THE OLD MAN GOES TO SCHOOL	1	"The Portmantle"	[A. III
		2	"John and Sally"	[A. III
		3	"The Old Roadman"	[A. III

Norton also gives a version, "Joseph o' Nuppits", from *Easther*, p. xxii (Almondsbury, Yorks.). "Nuppit" = a simpleton. Joseph died in 1794; he was a local idiot.

1382	THE PEASANT WOMAN AT MARKET		"The Puzzled Carter"	[A. III

Norton also gives "Horse and Cart", from Bacon and Parsons, p. 309, no. 102 (1899), Negro.

1383	THE WOMAN DOES NOT KNOW HERSELF		"Lawkamercyme"	[A. V

Norton also gives an Italian version, with incidental rhymes in English, quoted from C. R. H. Busk, who heard it in infancy. *Archivie per lo Studio delle Tradizioni popolari*, IX (Palermo 1890).

1384	THE HUSBAND HUNTS THREE PERSONS AS STUPID AS HIS WIFE	1	"*The Three Sillies*"	[A. III
		2	"The Three Noodles"	[A. III
		3	"Th' Lad 'at went oot to look for Fools"	[A. III

1408	THE MAN WHO DOES HIS WIFE'S WORK	1	"The Old Man in a Wood"	
		2	"The Old Man who Lived in a Wood"	[A. III
		3	"The Comical History of Simple John and his Misfortunes"	[A. III
		4	"Simple Simon's Misfortunes"	[A. III

1409*	THE WOMAN COOKS DOG FOR DINNER	1	"Wise Men of Gotham"	[A. III

1415 and 1653	LUCKY HANS	1	"Mr. Vinegar"	[A. II
		2	"Jack's Wonderful Bargains"	[A. II
Distant variant			"The Hedley Kow"	[B. V

Norton also quoted a version, "The Foolish Trader", from Boggs, *N. Carolina*, p. 307.

1416	THE MOUSE IN THE SILVER JUG	1	"A Son of Adam"	
variants		2	"Bob Appleford's Pig"	[A. III
		3	"The Clock"	[A. III
			"That's None of Your Business"	[A. III

Norton also gives a version from *Folk-Lore*, XXIV, p. 517, "Breconshire Village Folklore", from Miss E. B. Thomas, of Llanthomas, Llanigon, told by Anne Thomas, gardener's wife, who died in 1905, aged 91.

1417	THE CUT-OFF NOSE	"Wise Men of Gotham"	[A. III
1419C	THE RETURNING HUSBAND HOODWINKED	"The Returning Husband"	[A. III
1419H	WOMAN WARNS LOVER OF HUSBAND BY SINGING SONG	1 "The Exorcism" 2 "The Untrue Wife's Song"	[A. III
1423	THE ENCHANTED PEAR-TREE	"The Bewitched Tree"	[A. III
1430	THE MAN AND HIS WIFE BUILD AIR-CASTLES	"Buttermilk Jack"	[A. I

Norton (v, p. 51), quotes Stapleton, second edn, p. 61, which refers to *Notes about Notts.* (1874), p. 148: a story of two brothers, who quarrelled about pastures in the sky.

1431	THE CONTAGIOUS YAWNS	"The Flight of Birds"	[A. II
1439 (c.)	THE LAZY WIFE	"The Lazy Wife"	[A. III
1452* (variant) BRIDE-TEST		"The Choice of a Servant"	[A. I
1476A	THE PRAYER FOR A HUSBAND	1 "The Maid who wanted to Marry"	[A. III
		2 "Nowt but a Tailor"	[A. III
		3 "Praying for a Husband"	[A. III
variant		4 "MacCulloch's Courtship"	[B. VIII
1510	THE MATRON OF EPHESUS	"Old John and Young John"	[A. II
1525	THE MASTER THIEF	1 "Canny Jack"	[A. IV
		2 "Clever Jack"	[A. IV
		3 "Jack and his Master"	[A. IV
		4 "Jack the Robber"	[A. III
		5 "How Jack Became a Master Thief and Married his Master's Daughter"	[A. IV
		6 "Skelton, IX"	[A. III
		7 "The Boy who outwitted the Robber"	[A. IV
		8 "Lothian Tom"	[A. III
		9 "The Maltman and the Poller"	[B. VIII
1525B	THE HORSE STOLEN	"Dicky of Kingswood"	[A. III
1525H	THIEVES STEAL FROM EACH OTHER	"A Robber is Cunning against Robbers"	[A. III
1529	THE PEASANT BETRAYS THE JEW THROUGH THE SUBSTITUTION OF A HORSE	1 "The Pedlar's Ass' 2 "The Metamorphosis"	[A. III [A. III

1533	THE WISE CARVING OF THE FOWL	"Master John Scot"	[B. VIII
1529A	THE EXCHANGE OF HORSES	"Rob Hall and the Gentleman"	[A. III
1535	THE RICH AND THE POOR PEASANT	"Sheep for the Asking"	[A. III
1536B	THE THREE HUNCHBACK BROTHERS DROWNED	"The Baker and Jack the Fool"	[A. III

Norton (v, pp. 81–2), also gives one American and two Irish versions. Cf. also "The Cobbler and the Calf" in "The Comical Tricks of Lothian Tom". Another version of this in W. A. Clouston, *Popular Tales and Fictions*, II, pp. 43–4. Found in a fragment of a magazine c. 1820, Norton v, p. 81.

1525H	THE THEFT OF A SHEEP	1	"A Robber's Cunning against another Robber"	[A. III
		2	"The Two Pickpockets"	[A. III
1526A	SUPPER WON BY A TRICK		"Tom Tram's Merry Tales"	[A. III
1537	THE CORPSE KILLED FIVE TIMES		"The Monk of Leicester, who was Five Times Slain and Once Hanged'	[A. III
1539	CLEVERNESS AND GULLIBILITY	1	"The Irishman's Hat"	[A. III
		2	"The Cap that Paid"	[A. III
1539B	THE RABBIT AS LETTER-CARRIER		"The Wise Men of Gotham"	[A. III
1540	THE STUDENT FROM PARADISE	1	"Jack Hannaford"	[A. III
1541	FOR THE LONG WINTER	1	"Good Fortune"	[A. III
		2	"Herafterthis"	[A. III
		3	"The Miser and his Wife"	[A. III
		4	"The Thriftless Wife"	[A. III
		5	"Hoyik and Boyik"	[A. III
1548	THE SOUP-STONE		"The Fryer and the Whetstone"	[A. III
1551	THE WAGER THAT SHEEP ARE HOGS		"Hogs or Sheep?"	[A. III

Norton (v, p. 107c) also gives a version, "What Shift Scogin and his Fellow made when they lacked Money", from *Scoggins Jests* (1926), Hazlitt, II, pp. 56–8.

1556	THE DOUBLE PENSION (BURIAL MONEY)		"The Baker and Jack the Fool"	[A. III
1557	BOX ON THE EAR RETURNED		"Box about"	[A. III
1560	MAKE-BELIEVE EATING, MAKE-BELIEVE WORK	1	"The Farmer and his Man"	[A. III
		2	"Mr. Pengelly and the Tramp"	[A. III

1561	THE LAZY BOY: EATS BREAKFAST, DINNER AND SUPPER, ONE AFTER THE OTHER	1 "The Lad who was never Hungry" 2 "A Useful Appetite"	[A. III
1562	"THINK THRICE BEFORE YOU SPEAK	1 "Father, I think..."	[A. III
1562 (variant)		2 "King Edward VII and the Salad" 3 "They Took his Word!"	[A. III [A. III
1567	HUNGRY SERVANT REPROACHES STINGY MASTER	"Take a Pinch of Salt with It"	[A. III
1567G	GOOD FOOD CHANGES SONG	1 "The Hungry Mowers" 2 "The Rate for a Job"	[A. III [A. III
1570*	GORGE SILENTLY	"John Drew the Shoemaker",	[A. III

Norton also gives "The Tailor and his Apprentice" under this type-number, see 1575*.
[A. II

1571*	THE SERVANTS PUNISH THEIR MASTER	"The Tailor, the King and his Servants"	[A. III
1572*	THE HAIR-CUT	"The Hair-Cut"	[A. III

A Westmorland version in Norton V, p. 122, is from E. M. Wilson, "Some Humorous English Folk-tales", II, p. 282, no. 20. From Richard Harrison, December 1937. Heard from a local farmer.

1575*	THE CLEVER SHEPHERD	"The Tailor and his Apprentices"	[A. III
1585	THE LAWYER'S MAD CLIENT	"Pierre Patelin", or, "Of Him that paid his Debt by crying 'Bea'."	[A. III
1589	THE LAWYER'S DOG STEALS MEAT	1 "The Lawyer's Dog steals Meat" 2 "The Case is Altered"	[A. III [A. III
1590	THE TRESPASSER'S DEFENCE	"George Buchanan and the King"	[A. III

Norton also gives a version from *JAFL*, p. 371.

1591	THE THREE JOINT DEPOSITORS	1 "The Three Joint Depositors" 2 "George Buchanan as Advocate"	[A. III [A. III
1600	THE FOOL AS MURDERER	1 "Silly Jack and the Factor" 2 Second version, also from Aberdeenshire, from Bella Higgins.	[A. III

1611 CONTEST IN CLIMBING THE   "Do that if you Can"   [A. III
     MAST

1612 THE CONTEST IN SWIMMING   "George Buchanan and the Drover"
                                                                  [A. III

1613 PLAYING-CARDS ARE MY   *The Perpetual Almanack, or*
     CALENDAR AND PRAYER-BOOK   *Gentleman Soldier's Prayer-Book*
                                                                  [B. VIII

Norton v, p. 140 gives "A New Game of Cards", pp. 323–4, "Cards Spiritualized", from Taylor, *The History of Playing Cards*, "The Religious Card Player," an American version. Modern printed versions were examined by E. M. Wilson in *Folk-Lore*, L (September, 1939); *Derby Folk-Lore Journal* (1889), VII, pp. 315–16.

1615 (variant) THE HELLER THROWN   "The Fisherman and the Piskies"
               INTO OTHERS' MONEY   [B. V

1626 and 1319A*   1 "The Three Irish Tramps"
     DREAM BREAD. THE WATCH   [A. III
     MISTAKEN FOR THE DEVIL'S EYE   2 "Dream Bread"
                                    3 "Of the Faith of Three Fellows"
                                                                  [A. III

Norton also gives a version from *JAFL*, XXX (1917), p. 403.

1628 THE LEARNED SON AND THE   "The Rich Man's Two Sons" [A. III
     FORGOTTEN LANGUAGE

1640 THE BRAVE TAILOR   1 "John Glaick, the Brave Tailor"
                                                                  [A. II
                                    2 "Johnny Gloke"   [A. II
                                    3 "Jack the Giant-Killer" [A. II

1641 DOCTOR KNOW-ALL   1 "The Conjuror, or, The Turkey
                                       and the Ring"   [A. III
                                    2 "The Clever Gypsy"   [A. III
                                       "Old Woman and the Three
                                       Kippers"   [A. III
1641 (variant)   3 "The Three Kippers"   [A. III
1641   4 "The Clever Irishman"   [A. III

Norton quotes also an Irish version, from Kennedy, *Fireside Stories*, pp. 116–19.

1642 (variant) THE GOOD BARGAIN   "The Princess of Canterbury" [A. II

1645 THE TREASURE AT HOME   1 "The Pedlar of Swaffham" [B. IX
                                    2 "The Lambeth Pedlar"   [B. IX
                                    3 "The Swaffham Tinker"   [B. IX

Norton also (v, pp. 172, 175), gives two versions from *Antiquary*, XI, p. 168 (from W. E. A. Axon), two (pp. 177, 183) from Gomme, *Folklore as an Historical Science*, pp. 17–18, 19–20; one from John Noakes, *The Rambler in Worcestershire* (1848), pp. 48–9; and two in verse, one from Yorkshire, the other from Norfolk.

1651	WHITTINGTON'S CAT	1	"Dick Whittington and his Cat"	[B. VIII
		2	"The History of Sir Richard Whittington"	[B. VIII
1653	THE ROBBERS UNDER THE TREE	1	"The Tinker's Wife"	[A. III
		2	"The Thriftless Wife"	[A. III
		3	"Hereafterthis"	[A. III
1656 (variant)	HOW THE JEWS WERE DRAWN FROM HEAVEN	1	"Cause Bob"	[A. III
1676	JOKER POSING AS GHOST PUNISHED BY VICTIM	1	"The Croydon Devil Claims his own"	[B. III
		2	"The Chivalrous Devil"	[B. II
		3	"The Netherbury Churchyard Legend"	[B. IX
1676A	BIG 'FRAID AND LITTLE 'FRAID	5	"Run Black Devil! run White Devil!"	[B. II
		6	"Mock Ghost and Real Ghost"	[B. VI
1678	THE BOY WHO HAD NEVER SEEN A WOMAN	1	"Women or Devils?"	[A. III
		2	"Jacky Gahs Coortin"	[A. III
1681 (variant)	THE BOY'S DISASTERS		"Coat o' Clay"	[A. III
1682	THE GROOM TEACHES HIS HORSE TO LIVE WITHOUT FOOD	1	"Training a Donkey"	[A. III
		2	"Training a Cow"	[A. III
1685	THE FOOLISH BRIDEGROOM	1	"The Foolish Bridegroom of Gotham" "The Wise Men of Gotham"	[A. III
		2	"Billy Tyson's Coortin'"	[A. III
1687	THE FORGOTTEN WORD		"Stupid's Cries"	[A. III
1691* (variant)	PLUMS WITH LEGS		"Has Plummocks Legs?"	[A. III

Norton quotes other versions in dialect from Shropshire, Exmoor, Cornwall, Leicestershire and Rutland, also Scotland. One from *JAFL*.

1693*	THE LITERAL FOOL	1	"The Sheep's Head and Dumplings"	[A. III
		2	"The Sheep Head"	[A. III
		3	"The Restless Haggis"	

Norton (v, p. 214) also quotes another version from E. S. Hartland, in *Folk-Lore*, vi, p. 86; also versions from E. G. Bales, *Folklore from West Norfolk*, p. 73; Baldry, *The Rabbit-Skin Cap*, p. 49; (Norfolk) *The Scotch Haggis*, pp. 12–13; and *Scottish Jests* (1838), pp. 204–5. One version from Texas.

| 1694* | THE BOY IN THE RAIN | | "The Boy in the Rain" | [A. III |

Norton also gives a version from *Joe Miller's Jest-Book* (1836), p. 175, no. 1006.

1696   WHAT SHOULD I HAVE SAID   1   "Stupid's Mistaken Cries"   [A. III
           (DONE)?   2   "Jock and His Mother"   [A. III
                                           3   "Lazy Jack"   [A. III
                                           4   "Jack's Rewards and What he
Did with them"   [A. III
"Johnnie Raggie's Errand"   [A. III

Other versions given by Norton (v, pp. 223–39) are: "Biddable Jock", from *Miscellanea of the Rymour Club*, II, pp. 66–8; from Kirkcudbrightshire; one from A. Williams, *Round about the Upper Thames*, p. 67; from Mr M. F. C. Morris, *Yorkshire Reminiscences* (1922), p. 329; one from Ontario; one from *JAFL*; two from Ireland; one from Virginia. Variant in Chase, *Grandfather Tales*, p. 130; and in *Tales from Cloud-Walking Country*.

1697   WE THREE: FOR MONEY   1   "We Three"   [A. III
                                           2   "The Three Foreigners"   [A. III
                                           3   "The Purse and the Penny
Siller"   [A. III
                                           4   "We Three Hielandmen"   [A. III

1698C   DEAF PERSONS AND THEIR   "The Deaf Man and the Pig-
          FOOLISH ANSWERS   Trough"   [A. III

1698G   MISUNDERSTOOD WORDS   "Englishman and Highlandman"
          LEAD TO COMIC RESULTS   [A. III

1698K   THE BUYER AND THE DEAF   3   "The Buyer and the Seller"
          SELLER   [A. III

Norton (VI, p. 8) also quotes from E. M. Wilson (see 1, above) a version in Westmorland dialect, and (p. 10) one from *Texas Folk-Lore Society Publications*, XV (1939), pp. 82–3.

1699 (misunderstood) see 1319 (variant)   "We Killed Him"   [A. III
          MISUNDERSTANDING OF A FOREIGN
          LANGUAGE (PUMPKIN SOLD AS AN
          ASS'S EGG)

1705 (variant)   TALKING HORSE AND   "The Farmer and his Ox"   [A. I
                              DOG

1735A   THE BRIBED BOY SINGS THE   1   "The Man that stole the
          WRONG SONG   Parson's Sheep"   [A. III
                                           2   "The Wee Boy and Minister
Gray"   [A. III
                                           3   "The Parson and the Shepherd
Lad"   [A. III

Other versions given by Norton (VI, pp. 24–6) are "The Parson's Sheep", from S. Hewett, *The Peasant Speech of Devon*, p. 24; from Dallington, Sussex; and one from Boggs, *N. Carolina*.

1737   THE PARSON IN A SACK TO   1   "The Incorrigible Youth"   [A. III
          HEAVEN   2   "Canny Jack"   [A. IV

1738   ALL PARSONS IN HELL   1   "Old Charley Creed"   [A. III
                                           2   "The Parson's Meeting"   [A. III

		3	"Black John's Dream"	[A. III
		4	"Crowdy of Highworth"	[A. III
		5	"Skelton XI"	[A. III
1791	THE SEXTON CARRIES THE PARSON	1	"The Two Tailors"	[A. III
		2	"Bodysnatcher and Ram"	[A. III
		3	"The Bag of Nuts"	[A. III
		4	"The Churchyard"	[A. III
		5	"Mother Elston's Nuts"	[A. III
		6	"The Old Woman who crack'd Nuts"	[A. III
		7	"The Black and his Master"	[A. IV
(variant)		8	"Three in One"	[A. III
1800	JOKES ABOUT CONFESSION		"The Welchman and the Friar"	[A. III
1824	PARODY SERMON	1	"Tom's Conversion"	[A. III
		2	"A Sermon upon Malt"	[B. VIII
1827A	CARDS FALL FROM THE SLEEVE OF THE PREACHER		"The Parson and the Cards"	[A. III
1828 (variant)	THE COCK IN CHURCH CROWS		"A new Way to wauken Sleepers in Church"	[A. III
1830	IN TRIAL SERMON, PARSON PROMISES THE LAYMEN THE WEATHER THEY WANT		"Promising Candidate"	[A. III
1831A	INAPPROPRIATE ACTIONS IN CHURCH		"The angry Choirmaster"	[A. III
1832*	THE BOY ANSWERS THE PRIEST	1	"The Boy and the Parson"	[A. III
		2	"Breaking the Commandments"	[A. III
1833	THE BOY APPLIES THE SERMON	1	"Philip Spencer"	[A. III
		2	"The Curate and the Fool"	[A. III
		3	"The Parson and the Parrot"	[A. III
		4	"Skelton", III	[A. III
1833*	OTHER ANECDOTES OF SERMONS	1	"Parson Spry's Sermons"	[B. IX
		2	"The Devil defined"	[A. III
		3	"The Parson's Prayer"	[A. III
		4	"A Long-winded Preacher"	[A. III
		5	"Wanted, a Pup"	[A. III

1835 D*   WAGER: PARSON TO READ   "The Ploughman's Paternoster"
          PRAYERS WITHOUT THINKING   [A. III
          OF ANYTHING ELSE

1839 (variant)   THE CARD-PLAYING   1   "The Cock-fighting Parson"
                 PARSON   [A. III
                                       2   "Wold Forred"   [A. III
                                       3   "The Parson and his Boon-
                                           companions"   [A. III
(variant)   4   "Parson calls out Cards"   [A. III

1840 B   THE STOLEN HAM   1   "The Miller's Eels"   [A. III
                                       2   "Poetic Truth"   [A. III

1843   THE PARSON VISITS THE DYING   "An Honest MacGregor"   [A. III

1847*   BIBLICAL REPARTEE   "The Thieves and the Apples''
                                                                       [A. III

1848 A   THE PARSON'S CALENDAR   "Resurrexi"   [A. III
1848 B   BEANS IN THE POCKET   "The Priest who made Baskets"
                                                                       [A. III

1862 C   IMITATION, OR, DIAGNOSIS   "The Doctor's Apprentice"   [A. III
         BY OBSERVATION

1875 (variant)   THE BOY ON THE   "The Tin Can on the Cow's Tail"
                 WOLF'S TAIL   [A. III

1881   THE MAN CARRIED THROUGH   "The King of the Liars"   [A. IV
       THE AIR BY GEESE

1881*   PARROTS FLY AWAY WITH TREE   "The Crows fly away with the
                                           Pear-trees"   [A. III

1886*   FIGHTING SHEEP BUTT EACH   "Down Underground"   [A. III
        OTHER

1889   MÜNCHHAUSEN TALES   1   "A Lying Tale"   [A. V
                                       2   "Appy Boz'll"   [A. III

A variant "Appy Boz'll" in the T. W. Thompson *Notebooks*, from Gus Gray, Cleethorpes,
26 September 1914.

1889 (variant)   3   "The Sevenfold Liar"   [A. V
                                       4   "The Dog and the Hares"   [A. III
                                       5   "Appy Boz'll's Monkey"   [A. III
                                       6   "Five Men"   [A. V
                                       7   "The Pynots in the Crab-Tree'
                                                                       [A. III
                                       8   "The Basket-Maker's Donkey"
                                                                       [A. III

1889 D   TREE GROWS OUT OF HORSE   "Wool and Withies''   [A. III

1889L THE SPLIT DOG	"The Dog and the Hares"	[A. III
1890 THE LUCKY SHOT	"John of Horsill I"	[B. IX
1894 THE MAN SHOOTS A RAMROD FULL OF DUCKS	"Shooting Finches"	[A. III
1893A TWO HARES RUN INTO ONE ANOTHER	1 "The Two Hares" 2 "The Two Hares"	[A. III [A. III
1911A THE HORSE'S NEW BACKBONE	"The Basket-Maker's Donkey"	[A. III
1920 CONTEST IN LYING	1 "The Turnips" 2 "Mark Twain in the Fens" 3 "The Cole-Wort" 4 "The Four Fellows and their Three Dogs" 5 "The Man who Bounced" 6 "The Prize for Lying"	[A. III [A. III [A. III [A. III [A. III [A. III
1920F SKILFUL HOUNDS	"Dr. Fell's Dog"	[A. III
1930 SCHLARAFFENLAND	1 "Rabbits Baste Themselves" 2 "The Wee Yowe" 3 "Doun on Yon Bank" 4 "Down Underground" 5 "Sir Gammer Vans" 6 "Jack the Giant-Killer: B" 7 "Mother Shipton's House" 8 "I Saddled my Sow" 9 "A Thrawn Sang"	[A. III [A. V [A. V [A. III [A. V [A. II [A. V [A. V [A. V
1940 THE EXTRAORDINARY NAMES	1 "Tom Per Cent" 2 "Don Nippery Septo" 3 "Easy Decree" 4 "Master and Servant" 5 "Master of all Masters" 6 "The Clever Apprentice"	[A. III [A. III [A. III [A. III [A. III [A. III

Norton (VI, pp. 87–104) also gives the following: (3); "Maister Domine"; "Dominy Doster"; "Domine Hector"; "Mr Ord and Mrs Easy"; "Sir Augustus a Domino"; "Master and Servant", (second version); "Domine Sceptre"; "Master above a Master" (Chambers); and two American versions.

1950 THE THREE LAZY ONES	1 "Three Lazy Ones" 2 "Three Lazy Men at Fimber" 3 "The Three Lazy Ones"	[A. III [A. II [A. III
1950 (variant)	4 "The Lazy Fellow"	[A. III

1960	THE GREAT ANIMAL OR GREAT OBJECT	"Finn and the Dragon"	[A. II
1960B	THE GREAT FISH	"Apply Boswell Stories"	[A. III
1960D	THE GREAT VEGETABLE	1 "The Great Turnips"	
		2 "The Three Turnips"	[A. III
		3 "Giant Parsnips"	[A. III
1960Z	THE GREAT WIND	"The Great Wind"	[A III
2010	THE ANIMALS WITH QUEER NAMES	1 "Henny-Penny"	[A. V
		2 "The Hen and her Fellow-Travellers"	[A. V
2012	THE FORGETFUL MAN COUNTS THE DAYS OF THE WEEK	"The Priest who made Baskets"	[A. III
2014	THE HOUSE IS BURNT DOWN	1 "Good and Bad News"	[A. III
		2 "The House is Burning"	
2015* or 2016	THE GOAT WHO WOULD NOT GO HOME	"The Wee, Wee Mannie"	[A. V
2022	THE DEATH OF THE LITTLE HEN	1 "Titty Mouse and Tatty Mouse"	[A. V
		2 "Da Flech an' da Loose shackin' dir Sheets"	[A. v[

Norton (VI, pp. 128–32), also quotes: "The Mouse, the Grouse and the Little Red Hen", from *JAFL*, XII, pp. 291–2; "The Deukie and the Tod", from *Folk-Lore Journal*, III, W. Gregor, "Some Folk-tales and Jingles from Aberdeen and Banffshires", pp. 271–2. From the Misses Robertson, of Fraserburgh, who learnt it in Banff. Imperfect at the beginning. Also a version from Leyden, p. 318.

2925	THE PANCAKE	1 "The Wee Bannock"	[A. V
		2 "Johnny Cake"	[A. V
		3 "The Little Cake"	[A. V
2027 (variant)	THE FAT CAT	"The Whale that Followed the Ship"	[A. III
2030	THE OLD WOMAN AND HER PIG	1 "The Old Woman and her Pig"	[A. V
		2 "The Wife and her Bush of Berries"	[A. V
		3 "I Went to Market"	[A. V
		4 "The Cat and Mouse"	[A. V

Norton VI also gives four American versions.

2032	THE COCK'S WHISKERS (The Mouse's Tail)	1 "The Cat and the Mouse"	[A. V
2033	A NUT HITS THE COCK'S HEAD	1 "The Story of Chicken-Licken"	[A. V

	2 "Henny-Penny"	[A. V
	3 "Chickie Birdie"	[A. V
	4 "The Hen and her Fellow Travellers"	[A. V

Cf. "Smereree" (2033 and 130), S. Morison, *Manx Fairy Tales*.

2035	HOUSE THAT JACK BUILT	1 "The House that Jack Built"	[A. V
		2 "The Key of the King's Garden"	
2040	THE CLIMAX OF HORRORS	"News!"	[A. III
2204 (variant)	THE DOG'S CIGAR	"The Two Rings"	[A. III
2300	THE ENDLESS TALE	"The Endless Tale"	[A. V
2320	ROUNDS	"It was a dark and stormy Night"	[A. V
2335	TALES FILLED WITH CONTRADICTIONS	"Five Men"	[A. V
2401	THE CHILDREN PLAY AT HOG-KILLING	"The Three-Legged Hare"	[B. III

B MIGRATORY LEGENDS

3000	ESCAPE FROM THE BLACK SCHOOL OF WITTEBERG	"The Laird of Pitarro"	[B. XIII
3015	THE CARDPLAYERS AND THE DEVIL	1 "The Devil at the Card-Party"	[B. III
		2 "The Card-Player and the Devil"	[B. III
3020	INEXPERIENCED USE OF THE BLACK BOOK. ROPES OF SAND	"Master and Pupil"	[A. II
3021*	TASK SET TO EVIL SOUL	1 "The Demon Tregeagle"	[B. VI
		2 "Sir Robert Chichester of Martinhoe"	[B. VI
3025	CARRIED BY THE DEVIL OR BY EVIL SPIRITS	"St Adelme"	[B. XI
3026*	CONTEST BETWEEN MAGICIANS	1 "Bayard's (Byard's) Leap"	[B. XIII
		2 "The Two Magicians"	[B. XIII
		3 "The Witch of Fraddam and the Enchanter of Pengerswick"	[B. XIII
		4 "Blind Bizard", Addy	[B. XIII

4070 THE SEA-SPRITE HAUNTING   "The Mermaid and the Laird of
THE FISHING-BOAT   Lorntie"   [B. V

4075 VISITS TO FAIRYLAND
  1   "A Boy at Borgue"   [B. V
  2   "The Fairies in the Mill"   [B. V
  3   "Elidor and the Golden Ball"
   [B. V
  4   "The Fairy Widower"   [B. V
  5   "Cherry of Zennor"   [B. V
  6   "The Sautman o'Tullybody"
   [B. V
  7   "The Fairy Boy of Leith"   [B. V

4077* CAUGHT IN FAIRYLAND
  1   "Robert Kirk in the Fairy
  Knowe"   [B. V
  2   "The Fairy Dwelling on Selena
  Moor"   [B. V

4080 THE SEAL WOMAN
  1   "The Goodman of Wastness"
   [B. V
  2   "Johnny Croy and the
  Mermaid"   [B. V
  3   "The Mermaid Wife"   [B. V
  4   "John Reid and the Mermaid"
   [B. V
  5   "The Old Man of Cury"   [B. V

4081* THE WOUNDED SEAL
  1   "The Seal-Catcher's Adventure"
   [B. V
  2   "Gioga and Ollavitanus"   [B. V
  3   "The Mermaid and the Selkie"
   [B. V

5005 A JOURNEY WITH A TROLL
  1   "Blue-Cap"   [B. V
  2   "The Boy and the Fairies"   [B. V
  3   "The Poor Man of Peatlaw"
   [B. V
  4   "The Black Laird of Dunblane"
   [B. V
  5   "The Piskies in the Cellar"   [B. V
  6   "Horse and Hattock"   [B. V
  7   "Hupp, Horse, Handocks"   [B. V

5010 THE VISIT TO THE OLD   "The Pechs"   [B. VIII
TROLL. THE HANDSHAKE

5020 TROLL MAKING A CAUSEWAY
  1   "The Rollright Stones"   [B. IX
  2   "The Giants of Stokesay"   [B. VII
  3   "The Origin of the Wrekin"
   [B. VII
  4   "The Curious Cat"   [B. III

5020 (variant)		5 "The Devil's Porterage"	[B. III
		6 "The Giants of Castle Treen"	
			[B. VII
		7 "The Giant of Grabbist"	[A. II
		8 "The Devil's Ditch"	[B. III
		9 "Wade and his Wife"	[B. VII
5050	THE FAIRIES' PROSPECT OF SALVATION	1 "The Fairy's Enquiry"	[B. V
		2 "The Fairy and the Bible-Reader"	[B. V
5070	MIDWIFE TO THE FAIRIES	1 "The Midwife"	[B. V
		2 "Tam Scott and the Fin Man"	[B. V
		3 "Marie Kirstan the Midwife"	[B. V
		4 "Fairy Ointment"	[B. V
		5 "The Fairy Midwife"	[B. V
		6 "Minehead Market Pixies"	[B. V
5071	THE FAIRY MASTER	1 "The Fairy Master, or Bob o' the Carn"	[B. V
		2 "Cherry of Zennor"	[B. V
5075	REMOVING A BUILDING SITUATED OVER THE HOUSE OF THE FAIRIES	"Sir Godfrey Macculloch"	[B. V
5076*	THE FAIRY HELPER	"The Laird o' Co"	[B. V
5080	FOOD FROM THE FAIRIES	1 "The Broken Ped"	[B. V
		2 "The Broken Bilk"	[B. V
		3 "The Fairy's Spade"	[B. V
		4 "The Fairy's Kirn-Staff"	[B. V
		5 "The Fairy's Peel"	[B. V
		6 "The Ploughboy at the Fairy Feast"	[B. V
5081*	THE STOLEN OX	1 "The Tacksman's Ox"	[B. V
		2 "The Trow Boys and the Cow"	[B. V
		3 "The Three Cows"	[B. V
		4 "Da Trow-Shot Cow"	[B. V
5082*	FAIRY BORROWING	1 "Fairy Borrowing"	[B. V
		2 "The Fairy and the Miller's Wife"	[B. V
5085	THE CHANGELING	1 "The Changeling"	[B. V
		2 "The Fairy Changeling"	[B. V

5085 *cont.*

3 "Fairy Theft" [B. V
4 "A Fairy Changeling" [B. V
5 "The Changeling of Brea Venn"
[B. V
6 "Johnnie in the Cradle" [B. V
7 "The Caerlaverock Changeling"
[B. V
8 "Brewery in an Eggshell" [D. V
9 "The Changeling" [B. V
10 "The Tailor and a Baby" [B. V
11 "The Tailor of Kintalen" [B. V
12 "The Fairy Hill A' Lowe" [B. V

5086* RELEASED FROM FAIRYLAND

"Released from Fairyland" [B. V

5087 THE TROWS' BUNDLE

1 "The Trows' Bundle"
2 "The Lothian Farmer's Wife"

5088* THE TROW'S REVENGE

1 "The Trow's Revenge" [B. V
2 "The Neglected Trow's
Revenge" [B. V

6010 THE CAPTURE OF A FAIRY

1 "Colman Gray" [B. V
2 "The Pixy at the Ockerry" [B. V

6010 (variant)

3 "Skilly-Widden" [B. V
4 "Brother Mike" [B. V

6010 (variant)

5 "Taimi's Visit to the Fairies"
[B. V

6015A THE CHRISTMAS PARTY OF THE FAIRIES

"Thom and Willie" [B. V

6020 THE GRATEFUL FAIRY MOTHER

"Fairy Friends" [B. V

6035 FAIRIES ASSIST A FARMER AT HIS WORK

1 "The Pixy Threshers" [B. V
2 "The Fairy Threshing" [B. V
3 "Da Park at Windhus" [B. V
4 "Thomas Stonehouse and the
Hob" [B. V
5 "Skjaere, Skjaere" [B. V
6 "Robin Roundcap" [B. V

6045 DRINKING CUP STOLEN FROM THE FAIRIES

1 "Pixy Fair" [B. V
2 "The Fairy Horn" [B. V
3 "The Luck of Edenhall" [B. V
4 "The Fairies' Cauldron" [B. V
5 "The old Woman who turned
her Shift" [B. V
6 "The Fairy Banquet" [B. V

6060	THE FAIRY BULL		"The Elf Bull"	[B. V
6070	THE FAIRIES SEND A MESSAGE		"Tuna Tivla"	[B. V
6070B	THE KING OF THE CATS	1	"King o' Cats"	[B. V
		2	"Molly Dixon"	[B. V
		3	"The King of the Cats"	[B. V
		4	"Dildrum, King of the Cats"	
				[B. V
		5	"The Gudeman of Siggie Taft"	
				[B. V
7005	THE HEAVY BURDEN	1	"The Invisible Burden"	[B. V
		2	"I Weat, You Weat"	[B. V
		3	"Brother Mike"	[B. V
7010	REVENGE FOR BEING TEASED	1	"The Brownie of Cranshaws"	
				[B. V
(variant)		2	"Donald Cameron and the Brownie"	[B. V
7011*	THE BROWNIE AND THE MILK-BOWL		"The Brownie and the Milk-Bowl"	[B. V
7012*	REVENGE FOR NEGLIGENCE	1	"Lazy Molly"	[B. V
		2	"The King of the Fairies"	[B. V
		3	"Tarr Ball and the Farmer"	[B. V
7015	THE NEW SUIT	1	"The Pixy Threshers"	[B. V
		2	"The Fairy Threshers"	
		3	"The Cauld Lad of Hilton"	[B. V
		4	"The Piskey of Boston"	[B. V
		5	"A Brownie Legend from Lincolnshire"	[B. V
		6	"The Withypool Ding-Dongs"	
				[B. V
		7	"The Kind Pixy"	[B. V
		8	"Broonie"	[B. V
7016*	LAYING A BROWNIE		"The Brownie and the Midwife" ("The Brownie of Dalswinton")	[B. V
7020	VAIN ATTEMPT TO ESCAPE FROM THE NISSE	1	"The Farndale Hob"	[B. VI
		2	"The Saut-Box"	[B. V
		3	"The Boggart"	[B. II
		4	"The Oughtreds, their Hob and Peggy Flaunders"	[B. XIII
7060	DISPUTED SITE FOR A CHURCH	1	"Winwick Church"	[B. IX
(variant)		2	"The Building of Bideford Bridge"	[B. III

706 cont.

3 "Mauldslie Castle" [B. IX
4 "The Building of St Chad's" [B. IX
5 "Crooked Crookham" [B. IX
6 "Barnoldswick and Kirkstall Abbey [B. IX
7 "Callaly Castle" [B. IX
8 "The Castle of Melgund" [B. IX
9 "The Church of Fordoun" [B. IX
10 "The Spectral Cat" [B. IX
11 "Rochdale Church" [B. IX
12 "North Otterington Church" [B. IX
13 "The New Church at Marske" [B. IX
14 "The Church of Old Deer" [B. IX
15 "Garmstone Castle" [B. IX
16 "Cowthally Castle" [B. IX
17 "Glamis Castle" [B. IX
18 "Godshill" [B. IX
19 "The Devil on Brent Tor" [B. III

(Variant)

20 "The Fairies and Langton House" [B. V

7061* THE UNFINISHED BRIDGE

"William of Lindholme" [B. III

7070 LEGENDS ABOUT CHURCH BELLS: PROTESTING AGAINST REMOVAL

1 "The Bells of Forrabury Church" [B. IX
2 "The Bells of Whitby Abbey" [B. IX
3 "Kentsham Bell" [B. IX
4 "The Bells of Brinkburn" [B. IX
5 "Barlinch Bell" [B. IX
6 "Rivington Pike" [B. III

7080 LEGENDS CONCERNING THE GREAT PLAGUE

1 "A Tale of the Plague in Edinburgh" [B. XII
2 "Bessie Bell and Mary Gray" [B. IX

8000 WARS OF FORMER TIMES

1 "The Black Douglas" [B. VIII
2 "Hereward the Saxon" [B. VIII
3 "Goose Feathers" [B. VIII
4 "Folk Memories of Cromwell" [B. VIII
5 "Charles I and the Southwell Shoemaker" [B. VIII

		6 "The Fate of a Rebel" [B. VIII
		7 "The Earl of Traquair" [B. VIII
		8 "The Puppy under the Table" [B. VIII
8005	THE SOLDIER'S RETURN	"Drake's Cannon-ball" [B. VIII
8010	HIDDEN TREASURE	1 "The Gold of Craufurdland" [B. VI
		2 "The Gold of Largs Law" [B. IX
		3 "The Gold of Tentsmuir" [B. IX
		4 "Willy-Howe" [B. XII
		5 "The Treasure of Castle Rach" [B. III
		6 "The Treasure of Berry Pomery Castle" [B. IX
		7 "How Sampson was Punished for Swearing" [B. XII

INDEX TO STORY-TITLES IN PART A

6-2

I FABLES AND EXEMPLA

FABLES AND EXEMPLA

In the Aarne–Thompson classification the animal tales have been put together into one section, only subdivided into the kinds of animals that appear in them. I have chosen rather to put together fables after the manner of Aesop, which carry a moral applicable to humanity, and to class with them the brief tales with a moral or satiric intention.

The fables of Aesop had a great influence in early times. A detailed study of their transmission by Bengt Holbek forms the second volume of his facsimile of *Aesops Levned og Fabler*, printed from the manuscript of Christiern Pedersen in 1556. The fables are very ancient, the earliest possibly dating from the fifth century B.C.; the oldest surviving collection is dated in the first century A.D. and is contemporary with the *Aesop Romance*. This is a verse collection by Phaedrus, in Greek, and that of Babrius is possibly contemporary with it, though its date is uncertain. The Greek collections contain many tales of men and gods, but the *Romulus*, a Latin version of probably the sixth to the eighth centuries, contains almost exclusively the anthropomorphizing "Aesop's Fables" as we know them. A lost book of Alfred the Great introduced Aesop's Fables into England with new native material added, and a popular European addition to the corpus was the Reynard the Fox cycle. Avianus' fables in verse (*c.* A.D. 400) were the chief source of the medieval fables. *The Boke of Subtyl Historyes and Fables of Esop* was printed by Caxton in 1484; new versions and translations continued to come out all through the sixteenth and seventeenth centuries.

This number of editions shows the prestige in which the fables were held, and indeed the knowledge of them was widely diffused, as is shown in the nickname of "Archibald Bell-the-Cat"; but they were not far removed from literature, and soon returned to it again. They have been fortunate in their literary treatment. There are Henryson's lively fables, with the particularly pleasing "Taill of the Uplandis Mous and the Burges Mous" and there is Chaucer's delightful version of "The Fox and the Cock". In the seventeenth century there is a poem of type 283c*, "The Spider and the Gowt", included in *Churchyard Chippes* by Thomas Churchyard. It gives us a picture of the merry, active chambermaid, who gives her master leisure to lay up a store of gout but allows no peace to spiders. The tale is in oral tradition in Belgium, and was no doubt known in England before Churchyard used it, but I have found no trace of it in modern folk tradition, not even in a proverb.

Fables were used either as rhetorical devices or to enforce arguments, in the same way as "Belling the Cat" was used in the discussion on dealing with Cochran. An example is to be found in a letter from Lady Alington,

Sir Thomas More's stepdaughter, to Margaret Roper, describing how she
had tried to move interest for Sir Thomas More with the new Lord
Chancellor, and how she had been fobbed off with fables. (Letters
appended to Roper's *Life of Sir Thomas More* in the King's Classics
Series (1903), pp. 114 ff.)

And in good faith (said my Lord) I am very glad that I have no learning, but in a few
of Aesop's fables, of the which I shall tell you one. There was a country in the which
there were almost none but fools, saving a few which were wise, and they by their
wisdom knew that there should fall a great rain, the which should make all them
fools that should be fouled or wet therewith. They, seeing that, made them caves
under the ground, till all the rain was past. Then they came forth, thinking to make
the fools do what they list, and to rule them as they would. But the fools would none
of that, but would have the rule themselves, for all their craft. And when the wise
men saw that they could not obtain their purpose they wished they had been in the
rain and had fouled their clothes with them....And then he told me another fable
of a Lion, an Ass and a Wolf, and of their confession. First the Lion confessed that
he had devoured all the beasts he could come by. His confessor assoiled him because
he was a king, and also it was his nature so to do. Then came the poor Ass, and said
that he took but one straw out of his master's shoe for hunger, by the means whereof
he thought that his master did take cold. His confessor could not assoil this great
trespass but by and by sent him to the bishop. Then came the Wolf and made his
confession, and he was straitly commanded that he could not pass sixpence at a meal.
But when the said wolf had used this diet a little while, he waxed very hungry, in so
much that, on a day when he saw a cow with her calf come by him, he said to
himself, I am very hungry, and fain would I eat but that I am bound by my ghostly
father. Notwithstanding that, my conscience shall judge me. And then if that be so,
then shall my conscience be thus that the cow doth seem to me now to be but worth
a groat. And then if the cow be but worth a groat, then is the calf but worth two
pence; so did the wolf eat both the cow and the calf.

When More was shown Lady Alington's letter by his daughter Margaret
he proved to be already familiar with the fables. That about the rain he
had often heard at the King's Council from Cardinal Wolsey. The
second one, as he shrewdly deduced, could not be a genuine fable of
Aesop's, since Aesop was a pagan slave and this dealt with Christian
confession. But, as he truly said, neither tale was applicable to his own
case. The whole incident shows how commonly these fables were cited
in royal council chambers and places where matters of importance were
debated. The number which passed into proverbial phrases, such as
"dog in the manger", "sour grapes", and so on, shows how much they
were used. The tales are still generally known, but they are so widely
diffused in literature that it is difficult to assess the part which oral
tradition plays in the knowledge. The habit of citing fables in argument
or for illustration seems to have waned in the seventeenth century after
the Authorized Version of the Bible was universally known, the English

becoming the "People of a Book". Nowadays jocular references, such as that to Mrs Parton and her broom, are more often used in political argument than Aesop's fables.

The different kinds of tale contained in this group are: (*a*) The true Aesop fable, in which human characters are personified as animals, generally with satiric intentions. Modern traditional versions are "The Bum Bee", a lively variant on "The Ant and the Cricket", with an amended ending in which the Ant is punished for his churlish behaviour, "The Hare and the Prickly Backed Urchin", an international type, and "The Yaller-Legg'd Cock'ril", which shows a closer observation of animal behaviour than most of the fables. (*b*) The mock origin myths, which were never seriously believed, but which generally have some implicit moral, as, for instance, "The Wood-Pigeon's Nest". (*c*) The exemplary tale with a supernatural element, when the moral is pointed by a miracle. This is often a kind of origin myth, as in "The Greedy Peasant Woman" and "The First Cornish Mole". Many of the exemplary tales may be found among the saints' legends, the deciding factor being whether these tales were told by people who believed them. Tales of judgements count as legends, but might well be exemplary tales. (*d*) The simple moral tale, such as "The Choice of a Servant". Even the tales with no explicit moral generally embody a social comment.

BELLING THE CAT

Many of the nobility and barons held a secret council in the church of Lauder, where they enlarged upon the evils which Scotland sustained through the insolence and corruption of Cochran and his associates. While they were thus declaiming, Lord Gray requested their attention to a fable. "The mice," he said, "being much annoyed by the persecution of the cat, resolved that a bell should be hung about puss's neck, to give notice when she was coming. But though the measure was agreed to in full council, it could not be carried into effect, because no mouse had courage enough to undertake to tie the bell to the neck of the formidable enemy." This was as much as to intimate his opinion that though the discontented nobles might make bold resolutions against the King's ministers, yet it would be difficult to find anyone courageous enough to act upon them.

Archibald, Earl of Angus, a man of gigantic strength and intrepid courage, started up when Gray had done speaking. "I am he", he said, "who will bell the cat"; from which expression he was distinguished by the name of Bell-the-Cat to his dying day.

From *Tales of a Grandfather*, Sir Walter Scott, first series, ch. XXII, p. 222.
TYPE 110. MOTIF J.671.1 [*Belling the Cat*].
¶ Aesop: Jacobs, *The Fables of Aesop* (New York, 1894), no. 67. Turkish, Wesselski, *Hodscha Nasreddin*, I, no. 213. American Negro, Joel Harris, *Nights with Uncle Remus* (Boston, 1883). Irish, seven examples.

This anecdote about the conspiracy of the Scottish nobles against the favourites of James III shows that the fable was familiar in Scotland as early as 1482.

THE BUM BEE [summary]

The Queen of the Bumble Bees went out one day to get food for her children, and she was overtaken by a terrible storm. When it was at its worst, she saw ahead of her the palace of the King of the Pismoules, so she knocked at the door. A maidservant came to the door and the Bum Bee said, "Will you ask the King if the Queen of the Bum Bees can get shelter for the night out of the storm?" The maid shut the door and went to ask the King of the Pismoules. "Oh no," said the King. "She'll not get shelter here. Tell her, 'Where you made your summer's honey, go and make your winter's quarters.'" So the maid took the King's message, and went and shut the door on her, and the poor Queen of the Bum Bees struggled on through the storm, and at long last, more dead than alive, she got home, and told her children how the King of the Pismoules had refused her shelter and said; "Where you made your summer's honey, go and make your winter's quarters." And she said, "If the King of the Pismoules comes here seeking hospitality when I'm out, mind and pour boiling water on him." So the next summer the King of the Pismoules was out hunting, and he was overtaken by a terrible storm of rain, and he lost his party and his horse threw him and he hurt his leg. So he went to the Queen of the Bum Bees' palace to ask for shelter. But when she looked out and saw who it was she said; "Do you mind how you told me when I was near dead in the storm, 'Where you made your summer's honey, there make your winter's quarters'?" And she had a big kettle of boiling water and she poured it over the King of the Pismoules. And for all I know, it killed him.

The School of Scottish Studies, Maurice Fleming, from Bella Higgins, Perthshire. Has been compared to TYPE 280A, MOTIF J.711 [*In time of plenty, provide for want*], but it might rather be considered as half of TYPE 750*. MOTIFS Q.2 [*Kind and Unkind*]; B.857 [*Revenge taken for injury by one animal on another*].
¶ No exact parallel to this can be found. See "The Fox and the Magpie".

BUTTERMILK JACK

Ther wur an owld 'oman as had but one son,
And thay lived together as you med zee;
And they'd nought but an owld hen as wanted to sett,
Yet somehow a landlord he fain would be.

"Oh, I've been and begged me some buttermilk, mother,
Off of an owld 'oman as has girt store:
And I shall well rewarded be,
Vor she's gin me haf a gallon or mwore.

"Oh mother, my buttermilk I will sell,
And all for a penny, as you med zee:
And with my penny then I will buy eggs,
Vor I shall have seven for my pennèy.

"Oh mother, I'll set them all under our hen,
And seven cock chickens might chance for to be;
But seven cock chickens or seven cap hens,
There'll be seven half-crownds for me.

"Oh, I'll go carry them to market, mother,
And nothing but vine volk shall I zee:
And with my money then I will buy land,
Zo as a landlord I med be."

> "Oh, my dear zon, wilt thee know me,
> When thee hast gotten great store of wealth?"
> "Oh, my dear mother, how shall I know thee,
> When I shall hardly know my own self?"
>
> With that, the old 'oman she flew in a passion,
> And dashed her son, Jack, up agin the wall,
> And his head caught the shelf where the buttermilk stood,
> So down came the buttermilk, pitcher and all.
>
> Zo aal you as has got an old hen for to sett,
> Both by night and by day mind you has her well watched,
> Lest you should be like unto Buttermilk Jack,
> To reckon your chickens before thay are hatched.

T. Hughes, *The Scouring of the White Horse*, p. 171, Norton Collection, V, pp. 49–50
Berkshire.

TYPE 1430. MOTIFS, J.2060.1 [*Quarrel and fight over details of air-castles*]; J.2061.2
[*Air-castle: Pail of milk to be sold*].

¶ Aesop: Jacobs, no. 77. Wessleski, *Hodscha Nasreddin*, I, p. 249. Bødker, *Exemplar*
300, no. 55.

The tale is widely dispersed through Europe and in India, China, Indonesia, etc.
Stapleton in *All about the Merry Tales of Gotham*, second ed. p. 61, cites a similar
story about two brothers. In *NQ* VII and VIII, p. 222, Clouston mentions "our
nursery tale" as very like La Fontaine's "La Laitière et le pot au lait".

THE CHOICE OF A SERVANT

A farmer's wife was in need of a maidservant, so she asked a number of
girls to come to her house that she might choose the one that seemed
most likely to suit her. Now, when the farmer's manservant heard what
his mistress was going to do, he said to her, "I will show you how to
choose a good one."

"Very well," said the farmer's wife.

So the manservant laid a besom across the path by which the girls
had to come to the house, and he and his mistress watched them as they
came near.

The first girl who came kicked the besom aside. Then the farmer's
man said, "She's an idle slut, and can't bend her back."

The next girl who came jumped over the besom, and the farmer's
man said, "She won't do: she'll skip her work."

The last girl who came picked the besom up, and reared it up in a
corner out of the way. Then the farmer's man said, "That's the girl for
me: she'll be careful, industrious, and tidy."

So the third girl was chosen.

S. O. Addy, *Household Tales*, p. 13, North Derbyshire. Compare Grimm 155, "Looking for a Bride".

¶ A similar story of an office boy, chosen because he alone picked up a piece of paper, appeared in *The Children's Encyclopaedia*. See "Choosing a Worker", section III, Jocular.

CHRIST AND THE PEAS

(Christ) once went to a poor woman's door: whom he asked for food. She replied that even then she was boiling stones in the pot to make her children believe they were peas. Christ replied by telling her to lift the lid, which she did, and found the pot full of peas.

Norton Collection, II, p. 218, S.E. Lancashire; N. W. Thomas, *Folk-Lore*, VIII (1897), p. 379.

TYPE 750B (variant).

¶ "In 1869 a lady visiting a poor woman in S.E. Lancashire turned the conversation to Christianity. The woman said she had never heard of Christ. Afterwards she asked if it were not he who once went to a poor woman's door, etc." Another tale which begins in the same way with a starving woman boiling stones for her children is "The Poor Widow and her Son", section II.

THE FARMER AND HIS OX

There were a zurly old varmer and 'e 'ad a girt ox. One day 'e said to it, "Thee girt orkurd vule. Stupid vule thou be. I wonder who taught thee to be zo orkurd!"

And the ox 'e turn round to varmer, and 'e say, "Why, it were thee, tha' girt stupid vule!"

Ruth L. Tongue, *Folktales of England*, p. 140.

TYPE 1705 (variant). MOTIFS B.211 [*Animal uses human speech*], B.211.1.5.1 [*Speaking ox*].

¶ Baughman records only American versions, the earliest in 1925. Text from South Carolina. This could be classified as a Shaggy Dog story, but the brevity and the moral both qualify it to be considered as a fable.

THE FIRST CORNISH MOLE [summary]

Alice of the Combe, of noble birth, the only child of her mother, lived among the hills of Morwenna, near the Severn Sea. She was tall, blue-eyed, and very beautiful, but she was proud. She would pass whole days in choosing rich apparel, jewels and gold.

She rejected many suitors, for her heart was set on one man—Sir Beville of Stowe, a Granville, and one of the most renowned and faithful of the followers of the Stuart cause.

At last, Sir Beville was to give a ball and a banquet. For this, Alice spent many hours at her mirror, and when all was prepared, she descended to the hall, where her mother sat at her spinning, praying, as ever, for her daughter's success: for she longed to see her wedded, and to hold her children on her knee. Alice's robe was of rich dark velvet, jewels sparkled in her dark hair, and on her hand she wore a great, shining ring. But she felt no need of her mother's prayers, so secure was she in the power of her own beauty. "I lack no prayers," she said scornfully. But at the words, a burst of wild music and a flash of light filled the air: the girl shrieked in terror, and was gone. No search availed, for many days no sign nor trace of her could be found: until one evening a gardener, leaning on his spade, noticed a small heap of earth at his feet, and on its loosened surface gleamed the very ring which Alice had worn.

Their earnest scrutiny revealed a small, fine inscription on its inner surface, in the old Cornish tongue:

> Beryan erde
> Oyn und perde!

And this the priest at Morwenna, a learned, grey-headed man, interpreted:

> "The earth must hide
> Both eyes and Pride!"

As he spoke the words a little sound at his feet drew the eyes of all to the ground: and there stood a small dark creature, clothed like Lady Alice in soft velvet: but sightless, for her great blue eyes had been sealed for ever, and for her pride she had become a mole—the first ever to be found in Cornwall.

R. S. Hawker, *Footprints of Former Men in Far Cornwall*, p. 27 (John Lane, London, 1903).
Distant variant of TYPES 836 and 751. MOTIF A.1893.2* [*Girl proud of silky skin turned into mole*]. Cornwall, *Choice Notes*, XLVIII (1959). Courtney, *Cornish Feasts and Folklore* (1890), p. 111.
¶ The tradition also existed in Berkshire. In "Folk-Lore of the Kennet Valley" (*Folk-Lore*, XIII, p. 622), L. Salmon says: "Mrs Collins also told me a legend of the mole—that it was once a fine lady, so fine that the earth was not good enough to walk upon, so she was made to walk underground—as punishment for her pride, one concludes." This follows a version of 751. See "The Greedy Peasant Woman".

THE FOX AND THE HEDGEHOG

Another pretty numerous class of our popular stories consists of those in which animals are the actors. One of the most common of these relates to the strife between the fox and the hedgehog, who, according to the good people of Northamptonshire, are the two most astute animals in creation.

How a couple of these worthies once fell out as to which was the swifter animal: and how, when they had put their speed to the trial, the cunning urchin contrived to defeat Reynard by placing his consort in the furrow which was to form the goal; so that when her mate had made a pretence of starting, she might jump out and feign to be himself just arrived. And how, after three desperate runs, the broken-winded fox fell a victim to the deceit, and was compelled to yield to his adversary: who, ever since that day, has been his most inveterate enemy.

(Northamptonshire. T. Sternberg.) *NQ*, v, p. 364.
Norton Collection, III, p. 64.
TYPE 1074 or 275 A. MOTIF.KII.I [*Race won by deception: relative helpers*].
¶ See also "The Hare and the Prickly-backed Urchin", "How the Hedgehog ran the Devil to Death".

THE FOX AND THE MAGPIE

Once a fox and a magpie agreed to go a-robbing together on the King's highway. They overtook a girl with a basket of eggs and butter. "We cannot manage this," said the fox. "Oh, yes, we can," said the magpie. "I'll go and peck her nose, while you pick up the basket." But when the fox had the basket safe, he carried it off to his hole, and the magpie could get no share of the eggs and butter. "I'll serve him out for this," he thought to himself.

So a little time after, he went to the fox and said, "I know where to find some horseflesh, but it's no good to tell you, you'll keep it all yourself." "No, I won't," said the fox, "I promise you it shall be all right this time."

So away they went, over hedges and ditches, one flying, the other jumping, till they came to a high wall. "Now," says the magpie, "you jump, I'll fly."

The fox jumped, cleared the wall, and fell into the midst of a pack of hounds. As the magpie flew overhead, he cried, "What about eggs and butter now?"

E. M. Leather, *Folk-Lore of Herefordshire* (1912), p. 177.
Variant of TYPES 56B and 176*. MOTIF B.857. [*Revenge taken for injury by one animal on another*].
¶ Plot similar to "The Bum Bee".

THE FROG AND THE CROW

There was a jolly frog in the river did swim, O!
And a comely black crow lived by the river brim, O!
    Come on shore, come on shore,
    Said the crow to the frog, and then, O!
    No, you'll bite me, no, you'll bite me,
    Said the frog to the crow again, O!

But there is sweet music on yonder green hill, O!
And you'll be a dancer, a dancer in yellow,
    All in yellow, all in yellow,
    Said the crow to the frog, and then, O!
    All in yellow, all in yellow,
    Said the frog to the crow again, O!

Farewell, ye little fishes, farewell, every good fellow,
For I'm going to be a dancer, a dancer in yellow.
    Oh beware, take care,
    Said the fish to the frog, and then, O!
    All in yellow, all in yellow,
    Said the frog to the fish again, O!

The frog he came swimming, a-swimming to land, O!
The crow he came hopping to lend him a hand, O!
    Sir, I thank you, sir, I thank you,
    Said the frog to the crow, and then, O!
    You are welcome, most welcome,
    Said the crow to the frog again, O!

But where is the music on yonder green hill, O?
And where are the dancers, the dancers in yellow?
    All in yellow, all in yellow,
    Said the frog to the crow again, O!
    They are here, said the crow,
    And ate him up there and then, O!

I. and P. Opie, *The Puffin Book of Nursery Rhymes*, p. 138.
TYPE 242, MOTIF K. 815 [*Victim lured out by kind words is killed*].
¶ Aesop, Spanish, Indian, African, West Indian versions. Crane, *The Baby's Opera*.
Traditional from Mrs Lewis Turnbull. Versions of the song known in the seventeenth century. See notes in *Puffin Book of Nursery Rhymes*.

THE GRATEFUL BEASTS

About this time a remarkable circumstance happened to a rich and miserly Venetian, which we think it worth while to insert in this place; his name was Vitalis: and when he was on the point of giving his daughter in marriage, he went into a large forest near the sea to provide delicacies for the table. As he wandered alone through the forest, with his bow and arrows ready, and intent on taking venison, he suddenly fell into a pit-fall which had been cunningly set for the lions, bears and wolves, out of which he found it impossible to escape, because the bottom of it was so wide and the mouth so narrow. Here he found two fierce animals, a lion and a serpent, which had also by accident fallen in: and Vitalis signing himself with the cross, neither of them, though fierce and hungry, ventured to attack him. All that night he spent in this pit, crying and moaning, and expecting with lamentations the approach of so base a death. A poor wood-cutter, passing by chance that way to collect faggots, heard his cries, which seemed to come from beneath the ground, and following the sound till he came to the pit's mouth, he looked in, and called out, "Who is there?" Vitalis sprang up, rejoiced beyond measure, and eagerly replied, "It is I, Vitalis, a Venetian, who knowing nothing of these pit-falls, fell in, and shall be devoured by wild beasts, besides which I am dying of hunger and terror. There are two fierce animals here, a lion and a serpent, but, by God's protection and the sign of the cross, they have not yet hurt me, and it remains for you to save me, that I may afterwards show you my gratitude. If you will save me, I will give you half of all my property, namely five hundred talents; for I am worth a thousand." The poor man answered, "I will do as you request, if you will be as good as your word." Upon this Vitalis pledged himself on oath to do as he had promised. Whilst they were speaking, the lion, by a bland movement of his tail, and the serpent by a gentle hissing, signified to the poor man their approbation, and seemed to join in Vitalis's request to be delivered. The poor man immediately went home for a ladder and ropes, with which he returned and let the ladder down into the pit, without anyone to help him. Immediately the lion and serpent, striving which should be first, mounted by the rounds of the ladder, and gave thanks to the poor man, crouching at his feet, for their deliverance. The wood-cutter, approaching Vitalis, kissed his hand, saying, "Long live this hand! I am glad to say that I have earned my bargain," and with these words he conducted Vitalis to a road with which he was acquainted. When they parted, the poor man asked when and where Vitalis would discharge his promise. "Within four days," said Vitalis, "in Venice, in my own palace, which is well known and easy to find." The countryman returned home to dinner, and as he was sitting at table, the lion entered with a dead goat, as a present in return for his deliverance, and having laid it down, took his leave without doing any hurt. The countryman, however, wishing to see where so tame an animal lay, followed him to his den, the lion all the time licking his feet, and then came back to his dinner. The serpent now came also, and brought with him in his mouth a precious stone, which he laid in the countryman's plate. The same proceedings again took place as before. After two or three days, the rustic, carrying the jewel with him, went to Venice, to claim from Vitalis his promise. He found him feasting with his neighbours in joy for his deliverance and said to him, "Friend, pay me what you owe me." "Who art thou?" replied Vitalis, "and what dost thou want?" "I want the five hundred talents you promised me." "Do you expect", replied Vitalis, "to get so easily the money which I have had so much difficulty to amass?" and as he said these words he ordered his servants to cast the rash man into prison.

But the rustic, by a sudden spring, escaped out of the house and told what had happened to the judges of the city. When, however, they were a little incredulous, he showed them the jewel which the serpent had given him, and immediately one of them, perceiving that it was of great value, bought it of the man at a high price. But the countryman further proved the truth of his words, by conducting some of the citizens to the dens of the lion and the serpent, when the animals again fawned on him as before. The judges were thus convinced of his truth, and compelled Vitalis to fulfil the promise which he had given, and to make compensation for the injury which he had done the poor man.

Roger of Wendover, *Chronicle*, II, p. 143 (footnote).
TYPE 160, MOTIFS W.154.8 [*Grateful animals, ungrateful man*], B.361 [*Animals grateful for rescue from pit*].
¶ Type Index cites examples from Bolte-Polivka IV, 139, 2 Finnish, 1 Latvian, 1 Norwegian, 6 Danish, 2 French, 1 Catalan, 1 German, 1 Italian, 1 Hungarian, 1 Polish, 1 Greek, 2 Turkish, 10 Indian, 9 African.
The tale occurs in the *Gesta Romanorum* (Oesterley, no. 119).

THE GREEDY PEASANT WOMAN

Our Lord went to a baker's shop to ask for something to eat, and the woman there began making him a cake. But each time she put a handful of flour into the pan, she took some out, saying, "Oo-ooh, that's too much". And he said to her,

> Owl thou art and owl thou shalt be,
> And all the birds of earth shall peck at thee.

Norton Collection, II, p. 227, from Berkshire, Kennet Valley.
"Folklore in the Kennet Valley", L. Salmon, *Folk-Lore*, XIII, p. 421. From a Mrs Collins.
TYPE 751A, MOTIFS K.1811 [*Gods (saints) in disguise visit mortals*], D.1652.1.2 [*Halved cake grows miraculously larger*], Q.1.1 [*Inhospitality punished*].
¶ Norwegian, Dutch, Irish, French, Spanish, Italian, Rumanian, Hungarian, and Slovenian versions known.
    See "The Owl was a Baker's Daughter", *The Gentleman's Magazine* (November 1804), p. lxxiv.

THE HARE AND THE PRICKLY-BACKED URCHIN

It war yaa Sunday mornin' i' Summer, just aboot t' time when t' buttery bushes blooms. T' sun, war shinin' breet up i' t' sky, bees war bisy i' t' buttery blossoms, skylarks war singin' up aloft, as fowks war traipsin' eff tae t' chotch. All creation war happy, and t' prickly-backt urchin and all.

    T' urchin war standin' by his deär, sniftin' t' mornin' breeze, and hummin' a laatle song tiv hissen, as fowks does when they lewk oot eva fine Sunday mornin'. Whilst he war tunin' up, t' idee cam intiv his heäd as he mud just as weel hev a stroll oot, whilst his wife war washin' up, tae see hoo his tonneps war deein'. T' tonneps war t' next field tiv his hoos, and him and his family used t' hev a bite noo and agen. That war why he called 'em *his* tonneps. Seä he sneckt t' deär efter him, and set off up t' headland. He'd just gotten as far as t' bullas-bush at stands i' t' angle o' t' tonnep field, when he jumped wi' t' awd hare. T' hare war on t' same job. He war strollin' round, seein' his cabbishes.

    When t' urchin cam up wi' t' hare, he nodded and said: "Noo mate, what cheer?" But t' hare raither fancied hissen, an' stedd o' saying'; "Middlin', thankee, hoo's thysen?" he nobbut said, short like: "What's thoo doin' up here, all by thysen o' this fine mornin'?" "Oh, I's nobbut hevin' a stroll roond," said t' prickly-backt urchin. "Hevin' a stroll roond," laughed the hare, "I sud ha' thowt thoo cud ha' fun' summat better tae deä fer thy awd bandy legs nor tae come spyin' round my cabbish."

    Noo this answer nettled t' prickly-backt urchin, a vast. He cud stand a bit, but he warn't gyin' fur tae stand nowt said again his legs, for they war a bit crewkt, and he knew they war. Seä he answered: "Thoo talks as if thoo'd gotten a better set thysen." "Why, I sud be reet put oot, if I hedn't", said t' hare. "Weel", said t' urchin, "that depends. I lay I cud just aboot show thee t' culler o' my tail iv a race." "Why, thoo's daft," said t' hare, "thoo and thy bandy legs. But I deän't mind showing

thoo a thing or tweä, since thoo's sae keen aboot it. W'at's t' stakes?"
"I'll lay thee a guinea, and a bottle o' gin," said t' prickly-backt urchin.
"Deän", said t' awd hare. "Come on then, and let's have it oot nooe!"
"Nay, there's neä great hurry," answered t' urchin, "I's nut quite fit.
I hate tae deä things iv a despert hurry. I'll just gang away yam, and hev a
bit, and I'll meet thee up here iv aboot hauf an hour." Weel, t' awd
hare agreed tae this, an' t' prickly-backt urchin cantered away eff heäm,
thinkin': "He goods hissen aboot his lang legs, but I'll insnse him, I'll
show him hoo it's deän." When he gat yam, he said tiv his wife, he said:
"Missis, busk thysen, and lewk sharp aboot it, and come on oot wi' me."
"Why! whativir's up?" says she, "thoo hasn't been oot for a walk
wi' me, sin I deänt knaw t' time when." "Niver thoo bother aboot that,"
says he, "but come thoo oot wi' me. I've a bet on of a guinea and a
bottle o' gin wi' t' hare, and I want thee wi' me." "Thoo's gyin' tae run
t' awd hare! Why, thoo's lost thy wits! Hoo can thoo race wi' him? Thoo
knaws weel ineäf 'at he can gang ten-times faster ner thoo." "Noo,
missis," he says, kind but firm like, "this is my job. Just thoo get thysen
fit, and come oot wi' me." Noo, what cud t' prickly-backt urchin wife
deä? She cam wiv him, o' course.

As they war gyin' up tae t' bullas-bush, which war t' spot where they'd
arranged tae meet, t' prickly-backt urchin says tae his wife: "Noo, hod
thy noise a minit, and let *me* talk. I's gyin' tae fettle this race i' t' tonnep
field. I sal run i' yaa furrow and t' hare in t' next yan, noo wat thoo's
got tae deä is tae parzle off up tae t' top end o' t' furrow, ower anenst t'
bullas-bush, and sit there. We sal start frae this end o' t' field, and when
t' awd hare comes up at yon end, all that thoo has tae deä is tae jump up,
and mal oot: "Here I is."

Seä, t' prickly-backt urchin wife went on tae t' furrow ower anenst t'
bullas-bush, and efter he'd gi'en her time tae git there, t'awd urchin
went on tae t' bullas-bush. There war t' awd hare a-waitin' for tae win
his guinea and his bottle o' gin, and he said, as t' prickly-backt urchin
cam up: "Istä fit?" "Ay, lad," answered t' urchin. "Then come on."
And both of them tewk his stand iv his furrow.

T'awd hare coonted "Yan, tweä, three, away", and off he went
Hyder Ali up t' furrow, as hard as iver he cud gang. But t' awd urchin
nobbut ran a few yeds and then cam back and clapped hissen doon
amang t' tonneps at t' beginning o' t' furrow, and waited. T' hare went
loupin' up t' field like a steäm-ingen, and when he cam tae t' top, up
jumps t' prickly-backt urchin wife, and mals oot: "Here I is." It war
raither a cu-doon for t' awd hare, for he reckoned at t' urchin war a
hunthed yeds behint, but he misdooted nowt, 'cos t' prickly-backt urchin
wife lewkt just for all the world like t' awd prickly-backt urchin. He
thowt tiv hissen: "This is a queer job," but he said: "Come on back,

then," and off he went Hyder Ali, back agen doon t' furrow, like a steäm-ingen. But t' prickly-backt urchin wife stopped iv her spot. When t' awd hare gat tae t'other end o' t' field, up jumped t' urchin, and belled oot: "Here I is." And t' hare, fair beside hissen wi' rage, yelled back; "Then come on agen." "All reet," says t' urchin, "as oft as ye like for my sake." And off t' awd hare went again. This happened ninety-nine times, and t' prickly-backt urchin war allus even wi' him. Ivery time at t' awd hare cam to t' top or t' boddom o' t' furrow, t' urchin or his wife shouted, "Here I is."

And at t' hundedth lap, t' awd hare was fair bet wi' t' job. Aboot hauf-way doon t' field, he tumbled doon, and hed a stroke and deed. Seä t' urchin tewk t' stake from beside t' bullas-bush, a guinea and a bottle o' gin, he shooted for his wife tae come oot o' t' furrow, and off they went heäm, quite content wi' t' mornin''s wark. And if they ain't deed sin then, they're wick yet.

That's hoo t' prickly-backt urchin ran t' hare on Ganton Wold, and fairly ran him tae deäd, and sin that time neä hare has dared tae challenge t' Ganton urchins.

T' moral o' this tale is fost, that neäbody owt tae think hissen a better chap ner other fowk, and mak fun on 'em. And second, 'at men owt tae pick wives like theirsens, wives 'at can help 'em, and be use tiv 'em. Them 'at's urchins mun pick an urchin for a wife, and not a fond doe-rabbit, nor a bitin' rezzil.

Cowling, *Dialect of Hackness, N.E. Yorkshire* (1915), pp. 165–71.

TYPE 1074. See also 275 A and 275 A*. MOTIF K.11.1 [*Race won by deception*].

¶ Grimm, no. 187. American Negro, Dorson, 404 (North Carolina). American, Finnish, Estonian, Swedish, Spanish, Flemish, German, Austrian, Russian, Turkish, African versions known.

Norton Collection, III, p. 65, Yorkshire. Literary treatment, Walter de la Mare, *Told Again*. See also "The Fox and the Hedgehog", "How the Hedgehog ran the Devil to Death".

THE HARNIT AND THE BITTLE

A Harnit zet in a hollur tree,
A proper spiteful twoad was he:
And a merrily zung while he did zet
His stinge as shearp as a baggonet:
 "Oh, who so vine and bowld as I,
  I vears not bee, nor waspe nor vly!"

A bittle up thuck tree did clim,
And skornfully did look at him;

Zays he, "Zur Harnet, who give thee
A right to zet in thuck there tree?
    Vor aal you zings so nation vine,
    I tell 'e 'tis a house o' mine."

The harnit's conscience velt a twinge,
But growin' bowld wi' his long stinge,
Zays he, "Possession's the best laaw,
Zo here th' sha'sn't put a claaw!
    Be off, and leave the tree to me,
    The mixen's good enough for thee!"

Just then a yuckle passin' by
Was axed by them the cause to try:
"Ha! ha! I zee how 'tis!" zays he,
"They'll make a vamous munch vor me!"
    His bill was shearp, his stomach lear,
    Zo up a snapped the caddlin pair.

Moral:

All you as be to laaw inclined
This leetle stowry bear in mind:
Vor if to laaw you aims to gwo,
You'll vind thy'll allus zarve 'e zo:
    You'll meet the vate of these here two,
    They'll take your cwoat and carcass too!

Thomas Head, *Legends, Tales and Songs in the Dialect of the Peasantry of Gloucester-shire* (Cirencester, 1900), pp. 20–1. [Yuckle = woodpecker.]
TYPE 113B variant. MOTIF K.452 [*Unjust umpire misappropriates disputed goods*].
¶ It is strange that there is no type allotted to this tale, which seems a common enough theme. Lewis Carroll uses it in "Fury said to a mouse".

HOW THE HEDGEHOG RAN THE DEVIL TO DEATH

A hedgehog made a wager with the Devil to run him a race, the hedgehog to have the choice of time and place. He chose to run up and down a ditch at night. When the time came, the hedgehog rolled himself up at one end of the ditch, and got a friend to roll himself up at the other: then he started the Devil off. At the other end of the ditch, the friend said to the Devil—"Now, we go off again". Each hedgehog kept repeating this formula at his own end of the ditch, while the Devil ran up and down between them, until they ran him to death.

Norton Collection, III, p. 67, Worcestershire. Obtained from the Rev. T. H. Philpott of Hedge End, Botley, who learned it from his mother in Worcestershire. This story would be introduced by the remark, "Now we go off again, as the hedgehog said to the Devil." It also appeared in *Folk-Lore*, XXXVII, p. 298, the same version with minor alterations in wording, but given as obtained by T. H. Philpott from an old man near Malvern.

TYPE 1074. MOTIF K.11.1 [*Race won by deception; relative helpers*].

¶ Worcestershire. E. M. Leather, *Folk-Lore*, XXIII, p. 357. See also "The Fox and the Hedgehog" and "The Hare and the Prickly-Backed Urchin".

THE KING OF BEASTS

There was once a King, who determined to have the question decided as to which of the animals should be called the "King of Beasts". So on a certain day he had all the different kinds assembled and turned into a large arena. He then had it proclaimed that at a given signal they might all fall to fighting and that the one who survived should win the title of "King of Beasts" for his descendants for ever.

The word was given; all the animals began fighting furiously, and as one was slain the victor would seek another antagonist. At length the Lion, crippled, bleeding, and scarcely able to stir, thought himself to be the sole survivor, but on looking round to make sure that this might be so, he espied an old Donkey standing with his head thrust into a corner of the arena. The Donkey had run thither in very great fright at the commencement of the fray. The maimed Lion with great difficulty crawled along to where the Donkey was standing. The latter waited his opportunity, and when the Lion came close up to him, lashed out with both his heels, striking the Lion full on the head, and rolling him in the dust.

The Donkey, therefore, became "King of Beasts".

Lowsley, *A Glossary of Berkshire Words and Phrases* (1888), p. 28.
MOTIF B.236.0.1 [*Animal king chosen as result of contest*].

THE KING OF BIRDS: I

The eagle summoned all kinds of birds together, to choose their king; it was agreed that the one which could fly highest should be elected.

The Rook flew so high, that he called out,

"Caw, caw, caw,
I can zee it all."

The Lark flew quite up to heaven's gate, and there sang a sweet song of triumph.

But whilst these trials were going on the little blue Tit-mouse crept under the feathers of the eagle and hid itself there. When the eagle's turn came, he soared far higher than any of the others and remained stationary at that point, looking proudly downwards. At length when quite exhausted with the prolonged effort, he was obliged to commence to descend—at that moment the little blue Tit-mouse flew out and mounted still higher than the eagle had done, with its pert note of

"Tit, tit,
Higher it,
Tit, tit,
Higher it."

All the birds were therefore obliged to acknowledge that the little blue Tit-mouse must be their King.

Norton Collection, I, p. 57, from Berkshire; Lowsley, *A Glossary of Berkshire Words and Phrases* (1888). [Higher it = higher yet.]
TYPE 221, MOTIFS B.236.1 [*Election of king of birds*], K.25.1 [*Flying contest won by deception: riding on the other. Wren hides in eagle's wings*], B242.1.2 [*Wren king of the birds; wins contest for Kingship.*]
¶ "Wren king of the birds", J. O. Halliwell, *Nursery Rhymes*, pp. 165–6.
A similar story and verse, with a mention of a wren-building ceremony in Pembroke-shire. An Irish version of the legend is given in *Folk-Lore*, V, p. 197. Henderson, second edn p. 125, gives an Essex example of the ceremony. Chambers, p. 37, gives the wren boys' rhyme, and a note on the custom in the Scottish Lowlands. *Word-Lore* I, pp. 77–8, gives a version of Irish origin by H. C. D. Lewis of Langport. Hone's *Year-Book* (1832), p. 1608. An Ulster version was published by T. G. F. Paterson in "Contributions to Ulster Folk Life". The wren-hunting time is St Stephen's Day. Wren-hunting also in the Isle of Man, but the persecution is accounted for by a different story, that of a wicked fairy forced to assume a wren's form, W. W. Gill, *Second Manx Scrapbook*, p. 360. In a version given in the *Journal of American Folk-lore*, XII, p. 229, the wren is punished for its trickery, not by persecution but by only being able to fly low and flutteringly. The story is widespread. Grimm (no. 171). Modern oral versions as noted in the Aarne–Thompson Type Index. Finnish–Swedish, 1; Latvian, 2; Estonian 2; Swedish, 7; Norwegian, 1; Scottish, 2; Irish, 9; French, 10; Catalan, 1; Dutch, 6; Flemish, 14; German, 42; Italian, 3; Hungarian, 2; Polish, 6; Russian, 5; Greek, 2; Indonesian, 1; Franco-American, 1; African, 12.

THE KING OF THE BIRDS: II

"THE GATHERIN' OF THE BIRDS"

There was a gatherin' of all the birds of the air one day, to houl' a contest as to which would be king among them. Many a time I heared the story. They wur all there, big, small, great and little and some wur gay wi' colour, like the kingfisher and others sober coloured like the wee jinny wran.

There wus a great contention as to how the matter wud be decided but in the end it wus arranged that the one that cud rise the highest wud be the king.

They wur all there and they started. The lark soared into the sky, but it wus soon passed be the hawk and the eagle. Soon the eagle left them all behine and in no time was high as the sun itself. There and then it proclaimed itself king of the air but as sure as to-morrow a wee wran had hid itself in the topney of the eagle unknownst, from which it rose and continued upwards singing "I'm your king, king of the air am I." The eagle wus sore put out but it wus too tired to follow and the wran won. It's a right cute wee bird the same wran.

T. G. F. Paterson, contributions to *Ulster Folk-Life*. Crossmaglen, aged about eighty. Literary treatment: Pliny and Aristotle.

¶ T. F. Thistleton-Dyer in *Folk-Lore of Shakespeare* (1883), p. 110, quotes an Irish version from Kelly's *Indo-European Folk-Lore*, pp. 75, 79. "The birds all met together one day, and settled among themselves that whichever could fly highest was to be the king of them all. Well, just as they were starting, the little rogue of a wren perched itself on the eagle's tail. So they flew and flew and flew ever so high, till the eagle was miles above all the rest, and could not fly another stroke for he was so tired. 'Then,' says he, 'I'm the King of the birds,' says he, 'hurroo!' 'You lie,' says the wren, darting up a perch and a half above the big fellow. The eagle was so angry to think how he was outwitted by the wren, that when the latter was coming down, he gave him a stroke of his wing, and from that day the wren has never been able to fly higher than a hawthorn bush."

THE LABORER AND THE NIGHTINGALE

Sometime there was a laborer, which had a garden well pleasant and much delicious, into which he oft went for to take his disport and pleasure. And on a day at evening...when he entered into his garden and set himself down under a tree, he heard the song of a nightingale.

And for the great pleasure and joy which he took thereof, he sought and at the last found the means for to take the nightingale, to the end that yet greater joy and plaisance he might have of it.

And when the nightingale was taken, he demanded of the laborer, "Wherefore hast thou taken so great pains for to take me? For well thou knowest that of me thou mayst not have great profit."

And the villein answered thus to the nightingale; "For to hear the song of thee I have taken thee."

And the nightingale answered; "Certainly in vain thou hast pained and labored, for, for no good I will sing while that I am in prison."

And then the laborer or villein answered: "If thou singest not well, I shall eat thee."

And then the nightingale said to him: "If thou put me within a pot for to be sodden, little meat shalt thou then make of my body. And if thou settest me for to be roasted, less meat shall be then made of me. And therefore neither boiled nor roasted shall not be thy great belly filled of me. But if thou let me flee, it shall be to thee a great profit. For three doctrines I shall teach thee, which thou shalt love better than three fat kine." And then the laborer let the nightingale flee.

And when he was out of his hands, and that he was upon a tree, he said to the villein in this manner: "My friend, I have promised to thee that I shall give to thee three doctrines, whereof the first is this—that thou believe no thing which is impossible. The second is that thou keep well what thine is. And the third is that thou take no sorrow of the thing lost which may not be recovered."

And soon after, the nightingale began to sing, and in his song said thus: "Blessed be God Which hath delivered me out of the hands of this villein or churl, which hath not known, seen, nor touched the precious diamond which I have within my belly. For if he had found it, he had been much rich and from his hands I had not escaped."

And then the villein which heard this song began to complain and to make great sorrow and after said: "I am well unhappy that have lost so fair a treasure which I had won. And now I have lost it."

And the nightingale said then to the churl: "Now know I well that thou art a fool, for thou takest sorrow of that whereof thou shouldst have none, and soon thou hast forgotten my doctrine, because that thou weenest that within my belly should be a precious stone of more weight than I am. And I told and taught to thee that thou shouldst never believe that thing which is impossible. And if that stone was thine, why hast thou lost it? And if thou hast lost it and mayst not recover it, why takest thou sorrow for it?"

And therefore it is folly to chastise or to teach a fool, which never believeth the learning and doctrine which is given to him.

From *A Hundred Merry Tales*, ed. Zall, pp. 25–7.

TYPE 150, MOTIFS K.604 [*The three teachings of the bird*], J.21.14 [*Never try to reach the unobtainable*], J.21.12 [*Rue not the thing that is past*].

❡ Aarne–Thompson Type Index notes oral versions: Finnish, 39; Finnish–Swedish, 3; Estonian, 30; Irish, 1; French, 2; Flemish, 1; Italian, 1; Czech, 1; Russian, 1; Greek, 4; Turkish, 1; Arab, 1; Jewish, 1; Indian, 1; Indonesian, 1. Literary source: Aesop. See also "The Three Good Advices", type 910, "The Tale of Ivan", A. IV, "Master Vavasour and Turpin his Man", A. III.

LAPWING AND RINGDOVE

The common people in the North Riding of Yorkshire believe that at one period the cushat, or ringdove, laid its eggs upon the ground, and that the peewit, or lapwing, made its nest on high: but that some time or other an amicable arrangement took place between these birds, exchanging their localities for building. The peewit accordingly expresses its disappointment at the bargain as follows:

> "Pee-wit, pee-wit,
> I coup'd my nest and I rue it."

While the cushat rejoices that she is out of the reach of mischievous boys—

> "Coo, coo, come now,
> Little lad
> With thy gal,
> Come not thou!"

Halliwell, *Nursery Rhymes and Popular Tales*, p. 260.
TYPE 240 (variant), MOTIF A2247.4 [*Dove and magpie exchange eggs*].
¶ A comparable Highland tale, collected by Miss A. V. Stuart, is "The Legend of the Oystercatcher", in which the oystercatcher lent its power of swimming to the gull and never got it back.

The usual type is an egg-substitution, not a nest-substitution. The oral versions noted in the Aarne–Thompson Type Index are mainly northern: Finnish, 94; Finnish–Swedish, 1; Estonian, 11; Swedish, 52; Russian, 1.

THE LION, THE LEPER, AND THE TOD

There wiz ance a man traivllin in a hill, and he gede will (lost his way), an he gede an he gede (went) till he saw a bonnie clear lichtie, an he gede till he cam till't. Fin (when) he cam up till't, it wiz in a hoosie, an he gede in.

It wiz clean swypit, an there wiz a green bink, an there wiz a steel (stool), an there wiz a cheer (chair) in't, an there wiz a bonnie clear burnin' fire. He took a seat, an sat doon at the firie t'keep himsel warm. Bit he hidna sitten lang fin he hears a whiskan, whiskan like aboot the door, an he grew fleyt (afraid), an ran an haid himsel. In comes the tod (fox) whiskin, whiskin, an he sits doon o' the green bink. In comes the lion niest, an he sits doon o' the steel, an in comes the leper (leopard) niest, an sits doon o' the cheer, an they fell to newsan (conversation) amo' themsels, an they set t'brack——'s faul (fold), an tak oot a sheep. Sae the man slippit oot, an he wiz awa afore them, an taul the fouck (folk) faht he hid hard (had heard), an the fouck wiz afore them at the

121

faul, an they were forct t' come hame. The man cam hame afore them. They sat doon in their seats again, the tod on's green bink, the lion on's steel, an the leper on's cheer. They yokit wi ane anither, an said it some o' them hid be en clashin (telling tales). The leper said it wizna him, an the lion said it wizna him. Sae the blame lichtit o' the tod, for they said he wiz aye a fool (foul) clashin brute. He hid to be smackit for devulging their seicret. They took t' smack 'im, an he ran a'wye to hide, an he cam upo' the man. "Ha, ha!" said he,

> "Here's Lugie at the wa',
> An' he's cairrit a' the tales awa."

Collected by W. Gregor, *Folk-Lore Journal*, III, p. 269.

THE LION, THE LEOPARD, AND THE FOX [anglicized]

There was once a man travelling on a hill, and he lost his way, and he gaed and he gaed, until he saw a wee small light in the distance, and he gaed till he came to it. When he came to it, it was a housie, and he gaed in. It was clean sweepit, and there was a green bench, and a stool and a chair in it, and a clear fire burning. He took a seat, and sat down to warm himself at the fire. But soon he heard a whisking, whisking sound at the door, and he was feared, and ran and hid himself. In came a fox, whisking, whisking, and he sat down on the green bench. In comes the lion next, and then in comes the leopard, and they fell to newsing among themselves, and they settled it that they'd go and rob a neighbour's sheepfold. But the man slipped out before them, and away to the neighbours, and told them what he had heard, so the neighbours were before them at the fold, and they came home with nothing. The man slipped home before them, and hid again, to hear what he could hear. They sat down and argued together, as to who could have let it out. The leopard said it was not him, and the lion said it was not him, and the two of them fixed it on the fox, for he had a tongue that was aye wagging. So they went for him to skelp him, and he ran to hide, and came upon the man. "Ha, ha!" says he,

> "Here's Lugie at the wa',
> An' he's cairrit a' the tales awa'."

TYPE 613 (variant). MOTIFS B.235 [*Secrets discussed in animal meeting*], N.451 [*Secrets overheard from animal conversation*].

¶ F. J. Norton conjectures that this is a broken-down version of type 613, "The Two Travellers". In this case the man's second visit ought really to be the visit of a second man. The only approach to this theme in our native stories is in "The Apple-Tree Man".

THE MAGPIE'S NEST

All the birds asked the magpie to teach them to build their nests. So first she made a round cake of mud, and this was enough for the thrush, who made her nest of mud ever afterwards. Next she fixed some twigs in the mud, which satisfied the blackbird. She added another layer of mud, and this contented the owl. She lined the outside with more twigs, and the sparrow went off and did the same. The inside she lined with feathers, and the starling went and did the same. Thus every bird learnt something of the art from the magpie, until there was only the turtle-dove left, and she kept singing her usual song, "Take two, Taffy Take two-o-o-o". The magpie answered "One's enough!", but the turtle-dove kept on with her croon, until the angry magpie flew off, refusing to help the birds any more. That is why different birds build different nests.

Halliwell's *Nursery Rhymes*, p. 257; Jacobs, *English Fairy Tales*, no. 36. Derived from Swainson's *Folk-Lore of British Birds*, pp. 80 and 166.
TYPE 236 (variant). MOTIF A2271.1 [*Thrush teaches dove to build nest*]. See "Wood-pigeon's Nest".

THE MAN IN THE MOON

The "man in the moon" is said to have a bundle of sticks on his back, and it is said that he was put there because he gathered sticks on Sunday.

Addy (1895), p. 59.
MOTIF A.751.1 [*Man in the moon put there as a punishment.*]
C.631 [*Tabu: breaking the Sabbath*]. Thistleton Dyer, *Folk-Lore of Shakespeare*, pp. 65–6.
 Literary: Chaucer, *The Testament of Cresside* (Quoted by Baring-Gould, *Curious Myths of the Middle Ages*, p. 195).

> Her gite was gray and full of spottis blake,
> And on her breste a chorle painted good even,
> Bering a bush of thornis of his backe,
> Whiche for his theft might clime so neare the heaven.

MOTIF A751.1.4 [*Man in the moon banished there for stealing bundle of thorns*].
¶ Shakespeare, *A Midsummer-Night's Dream*, V; *The Tempest*, II, ii, "My mistress shewed me thee, and thy dog and bush."
 Baring-Gould, loc. cit., pp. 191–2, gives a German version very near to what the sparsely summarized English version must have been:
 "Ages ago there went one Sunday morning an old man into the wood to hew sticks. He cut a faggot and slung it on a stout staff, cast it over his shoulder, and began to trudge home with his burden. On his way he met a handsome man in Sunday suit, walking towards the church; this man stopped and asked the faggot-bearer, 'Do you know that this is Sunday on earth, when all must rest from their labours?'
 "'Sunday on earth, or Monday in heaven, it is all one to me,' laughed the wood-cutter.

"'Then bear your burden for ever,' answered the stranger; 'and as you value not Sunday on earth, yours shall be a perpetual Moon-day in heaven; and you shall stand for eternity in the moon, a warning to all Sabbath-breakers.'

"Thereupon the stranger vanished, and the man was caught up with his stock and his faggots into the moon, where he stands yet."

THE OWL WAS A BAKER'S DAUGHTER

Our Saviour went into a baker's shop where they were baking, and asked for some bread to eat. The mistress of the shop immediately put a piece of dough into the oven to bake for him: but was reprimanded by her daughter, who, insisting that the piece of dough was too large, reduced it to a very small size. The dough, however, immediately afterwards began to swell, and presently became of a most enormous size. Whereupon, the baker's daughter cried out, "Heugh, heugh, heugh", which owl-like noise probably induced our Saviour for her wickedness to transform her into that bird.

Norton Collection, II, p. 226.

TYPE 751.

¶ Staunton's *Shakespeare*, III, p. 403, note to *Hamlet*, IV. v. Described as *c.* 1860, still current in the country.

Copied verbatim from Malone's *Shakespeare*, where it is called a common Gloucestershire story. Given as from Douce, but not in Douce's *Illustrations*. Perhaps communicated by him. Malone, VII, p. 426: "They say the owl was a baker's daughter."

It is this version of the tale that Walter de la Mare retells in the notes to *Come Hither* (1923), pp. 540–1. See also "The Greedy Peasant Woman" (A. I) and "The Owl was a Baker's Daughter" (A. II).

WHY THE ROBIN'S BREAST IS RED

A. The robin and the wren are both connected with fire, and an old legend tells how the wren braved the dangers of Hell to bring fire to mankind. He returned in flames, and the robin wrapped himself round the burning bird, and so scorched himself that his breast has remained red ever since.

Another story says the robin got his crimson breast by trying to draw a thorn from the Crown of Thorns: a drop of Our Lord's blood fell on him, and dyed his breast feathers for ever.

Hole, *English Folk-Lore*, p. 74.

B. The robin is regarded as a sacred bird, though it is doubtful whether its sanctity goes back to pre-Christian times. The tales and rhymes about it have a Christian flavour. It is said, for instance, that the robin's breast was once white, but that he flew through the fires of Hell to bring a drop of water on his beak to Our Lord on the Cross, and that his breast was scorched red as he went through: or, alternatively, that he tried to pull out the thorns from the crown of thorns, and his breast was dyed with the blood.

Ruth L. Tongue, *Somerset Folklore*, p. 45.
MOTIF A.2221.2.2 [*Blood from Cross on robin's breast*], Addy, p. 66; *Choice Notes*, pp. 183–4.

THE WOLF, THE LABORER, THE FOX AND THE CHEESE

Sometime was a laborer which unnethe [= scarcely] might govern and lead his oxen because that they smote with their feet. Wherefore the laborer said to them: "I pray to God that the wolf may eat you." The which words the wolf heard, wherefore he hid himself nigh them until the night, and then came for to eat them.

And when the night was come, the laborer unbound his oxen and let them go to his house. And then when the wolf saw them coming homeward, he said: "O thou laborer, many times on this day thou didst give to me thine oxen, and therefore hold thy promise to me."

And the laborer said to the wolf: "I promised to thee nought at all, in the presence of whom I am obliged or bound. I swore not neither to pay thee."

And the wolf answered: "I shall not leave thee go without that thou hold to me, that that thou promised and gavest to me." And as they had so great strife and dissension together, they remitted the cause to be disputed or pleaded before the judge. And as they were seeking a judge, they met with a fox to whom they recounted or told all their difference and strife.

Then said the fox unto them: "I shall accord you both well and I shall give on your case or plea a good sentence. But I must speak with each one of you both apart or alone." And they were content.

And the fox went and told to the laborer: "Thou shalt give to me a good hen and another to my wife, and I shall it so make that thou with all thine oxen shalt freely go unto thy house." Whereof the laborer was well content.

And after, the fox went and said to the wolf: "I have well labored and wrought for thee, for the laborer shall give to thee therefore a great cheese, and let him go home with his oxen." And the wolf was well content.

And after, the fox said to the wolf; "Come thou with me, and I shall lead thee whereas the cheese is." And then he led him to and fro, here and there, unto the time that the moon shined full brightly, and that they came to a well. Upon the which, the fox leaped and showed to the wolf the shadow of the moon, which reluced in the well, and said to him: "Look now, godsip, how that cheese is fair great and broad. Hie thee, now, and go down, and after take that fair cheese."

And the wolf said to the fox: "Thou must be the first of us both that shall go down, and if thou mayst not bring it with thee because of its greatness, I shall then go down for to help thee." And the fox was content, because that two buckets were there, of which as the one came upward the other went downward, and the fox entered into one of the same buckets and went down into the well.

And when he was down, he said to the wolf: "Godsip, come hither and help me, for the cheese is so much and so great, that I may not bear it up." And then the wolf was afraid that the fox should eat it and entered within the other bucket. And as fast as he went downward the fox came upward. And when the wolf saw the fox coming upward, he said to him: "My godsip, ye go hence?"

"Thou sayest true," said the fox. "For thus it is of the world. For when one cometh down, the other goeth upward." And thus the fox went away and left the wolf within the well.

And thus the wolf lost both the oxen and the cheese. Wherefore it is not good to leave that which is sure and certain for to take that which is uncertain. For many a one has been thereof deceived by the falsehood and deception of the advocate and of the judge.

From *A Hundred Merry Tales*, ed. Zall, pp. 30–1.
TYPE 34, MOTIF J.1791.3 [*Diving for cheese*].
¶ Clouston, *Noodles*, p. 44. Aarne–Thompson Type Index notes 2 Latvian examples, 13 Swedish, 4 Danish, 11 Irish, 6 English, 4 French, 4 Spanish, 1 Catalan, 3 Flemish, 4 German, 1 Hungarian, 4 Slovenian, 8 Serbo-Croatian, 11 Polish, 1 Turkish, 2 Franco-American, 3 Spanish-American, 3 West-Indian, 1 American Indian, 2 African.

THE WOOD-PIGEON'S NEST

The Magpie has always been the highest authority amongst the Birds in the art of nest-building. Its own extensive nest of twigs is not surpassed by anything of the kind in the woods, the "Squirrels' Draw" alone approaching it in appearance.

The poor Wood-Pigeon knew not how to build a nest at all, and in her tribulation besought the Magpie to teach her. The Magpie consented, so some sticks were collected, and the lesson began.

"One stick this waay, t'other stick that waay, one stick a-thurt, t'other stick across," chattered the Magpie.

"That 'ooll do-o-o-o-o, that 'ooll do-o-o-o", coo'd the Wood-Pigeon, highly pleased with what had been done, and feeling that this was as much as she could possibly manage to remember.

"No t'wunt, no t'wunt, one stick here, t'other stick there, and one betwixt," replied the Magpie, suiting the action to the words.

"That 'ooll do-o-o-o, that 'ool do-o-o-o," said the poor Wood-Pigeon again, now quite confused, and unable to follow the teaching any longer.

"Well, if 't'ool for thee, 'twunt vor I," responded the Magpie, out of patience with so inapt a pupil, and off she flew.

Thus it arises that the Wood-Pigeon's nest has never been properly constructed, and that it consists of only a few twigs roughly laid across each other.

Norton Collection, I, p. 64. Lowsley, *Berkshire*, pp. 28–9.

Soon after the creation of the world all the birds wanted to learn how to make nests. So they asked the magpie, who was the cleverest of them all, to teach them how to do it. The magpie builds a domed nest, and he showed the Jenny-Wren and Long-tailed Capon how to make one like his, but smaller and neater. The other birds he taught according to their capacity to make neat cups lined with feathers or mud or grass. At last he came to the Wood-Pigeon, which was so lazy and careless that he would not attend but kept singing out: "What, athurt and across! What zoo! What zoo!—athurt and across! What zoo! What zoo!" At last the magpie lost patience, and flew away, leaving the Pigeon to build its nest as best it could.

In a Suffolk version, given by Montagu, the pigeon irritated the magpie by calling out, "Take two, Taffy! Take two!" all the time the magpie was teaching it. At length the magpie lost his temper, and said: "Take two! I say that one at a time's enough. But if you won't learn you may do it your own way!" And off he flew.

In some versions it was the Magpie who was too self-satisfied to learn, and has had to be content with a bundle of sticks ever since.

Halliwell's *Nursery Rhymes and Popular Tales*, Isle of Wight.
TYPE 236, MOTIF A2271.1 [*Thrush teaches dove to build nest*].
¶ In another version (Halliwell) it is the Magpie who is unteachable. Versions of this tale are found in Finland, Lithuania, Latvia, Sweden, Denmark, Belgium, Germany (45), Hungary, Poland, and Russia. Also in Ireland.

THE WREN THE KING OF THE BIRDS

Once, long ago, the birds met to choose a King. After some dispute they decided that he who could fly highest should be king. Up they all sprang from the earth, and soon one after another dropped again, but still the eagle soared higher and higher, until it was above all others. Just as it was going to dart triumphantly back to earth, a little feathered ball flew twittering from its back. It was the wren, who had hidden among the eagle's feathers, and now began to soar up as fast as its little wings could carry it. The eagle beat its way upwards again, but by this time it was exhausted, and, try as it would, the tiny bird was still above it. So the eagle sank down to the earth in disgust, and the birds held to the letter of their decision, and crowned the Wren King of the birds. But some shade of dishonour for sharp dealing clings to it still.

Halliwell's *Nursery Rhymes.*
¶ See "The King of the Birds".

THE YALLER-LEGG'D COCK'RIL

He's a good hand at swaggerin' hissen off, he is. Bud it'll be happenin' to him as it happen'd to th' yaller-legg'd cok'ril, if he doesn't mind what he's aboot.

What soort'n a taale's that, do ye saay? Why, it's a peäce 'at my gran'-feyther offens tell'd me when I was a little lad at hoäme.

Yaller-legg's cock'ril liv'd i' frunt yard wi' owd white cock 'at was his feyther, an' red cock liv'd o' steäm-hoose side o' yard. An' won daay, when owd cock's sittin' crawin' upon crew-yard gaate, cock'ril gets up an' begins to craw an' all.

"Cock-a-doodle-doo," says owd cock. "Kick-a-ee-a-ee", says cock'ril: he couldn't craw plaain yit, he was ower yung. "Houd thy noise," says owd cock, as couldn't abeär to hear him skreelin' like yon. "Houd thy noise, bairns should be seän an' not heerd." Soä cock'ril, 'at thinks as he's doin' on it fo'st raate, has to get off gaate an' tek up wi' th' hens an' chickens agaan. An' owd cock craws an' craws, till at last cock fra t'uther side o' yard cums to knaw what's up. Bud when he seäs who it is 'at's makkin' all to-do, he reckons 'at he's nobbut dropp'd in by chanche, an' passes time o' daay: an' then says as how he mun goä and seä if garthman isn't sarvin' pigs, an' if he hasn't slatter'd a few taaties an' things 'at'll mak a dinner fer that theare last cletch 'at graay hen's browt off. An' soä he taks his hook back agaain to steäm-hoose yard.

Bud daay efter, when owd cock's gone a peäce o' waay doon sandy laane wi' a pullet 'at's lookin' fer a nest, cock'ril flies upo' gaate agaan, an' claps his wings an' craws till th' hens is o'most stoäne-deäf. Fo'st won on 'em tell'd him to cum doon, an' then anuther, bud it wasn't noa good: he was that setten upo' hearin' hissen 'at he niver hed noä time to listen to onybody else. Awiver, just when he reckon'd 'at he'd gotten to do it o'most as well as his feyther, or mebbe a bit better, up cums cock fra t'uther side o' yard wi' all his neck-feathers up, an' he says to cock'ril, "I thowt I heerd ye at it yesterdaay, an' noo I knaw I did: cum on." An' afoor cock'ril could get oot anuther craw, red cock hed him off gaate an' doon i' crew-yard. An' when he'd gotten him theare, he wasn't long afoor he'd made an end o' him. An' when owd cock cum'd hoäm he fun' pigs just finishin' cock'ril's yaller legs, an' he heerd red cock crawin' like mad upo' steäm-hoose wall. "A-deary-me", says he, "I knaw'd how it would be if he wouldn't keäp his tung still. Well, you uther chickens mun tak warnin' by him, an' mind what I tell ye; niver craw till yer spurs is grawn."

M. Peacock, *The Lindsey Folk-Speech*, p. 105.
MOTIF Q 331 [*Pride punished*].

II FAIRY TALES

FAIRY TALES

By the term "Fairy Tales" I indicate the class which the Type Index describes as "Ordinary Folk-Tales", that is, those folk fictions of which magical or supernatural episodes are a necessary part. As I have already said, the distinction between Fairy Tales and Novelle is rather doubtful, but there is generally enough difference in mood and style to justify discrimination between them. A great many of the fairy tales still known throughout Europe have been lost in England. Literary references show that many once existed, and some not found in England are still extant in the Lowlands of Scotland and among the gypsy people. There are one or two stories known to this country which resist international classification, and these are often tales of peculiar beauty. Examples of these are "Kate Crackernuts", "Tattercoats" and "The Green Mist". All of them have motifs in common with widespread tales, but they have a local twist and often a free use of legendary beliefs.

All the Aarne–Thompson subdivisions of this class are represented among the British tales, either fully or slightly. *The Supernatural Adversary* (types 300–82) is well represented with "St George and the Dragon", "Jack the Giant-Killer", "Mallie Whuppie", and many others. Types 400–49 (*The Supernatural Husband or Wife*) contain some of our best tales, "The Black Bull of Norroway", "Nicht Nought Nothing", "Jack and the Puddock" and "Allison Gross". *Supernatural Tasks* (460–99) is a rather miscellaneous collection in the Type Index and is best represented in English by variants of 480 (*The Spinning Women at the Well*) such as "The Glass Ball", "The Three Heads in the Well", "The Green Lady". We have, besides, stories of the supernatural passage of time (*The Monk and the Bird*, 471 A), of which a notable example is "The Noon-Tide Ghost". We are rich in the section types 500–59 (*Supernatural Helpers*); types 500 and 501 are very numerous; and there are many variations, close or remote, on the Cinderella theme. The theme of *The Grateful Dead*, which is common in the Celtic tales, occurs in the English ones chiefly in a residual form, as for instance in the chap-book form of "Jack the Giant-Killer". "The Ass, the Table and the Stick" (type 563) is one of the commonest of *Magic Objects* (types 560–649). "Fortunatus" is perhaps a rather literary version of 566 (*The Three Magic Objects*). It was so well known in chap-book versions in the eighteenth and nineteenth centuries as to become proverbial, and it has therefore been included. Types 650–99 (*Supernatural Power or Knowledge*) are represented by such tales as "Tom Hickathrift" (650) and a gypsy version of "The Three Doctors".

That miscellaneous group, *Other Tales of the Supernatural* (700–49), has three strong representatives in "Tom Thumb" (700), "The Rose Tree" (720) and "The Oldest on the Farm" (726). There are Scottish and gypsy versions of "The Maiden without Hands" (706), "The Wonder Child" (708) and "Snow-White" (709).

In the Type Index the tales of *The Stupid Ogre* have a group of their own, while "The Giant-Killer" and "The Boy Steals the Giant's Treasure" are put into different groups. In the same way in the Dictionary some of the stories about giants are to be found among the Fairy Tales and some among the Legends (B Giants). It is sometimes difficult to determine into which category they should be put. "The Giant of Grabbist", for instance, might well go among the Legends because of its strong local flavour and the stone-throwing contests between the Giant and the Devil. The humorous twist that is given to the whole, however, marks it as belonging to the age of incredulity.

ALLISON GROSS [summary]

Allison Gross, "the ugliest witch i' the north country", lured a young man into her bower and with many fair speeches tried to persuade him to become her "lemman so true". He withstood all her bribes and blandishments, for first she promised him a scarlet embroidered mantle, then a "sark o' the saftest silk", wrought with pearls, then a cup of red gold. But he would not so much as give her one kiss, and at last she blew three blasts on a grass-green horn and, taking a silver wand in her hand, turned round three times, muttering words that chilled the blood till the youth fell down senseless and she changed him into a worm,

"And gard me toddle about the tree."

Every Saturday night his sister Maisry came with a silver basin and silver comb, and took the worm's head on her knee and tended it. There seemed to be no remedy against the enchantment, until at last, on Hallowe'en, the fairy court rode by, and the queen, alighting near the tree where the worm lay coiled, took it up in her hand, and stroked it three times over her knee, and the worm was restored to its own shape.

Child, *The English and Scottish Ballads*, I, pp. 313–15.
TYPE 303, parts III and V (distant variant), or TYPE 450A (variant). MOTIFS: D.683.2 [*Witch transforms*]; D.700 [*Disenchantment*]; G.269.4 [*Curse from disappointed witch*]; G.275.8.2 [*Witch overcome by help of fairy*].
¶ There is no motif in the Index for the turning of a man or woman into a monster, though this occurs in "The Loathly Lady" type. See also "The Laidly Worm of Spindlestone Heugh", "The Lailey Worm".

THE APPLE-TREE MAN

There was a hard-working chap as was eldest of a long family, see, so when his Dad did die there was nothing left for he. Youngest gets all, and he do give bits and pieces to all his kith, but he don't like the eldest, see, spoilt young horsebud he was; so all he do let he have is his Dad's old dunk (donkey) and a ox that's gone to a natomy (skeleton), and a tumble-down cottage with two-three ancient old apple trees where his Dad had lived to with his granfer. The chap don't grumble, but he goes cutting grass along lane, and old dunk began to fatten up, and he do rub ox with herbs and say the words, and old ox do pick up hisself and walk smart, and then he'd turn they beasties into orchet, and they old apple trees flourish a marvel. But it don't leave him no time to find the rent. Oh yes, the youngest was bound to have his rent. Dap on the dot too! Then one day he come into orchet and say: "'Twill be Christmas

Eve come to-morrow when beasts do talk. There's treasure hereabouts we've all heard tell, and I'm set to ask your dunk when beasts do talk, cause he mustn't refuse to tell me. Yew wake me just afore midnight and I'll take sixpence off your rent."

Come Christmas Eve the chap do give old dunk and ox a bit extra, and he do hang a bit of holly in the shippon, and he gets his last mug of cider and mulls it by ashen faggot and outs to the orchet to give it to the apple trees. Then the Apple Tree Man he calls to'n and say: "Yew take a look under this gurt diddiky (rotten) root of ours." And there was a box full of richest gold. "'Tis yours and no one else," say the Apple Tree Man. "Put'n away safe, and bide quiet 'bout 'un." So he done that. "Now," say the Apple Tree Man, "yew can go and call your dear brother. 'Tis midnight."

So the youngest brother he do run out in a terrible hurry-push, and sure enough the dunk's a-talking to the ox.

"Yew d'know this gurt greedy fule that's a listening to we so unmannerly. He d'want us to tell where treasure is."

"And that's where he won't never get it," say the ox. "Cause someone have a took't it already."

Recorded by Ruth L. Tongue, 26 September 1963, as she heard it from an old man at Pitminster, Somerset, about 1920.

Miss Tongue's note: "Pitminster was the place where, in my childhood, I was gravely and proudly conducted by a farm-child to a very old apple-tree in their orchard, and told mysteriously that it was 'the Apple-tree Man'. In 1958 I heard of him again on the Devon–Somerset borders."

MOTIFS: B.251.1.2 [*Animals speak to one another at Christmas*]; N.541.1 [*Treasure reveals itself only on Christmas at midnight*]; N.511.1.9 [*Treasure buried under tree*]; N.471 [*Foolish attempt of second man to overhear secrets*].

¶ American legends concerning B.251.1.2 are known from North Carolina (*Brown Collection*, I, p. 637) and Mississippi (Dorson, *Negro Tales in Michigan*, pp. 152–3).

"Borough English" was a local inheritance custom in country districts, by which the farm came to the youngest son instead of to the eldest, who was supposed to have already made his way in the world. It has sometimes been suggested that it was this custom which made it seem right to folk storytellers that the youngest son of the king should inherit the throne. It is clear, however, from this story, that this system aroused some criticism.

"Horse-bud" or "hose-bird" means bastard or rascal.

For another mention of the Apple-Tree Man see "Tib's Cat and the Apple-tree Man".

ASHEY PELT

Well, my Grandmother she told me that in them auld days a ewe might be your mother. It is a very lucky thing to have a black ewe. A man married again, and his daughter, Ashey Pelt, was unhappy. She cried alone, and the black ewe came to her from under the grey-stone in the field, and said, "Don't cry, go and find a rod behind the stone and strike it three times, and whatever you want will come." So she did as she was bid.

She wanted to go to a party. Dress and horses all came to her, but she was bound to be back before twelve o'clock or all the enchantment would go, all she had would vanish.

The sisters, they didna' like her, she was so pretty, and the stepmother, she kept her in wretchedness just.

She was most lovely. At the party the Prince fell in love with her, and she forgot to get back in time. In her speed a-running, she dropped her silk slipper, and he sent and he went over all the country, to find the lady it wad fit. When he came to Ashey Pelt's door he did not see her. The sisters was busy a-nipping and a-clipping at their feet to get on the silk slipper, for the king's son he had given out that he loved that lady sae weel he wad be married on whaever could fit on that slipper.

The sisters they drove Ashey Pelt out bye to be out of the road, and they bid her mind the cows. They pared down their feet till one o' them could just squeeze it on. But she was in the quare agony I'm telling you.

So off they rode away: but when he was passing the field, the voice of the auld ewe cried on him to stop, and she says, says she—

> "Nippet foot and clippet foot
> Behind the king's son rides,
> But bonny foot and pretty foot
> Is with the cathering hides."

So he rode back and found her among the cows, and he married her, and if they live happy, so may you and me.

Norton Collection, II, p. 78. *Folk-Lore*, VI (1895), pp. 305–6, contributed by M. Damant. "The following tale was told me by a woman now living, a native of Ulster, aged about 60."
TYPE 510.
¶ See "Ashpitel".

ASHPITEL

Very many years ago there lived a gentleman and a lady in a very beautiful part of the country. They had only one little girl, who was very pretty and very good, and her father and mother were very fond of her. When the little girl was about five years old her mother died. The father was nearly heart-broken about the loss of his wife, and left the little girl pretty much to herself. She cried a good deal and could not understand where her mother had gone that she did not come to her.

After a while her father married a widow lady, who had two daughters, both older than the little girl. They were both very plain, and were jealous of the beauty of their little step-sister. They resolved to try and banish her to the kitchen along with the servants, but the mother was afraid to do that, for fear of her husband. She at last devised a plan, by which she thought in time to cause her step-daughter's death.

The little girl was very fond of the fields and flowers and sheep. The sheep had found a hole leading into the garden, and the mother told the little girl that she must stay and watch the hole, and not let the sheep through, and she would send her some dinner. When dinner-time came, she sent her out a thimbleful of broth, a grain of barley, a thread of meat, and a crumb of bread.

The little girl was not long till she had finished that, and felt just as hungry as if she had not had anything. She did not dare to go home, as she had been told to stay out till night.

She began to cry: and as she sat crying, a little black lamb came up to her, and wanted to know what was the matter with her. So she told it she had had no dinner and was very hungry.

The little black lamb told her not to cry, but to put her finger into its ear, and see what she could find. So she put her finger in, and got a big piece of bread, and the little lamb told her to put her finger in the other ear, and she did so, and got a big piece of cheese, and had a good dinner, and felt quite happy.

In the evening, instead of being tired and hungry, as her stepmother had expected, she was quite bright and cheerful. Next day she was told to go out again, and her stepmother told her she would not send her any dinner. But the little lamb came again, and gave her some more bread and cheese. So the stepmother began to think there was more in it than she knew of; so she sent a man to watch next day.

He saw the black lamb feed the little girl with bread and cheese, and went home and told the stepmother. Then she said to her husband she would like to have one of the sheep killed, and he told her she could kill any one she wished. So she had the little black lamb killed.

Next day, when the little girl was sitting crying in the field, a funny little old woman came up and asked her what was the matter; and when the little girl told her about the lamb, she told her not to cry, but to go gather all the bones and bring them to her. She gathered all the bones: but one shank-bone she could not find, and so she gave all the others to the little old woman.

When Sunday came, the girl was left to cook the dinner while all the others went to church. The stepmother only left her a thimbleful of water, a grain of barley, and a crumb of bread, and told her she was to make a big pot of soup. The little girl did not know what to do, and she was sitting crying and wishing for her little lamb; she was sure it would have helped her.

Then in came the little black lamb, limping, limping, because a shank-bone was a-wanting, and told her not to cry, but to get dressed and go to church, and it would cook the dinner, but to be sure to leave before the church was out. So she went and dressed herself, and put on a pretty pair of glass slippers she had.

When she reached the church, service had commenced, and she sat near the door. It happened that there was a young Prince near her, and he was so struck with her beauty he thought he would follow her and see where she lived. But she went out before him, and he was too late. When she came home, she put on her old clothes: and her stepmother and sisters were astonished to find the dinner ready.

Next Sunday she was again left at home, and the lamb came again, and sent her off to church. This Sunday the Prince followed her; and in her haste to get away, she left one of her slippers. The Prince picked it up and put it in his pocket, finding he could not follow her. The next day he sent out a proclamation that he would marry whoever could get the slipper on. In course of time he came to the house where the little girl lived, and one of her step-sisters said that she could get the slipper on. So she took a chopper and chopped off her toes, and a piece of her heel, and put the slipper on.

The Prince put her on his horse behind him, to take her away to his castle, where he was to marry her. On the road they had to pass some trees. On the first tree there was a raven which said:

> "Haggit-heels and Hewed-toes
> Behind the young Prince rides.
> But Pretty-foot and Bonnie-foot
> Behind the caldron hides."

Then the Prince said: "What did that bird say?"

"Oh", said she, "never mind it! It is only talking nonsense."

However, on the next tree another bird—also a raven—said the same thing. Then the Prince got off and looked at her foot, and found it all blood. He then said he was sure the slipper did not belong to her.

So he took her back to her mother, and insisted on looking behind the caldron, and there he saw the little girl. She asked to go and change her dress, and get the other slipper: and she came down with it on. The Prince recognised her at once, and took her away on his horse, behind him.

When they were passing the first tree, the bird said:

> "Pretty-foot and Bonnie-foot
> Behind the young Prince rides.
> But Haggit-heels and Hewed-toes
> At home with Mamma bides."

They rode on, and reached the castle, and lived happily ever after, and if they are not dead, they are living yet.

Norton Collection, II, p. 75. Melbourne, told by a woman from a small town near Glasgow, 1888. In "A fresh Scottish Ashpitel and glass shoe tale", by Karl Blind, *Archaeological Review*, III (March 1889), pp. 24–7.

TYPE 510. MOTIFS: S.31 [*Cruel stepmother*]; L.55 [*Stepdaughter heroine*]; B.313.1 [*Helpful animal reincarnation of parent*]; B.335 [*Helpful animal killed*]; E.33 [*Resuscitation with missing member*]; N.711.4 [*Prince sees maiden at grave, and is enamoured*]; F.823.2 [*Glass shoes*]; H.36.1 [*Slipper test*]; K.1911.3.3.1 [*False bride's mutilated foot*]; B.143.1 [*Bird gives warning*].

¶ This is a particularly full example of the earlier form of the Cinderella story, with the helpful animal and the resuscitated bones. This version is described as type AB by Anna Birgitta Rooth in *The Cinderella Cycle* (Lund, 1951). The various forms of 510, which have an almost universal distribution, are examined in her book, and in the earlier *Cinderella* by Marion Roalfe Cox, which is full of good material but has not the advantages of modern methods of research of which A. B. Rooth has availed herself.

ASHYPELT [summary]

An old man & woman in the forest of Dean had twelve sons, & the youngest, whom all despised, was called Ashypelt, because he always lived in the esshole beneath the fire.

The others worked hard at felling timber, & brought home so much money to their parents that at last they needed no more help, & being wicked old people they decided to shut them up in the barn under pretence of hiding them from the press-gang, & then burn them to death. But Ashypelt warned his brothers & they all escaped & set out by twelve roads to seek their fortunes, agreeing to meet again after a year & a day.

Ashypelt, dazzled by the unaccustomed sunlight, crept on up a muddy lane, till he met a man living in a new house, who promised him fifty pounds, a bag of nuts, plenty of tobacco, & a warm fire, if he would sleep all night in the nearby castle. Ashypelt agreed, & at midnight a naked man entered the room. Ashypelt invited him to come & warm himself at the fire. The ghost ended by eating all his nuts & smoking all his tobacco & only went away at two o'clock in the morning. The next two nights the same things happened, & in the daytime in between, Ashypelt learnt gardening in his employer's new garden. But there were more ghosts on the second night, & one of them fell to pieces at Ashypelt's touch, & while he was putting him together the others ate the nuts & smoked the tobacco. The third night the ghost which came in had its throat cut from ear to ear, & it told Ashypelt that it was his employer's elder brother, & that they had quarrelled over the inheritance of the castle. The ghost said that he was the same man whose skeleton had fallen to bits the previous night, & showed Ashypelt a great bag of spade-ace guineas buried under a heavy stone, & promised him the castle for life if he would inform the magistrates of the truth. Ashypelt thus got the wicked brother convicted, the ghost appearing as witness at the critical moment of the trial, & the convicted brother received a life sentence, & soon afterwards died of a broken heart. At the appointed day Ashypelt returned to join his brothers, who did not recognise him in his new grandeur, until he shewed them the birthmark on his arm, & gave them each a suit of new clothes. They returned home & Ashypelt accused his mother of having tried to burn all her sons to death in the barn. But she denied it.

Gypsy Folk-Tales, selected by Dora E. Yates (London, Phoenix House, 1948).
TYPE 326 (variant). MOTIFS: L.131.1 [*Ashes as hero's abode*]; R.155.1 [*Youngest rescues his elder brothers*]; H.1462.1 [*Youngest son alone endures frightful experiences*]; E.578.1 [*Revenants want to warm themselves*]; H.1411 [*Staying in haunted house*]; E.281 [*Ghosts haunt house*]; E.231 [*Return from dead to reveal murder*].
¶ This tale is somewhat slenderly related to type 326, because the hero has no desire to learn what fear is. The theme of the avenging ghost in the haunted house and then in the law court appears in Douglas Hyde's "The Trunkless Corpse".
  See also "The Cutler and the Tinker", "The Black Cat", "The Golden Ball".

THE ASS, THE TABLE AND THE STICK

A lad named Jack was once so unhappy at home through his father's ill-treatment, that he made up his mind to run away and seek his fortune in the wide world.

He ran, and he ran, till he could run no longer, and then he ran right up against a little old woman who was gathering sticks. He was too much out of breath to beg pardon, but the woman was good-natured, and she said he seemed to be a likely lad, so she would take him to be her servant, and would pay him well.

He agreed, for he was very hungry, and she brought him to her house in the wood, where he served her for a twelvemonths and a day. When the year had passed, she called him to her, and said she had good wages for him. So she presented him with an ass out of the stable, and he had but to pull Neddy's ears to make him begin at once to ee--aw! And when he brayed there dropped from his mouth silver sixpences, and halfcrowns, and golden guineas.

The lad was well pleased with the wage he had received, and away he rode till he reached an inn. There he ordered the best of everything, and when the innkeeper refused to serve him without being paid beforehand, the boy went off to the stable, pulled the ass's ears, and obtained his pocket full of money. The host had watched all this through a crack in the door, and when night came on he put an ass of his own for the precious Neddy of the poor youth. So Jack, without knowing that any change had been made, rode away next morning to his father's house.

Now, I must tell you that near his home dwelt a poor widow with an only daughter. The lad and maiden were fast friends and trueloves: but when Jack asked his father's leave to marry the girl, "Never till you have the money to keep her," was the reply. "I have that, father," said the lad, and going to the ass, he pulled its long ears: well, he pulled, and he pulled, till one of them came off in his hands: but Neddy, though he hee-hawed and he hee-hawed let fall no half-crowns or guineas. The father picked up a hayfork and beat his son out of the house. I promise you he ran. Ah! he ran and ran till he came bang against the door, and burst it open, and there he was in a joiner's shop. "You're a likely lad," said the joiner, "serve me for a twelvemonths and a day, and I will pay you well." So he agreed, and served the carpenter for a year and a day. "Now," said the master, "I will give you your wage;" and he presented him with a table, telling him he had but to say, "Table, be covered," and at once it would be spread with lots to eat and drink.

Jack hitched the table on his back, and away he went with it till he came to the inn. "Well, host", shouted he, "my dinner today, and that of the best."

"Very sorry, but there is nothing in the house but ham and eggs."

"Ham and eggs for me!" exclaimed Jack. "I can do better than that.—Come, my table, be covered!"

At once the table was spread with turkey and sausages, roast mutton, potatoes and greens. The publican opened his eyes, but he said nothing, not he.

That night he fetched down from his attic a table very like that of Jack and exchanged the two. Jack, none the wiser, next morning hitched the worthless table on to his back, and carried it home. "Now, father, may I marry my lass?" he asked.

"Not unless you can keep her," replied the father.

"Look here!" exclaimed Jack. "Father, I have a table which does all my bidding."

"Let me see it," said the old man.

The lad set it in the middle of the room, and bade it be covered: but all in vain, the table remained bare. In a rage, the father caught the warming-pan down from the wall, and warmed his son's back with it so that the boy fled howling from the house, and ran and ran till he came to a river and tumbled in. A man picked him out and bade him assist him in making a bridge over the river: and how do you think he was doing it? Why, by casting a tree across; so Jack climbed up to the top of the tree, and threw his weight on it so that when the man had rooted the tree up, Jack and the tree-head dropped on the farther bank.

"Thank you," said the man; "and now for what you have done I will pay you;" so saying, he tore a branch from the tree, and fettled it up into a club with his knife. "There," he exclaimed, "take this stick, and when you say to it, 'Up stick and bang him,' it will knock anyone down who angers you."

The lad was overjoyed to get this stick,—so away he went with it to the inn, and as soon as the publican appeared, "Up stick, and bang him!" was his cry. At the word, the cudgel flew from his hand and battered the old publican on the back, rapped his head, bruised his arms, tickled his ribs, till he fell groaning on the floor; still the stick belaboured the prostrate man nor would Jack call it off till he had got back the stolen ass and table.

Then he galloped home on the ass, with the table on his shoulders, and the stick in his hand. When he arrived there, he found his father was dead, so he brought his ass into the stable, and pulled its ears till he had filled the manger with money.

It was soon known through the town that Jack had returned rolling in wealth, and accordingly all the girls in the place set their caps at him.

"Now," said Jack, "I shall marry the richest girl in the place; so to-morrow do you all come in front of my house with your money in your aprons."

Next morning the street was full of girls with aprons held out, and gold and silver in them; but Jack's own sweetheart was among them, and she had neither gold nor silver, nought but two copper pennies, that was all she had.

"Stand aside, lass," said Jack, speaking to her roughly. "Thou hast no silver nor gold—stand off from the rest." She obeyed, and the tears ran down her cheeks, and filled her apron with diamonds.

"Up stick and bang them," exlaimed Jack: whereupon the cudgel leaped up, and running along the line of girls, knocked them all on the heads and left them senseless on the pavement. Jack took all their money and poured it into his truelove's lap. "Now, lass," he exclaimed, "thou art the richest, and I shall marry thee."

Jacobs, *English Fairy Tales*, pp. 206–16, from Baring-Gould in Henderson's *Folk-Lore of the Northern Counties*, first edition, pp. 327–9, second version, pp. 329–31.
TYPE 563.
MOTIFS: S.327 [*Child cast out because of his stupidity*]; B.103.1.1 [*Gold-producing Ass*]; D.861.1 [*Magic object stolen by host at inn*]; D.1472.1.22 [*Magic bag supplies food*]; D.1651.2 [*Magic cudgel works only for master*]; D.881.2 [*Recovery of magic object by use of magic cudgel*].
¶ Very widely spread: Scandinavia, Germany, France, Russia, Italy, the Balkans, America, West Indies, Africa, etc. See also "The Seven Mysteries of the Luck", "The Boy and his Wages".

ASSIPATTLE AND
THE MESTER STOORWORM [summary]

The goodman of Leegarth, a well-to-do Udaler, owned a farm in a fertile valley, sheltered by surrounding hills. His thrifty and active wife bore him seven sons and a daughter. The youngest son, Assipattle, was scorned by his brothers, for he did little work, and ran about all day, ragged and unkempt; and in the evenings he would lie among the ashes on the hearth. All the small, degrading jobs were given to him to do, and he was the laughing-stock of all except his sister. She would listen by the hour to the long stories he told, of trolls and giants, in all of which he himself was the hero. This all added to his brothers' provocation, and made them more unkind to him.

In time his sister received a summons from the king himself, bidding her to go and live in the palace, and be maid to the king's only daughter, the princess Gemdelovely.

Her father made her a pair of rivlins, for she had always hitherto gone barefoot, and dressed in her best, the maid rode away on a pony; and Assipattle became more lonely and dull than ever.

Presently it was rumoured that the Stoorworm was approaching that land, the largest, and the Father of all the Stoorworms; for which reason he was known as the Mester Stoorworm. His breath could kill every living thing, and wither up every thing that grew.

And the Stoorworm came, and the land was full of lamentation. There was a powerful sorcerer living there, who, it was said, knew everything, but the king was unwilling to consult him, for he thought him a deceiver.

So he took counsel with the Thing; but at the end of three days, they could come to no device; and then the Queen entered the Thing, a tall, man-like woman, and mocked the Thing-men, bidding them go for counsel to the sorcerer, whose wisdom, she said, would conquer where strength failed. The sorcerer was sent for, and promised to give them an answer by sunrise the following day. The next day he told the Thing that the Stoorworm could only be satisfied by the sacrifice of seven virgins once every week. If this did not suffice, there was a further way, but it was too terrible to be revealed except in the direst necessity. So each week seven maidens were brought to where the monster lay, and it stretched forth its terrible tongue, and swept them all together into its horrid mouth. All the people wept and lamented at the sight, but one day Assipattle said, "I'm not afraid. I would willingly fight the monster." But his eldest brother gave him a kick, and drove him home to his ash-hole. That night, when the mother sent him into the barn, to call his brothers to supper, they threw him to the ground, and half smothered him with the straw from their threshing. His father came to his rescue, but Assipattle said he could have beaten them all, but he was saving his strength to fight the Stoorworm.

At last the Thing-men asked the sorcerer to name his second remedy. He replied that the Stoorworm would only go away if the princess Gemdelovely herself were given to him.

The king, in deep sorrow, promised to let this be done, but begged for three weeks' respite, that he might proclaim that whoever could slay the monster should have his daughter in marriage, the kingdom to which she was heir, and the magic sword, Sickersnapper, as his reward. The king's Kemperman added, that if even this remedy did not cause the Stoorworm to depart, the sorcerer himself should be its next victim, and this was hailed with a shout of approval.

The only person who was not grief-stricken by this doom was the queen, who was Gemdelovely's stepmother. Thirty-six champions came to try for the prize, but twelve of them fell sick at the sight of the monster, and had to be carried home: twelve more ran away, and twelve, with sinking hearts, remained in the king's house. And though the king made them a great feast on the night before the ordeal, there was no merriment, and when they had all gone to bed, the king drew Sickersnapper from the chest in which it lay, and told his Kemperman, that for all his ninety-six years, he himself would strike a blow for his daughter's life on the next day. He bade the Kemperman launch his boat, and guard it until day-break.

At Leegarth the whole family was preparing to go and view the sacrifice of the princess, except Assipattle, who was to stay and herd the geese. As he lay in the ashes that night, he overheard his father telling his wife that she should ride behind him on his horse Teetgong, who was the fastest horse in all the land. But she begged him to tell her the secret of Teetgong's swiftness, or else, she said, she would never believe he loved her as a true husband should. At last he consented...one clap on the left shoulder meant "Stand still", two on the right shoulder, "Fairly fast"; and a blast through the wind-pipe of a goose, "Full speed".

When the old people were asleep, Assipattle stole the "goose-thrapple" from his father's pocket, saddled Teetgong, and escaped on his back from the stable. But Teetgong, knowing it was not his master, gave a loud neigh, which woke the goodman, who roused his sons, and they all set out in pursuit, the goodman roaring,

"Hie, hie, ho!
Teetgong, wo!"

Teetgong stopped dead. But Assipattle blew on the goose-thrapple, and off he went again like the wind. The pursuers gave up in despair, and went sadly home.

At dawn, Assipattle reached the shore. He crept into a cottage, and stole an old pot, into which he put a live peat from the fire. The old woman sleeping there did not awake, and Assipattle went softly to where the king's boat was moored, with the man on duty sitting in it. Assipattle lured him on shore, by pretending to have found gold in a hole he was digging to cook his breakfast of limpets. As soon as the boat was empty, he seized his pot, jumped into the boat with it, and sailed away towards the Stoorworm's head. It lay like a mountain, stretched half across the world. Its tongue, hundreds of miles long, could sweep towns, trees, and hills into the sea. It used its forked tongue like tongs, to grasp and crack its prey. But Assipattle sailed up to its right side, shipped his oars, and lowered his sail, and when the sun struck the Stoorworm's eyes, it yawned the first of the seven great yawns which it always yawned before breakfast. A great surge of water flowed into its mouth, and swept Assipattle and his boat into the bottomless pit of its throat, until at last the boat's mast caught fast in the roof of the gullet. Out jumped Assipattle with his pot, and ran till he came to the enormous liver. In this he dug a hole and placed the live peat in the hole, then rushed back to his boat, and made his escape, just in time to avoid the torrents of water, fire and smoke which now gushed forth from its mouth. The oil in the liver had kindled, and the monster was slowly burnt up from inside, and disintegrated. Its forked tongue, flung up in agony, caught in one of the horns of the moon, and then fell to earth with a crash which clove out the sea that now divides Denmark from Sweden and Norway. As it tossed its head in torment, the teeth fell out, and became, some the Orkneys, some the Shetlands, and some the Faroe Islands. The Stoorworm then coiled itself into one huge lump, which is now Iceland, but the inner burning continued, and that is why there are volcanoes there still.

The king blessed and kissed Assipattle and gave him his daughter, and the other rewards. He mounted on Teetgong, and rode off with Gemdelovely at his side. As they rode, Assipattle's sister ran to meet them, with the news that the sorcerer had been making love to the queen, and that they had fled on the two swiftest horses in the stable.

Assipattle blew on his goose-pipe, and Teetgong soon brought him up with the two fugitives. The sorcerer drew his sword, believing himself to be invulnerable. But the magic sword, Sickersnapper, drove straight through his heart, and his black blood ran out. The queen was imprisoned for the rest of her life in a high inaccessible tower.

After that, there was a great wedding feast, and Assipattle and Gemdelovely were made king and queen: and if not dead, they are still alive.

Douglas, *Scottish Fairy and Folk-Tales*, p. 58.
TYPE 300, MOTIFS: L.131.1 [*Ashes as hero's abode*]; B.11.10 [*Sacrifice of human being to dragon*]; T.68.1 [*Princess offered as prize to rescuer*]; B.11.2.12 [*Dragon of enormous size*]; B.184.1.1 [*Horse with magic speed*]; B.11.2.11.2 [*Breath of dragon kills*]; A.2468.3 [*Why dragon dies by means of fire*]; H.335.3.1 [*Suitor task: killing dragon to whom princess is to be sacrificed*]; D.429.2.2 [*Transformation of dragon to stone*]; R.227 [*Wife flees husband*].
¶ An unusual and rather literary version of a widespread tale. See also "The Little Bull-Calf".

THE BIG WIND [summary]

An old woman and her son lived in a lonely wee house on the hillside with one cow, and a pig and a few hens. The son worked hard at reaping their little field, and had all their corn stacked, when, at the back end of the year, a Big Wind arose, so strong that it lifted the thatch off their house, and when Jack went out to feed the cow, he found every bit of corn and straw had been blown away by the Big Wind. So he was very angry, and he set out to look for the Big Wind, and call him to account for the damage he had done. He walked on and on, till at last he came to a farm, and he asked the farmer if he had seen The Big Wind. "I should just think I have," said the farmer. "He's lifted everything off me. I'm fair ruined." "Well," said Jack, "I'll add your account to mine, and I'll make him sorry for it. Which way did he go?"

"He went that way," said the Farmer, "but it's an awful desolate road. It'll be maybe two days before you come to another house." He gave Jack something to eat, and Jack went on, on and on for two days, and then he saw a farmhouse, and a King's Castle just beyond it. He asked at the farmhouse, and the farmer told him to go up to the King's Castle, and he would get news of The Big Wind. The King had him in, and said: "I'd be more than delighted if anyone could reckon with The Big Wind. He's done more damage in my kingdom than anyone else in the earthly world. He's a two-headed giant, and he lives on that Island away over there in a ruined castle. And anyone that could kill him should have my daughter in marriage." So they gave Jack a sword and a knife, and gave him a boat to row across to the Island. And he got to the Island, and went up to the Castle, and he heard a great roar, and there was the giant. And the Giant said: "I'm going to kill you this moment". And Jack said: "I'm not so sure of that. I've come to call you to account for all the mischief you've done." "No, but I will kill you," said the Giant, "unless you can win above me in the challenges I set you. If I win, I'll have your head, and if you win, I'll give you a bag of money."

"Well, what are the challenges?" said Jack. "The first is for me to eat against you." "I'll try that," says Jack. Now Jack had a long bag that his mother had given him to carry his bannocks in, and he tucked it under his clothes, and sat down to table. The Giant's old wife cooked them a great hogshead of porridge, and they set to and ate and ate, at least the Giant ate, and Jack popped his into the bag. And in the end the Giant began to be full, and Jack still shovelled away at the porridge. "Come on, man," said Jack at length. "Are you full already? Why, I could eat as much again. I just have to let out what I've ta'en in, and I'm ready to start all over again." With that he took his sharp wee knife, and slit the bag open with a great wheedge! and out came all the porridge. "Oh, thank you," said the Giant, "for teaching me that. Can anyone do it?" With that, the Giant took his great knife, and he stuck it wheedge! into his own belly, and split himself from side to side, and fell down dead.

So Jack cut off his two heads, and took them back to the King's Castle, and he married the King's daughter, and they lived happily all their days.

School of Scottish Studies, Maurice Fleming, from Bella Higgins.
TYPE 1088. This begins with the quest of Wind to exact payment for damage; something like "Boots and the North Wind" (Dasent).
    MOTIFS: T.68 [*Princess offered as prize*]; K.81.1 [*Deceptive eating contest*]; G.524 [*Ogre deceived into stabbing himself*]; L.161 [*Lowly hero marries princess*].
¶ A wide distribution. See "Jack the Giant-Killer".

BILLY BITER AND THE PARKIN

Here be a tale young Charley, the Yorkshire undergroom, used to tell.
    There was a Dragon who lived in a deep gully and no-one else cared about living near him except him except old Mrs Greenaway, in a cottage

in the woods above, and she were a "gifted" woman as had a way with warts and such like so maybe she had a way with a Dragon—anyway up there she stayed safe and sound, and down there he stayed too, getting hungrier and hungrier. The farmers had moved backalong over the hill to the village with all their stock. The hill grazing was rich but no-one with their full senses let good beasts fatten to feed a dragon. For that matter an angry sturdy farmer would come a tasty snack like.

On t'other side of gully right atop the hill were Billy Biter, the travelling tailor, and folks kept a-telling Billy 'twere real dangerous to live there. They all had a liking for Billy Biter and not one a good word for Hepzibah, his wife, and her girt black—jack. Billy's cottage had been the most welcoming in the parish while his old mother lived. All the folks found some excuse to go a-visiting up the hill. There were always a kettle ready to boil hanging on the crook, and a good back log burning in hearth and old Tom Puss a-washing himself in the chimbley corner. They brought in the logs and carried fresh water in for her when Billy was away on his tailoring, and 'twas believed old Mrs Greenaway kept an eye on the dear soul too. Anyway the corrage were a picture while she lived but when she died things was very different.

A man needs a home to come back to after his day's labour so poor Billy he went and married Hepzibah and everyone said she proper terrified him into it. He were only a little fellow, kind as they come, and she were six feet high and so thin as a yard of pump-water—but 'twarn't pump-water as Hepzibah were always apouring down her gullet from her black-jack. The folk reckoned she only married Billy because the cottage wasn't half a mile down to the Inn and every day Hepzibah would come a-staggering and all a draggle tail to get black-jack filled and if she got back up whoame 'twas a month's wonder. There wadn't no fire till Billy trudged home and a faggot with him. He'd fetch water for the kettle and swept up a bit, and old Tom Puss could sit in a warm chimbley-corner for a two-dree minutes afore Billy took the wheelbarrow and went to look for Hepzibah.

There were times when she were fast asleep half-way whoame, and black-jack were empty beside her, times when she were nearly whoame and not such a troublesome load for a bone-weary little man, and times when she was really to whoame, and all a spread in old Mrs Biter's rocking-chair that Hepzibah had sat right through the seat of, and then Billy and Tom Puss went a-tiptoe while they kept one eye open in case she moved.

When she moved a foot they was both out of the door and atop of the roof she were too bone-idle to reach, and there they sat the whole night cuddled to chimney for a bit of warmth. Folks talked and Billy went on same way, too tired to do aught about it until one day he met

Mrs Greenaway. "Where be your pay-money, Billy?" she say and somehow Billy give it over—she give him a silver sixpence back. "That'll all be down Hepzibah's droat by tomorrow," she say. "Get this bite of bread and cheese inside you." And Billy Biter went a home feeling fine. He give Hepzibah the sixpence and then he joined Tom Puss up against the chimney pot. Hepzibah were too handy with a broom handle for comfort and she could run a deal too fast for his thin liddle tailor's legs. Bye and bye there was no smoke up chimney and cottage windows was dark and old Mrs Greenaway noted it—and the Dragon below give a girt groan he were that hungry but he didn't stir out for all that.

Next night 'twas the same—Hepzibah were a-spread across drashel so Billy went up on roof to join Tom Puss and sat there in the rain and Mrs Greenaway noted that too and the Dragon give another girt hollow groan but he didn't stir neither.

The third night they give Billy Biter a good Yorkshire tea at the farm afore sending him on his way and he'd kept back a bit in his pocket for Tom Puss, but Varmer's wife had her own notions. They was all fond of Billy Biter. He had been a merry little soul, he could sing tunable at his work and dance dapper and laugh like a pixy, so now she had packed him a load of good vittles. "If Hepzibah can't trouble herself to cook 'en, you up and vind a time and place," she said, and Varmer bound a good dry faggot atop. "Tidn' so heavy as wheelbarrow load," he say, and watch Billy Biter go into the vog looking like a walking hod-me-dod (snail). Hod-me-dod or no, Billy made good time until he smelled summat so good it somehow brought him out of his way to Mrs Greenaway's wood. She come to her door. "Come in, Billy Biter, you and your good vittles and faggot. Hepzibah won't be wanting 'en. Hand over." Well, she was old and had been good to his old mother, and 'twas cruel hard to go hungry, as Billy well knew but for all that he hands over the load. But Mrs Greenaway she don't trouble herself to undo it, she just shakes summat like vlour over it. "I been a bakin'," she say. "Can 'ee smell my parkin?"

(Parkin, Charley say, be a Yorkshire girt square ginger cake. He don't think much of our thin gingerbread—he say it should be square and sticky, but for all that he eat enough of it.)

Billy could smell nothing else nor could the hungry Dragon far below.

"I'll give 'ee a mouthvill to warm your road whoame," and with that she cut a huge slice for Billy from the square baking sheet on the hearth. "A bit for Tom Puss to go in your pocket so well—and this in corner be for Hepzibah *alone*—no-one else, mind." And with that she broke off a girt corner, wrapped it up in clean leaves and laid it on the load. "'Tisn't vor such as you and Tom Puss, mind now—on your way and sleep well tonight." And out went Billy full of good food and with his own girt wedge of warm parkin to nibble on his trudge on home. He were even full of hope that Hepzibah might take a fancy to a hot meal and cook'n vor the once and so 'twas no wonder that mistymoisty night he step right over the edge of the Dragon's gully, and down he went arsey-varsey almost down his gullet too. He landed on his load, which were softer than all the oven–hot rock down there and up against a girt red light that blinked. "That be my eye you be poking your faggot in," said Dragon. "Let's have a proper look at what I'm to dine on." Poor Billy's knees chattered and he dropped his wedge of parkin afore Dragon's nose—out come a girt hot tongue and golloped it while even Tom Puss half a mile uphill could hear the clatter of Billy Biter all a-tremble below—But the parkin just wouldn't gollop—it stuck to Dragon's teeth and he vound it so welcome as vlowers in May. "What do 'ee call this?" he say droo the sticky chumble. "P-p-parkin," say Billy still a-twitter and all adrench wi' cold sweat. For all that his load were beginning to scorch gentle. "Then go back and bring me some more," say Dragon, sneezing out a crumb as were tickling his gullet. That sneeze fair blew Billy Biter clean out of the gully and atop of Tom Puss by the cold cottage chimney and rope on his load were so scorched droo that it broke and down inside chimney tumbled the whole load on the dying embers. It just passed Hepzibah's head where she lay all a-spread, her shoes all untied, her skirts a-tatter and greasy, and black-jack empty alongside. The smell of her own girt corner of parkin made her nose twitch and she sat up to gobble it, then she got up and kicked faggot which were beginning to catch and crackle a bit. "You come down here, Billy," she yelled up chimney. "Drowing cake at your poor wife. What be it anyway?" 'P-p-parkin," say Billy, coming down carefully. Tom Puss he didn't stir, not he. "Parkin," yells Hepzibah. "Give I the sack, I'll show thee how to bake parkin." And she did too; Billy were kept on the gallop filling pigtrough with the dough, she kicked and trampled till it were ready to use and Tom Puss watched down the chimney in between the smoke. She've a girt dollop of dough on a baking sheet so long and round as a wagon wheel and 'tis still swellin'. "Parkins is square," whispered Billy. "I'm biding here." "When 'tis cooked us'll see," say Hepzibah. Believe it or no, in two minutes that girt round parkin were baked and smelling rich and strange. Billy took to the roof when Hepzibah hauled the hugeous round out of the blaze without a burn to it. "I'll show 'ee broom end," shrieks Hepzibah, "when I come back from showing the old witch how to bake parkin." And she tumbled over a shoe-lace and out of the door. She lost one shoe, then she lost t'other, then she lost the girt round parkin and it went a-bowling and a-rolling downwards towards gully where Dragon were still waiting hopevil and Hepzibah staggered after it yelling like a flock of crows—the village come out to look-see. They seed Billy's cottage lit up and they seed the girt round parkin a-bouncing and a-jouncing down over and they seed Hepzibah run right over the edge of the gully and they heard Dragon give a gollup as he swallowed her. "'Twadn't a very tasty morsel," he say and then the girt round parkin what had been a-spinning and wig-wagging on the edge above plump down afore his nose. "Cor!" say Dragon, and he bit into it hearty that he couldn't say no more and he never didn't on account his teeth were that stuck he couldn't only snort. When the folk seed what come of it they all runned for sledge-hammers, and pickforks and axes and such, but how to get into gully without being fried they couldn't tell. Dragon he settled it vor 'en nicely. He took off away down to the sea to wash the girt round parkin vrom between his teeth where it were clinging so loving as an ivy-bine. Well, the folk followed and they was just in time to see Dragon ker-vlop right down in deep water and stick his head under; then they run and give his nose arf-dozen whister-poops as stopped his breath and run back to safety, and avore Dragon come to there were a girt oncome of waves and he drounded then and there.

When folks come rejoicing back past Billy's cottage, door were wide open, house were all clean and tidy—there was vittles on table, a kettle on the crook, Tom Puss a-washing himself in chimbley corner, and a nice square parkin on baking sheet avore the vire, and Billy mending the seat of the rocking-chair—and I don't doubt old Mrs Greenaway saw that too.

Charley say Dragon's bones turned into a long stretch of rock folk up there call Filey Brigg—but I never heard of 'en.

Ruth L. Tongue, tape-recorded 1967. A Yorkshire folk-tale recovered from a Somerset stable (about 1905–7).
MOTIFS: B.11.12.3 [*Fiery dragon*]; N.828 [*Wise woman as helper*]; B.11.10.2 [*Dragon eats people*]; Q.304 [*Scolding punished*]; D.429.2.2 [*Transformation: dragon to stone*].

BINNORIE [summary]

There were two sisters in a bower: a knight came to court the first, but he loved the second. The elder sister was sorely vexed at it, and one day she said: "Come down with me to the strand and see our Father's ships coming to shore."

The younger stood on a stone, and the elder pushed her in.

"Oh, sister, reach out your hand, and you shall be heir of all I have!"

"If I leave you to sink I shall still be your heir."

"Oh sister, reach me your glove and Sweet William shall be yours!"
"He will be mine if I leave you to sink. It was your cherry cheeks and golden hair that parted us."

The younger sister was tossed up and down till she was drifted into the Mill-dam of Binnorie. The miller's daughter saw something white in the water, and called to her father to draw the dam, thinking a mermaid was there, or a swan. But they only drew out a drowned woman in silk and jewels. The king's harper was passing by: he grieved at the sight, and made her breast-bone into a harp and strung it with her golden hair.

When he got to the King's Hall he set the harp on a stone, and it played and sang of its own accord. It sang: "There sits my Father the King and my Mother the Queen! There stands my Brother Hugh and True-Love William!" But the last song it sang was, "Woe to my sister, False Helen!"

From Child's *English and Scottish Popular Ballads* I, p. 128.

This is Version C in Child, taken from Scott's *Minstrelsy*, where it is a combination of two fragments. Jacobs retold the tale in *English Fairy Tales* (p. 44), apparently using this version as his source.

TYPE 780, MOTIFS: K.2212 [*Treacherous elder sister*]; E.632 [*Reincarnation as musical instrument. The singing bone*]; N.271 [*Murder will out*].

❡ Widespread. Grimm, no. 28; common through Europe; African and American versions. There are many variants of the ballads in English but the basic story is the same, though in some the miller draws out the younger daughter still alive, robs her and pushes her back into the water.

BLACK BROTTIE

There wiz a wife, an she hid three sins, an the twa aulest geed awa t'push their fortun, an Black Brottie, the little een, he followt aifter them, an she geed t' tack 'im back, and she said, she wiz gyaain t' mack a ban-nockie an roast a fishie, an he wid get a bit o' a' that gehn he wid come back. Bit he widna come back, bit followt aifter them, an they took 'im an set 'im in a tree. An there cam a man bye fin he wiz sitting' i' the tree, an he said: "Gehn ye wid tack me doon, I wid set you up, and ye wid see faht I see." He took 'im doon, bit he didna set 'im up, an geed aff aifter his breethirs. An they war a' lodged in ae hoose, an the wife ordert his twa breethirs t' lie wi' her ain sins, an Black Brottie t' lie wi' the dog. Sae aboot the middle o' the nicht the wife tied red threeds aboot her ain sins' necks. An syne fin it cam near mornin, Black Brottie saw faht she did, an he raise an he took aff the red threeds, an pat them aboot's ain breethirs' necks. An the wife raise aboot the dawnin o' the mornin, an cuttit the throats it hidna the red threeds, an syne fin daylicht cam in, she saw it she hid cuttit her ain sins' throats, bit she said Black Brottie wizna awa fae the hoose yet. An she said it hid been a bleedy mornin. An she said t' the uman (the female servant) t' gyang awa' t' the wall for pottage bree, an Black Brottie followt 'er, an pat 'er in o' the wall, an the buckets abeen 'er, an he geed back again. An the wife said, "Faht wid ye dee t'me, an I hid deen t' you as ye hae deen t' me?" He said: "I wid gaither a' the siller an a' the pyouter (pewter) it's i' the hoose, an pit it intil a saick, an you in amon't, an I wid tie the mooth o' the saick wi' a bleedy puthin (pudding), an I wid gyang t' the wid (wood) for as big a tree as I cud trail hame, an I wid lay on you as lang as you were livin." "Weel", she said, "I'll jist dee that t'you," an' so she pat in a' her siller an a' her pyouter into the saick an him in amon't, an tied the mooth wi' a bleedy puthin, an geed t' the wid, an cam hame wi' a stick. Bit fin she wiz awa, he cam oot o' the saick, an took a' the siller an a' the pyouter, an he pat in the cat an the dog. An she cam hame an her stick thegeether (together), an she laid o' them, an the dog bow-wowt, an the cat myawt, bit she said she sud gar'im bow-wow an myawve tee (too) afore she leet 'im oot o' that.

BLACK BROTTIE [anglicized]

There was a woman who had three sons; the two eldest went away to push their fortunes, and Black Brottie, the little one, followed after them; and she went to get him back, and she said she was going to bake a bannock, and roast a fish, and he would get a bit of all that if he would come back. But he would not come back, but followed after them, and they took him and set him up in a tree. And there came a man by as he was sitting in the tree, and he said, "If you would take me down, I would set you up, and you would see what I see." He took him down, but he did not set him up, and went off after his brothers. And they were all lodged in one house, and the wife ordered the two brothers to lie with her own sons, and Black Brottie to lie with the dog. So, about the middle of the night, the wife tied red threads about her own sons' necks. And presently, when it came near morning, Black Brottie saw what she did, and he rose, and took off the red threads, and put them around his own brothers' necks. And the wife rose about the dawning of the morning, and cut the throats that had not the red threads, and then, when daylight came in, she saw that she had cut her own sons' throats, but she said Black Brottie was not away from the house yet. And she said it had been a bloody morning. And she told the servant to go to the well for water for the broth, and Black Brottie followed her, and put her into the well, and the buckets on top of her, and he went back again.

And the wife said, "What would you do to me, if I had done to you as you have done to me?" And he said, "I would gather all the silver and pewter that is in the house, and put it into a sack, and you in among it, and I would tie the mouth of the sack with a blood pudding, and I would go to the wood for as big a stick as I could drag home, and I would lay on you as long as you were alive."

"Well," she said, "I'll just do that to you," and so she put all her silver and all her pewter into the sack, and him in among it, and tied the mouth of it with a blood pudding, and went to the wood, and came home with a stick.

But while she was away, he came out of the sack, and took all the silver and the pewter, and he put in the cat and the dog. And she and her stick came home together, and she laid on them, and the dog bow-wowed, and the cat miaowed, but she said she would make him bow-wow, and miaow too, before she let him out of that.

Collected by W. Gregor, *Folk-Lore Journal*, III, p. 270.

Told by Mrs Scott, a small farmer's wife in the parish of Pitsligo, originally from Aberdour, an adjoining parish. She was over seventy years old.

TYPE 327B or 1119, MOTIFS: K.1611 [*Ogre kills his own children*]; K.526 [*Captor's bag filled with animals or objects while captives escape*].

This is a truncated version of "Hop o' My Thumb" or "Mally Whuppie".

¶ The tale has a very wide distribution; the best-known version is "Le Petit Poucet" of Perrault. See also "Mally Whuppie", "The Enchanted Mountain", "Fairy Jip and Witch One-Eye", "Jack the Buttermilk".

THE BLACK BULL OF NORROWAY

In Norroway, long time ago, there lived a certain lady, and she had three daughters. The oldest of them said to her mother: "Mother, bake me a bannock, and roast me a collop, for I'm going away to seek my fortune." Her mother did so; and the daughter went away to an old witch washerwife and told her purpose. The old wife bade her stay that day, and look out of her back-door, and see what she could see. She saw nought the first day. The second day she did the same, and saw nought. On the third day she looked again, and saw a coach and six coming along the road. She ran in and told the old wife what she saw. "Well," quoth the old woman, "yon's for you." So they took her into the coach, and galloped off.

The second daughter next says to her mother: "Mother, bake me a bannock, and roast me a collop, for I'm going away to seek my fortune." Her mother did so; and away she went to the old wife, as her sister had done. On the third day she looked out of the back-door, and saw a coach-and-four coming along the road. "Well," quoth the old woman, "yon's for you." So they took her in, and off they set.

The third daughter says to her mother: "Mother, bake me a bannock, and roast me a collop, for I'm going away to seek my fortune." Her mother did so, and away she went to the old witch. She bade her look out of her back-door, and see what she could see. She did so: and when she came back, said she saw nought. The second day she did the same, and saw nought. The third day she looked again, and on coming back said to the old wife she saw nought but a great Black Bull coming crooning along the road. "Well," quoth the old witch, "Yon's for you." On hearing this she was next to distracted with grief and terror: but she was lifted up and set on his back, and away they went.

Aye they travelled, and on they travelled, till the lady grew faint with hunger. "Eat out of my right ear," says the Black Bull, "and drink out of my left ear, and set by your leaving." So she did as he said, and was wonderfully refreshed. And long they rode, and hard they rode, till they came in sight of a very big and bonny castle. "Yonder we must be this night," quoth the Bull, "for my old brother lives yonder;" and presently they were at the place. They lifted her off his back, and took her in, and sent him away to a park for the night. In the morning, when they brought the Bull home, they took the lady into a fine shining parlour, and gave her a beautiful apple, telling her not to break it till she was in the greatest strait ever mortal was in in the world, and that would bring her out of it. Again she was lifted on the Bull's back, and after she had ridden far, and farther than I can tell, they came in sight of a far bonnier castle, and farther away than the last. Says the Bull to her: "Yonder we must be this night, for my second brother lives yonder;" and they were at the place directly. They lifted her down, and took her in, and sent the Bull to the field for the night. In the morning they took the lady into a fine and rich room, and gave her the finest pear she had ever seen, bidding her not to break it till she was in the greatest strait ever mortal could be in, and that would get her out of it. Again she was lifted and set on his back, and away they went. And long they rode, and hard they rode, till they came in sight of the far biggest castle, and far farthest off they had yet seen. "We must be yonder to-night," says the Bull, "for my young brother lives yonder;" and they were there directly. They lifted her down, took her in, and sent the Bull to the field for the night. In the morning they took her into a room, the finest of all, and gave her a plum, telling her not to break it till she was in the greatest strait mortal could be in, and that would get her out of it. Presently they brought home the Bull, set the lady on his back, and away they went.

And aye they rode, and on they rode, till they came to a dark and ugsome glen, where they stopped, and the lady lighted down. Says the

Bull to her: "Here ye must stay till I go and fight the Old Un. Ye must seat yourself on that stone, and move neither hand nor foot till I come back, else I'll never find ye again. And if everything round you turns blue, I have beaten the Old Un; but should all things turn red, he'll have conquered me." She set herself down on the stone, and by-and-by all round her turned blue. Overcome with joy, she lifted one of her feet, and crossed it over the other, so glad was she that her companion was victorious. The Bull returned and sought for her, but never could find her.

Long she sat, and aye she wept, till she wearied. At last she rose and went away, she didn't know where. On she wandered, till she came to a great hill of glass, that she tried all she could to climb, but wasn't able. Round the bottom of the hill she went, sobbing and seeking a passage over, till at last she came to a smith's house; and the smith promised, if she would serve him seven years, he would make her iron shoon, wherewith she could climb over the glassy hill. At seven years' end she got her iron shoon, clomb the glassy hill, and chanced to come to the old washerwife's habitation. There she was told of a gallant young knight, that had given in some clothes all over blood to wash, and whoever washed them was to be his wife. The old wife had washed till she was tired, and then she set her daughter at it, and both washed, and they washed, and they washed, in hopes of getting the young knight; but all they could do, they couldn't get out a stain. At length they set the stranger damosel to work; and whenever she began, the stains came out pure and clean, and the old wife made the knight believe it was her daughter had washed the clothes. So the knight and the eldest daughter were to be married, and the stranger damosel was distracted at the thought of it, for she was deeply in love with him. So she bethought her of her apple, and breaking it, found it filled with gold and precious jewellery, the richest she had ever seen. "All these", she said to the eldest daughter, "I will give you, on condition that you put off your marriage for one day, and allow me to go into his room alone at night." So the lady consented; but meanwhile the old wife had prepared a sleeping drink, and given it to the knight, who drank it, and never wakened till next morning. The life-long night the damosel sobbed and sang:

> "Seven long years I served for thee,
> The glassy hill I clomb for thee,
> Thy bloody clothes I wrang for thee;
> And wilt thou not waken and turn to me?"

Next day she knew not what to do for grief. She then broke the pear, and found it filled with jewellery far richer than the contents of the apple. With these jewels she bargained for permission to be a second night in the young knight's chamber; but the old wife gave him another sleeping drink, and he again slept till morning. All night she kept sighing and singing as before:

> "Seven long years I served for thee,
> The glassy hill I clomb for thee,
> Thy bloody clothes I wrang for thee;
> And wilt thou not waken and turn to me?"

Still he slept, and she nearly lost hope altogether. But that day, when he was out hunting, somebody asked him what noise and moaning was that they heard all last night in his bedchamber. He said, "I haven't heard any noise."

But they assured him there was; and he resolved to keep waking that night to try what he could hear. That being the third night, and the damosel being between hope and despair, she broke her plum, and it held far the richest jewellery of the three. She bargained as before; and the old wife, as before, took in the sleeping draught to the young knight's chamber; but he told her he couldn't drink it that night without sweetening. And when she went away for some honey to sweeten it with, he poured out the drink, and so made the old wife think he had drunk it. They all went to bed again, and the damosel began, as before, singing:

> "Seven long years I served for thee,
> The glassy hill I clomb for thee,
> Thy bloody clothes I wrang for thee;
> And wilt thou not waken and turn to me?"

He heard and turned to her. And she told him all that had befallen her, and he told her all that had happened to him. And he caused the old washerwife and her daughter to be burnt. And they were married, and he and she are living happy to this day, for aught I know.

Jacobs, *More English Fairy Tales*, p. 20. Anglicized from Chambers, *Popular Rhymes of Scotland*, p. 95.

TYPE 425, MOTIFS: C.932 [*Loss of husband for breaking tabu*]; H.1385.4 [*Quest for vanished husband*]; H.1114 [*Climbing glass hill*]; Q.482.1 [*Princess serves as menial*]; D.2006.1.4 [*Forgotten fiancée buys place in husband's bed*].

¶ Swahn in "The Tale of Cupid and Psyche" makes a detailed study of this type. See also "The Glass Mountain", "The Red Bull of Norroway", "The Three Feathers", and (a more distant connection) "Nicht, Nought, Nothing".

THE BLACK CAT

In Fifeshire there lived a farmer who had a lazy son, unwilling to do anything but list as a common soldier. After having taken the bounty and squandered it away, his colonel, who was a very harsh man, ordered him abroad, where the governor of the place treated him very ill. Tom (for that was the soldier's name), deserted from the regiment, and fled to a distant part of the country, where he met with an old woman to whom he told his tale of woe. She advised him to go to the king, and lay his case before his majesty, who would redress all his wrongs. He having done as requested by the old woman, he was sent away to a castle at a little distance to sleep, where he again met with the old woman, who told him to speak to and tell his wants to a black cat, which would come in and follow his commands. About the middle of the night, as the soldier sat pensive and uneasy, the cat, as foretold by the old woman, came in, when he said, come away my bonny cat, I have long been waiting you. She said, who bade you speak? He told her. She said: There will two men come in, but never do anything they request of you, till one of a higher deportment arrive, and when I touch you, do as he bids you. In a little time in came three men, who said rise and let us sit down; but he paid no attention to them. Another who came in said, Follow me, then the black cat touched him, so he followed the stranger, who spoke to him thus:– I was king of this castle, but was murdered by my steward who fled abroad, and is now your governor. Tell this to my son the king, who will bring him to punishment, and we will never trouble the castle any more. The three men you saw were my murderers, and they do all the mischief that lies in their power. They then vanished, and the man went and told the king, who gave him a letter to the commander-in-chief. He went as directed, and arrived safe at the place, who, when he was recognized by a fellow-soldier, was much pitied, as he feared he would have to undergo some dreadful punishment for his desertion. An officer next met him who gave orders to place him in close confinement, and afterwards sentenced him to die; but having sent to the commander-in-chief the king's letter, was soon after set at liberty. The governor was then secured, sent to the king with a strong guard who commanded him to be beheaded without judge or jury, and Tom made governor in his place. Tom having now power, reduced the officer to a private, and the private to be officer; sent for his father, and lived happy.

Norton Collection, I, p. 168; from Buchan, *Ancient Scottish Tales*, pp. 51–2, 181–2. TYPE 326A*, MOTIFS: H.1411.2 [*Staying in haunted house infested by cats*]; E.281 [*Ghosts haunt house*]; E.231 [*Return from dead to reveal murder*].
¶ See also "Ashypelt".

THE BLACK CLOAK [summary]

There was a widow with three sons, Tom, Harry and Jack. They went
in turns to seek their fortune. Big bannock or blessing? The first two
chose the first. Jack, who was simple, begged to go, but for long was
refused. A little man appeared in a dream, and advised him to take the
little bannock and the blessing. He did so. On his way, the little man
appeared to him and gave him a magic whistle. He arrived at a castle,
where he was given three tasks, and recognized his brothers' heads on
spikes on the gates. The first task was to kill a three-headed giant. He
blew the whistle, and the little man appeared and told him to take pebbles
and climb the highest tree on the giant's mountain. He did so, and the
giant appeared, sat down, and fell asleep.

Presently a second giant appeared and fell asleep too. Jack dropped the
pebbles on both of them, so that they fought, and one killed the other.
Jack cut off the three heads, and took them back. That night the Princess
came and spoke to him, and said she had sent the little man. His next
task was to kill a monstrous bull. She gave him a handful of corn. He
spilled this before the bull when it charged him, and it ate it and died. The
Princess did not know what the third task would be, but she gave him
a magic reel of yarn. He was to fetch a feather from the Black Man's
cloak. The Princess gave him some food for his journey. On the way he
sat down to eat it, and the little man came and begged for some. He gave
him help. Then the little man told him what he must do. He must go
on to a wide river. Three swans would offer themselves to carry him
across. The first two he must refuse, and take the third. So it happened,
and the third swan told him what he must do. He must go on far and far,
to Doom Castle, but the reel of yarn would shorten his way. When he
got to the castle he must turn quickly to the right, and snatch up a black
cloak lying in the right-hand chamber, and put it on, and he would
break the spell under which the Princess lay. He did as he was told, and
as he put the cloak round him, the Lord of the Castle came in, and they
fought, and the Black Lord was killed, and the Princess woke from her
enchanted sleep, and she was none other than the Princess who had
helped him before. So they went back over the long, long road, till they
got to the Castle, and there they reigned together.

And I went to the wedding, and had a rare drink.

RUN: "He tramped over the road as far as I can tell you or you can tell me, through all
the birks, brakes and over all the hills in Yarrow."

School of Scottish Studies, Hamish Henderson. Willie Johnson (from his grandmother).

TYPE 313 (variant), MOTIFS: L.101 [*Unpromising hero*]; J.229.3 [*Bannock or blessing*];

D.1814.2 [*Advice in dream*]; D.810 [*Gift of magic object*]; D.1225 [*Magic whistle*]; H.901.1 [*Heads on stakes*]; H.335 [*Tasks assigned to suitors*]; G.512 [*Ogre killed*]; K.1082 [*Ogres duped into fighting each other*]; H.1174 [*Suitor test: killing monster*]; H.335.0.1 [*Bride helps suitor*]; H.1161.2.2 [*Task: killing fierce bull*]; D.1184.1 [*Magic ball of thread*]; Q.40 [*Kindness rewarded*] (this comes late in story); H.1274 [*Quest to hell for three dragon's feathers*]; D.1053 [*Magic cloak*]; B.469.2 [*Helpful swan*]; F.141.1 [*River as barrier to other world*]; D.700 [*Person disenchanted*]; L.10 [*Victorious youngest son*].

❡ The motif of the Bannock and the Blessing occurs in a number of different types of Scottish fairy tale. This is a widespread tale. One of the best-known versions is the Scandinavian "Master Maid".

See also "Nicht Nought Nothing", "The Green Man of Knowledge", "Daughter Greengown", etc.

THE BLACK DOG OF THE WILD FOREST [summary]

Son born to King and Queen on condition that when 21 he should be surrendered to Black Dog of Forest. After son's birth, King goes away to a house, and shuts himself up. At 21 the son goes to find him, and finds him very old man with beard reaching to ground. The King tells him to get horse and go. He hears the Black Dog roaring behind him, but reaches giant's house before six o'clock.

He pets a little white dog, Hearall. It is given to him. The Black Dog comes, is heard by Hearall, who fights it so that it retires to get more strength.

Next day the Prince goes on, followed by Hearall. Next giant's house; given second white dog, Seeall, and bottle of elixir to treat dogs. Black Dog comes. Fought by two dogs, and driven back. Third day to third giant; given third dog, Fightall. All these fight Black Dog. Next day all cross the Black River of Jordan, closely pursued by the Black Dog, which cannot cross.

New country: two princesses; Jack loves one, another wants him. Jealous; she goes to a magician for help. Told to cross the Black River of Jordan and carry over small dog. It is the Black Dog: Hearall hears him, Seeall sees him, Fightall leads them to fight. Black Dog killed, as he cannot cross river.

Princess returns to wizard; told to take Black Dog's bone, and lay it over Prince as he is sleeping. Dogs pull off bone, Princess kills the dogs, but Prince brings them back to life with the elixir. Princess gives it up, and the Prince marries his true love.

Thompson Notebooks, IX (also fuller version in *Notebook*, D). Collected in outline from Pat, Reuben and Shanny Smith, Oswaldtwistle, 11 January 1915. Supposed to be Abraham Lee's story.

TYPE 313 variant, MOTIFS: S.223 [*Childless couple promise child to devil if only they may have one*]; H.1235 [*Successive helpers on quest*]; B.312.1 [*Helpful animals a gift*]; G.303.16.19.13 [*Devil cannot follow man over running water*]; B.524.1.1 [*Dogs kill attacking cannibal or dragon*]; B.333.3 [*Unsuccessful attempt to kill helpful animal*].

THE BLACK KING OF MOROCCO

One of those farmers in the North of Scotland, who delight in educating their sons, had a favourite son who had got all the education that that part of the country could bestow; his father thought of improving it still a little farther by travel. Accordingly the father and son set off together, to procure more knowledge, when they met with a stranger, who, in a familiar manner, asked where they were going? The old farmer told him that he was going in quest of knowledge to his son, who had been tutored in the best schools in Scotland, but was still deficient in the principal requisites of human education. The stranger then said, that if he would entrust him to his care, he would complete his education, and make him perfect in all that was necessary for any of the learned professions in the course of seven years. To this the old man consented, having himself a thirst for knowledge, but asked, at the expiry of the term, where he would find his son. The stranger then replied that, if he did not get him ere the seven years were expired, he would not get him at all; and where he was to find him he did not let him know. They then went their several ways, the farmer back to his farm, and his son and teacher to a place beyond the ken of man. Before the end of seven years the farmer began to weary for the return of his son, so went in pursuit of him. When travelling in a solitary part of the road, in an uninhabited part of the country, he met with an old man drest in pilgrim's weeds who said he knew his errand, and desired him to go to Dr Brazen-nose of Cambridge, who can inform you of your son, as it was he who gave him to the black King of Morocco, where, I fear, you will have to go before you receive your son. On arriving at Cambridge, he was told by the Doctor that he would get his son if he could find him. This was all the information he received from the learned Brazen-nose; so he set off for the court of the black king, where he arrived, after having seen many strange sights, in safety. Here he asked for his son, when seven doves were set before him, and he was desired to make his choice; he did so, and made choice of one with a broken wing, which chanced to be his son in the likeness of a dove. Happy to meet again, they now took leave of the black king's court, and pursued their journey homewards with all the speed they may. On their way home, hunger began to prey upon their vitals; but having no money wherewithal to pay for meat, the son said he would turn himself into a horse, which he could sell at the first market, but to be sure to be on his guard not to let the bridle slip out of his hand, for if he did, the consequence might be fatal to him. The old man promised, but thoughtlessly forgot the serious injunction, and let the bridle fall from his hand, which put the young man into much danger, being pursued by the king and his companions. The young man then changed himself into an eel, which the king observing, who with six of his nobles, turned themselves into seven sharks, and pursued the eel. Being hard beset, he next changed himself into a bird, when they did the same into eagles, and gave him chase, till he took shelter in a lady's window, and became a ring on her finger. When night came, he became a man, which put the lady in great fear. He told her the danger he was in, and begged her assistance in making his escape from the king and his nobles, who were his pursuers, and were at that time at her gate as musicians, who would ask nothing of her but the ring; but instead of complying with their request, throw me into the fire, and I will save myself. Accordingly as he had said, they asked of her the ring, but she threw it into the fire, which they observing, they became goldsmiths in order to beat the ring. He next turned himself into a sack of barley, when they became geese to eat the barley; but instead thereof, he immediately turned himself into a fox, and ere they wist, devoured them all, which put an end to his troubles. He then married the lady, and went in search of his father, who had caused him so much pain. On his travels, he happened to see a man who had two old wives whom he asked what he was going to do with them, but receiving no answer, he said he could grind them together, and out of the two, produce a beautiful young one. This he did, to the astonishment of every beholder. He next made a fine young horse out of two useless old ones, which two men observing, would need try the same, but out of two produced nothing. One man also would go try the making of a young woman out of two old ones which he had, but was still more unfortunate than the former, for they only lost their horses, but he lost his wives, and was condemned to death for murder. At length he put all things to right again, found his father, went back to his wife, and for many years lived happily and peaceably, much and justly esteemed by all who knew him, for his great learning.

Norton Collection, I, p.149, from Buchan, *Ancient Scottish Tales*, pp. 59–60, 189–90. TYPE 325, MOTIFS: D.1711.0.1 [*Magician's apprentice*]; H.62.1 [*Recognition of person transformed*]; D.1721 [*Magic power from magician*]; D.100 [*Transformation of man to horse*]; C.837 [*Tabu: losing bridle in selling man transformed to horse*]; D.615.2 [*Transformation contest between master and pupil*]; D.641.1 [*Lover as bird visits mistress*]; L.142.2 [*Pupil surpasses magician*]; D.1880 [*Magic rejuvenation*]; D.1868.1 [*Broken-down nag becomes magnificent horse*]; J.2411.1 [*Unsuccessful imitation*].

¶ A widespread tale in German, French, Balkan, Russian, Indian, Jamaican, American Negro examples, etc. Examples in Ireland and the Scottish Highlands, e.g. "The Magician's Ghillie", J. G. Mackay. See also "The King of the Black Art".

THE BLACK YOW

This is the story of Cinderella. When the stepmother goes with her two daughters to the ball on the first night, she tells Cinderella to make some good soup by the time they return, but gives her only one small carrot, turnip, onion, and a bone to make it of. While she is lamenting in comes a black yow, undertakes the soup, changes Cinderella's dress, and sends her to the ball. The second night the same thing happens, only the stepmother gives a smaller quantity than before, and the black yow says: "If anything should happen to me, take up my bones and bury them."

The stepmother kills the yow, and while Cinderella is burying it, a dog runs away with one shank.

The third night the stepmother and sisters go off as before, and Cinderella is in despair, because the yow is dead, and cannot come to her help. But presently, while she is lamenting,

> In came the black yow,
> Limping, lamping,
> With one shank wanting.

Cinderella goes again to the ball, and loses her shoe. The next day, the prince himself comes round with it to find the owner.

The eldest girl tries it on, and can get in all but her heel, so she cuts off a bit, and the prince takes her up behind him on his horse. But as they ride along a bird in a bush sings:

> "Nippit foot and clippit foot
> Ahint the young prince rides,
> But bonny foot and pretty foot
> Ahint the cauldron hides."

"What does the birdie say?" said the prince.

"Who cares what a birdie says?" answers the girl. But the prince looks round, and seeing the blood running from her foot, feels sure there is something wrong, and goes back.

The second girl cuts off her toe, and the same thing happens. Then he goes behind the cauldron, and, half in joke, makes Cinderella try on the shoe. She produces the other. As she mounts behind him the black yow appears, changes Cinderella's dress, and is herself changed into a fairy.

Norton Collection, II, p. 79. (*NQ*, x, pp. 463–4. Told by a Scottish lady, who was familiar with it in her childhood in Dumbartonshire.) Contributed by Selina Gaye. TYPE 510.

¶ See also "Ashpitel", etc.

THE BLACKSMITH FROM IRELAND

There was an Irish blacksmith that had a great reputation, and an English goldsmith challenged him to work against him for three bags of gold and fetched him all the way to London. On the way a boy met him and said to him: "If I help you, will you give me the half of what you take?" "I will," said the smith. When he got to London, the goldsmith said to him: "Do you like to work alone or in company?" "I like to work alone," said the smith. So they weighed out a pound of iron each, and went each to his smithy. But the wee boy keeked through the goldsmith's keyhole and saw that he was making a ship to sail the Atlantic. So he went to the blacksmith, who was making a plough-colter. "The goldsmith is making a ship of iron," he said. "You'd better let me help you." So he made a ship that would sail faster than the goldsmith's ship. So that day he got the first bag of gold. The next day they weighed out a pound of iron apiece, and the blacksmith set out to make a plough-coulter, but the wee boy peeked into the goldsmith's room, and he was making a hare. So the wee boy made a greyhound. And in the evening they went up to the hill, and the goldsmith set down the hare, and it raced away, but the smith took out the greyhound, and it caught the hare in a few minutes. The next day they weighed out their iron again, and the smith set to on a plough-coulter, for he said, "I'm the best coult and sock-maker in the whole county of Mayo, and I can do with a pound of iron what no other mannie can do." But the wee boy keeked through the keyhole, and saw the goldsmith making an iron pigeon, and he set to to make an iron hawk, and they let the pigeon fly through the wood, but the hawk went after it, and brought it back; so the blacksmith got his third bag of gold. And as he was on his way home, the wee boy said to him: "Well, will you give me my half?" "You may whistle for it," said the smith. "You'll be sorry for that," said the wee boy, and away he went.

Well, the smith got home, and set to work again in his smithy, very well pleased with himself. One night there was a knock at the door, and a stranger came in with two withered old horses. "I've got two old horses," he said. "Will you make me one good one out of them?" "I'm the best, etc.", said the smith, "and if any man can do it, I can." But it puzzled him how to set about it. "I'd better show you," said the stranger. He put the two horses in the fire and hammered them, and a lovely young horse came out. The smith thought he could do as well as any man in Ireland, and he had two old horses, so he brought them in, and put them in the fire, but they just burnt up. The next day the stranger came again with a cross, ugly young woman and an old one. "I've a scolding wife, and an old mother-in-law," he said. "Will you make them into one lovely young woman for me?" The smith said, "I'm the best, etc." But he had no notion how to set about it, so the stranger set the pair on the fire, and with a stroke here and there, he turned them into a lovely young girl. The smith had a scolding wife and a mother-in-law of his own, so he thought he would do the same. But he only burned the pair of them into nothing. The next day the stranger came again and said: "I'm courting a lovely young woman up the road, but I'm getting old and feeble, and I want to renew my power. Blow up the fire." The smith blew up the fire, and the stranger thrust his member into it, gave it a tap or two, and away he went, with all the lusty vigour of a young man. The fool of a smith thought he could do the same, and he fairly sat on the fire, and burnt himself almost to death before he could get off it. He had just strength to stagger to his bed, and there he lay dying, when the stranger came in. "Will you give the wee boy his half now?" he said. "I will that," said the smith, and he told the stranger where the sacks of gold lay. The stranger divided it into two halves, but when he was done, there was some over. "Will this go to the wee boy, or to you?" he said. "To the wee boy," said the smith, "for he fairly earned it." "Well," said the stranger, "I'm the wee boy, and all shall be as it was before." And with that he went, and the smith got out of bed, and went up to his scolding wife, and ever after that he held to his promises.

RUN: "I'm the best coult and sock maker in the whole county of Mayo, and I can do with a pound of iron what no other mannie can do."
School of Scottish Studies, Hamish Henderson from Tom Wilson, Stirling. Told him by his grandfather from Stirling.
TYPE 753 (variant), MOTIFS: N.845 [*Magician as helper*]; D.1719.1 [*Contest in magic*]; K.231.2 [*Reward withheld*]; D.1886 [*Rejuvenation by burning*]; J.2411.1 [*Unsuccessful imitation*].

¶ As a religious tale this is widespread. It is possible that the little boy in this version may be Christ. There are 166 Irish, 59 Finnish, 44 French, 22 German, 6 Russian, 7 Italian examples. This is a fuller version than usual as it gives a first contest between magicians, in which an obstinately self-satisfied smith is aided, who refuses to acknowledge his obligation and is punished by the disastrous consequences of his own conceit, which are annulled after he has made proper reparation.

See also "The Old Smith" and "Will the Smith".

THE BLACKSMITH WHO SOLD HIMSELF TO THE DEVIL

There was once a blacksmith who had neither fire nor iron for his forge, and because things did not go according to his mind—

> He ripped and he tore
> And he cursed and he swore.

One day as he was grumbling about his want of work, a man, who was dressed in black, came to see him, and said to him, "What dost thou want?"

The blacksmith answered, "I want nought but iron and stuff for my fire."

The man in black said, "If thou wilt sell thyself to me thou shalt want nought for seven years."

So the blacksmith agreed to sell himself, and when he got back to his forge he found there was as much coal and iron there as he wanted, so that he had plenty of work and plenty of money for seven years. But when the seven years were ended he was downhearted, for then the devil came for him, and made a great hole in his garden and put a bridge over the hole. Then he said to the blacksmith, "Step on this ring," meaning on the bridge, for he wanted the blacksmith to fall into the hole and break his neck. But the blacksmith defied the devil, and said, "I won't. Take all thy coal and iron back to hell with thee."

So the devil went and left the man as poor as he found him.

When the blacksmith got back to his forge he found it was empty, but he vowed that he would go without fire, iron, or coal before he would have ought to with the devil again.

S. O. Addy, *Household Tales and Traditional Remains*, p. 17.
TYPE 810 (variant), MOTIF: M.211 [*Man sells himself to the devil*].
¶ In this tale the Devil is not cheated, but merely conquered by firmness, and persuaded to take back his gifts.

See "The Man who wouldn't go out at Night", "The Devil and the Tailor", "Dule upon Dun", etc.

THE BOTTLE OF WATER FROM THE WORLD'S END WELL [summary]

A King's daughter had a cruel stepmother, who set her menial tasks. One day she sent her to draw water in a sieve: a frog advised her to stop it with moss and clay, and she filled it. Next day, to wash black wool white: a bird advised her to dip it in a certain spring and wring it three times, and it came white. Next day, given a bottle, and told to fill it at the Well of the World's End; on the way found a shaggy pony, loosed it at its own request and it carried her to the Well. Too deep to dip: three dirty heads came up and asked her to wash them and brush them. She did so and they gave her three blessings: increase of beauty, a voice like silver bells, and gold out of her hair whenever she combed it. She went back with her bottle, and everything was as the three heads had promised.

The second sister went, refused to untether the pony and had to walk, refused to comb the heads, and they wished evil on her: that she should be ten times uglier, that dirt should drop from her mouth when she spoke, and that she should get a quart pot full of lice whenever she combed her hair. She returned home. A great King's son married the lovely Princess, but her stepsister was turned out of the palace, and an ugly old beggarman married her. The Queen died in despair.

Thompson Notebooks, IX, from Tommy Smith, Oswaldtwistle, 11 January 1915. TYPES 480, 1180, MOTIFS: H.1023.2 [*Task: carrying water in sieve*]; B.493.1 [*Helpful frog*]; H.1023.6 [*Task: washing black wool white*]; H.1192 [*Task: combing hair of fairies*]; D.1860 [*Magic beautification*]; Q.111 [*Riches as reward*]; Q.2 [*Kind and unkind*]; D.1870 [*Magic hideousness*].
¶ See "The Three Golden Heads", "The Wal at the World's End".

THE BOY AND THE MANTLE [summary]

King Arthur was holding court at Carlisle in the month of May. On the third of the month a boy came to court. His manners were courteous, and his clothing of silk, and he wore many rich jewels.

He greeted the King and Queen and their courtiers, and presented to the King a mantle of fairy work, so fine that he drew it out from between two nutshells.

The property of the mantle was that when any lady put it on it would show by its fit whether or not she was true to her husband. The boy suggested that the Queen should be the first to try: when she did so the mantle appeared to have turned to rags, as though shorn by a pair of shears: its colours were all changed and it fitted no part of her body. She turned red with shame, and fled to her chamber.

Next Sir Kay called to his own lady to try it, but for her it was shamefully short, and she too fled from the hall. Every knight in turn then tried the mantle on his lady, but none was found of perfect virtue. Sir Craddock's lady, at last, by confessing to a sin, made the mantle seem to fit her, but Queen Guenevere denounced her for a witch, saying she was the most unchaste of them all. The little boy rebuked the Queen for discourtesy;

then he went out, slew a wild boar, and brought its head into the hall. He said that no knight who was a cuckold would be able to carve it, sharpen his knife as he would; and when they tried, Craddock's knife was the only one that could pierce the flesh, and it carved it so neatly that every knight had a share.

Then the boy showed them his drinking-horn of red gold, and said that no one could drink from it without spilling, whose wife was not chaste. And again they all tried to drink. Some spilled the wine on their shoulders, some on to their knees, and some into their eyes. Only Craddock drank without spilling. The horn and the boar's head were given to him, and the silken mantle to his lady, to reward them for their faithfulness.

Child, *The English and Scottish Ballads*, I, pp. 257–74.
MOTIFS: H.410 [*Chastity test by magic objects or ordeals*]; H.411.4 [*Magic drinking-horn as chastity test*]; H.411.7 [*Mantle as chastity test*]; H.425.1 [*Cuckold's knife cannot carve boar's head*].

THE BOY AND HIS WAGES

A boy once had a very cruel stepmother; so cruel was she that the lad determined to run away. In the end he did so, and hired himself to a farmer. Now when a year had passed, the kind farmer gave the lad for his wages an ass which dropped gold. Off home went the boy, driving his ass in front of him. On coming to a wayside inn, the landlord asked him why he did not ride such a fine-looking ass. The lad in reply foolishly told Boniface that his ass was much too valuable a one to ride; adding, "Would you ride an ass that dropped gold?" To this the man asked him to make it drop gold where it stood. The boy wisely explained that it was only when nature's call had to be obeyed that it did so, and quite beyond his power to command it. Whilst the boy was having refreshment, the ass was put in the stable, the landlord keeping his eye on it; before the lad had eaten and rested, evidence was given that he had spoken nothing but the truth. It happened that the landlord had a very fine ass of his own; this he fetched from the field, and while the lad slept he groomed it, trimmed its ears and tail, and blacked its hoofs, till in the end, it exactly resembled the gold-dropping one. This he took away and hid, putting his ass in its place. The boy never noticed it was a changeling he was driving home. On his arrival, he told his stepmother what a treasure he had brought her.

Hearing such good news, she received him kindly, giving him a supper of fried eggs and bacon. For three days he was, as she told him, treated like a prince; but the third morning, instead of his breakfast, she gave him a worse thrashing than ever, and turned him to the door, calling him all the names she could lay her tongue to. He returned to his master, who kindly received him, and on the completion of his second year's labour, gave him for his wages a hamper, which every day, on the command being given to fill itself, would be found packed with choicest food, sufficient to feed a large household.

Again he stopped at the inn on his way home; calling for a glass of beer, he ordered the hamper to fill. On beholding such a wonderful hamper, the landlord determined to steal that also, so while the lad slept he took it away, replacing it with one of his own, exactly similar. To the lad's discomfiture, the fraud was discovered the moment he returned home. Once again he was severely beaten and turned adrift. Again his kind master took him in, and at the end of his third year gave him a bag containing a thick stick, which on the command being given, "Come out, stick, and bend yourself," would immediately leap out and unmercifully thrash the individual who at the time was holding the bag. On his way home, the landlord spied him approaching, and with smiles and kind words asked him in. "And pray, what does your bag contain?" asked he, as soon as the lad was seated. "The most wonderful thing you ever saw," said he; "but let me have a good dinner, and then I will show you." The landlord, thinking to have another good haul, served him with the best of everything, going so far, even, as to give him a glass of wine. All impatience, he waited until the repast was finished. "Now," said the youth, smacking his lips as he swallowed the last bite, "stand in the middle of the room, and hold the bag in your hand, and I'll promise you the biggest surprise you ever had in your life. That bag is just wonderful." Before the lad had finished speaking, the landlord had taken his place in the middle of the floor, holding the bag in his hand.

"Now, open it," said the boy—which Boniface did. "Why", said he, in a tone of great disappointment, "it is only a stick." "Yes," replied the boy, "but it is a wonderful stick. Now just watch what it can do"; and then he shouted, "Come out, stick, and bend yourself." Immediately the stick jumped out of the bag, and bent itself about the back of the landlord until he howled with pain. Do what he would, go where he might, the stick leapt after and beat him, till at last, almost dead, he cried out, "Put it in the bag again; I will return thee thy ass and hamper," which he did. On nearing home, the lad saw his cruel stepmother waiting for him, with a thick stick in her hand. "Wait a while," he called, "until you see what I have brought you in my bag."

Thinking it would be wiser to wait, she laid down her stick and let him enter. "Now, before I show to you what I have in my bag, give me a good tea; you can thrash me afterwards quite as well as now," said he. After his tea, he asked the cruel old dame to take hold of the bag and open it.

This she readily did, little dreaming of what was to follow. Again he shouted, "Come out, stick, and bend yourself"; and for once the old hag knew what a stick laid across the back meant. She begged, she implored, she promised she would be good and kind to him, if he would only call off the stick. At last, when he considered she had been sufficiently punished, he ordered the stick back into the bag.

And from that day she behaved herself in a decent manner.

Norton Collection, II, p. 134, from Blakeborough, *Wit, Character, Folk-Lore and Customs of the North Riding of Yorkshire*, pp. 255–7.
TYPE 563.
❡ See "The Ass, the Table and the Stick", "The Seven Mysteries of the Luck", etc.

THE BROKEN PITCHER

Once upon a time there were two sisters, one called Orange and the other Lemon. Their mother loved Lemon much more than Orange, and made Orange do all the hard work in the house, and fetch water from the well every day. One day Orange went to the well as usual, taking her pitcher with her, and as she was stooping down to fill it with water the pitcher fell out of her hand into the well and was broken. Then Orange was very grieved, and dared not go home; so she sat down on the grass and cried.

After she had cried awhile, she looked up from the ground and saw a beautiful fairy standing near her. And the fairy said, "Why dost thou cry, little Orange?"

Orange said, "Because I have broken our pitcher, and mother will beat me."

"Dry up thy tears," said the fairy, "and see, I live in the well, and know all about you, and I will help you, because thou art such a good little girl, and so ill-used."

Then the fairy struck the ground, and the pitcher came back out of the well, sound and whole, and just as it was before, except that it had arms and legs.

"See," said the fairy, "this little pitcher shall always be thy friend, and now it will walk home with thee and carry the water itself. Go home now, tell it to nobody and be a good little girl." Having said this the fairy disappeared down the well.

After this Orange soon dried up her tears, and, taking hold of the pitcher's hand, she and the pitcher walked home together. But when they got to the door of her mother's house the arms and legs of the pitcher were gone. Then Orange took the pitcher into the house, and, remembering what the fairy had said, told what had happened to nobody.

The next morning Orange awoke very early, as she always did, and said to herself, "How tired I shall be before night comes, for there is so much work to do in the house."

So she got up, and when she came downstairs she found the pitcher, with its arms and legs on, sweeping the kitchen, and doing all the hard work, and ever after the pitcher was her faithful and helpful friend.

S. O. Addy, *Household Tales*, p. 29.

TYPE 510 variant, MOTIFS: L.52 [*Abused youngest daughter*]; N.815 [*Fairy as helper*]; D.813 [*Magic object received from fairy*].

¶ It is possible that this tale is literary in origin. A tale very like it, "Patty and her Pitcher", was published by Kegan Paul in *Mother Goose's Nursery Rhymes and Fairy Tales, c.* 1880. It is, however, longer. It seems as if someone had remembered and retold the beginning.

THE BROOMFIELD HILL [summary]

A knight and his lady made a tryst to meet at the Broomfield Hill, but he warned her that she would not return home from the tryst a maid. She vowed that she would, and they made a wager on it. The girl went to a wise woman who bade her go late to the tryst, and she would find her lover sleeping on the hill. Then she must gather the flowers of the broom, scatter them over him as he lay, and his sleep would be so deep that she could come and go without his knowing.

The knight reached the hill early in the morning, but when the lady did not come he lay down to wait, and fell asleep. In the afternoon the girl came, scattered the broom blossom over him, and left tokens to show him that she had indeed been there: her rings, which she placed on his fingers, and her girdle, which she laid on his breast. Then she stole away.

When the knight awoke, he cried to his horse:

> "O where were ye, my milk-white steed,
>   That I hae coft sae dear,
> That wadna watch and waken me,
>   When there was maiden here?"

> "I stamped wi my foot, master,
>   And gard my bridle ring,
> But na kin thing wald waken ye,
>   Till she was past and gane."

Next he chided his goshawk in the same words, but it replied:

> "I clapped wi my wings, master,
>   And aye my bells I rang,

And aye cried, 'Waken, waken, master,
  Before the ladye gang.'"

Then he reproached the young men of his company, but they all said
they had tried in vain to wake him. He cried out that if he had but once
had his will of the lady, the small birds might have had her afterwards
for their prey for aught he cared.

The lady heard him, for she was hidden behind a bush of broom, and
she went home singing for joy that she had won her wager and remained
a maid.

Child, *English and Scottish Popular Ballads*, I, pp. 394–9.
MOTIFS: K.1210 [*Humiliated or baffled lover*]; D.1814.1 [*Advice from magician*];
D.1364.3 [*Flowers produce magic sleep*]; B.211.1.3 [*Speaking horse*]; B.211.3
[*Speaking bird*].

BROWN ROBYN'S CONFESSION

It fell upon a Wodensday
  Brown Robyn's men went to sea,
But they saw neither moon nor sun,
  Nor starlight wi' their ee.

"We'll cast kevels us amang,
  See wha the unhappy man may be";
The kevel fell on Brown Robyn,
  The master-man was he.

"It is nae wonder," said Brown Robyn,
  "Altho I dinna thrive,
For wi my mither I had twa bairns,
  And wi my sister five.

"But tie me to a plank o wude,
  And throw me in the sea;
And if I sink, ye may bid me sink,
  But if I swim, just lat me bee."

They've tyed him to a plank o wude,
  And thrown him in the sea;
He didna sink, tho they bade him sink:
  He swimd, and they bade lat him bee.

He hadna been into the sea
  An hour but barely three,
Till by it came Our Blessed Lady,
  Her dear young son her wi.

"Will ye gang to your men again,
    Or will ye gang wi me?
Will ye gang to the high heavens,
    Wi my dear son and me?"

"I winna gang to my men again,
    For they would be feared at mee.
But I would gang to the high heavens,
    Wi thy dear son and thee."

"It's for nae honour ye did to me, Brown Robyn,
    It's for nae guid ye did to mee:
But a' is for your fair confession
    You've made upon the sea."

Child, *English and Scottish Popular Ballads*, II, p. 16.
TYPE 973, MOTIFS: N.271.10 [*Ship will sink if murderers aboard*]; S.264.1 [*Man thrown overboard to appease storm*]; V.21 [*Confession brings forgiveness of sin*].

THE BULL, THE TUP, THE COCK
AND THE STEG

A bull, a tup, a cock, and a steg* set out together to seek their fortune. When it got to night, they came to a house, and asked for a night's lodging, but the folks said no. However, at last they were let come into the kitchen. The bull said he would lie on the floor, the tup said he would lie by his side, the cock would perch on the rannel bank, and the steg would stand at t' back of the door. At midnight, when all was quiet, two men, meaning to rob the house, were heard parleying outside which should go in, and which watch outside. One went in, the bull got up and knocked him about, the tup did the same, and the cock said, "Fetch him here, I'll pick out his eyen." So he says, "I'd best be out of this." As he went to the door, the steg took him by the nose with its neb, and beat him with its wings. The other said when he got out, "What have you done?" "Done," says he, "the devil knocked me about; when he'd done, one of his imps set on. A thing wi' glowering eyen said, 'Fetch him here', etc. and when I got to the door, a blacksmith took me by the snout with his tongs, and flapped me by the lugs with his leather appron."

Norton Collection, I, p. 55. *Folk-Lore*, XX (1909), pp. 75–6. Collected in Gainford, Co. Durham, by Miss Alice Ecleston, 1893 or earlier.
TYPE 130, MOTIFS: B.296 [*Animals go a-journeying*]; K.1161 [*Animals hidden in various parts of a house attack owner (thief) with their characteristic powers*].
❡ See also "Mr Korbes the Fox" (A. V) and "How Jack went to seek his Fortune".

* steg = gander.

CAPTAIN MURDERER

The first diabolical character who intruded himself on my peaceful youth...was a certain Captain Murderer. This wretch must have been an offshoot of the Blue Beard family, but I had no suspicion of the consanguinity in those times. His warning name would seem to have awakened no general prejudice against him, for he was admitted into the best society, and possessed immense wealth. Captain Murderer's mission was matrimony, and the gratification of a cannibal appetite with tender brides. On his marriage morning, he always caused both sides of the way to church to be planted with curious flowers; and when his bride said, "Dear Captain Murderer, I never saw flowers like these before: what are they called?" he answered, "They are called Garnish for house-lamb," and laughed at his ferocious practical joke in a horrid manner, disquieting the minds of the noble bridal company, with a very sharp show of teeth, then displayed for the first time. He made love in a coach and six, and married in a coach and twelve, and all his horses were milk-white horses, with one red spot on the back, which he caused to be hidden by the harness. For, the spot *would* come there, though every horse was milk-white when Captain Murderer bought him. And the spot was young bride's blood. (To this terrific point I am indebted for my first personal experience of a shudder and cold beads on the forehead.) When Captain Murderer had made an end of feasting and revelry, and had dismissed the noble guests, and was alone with his wife on the day month after their marriage, it was his whimsical custom to produce a golden rolling-pin and a silver pie-board. Now, there was this special feature in the Captain's courtships, that he always asked if the young lady could make pie-crust; and if she couldn't by nature or education, she was taught. Well! When the bride saw Captain Murderer produce the golden rolling-pin and silver pie-board, she remembered this, and turned up her laced-silk sleeves to make a pie. The Captain brought out a silver pie-dish of immense capacity, and the Captain brought out flour and butter and eggs, and all things needful, except the inside of the pie; of materials for the staple of the pie itself, the Captain brought out none. Then said the lovely bride, "Dear Captain Murderer, what pie is this to be?" He replied, "A meat pie." Then said the lovely bride, "Dear Captain Murderer, I see no meat." The Captain humorously retorted, "Look in the glass."

She looked in the glass, but still she saw no meat, and then the Captain roared with laughter, and, suddenly frowning and drawing his sword, bade her roll out the crust. So she rolled out the crust, dropping large tears on it all the time, because he was so cross, and when she had lined the dish with crust, and had cut the crust all ready to fit the top, the Captain called out, "*I* see the meat in the glass!" And the bride looked up at the glass, just in time to see the Captain cutting her head off; and he chopped her in pieces, and peppered her, and salted her, and put her in the pie, and sent it to the baker's, and ate it all, and picked the bones.

Captain Murderer went on in this way, prospering exceedingly, until he came to choose a bride from two twin sisters, and at first didn't know which to choose. For, though one was fair, and the other dark, they were both equally beautiful. But the fair twin loved him, and the dark twin hated him, so he chose the fair one.

The dark twin would have prevented the marriage if she could, but she couldn't; however, on the night before it, much suspecting Captain Murderer, she stole out and climbed his garden wall, and looked in at his window through a chink in the shutter, and saw him having his teeth filed sharp. Next day she listened all day, and heard him make his joke about the house-lamb. And that day month he had the paste rolled out, and cut the fair twin's head off, and chopped her in pieces, and peppered her, and salted her, and put her in the pie, and sent it to the baker's, and ate it all, and picked the bones.

Now, the dark twin had had her suspicions much increased by the filing of the Captain's teeth, and again by the house-lamb joke. Putting all things together, when he gave out that her sister was dead, she divined the truth, and determined to be revenged. So, she went up to Captain Murderer's house, and knocked at the knocker, and pulled at the bell, and when the Captain came to the door, said, "Dear Captain Murderer, marry me next, for I always loved you, and was jealous of my sister." The Captain took it as a compliment, and made a polite answer, and the marriage was quickly arranged. On the night before it, the bride again climbed to his window, and again saw him having his teeth filed sharp. At this sight she laughed such a terrible laugh at the chink in the shutter, that the Captain's blood curdled, and he said, "I hope nothing has disagreed with me." At that, she laughed again, a still more terrible laugh, and the shutter was opened and a search made, but she was nimbly gone, and there was no one. Next day they went to church in a coach and twelve, and were married. And that day month she rolled the pie-crust out, and Captain Murderer cut her head off, and chopped her in pieces, and peppered her and salted her, and put her in the pie, and sent it to the baker's, and ate it all, and picked the bones.

But, before she began to roll out the paste, she had taken a deadly poison of a most awful character, distilled from toads' eyes and spiders' knees; and Captain Murderer had hardly picked her last bone, when he began to swell, and to turn blue, and to be all over spots, and to scream. And he went on swelling, and turning bluer, and being more all over spots, and screaming, until he reached from floor to ceiling, and from wall to wall; and then at one o'clock in the morning, he blew up, with a loud explosion. At the sound of it, the milk-white horses in the stables broke their halters and went mad, and then they galloped over everybody in Captain Murderer's house (beginning with the family blacksmith who had filed his teeth) until the whole were dead, and then they galloped away.

Charles Dickens, *The Uncommercial Traveller* (London, Chapman and Hall, 1892), p. 72. Story told to Dickens in childhood by a nursemaid.
TYPE 311 (variant), MOTIFS: G.81 [*Unwitting marriage to cannibal*]; G.77 [*Husband eats wife*]; G.303.7.3.4 [*Devil with carriage drawn by four white horses*]; G.303.7.3.5 [*Devil travels in coach drawn by four blood-red horses*]; G.83.1 [*Ogre whets teeth in preparation for eating captive*]; Q.211.3 [*Uxoricide punished*].
¶ See "Mr Fox", "The Cellar of Blood", etc. for an allied type.

CATSKIN: I

THE WANDERING GENTLEWOMAN'S GARLAND [summary]

A great gentleman longed for an heir to his estates, but his wife bore him only daughters for a long time. At last the lord declared that if their next child proved to be a girl also, he would disown her. To his wife's distress, this was what happened, and the child was sent away to be nursed, without ever being seen by its father. She was well cared for by the nurse, and wanted for nothing, but at the age of fifteen when she left school she determined to seek service. She rolled up her grand dresses in a bundle, which she hid in a forest, and put on a robe made of catskin. When she came to a certain castle she knocked at the gate, and begged to be taken in and given some work. The lady of the castle was greatly taken by the girl's beauty and manners, but said she could only employ her as a scullion to serve under the cook. The girl became known to her fellow-servants as "Catskin"; they were envious and the cook was cruel, and used to beat her about the head with a ladle, so her life was very unhappy.

One day when a great ball was to be held at the castle, Catskin said to the cook how much she would like to be there. But the cook jeered at her, and dashed a basin of water in her face. Catskin only shook her ears and ran away to the forest, where she took out her bundle of clothes, washed herself in a stream, and put on one of her beautiful dresses. She went to the ball, and all the ladies gazed at her in astonishment at her beauty. The young lord of the castle instantly fell in love with her, and would dance with no one else all night. At the end of the ball, he begged her to tell him where she lived, but she only answered,

"Kind sir, if the truth I must tell,
At the sign of the basin of water I dwell."

She fled from the room, changed into her catskin dress, and slipped back into the castle before the cook and the other servants were awake.

The young lord, however, was so much in love with her that he told his mother the next day that he would not rest until he discovered where the beautiful girl lived. In the hope of finding her, another ball was held, and everything went as before except that this time the cook broke a ladle over Catskin's head, so that when the young lord asked her for her address, she replied,

"Kind sir, if the truth I must tell,
At the sign of the Broken Ladle I dwell."

This time she was wearing an even lovelier dress and appeared even more beautiful than before, so the young lord was even more deeply in love than before, and told his mother that he could never be happy again if she did not become his wife. So another great ball was proclaimed and, as before, Catskin went to it, after the cook had broken a skimmer about her ears.

She was wearing her most beautiful dress of all, and the young master resolved that this time she should not escape him. Again he asked her where she lived, and she told him,

"Kind sir, if the truth I must tell,
At the sign of the Broken Skimmer I dwell."

But when she fled from the room, he followed her secretly, and saw her change back into her catskin robe, so now he knew who she was.

The next morning he was too ill to get up, and when the doctor came, he begged that none but Catskin should wait on him in his illness. The kind old doctor spoke to the lady of the castle, who at last unwillingly gave her consent to her son's marriage with Catskin. They were married, and soon afterwards Catskin bore her husband a son.

When the baby was out one day with his nurse, a wayfaring woman with a child was to be given some alms, sent by the lady of the castle. The lord's baby handed the alms to the other baby, whereupon the woman exclaimed, "See how the beggars' brats take to each other!" When Catskin heard this she begged her husband to send in search of her own parents, and they set out together to the town where her father was known to live. They found him, now an old man and childless, for her sisters had all died. The young lord asked him kindly whether he had not another child, whom he had never seen nor owned. The old man replied that it was true, and that he now deeply repented of his wicked act and would give all his possessions to see his child.

Then the young lord brought in his wife and child, to the joy of the old man, and of Catskin and all her people.

Halliwell, *Nursery Rhymes and Tales*, p. 10.

This broadside is a bowdlerized version of the tale, in which motifs T.411.1 [*Lecherous father*] and T.311.1 [*Flight of maiden to escape marriage*] are suppressed, and motif S.322.1 [*Father casts out daughter*] substituted; but K.521.1 [*Escape by dressing in animal skins*] is retained.

TYPE 510B, MOTIFS: L.102 [*Unpromising heroine*]; N.711.6 [*Prince sees heroine at ball and is enamoured*]; R.221 [*Heroine's threefold flight from ball*]; H.151.5 [*Attention attracted by hints dropped by heroine as menial*]; H.151.6 [*Heroine in menial disguise discovered in her beautiful clothes*]; K.1816.0.2 [*Girl in menial disguise at lover's court*].
¶ For a full version of this type see "Mossycoat". See also "Cap-o'-Rushes" and "Rashen Coatie". Compare Professor Jacobs' notes in "Catskin" in *More English Fairy Tales* (London, 1894), pp. 240–1.

The following fragmentary version from Cornwall gives the unbowdlerized motif, which is variously transformed in the Irish "Princess in the Catskins" (Kennedy, *Old Fireside Stories*) and in the American "Old Catskins" (*JAFL*, XXXVIII).

CATSKIN: II
THE PRINCESS AND THE GOLDEN COW

"Once there was a King who had a daughter, being very beautiful, and he loved her so much he wanted to marry her." (Details forgotten.) But the princess was in great trouble, especially as she loved a prince who lived a long way off, and he loved her. She had made (or got her father to give her) "a beautiful golden cow as large as a real one". She made arrangements in some manner (details forgotten) to have the golden cow conveyed under pretence of its being a parting gift or token of remembrance to the prince. She got inside it, and went in the cow a long journey by sea. There was a signal prearranged (details forgotten) of three knocks on the cow to show when she could come out safely. But when she had gone a long way the cow was landed (I think the captain of the ship was in the secret, and was told to see to her reaching the prince), but people came to see the cow, for it was very curious, amongst them three gentlemen who wanted to be able to say they had touched it, "and one poked it with his umbrella, and said, 'I've touched the golden cow,' and the next poked it with his umbrella, and said, 'I've touched the golden cow,' and the third poked it with his umbrella, and said, 'I've touched the golden cow.' With that, the princess opened the door and came out, for she thought those three knocks were the signal." Then the prince turned up, after some adventures that I have forgotten, and all ended happily.

Norton Collection, II, p. 95. *Folk-Lore*, I (1890), p. 149 of Appendix, note to "La Candeliera" by Isabella Barclay: told to her and her sisters as children by a servant from the Lizard district of Cornwall.
TYPE 510B.

CHILD ROWLAND

"(King Arthur's sons o' merry Carlisle)
      Were playing at the ba'
   And there was their sister Burd Ellen,
      I' the mids amang them a'.

"Child Rowland kicked it wi' his foot,
      And keppit it wi' his knee:
   And ay, as he play'd out o'er them a'
      O'er the kirk he gar'd it flee.

"Burd Ellen round about the aisle
      To seek the ba' is gane:
   But they bade lang and ay langer,
      And she camena back again.

"They sought her east, they sought her west,
      They sought her up and down;
   And wae were the hearts (in merry Carlisle)
      For she was nae gait found!"

At last her eldest brother went to the Warluck Merlin (Myrddin Wyldt), and asked if he knew where his sister, the fair burd Ellen, was. "The fair burd Ellen," said the Warluck Merlin, "is carried away by the fairies, and is now in the castle of the king of Elfland; and it were too bold an undertaking for the stoutest knight in Christendome to bring her back." "Is it possible to bring her back," said her brother, "and I will do it, or perish in the attempt." "Possible indeed it is," said the Warluck Merlin; "but woe to the man or mother's son who attempts it, if he is not well instructed beforehand of what he is to do."

Inflamed no less by the glory of such an enterprise, than by the desire of rescuing his sister, the brother of the fair burd Ellen resolved to undertake the adventure; and after proper instructions from Merlin (which he failed in observing), he set out on his perilous expedition.

"But they bade lang and ay langer,
      Wi' dout and mickle maen:
   And wae were the hearts (in merry Carlisle),
      For he camena back again."

The second brother in like manner set out; but failed in observing the instructions of the Warluck Merlin; and

"They bade lang and ay langer,
      Wi' mickle dout and maen:

And wae were the hearts (in merry Carlisle),
For he camena back again."

Child Rowland, the youngest brother of the fair burd Ellen, then resolved to go; but was strenuously opposed by the good queen, who was afraid of losing all her children.

At last the good queen gave him her consent and her blessing; he girt on (in great form, and with all due solemnity of sacerdotal consecration) his father's good claymore, that never struck in vain, and repaired to the cave of the Warluck Merlin. The Warluck Merlin gave him all necessary instructions for his journey and conduct, the most important of which were, that he should kill every person he met with after entering the land of Fairy, and should neither eat nor drink of what was offered him in that country, whatever his hunger or thirst might be; for if he tasted or touched in Elfland, he must remain in the power of the Elves, and never see *middle eard* again.

So Child Rowland set out on his journey, and travelled "on and ay farther on", till he came to where (as he had been forewarned by the Warluck Merlin) he found the king of Elfland's horseherd feeding his horses. "Canst thou tell me," said Child Rowland to the horse-herd, "where the king of Elfland's castle is?" "I cannot tell thee," said the horse-herd; "but go on a little farther, and thou wilt come to the cow-herd, and he perhaps may tell thee." So Child Rowland drew the good claymore that never struck in vain, and hewed off the head of the horse-herd. Child Rowland then went on a little farther, till he came to the king of Elfland's cow-herd, who was feeding his cows. "Canst thou tell me," said Child Rowland to the cow-herd, "where the king of Elfland's castle is?"—"I cannot tell thee," said the cow-herd; "but go on a little farther, and thou wilt come to the sheep-herd, and he perhaps may tell thee." So Child Rowland drew the good claymore that never struck in vain, and hewed off the head of the cow-herd. He then went on a little farther, till he came to the sheep-herd.

[*The sheep-herd, goat-herd, and swine-herd are all, each in his turn, served in the same manner; and lastly he is referred to the hen-wife.*]

"Go on yet a little farther," said the hen-wife, "till thou come to a round green hill surrounded with rings (terraces) from the bottom to the top; go round it three times *widershins*, and every time say, 'Open, door! open, door! and let me come in'; and the third time the door will open, and you may go in." So Child Rowland drew the good claymore that never struck in vain, and hewed off the head of the hen-wife. Then he went three times *widershins* round the green hill, crying, "Open, door! open, door! and let me come in;" and the third time the door opened, and he went in. It immediately closed behind him; and he proceeded through a long passage, where the air was soft and agreeably warm like a May evening, as is all the air of Elfland. The light was a sort of twilight or gloaming; but there were neither windows nor candles, and he knew not whence it came, if it was not from the walls and roof, which were rough and arched like a grotto, and composed of a clear and transparent rock, incrusted with *sheeps silver* and spar, and various bright stones. At last he came to two wide and lofty folding-doors, which stood ajar. He opened them, and entered a large and spacious hall, whose richness and brilliance no tongue can tell. It seemed to extend the whole length and height of the hill. The superb Gothic pillars by which the roof was supported were so large and so lofty (said my seannachy), that the pillars of the Chanry Kirk, or of Pluscardin Abbey, are no more to be compared to them, than the Knock of Alves is to be compared to Balrinnes or Ben-a-chi. They were of gold and silver, and were fretted like the west window of the Chanry Kirk, with wreaths of flowers composed of diamonds and precious stones in the same manner. And from the middle of the roof, where the principal arches met, was hung by a gold chain, an immense lamp of one hollowed pearl, perfectly transparent, in the midst of which was suspended a large carbuncle, that by the power of magic continually turned round, and shed over all the hall a clear and mild light like the setting sun; but the hall was so large, and these dazzling objects so far removed, that their blended radiance cast no more than a pleasing lustre, and excited no other than agreeable sensations in the eyes of Child Rowland.

The furniture of the hall was suitable to its architecture: and at the farther end, under a splendid canopy, seated on a gorgeous sopha of velvet, silk and gold, and "Kembing her yellow hair wi' a silver kemb,"

> There was his sister burd Ellen:
> She stood up him before.

Says,
> "God rue on thee, poor luckless fode !*
> What hast thou to do here?

> "And hear ye this, my youngest brither,
> Why badena ye at hame?
> Had ye a hunder and thousand lives,
> Ye canna brook ane o' them.

> "And sit thou down; and wae, O wae
> That ever thou was born;
> For come the king o' Elfland in,
> Thy leccam† is forlorn !"

A long conversation then takes place; Child Rowland tells her the news, and of his own expedition; and concludes with the observation

* fode = man.   † leccam = body.

that, after his long and fatiguing journey to the castle of the king of Elfland, he is *very hungry*.

Burd Ellen looked wistfully and mournfully at him, and shook her head, but said nothing. Acting under the influence of a magic which she could not resist, she arose, and brought him a golden bowl full of bread and milk, which she presented to him with the same timid, tender, and anxious expression of solicitude.

Remembering the instructions of the Warluck Merlin, "Burd Ellen," said Child Rowland, "I will neither taste nor touch till I have set thee free!" Immediately the folding-doors burst open with tremendous violence, and in came the king of Elfland.

> "With *fi, fi, fo*, and *fum*!
> I smell the blood of a Christian man!
> Be he dead, be he living, wi' my brand
> I'll clash his harns frae his harn-pan!"*

"Strike, then, Bogle of Hell, if thou darest!" exclaimed the undaunted Child Rowland, starting up, and drawing the good claymore that never struck in vain.

A furious combat ensued, and the king of Elfland was felled to the ground; but Child Rowland spared him on condition that he should restore to him his two brothers, who lay in a trance in a corner of the hall, and his sister, the fair burd Ellen. The king of Elfland then produced a small crystal phial, containing a bright red liquor, with which he anointed the lips, nostrils, eyelids, ears, and finger-ends of the two young men, who immediately awoke as from a profound sleep, during which their souls had quitted their bodies, and they had seen &c. &c. &c. —So they all four returned to merry Carlisle.

H. W. Weber, R. Jamieson and Sir Walter Scott, *Illustrations of Northern Antiquities* (Edinburgh, 1814), p. 398. The outline of the Romance of Child Rowland as told to the writer by a country tailor at work in his father's house, when he was a child of seven or eight. "It was recited in a sort of formal, drowsy, measured, monotonous recitative, mixing prose and verse, in the manner of the Icelandic sagas; and as is still the manner of reciting tales and *fabulas aniles* in the winter evenings, not only among the Islanders, Norwegians, and Swedes, but also among the Lowlanders in the North of Scotland, and among the Highlanders and Irish...of the *verses* which have been introduced, I cannot answer for the exactness of any, except the stanza put into the mouth of the king of Elfland, which was indelibly impressed upon my memory, long before I knew anything of Shakespeare, by the odd and whimsical manner in which the tailor curled up his nose and sniffed all about, to imitate the action which 'fi, fi, fo, fum!' is intended to represent."
TYPE 312D, MOTIFS: R.11.1 [*Princess abducted by ogre*]; H.1385.1 [*Quest for stolen*

*harn = brain.

183

Princess]; H.1242 [*The youngest brother succeeds on quest*]; R.III.2.1 [*Rescue of Princess from lower world*]; D.763.2 [*Disenchantment by single combat with enchanter*]; D.711 [*Disenchantment by decapitation*]; D.771.6 [*Disenchantment by medicine* (D.1242, *magic fluid*)].

CHIMBLEY CHARLIE

There was a poor widow up over, with just the two liddle trots, sco, and she was took proper poorly. Nothing 'ood better her than a cup of cold water from the Spring up the hill, and there wasn't no one to send get'n, let alone they daredn't. There was a bad name to it!

But that water she must have or she knew she'd die, so at the last she calls her Jacky and her Jenny and d'send 'n along, a-praying vor'n every step they took.

Well, they gets the 'ooden pail, near as big as the both on 'en, and heavy tew, and they doesn't want to goo all up there to thic unket Spring but, bless their hearts, the dear liddle souls they does it vor their loving mother. But vurst they goo into kitchen to tell it up chimbley to Chimbley Charlie. They be zuch liddle young trots they can a-zee him plain. He were a-croopy down, as he's blowing up each log vor to vlame under kettle.

"Oh, Chimbley Charlie," they both d'say, "we'm got to get up to the Spring vor our Mammy—and, Chimbley Charlie, we'm terrible afeared!"

Then Chimbley Charlie he d'zay, "Take and go, but never you speak a word till I tell. I'll watch 'ee from roof-top." So they up and went.

Their poor liddle arms and legs ache terrible, and when they got to Spring there was a tree with gingerbread vairings on it! Jenny she did clap her liddle hands, but Jacky he remember in time, and hand her a nudge, and Chimbley Charlie away down below on roof-tree call out, "Remember now!" and Jenny never give out a sound.

Then the wicked witch come out vrom behind the tree, and she's awaiting to catch they two, and make'n her Lost Souls vor Down Below if they speaks. So she smile and say, "Would 'ee like a bit o' gingerbread?"

And they nods! So she *had* to give 'n each a cake, vor they've answered and never spoke. Jacky's his were a crown, and Jenny's hers were a pony all gilt-like.

Then the witch she try again. "Do 'ee want some water vrom my Spring?"

And they nod again, and she *have* to get it vor'n.

Then she have a third try—and this'n's her last, or she'll have to go be a soul-slave herself.

"You'm hungry, I know. Why don't 'ee eat your gingerbread?"

But Chimbley Charlie calls to 'en, "Ask her to eat some herself!"

So they done just that, and she *had* to, and she give a girt skreek, and disappear Down Below to be a lost soul, and the Spring dried up, and there's nothing but mist. . . .

2ND OLD MAN. 'Tis there always!

3RD OLD MAN. And they valled down 'ill, and spilt the water all abroad, and Jacky broked 'is crownd, is the way my missus tell it. . . .

2ND OLD MAN. Yewr missus be a voreign woman [*she came from Ilminster*]. 'Tis all a make-game that! They gets to whoam, and Chimbley Charlie swing on crook, to boil the soup kettle, vor'n, and their mammy get well. . .and then he goo and a-zit all in the mist tew cool hisself.

1ST OLD MAN. The mist be always thereabouts. I've a-seed it, but I never goo near. Charlie bides there when 'ee d' wish vor a bit of quiet.

3RD OLD MAN [*determined to get his version in*]. That idn' the proper end of the tale. They did eat the pony-cake, and glad of it, they was starving, but the Higgler he come by, and he catch sight and see the gilt crown, and he thinks he'll zell 'n vor a whole zixpence down here in Market Place, so he give Jacky a varden vor'n. But when he go to come out of cottage, the pony's head have been a-turned round, and 'tis stood tail to head in the shafts, nor he couldn't unbuckle harness at all. So he shout, "I'll give 'ee a penny as well!" but 'twasn't no manner of use: he had to go on till he shouts, "Shillun! I'll give 'ee a shillun! Or I'll be too late vor market!" And then Chimbley Charlie, he let him goo. Higgler he turned pony back round in shafts, and let out vor Ta'nton like he and the cart and the crown was afire.

CHUCKLING CHORUS. But they vound the shillun 'andy come rent time!

From Ruth L. Tongue, told by three old men at Taunton Market in 1907, by Blagdon Hill W.I., 1930–62, and Churchinford W.I., 1964.

MOTIFS: D.926 [*Magic well*]; D.927.2 [*Magic spring guarded by demons*]; F.347 [*Fairy adviser*]; C.401 [*Tabu: speaking during certain time*]. The tree hung with gingerbread is akin to the gingerbread house which allures children (G.412.1). G.273 [*Witch rendered powerless*].

¶ There is something rather literary about the linking of this tale with the nursery rhyme of Jack and Jill, but the various sources show it to be truly in oral tradition.

CHIPS AND THE DEVIL

There was once a shipwright, and he wrought in a Government Yard, and his name was Chips. And his father's name before him was Chips, and *his* father's name before *him* was Chips, and they were all Chipses.

And Chips the father had sold himself to the Devil for an iron pot and a bushel of tenpenny nails and half a ton of copper and a rat that could speak; and Chips the grandfather had sold himself to the Devil for an iron pot and a bushel of tenpenny nails and half a ton of copper and a rat that could speak; and Chips the great-grandfather had disposed of himself in the same direction on the same terms; and the bargain had run in the family for a long long time. So, one day, when young Chips was at work in the Dock Slip all alone, down in the dark hold of an old Seventy-four that was haled up for repairs, the Devil presented himself, and remarked:

> "A lemon has pips,
> And a Yard has ships,
> And *I*'ll have Chips!"

Chips looked up when he heard the words, and there he saw the Devil with saucer eyes that squinted on a terrible great scale, and that struck out sparks of blue fire continually. And, whenever he winked his eyes, showers of blue sparks came out, and his eyelashes made a clattering like flints and steels striking lights. And hanging over one of his arms by the handle was an iron pot, and under that arm was a bushel of tenpenny nails, and under his other arm was half a ton of copper, and sitting on one of his shoulders was a rat that could speak. So, the Devil said again:

> "A lemon has pips,
> And a Yard has ships,
> And *I*'ll have Chips!"

So, Chips answered never a word, but went on with his work. "What are you doing, Chips?" said the rat that could speak. "I am putting in new planks where you and your gang have eaten old away," said Chips. "But we'll eat them too," said the rat that could speak, "and we'll let in the water and drown the crew, and we'll eat them too." Chips, being only a shipwright, and not a Man-of-war's man, said, "You are welcome to it." But he couldn't keep his eyes off the half a ton of copper, or the bushel of tenpenny nails; for nails and copper are a shipwright's sweethearts, and shipwrights will run away with them whenever they can. So, the Devil said, "I see what you are looking at, Chips. You had better strike the bargain. You know the terms. Your father before you was well acquainted with them, and so were your grandfather and great-grandfather before him." Says Chips, "I like the copper and I like the nails, and I don't mind the pot, but I don't like the rat." Says the Devil fiercely, "You can't have the metal without him—and *he's* a curiosity. I'm going." Chips, afraid of losing the half a ton of copper and the bushel of nails, then said, "Give us hold!" So, he got the copper and the nails, and the pot and the rat that could speak, and the Devil vanished. Chips sold the copper, and he sold the nails, and he would have sold the pot; but, whenever he offered it for sale, the rat was in it, and the dealers dropped it, and would have nothing to say to the bargain. So, Chips resolved to kill the rat, and, being at work in the Yard one day with a great kettle of hot pitch on one side of him, and the iron pot with the rat in it on the other, he turned the scalding pitch into the pot, and filled it full. Then, he kept his eye on it till it cooled and hardened, and then he let it stand for twenty days, and then he heated the pitch again, and turned it back into the kettle, and then he sank the pot in water for twenty days more, and then he got the smelters to put it in the furnace for twenty days more, and then they gave it him out, red-hot, and looking like red-hot glass instead of iron—yet there was the rat in it just the same as ever! And the moment it caught his eye, it said with a jeer;

"A lemon has pips,
And a Yard has ships,
And *I*'ll have Chips."

Chips now felt certain in his own mind that the rat would stick to him; the rat, answering his thought, said, "I will—like pitch!"

Now, as the rat leaped out of the pot when it had spoken, and made off, Chips began to hope that it wouldn't keep its word. But, a terrible thing happened next day. For, when dinner-time came, and the Dock-bell rang to stop work, he put his rule into the long pocket at the side of his trousers, and there he found a rat,—not that rat but another rat. And in his hat he found another; and in his pocket-handkerchief, another; and in the sleeves of his coat, when he pulled it on to go to dinner, two more. And from that time, he found himself so frightfully intimate with all the rats in the Yard, that they climbed up his legs when he was at work, and sat on his tools while he used them. And they could all speak to one another, and he understood what they said. And they got into his lodging, and into his bed, and into his teapot, and into his beer, and into his boots. And he was going to be married to a corn-chandler's daughter; and when he gave her a workbox he had himself made for her, a rat jumped out of it; and when he put his arm round her waist, a rat clung about her; so the marriage was broken off, though the banns were already twice put up—which the parish clerk well remembers, for, as he handed the book to the clergyman for the second time of asking, a large fat rat ran over the leaf.

You may believe that all this was very terrible to Chips: but even all this was not the worst. He knew besides, what the rats were doing, wherever they were. So, sometimes he would cry out, when he was at his club at night, "Oh! Keep the rats out of the convicts' burying-ground! Don't let them do that!" Or, "There's one of them at the cheese downstairs!" Or, "There's two of them smelling at the baby in the garret!" Or, other things of that sort. At last, he was voted mad, and lost his work in the Yard, and could get no other work. But, King George wanted men, so before very long he got pressed for a sailor. And so he was taken off in a boat one evening to his ship, lying at Spithead, ready to sail. And so the first thing he made out in her as he got near her, was the figure-head of the old Seventy-four, where he had seen the Devil. She was called the Argonaut, and they rowed right under the bowsprit where the figure-head of the Argonaut, with a sheepskin in his hand, and a blue gown on, was looking out to sea; and sitting staring on his forehead was the rat who could speak, and his exact words were these: "Chips ahoy! Old boy! We've pretty well eat them too, and we'll drown the crew, and will eat them too."

The ship was bound for the Indies; and if you don't know where that is, you ought to, and angels will never love you. The ship set sail that very night, and she sailed, and sailed, and sailed. Chip's feelings were dreadful. Nothing ever equalled his terrors. No wonder. At last one day he asked leave to speak to the Admiral. The Admiral giv' leave. Chips went down on his knees in the Great State Cabin. "Your Honour, unless Your Honour, without a moment's loss of time, makes sail for the nearest shore, this is a doomed ship, and her name is the Coffin." "Young man, your words are a madman's words." "Your Honour, no: they are nibbling us away." "They?" "Your Honour, them dreadful rats. Dust and hollowness where solid oak ought to be. Rats nibbling a grave for every man on board. Oh! Does Your Honour love your Lady and your pretty children?" "Yes, my man, to be sure." "Then, for God's sake, make for the nearest shore, for at this present moment the rats are all stopping in their work, and are all looking towards you with bare teeth, and are all saying to one another that you shall never, never, never, never, see your Lady and your children more." "My poor fellow, you are a case for the doctor. Sentry, take care of this man!"

So, he was bled and he was blistered, and he was this and that, for six whole days and nights. So, then he again asked leave to speak to the Admiral. The Admiral giv' leave. He went down on his knees in the Great State Cabin. "Now, Admiral, you must die! You took no warning; you must die! The rats are never wrong in their calculations, and they make out that they'll be through, at twelve to-night. So, you must die!— With me and all the rest!" And so at twelve o'clock there was a great leak reported in the ship, and a torrent of water rushed in and nothing could stop it, and they all went down, every living soul.

And what the rats—being water-rats—left of Chips, at last floated to shore, and sitting on him was an immense overgrown rat, laughing, that dived when the corpse touched the beach, and never came up. And there was a deal of seaweed on the remains. And if you get thirteen bits of seaweed, and dry them, and burn them in the fire, they will go off like, in these thirteen words, as plain as plain can be:

> "A lemon has pips,
>   And a Yard has ships,
>   And *I*'ve got Chips!"

From *The Uncommercial Traveller*, Charles Dickens, chapter xv. Heard in childhood from a nursemaid.

TYPE 813C variant, MOTIFS: G.303.4.1.2.4 [*Devil has saucer eyes*]; M.211 [*Man sells soul to devil*]; G.303.3.3.2.4 [*Devil in form of mouse*]; G.303.25.9 [*Ship with devil aboard sinks*]; B.211.2.9 [*Speaking rat*].

¶ There are many folk-tales in which the devil is worsted, fewer in which he is triumphant. See "The Witch of Berkley" and "The Devil and the Muff", both among the Legends.

THE CLEAN FAIRY AND THE DIRTY FAIRY

Once upon a time a dirty fairy stole a little girl and took her to a hill in which she lived a long way off. When the little girl had been there some time the dirty fairy went out one day, leaving the little girl at her house in the hill, and telling her that she must put many thousands of pins straight upon a paper before she came back.

Then the little girl began to cry because she saw that she could not put the pins back straight before the dirty fairy came back. Whilst she was crying a clean fairy came into the house in the hill with a wand in her hand, and said, "Why do you cry?"

The little girl said, "I've all these pins to put straight before the dirty fairy comes back, and I can't do it." "Don't cry," said the clean fairy, "and I will put them straight for you."

Then the clean fairy passed her wand across them, and they became straight in a moment. So the little girl waited until the dirty fairy came back.

When the dirty fairy came back, and found that the pins were all put straight, she said, "Well, never mind, I'll set you a job to-morrow that you can't get done."

So the next day she gave the little girl twice as many needles as she had given her pins to put straight on the paper. And then when the dirty fairy had gone, the little girl cried, and the clean fairy came as before, and put the needles straight with her wand. And as soon as the dirty fairy had come back she said to the little girl, "Let me see the needles," and she saw that they were all in their places. When the dirty fairy saw that, she said, "I'll set you a job that I know you can't get done."

So the next day the dirty fairy brought a great paper full of beads of many kinds, and told her to thread them in a certain way that was very hard to do. But the clean fairy came as before and threaded all the beads by waving her wand across them.

S. O. Addy, *Household Tales*, p. 16. A fragmentary tale.
MOTIFS: F.321 [*Fairy steals child from cradle*]; H.1091 [*Sorting large amount of beads in one night*]; H.935 [*Witch assigns tasks*]; H.973.1 [*Task performed by fairy*]; N.815 [*Fairy as helper*].

THE CLEVER LITTLE TAILOR [summary]

Three children, two brothers and a sister, had promised their father always to keep together. They went together to a reported festivity, and found nothing. Elder brother ran towards a light he saw, and the sister was carried away.

The two brothers dug down into a subterranean land in search of her, and found her abducted by a two-headed giant, who wished to marry her. She hid her brothers, but finally told her giant lover that they were there. He blackmailed her into marrying him, and tolerated her brothers for a time, but disliked the younger (a dwarf), and had him stripped, tied down by the seaside, and blinded by his own sister with red-hot irons. He was left to die, but some monkeys took pity on him, and carried him across the water to a "High Institution", where the blinded and crippled were healed. They healed his illness, but could not heal his blindness. He dreamt of a well which would cure his blindness if he could find it. The giant and his wife were periodical visitors to the High Institution. When the giant came, the dwarf tried to persuade him to find the well, but he said there was no such place. With the sister's help, however, he found the well and was cured. He left the island and tried to practise his trade of tailor. Went to a giant's house, but no tailor was needed.

The giant set him to farm work. The giant's wife, frightened of humans, persuaded the giant to kill him at night with a club. He overheard, and substituted a calf. Giants more frightened than ever. Hammer-throwing contest: dwarf to throw hammer to America. Eating contest: tailor put the food in a bag which he slit open. Ogre killed himself.

Afterwards, the tailor rescued his brother and sister by unspecified means.

Thompson Notebooks, from Taimi Boswell, Oswaldtwistle, 11 January 1915.
TYPES 312D (variant), 327B, 1063A, 1088, MOTIFS: H.1385.6 [*Quest for lost sister*]; S.0 [*Cruel relative*]; B.441.1 [*Helpful monkeys*]; D.1814.2 [*Advice in a dream*]; D.2161.4.0 [*Cure after following instructions received in a dream*]; K.525 [*Escape by use of substituted object*]; K.18.1 [*Throwing contest: trickster shouts to warn people across the sea*]; K.81.1 [*Deceitful eating contest*]; G.551 [*Brother rescues sister from ogre*].
¶ This is a curious mixture of types. The sister's treachery is more usually that of a

mother, with a wicked or monstrous lover. Among the odd strains in this tale are the helpful monkeys—more appropriate to an Indian than an English tale—and the curiously modern "High Institution", with the giant and his wife as visitors—a naïve, gypsy touch. More interesting is the giant's fear of the sly humans, in which there is a touch of perceptive psychology.

CLEVER PAT

The' was wonst a big lord—a king he was in fact—what put a 'vartisement into the papers, saying as how he was in want of a man, an' this man he was to be a spicially good driver. Now this king he had a very crooked road, and it was very narrow as well this road was, an' falled away right steep on both sides; he'd had it made this way on purpose. Whatever to you, an Englishman an' an Irishman replies for the job. An' first the Englishman comes. "Can you drive?" the king axes him. "Yes, sir," he says, "I think I can drive pretty well." "That won't do," says the king. "You must *know*." Whatsumever, he gi'es him a carriage an' pair, an' tells him to drive along this crooked road n' his. He starts off, the Englishman does, driving very careful—he was a good stidy driver, mind, an' knowed how to handle a pair o' horses—but he hadn't gone far afoare he has the carriage over, an' it an' the horses an' all goes rowling down the bank by the side n' the road. Then the Irishman comes. "Can you drive?" the king axes him. "Yes, yer honour," says Pat, "I can drive on the top 'n a needle as straight as a pin." So the king set him the same to do as the Englishman had failed at. Now Pat, he starts off full gallop, an' he does it as azy as winking. "That's very good," says the king, "an' you're a won'erful clever fellow."

"Now, what else is the' you can do?" he axes Pat. "I can do annythink in the world, yer honour." "Well, then," says the king, "go and count all my cattle an' sheep." "Right ye are, yer honour", says Pat, an' away he goes. Now a'ter a bit he comes back wid the number, an' tells it to the king. "The's sich an' sich a number, yer honour," he says. "No," says the king, "that won't do at all: it's ten behind." "Shure, yer honour," says Pat, "an' why not ten in front?" "You don't take my meaning," says the king, "it's ten too few." "Oh! now I see, yer honour," says Pat, "I ha'n't fun 'em all." "That's it," says the king. "But have you looked," he axes, "in that little wood over yonder? They sometimes gets there,—leastways the cattle does for sake 'n the flies." Pat hadn't looked there, so away he goes, an' he hunts about, an' he hunts about, till he finds all save one. Presently he comes back, an' he tells the king as he's now f'un' all the tothers saving one. "That won't do," says the king, "not yet; you must find the one what is missing."

Now Pat was just going off agen, when the king calls him back.

"Pat," he says, "to-night I'm to hold a grand ball at nine o'clock," he says, "an' I wants you to come an' throw eyes at me, so as to gi'e me a bit of encouragement like when I'm dancing wid the ladies." "Very good, yer honour", says Pat, "I shall be there." "An' now, Pat," says the king, "you must come an' have somethink to eat 'an drink," an' he takes Pat, an' gi'es him vittles an' drink, plenty an' to spare. Now, a'ter when he has had a bellyful, what does Pat do but he goes an' cuts the eyes out'n all the king's cattle an' sheep, an' stuffs his pockets cram full o' these eyes, till they're bulging out, an' won't hold not another one.

So whatever to you, just afoare nine o'clock Pat goes into the ballroom wid these eyes in his pocket, an' as soon as ever the king catches sight 'n him he nods an' winks to Pat, an' Pat nods 'n winks back at him. Then he comes over to where Pat is stood, the King does, an' 'minds him what he's got to do. "You'll be sure", he says, "an' throw eyes at me, every time as I comes past wid a lady." "You can trust me for that, yer honour," Pat tells him.

It wan't long now afoare the musicianers starts playing, an' the dancing begins. The king comes round tripping it wid some grand lady, an' as he passes close by to Pat, Pat puts his hand in his pocket, an' pulls out an eye, an' throws it at him. An' the king he winks an' smiles at Pat, very pleased-like, an' Pat he winks an' smiles back at the king. Now, a'ter this the same thing happens every time as the king comes round, till Pat he ha'n't not a single eye left; an' the floor got that slippy wid all the eyes Pat had throwed, 'at the dancers started tum'ling down. Now a'ter when the ball is over, an' all the guests is gone, the king he comes to Pat. "Pat," he says, "that was very nice indeed; you throwed eyes at me ancommon well". "Yes, yer honour," says Pat, "your own sheep's an' cattle's." But the king he didn't take his meaning a bit, though he thought it a very funny saying.

Whatsumever to you, next morning the king sends for Pat again. "Pat," he says, "if you can bring all my cattle an' sheep together into the yard here, an' count 'em back'ards, then", he says, "you shall have my da'ghter." So Pat goes, an' he gathers all the king's cattle an' sheep together into the yard, an' begins counting 'em back'ards. And the king he comes out to inspect 'em. First of all he goes to his prize bull. "O—h!!!" he says, as soon as ever he sets eyes on it. "Whatever is up? Here's my prize bull wid its two eyes cut out." Then he goes and he looks at all the tothers, an' he finds ne'er a one 'n they but what has its two eyes cut out! An' he calls for Pat to come. "However can sich a thing have happened, Pat?" he axes. "I've never heard in all my life of annythink like it." "Well, yer honour," says Pat, "if you mind it rightly, you towld me to throw eyes at you at the ball last night." "Yes," says the king, "I did." "An' shure, yer honour," says Pat, "wherever should

I get so many eyes, 'cepting from your own cattle an' sheep?" "You fool," says the king, "what I meant for you to do was to wink an' smile at me an' that. But now," he says, "for this thing what you done—blinded all my cattle an' sheep—you shall be 'headed."

So whatever to you, it wa'n't so very long afoare the king sent for Pat agen. "Pat," he says, "I'm now going to gi'e you one moare chance: I'm going to set you", he says, "one moare thing to do, an' if you comes through all right, then I shan't have you 'headed, an' you shall marry my da'ghter just the same; but if you don't," he says, "then for certain you shall be 'headed." "Yer honour is very good to me," says Pat. "An' now, what is it yer honour would set me to do?" "Well," says the king, "I got five pigeons, an' the task you must reform is to catch these pigeons —all the five 'n they, mind—an' a'ter when you catched 'em you got to bring 'em an' show 'em to me." An' he axed Pat if he un'erstood his meaning this time, an' Pat said as he did. Now these here five pigeons was his five da'ghters what had been 'chanted.

Well, the first thing Pat did was to fill his pockets full wid corn, an' then he goes into the barn, an' he throws down a few grains near by to the doar. Two 'n the pigeons comes an' eats this, so Pat throws 'em a bit moare farther in, an' then a bit moare, farther in agen, till he 'tices 'em right in. Then he does the same by the tother three, an' all the while he keeps throwing a bit o' corn to the ones as he's got in, till at last he has all the five 'n they inside the barn.

Still he goes on feeding 'em, a bit at a time, an' then a bit moare, an' wid every lot he throws down he creeps a bit nearer to the doar, till in the end he has 'em safe shut in. Then he catches the five pigeons an' puts them in a basket, an' off he goes wid 'em to the king. An' he is pleased wid hisself for sure.

The king is standing in his big hall, wid his sword in his hand, ready to 'head Pat. "Well, Pat," he says, "have you catched 'em?" "Yes, yer honour," says Pat. "But have you catched all the five 'n they?" the king axes. "Yes, yer honour," says Pat, "I got the lot here in this basket." "Well, open it then," the king tells him, "an' let me see for myself." So Pat opens the basket, an' the pigeons flies out. "The's only but four here, Pat," he says. "Faith, yer honour," says Pat, "I catch all the five 'n they." "That don't signify," says the king. "You've only fetched me four. You must go an' catch me the other one," he says, " or I shall 'head you."

Now Pat, he wa'nt telling no lies: he had catched all the five 'n they right enough: but one 'n the king's da'ghters had fell in love wid him, see? an' she was that shy 'n him 'at somehow or another she'd got away from him agen, a'ter when he'd put her in the basket.

Whatever to you, Pat now goes to catch this one pigeon what was missing, an' he tries an' he tries for two or three days till at last he gets it. Then he takes it to the king, an' the king he's very pleased, an' says as he shall make a big feast in honour 'n the 'casion.

Now, a'ter when the king has gone out 'n the room, this pigeon it flies an' parches itself on the throne, an' when Pat looks what does he see sitting there but the most beautiful lady you ever set eyes on, all dressed in fine clothes an' jewels, an' wid a gowlden crown on her head. An' she speaks to Pat, "Pat," she says, "you're the luckiest man in the world, for I fell in love wid you, as soon as ever I set eyes on you."

Well, soon a'ter that Pat was married to the King's da'ghter, an' the owld King, he gi'ed up his palace an' all his lands to Pat an' his da'ghter, an' they lived happy there in the palace ever a'ter.

Norton Collection, I, pp. 142–4, from the *Journal of the Gypsy Lore Society*, n.s. VIII, pp. 219–23. Also in T. W. Thompson, *Notebook* E.
TYPES 313 and 1006, MOTIFS: K.1442 [*Casting eyes*]; H.901 [*Tasks imposed on pain of death*]; D.361.1 [*Swan maiden*].
¶ This is a rather confused and broken-down version of the "Nicht Nought Nothing" tale, beginning with the common motif (not recorded in the Motif-Index) of the Choice of a Servant, and going on with a suggestion of the Anger Bargain, before the supernatural motif of the Wizard's Daughters as Pigeons turns the story into type 313.
See also "Nicht Nought Nothing", etc.

THE COAT or THE TASK [shortened version]

A poor man met a stranger, who gave him a coat which had endless money in its pockets, on condition that he did not wash, shave, or take off his coat for a year and a day. As he was going along one day he met a poor man who was worried about his rent, and gave him a handful of money to pay it. The man asked him home, and called in his three daughters to give the stranger something to eat. The two eldest were scared by his looks, but the youngest was sorry for him, and came up and talked to him, and the days that he stayed there they got fond of each other, and parted a token between them. And now the man was very uneasy in his mind, and wanted to be rid of his bargain, for it had come into his head that the strange gentleman was none other than the devil. So he went to a wise man and asked him what he could do to be quit of it. The wise man gave him a circle to stand in and a Bible to read, and told him to go into a wood at midnight, and get into his circle and read the Bible, and neither look up nor stir for whatever he heard. So he did that, and the strange gentleman came up, but he couldn't touch him, because of the circle. Then a bee came buzzing round, and then a fly. Then he heard a sound like the roaring of a lion, but he didn't look up, but read on. Then he heard a hissing like a snake, but he didn't look up, and then he saw a flashing round him like fire, but he read on.

Then all was still and silent, but he still read on till morning; and when he looked up the gentleman and the coat were gone, but there was a bag of gold in the ring beside him. So he picked it up, and went and bought himself new clothes, and he had a wash and comb and shave, and went back to the old man's house. They did not know him. He said, "I'm engaged to your youngest daughter."

The old man said, "I never saw you in my life". Then he took out the token, and the youngest daughter knew him, and very glad she was to see what a fine-looking fellow he had become. So they were married.

School of Scottish Studies, Maurice Fleming, from Mrs Reid.
TYPE 361, MOTIFS: M.211.1 [*Man unwittingly sells soul to the Devil*]; C.721.1 [*Tabu: bathing during certain time*]; C.723.1 [*Tabu: combing hair during certain time*]; D.1381.11 [*Magic circle protects from devil*]; G.303.3.3.2.5 [*Devil in form of lion*]; G.303.3.4 [*Devil in form of insect*]; L.54.1 [*Youngest daughter agrees to marry monster*].

CROOKER

A traveller was on his way to Cromford late in the evening when an old woman came from the hillside and met him. "And where are you bound for so late?" she asked. "The sun has gone down, and it will soon be dark. This is no road to travel late at night."

He was silent, and then she said, "I see you are wise enough not to speak and put yourself in danger, but I doubt if you'll be safe from Crooker without any of the right kind of help." He looked at her in the after light and saw she was holding out a posy to him. He hesitated, for it seemed as if she were dressed in green but then he saw the posy was St. John's Wort. The old woman nodded. "I wish you well," she said. "You once freed a bird from a fowler's net. I know that bird. Take the posy and when you travel Cromford Road show it to Crooker." "Who is Crooker?" said the traveller. But the old woman was gone. He was all alone with the posy in his hand.

"That was an honest warning," he thought. "But I must go on to Cromford for all that." And he went on his way.

Another old woman was waiting for him on the lane side and tho' it was getting dark he thought she was dressed in green and held a posy of primroses. "No one travels Cromford Road at night," she said. "I must," he said, for he knew by the posy she wished him well. "My old mother is ill and needs me." "Then show these to Crooker," said she as he took the second posy. "You freed a rabbit from a snare. I know that rabbit. And you need the right kind of help." "Who is Crooker?" asked the traveller.

But she too was gone and he was all alone.

"It will be dark before moonrise", said the traveller. "I doubt I'll need my two posies on the road. That was some more honest help but I'd feel even safer with three. I must hasten." And he went into the dark.

At the corner of the lane he met a third old woman in green holding a posy of daisies. "'Tis a dark and dangerous time to travel Cromford Road," she said. "You can do with the right kind of help. Take the posy and show it to Crooker." "Who is Crooker?" asked the traveller, but she did not answer, but said, "You freed a vixen and her fox-cub from a trap. I know that fox-cub and that vixen. So here's a second bit of advice. Keep as far from the Darrent River as you can and Cromford Road runs beside it. You must be on Cromford Bridge before the moon rises."

And then she too went away into the hill and there he was all alone with his three magic flower posies. "I'll need these," he thought. "Honest help never comes amiss. But I am so weary I doubt if I'll reach the shrine on Cromford Bridge before moonrise. I'd be glad of its light, for they say Darrent runs fast and deep and I'd not like to miss my footing and fall in."

But when at last he came to Cromford Road the moon was high overhead and very bright. The river swirled by just below and there were great trees on the bank above the road. They cast strange muddling shadows that moved in the breeze. "I don't like the look of those moving branches," said the traveller. "There's one tree all by itself that frightens me; its shadow looks like skinny clutching hands. I'm close to Cromford Bridge now. I'll run past it." And for all his weariness he did.

Then the river began to ripple loudly as if it were crying "Hungry" and on the moonlit road before him he saw the chasing shadow of long crooked hands like branches. "Crooker," gasped the traveller and without looking back he hurled the posy of daisies over his left shoulder on to the road. The shadow disappeared. Darrent River cried "Give" and there was a splash.

The terrified traveller began a hobbling run for the safety of the Bridge and its shrine, but once more the chasing shadow of Crooker came on to the road in front of him and he hurled the posy of primroses over his left shoulder. Crooker stopped; Darrent River cried "Give" and there was a second splash. Fear lent wings to the traveller's weary feet. He was almost at the Bridge itself when once more the clutching shadow lay across his way. With his last strength he turned right round and flung the posy of St. John's Wort straight at the wicked tree. It cried out terribly as the traveller gave a despairing leap on to Cromford Bridge and fell in a swoon at the foot of the shrine.

Darrent River roared and moaned and the good people of Cromford looked at each other white-faced. "Darrent and Crooker", they whispered. "We must go at sunrise and get the Priest. There'll be another dead for Churchyard."

"D'you remember the old beggar woman we found with a broken neck, drowned in Darrent one night she was? He roared then."

But when they came to Cromford Bridge in bright sunlight there was a pale footsore traveller saying his prayers at the shrine. He got up stiffly and hobbled on his way to the village, while Darrent River ran shallow and sunny below the bank where a great ash tree stood.

Ruth L. Tongue, from Cromford Bridge, Derbyshire.

MOTIFS: V.1.7 [*Worship of trees and plants*]; F.402.6.1 [*Demon lives in tree*]; F.236.1.6 [*Fairy in green clothes*]; F.330 [*Grateful fairies*]; N.815 [*Fairy as helper*]; Q.10 [*Deeds rewarded*].

Traditions of malignant and benevolent trees are widespread in England, but are hardly treated in the Motif-Index.

THE CRUEL STEPMOTHER

About the year 800, there lived a rich nobleman in a sequestered place of Scotland, where he wished to conceal his name, birth, and parentage, as he had fled from the hands of justice to save his life for an action he had been guilty of committing in his early years. It was supposed, and not without some good show of reason, that his name was Malcolm, brother to Fingal, King of Morven. Be this as it may, it so happened that he had chosen a pious and godly woman for his consort; who, on giving birth to a daughter, soon after departed this life. Malcolm (as we shall call him, for the better understanding of his history) lived a widower for the space of sixteen years, when, he thought that his daughter had now become of such age as to leave him, if she got a good offer. With these thoughts full in his head, he went to a distant place of the country where the thane of Mull dwelt, and made love to one of his daughters, whom he afterwards married and brought to his own domain. The new bride had no sooner fixed her eyes on Beatrix (for that was his daughter's name), than she conceived the most deadly hatred imaginable; so much so, that it almost deprived her of her rest, meditating schemes how to get rid of her, as she envied her for her superior beauty. One day on her husband going a-hunting, she took the young lady, and bound her by an oath that whatever she saw or heard her do or say, she would conceal the same from her father. The oath being extorted from her by threatening her with death and destruction, if she did not comply.

The first act of the stepmother was to go into the garden, and cut down a favourite tree, which was in full blossom, and so destroyed the root and beauty of the branches by burning the same. On Malcolm's return, he immediately discovered the want of his favourite tree, and getting into such a passion, few could approach the place where he was for a considerable length of time. When his passion had somewhat subsided, he asked his wife what had become of it, or how it had been destroyed, but she desired him to ask his daughter, as she knew nothing about it herself. Beatrix was then summoned before him, and interrogated with all the vigour of a passionate father, as to her knowledge of the destruction of his tree. Her only answer was, that He was above who knew all about it.

No more satisfaction would she give him. A second time he went from home, and on his return, found his favourite hound weltering in his blood. This again renewed his passion, but who was the guilty person he could never learn; on enquiring at his daughter, he received the same answer as formerly. A third time he went a-hunting, and on his return found his favourite hawk lying dead; but the perpetrators of these horrid deeds he could not discover. On applying to his wife, he was requested to ask his daughter; and on consulting her, her answer was as at the first. His wife thereby seeing that all the stratagems which she had devised for her destruction had proved abortive; to gratify her mortal hatred, rather than suffer her to live, she would sacrifice everything she had in the world. One year had scarcely passed in this disagreeable manner, when the lady was delivered of a fine boy, which soon became the darling of his father. This was too glaring not to be perceived by the mother; but rather than live the life which she had done since they had been married, with the envious venom rankling in her breast, she would destroy her own child and offspring. This being determined upon, one night when Beatrix was in bed soundly sleeping, dreading no harm, this bad woman, her stepmother, took a knife, bereaved the sweetly smiling young thing of its life, and laid it, with the knife reeking in gore, into the arms of the innocent Beatrix. After having been in bed for some time with her husband, she started as from some frightful dream, crying, O, my child, what has become of my lovely child! This alarmed the father, who, on looking for the child, it was not to be found. The mother then said, she was much afraid that Beatrix had stole it away from them while they slept, and had murdered it. The father by no means could be made to believe this; but upon examining her bed, the child was found horribly mangled, and the knife beside it. He was now petrified with horror, and could ask nor answer anything.

It was in vain for the young lady to plead ignorance, or deny the guilty deed, the proofs were too strong, as certainly no one could have suspected the unnatural mother of such cruel barbarity; and no one else had access to the place where it lay but Beatrix. Her father then, having determined to put her to the most cruel torture for the death of his beloved child, she was now charged with all the other bad deeds which had been committed for the space of the bygone twelve months in his house and premises, which caused him to take her to a wood, and after having cut off her right hand and arm, he next cut off her right leg. She still pleaded her innocence, but rather than perjure herself, she would suffer all that he choosed to inflict upon her; but as proof of her innocence, she told him on his way homewards, a thorn would so stick in his feet that none but herself could extract, and that only after her arm and leg had been reunited to her body, as before. He paid no attention to this, but next cut out her tongue, and left her to perish, or to be destroyed by wild beasts in the wood. She had not, however, lain long in this humiliating posture, till a knight came riding that way, when, on observing her, he alighted from his horse, and enquired the nature of her sufferings. As she could not speak, she made signs to him for pen, ink, and paper, when she wrote an account of the whole. He then took her on his horse behind him, and carried her home to his mother, who being acquainted with the virtues of a particular well nearby, she soon restored to her the full use of her amputated limbs; but her tongue still continued useless. The knight, notwithstanding the deficiency of the want of her tongue and speech, took such a liking to her that they were shortly after married, and lived in the greatest peace and pleasure, till one day that he was necessitated to leave his country on some very urgent business. Previously to his setting off, he had matters so arranged that by giving certain directions to his wife, she might write to him by her page. All things being prepared, the knight went away with a sorrowful heart. He had not been long away till his wife became sick at heart (being pregnant), and longed to see her esteemed lord. A message was then sent to the place of his residence, with a request that he would return immediately home. The messenger was her own page, who was enjoined to make every dispatch, and not to tarry on the way; but these instructions he soon forgot, when out of sight and reach of his mistress. As he journeyed on his way, it so happened that he should take up his abode for the night in the very house of Beatrix's father. His lady, observing the stranger, was desirous of knowing his errand, and so prevailed on him to give her a sight of the letter which he carried from Beatrix to her husband. By her fair speeches she so won his heart, that he gave it to her. On opening it, she soon discovered from whom it came, and tore it, and wrote in its place one, as if come from his mother, requesting him to put away or destroy the bad woman he had brought unto her. To this letter he made no reply, when a second one was written by his wife, not knowing the cause of his delay; but it shared the same fate as the former, and another of like tenor, breathing the bitterest enmity and hatred against his beloved and virtuous wife, put in its place. On receiving this second menacing letter, he hurried home, and finding his wife in the house, without any provocation or enquiry, he immediately dragged her forth, and abused her very unmercifully, till having driven her into a ditch, to get quit of her altogether, a powerful herb happened to get into her mouth, in the course of her struggle, which at once restored to her the use of her speech. It now became her turn to interrogate him, and ask why he had used her so cruelly without a cause. He then showed her the letters which he had received, purporting to be from his mother. She said they were not written by his mother, as they lived on the most friendly terms imaginable.

It was then referred to his mother, who, on seeing them, was no less surprised than vexed at them, and at his maltreating his wife so basely. The page was then called and examined, when he confessed what he had done. The knight, without further enquiry into the matter, took his sword, and cut off his head, and threw it away as a warning to all others, not to betray their trust, but behave in a more upright and honourable manner. As it was at length discovered that the cruel stepmother had been the cause of the whole of Beatrix's misfortunes, she was adjudged to be put to an ignominious death by the most cruel torture, which was put into execution immediately after, as a just reward for her hatred and cruelty. Beatrix then relieved her father from the pain which he suffered in his foot by a thorn which stuck in it and baffled all the medical skill of that part of the country. They afterwards lived to a good old age, and died in peace.

Norton Collection, II, pp. 177–9. Buchan, *Ancient Scottish Tales*, pp. 125–8.
TYPE 706, MOTIFS: S.31 [*Cruel stepmother*]; K.2110 [*Slanders*]; Q.451.1 [*Hands cut off as punishment*]; Q.451.2.3 [*Foot cut off as punishment for murder*]; Q.451.4 [*Tongue cut off as punishment*]; N.711.1 [*King finds maiden in woods and marries her*]; E.782.1 [*Hands restored*]; K.2117 [*Calumniated wife, substituted letter*]; E.782.5 [*Substituted tongue*]; S.451 [*Outcast wife united with husband*].

See "Daughter Doris."

❡ Daumling has made a study of this type (*Studie über den Typus des Mädchens ohne Hände*, 1912). The story is very widespread over the whole of Europe, North and South America, Africa, and the West Indies.

THE CUTLER AND THE TINKER [summary]

A cutler and a tinker travel together, and sleep in an empty haunted house for a reward. They are beset by ghosts and spirits of murdered ladies and gentlemen, and the inferior, the tinker, shows the more courage, and is the hero. He goes into the cellar to draw beer, and there he finds a little chap, a-sittin' on a barrel with a red cap on 'is 'ed: and he sez, sez he, "Buzz!" "Wot's buzz?" sez the tinker. "Never you mind wot's buzz," sez he. "That's mine. Don't you go for to touch it." etc. etc. etc.

Norton Collection, I, p. 162, from J. F. Campbell, *Popular Tales of the West Highlands*, collected by him at Westminster from a tinker. A fragmentary summary of a tale. TYPE 326A*, MOTIFS: H.1400 [*Fear test*]; H.1411.1 [*Staying in haunted house*].

See also "The Dauntless Girl", "The Boy who feared Nothing", "A Wager Won", "The Gibbet", "A Wager Lost", "The Devil and the Hogshead", "Ashypelt", "The Black Cat", "The Golden Ball".

¶ Full example of Grimm 41. Very wide dispersion. An analysis of the tale by Kurt Ranke, Irish versions dealt with in Ó' Súilleabháin's *Handbook*. Rather loose variants to be found all over the world. Many American versions, four noted by Boggs in *N. Carolina Folklore*, pp. 300–21.

DAUGHTER DORIS [summary]

There was once a King's daughter, who had a stepmother. The mother was fetching water one day and she broke the pitcher, and put the blame of it on the girl. The father was so angry that he turned the girl away, and she married a soldier, and had a baby, but before the baby was born the soldier was sent away to the wars, and the girl was left alone. One day as she was walking with the baby in her arms she saw her father, and he was very angry at the sight of her. "Daughter Doris," he said, "do you see this sword? It's going to cut off your right arm." He cut if off, and he said: "Daughter Doris, is that sore?" "Aye," she said, "it's very sore." "Not so sore as what you did to my pitcher," he said. Then he cut off her left arm and her right leg and her left leg, and each time he asked, was it sore? And so she was lying on the road, bleeding, and she asked how she could carry her babe without arms or legs, and he was to be a great champion when he grew to be a man. "He'll not grow to be a man," he said, "for I'll cut off your breasts." And he cut off her breasts, and mounted his horse. But as he mounted she said: "I wish you a black thorn in your foot, and that no man at all can take it out, except this baby by my side." And when he was gone she took the baby in her teeth, and struggled and rolled off the road into an orchard. And she was bleeding to death. And she took an apple in her teeth and chewed it to feed her baby. And as she did so an old man with a long white beard came up to her. And he said, "Lift up your baby, Daughter Doris." "How can I lift him up", she said, "when my arms are cut off?" "Try," he said, "just try." She tried, and she had arms again. "Stand up, Daughter Doris," he said, "and carry your baby." "How can I", she said, "when I have no legs?" "Try," he said, and she tried, and her legs came back to her. "Feed your baby, Daughter Doris," he said. "How can I", she said, "when my breasts are cut off?" "Try", he said, "just try." And she had her breasts again. So she thanked the old man a thousand times, and went on her way.

After a time she met a handsome young man who married her and they lived happily for fourteen years. Then notices were posted up everywhere, to say that the king was ill with a poisoned foot and offering a reward to anyone who could cure him. They went along to the Palace, and the King recognized his daughter. She said to him, "My son is the only man who can cure you, and the sword you wounded me with is the only one that can take out the thorn."

So the son took the sword, and cut off the King's leg, and put it in a bin.

And he got a toad, and put it in the bed with the King, and it licked his leg and it grew whole again. Then the king said: "You are my grandson, who has cured me. You shall have my place, and I will have yours." So the grandson reigned in the King's place, and he was a great hero.

School of Scottish Studies, Hamish Henderson, from Davie Stewart. A second version collected by Maurice Wilson from Mrs Reid: The father's pony broke his leg whilst she was riding it and the father cut off his daughter's limbs and breasts as a punishment. TYPE 706, MOTIFS: S.31 [*Cruel stepmother*]; S.11.1 [*Father mutilates children*]; M.431.5 [*Curse: wound not to heal*]; E.782.1 [*Hands restored*].
¶ The guilty father's festering wound, only to be cured by his daughter or grandson, is a common feature in these two tales. A motif is not given in the Aarne–Thompson summary of the type. See "The Cruel Stepmother".

DAUGHTER GREENGOWN [summary]

Handsome young gentleman, fond of gaming. Late at night, when all had gone home, an old gentleman in full evening dress (the devil) appeared and challenged him to play. Young man won, and asked for house with walls of diamond and floors of gold and got it. His father warned him against playing again, but the next night the old gentleman challenged him again, and this time he lost. So he forfeited his gains, and had to search for the devil for a year and a day, and if he didn't find him he would be the devil's. So he set out on the search, found a great tree a million years old, who directed him to go to his brother, three million years old, and gave him twenty-mile boots to go in. Well received, sent on to next brother, seven million years old. Well received, and directed to a castle with a moat, where three geese bathed. To steal a feather from one. He arrived, sent back the boots, stole feather from smallest goose, and only returned it on condition of help. She took him on her back, and promised help. Three tasks set. First: to clear stable with a needle; helped by daughter Greengown; denied knowledge of her to devil. Second: to make bricks and build castle; helped again. Third: to climb a glass mountain and fetch down three eggs from a nest: steps made by daughter's bones, little finger broken; keeps the eggs. Task to pick out Greengown from her sisters, as a walnut, and then a pigeon; chooses right. To be married to Greengown, but his death still intended. Flight on the goose's back, soon followed by a black cloud, the devil and his daughters. Killed by the three eggs.

Hero returns home. Prohibition against kiss. His dog licks face and he forgets Greengown. She lodges with an old cobbler, and the young men come to court her, among them her lover. She pretends to be a harlot, but by magic keeps him locking the door all night. Another suitor kept shooing out the hens. The lover to be married to a neighbouring girl. As they pass the cobbler's, Greengown halts the coach, and no one can move it until she does so. Invited to the wedding. Stories told round. Greengown tells hers, and the hero remembers. Question of old master key and new keys. New bride sent home, Greengown married.

In Taimi Boswell's version they play three times, Jack wins, and the third time has to seek the gentleman's estate, which he has won. Inconsistent with the rest of story. The three geese are three swans. The helpers: the first a tree, his three brothers, hares, of which the youngest helps the hero. The old men to whom he is sent are giants. In the wizard's castle he is fed on bread and water, and put in hazardous beds. A substitution of eggs. Transformation flight, into a gate and a gate-keeper. Master-maid trick played with the groom, not the hero.

Collected by T. W. Thompson from Reuben Gray at Old Radford, Nottingham, 21 December 1914. Another version, with slight variations, told by Taimi Boswell, Oswaldtwistle, 8 January 1915 (*Thompson Notebooks*, III, VI, and VII).
TYPE 313, MOTIFS: N.2.0.1 [*Play for unnamed stakes*]; K.2378.1 [*Person allowed to win first game, so that he will play for larger stakes*]; H.1219.1 [*Quest assigned as payment for gambling loss*]; D.1521.1 [*Seven-league boots*]; D.361.1 [*Swan maiden*]; D.721 [*Disenchantment by removing skin*]; H.1010 [*Impossible tasks*]; H.1102 [*Task: cleaning Augean stables*]; H.1104.1 [*Task: building a lodge of birds' feathers in one night*]; F.751 [*Glass mountain*]; F.848.3 [*Ladder of bones*]; E.33 [*Resuscitation with missing member*]; H.57.2 [*Recognition by missing finger*]; D.670 [*Magic flight*]; D.651.1 [*Transformation to kill enemy*]; D.2004.2 [*Kiss of forgetfulness*]; D.2004.2.1 [*Dog's licking produces forgetfulness*]; D.2006.1.1 [*Lovers magically detained*]; H.151 [*Attention drawn: recognition follows*]; D.2006.1.5 [*Forgotten fiancée magically stops wedding-carriage of new bride*].
❡ There are many versions of this type. See "Nicht Nought Nothing", "The Green Man of Knowledge".

THE DAUNTLESS GIRL

She lived first with a farmer, and he and his friends were a-drinking one night and they ran out of liquor. So the farmer he up and say, "Never you mind, my girl will go down to the public and bring us up another bottle." But the night was very dark, so his friends they say, "Surelie she'll be afeard to go out such a dark night by herself all alone." But he say, "No she won't, for she's afeard of nothing that's alive nor dead." So she went and she brought 'em back their licker, and his friends they say it was a wery funny thing she shewd be so bold. But the farmer he say, "That's nuthin at all, for she'd go anywhere day or night for she ain't afeared of nothing that's alive or dead." And he offered to bet a golden guinea that none of 'em could name a thing she would not dew. So one of 'em agreed to take the bet and they were to meet the same day as it might be next week and he was to set her her task. Meanwhile he goes to the old passon and he borrows the key of the Church and then he goes to the old sexton and right-sided it with him for half the guinea to go into the church and hide himself in the dead house so that he was to frighten the Dauntless Girl when she came.

So when they all met together at the farmer's he say, "*This* is what the Dauntless Girl *won't* dew—she won't go into the Church alone at midnight and go into the dead house and bring back a skull bone." But she made no trouble about it and up and went down to the church all along of herself and she opened the door of the dead house and she picked up a skull bone.

Then the old sexton behind the door he muffled out, "Let that be, that's my mother's skull bone." So she put it down and picked up another. Then the old sexton he muffled out again, "Let that be, that's my father's skull bone." So she put that down tew, and took up still another and she say out loud, for she'd lost her temper, "Father or mother, sister or brother, I *must* hev a skull bone and that's my last word," and so she up and walked out with it, and she locked the door of the dead house behind her and she come home, and she put the skull bone on the table and she say, "There's your skull bone, master," and she was for going back to her work.

But him as had made the bet he up and say, "Didn't yew hear nothing, Mary?" "Yes," she say, "some fule of a ghost called out to me, 'Let be, that's my father's skull bone, and let be, that's my mother's skull bone,' but I told him right straight that father or mother, sister or brother, I *must* hev a skull bone, so I tuk it and here't be, and then as I was goin' away arter I had locked the door, I heard the old ghost a-hallering and shrieking like mad."

Then him as had made the bet was rarely upset, for he guessed it was the old sexton a-hallerin' about for fear of being locked up all alone in the dead-house. And so it was, for when they ran down to let him out they found him lying stone dead on his face a dead-o-fright.

And it sarved him right to try and terrify a poor mawther. But her master he gave her the golden guinea he had won.

A little while after down in Suffolk there was a squire and his mother, a very old lady and she died and was buried. But she would *not* rest and kept on coming into the house "specially at meals". Sometimes you could see all of her, sometimes not all, but you'd see a knife and fork get up off the table, and play about where her hands should be. Now this upset the servants so much that they would *not* stop, and the Squire was sadly put to, to know what he should do. One day he heard of the Dauntless Girl, tree villages off, who was feared at nowt. So he rode over, and told her all about it, and asked her if she would come as servant, and she said she paid no regard to ghosts so she would come, but that it ought to be considered in her wages. And so it was and she went back with the Squire. First thing she did was to allus lay a place regular for the ghost at meals, and took great care not to put the knife and fork criss-cross way. And she used to hand her the vegetables and the rest just as if she were real. And would say, "Peppaw, mum," or "Salt, mum" as it might be. This fared to pleased the old ghost, but nothing come of it, till Squire had to go up to London on some law business.

Next day, the Dauntless Girl was down on her knees a-cleaning the parlour grate when she noticed a thin thing push in through the door, which was just ajar and open out wide when it got into the room, till she turned out to be the old ghost.

Then the ghost she up and spoke for the first time and she say, "Mary, are you afeared of me?" and the girl say, "No, mum, I've no call to be afeared of yew, for *yew* are dead, and *I'm* alive," which fairly flummoxed the old ghost, but she went on and say, "Mary, will yew come down into the cellar along o' me—yew musent bring a light but I'll shine enow to light you." So they went down the cellar steps, and she shone like an old lantern, and when they got down she pointed out to some loose tiles and said, "Pick yew up those tiles." So she did, and there were tew bags of gold, one a big 'un, and one a little 'un, and she said, "Mary, that big bag's for your master, and that little bag's for yew, for you are a dauntless girl, and desarve it." Then off went the old ghost and never was seen no more and the Dauntless Girl she had a main o' trouble to find her way up in the dark out of the cellar.

Then in tree days' time, back there came the Squire and he said, "Morning, Mary, hae yew seen anything of my mother since I've been away?" and she said, "Iss, sir, that I hev, and if yew ain't afraid of coming down into the cellar, along o' me, I'll show yew something." And he larfed, and said *he* wornt afraid if *she* wornt, for the Dauntless Girl wor a very pretty girl.

So they lit a candle and went down and she opened up the tiles and she say, "There are the tew bags of gold, the *little* one is for yew, and the big 'un is for *me*." And he say, "Lor!" for he thought his mother might have given *him* the big one (and so she had), but he took what he could. And the Dauntless Girl she ollus afterwards crossed the knives and forks, to keep the ghost from telling what she had done. But after a while the Squire thort it all over, and he married the Dauntless Girl, so arter all he got both bags of gold, and he used to stick-lick her whenso-ever he got drunk. And I think she desarved it, for deceiving the old ghost.

Norton Collection, I, pp. 152–4, from Rye, *Recreations of a Norfolk Antiquary*, pp. 22–6, presumably from an oral source.
TYPE 326, MOTIFS: H.1400 [*Fear test*]; H.1435 [*Fetching skulls from a charnel-house*].
¶ See "The Golden Ball", "The Cutler and the Tinker", "Ashpelt", etc.

THE DEAD MOON [dialect modified]

Long ago the Lincolnshire Cars were full of bogs and it was death to walk through them, except on moonlight nights, for harm and mischance and mischief, Bogles and Dead Things and crawling horrors came out at nights when the moon did not shine. At length the Moon heard what things went on in the bog-land when her back was turned, and she thought she would go down to see for herself, and find what she could do to help. So at the month's end she wrapped a black cloak round her, and hid her shining hair under a black hood, and stepped down into the boglands. It was all dark and watery, with quaking mud, and waving tussocks of grass, and no light except what came from her own white feet. On she went, deep into the bogland and now the witches rode about her on their great cats, and the will-o'-the-wykes danced with the lanterns swinging on their backs, and dead folks rose out of the water, and stared at her with fiery eyes, and the slimy dead hands beckoned and clutched. But on she went, stepping from tuft to tuft, as light as the wind in summer until at length a stone turned under her, and she caught with both hands at a snag nearby to steady herself; but as soon as she touched it it twisted round her wrists like a pair of handcuffs and held her fast. She struggled and fought against it but nothing would free her. Then, as she stood trembling she heard a piteous crying, and she knew that a man was lost in the darkness, and soon she saw him, splashing after the will-o'-the-wykes, crying out on them to wait for him, while the Dead Hands plucked at his coat, and the creeping horrors crowded round him, and he went further and further from the Path.

The Moon was so sorry and so angry that she made a great struggle, and though she could not loose her hands, her hood slipped back, and the light streamed out from her beautiful golden hair, so that the man saw the bog-holes near him and the safe path in the distance nearly as clear as by day. He cried for joy, and floundered across, out of the deadly bog and back to safety, and all the bogles and evil things fled away from the moonlight, and hid themselves. But the Moon struggled in vain to free herself, and at length she fell forward, spent with the struggle, and the black hood fell over her head again, and she had no strength to push it off. Then all the evil things came creeping back, and they laughed to think they had their enemy the Moon in their power at last. All night they fought and squabbled about how best they should kill her, but when the first grey light before dawn came they grew frightened, and pushed her down into the water. The Dead Folk held her, while the Bogles fetched a great stone to put over her, and they chose two will-o'-the-wykes to guard her by turns, and when the day came the Moon was buried deep, until someone should find her, and who knew where to look?

The days passed, and folk put straws in their caps, and money in their pockets against the coming of the new Moon, and she never came. And as dark night after dark night passed, the evil things from the bogland came howling and screeching up to men's very doors, so that no one could go a step from the house at night, and in the end folk sat up all night, shivering by their fires, for they feared if the lights went out, the things would come over the thresholds.

At last they went to the Wise Woman who lived in the old Mill, to ask what had come of their Moon. She looked in the mirror, and in the brewpot, and in the Book, and it was all dark, so she told them to set straw and salt and a button on their door-sills at night, to keep them safe from the Horrors, and to come back with any news they could give her.

Well, you can be sure they talked, at their firesides and in the Garth and in the town. So it happened one day, as they were sitting on the settle at the Inn, a man from the far side of the bogland cried out all of a sudden, "I reckon I know where the Moon is, only I was so mazed I never thought on it." And he told them how he had been all astray one night, and like to lose his life in the bog-holes, and all of a sudden a clear bright light had shone out, and showed him the way home. So off they all went to the Wise Woman, and told what the man had said. The Wise

Woman looked in the Book, and in the pot, and at last she got some glimmer of light and told them what they must do. They were to set out together in the darkness with a stone in their mouths and a hazel twig in their hands, and not a word must they speak till they got home; and they must search through the bog till they found a coffin, and a cross, and a candle, and that was where the Moon would be. Well, they were main feared, but next night they set out and went on and on, into the midst of the bog.

They saw nothing, but they heard a sighing and whispering round them and slimy hands touching them, but on they went, shaking and scared, till suddenly they stopped, for half in, and half out of the water they saw a long stone, for all the world like a coffin, and at the head of it stood a black snag stretching out two branches, like a gruesome cross, and on it flickered a tiddy light. Then they all knelt down and they crossed themselves and said the Lord's Prayer, forward for the sake of the cross, and backward against the Bogles, but all silently, for they knew they must not speak. Then all together they heaved up the stone. For one minute they saw a strange beautiful face looking up at them and then they stepped back mazed with the light, and with a great shrieking wail from all the horrors, as they fled back to their holes, and the next moment the full moon shone down on them from the Heavens, so that they could see their path near as clear as by day.

And ever since then the Moon has shone her best over the boglands, for she knows all the evil things that are hid there and she remembers how the Car men went out to look for her when she was dead and buried.

Mrs Balfour, "Legends of the Cars", *Folk-Lore*, II. An unusual mythological theme. The plot corresponds to an Indian motif, A.754.1.1; it is uncommon in European folk-tales.

MOTIFS: A.106.2.1.1 [*Banished devil appears on earth only on day of dark moon*]; A.753 [*Moon as a person*]; A.758 [*Theft of moon: stolen and brought to earth*]; A.754.1.1 [*Moon falls into a pit, but is rescued by man*].

THE DEVIL AND THE FARMER

The devil once called on a farmer and exed 'im if he could give him a job.

"What can'st do?" said the farmer. "Oh! enything about a farm," said the devil. "Well, I wans a man to 'elp mŭ to thresh a mow o' whate," sez the farmer. "All right," sez the devil, "I'm yer mon." When they got to the barn, the farmer said to the devil, "Which oot thee do, thresh or thraow down?" "Thresh," said the devil. So the farmer got o' top o' the mow, and begun to thraow down the shuvs of whate on to the barn flur, but as fast as 'e cud thraow 'em down, the devil ooth one stroke uv 's nile, knocked all the carn out on um, an' send the shuvs flying out o' the barn dooer. The farmer thought he had got a queer sart uv a thresher-mon; un as he couldn't thraow down fast enough far 'im, 'e sez to 'im, "Thee come un thraow down oot?" "All right," sez the devil. So the farmer gets down off the mow by the ladther, but the devil 'e just gives a lep up from the barn flur to the top o' the mow, athout waiting to goo up the ladther. "Be yŭ ready?" sez the devil. "Iss," sez the farmer. Ooth that the devil sticks 'is shuppick into as many shuvs as ood kiver the barn flur, an throaws um down. "That'll do fur a bit," sez the farmer, so the devil sat down un waited t'll the farmer'ud threshed that lot, an when a was ready agyun, 'e thraowed down another flur full; un afore night they'd finished threshin' the whole o' the mow o' whate. The farmer couldn't 'elp thinkin' a good dyull about 'is new mon, fur 'e'd never sin sich a one afore. ('E didn't knaow it was the devil, thŭ knaowst, 'cos 'e took keer not to let the farmer see 'is cloven fut.) So in the marnin' 'e got up yarly un went un spoke to a cunnin' mon about it. The cunnin' mon said it must be the devil as 'ad come to 'im, un as 'e 'ad exed 'im in, 'e couldn't get shut on 'im athout 'e could give 'im a job as 'a couldn't do. Soon atter the farmer got wum agyun, 'is new mon wanted to knaow what he wus to do that day, and the farmer thought he'd give 'im a 'tazer; so 'e sez, "Goo into the barn, look, un count the number o' carns there be in that yup o' whate as we threshed out istaddy." "All right," sez Old Nick, un off a went. In a faow minutes 'e comes back un sez, "Master, there be so many" (namin' ever so many thousan' or millions un odd, I d'na'ow many). "Bist sure thee'st counted um all?" sez the farmer. "Every carn," sez Satan. Then the farmer ardered 'im to goo un fill a hogshead barrel full o' water ooth a sieve. So off 'e shuts agyun, but soon comes back un tells the farmer 'e'd done it; un sure enough a 'ad; un every job the farmer set 'im to do was the same. The poor farmer didn't know what to make on it, fur thaough 'e wus agettin' 'is work done up so quick, 'e didn't like 'is new mon's company. 'Owever, the farmer thought 'e'd 'ave another try to trick 'im, un told the devil 'e wanted 'im to goo ooth 'im a mowin' next marnin'. "All right", sez the old un. "I'll be there, master." But as soon as it was night, the farmer went to the fild, un in the part the devil was to mow 'e druv a lot o' horrow tynes into the ground amongst the grass. In the marnin' they git to the fild in smartish time, un begun to mow; the farmer 'e took 'is side, and told the devil to begin o' the tother, where 'e'd stuck in the horrow tynes, thŭ knaowst. Well, at it went the devil, who but 'e, un soon got in among the stuck-up horrow tynes, but they made no odds, 'is scythe went thraough them all, un the only notice on 'em 'e took wus to say to the farmer every time 'ed cut one on 'um thraough, "A burdock, master", un kep on just the same. The poor farmer 'e got so frightened at last, 'e thraughed down 'is scythe, un left the devil to finish the fild. As luck ood 'ave it, soon atter 'a got wum, a gipsy ooman called at the farm 'ouse, and seein' the farmer was in trouble, exed 'im what was the matter; so 'e up un tell'd 'er all about it. "Ah, master," 'er sez to 'im when 'e 'ad tell'd 'er all about it, "you 'a got the devil in your 'ouse sure enough; un you can only get shut on 'im by givin' 'im summut to do as 'a caunt manage." "Well, ooman," sez the farmer, "What's the use o' tellin' mŭ that? I a tried everything I con think on, but darned uf I con find 'im eny job as 'a caunt do." "I'll tell you what to do," sez the gipsy ooman: "When 'a comes wum, you get the missus to give 'im one uv 'er curly 'airs; un then send 'im to the blacksmith's shap, to straighten 'un on the blacksmith's anvil. 'E'll find 'a caunt do that, un 'e'll get so wild over it, as 'e'll never come back to yu agyun." The farmer was very thenkful to the gipsy ooman, and said 'e'd try 'er plan. So bye'n bye in comes the aowd fella, un sez, "I a finished the mowin', master; what else 'a you got fur mu to do?" "Well, I caunt think uv another job just now," sez the farmer, "but I thinks thee missis a got a little job fur thu." So 'e called the missis, un 'er gan the devil a curly 'air lapped up in a bit o' paper, un tell'd 'im to goo to the blacksmith's shop, un 'ommer that there 'air straight: un when a was straight, to bring 'im back to 'er. "All right, missis," the devil sez, un off a shut. When a got to the blacksmith's shop, 'e 'ommered un 'ommered at that there 'air on the anvil, but the more 'a 'ommered the cruckeder the 'air got; so at last 'e thraowed down the 'ommer and the 'air, un baowted, un never went back to the farmer agyun.

Norton Collection, III, pp. 94–5, J. Salisbury, *South-East Worcestershire Glossary*, pp. 73–5 (told to him when a boy by a thresher at Little Comberton, 1850).
TYPE 1175, MOTIFS: G.303.3.1.10 [*Devil as peasant*]; G.303.9.3.1 [*Devil hires out to a farmer*]; H.1023.4 [*Straightening curly hair*].
¶ Irish version by Ó Súilleabháin.
See also "Yallery Brown", "The Man who wouldn't go out at Night".

THE DEVIL AND THE TAILOR

There was a tailor at Kingston who was always cursing and swearing. It was before the days of railways, and he had to go by road to Glee Hill by Ludlow, to get a load of coal. He met a man who wanted to be measured for a suit of clothes; measuring from his shoulders down, he came at last to two feet, cleft like cows' feet. Then he knew what his cursing had brought him to. The "auld chap" appointed a meeting-place, and a certain time, at which the suit must be ready. The tailor was there in time with the suit, but he took a parson with him, who stood on the other side of the hedge, praying hard all the time; he had wanted the tailor to take no payment from the "Old 'Un" for his work. As soon as the suit was handed over, the Devil held out a handful of money, and tried to make him take it; if he had, it would have been selling his soul. But the parson went on praying hard till the cock crew, and the tailor held out, and got safe away. He never cursed no more after.

"And that", added my informant, "is as true as I'm standin' here, holding this 'ere hop-pole."

E. M. Leather, *Folk-Lore of Herefordshire*, p. 41, told by a Radnorshire man in Homme hop-yard, Weobley, 1908.
TYPE 815*, MOTIF: K.218 [*Devil cheated by religious means*].

THE DEVIL AND THE TAILOR

There was a tailor in our town,
Who was a worthy wight;
   All through the day
   He worked away,
And halfway through the night.

He had a wife whom he did love,
And he had children bright;
   To find the meat
   For them to eat,
Did puzzle the tailor quite.

One day as on the board he sat,
When cupboard and shelf were bare,
   The children cried,
   Unsatisfied
With feeding on the air.

Oh! then unto himself he said,
"Ah! would that I were rich,
   With meat galore,
   And money in store,
And never a coat to stitch."

"If Old Nick now to me would say,
'In riches you may roll,'
   I'm sure I'd sell
   To the Lord of Hell
Myself, both body and soul."

The Devil unto the tailor came,
And thus to him said he,
  "This bag of gold
  Is wealth untold,
And emptied ne'er shall be.

Exhaustless is its boundless store,
And it shall all be thine
  Whilst thou hast breath,
  But at thy death
Thy soul shall then be mine."

"Nay, put the matter as a bet,
Thy bag against my soul;
  We each will take
  A coat to make,
The quickest to take the whole."

Old Nick to this at once agreed,
And thought the tailor to wheedle;
  "My sight is bad,
  So I'll be glad,
If you will thread my needle."

"A needleful I'll put you in,"
The tailor said, "with pleasure,
  Sound and true,
  To last all through
The job we are to measure."

A needleful he put him in,
The tailor did, with pleasure,
  Sound and true,
  To last all through
A hundred yards by measure.

To work the two did settle then:
The tailor worked in dread;
  The Devil flew
  The room all through,
With his hundred yards of thread.

But though the Devil beat his wings,
And panted fit to burst,
  With shorter thread,
  And clearer head,
The tailor finished first.

Thus was the Devil overcome,
And fairly left i' the lurch;
   The tailor wight
   Became a knight,
And always went to church.

He patronized charities,
And never joined a revel;
   To end my song,
   I think it wrong
To swindle—e'en the Devil.

Norton Collection, III (Lancashire), W. E. A. Axon, *The Black Knight of Ashton*,
pp. 36–9.
TYPE 1096, MOTIF: K.47.1 [*Sewing contest won by deception: long thread*].
¶ Finnish, Estonian, Swedish, Danish, German, Italian, Hungarian, Slovenian,
Indian versions cited in Aarne–Thompson Type-Index.
   See also "Dule upon Dun" and "The Tailor of Clitheroe" and also the section
"The Devil" in Legends, part B.

THE DEVIL'S RIDDLES

There was a knicht riding frae the east,
   Sing the Cather banks, the bonnie brume
Wha had been wooing at monie a place,
   And ye may beguile a young thing sune.

He came unto a widow's door,
   And speir'd whare her three dochters were.

The auldest ane's to a washing gane,
   The second's to a baking gane.

The youngest ane's to a wedding gane,
   And it will be nicht or she be hame.

He sat him doun upon a stane,
   Till thir three lasses came tripping hame.

The auldest ane's to the bed making,
   And the second ane's to the sheet spreading.

The youngest ane was bauld and bricht,
   And she was to lye with this unco knicht.

"Gin ye will answer me questions ten,
   The morn ye sall be made my ain."

"O what is heigher nor the tree?
   And what is deeper nor the sea?

213

"And what is heavier nor the lead?
  And what is better nor the breid?

"O what is whiter nor the milk?
  Or what is safter nor the silk?

"Or what is sharper nor a thorn?
  Or what is louder nor a horn?

"Or what is greener nor the grass?
  Or what is waur nor a woman was?

"O heaven is higher nor the tree,
  And hell is deeper nor the sea.

"O sin is heavier nor the lead,
  The blessing's better nor the breid.

"The snaw is whiter nor the milk,
  And the down is safter nor the silk.

"Hunger is sharper nor a thorn,
  And shame is louder nor a horn.

"The pies are greener nor the grass,
  And Clootie's waur nor a woman was."

As sune as she the fiend did name,
  He flew awa in a blazing flame.

Child, *The English and Scottish Popular Ballads*, I, p. 4.
TYPE 812, MOTIFS: H.660 [*Riddles of comparison*]; G.303.16.19.9 [*Devil becomes powerless when called by name*]; L.50 [*Victorious youngest daughter*].

Other songs on this theme are: "Lay the Bent with the Bonnie Broom", "The Riddling Knight" (Child).

"DOCTOR FORSTER" [summary]

About half-way along a lonely twenty-mile stretch of tree-enclosed road in the south of England, stood a great hotel. Coaches used to change horses there, and it was known far and wide for its hospitality of every kind.

The landlord and his wife had a son and a daughter. The daughter used to serve in the select bar where the great folk went, and many of them used to talk to her. She was twenty-two, and her name was Lily.

One of the most regular customers at this bar was Squire King Kaley. He took to spending most of his time there. Well mannered, well dressed, and rich, he became a favourite with the ostlers, and with the other guests, for he was generous with his tips and treats. He and Lily became almost sweethearts, though she had never been out with him, until one day he told her that his mother and sisters were longing to meet her, and asked her to come to dinner next day. To show her the way, he would kill a pig, and lay a trail of blood-spots. This seemed strange, but Lily wanted to go, and her brother was enthusiastic. She obtained a very unwilling consent from her parents, dressed in her smartest black riding-habit, and rode off on her mare Bessy.

The bloodstains led her clearly enough, but it was over thirty miles before they brought her to a gate leading into open fields, at the end of which was a high hedge, and a ditch beyond it, over which Bessy jumped beautifully. The marks ended here, and she found herself before a large brick house, on the gate of which was a brass plate, "Doctor Forster". No one was about, and the startled Lily found her own way to the stables. They were bare, and Bessy had to do without either hay or straw. Crossing the yard again, she saw a huge dog-kennel, with an enormous dog in it, which neither barked nor moved. She entered the house, and saw only an old, shrivelled, dirty woman, who was trying to blow up a wretched little fire of damp sticks. She made no reply to Lily's questions, so the girl went on into the house, more and more mystified, and found a parrot in a gilt cage.

She coaxed it to speak, and at last it said, "If Doctor Forster catch you here he'll mek your blood run cold. Pretty lady, fair lady, go home!" "Polly, pretty Polly, where's master?" But all the reply was again, and again, "Pretty fair lady, go home!" After much coaxing, it said, "If you don't believe me now, open that little trap-door, and see what it'll show. Then, pretty fair lady, go afore it's too late." She opened it, and saw a great cellar full of blood. She shrieked, and rushed from the house, and round to the stables to find Bessy. Just then she heard the gate bang, and saw Squire King Kaley himself ride in. He was "Doctor Forster". She slipped into the quiet dog's kennel before he could see her, and as he rode past, he threw in a lady's hand. So she knew he was a body-snatcher.

She coaxed the dog with cakes she had brought as a gift to her lover's mother, and it gave up the hand, which she hid in the bosom of her dress. Then she leapt on to Bessy's back, and rode off. In a minute she heard the man pursuing her, for he had found from the old woman, who was his mother, that she had been there. But Lily was too quick for him, and he had to turn back.

When she told her story at home, her father told her to take no notice next day, but behave to Squire King Kaley as though nothing had happened, but she had had to stay with her mother, who had been taken suddenly ill.

She managed this, and he told her that his mother and sisters had ridden out ten miles along the road to meet her, and how disappointed they had all been. Then her father came in and said that he wanted to give one of the great parties for which the hotel was famed, and proposed for a novelty that each of the guests should recount a dream. This was planned for two days ahead. In the meantime the father had telephoned the whole story to Scotland Yard, and it was arranged that five detectives, disguised as farmers, should be at the feast. Lily was to dress up as a young man, and tell as her dream the whole adventure of her visit to Doctor Forster.

All went well, and Lily's tale was the last. Several times "Doctor Forster" tried to interrupt her, or to make his escape, but they held him there, until she produced the hand. Then one of the guests recognized by the ring on one finger that it belonged to his sweetheart, and he would have shot the guilty man on the spot, but the detectives prevented him, and led their prisoner away to be hanged.

Thompson Notebooks, D, from Eva Gray at Grimsby, 18 November 1914.
TYPE 955, MOTIFS: B.143.1.3 [*Warning parrot*]; J.1147 [*Detection through feigned dream*]; H.57.2.1 [*Severed finger a sign of crime*]; K.1916 [*Robber bridegroom*].
¶ There are many versions of this Robber Bridegroom tale in England. See "Mr Fox", "Mr Fox's Courtship". Allied to it are the tales of "The Girl who climbed up a Tree", "The Girl who had her Grave dug", "The Oxford Student". These are to be found among the Legends.

THE DRÄGLIN HOGNEY

Once upon a time there was a man, and he had three sons. The eldest said to his father: "Father, if you'll give me a hound, a hawk, and a horse to ride on, I'll go an' seek my fortune." So his father gave him a hound, a hawk and a horse to ride on, and he gaed out to seek his fortune.

He rade an' he rade far and far'er than I can tell, till he came to a thick wood and lost his way, and night came on. Then he saw a light, and coming nearer found a splendid castle. He blew the horn, the door opened, but nobody was to be seen. He went in, and found in the hall a fine supper set ready, and a large fire burning.

He ate his supper, and sat down by the fire to dry his wet clothes; still nobody came.

At last twelve o'clock struck, the door opened, and in came the Dräglin Hogney.

He sat down over against the young man, and glowered at him. Then said the Dräglin Hogney: "Does yer horse kick ony?"

"Ow, ay," said the young man.

"There's a hair to fling ower him." The young man flung it ower his horse.

"Does yer hund bite ony?"

"Ow, ay," said the young man.

"There's a hair to fling ower him."

Again, "Does yer hawk pick ony?"

"Ow, ay," said the young man.

"There's a hair to fling ower him."

With that, the Dräglin Hogney whiecked frae the tae side to the tither, till he fell upon the young man and killed him.

The second son then makes the same request to his father, with the same result.

The third son, finding neither of his brothers return, goes out to seek them, finds, of course, the same castle and a similar entertainment, but when the Dräglin Hogney begins to work his spell, by asking, "Does yer horse kick ony?" and giving the hair to fling over him, the young man flings it in the fire.

"What's that crackin'?" says the Dräglin Hogney.

"It's the the craps o' the green wud come yer waysay," said the young man.

Again, "Does yer hund bite ony? Does yer hawk pick ony?"

The hairs are thrown on the fire. "What's that crackin'?" is asked again.

"It's the craps o' the green wud come yer waysay", is again repeated.

Whereupon the Dräglin Hogney whiecked frae side to side, but the young man called to his horse to kick, and his hound to bite, and his hawk to pick, and they slay the Dräglin Hogney.

The young man then ransacks the castle, finds the enchanter's wand, disenchants his brothers, their horses, hawks, and hounds, and divides the spoil, sends for their father, and, in the old wind-up of a Scotch fairy-tale, "they live happy, and dee happy, and never drink out of a dry cappy". Which I take to be the equivalent of the English "live happy ever after".

A. Lang, *Folk-Lore*, I, pp. 310–12 (here first published), Orkney.

TYPE 303, III; MOTIFS: G.263 [*Witch injures or enchants*]; G.275.2 [*Witch overcome by helpful dogs of hero*]; G.551.4 [*One brother rescues another from ogre*]; D.771.4 [*Disenchantment by using wand*]; L.10 [*Victorious youngest son*].

§ See "The Witch of Laggan", B. Witches.

DUFFY AND THE DEVIL [shortened version]

Squire Lovel of Trove, or Trewoof, rode up to Burian Churchtown at cider-making time, to hire some lads and girls to pick and carry the apples. Passing Janey Chywin's cottage, he heard scolding and cries, and found Janey beating her step-daughter, Duffy, about the head with the gown in which she had been carrying out the ashes. The cloud of

dust almost blinded the Squire, but he discovered at last that the trouble
was that Janey accused Duffy of being idle, and running after the boys,
instead of staying at home to cook and knit and spin. Duffy protested
that her knitting and spinning were the best in the countryside, so the
end was that the Squire took Duffy to his home, to help his old housekeeper, and bring peace to Janey. Duffy rode home behind him, and the
housekeeper, who was almost blind, was glad to welcome her. She soon
took Duffy up to the garret where the wool was, and asked her to set to
work at once.

But in truth Duffy was as idle as her stepmother had said. She could
neither knit nor spin, and she looked in despair at the piles of fleeces, and
cried out:

"Curse the spinning and knitting! The devil may knit and spin for the
Squire, for what I care."

From behind the wool-packs stepped out a dapper little man, with
strange flashing eyes, a knowing twist to his mouth, and a hooked,
intelligent-looking nose. He wore black, and as he came towards Duffy,
something tapped against the floor at every step.

"Duffy, my dear," he said, "I'll do all the spinning and knitting for
you, and you shall become a fine lady; but at the end of three years you
must go away with me, unless you can guess my name." Duffy idled
away the rest of the day, and at the end of it she wished for some yarn,
took it to the housekeeper, who had never seen yarn so beautifully spun,
and next day gave her the yarn back to be knitted into stockings. So things
went on. The Squire was delighted with her work and for fear of losing
Duffy, he married her. She had only to wish, and knitted garments of
every kind appeared to fill her drawers, and satisfy her husband.

She spent much time at the mill, dancing and gossiping with the
women who were waiting to have their corn ground. In this way she
became fast friends with the miller's wife, Old Bet, who was a witch.
Old Bet discovered who did Duffy's work for her, but she never betrayed
her, nor did she tell anyone that the stockings were never quite finished.
There was always one stitch down!

But the three years drew to an end, and Lady Lovel, or Duffy Lady, as
she was more often called, grew anxious, for she did not want to be taken
off by the strange little man. But she had no way of finding out his name.
Old Bet promised that at the last minute she would come to her aid,
but the little man began to haunt Duffy, and jeer at her so that she grew
sad and lost all her merry ways.

When only one day remained, Old Bet told Duffy to bring down to
the mill that evening a jack of the strongest ale; then she was to stay
up till the Squire returned from hunting, however late it might be; and
whatever he might tell her, she was to make no remark in reply.

When Duffy had left the mill, Old Bet turned off the water of the mill-wheel, shut the door behind her, and was seen by passers-by tramping off into the Downs, but no one saw where she went after that.

Very late that night, the Squire's dogs came home alone, covered with foam, and with their tongues hanging out, so that the servants all said they must have met the devil's headless hounds.

Much later, after midnight, came the Squire, wildly singing, though he was not drunk:

> "Here's to the devil,
> With his wooden pick and shovel."

At last, growing somewhat calmer, he told Duffy that though she had not smiled for so long, he would now tell her something at which she could not but laugh, even if she were dying.

He said that all day his hunting had been without success, till at nightfall, at Dawnse Main, up on Brene Downs, up started a fine hare. She passed the Pipers, and down through the Reens, with the dogs so close that they almost had her a dozen times, yet always she gave them the slip, and at last she took refuge in the Fugoe Hole. The dogs followed, and so did the Squire, with owls and bats still flying round his head. They ran a mile or more, through water and mud, till they came to a wide pool, and there the dogs lost the scent. They turned, and ran back in terror, past the Squire, and so home. But he went on, and round the corner, where he saw a fire glimmering, and the St. Leven witches in scores, and among them was Old Bet of the mill, with her "crowd" in her hand, and the Squire's own blackjack slung over her shoulders.

They blew up their fire till it burned with a strange blue flame, and from the flames came a queer little man in black, with a long, forked, twirling tail.

Then they all danced, while Bet beat out the time with her crowd, and sang:

> "Here's to the devil,
> With his wooden pick and shovel,
> Digging tin by the bushel,
> With his tail cocked up!"

Each time the little man passed Bet in the dance, he took a pull at the black jack, till at last he seemed to have lost his head, for he jumped up and down, turning and twisting, and roaring out:

> "Duffy, my lady, you'll never know—what?
> That my name is Terrytop, Terrytop—top!"

Duffy turned pale and red by turns, but she said nothing, and the Squire told how the witches again blew up the fire to blue flame, and the devil danced and sprang among the witches, till, forgetting himself, the Squire cried out aloud, "Go it, old Nick!" At once the lights went out, and every witch turned to pursue him. But he fled away home, and now at last Duffy laughed heartily at and with her husband.

Within an hour the little black man appeared. Duffy was up in the wool-chamber, trying to cram all the woollen garments she had wished for into a great chest, so that her husband should never discover how she had tricked him, when there the little man was, bowing very offensively to the ground, and leering at her. He challenged her to guess his name, and, enjoying her secret, she said, "Maybe your name is Lucifer?" He stamped his foot and grinned. "Lucifer! He's no more than a servant to me. I would scarcely be seen speaking to him at court."

"Perhaps it may be Beelzebub?" He grinned and shook with laughter.

"Beelzebub! A common devil! I believe he's some sort of a Cornish cousin." He was about to seize her roughly, when she cried out: "Stop, stop! Perhaps you will be honest enough to own that your name is Terrytop!"

He would not deny it, but exclaimed: "The pleasure of your company is merely postponed." He departed in a flame of fire, and all his knitting turned suddenly to ashes. The Squire was away hunting on the moors. It was a cold, windy day, and suddenly the homespun dropped from his back, and the stockings from his legs. He came home half dead with cold with nothing but his shirt and his shoes.

Luckily for Duffy, he attributed all this to the vengeance of Old Bet, who he thought was angry with him for pursuing her in the form of a hare, with his hounds.

Hunt, *Popular Romances of the West of England*, pp. 239 ff.
TYPE 500.
MOTIFS: H.915 [*Tasks assigned because of girl's own boast*]; G.303.9.8.1 [*The devil spins and knits*]; H.521 [*Guessing unknown propounder's name*]; H.512 [*Guessing with life as wager*]; N.475 [*Secret name overheard by eavesdropper*]; C.432.1 [*Guessing name of supernatural creature gives power over him*].

The most famous English version of this story is "Tom Tit Tot". This version is one of the long-wandering Cornish drolls, of which Hunt collected the last. They were often presented in dramatic form, and would last a long winter's night.

See also "The Legend of Titty Tod", "Whuppity Stoorie". A parallel Welsh legend is "Tryten a Tratyn".

❡ A detailed study of the whole type was made by Edward Clodd in "Tom Tit Tot".

DULE UPON DUN [summary]

There was once a tailor in Clitheroe who sold his soul to the Devil, but like many others he got very little good of his bargain. The allotted years passed by and he was still beggarly and poor. At length the Devil came to carry off the tailor body and soul, and the tailor bitterly reproached him for the non-performance of his part of the bargain. "The least you can do", he said, "is to grant me one last wish before you carry me away." The Devil feared for the loss of his credit, so he agreed.

There was an old dun horse grazing in the field nearby and the tailor said, "Then I wish that you may mount on that horse, and ride off to Hell, and never more come back to trouble any man in bodily form."

At that the Devil, with a fearful yell, leapt on the horse and vanished away, and since that time he has never more come to tempt men in bodily form.

The tailor got some profit from the transaction, for so many people came to hear the story and to rejoice at the Devil's defeat that he set up an inn to receive them and called it *Dule upon Dun*, and there it stood in Clitheroe for many years, with a painted sign which showed the Devil riding away on horseback, and a tailor, with his shears in his hand, capering for joy.

Henderson, *Folk-Lore of the Northern Counties*, p. 279.
TYPE 330, variant, MOTIFS: M.211 [*Man sells his soul to devil*]; M.223 [*Wish granted without hearing it*].
¶ See also "The Man Who Wouldn't Go out at Night", "St Dunstan and the Devil" (Part B, Saints), "Will the Smith".

THE EARL OF MAR'S DAUGHTER [summary]

Earl Mar had a lovely daughter, and wished her to make a grand marriage. But the girl refused all her suitors, and cared only for a dove, which she had first seen perched on a tower, as she was playing in her garden. She called to the dove, and it came down and lighted on her head. She took it to her chamber, and tended it, and at night the dove became a handsome youth, who told her that his mother, an enchantress, had changed him to a dove, that he might charm some beautiful maid, and that as soon as he set eyes on her, he knew that it was with her that he must live and die. For seven years she bore him a son every year; and as soon as the children were born, the dove carried them away over the sea to his mother, who kept them safe, and brought them up. But at the end of twenty-three years, Earl Mar swore that his daughter should be married to a great lord who was seeking her hand.

The dove, in his cage, heard the oath which the Earl swore, and his wife's reply, "I am content to live alone with my dove". The Earl in a rage, vowed to kill the dove, before he should eat or drink on the next morning. But the dove escaped, and flew to his mother, who rejoiced to see him home, and would have prepared a great feast, but he bade her instead to change twenty-four of her men into grey storks, and his seven sons into seven swans, and himself into a gay goshawk. This was more magic than his mother could command, but she applied to a wise woman of greater skill than her own, and the flock of birds alighted in the trees round Earl Mar's castle, as the dancers were celebrating his daughter's marriage. They stood gazing at the birds, until they all flew down among the crowd of nobles. Some of the storks seized the strongest of the men, the seven swans bound the best man to an oak tree, and the rest seized the bride, and carried her high into the air, and away over the sea to safety. Earl Mar, when he found out the truth, was reconciled.

Child, *The English and Scottish Popular Ballads*, v, pp. 38–42.
TYPE 432 I, MOTIFS: D.150 [*Transformation: man to bird*]; D.641.1 [*Lover as bird visits mistress*]; B.642 [*Marriage to person in bird form*]; D.671 [*Transformation flight*]. ¶ The full story of this type is "The Blue Bird" (Perrault). This ballad only uses one strand of the story, the lover's transformation into a dove, and has a different ending in the transformation flight. The enchantress who turns the Prince into a bird is not in this version a jealous stepmother, but an indulgent mother.

THE ENCHANTED MAN [summary]

There were two brothers, and they were very handsome and gentlemanly in appearance, but they hadn't got much money where they lived. One said to the other: "We'll travel to such and such a castle, and we'll get good money there. You can be gardener, and I'll be coachman." The other said that he was agreeable to go with him. "I think it will be better for us to go." So they packed their things, and went off in the morning, far further than I'll tell you or you'll tell me.

Night came on. They came to a wild forest. One said to the other: "We are fatigued; the night is good. Let us have a night's rest." They took some refreshments, and fell into a slumber, and dreamed that they would come to a castle where everything would be better for them. One woke the other, and they decided to go and find the place, and after a very long journey they did find it.

They entered and looked around, but though everything seemed prepared for their coming they found no one to wait upon them. The teapot poured out tea by itself, and when they were satisfied, a candle and candlestick rose from the table, and led them away to their room. A bed was folded down ready for them, and they slept well that night.

In the morning there was still no one to be seen. They breakfasted, and went on their way. At nightfall they came to another and larger castle. There, as before, everything seemed to be waiting for them, but the table was laid for a larger number of guests, and though they saw no one, the plates and dishes were being emptied as they watched, as fast as their own. Again a candle and candlestick showed them the way to bed, and again they slept well and peacefully.

But in the morning when they came downstairs, there was a lady, all black except for her white face, who waited until they had eaten, and then said: "You were in my sister's house last night; you are in my house tonight; you'll be in another sister's tomorrow night. Tell her that you saw me, and that I spoke to you." They asked her how far it would be, and she told them, "Something like a hundred and fifty miles, but you will not be long in doing that."

When they came to this third palace, it was so beautiful that they were afraid to enter by the front door. But, finding no other, they did at last go in, and found everything more magnificent even than before. But all the events were the same, and when they came down in the morning, again a lady came to them, black all except her face and neck, who told them that they must now return by the way they had come, stay again with her two sisters, and remain in the last house they entered. There they would find work.

So they returned that night to the second of the three inns, or castles. Again they could find no entrance but by the front door, and again they found a sumptuous meal waiting for them. Some bottles of wine were on the table, but these they decided not to touch, out of modesty.

In the morning, a lady all white down to her breast, came and talked to them, and told them that that night they would reach the third sister's house again, and that they might stay there. One of them was to be coachman, and the other gardener, but there was an enchantment that they must break.

They arrived at the inn, or castle, and noticed, as they had noticed in the others, that a sort of "Waff" went through the place as they entered, but no one was to be seen, and as before the only way in was by the front door.

Once more they were fed and guided to bed by invisible hands, and slept in a splendid bed, and in the morning a young lady, white all over, came to them.

She said they were the noblest young men who had ever entered her kingdom, and told the brother who was to be the coachman that the horse he had to drive was enchanted. He was really her elder brother, and only one special rod could break the enchantment. In the garden were some trees to be uprooted, and some parts that were not to be

223

touched at all. The brothers agreed, and the coachman went to look at the horse and his manger. In the manger lay a small, white peeled rod. Thinking it was just right to serve him as a whip, he took the rod and prepared the carriage to take the sisters for a drive. All nine got into the carriage (for there were nine sisters altogether, three to each castle).

"Where shall we go?" he asked them. They told him, "To such and such a place, provided man and horse keep good." "My horse will keep good", he replied.

After about a mile, he touched the horse with the rod, and a man's shoulder appeared. The next time he touched it, a hand appeared. And so, by little and little, as they approached their destination, the horse became less and less a horse, and more and more a man. When he had struck it eight times, the horse fell down. The coachman apologized to the ladies, but they got out of the carriage, and one by one they dropped something into his pocket. First one and then another told him to put his hand into his pocket and find something to throw over the horse, and when he did so —first a stalk of corn, then a head of wheat, and so on—the horse gave a kick and a cry. As the last of the nine gifts touched him, one from each sister, he sprang up, and was a whole man again.

So the enchantment was broken.

Dora E. Yates, *Gypsy Folk-Tales*, p. 168.
MOTIFS: D.1814.2 [*Advice from dream*]; D.6 [*Enchanted castle*]; D.131 [*Transformation, man to horse*]; D.771.4 [*Disenchantment by using wand*].
¶ Another variation on this theme is "The Singing Bride".

THE ENCHANTED MOUNTAIN

One Sunday afternoon, as two children, named Kate and Willie, came out of church, they agreed to go for a walk together. So they walked on until they came to a large mountain, which made everyone who went near it go to sleep. As they drew near to the mountain they began to be sleepy, and at last they both fell asleep at the foot of the mountain. After they had lain there awhile a giant came by, and woke the children up, saying that he would take the boy and kill him, and keep Kate to clean his four-and-twenty-league boots. So he took them to his castle, which was on the top of the mountain, and gave them in charge of the old woman who kept house for him.

Willie soon escaped from the castle, but Kate could not find her way out. When the giant arose the next morning and found the boy gone, he was very angry, and the first thing that he did was to make Kate clean his boots. After the boots were cleaned he said, "I will go and bathe me in the river, and thou, Kate, shalt go with me, and hold in thy hands this golden ring and golden ball." Now Kate knew that if you put the ball inside the ring and wished something your wish would be granted.

When the giant had got well into the water, Kate slipped the ball into the ring, and wished that the giant were leagues away, and herself safe in her own village.

Immediately she found herself walking up the village street, and meeting her father and mother and Willie coming out to seek her. And so Kate became the owner of the ring and the ball, and whenever after that she wished for anything her wish was granted.

S. O. Addy, *Household Tales and Traditional Remains*, p. 6.
TYPE 328 (variant).
MOTIFS: G.610 [*Theft from ogre*]; D.1065.1 [*Magic boots*]; G.501 [*Stupid ogre*]; D.833 [*Magic object acquired through tricking giant*].
    See "Jack and the Beanstalk", "Mally Whuppie", etc.
¶ This is a fragmentary and unsatisfying tale using a few familiar motifs.

FAIREST OF ALL OTHERS [summary]

A poor fisherman found a floating box with a baby girl in it. Took it to wife who reared it as theirs, though they were eighty and seventy-five years old. People came from all round to see the marvel, among them a squire's son who offered to read her horoscope. He found the child was destined to wed him, and determined to prevent it. Offered to adopt the baby. He gave £200. Carried the baby away, had a box made, cut a large cross on the baby's cheek to mark it, put it into the box and threw it into the sea. The box was found by the same fisherman. The baby brought up till it was seventeen, very beautiful in spite of scar. The Squire's son heard of the child again, went to house unrecognized, and engaged the girl as cook. Took her to lonely place by seaside, and drew out his sword to kill her. She begged for her life. He relented, took a ring from his finger, threw it into sea, and said if he saw her again, he would kill her unless she brought him the ring. Left her. She made her way to a lodge where she was taken in, and finally engaged as cook by a grand lady. Her beauty became famous, and she was called Fairest of All Others. One day a man came to sell fish. She bought a few, and while cleaning the last one, found the ring. Many visitors came to see the beautiful cook, among them the Squire's son, who knew her by the scar. He drew his sword to kill her. She produced the ring. He submitted to Fate, and married her. They had many fine sons and fair daughters.

Collected by T. W. Thompson from Taimi Boswell at Oswaldtwistle, 9 January 1915.
TYPE 930A. MOTIFS: T.22.2 [*Predestined wife*]; M.370 [*Vain attempts to escape

fulfilment of prophecy]; s.331 [*Exposure of child in floating chest*]; R.131.4 [*Fisher rescues abandoned child*]; N.211.1 [*Lost ring found in fish*].

¶ See "The Fish and the Ring", "The Bride who had never been kissed", (A. Novelle) "The Prophecy".

THE FAIRY AND THE RING

There was once a wicked king who lived in a large castle which stood on a high hill in a lonely wood, and he had a son who was as wicked as himself. The castle was a very long way from any other house, and nobody ever ventured too far into the wood for fear of being caught by the king or his son, because they were very cruel, and kept prisoners at the castle. One fine day a pretty maid, who had been wandering about the wood, lost her way; but after a time she came in sight of the castle. As darkness was coming on she began to get frightened, and ran up to the castle to enquire the way home. When she got there she knocked at the door, which was opened by a very rough-looking servant.

"Can you tell me my way home?" said the maid.

"No, I can't", said the rough-looking servant; "but I'll fetch my master."

So the servant slammed the door, and went away, and soon after a strong, wicked-looking man came down and said to the maid, "You are a long way from home, and it is dark, so you can't go back now, but follow me, and you shall have a night's lodging."

So the maid followed him, and he led her through a long, dark passage, which brought them to a dimly-lighted room, which was beautifully furnished. There were two servants in the room, and the wicked-looking man, who was the king, told them to give the maid some supper and then show her to her bedroom. So when she had eaten her supper, she was taken into her bedroom, and left alone.

The bedroom was very comfortable, but she began to think about home, and how troubled her father and mother would be about her. "I wonder what will become of me," she said to herself. "I don't like that big, rough man, and oh! it is very lonely here." Then the tears began to fall from her eyes, and she sobbed and could not sleep.

The next morning, when the maid came downstairs, she met the king and his son, and they asked her to take breakfast with them; but she refused, and said, "I want to go home to my father and mother, for they will be grieved about me."

Then the king was angry, and would not let her go, but told the servants to lock her up in a room until they had finished breakfast. After breakfast was done the king and his son went into the maid's room, and she said to them, "I pray you let me go home."

But the king said, "You shall not go home, for I want you to marry my son."

But the maid said, "I will not marry him," and though the king asked her again and again, and offered her all sorts of presents, she still refused.

Then the king grew very angry, and ordered her to be locked up in one of the rooms of the castle until she consented, and to be fed on bread and water. And he said, "Unless you will marry my son, you will be put to death."

So when the maid found herself locked up alone she began to cry bitterly, and call for help. And as she was crying she heard a slight tapping at the little window of her room. On looking up she saw a beautiful woman standing on a large stone which projected out of the wall. The beautiful woman asked the maid why she wept. The maid said, "I am a prisoner in this castle, and to-morrow I am to be killed because I will not marry the king's son."

But the beautiful woman said, "Weep no more, but follow me." Then she came through the window, opened the door, and led the way down a dark passage that brought them to the gates of the castle, which were lying open. They walked through the gates unseen by anyone, and the maid found that she was once more in the wood in which she had lost her way.

Soon after the maid had gone, the king sent one of his servants up to the room in which she had lain, to ask her if she had changed her mind, and was ready to marry his son. But when the servant entered the room he found that she had gone. Then the king was very angry, and fetched his dog, and began to search for her in the wood.

When they got out of the castle the maid asked the beautiful woman what her name was, and thanked her for her great kindness. The beautiful woman said, "I am a fairy, and heard thee calling for help, so I came to help thee. But now I must leave thee here."

But the maid was troubled at these last words, and said, "I don't know which way to go. Wilt thou not show me my way home?"

Then the fairy gave her a ring, and said, "See, take this ring, and tie a piece of ribbon to it. Then hold it in front of thee, and it will lead thee home. But take care of it, for if thou shouldest lose it thou wilt lose thy way again, and the king will overtake thee." Then the fairy suddenly disappeared.

When the fairy had gone the maid was very sorry, but she did as the fairy had told her, and followed the ring, which floated before her in the air.

Thus the maid walked on, the ring going before her; but after a while she saw some pretty flowers growing in the wood, and stopped to gather them.

While she was gathering the flowers she lost the ring, and could not find it again. So she walked on without the ring, when she came to a river and wondered how she was to get across.

As she stood wondering by the river-side, she heard a dog barking, and also the voice of a man shouting, which she knew to be the king's voice. Then the maid was very frightened, and said to herself, "The fairy told me to take great care of the ring, and that if I lost it I should lose my way, and the king would overtake me. Now I shall be taken back to the castle." And again she wept as though her heart would break.

As she was weeping she heard the voice of one who was singing sweetly, and on looking round she again saw the same fairy who had delivered her from the castle. The fairy said, "Hast thou lost the ring that I gave thee?"

The maid said, "I stopped to gather some flowers, and then I lost the ring. And now I do not know which way to go, or how to cross this river, and the king and his dog are searching for me."

Then the fairy was angry, and said, "Thou hast been careless, and unmindful of what I told thee. But I will have pity on thee, and give thee another ring. Follow it, and it will lead thee home." Then the fairy disappeared.

By this time the king and the dog had got close up to her, but the maid followed the ring, which led her straight to a bridge which crossed the river.

Then she went over the bridge and found that she was close to her own home. When she got home she found that her father and mother had been greatly troubled, and wished to know everything that had happened. So she told them all that had happened, and how the fairy had saved her.

S. O. Addy, *Household Tales*, p. 30. This is a poor and uncharacteristic tale, probably a recollection of a nurse's improvised tale to a child.
MOTIFS: T.311.1 [*Flight of maiden to escape marriage*]; F.349.1 [*Fairy aids mortal in flight*]; D.813 [*Magic object received from fairy*]; D.1076 [*Magic ring*]; D.860 [*Loss of magic object*]; D.1384.7 [*Magic ring prevents one losing one's way*].

FAIRY JIP AND WITCH ONE-EYE

Once upon a time, just before the monkey tribe gave up the nauseous custom of chewing tobacco, there lived an old hag who had conceived an inordinate desire to eat an elf: a circumstance, by the way, which indubitably establishes that elves were of masticable solidity, and not, as someone has it, mere

"Shadowry dancers by the summer streams."

So the old lady went to the place where the fairies dwelt, and knocked at the hill-top. "Pretty little Jip!" said she; "come and see the sack of cherries I have brought thee, *so* large, *so* red, *so* sweet." Fairies, be it known, are extremely fond of this fruit, and the elf rushed out in eager haste. "Ha! Ha!" said One-eye, as she pounced upon him, and put him in her bag (witches always carry bags). "Take care the stones don't stick in thy throttle, my little bird." On the way home, she has to visit a place some distance from the road, and left Jip meanwhile in the charge of a man who was cutting faggots. No sooner was her back turned, than Jip begged the man to let him out; and they filled the bag with thorns. One-eye called for her burden, and set off towards home, making sure she had her dinner safe on her back. "Ay! ay! my lad," said she, as she felt the pricking of the thorns; "I'll trounce thee when I get home for stinging me with thy pins and needles." When she reached her house, she belaboured the bag with a huge stick, till she thought she had broken every bone in the elf's body; and when she found that she had been wasting her strength upon a "kit" of thorns, her rage knew no bounds. Next day she again got possession of Jip in a similar manner, and this time left him in care of a man who was breaking stones by the roadside. The elf makes his escape as before, and they fill the sack with stones. "Thou little rogue!" said the witch, as she perspired under the burden, "I'll soften thy bones nigh-hand." Her appetite was only whetted, not blunted, by these repeated failures; and, despairing of again catching her prey in the same way as before, she assumed the shape of a pedlar with a churn on his shoulder, and contrived to meet Jip in a wood. "Ah! Master Redcap," quoth she, "look alive, my little man, the fox is after thee. See! here he comes: hie thee into my churn, and I will shelter thee. Quick! Quick!" In jumped the elf. "Pretty bird!" chuckled the old Crocodile, "dost thee scent the fox?" This time she went straight home, and gave Jip to her daughter, with strict orders that she should cut off his noddle and boil it. When the time came for beginning the cooking, Miss One-eye led her captive to the chopping-block, and bade him lay down his head. "How?" quoth Jip, "I don't know how." "Like this, to be sure," said she; and, suiting the action to the word, she put her poll in the right position. Instantly the fairy seizes the hatchet, and serves her in the manner she intended to serve him. Then picking up a huge pebble, he climbs up the chimney to watch the progress of events. As he expected, the witch came to the fire to look after her delicacy; and no sooner does she lift up the lid of the pot, than "plop" came down Jip's pebble right into the centre of her remaining optic, the light of which is extinguished for ever; or, according to some versions, killed her *stone*-dead.

Norton Collection, I, pp. 196–7. Northamptonshire. T. Sternberg, *NQ*, V, 26 June 1952, pp. 601–2.

TYPE 327C. MOTIFS: G.10 [*Cannibalism*]; G.441 [*Ogre carries victim in bag*]; K.526 [*Captor's bag filled with objects while captives escape*]; G.526 [*Ogre deceived by feigned ignorance*]; G.512.3.2.1 [*Ogre's daughter burned in his own oven*]; G.512.8.2 [*Ogre killed by striking with stones*].

⁋ A slightly sophisticated version of type 327C (the witch carries the hero home in a sack), in which a fairy is substituted for a child.

THE FAUSE KNIGHT UPON THE ROAD: A

"O whare are ye gaun?"
  Quo the fause knicht upon the road:
"I'm gaun to the scule,"
  Quo the wee boy, and still he stude.

"What is that upon your back?"
  Quo the fause knicht upon the road:
"Atweel, it is my bukes,"
  Quo the wee boy, and still he stude.

"What's that ye've got in your arm?"
  Quo the fause knicht upon the road:
"Atweel, it is my peit,"
  Quo the wee boy, and still he stude.

"Wha's aucht they sheep?"
  Quo the fause knicht upon the road:
"They are mine and my mither's,"
  Quo the wee boy, and still he stude.

"How monie o' them are mine?"
  Quo the fause knicht upon the road:
"A' they that hae blue tails,"
  Quo the wee boy, and still he stude.

"I wiss ye were on yon tree,"
  Quo the fause knicht upon the road:
"And a gude ladder under me,"
  Quo the wee boy, and still he stude.

"And the ladder for to break,"
  Quo the fause knicht upon the road:
"And you for to fa down,"
  Quo the wee boy, and still he stude.

"I wiss ye were in yon sie,"
　Quo the fause knicht upon the road:
"And a gude bottom under me,"
　Quo the wee boy, and still he stude.

"And the bottom for to break,"
　Quo the fause knicht upon the road:
"And ye to be drowned,"
　Quo the wee boy, and still he stude.

Child, *English and Scottish Popular Ballads*, I, p. 22.

THE FAUSE KNIGHT UPON THE ROAD: B

"Why are you driving over my field?"
　said the carlin:
"Because the way lies over it," answered the
　boy, who was a little fellow.

"I will cut (hew) your traces,"
　said the carlin:
"Yes, you hew, and I'll build," answered the
　boy, who was a little fellow.

"I wish you were in the wild wood,"
　said the carlin:
"Yes, you in, and I outside," answered the
　boy, who was a little fellow.

"I wish you were in the highest tree-top,"
　said the carlin:
"Yes, you at the top, and I at the roots,"
　answered the boy, who was a little fellow.

"I wish you were in the wild sea,"
　said the carlin:
"Yes, you in the sea, and I in a boat," answered
　the boy, who was a little fellow.

"I'll bore a hole in your boat,"
　said the carlin:
"Yes, you bore, and I'll plug," answered the
　boy, who was a little fellow.

"I wish you were in hell,"
　said the carlin:

"Yes, you in, and I outside," answered the
   boy, who was a little fellow.

"I wish you were in heaven,"
   said the carlin:
"Yes, I in, and you outside," answered the
   boy, who was a little fellow.

Child, *English and Scottish Popular Ballads*, I, p. 21.

HARPKIN: C

Harpkin gaed up to the hill,
And blew his horn loud and shrill,
   And by came Fin.

"What for stand you there?" quo Fin:
"Spying the weather," quo Harpkin.

"What for had you your staff on your
   shouther?" quo Fin:
"To haud the cauld frae me," quo Harpkin.

"Little cauld will that haud frae you,"
   quo Fin:
"As little will it win through me,"
   quo Harpkin.

"I came by your door," quo Fin:
"It lay in your road," quo Harpkin.

"Your dog barkit at me," quo Fin:
"It's his use and custom," quo Harpkin.

"I flang a stane at him," quo Fin:
"I'd rather it had been a bane," quo Harpkin.

"Your wife's lichter," quo Fin:
"She'll clin the brae the brichter," quo Harpkin.

"Of a braw lad bairn," quo Fin:
"There'll be the mair men for the King's
   wars," quo Harpkin.

"There's a strae at your beard," quo Fin:
"I'd rather it had been a thrave," quo Harpkin.

"The ox is eating at it," quo Fin:
"If the ox were i the water," quo Harpkin.

"And the water were frozen," quo Fin:
"And the smith and his fore-hammer at it,"
   quo Harpkin.

"And the smith were dead," quo Fin:
"And another in his stead," quo Harpkin.
"Giff, gaff," quo Fin:
"Your mou's fou o draff," quo Harpkin.

Child, *English and Scottish Popular Ballads*, p. 21.
TYPE 1093. MOTIF: H.507 [*Contest in wit*].

The Appalachian folk-song "The False Knight upon the Road" (*English Folk-Songs from the Southern Appalachians*, collected by Cecil Sharp, edited by Maud Karpelcs, Oxford, 1932), is a version of the same tale.

The importance of having the last word in a contest with a supernatural adversary is also shown in the Highland story "Lochiel and the Witch" (J. G. Campbell *Witchcraft and Second Sight in the Scottish Highlands*, p. 198).

FINGER LOCK

There were three McCrimmon brothers, and two of them were great pipers, and used to go piping about everywhere, but they just kept the youngest one for a slave. Once at the time of the Games the youngest one asked if he might go too to hear the piping. The eldest hit him across the face, and told him to bide at home, and mind the cows. So the two went off and locked the door so that the laddie shouldn't steal any food and left him at the burnside watching the cows. He was lying there very sadly when a wee green man came up and asked him what was the matter. "I wanted to the games with my brothers, to hear the piping," said the laddie. "I'll give you piping," said the fairy, and he played the loveliest tune on a strae. "Now you play," he says. "I canna play," says the laddie, "not even the chanter, and my brothers has the pipes with them, and the door of the house is locked forbye." "That's easy enough," said the fairy. "Just blow in the lock, and put your wee finger in and turn it." The laddie did that and the door opened. "Look in the old kist," said the fairy, "and you will find your pipes."

There was an old kist there he had never seen before. He opened it, and there was a set of pipes mounted in gold, and the finest kilt you ever saw. The laddie put it on, and he looked grand.

"Play a tune on the pipes," said the wee green man. The laddie played, and a tune seemed to come out of his head, the like of which he'd never heard before. "The name of that tune is 'The Finger Lock'," said the wee green man.

He went off to the games, and everyone sat in a dream, listening to him playing "The Finger Lock". He got the prize above everyone, but the fairy had told him to be home early, so he slipped away, and when his brothers came back, everything was back in the kist, and there he was in his old clothes watching the cows by the burn. He asked his brothers how the playing had gone and they said the grandest piper had come and played the finest tune that ever was heard. "What was the name of it?" said the laddie. "It was called 'The Finger Lock'." "Ach!" says he, "I can play that tune mysell." "You!" they say. "You canna so much as play on the chanter." "Wait here a wee minute," he says, and he went off to the kist, and put on his kilt and took up the pipes, and played "The Finger Lock" over to them. After that the two elder McCrimmons never went to the Games and Gatherings, but the youngest went to them all and was the best piper of the three. And that was how "The Finger Lock" was first played.

The School of Scottish Studies, Hamish Henderson, told by Walter Johnson.
TYPE 510 (variant). MOTIFS: L.101 [*Unpromising hero, often youngest brother*]; D.813 [*Magic object received from fairy*]; D.996.1 [*Magic finger*]; D.1224 [*Magic pipe*].
¶ This fairy-story theme of the despised youngest given magic gifts by a fairy helper is attached to a famous family of pipers, the McCrimmons, and gives the origin of a well-known tune.

FINN AND THE DRAGON

"Finn met a dragon once. It wus nearly half as big as a mountain. But he had all his men with him and wusn't a bit afeard, so he give it battle. The head of it wus nearly as big as Sturgan, it's said, an' the mouth of it wus gaping open and full of teeth the size of trees. An' the tail of it wus high in the air—nearly out of sight it wus. An' with it it cud knock a cow or a man over as aisy as ye like. But it wus no match for Finn an' his band, though it swallowed them every one. Finn bedad, made an opening in the belly of it, with his sword an' out he hopped an' ivery man-jack after him. An' the brute was that put about it lay down an' died. Finn killed that one in Camlough, but sure there wur lots of them in them days." [Lislea.]

T. G. F. Paterson, *Contributions to Ulster Folk Life* (seen in manuscript).
TYPES 333 (variant) and 1960. MOTIFS: B.11.2.12 [*Dragon of enormous size*]; B.11.11 [*Fight with dragon*]; F.913 [*Victims rescued from swallower's belly*].

THE FISH OF GOLD [summary]

There was a poor freshwater fisherman lived with his wife in a little cottage. One day he caught a fish made all of gold in his net. It begged him to let it go, and it would turn his house into a castle, and on the table would be a magic cloth, which would give him anything he wanted to eat. So the fisherman let it go, and it warned him that he must tell no one of how he got his wealth, or it would all vanish away. So the fisherman went home, and found his wife richly dressed, and the magic cloth on the table, so that they feasted on everything that they liked to eat. But the wife was very curious to know how it happened, and nagged at her husband until he told her, and then all their riches vanished, and they were in their poor, bare cottage again. The husband had to go out fishing for food, and once again he caught the golden fish, and again it promised him the magic castle if he would let it go. They were as rich as before, and, as before, they lost their wealth through the wife's curiosity. The old man went out fishing again, and caught the fish a third time. The fish knew then that there was no resisting fate, and it told the old fisherman to cut it into three parts, and give one to his wife, one to his mare, and bury the third in the garden. In due time a golden boy was born to the wife, a golden foal to the mare, and a golden lily sprang up in the garden. When the boy grew up, he wanted to seek his fortune. His parents wanted him to stop at home, but he told them he would be safe as long as the lily flourished. If it drooped, his father was to pick a piece, and put it in his pocket, and it would help him on his way. So the boy set out, riding the golden horse. On his way he passed a great forest, where he was warned against a band of robbers. He disguised himself in rags, and covered his horse with sacking, and passed safely through. After a while he met a very pretty girl, who was a Princess in disguise. They loved each other, and were married, and then the Princess took him to her father's palace. The King was very angry, and would have had him killed, but the Princess begged for his life.

One day the King looked into his daughter's room, and saw there a golden lad instead of a beggar: so he was reconciled to the match. But the courtiers were jealous, and they told the golden boy of a deer in the forest whom no one could catch, and the golden boy went out to catch it. He followed the deer all day, and at night he lost it near a little hut. An old witch came to the door, and when he tried to go in, she touched him, and he turned to stone. The same day the lily fell flat in the garden. The old fisherman picked a piece of it, and mounted his old mare, with a gun in his hand. At once they were both filled with magic power, and he rode straight to where his son was enchanted, and held the gun to the witch, until she disenchanted him and his horse. They went back to the Princess, and the fisherman and his wife came to live in the palace. The King had the old witch killed, and the magic deer was never seen again.

Thompson Notebooks, C, from Johnny Smith, Kendal, 9 April 1924.
TYPE 303. MOTIFS: B.375.1 [*Fish returned to water: grateful*]; B.211.5 [*Speaking fish*]; B.505 [*Magic object received from animal*]; F.348.7 [*Tabu: telling of fairy gifts: the gifts cease*]; T.511.5.1 [*Conception from eating fish*]; T.589.7.1 [*Simultaneous*

birth of domestic animal and child]; E.761.3 [Life-token]; G.451 [Following witch's fire into her power]; D.231 [Transformation: man to stone]; E.761.3 [Life-token: flower fades]; D.700 [Disenchantment].

¶ This story follows type 303 (the twins, or blood-brothers), pretty closely, except that there is only one magically born son, and the old father takes the second twin's part. The beginning is reminiscent of "The Fisherman and his Wife" (type 555).

See also "The Two Brothers" and "The Ticky Wee Man"

THE FISH AND THE RING

Once upon a time, there was a mighty baron in the North Countrie who was a great magician that knew everything that would come to pass. So one day, when his little boy was four years old, he looked into the Book of Fate to see what would happen to him. And to his dismay, he found that his son would wed a lowly maid that had just been born in a house under the shadow of York Minster. Now the Baron knew the father of the little girl was very, very poor, and he had five children already. So he called for his horse, and rode into York, and passed by the father's house, and saw him sitting by the door, sad and doleful. So he dismounted and went up to him and said: "What is the matter, my good man?" And the man said: "Well, your honour, the fact is, I've five children already, and now a sixth's come, a little lass, and where to get the bread from to fill their mouths, that's more than I can say."

"Don't be downhearted, my man," said the Baron. "If that's your trouble, I can help you. I'll take away the last little one, and you won't have to bother about her."

"Thank you kindly, sir," said the man; and he went in and brought out the lass and gave her to the Baron, who mounted his horse and rode away with her. And when he got by the bank of the River Ouse, he threw the little thing into the river, and rode off to his castle.

But the little lass didn't sink; her clothes kept her up for a time, and she floated, and she floated, till she was cast ashore just in front of a fisherman's hut. There the fisherman found her, and took pity on the poor little thing and took her into his house, and she lived there till she was fifteen years old, and a fine handsome girl.

One day it happened that the Baron went out hunting with some companions along the banks of the River Ouse, and stopped at the fisherman's hut to get a drink, and the girl came out to give it to them. They all noticed her beauty, and one of them said to the Baron: "You can read fates, Baron. Whom will she marry, d'ye think?"

"Oh! that's easy to guess," said the Baron: "some yokel or other. But I'll cast her horoscope. Come here girl, and tell me on what day you were born?"

"I don't know, sir," said the girl, "I was picked up just here after having been brought down by the river about fifteen years ago."

Then the Baron knew who she was, and when they went away, he rode back and said to the girl: "Hark ye, girl. I will make your fortune. Take this letter to my brother in Scarborough, and you will be settled for life." And the girl took the letter, and said she would go. Now this was what he had written in the letter:

> "DEAR BROTHER,—Take the bearer and put her to death immediately.
> Yours affectionately,
> ALBERT."

So, soon after, the girl set out for Scarborough, and slept for the night at a little inn. Now that very night a band of robbers broke into the inn, and searched the girl, who had no money, and only the letter. So they opened this and read it, and thought it a shame. The captain of the robbers took a pen and paper, and wrote this letter:

> "DEAR BROTHER,—Take the bearer and marry her to my son immediately.
> Yours affectionately,
> ALBERT."

And then he gave it to the girl, bidding her begone. So she went on to the Baron's brother, at Scarborough, a noble knight, with whom the Baron's son was staying. When she gave the letter to his brother, he gave orders for the wedding to be prepared at once and they were married that very day.

Soon after, the Baron himself came to his brother's castle, and what was his surprise to find that the very thing he had plotted against had come to pass. But he was not to be put off that way; and he took out the girl for a walk, as he said, along the cliffs. And when he got her all alone, he took her by the arms, and was going to throw her over. But she begged hard for her life, "I have not done anything," she said. "If you will only spare me, I will do whatever you wish. I will never see you or your son again till you desire it."

Then the Baron took off his gold ring and threw it into the sea, saying: "Never let me see your face till you can show me that ring," and he let her go.

The poor girl wandered on and on, till at last she came to a great noble's castle, and she asked to have some work given to her; and they made her the scullion girl of the castle, for she had been used to such work in the fisherman's hut.

Now one day who should she see coming up to the noble's house but the Baron and his brother and his son, her husband. She didn't know what to do; but thought they would not see her in the castle kitchen. So she went back to her work with a sigh, and set to cleaning a huge big fish that was to be boiled for their dinner. And, as she was cleaning it, she saw something shine inside it, and what do you think she found? Why, there was the Baron's ring, the very one he had thrown over the cliff at Scarborough. She was right glad to see it, you may be sure. Then she cooked the fish as nicely as she could, and served it up.

Well, when the fish came on the table, the guests liked it so well that they asked the noble who cooked it. He said he didn't know, but called to his servants: "Ho, there, send up the cook that cooked that fine fish." So they went down to the kitchen, and told the girl she was wanted in the hall. Then she washed and tidied herself, and put the Baron's gold ring on her thumb, and went up into the hall.

When the banqueters saw such a young and beautiful cook, they were surprised. But the Baron was in a tower of a temper, and started up as if he would do her some violence. So the girl went up to him, with her hand before her with the ring on it; and she put it down before him on the table. Then at last the Baron saw that no one could fight against Fate, and he handed her to a seat and announced to all the company that this was his son's true wife; and he took her and his son home to his castle; and they all lived as happy as could be ever afterwards.

Joseph Jacobs, *English Fairy Tales*, p. 190, from Henderson, *Folk-Lore of the Northern Counties*, p. 326.
See also Homer, *Iliad*, VI, 170 ff. "The Story of Bellerophon" (in Rieu's translation, p. 121), for the death-letter motif.
TYPE 930D, MOTIFS: M.359.2 [*Prophecy of prince's marriage to common woman*]; M.370 [*Vain attempts to escape fulfilment of prophecy*]; K.2015 [*Child adopted by rich man in order to get rid of it*]; R.131.4 [*Fisher rescues abandoned child*]; K.511 [*Uriah letter changed*]; N.211.1 [*Lost ring found in fish*].
¶ See also "Fairest of All Others", "The Prophecy". This tale has been treated by Archer Taylor in "The Predestined Wife", *Fabula*, II, pp. 45–82.

THE FLIGHT OF BIRDS

There was once a farmer living in a wild part of the country, where strangers seldom came. His wife was very beautiful and a good wife to him, and her husband loved her so fondly and so jealously that he could hardly bear another man to set eyes on her. One night of great storm and wind a small boat was forced to seek shelter in the little bay near the farm, and a stranger came knocking at the door to ask for food and lodging. He was a fine-looking man, and as he sat warming himself by the fire, and glancing at the goodwife as she moved about the room, it came into the farmer's head that anyone who saw them would say that they would make a grand pair, and that he himself looked nothing beside them. A little thing is tinder to a jealous heart, and as he was thinking so, it chanced that the stranger yawned, and from the table where she was laying supper his wife yawned too. "Ah," thought the husband, "there is but one thought between them. Likely they are lovers from long syne, and he came here with no purpose but to lie with her."

No sooner did the thought pass through his head than he took it as proved, and all through supper he sat glowering there without a word to throw at a dog. If they had met on road or at market he would have fought the stranger and tried to kill him, but here he was a guest, and his life was sacred.

The stranger soon went into the bedroom they had left empty for him, and fell asleep; then the husband reached a hempen rope down from the rafters and took his wife by the wrist. "Come," he said, and led her out into the stormy night. "What's the matter? What are you wanting with me?" "I'm wanting to keep you an honest and true wife, and I see no way for it but to hang you. That'll be your old love, no doubt."

"I declare to God, I've never seen him till this day."

"Then the thought gaed quickly between you. What for did you gant when he ganted?" And for all his wife could say, she could not shake his belief, nor soften his heart. He put the rope round her neck, and led her towards the nearest tree. The wind was dropping, but it still blew hard, and they struggled against it towards a ragged wood that stood in a sheltered dean not far from the farm. As they went, a flock of small birds passed them, fluttering against the wind. The moon shone out fitfully as they reached the first tree, and the farmer threw up his rope over the lowest bough. It crossed it, but it did not lodge there, for the flight of birds landed on the branch, and it slid down over their beating wings. He tried again, but with no better success. "We'll leave that tree to the birds," he said, "and gang on to the neist." They moved on, but the flight of birds went with them, and when the farmer threw up the rope, it slid down once more. Then his wife spoke for the first time since they had set out:

"The birdies flee frae tree tae tree,
Sae ganting gangs frae Man tae me," she said.

But the farmer was obstinate. "We'll try't again," he said, and he went on, and the birds went with them. Then again as his rope slipped down his wife said:

"The birdies flee frae tree tae tree,
Sae ganting gangs frae Man tae me."

But he was obstinate still, and tried one tree after another all through the wood, and still the birds went before him. At last he said, "This wood is o'er full of birdies, but I mind me of an old fir tree, that stands its lane on the hillside a twa-three mile off. And the wind blows sae snell through it that nae birdies will light on it. We will gang there."

So they set off on the long tramp, and the birds left the wood, and soared high up into the air, and for a while they did not see them.

They went on and on, struggling against the wind, until they reached the one lonely pine on its hill top, and it was the grey light before dawn.

"There are no birdies here to save you," said the farmer, and flung the rope up at the nearest branch, high above them. But as he threw, there was a grand whirr of wings, and the birds swept down from the sky again, and the rope fell to the ground. And the first rays of the sun fell on the farmer's wife, as she said again:

> "The birdies flee frae tree tae tree,
> Sae ganting gangs frae Man tae me."

At the sight and the sound, the farmer's heart was softened, and he burst into tears. He knew that his wife was true to him, and he knew that if he had murdered her in his jealous anger, the birds would have followed him night and day, and he would have known no rest. He took the rope from his wife's neck, and they went back hand in hand; and so long as he lived the farmer never mistrusted her again.

Miss Naismith, from her mother, heard in 1917, Berwickshire.

TYPE 1431. MOTIFS: T.257 [*Jealous husband*]; B.131.7 [*Birds reveal innocence of suspect*].

¶ The foundation story of this type is a jocular tale of a jealous husband, very different in mood from this. Examples have been found in Finland, Estonia, Livonia and Sweden. In its present form it was printed in *Von Prinzen, Trollen und Herrn Fro*, II (1957).

FOOD AND FIRE AND COMPANY

An old woman lived in a cottage on a hillside. It was a very little cottage with a door and one window and a garden in which the old woman could grow a few herbs.

The cottage had a good stout door and a window and a roof of stone slabs that kept out the rain, and a well-swept floor. She was a very clean and tidy old woman and in the corner she had dry brushwood and some piles of turves which the farmer brought her when he remembered.

He was a kind man but forgetful. Besides the turves he sometimes brought her straw or hay to make her a soft bed in the other corner, and farmer's wife sent her an old stew-pot to hang on the crook in the chimney and a mended patchwork quilt for her bed.

So there she was with a warm, soft bed, and a fire, and four stout walls and a good roof overhead. She had a wooden bowl and two wooden spoons that farmer's boy had carved for her and oatmeal to sup when Farmer remembered.

Then one day the tinman came by with his loaded cart at a gallop. He was running away from the gamekeepers, for he had a load of ducks and rabbits under his tins.

The old woman went to her gate as the keepers came up and there on the road was a nice tin mug that had rolled off the cart.

"He won't come back this way any more", said the gamekeeper. "You'd best have it to put in your neat little house. Very clean and comfortable it is."

The old woman smiled at him and then she sighed a little. "I be very lucky, I am," she said, "I've four stout walls and a good roof and a good door, a warm bed and firing and I'm making me a twig broom to sweep the hearth—but I wouldn't mind a bit of company."

The gamekeepers went away again but first one brought in another armful of dry branches for her and the other took a flat cake from his wallet and put it on the window-seat. "Food and firing and company," he said, "and here you've got all three."

After they had gone the old woman broke the sticks neatly and put them in their corner and made up the fire and filled the stewpot with spring water and shook up the bed nicely and swept the floor with a bunch of fern, and everything was clean and tidy again. So she put her last handful of meal in the pot to make a warm gruel for the morning in case Farmer forgot to bring her sackful. "'Tis dusty stuff, meal," said the old woman. "I must make my twig broom tomorrow."

Then she drank some spring water from the tin mug and broke a bit off the flat cake and went to bed.

The next day Farmer came—his wife had remembered, and he brought meal, and a goosewing to sweep the hearth and a small gooseberry bush for the garden and a battered wooden bucket for the water, but it was half full of new milk.

"There," said Farmer, "now you've got four stout walls and a door, a good roof and a good fire, food and drink, and a soft bed. What more can you want?"

But he didn't remember to ask any rent, and he never did.

"What a busy time I'm having," said the old woman when he had gone. "Two visitors yesterday, and another to-day—but I'd dearly like them to stay a bit for company. I'll make a dish of milk porridge, that's what I'll do, and while it cooks I'll tidy up."

So she made enough porridge for two, and hung it to cook over the bright fire, and she swept the hearth with the goosewing and carried out her bed to air in the sun while she took a sharp stick and dug a hole for the gooseberry bush and planted it.

Then she carried back her hay bed in the quilt and shook it up in its corner and spread the quilt over it, and swept all the bits of hay off the floor with the goosewing into the fire, and then she was quite ready to sit in the window-seat and drink warm milk in a tin mug and nibble a bit more flat cake and count all her blessings.

"How lucky I am," she said. "I have a beautiful spring at my gate, and a gooseberry bush in my garden, a good door, four stout walls and a good roof, a good bed and a good fire, a crock of milk porridge and half of the gamekeeper's flat cake, a bowl and a tin mug and two spoons—but Farmer forgot the turves and there are only four left—I must be careful. The sun is warm, so I'll go to bed warm too." Then she said, "But I'd dearly like someone to come and share it." So before she went to bed she poured out half of the milk porridge into the bowl and set a bit of the cake beside it and put it outside the door and called out into the listening dark, "Come and eat a bit. You're very welcome whoever you are, but I'm afraid there isn't much."

When she opened the door in the morning the bowl was empty and the bit of cake was gone.

"Now, who took that, I wonder," she said, "They're very welcome—but I'd dearly like their company for a bit."

Now four miles away on the other side of the valley was the Manor House. It was hundreds of years old and folk said it was lucky. It had a great garden full of roses and the scent of the red ones came on the wind across to the old woman and was so lovely she could have stood sniffing it all day, but to-day there was no scent at all. "'Tis the rain maybe," she said, though she felt it wasn't. "I'll be soaked standing here."

And when Farmer came he was soaked too and so were the turves his wife had reminded him to bring, and of course he couldn't keep the cart-horse standing in the drenching rain, so he was off and away fast, but he did pass on a bit of news first.

"The old Squire died in London and a rich London nephew has come to the Manor with a parcel of fine city servants. The old servants won't work for him since he turned out the luck."

"Oh dear, whatever did he do?"

"He found the bowl of milk and a bit of bread put by for you know who, as has been done for hundreds of years and he threw it to his dog. Things won't prosper for him and he won't get any fine servants to bide there."

The old woman felt quite upset with the wet turves, and Farmer's boots had made such a mess and she was bent double too with the aches in her bones; it took her nearly all day.

"I'll bake a couple of flat cakes," she said. "'Twill take off my aches and pains." So she kneaded them and laid them to cook on the warm hearth.

Then she remembered to put out the tin mug of milk and the last of the keeper's cake, and call out her welcome. "I shall have porridge and cake of my own," she thought, but the rain fell and the turves wouldn't catch and the fire just smouldered and the old woman sat and shivered.

Then, out of the night came a strange voice and something scratched on her door.

> "Oh dear oh,
> Where can I go,
> In rain and snow?
> Oh dear oh,
> What can I do?
> Let me come in
> And stay with you."

"Poor thing," said the old woman. "I'll ask it in out of the rain." Then she thought a bit. "It may be a ghost! Well, the poor thing needs comfort instead of wandering about—or it may be summat else," but she called out bravely, "Come in and welcome whoever you are, tho' the fire don't burn very well." And a thin brown hand slid round the door and summat else slid round it too. The old woman hobbled to close the door and out of the corner of her eye saw something small and brownish slither along the wall and leap up into the chimney.

The rain poured in and the wind blew until she had barred the door. There was just a spark in the embers, so she blew them into a faint glow and crawled into bed.

"You chose a good spot if it's still warm," she called out. "But the fire won't light us and warm us tonight. I'm sorry there's no porridge for you." Then she shivered and went to sleep.

She woke suddenly and lay watching a warm light that glowed in the cottage and flickered on the rafters and the stag's-horn pegs that held the roof slabs in place.

Where did the light come from and what was that lovely smell of baking? She sat up, puzzled, and the fire was flaming, the porridge was cooking, the two cakes were brown and smelling lovely, there was a neat pile of brown dry turves stacked near the fire.

The old woman looked and looked and then she called out, "Thank you kindly, whoever you are, and now we'll have a bit of supper." Then she got up and poured out the milk porridge into two portions and she put one cake into one of the bowls to stand on the hearth and she ate the rest herself. Oh, she was hungry. Then she called out again, "Thank you kindly," and went back to bed and fell fast asleep. In the morning the sun was shining and there came a knock at the door and there was Farmer. "You sleep late," he said. "My missus wants to know if you've got such a thing as a rosebud in your hedge. She wants it for the Well

Dressing down in the village. 'Tis a pity you live so far out; with that flat rock over your spring you could make a fine picture in flower petals for the judges to see." The old woman sighed. "Ah, but I can't stoop to pick 'em and I can't climb to get 'em tho' I'd like fine to make a picture with flowers over my stream. Here's the rose for your Missus." When he went away she sighed again. "'I would have been something to think about and I do love flowers and the Well Dressing is very pretty to see. Dear, dear, how late it's getting—I must get tidied up and bake some more cakes when I've got the fire going." But when she went in the fire was burning. There were two cakes on the hearth, her bed was made and the floor swept. She was so surprised that she sat down and ate her breakfast without another word.

"I shall have time to do a bit in the garden," she said, when she had finished. "I wonder if I could find a flower or two for my rock." Then she opened the door again, and the cottage was filled with a lovely scent. "How beautiful those Manor roses scent this morning air. You could almost think they were at my gate." And that was exactly where they were, great piles of crimson petals, heaped neatly beside her spring.

There were other flowers too, blues and yellows and whites and pinks. The old woman gave a gasp of joy. Then she spread wet clay on the rock and set to work. "Nobody will come this way," she said, "but I'll just see if I can get finished before the church bells ring, but the judges won't see it," so she worked and she worked and somebody must have helped her, for she had just finished putting the last petal into place when the church bells rang out and she heard voices. It was the farmer's cart with the judges in it and he had brought them round this way to the village so the old woman might have a peep at them. (He was a very kind man.) They did more than take a peep. When they saw the rock and the spring and smelled the scent of the red rose petals they all said together it was beautiful. Then they went away.

In the evening they came back and some of the villagers too, and they gave the old woman the prize, three silver pennies. The farmer drove off with them. "You and your red rose petals," said the villagers, "if you could run about, I'd say you'd walked eight miles to pick those roses; there isn't a single red rose in all Manor gardens to-day, not one, and the new Squire is so angry that he went back to London after he'd given the judges lunch. He was so sure he was going to win the three silver pennies with all his great gardens against our little bits. I'm glad you got it, living all alone as you do."

The old woman just smiled at them and they went away. Then she went indoors again—she looked at the firelight, the steaming porridge, the cakes baking on the hearth, the pile of turves, and her neatly made bed. The floor had been swept. She put her three silver pennies on the window seat, and sat down to her supper. "How lucky I am," she said at last. "Here I sit with food and fire and company. Thank you kindly, whoever you are."

Ruth L. Tongue, Staffordshire/Derbyshire, 1962, near Tissington "well-dressing" area.
TYPE 503 (distant variant). MOTIFS: F.332 [*Fairy grateful for hospitality*]; F.343.19 [*Fairies give mortals fairy bread*]; F.346 [*Fairy helps mortal with labour*].

This tale treats of folk-beliefs and customs, but has been at some time a good deal dressed up. Probably told by an educated person to a child and remembered. According to some authorities it is unlucky to thank fairies.

FORTUNATUS [summary]

I

A rich merchant of Cyprus, named Theodorus, was so strongly addicted to pleasures of every kind that he soon spent all his fortune, and was reduced to great distress. His friends sought a remedy for him, and advised him to marry; and they found for him the daughter of another wealthy merchant, Gratiana, whom he married, and they had a son whom they named Fortunatus.

But Theodorus soon returned to his former way of life, and dissipated his wife's fortune, as he had done his own: so that when Fortunatus grew to be a comely youth, his father grieved for his poverty, and became so sad that the boy begged leave to go away and seek his own living.

He took service with the Earl of Flanders, who was about to be married to the daughter of the Duke of Cleves; and on their way home the earl bought rich jewels and embroideries for his lady, and Fortunatus, knowing the language of the merchants of Venice, was of great service to him. When they reached Flanders the earl gave Fortunatus the finest horse of all, except his own, to ride at the wedding.

Fortunatus soon became so great a favourite that the other servants became jealous; and their jealousy grew beyond all bounds when Fortunatus defeated all but one of the contestants in the jousting to celebrate the wedding, and so won one of the two precious jewels which were awarded as prizes. The other victor was one of the servants themselves, whose name was Timothy. So these two now entered the lists together and Fortunatus was again successful, and his master made him the chief chamberlain of his court.

But now the other servants made up a tale that the earl was preparing to make war on another great lord; and so that no one should do wrong to his lady in his absence, he intended to make eunuchs of all his officials who would be left behind, among them Fortunatus. This so terrified the young man that, without stopping to discover whether it was true, he escaped, and fled from the country, to his master's great grief and mystification.

II

He travelled to London and for a short time worked for a Florentine merchant in Lombard Street, but being accused of a robbery and murder, though innocent, he barely escaped with his life; and therefore took ship for France where, after many more adventures, he encountered in a huge forest a most beautiful lady, whose face was veiled, seated under a great beech-tree. She rose and took him by the hand and told him that she was Fortune, and was commissioned by the maker of all things to distribute from time to time six gifts, of which he might now choose one. They were Wisdom, Health, Long Life, Beauty, Strength and Riches. Fortunatus joyfully chose Riches, remembering his own and his father's great poverty; and the lady gave him a purse which, in whatever country he found himself, would always be filled with the money used there. This gift would last for the lifetime of himself and his sons, but no longer. He thanked her, but she stopped him, saying that it was her duty to distribute these things, and that her face was veiled that she might not see to whom she gave them. She bade him remember to share the riches he now possessed with the poor; and he willingly promised.

With the help of his purse he soon provided himself with a horse and trappings, and afterwards bought from an innkeeper three more horses, splendidly accoutred, which the man was hoping to sell for five hundred crowns to the Earl Rodolph. Fortunatus bought them and went on his way, but the earl was angry, and overtook him, accused him of having stolen the money for the horses, and put him to the rack. Fortunatus would again have perished had not many begged his life; but at last the earl relented and sent him on his way, giving him two gold crowns to help him on his way. But Fortunatus still had his purse. He journeyed to Angers, and thence, in company with an Irish gentleman, to England, Scotland, and Ireland. Their adventures were many but, surviving all hazards, they sailed again for Venice and Constantinople. In the city of the Great Turk, Fortunatus, remembering his promise to Fortune, inquired whether there was any marriageable virgin to whom he might give a portion. His evident wealth aroused the avarice of the landlord, who, in the night, crept into their room and stole the Irish gentleman's purse, with fifty crowns in it; but Fortunatus' purse appeared to be empty, so he angrily threw it under the bed, where Fortunatus thankfully found it the next morning. In the meantime a virgin had been found, and Fortunatus gave her four hundred gold crowns for her dowry. The next night the thieving landlord again crept into their room to seek for their riches; but this time the Irish gentleman was aroused. He seized his sword, and ran the landlord through the body, and called to the servants to carry it away and throw it down the well. In the darkness the servants did not know it was their own master's body which they were carrying, and in the morning Fortunatus and the Irishman gave them two ducats each, and rode away.

They made for Famagusta, where Fortunatus was eager to visit his parents; but he found that they were both dead. He erected a noble monument to them and built himself a splendid house, hired servants, and bought a coach, till all began to wonder how he, who had left the country so poor, had won such stores of wealth.

He soon became the most powerful and magnificent citizen in all Cyprus, and for his splendour and many good deeds, the king decided that it was time he should be married, and commanded him to wed Cassandra, the youngest and most beautiful of the three daughters of one of his greatest nobles. They were married with the utmost splendour at Famagusta, where, for nine days after the ceremony, all the citizens were entertained at the cost of Fortunatus; while the Irish gentleman who had for so long been his friend was established in great comfort in Cyprus. He sent for his wife and family to join him, but unhappily died of old age before they were able to arrive.

III

After some years two sons were born to Fortunatus and Cassandra, whom they named Ampedo and Andalosia. And after their birth Fortunatus again set out on his travels, having made ample provision for his wife and household in his absence. He came first to Egypt, where the Soldan befriended him, dazzled by the liberality of his gifts, and gave him letters to other monarchs, by the help of which he arrived at last at the court of Prester John, who had sixty-two kings among his subjects, and dwelt in a palace that shone like gold. In return for his rich gifts he showed Fortunatus all the wonders of his house, and his necromancers performed strange feats for their entertainment. At dinner the bottles and glasses danced on the table; then an orange-tree sprang up, and when some black men had gathered all the fruit, disappeared again. A stag followed by a pack of hounds rushed round the room two or three times and disappeared and there were other delights. But the magicians tried by their arts to discover the secret of Fortunatus' wealth and to steal his purse, so he left the place suddenly and returned through the Holy Land to Egypt. Here the Soldan again gave him great welcome and showed him all his treasures. In the last room of all he pointed to an old shabby hat, which he said was his greatest possession, for whoever put it on had only to wish and he would find himself in the place of his desire. Fortunatus asked if the hat with its wonderful property were not very heavy to wear. But the Soldan said it was not, and bade him put it on and try.

Fortunatus did so, and wished himself on board his ship in the harbour of Alexandria, on which he at once set sail for Famagosta and soon found himself at home. The Soldan vowed vengeance if he ever caught Fortunatus for stealing his hat, but the merchants of Alexandria were glad, for they knew that he would not return again to do harm to their traffic.

IV

When Fortunatus began to feel that the end of his life was near, he sent for his two sons and told them the truth about the purse and the hat, and bade them keep both secrets. Soon afterwards he died, and his wife quickly followed him to the grave, so that the two sons were left to divide their estate. They fell into sharp dispute, but in the end resolved that Andalosia should give his brother certain bags full of money from the purse, and also all the land and goods, and the wonderful hat besides; while he himself was to keep the purse for six years. After that they were to meet and, if his brother wished, he should then return the purse to him.

Andalosia travelled far and wide with his purse, and at last came to London, where he fell in love with the king's daughter. The king, desiring to know the source of his wealth, bade the princess discover it if she could, and at last he told her; and she stole the purse from him; so that to his great chagrin he had to return to his brother without it. But with the help of a holy hermit he discovered the virtue of the apples in the holy garden and, stealing the hat from his brother, he returned again to England and gave one of the apples to the princess, which caused great horns to grow on her forehead.

Andalosia now disguised himself as a doctor and, pretending to be curing the princess, he first sought for and found his purse and then, by means of the hat, transported them both to a distant land, where he revealed himself to her and charged her with perfidy.

He punished her by shutting her up in a nunnery; and himself returned home to his brother, who welcomed him, and so did the king. The king had heard so much of the beauty of this English princess, Agrippina, that he desired to marry her. He knew that her horns were due to an enchantment, and begged Andalosia to remove them. He did so, and the princess and the king were wedded.

His great wealth in time excited the envy of certain nobles of Cyprus, who laid a plot and murdered him. When his brother Ampedo heard of his death he burnt the hat, which therefore was never recovered by its rightful owner, the Soldan, and, since the virtue of the purse did not extend beyond their generation, the secret of their wealth perished at their death.

W. Carew Hazlitt, *National Tales and Legends*, p. 157.

This is a literary version of a widespread folk-tale, but the "Fortunatus Purse" is a reference so well known in England that it seemed best to give a summary of the tale. TYPE 566. MOTIFS: D.812 [*Magic object received from supernatural being*]; D.1451 [*Inexhaustible purse provides money*]; D.1520 [*Magic object affords miraculous transportation*]; D.861 [*Magic object stolen*]; D.1375.1.1 [*Magic fruit causes horns to grow on person's forehead*]; D.881.1 [*Recovery of magic object by use of magic apples*]; D.895 [*Removal of magic horns*].

¶ The motif of the fruit which causes horns to grow, or other magic deformity, is best known in Grimm no. 122. The tale has an almost world-wide dispersion.

FOUR EGGS A PENNY

Tom was very poor, and on market days he took eggs to sell. Sometimes there was only one, and he got a farthing for it. (If there were two, he'd leave one on the window-sill for the old beggarman who had nothing at all.) One day he was lucky, he found some nests, and he had twenty-four eggs to take, and that would be a silver sixpence for him. "I'll buy a whole loaf," said Tom. Then he thought of the old beggarman's egg. "Oh, well," said Tom, "I can get a piece of real bread for 5¾d. and perhaps a bit of butter to go on it, and if he comes by when I come back, we'll have a feast, and he'll make me laugh." So off he went to market, and there in the road outside the ale-house was the poor old beggarman lying dead.

Tom was very upset. "He owed me a penny," said the ale-wife. "He can lie in the dirt, for all I care." Tom gave her four eggs, and four more for the halfpennies to put on his eyes for St. Peter, then he went to the carpenter to make him a coffin, which was another four eggs. A farmer was kind, and took Tom and the dead man in his ox-cart to the Parson for nothing but thanks. "The old man made me merry often," he said, and Tom said so too. But the Parson and the Clerk, they wanted all the other eggs to bury the beggarman in a little dark corner of the church-yard on the north side. So Tom gave them his twelve eggs, and said a prayer for the old beggar, and came back home as hungry as he went. "There's one potato," he said. "No bread or butter for me to-day. It'll be 'pull in my belt' and 'potato and point'."

When he got in, there was a nice fire, and there on the table was a big loaf of bread, there was butter, and *twenty-four* eggs.

But there wasn't any egg on the window-sill.

Ruth L. Tongue, Somerset.

This is a short and homely variant of the tale of "The Grateful Dead". In this tale the dead man only makes restitution of what has been expended on him. TYPE 506 (variant). MOTIFS: Q.271.1 [*Debtor deprived of burial*]; E.341.1 [*Dead grateful for having corpse ransomed*].

¶ There are many Celtic versions of type 506, as, for instance, "The Barra Widow's Son" in Campbell's *Popular Tales of the West Highlands*. That the tale was also known in England is shown by its introduction into Peele's *Old Wives' Tale*, where the servant, Jack, is the ghost of the dead man buried by the hero. A disguised form of the story would be familiar to Englishmen in the Apocryphal "Tobias and the Angel".

THE FRIAR AND THE BOY

God that died for all give them a good life and long that listen to my tale!

There was a man in a certain country who in process of time had three wives. By the first he had a son, who was a light-hearted lad; but by the other twain, issue had he none.

His father loved this boy well; but his stepdame looked upon him with an evil eye, and stinted him in his victual, and did him many a shrewd turn.

At length she said unto the goodman: "I heartily pray you, sir, that you would put away this boy, who is a cursed plague to me, and let him serve someone else who will give him his desert."

Her husband answered her, saying: "Woman, he is but a child. Let him abide with us another year, till he is better able to shift. We have a man, a stout carl, who keeps our beasts afield; look, the boy shall take his place, and we will have the fellow in the stead of him at home."

To which the goodwife agreed.

So on the morrow, the little lad was sent to tend the sheep, and all the way he sang out of the gaiety of his heart; and his dinner he carried with him in a clout. But when he came to see what his stepdame had given him to eat, he had small lust thereto, and he took but little, thinking he would get more when he returned homeward at sundown.

The boy sat on a hillside, watching his sheep, and singing, when there came along an aged man, and stood still, when he espied the child, saying unto him, "Son, God bless thee!"

"Welcome, father," the boy replied.

The old man said, "I hunger sore; hast thou any food of which thou mightest give me even some?"

The child replied: "To such victual as I have, thou art welcome, father."

So he gave the old man the rest of his dinner, and thereof he was full fain. He ate, and grudged not. To please him was not hard.

Then, when he had finished, he said: "Gramercy, child; and for the meat which thou hast spared me I will give thee three things. Tell me now what they shall be."

The boy thought in his mind, and anon: "I would", he quoth, "have a bow, wherewith I could shoot birds."

"I will find thee incontinently," said the stranger, "one that shall last thee through thy whole life, and shall never need renewing. Thou hast but to draw it, and it will hit the mark."

Then he handed him the bow and the arrows; and when the child saw them, aloud he laughed, and was mightily content.

"Now", said he, "if I had a pipe, if it were ever so small, then I should be glad."

"A pipe I here give thee," the old man said, "which hath in it strange properties; for all whosoever, save thyself, shall hear it, when thou playest, must dance to the music perforce. I promised thee three things. Say, what is to be the last?"

"I seek nothing more," replied the boy.

"Nothing?" quoth the stranger. "Speak, and thou hast thy will."

"Well," said he, musing, "I have at home a stepdame—a shrewd wife she—and she oftentimes looks ill-favouredly at me, as though she meant me no love. Now, prythee, when she so looketh in that wise, let her laugh till she fall to the earth, and laugh still, unless I bid her to desist."

"It is granted," said the stranger. "Farewell!"

"God keep thee, sir," said the boy.

The evening drew on, and Jack wended homewards in great glee. He took his pipe and played it, and all his beasts and his dog danced to it in a row. He played as he went along, and the sheep and kine followed at his heels, and the dog, dancing all the way, till they came to his father's abode; and he put by the pipe, and saw that all was fast, and then walked he into the house.

His father sat at his supper, and Jack said unto him, "I am a-hungered, sir; my dinner I might not eat, and I have had charge of the beasts the whole day."

The husbandman threw a capon's wing toward him, and told him to eat it. The goodwife sorely grudged that he should have so fair a morsel, and eyed him sourly. But she straightway fell to laughing, and she laughed, and she laughed, till she could no longer stand or sit, and fell on the floor, laughing still, and she ceased not till she was half-dead; and then the boy said: "Dame, enough!" And she laughed not a whit more, which made them both amazed.

Now this goodwife loved a friar, who oftentimes came to the house; and when he next showed himself, she made complaint to him of the boy, and told him how Jack had caused her to laugh, and had mocked her, and she prayed this friar to meet him on the morrow and beat him for his pains.

"I will do thy pleasure as thou desirest," quoth the friar.

"Do not forget," quoth the goodwife. "I trow he is some witch."

So the morning following the boy went forth to drive his father's beasts to the field, and he took with him his bow and his pipe. And the friar rose betimes likewise, lest he might be too late, and he approached the boy, and thus he accosted him:

"What, forsooth, hast thou done by thy stepmother, Jack, that she is angered at thee? Tell me what it is; and if thou canst not satisfy me, surely I will beat thee."

"What aileth thee?" asked Jack. "My dame fares as well as thou. Have done with thy chiding. Come, wilt thou see how I can bring down a bird with my bow, and what other things I can do? Though I be a little fellow, I will shoot yonder bird, and yours it shall be."

"Shoot on," said the friar.

The bird was hit, surely enough, and dropped into a thorn bush.

"Go and fetch it," said Jack.

The friar stepped into the middle of the brambles, and picked up the bird. Jack put the pipe to his lips, and began to play. The friar let the bird fall, and set to dancing, and the louder the pipe sounded, the higher he leapt, and the more the briars tore his clothes and pierced his flesh. His dress was now in shreds, and the blood streamed from his legs and arms. Jack played all the faster, and laughed withal.

"Gentle Jack," gasped out the friar, "hold thy hand. I have danced so long that I am like to die. Let me go, and I promise thee I will never again offer thee harm."

"Jump out on the other side," quoth the boy, pausing, "and get thee gone."

And the holy man made all the haste he could for shame's sake; for the thorns had almost stripped him to the skin, and covered him with blood.

When he reached the house, they wondered where he had been, and how he had fallen into such a sorry plight. The goodwife said: "I see well, father, by thine array, that thou hast come to some mischief. What has befallen thee?"

"I have been with thy son," he replied. "The devil overcome him, for no one else may."

Then entered the goodman, and his wife said unto him: "Here is a pretty matter! Thy dear son hath well-nigh slain this holy friar. Alack! alack!"

The goodman said: "*Benedicite!* What hath the boy been doing to thee, friar?"

"He made me dance willy-nilly, among the briars, and by Our Lady, the pipe went so merrily that I might have danced till I burst myself."

"Hadst thou met with thy death so, father," said the goodman, "it had been a great sin."

At night, at the usual hour, the boy came back, and his father called him unto him, and questioned him about the friar.

"Father, I did nought, I tell thee, but play him a tune."

"Well," answered the goodman, "let me hear this pipe myself."

"Heaven forbid!" cried the friar, wringing his hands.

"Yes," quoth the goodman, "give us some music, Jack."

"If," entreated the friar piteously, "thou wilt indeed have him play, first bind me to some post. If I hear that pipe I must fain dance, and then my life is nought worth. I am a dead man."

They fastened him to a post in the centre of the hall, and they all laughed at his distress, and one said, "The friar is out of danger of falling now."

"Now, boy," said the goodman, "play on."

"That will I do, father," he replied, "till you bid me hold, and I warrant ye shall have music enough."

As soon as the boy took up his pipe and laid his mouth to it, all began to dance and jump, faster and faster, and higher and higher, as though they were out of their wits. Even the friar struck his head against the post, and screamed with pain. Some leapt over the table; some tumbled against the chairs; some fell into the fire. Jack passed out into the street, and they all followed him, capering wildly as they went. The neighbours started at the sound, and came out of their houses, springing over the fences; and many that had gone to rest jumped out of bed and hurried into the village, naked as they were, and joined the throng at Jack's heels. A phrenzy was upon them all, and they bounded into the air, and looked not whither they plunged; and some that could no longer keep their feet for lameness danced on all fours.

The goodman said to his son, "Jack, I trow it is best to give over."

"Let it be so," said the boy, and he desisted from his playing accordingly.

"This is the merriest sport", said the goodman, "that I have known this seven year."

"Thou cursed boy!" exclaimed the friar, when they returned to the house. "I summon thee before the judge. Look thou be there on Friday."

"Good," answered the boy, "I will. I would with all my heart it were already come."

Friday arrived, and Friar Topas and the stepdame, and the whole party appeared, and the judge was in his place, and there was a goodly gathering of people, for there were many other cases to be heard. The friar was fain to wait till his turn came, and then he addressed the judge, saying to him:

"See, my lord, I have brought a boy to thee, who hath wrought me and others many grievous trouble and sorrow. He is a necromancer such as in all this country hath not his like."

"I hold him for a witch," put in the goodwife, and scowled at Jack; and forthwith she set to laughing till she fell down, and none could tell what she ailed, or whence her great mirth arose.

"Woman," said the judge, "tell thy tale." But she could not utter another word, though Jack stayed her laughter, as he had power given to him to do so by the stranger on the hillside.

Then spoke Friar Topas, and said: "My lord, this boy will worst us all unless you soundly chastise him. He hath, sir, a pipe that will make you dance and hop till you are well-nigh spent."

The judge said, "This pipe I fain would see, and know what sort of mirth it maketh."

"Marry! God forbid!" quoth the friar, "till I am out of the hearing of it."

"Play on, Jack," said the judge, "and let me see what thou canst do."

Jack set the pipe to his lips, and blew, and the whole room was quickly in motion. The judge sprang over the desk, and bruised both his shins; and he shouted out to the boy to cease for God's sake and the love of the Virgin.

"Well," said Jack, "I will if they will promise me that they will never again do me trespass so long as I live."

Then as many as were there, the friar, the stepdame, and the rest, swore before the judge that they would keep the peace toward the boy, and help him to their power at all seasons against his enemies; and when they had done so, Jack bade the judge farewell, and all proceeded merrily home.

And thus it may be seen how the boy, because he was courteous and kind to the old man whom he met on the hillside while he tended his father's beasts, prospered, and kept everyone in his country in his fear for evermore. For the old man was in truth a magician.

W. Carew Hazlitt, *National Tales and Legends*, p. 17. Retold from "The Friar and the Boy" (1617).

TYPE 592. MOTIFS: S.322.4 [*Evil stepmother casts out boy*]; Q.42.1.1 [*Child divides last loaf with fairy*]; D.1761.0.2 [*Limited number of wishes granted*]; D.1415.2.4 [*Magic pipe causes dancing*].

This is cited by Herrick among the chapbooks he deplores: "The dancing Frier, tatter'd in the bush" (*Herrick's Poems*, Oxford, 1915, p. 155).

⁋ There is a Welsh version of this tale given by Eirwen Jones in *Folk Tales of Wales*, p. 22; also one from Kentucky in M. Campbell's *Tales of Cloud-Walking Country*.

FRIAR RUSH [summary]

I

"Friar Rush" was a devil, who presented himself in the guise of a young man at the gate of a certain religious house, and asked to be given work there. The monks had become rich and idle, and Lucifer had held an assembly of his chief devils and decided to send one of their number to work further evil among them.

The prior sent Rush to the kitchen to work under the master-cook until he could find him some other tasks; and after a few days he sought him out and asked, "Rush, can you couple hounds together?" "Yea, my lord," he replied, "and more than that; for I can couple men and women together, and I could convey a fair young woman to your chamber and bring her away in the morning, and no man should be privy thereto. And all your counsels I would keep." So the prior knew that in Rush he would have a servant after his own heart.

A few days later Rush brought to him, at his request, a lady whom he found sitting alone in her house, and she stayed with him all night. And it was not long before the other monks found that Rush was a discreet messenger, and sent him on many like errands.

II

One night the master-cook chided Rush for staying out late, and Rush, in anger, flung him into a cauldron of boiling water and went away on an errand for the prior. When he returned the monks had discovered the body of the master-cook in the cauldron, but having no reason to suspect Rush they agreed to make him master-cook in place of the dead man.

And this service he performed so well that at the end of seven years the prior made him one of their order, and though he continued as master-cook, he thereafter wore the proper dress of the house.

III

When his work was not pressing, Rush had many other occupations. Once he fashioned a number of truncheons of oak, one for each monk, which he said would be a protection for them against thieves. But soon after he contrived that a quarrel broke out among them concerning a woman whom both the prior and sub-prior desired; and the monks took sides in the matter. The next night at the midnight service the prior suddenly struck the sub-prior, the monks seized their cudgels, and to add to the confusion Rush blew out all the candles. So great a fight broke out that several monks were killed. After a time Rush returned to the chapel with a lighted candle, and pretended to have come to restore them to amity and peace. Filled with shame, the monks gave up their truncheons, buried their dead in secret, and stayed indoors until their wounds were healed.

IV

To make the prior angry, Rush purposely misunderstood an order to prepare a waggon for him, and see that the wheels were well greased. Instead Rush covered the whole waggon with tar so that the prior's clothes were smeared with it, and another waggon had to be found.

They went on their journey, but that night the prior allowed Rush no wine at dinner, though he himself drank of the best. Rush therefore ordered three more bottles for himself and his companions; and when the prior saw and questioned the bill, he replied that he and the others had drunk one bottle and given the other two to the horses because they had travelled far and were weary. After that, Rush was not again taken by the prior on his travels.

Later on, Rush was appointed sexton of the church. He had to ring the bell, light the candles, and call the friars to prayers; also to report to the prior any who were absent. Very soon he had reported them all, so that they became resentful against him. One night he removed the stairs of the dorter, then rang for matins, and as the friars hurried from their cells they fell in a great heap to the bottom. They crawled painfully into church, and there they had to remain all day, for the stairs were gone. Rush pretended to the prior that the weight of the hurrying monks had broken down the staircase, but the prior was beginning to be suspicious, and he removed Rush from the office of sexton and sent him back to the kitchen.

V

One night Rush was drinking in a village some miles from the convent, when he remembered that there was nothing at home for the monks' supper. He rose quickly, paid for his drink, and on his way home he saw a fat cow grazing in a field, and divided it in two. He left half in the field and carried the other half home, dressed the meat in various ways, and made excellent broth; so that the monks, who knew how late he had returned, were astonished. But the unhappy farmer late that night found his cow so strangely mangled that no human hand could have so treated it; and while he was still puzzling and grieving over his loss, he heard voices in the field. Lucifer was again holding an assembly, and the various devils each reported what evil he had done that day. Last came Rush, whom Lucifer commended more than any of the others.

The next day the farmer summoned up his courage to go and tell the prior what he had learnt; and his tale so opened the eyes of the prior that he repented of his evil ways, which had laid the whole house open to the temptations put in their way by Rush. He called all the brothers together and confessed all the truth, and they all fell on their knees and asked for God's grace and pardon.

The prior sought out Rush in the kitchen, and commanded him to take the form of a horse, and wait at the gate where he had first sought employment among them. There all the monks went to him, and asked why he had ever come among them. He replied that it was to work them all possible harm, and that in time they would all have been damned.

He promised to molest them no more and the prior allowed him to depart; and from that time the monks returned to their proper devotions and gave up their sinful habits.

VI

Lucifer now bade Rush find other work for himself. He took service with a husbandman, whose wife strongly resented his employing any man at all, contending that he was well able to perform the work alone. But when she found how useful and profitable Rush was, she became kinder to him. Rush would complete a whole day's work before breakfast, and the more his master gave him to do, the more he did. But Rush discovered an intrigue between the wife of his master and the parish priest, and would invent pretexts to return to the house when he knew the priest was there. Once it was to change his master's boots—and there was the priest hiding in the great chest where boots and shoes were kept.

Another day he came to clean out the stable—and the priest was hidden under a truss of straw. Rush threatened to make an end of him, but the priest begged for mercy, saying that if he ever found him there again he might do what he liked with him.

But he came again, and this time, hearing Rush enter the house, the wife hid him in the cheese-basket upstairs. Then Rush said he had come to clean out the cheese-basket, and he went up and cut the rope by which it was hanging from a window. The basket and the priest fell together into the pond below, and Rush tied a horse to the rope, dragged it several times up and down the pond and then through the town, pretending all the time not to know the priest was there. At last he looked in and saw him and cried out: "Thou shalt not escape me again!" But the priest gave him a hundred gold pieces and he let him go. Then Rush gave half the money to his master and went away to seek yet another service.

VII

He next entered a gentleman's house where the master was greatly distressed for his daughter, who was possessed by a devil. Rush bade him send her to the convent where he had formerly been employed, and there the prior and all the monks knelt and prayed for the girl and a great devil flew out of her mouth, and she was well.

Her father would have given the prior much gold in return for this service, but the prior asked instead for lead to cover the roof of the church, which was in sore need of repair. There was abundant lead in that part of the country, and the gentleman took the prior to a great heap and bade him take as much as he would. The prior turned to Rush, and bade him carry enough for the roof of his church. Rush again changed himself into a horse and, taking the lead on his neck, he was there in a quarter of an hour.

Then the prior transformed Rush to his right shape, and banished him to a castle far away in the forest, from which he has never returned.

W. Carew Hazlitt, *National Tales and Legends*, p. 136. (See Thorn's *Early English Prose Romances*.)
MOTIFS: K.1987 [*Devil disguised as man goes to church*]; G.303.9.4 [*The devil as a tempter*]; G.303.16.9 [*The devil is made impotent by confession*]; G.303.9.3.1 [*Devil hires out to a farmer*]; G.303.3.3.1.3 [*Devil as horse*]; G.303.25.19 [*Parliament of devils*].

THE FROG

There was a stepmother who was very unkind to her stepdaughter, and very kind to her own daughter; and used to send her stepdaughter to do all the dirty work. One day she sent her to the pump for some water when a little frog came up through the sink and asked her not to pour dirty water down, as his drawing-room was there. So she did not, and as a reward he said pearls and diamonds should drop from her mouth when she spoke. When she returned home it happened as he said; and the stepmother, learning how it had come about, sent her own daughter to the pump. When she got there, the little frog spoke to her and asked her not to throw dirty water down, and she replied: "Oh! you nasty, dirty little thing, I won't do as you ask me."

Then the frog said "Whenever you speak, frogs and toads and snakes shall drop from your mouth." She went home, and it happened as the frog had said. At night, when they were sitting at the table, a little voice was heard singing outside:

"Come bring me my supper,
My own sweet, sweet one."

When the stepdaughter went to the door, there was the little frog. She brought him in, in spite of her stepmother, took him on her knee and fed him with bits from her plate. After a while he sang:

> "Come, let us go to bed,
> My own sweet, sweet one."

So, unknown to her stepmother, she laid him at the foot of her bed, as she said he was a poor, harmless thing. Then she fell asleep and forgot all about him. Next morning there stood a beautiful prince, who said he had been enchanted by a wicked fairy and was to be a frog till a girl would let him sleep with her. They were married, and lived happily in his beautiful castle ever after.

Norton Collection, I, p. 288. (Holderness. W. H. Jones, in notes to *Folktales of the Magyars*, pp. 404-5, London, 1889. Told him by a nurse when a child, but he "heard the following version a short time ago in Holderness, and was informed it had been told thus for ages". The verse was sung to a traditional air.)

TYPE 440. MOTIFS: L.55 [*Stepdaughter heroine*]; F.451.4.4.3 [*Request: (not to pour down dirty water) to remove stable*]; Q.41 [*Politeness rewarded*]; D.1454.2 [*Treasure falls from mouth*]; Q.287 [*Refusal to grant request punished*]; M.431.2 [*Curse: toads from mouth*]; D.195 [*Transformation: man to frog*]; K.1361.1 [*Transformed person sleeps at foot of bed*]; D.734 [*Disenchantment of animal by admission to woman's bed*]; L.162 [*Lowly heroine marries prince*].

¶ There is an admixture of type 440 with 480. An unusual feature in this version is that the heroine admits the frog willingly, and is not forced to do so.

See also "The Paddo", "The Well of the World's End", etc.

THE FROG PRINCE

There was a farmer that had an only daughter; and she was very handsome, but proud. One day when the servants were all afield, her mother sent her to the well for a pitcher of water. When she had let down the bucket, it was so heavy that she could hardly draw it up again; and she was going to let loose of it, when a voice in the well said, "Hold tight, and pull hard, and good luck will come of it at last." So she held tight and pulled hard; and when the bucket came up, there was nothing in it but a frog, and the frog said, "Thank you, my dear, I've been a long while in the well, and I'll make a lady of you for getting me out." So when she saw it was only a frog, she took no notice, but filled her pitcher and went home.

Now, when they were at supper, there came a knock at the door, and somebody outside said:

> "Open the door, my dearest sweet one,
> And think of the well in the wood;

17-2

Where you and I were together, love a-keeping,
And think of the well in the wood."

So she looked out of the window, and there was the frog in boots and spurs. So says she, "I shan't open the door for a frog." Then says her father, "Open the door to the gentleman. Who knows what it may come to at last?" So she opened the door, and the frog came in. Then says the frog:

"Set me a chair, my dearest, sweet one,
And think of the well in the wood."

"I'm sure I shan't set a chair; the floor's good enough for a frog." The frog makes many requests, to all of which the lady returns uncivil answers.

He asks for beer, and is told, "Water is good enough for a frog;" to be put to bed, but, "The cistern is good enough for a frog to sleep in." The father, however, insists on her compliance; and even when the frog says, "Cuddle my back, my dearest, sweet one," orders her to do so. "For who knows what it may come to at last?" And in the morning, when she woke, she saw by her side the handsomest gentleman that ever was seen, in a scarlet coat and top-boots, with a sword by his side and a gold chain round his neck, and gold rings on his fingers; and he married her and made her a lady, and they lived very happy together.

Norton Collection, I, p. 287 (Oxfordshire), *NQ*, V (15 May 1852), p. 460.
TYPE 440. MOTIFS: B.211.7.1 [*Speaking frog*]; K.1361.1 [*Transformed person sleeps in the bed*]; D.734 [*Disenchantment of animal by admission to woman's bed*].
¶ See also "The Frog", "The Girl who fetched Water in a Riddle", "The Maiden and the Frog", "The Paddo", "The Prince Paddock", "The Well of the World's End".

THE FROG SWEETHEART [summary]

A King with three daughters fell ill. No doctor could help, but a wise man told him he could be cured by a draught of water from his own well, but it must be drawn by one of his own daughters.

The eldest and the second tried in vain, for the water was muddy and thick, and each time a frog jumped out, and promised clear water if she would be its sweetheart.

The girls refused, and the water remained muddy. Then the youngest went, and in fun promised the frog to be its sweetheart. The water cleared, the King drank it and was cured.

A few days later the princess heard the frog calling at her door, as she was about to get into bed. She let it in, and it lay on the foot of her bed all night; and was gone in the morning. It returned the next night;

but the third night, when it came again, she told it it was the last time. When she had fallen asleep, the frog crept up to her face, and lay half in and half out of the bed. When she awoke, she shrieked, and threw it on the floor. In its place appeared a handsome prince, who told her that he had been enchanted, and she had lifted the spell. He begged her to marry him, and the King consented, if he first returned home to make sure that all was well. He sent a groom with him, to find out what he could of the prince's homecoming, and return with the horses. The groom reported that the prince had been welcomed with the greatest joy, and that he and his father would be there in two days' time to claim the princess. So it fell out. They were married, and the wise man was found and richly rewarded.

Thompson Notebooks, F, told by John Lock, Clun Forest, Salop, August 1923. Rationalized version of type 440. See previous tales.

THE GAY GOSHAWK [summary]

A young lover in Scotland sent his goshawk with a letter tucked into its feathers to be carried to his lady in England. The goshawk asked how he could know this lady whom he had never seen, but the lover replied that she had the whitest skin, and the reddest lips and cheeks of any lady in England. When the goshawk reached her father's castle, it was to alight on the ash-tree and sing, and when the lady went into the castle, it was to follow her and sing to her again on the "whin".

When the lady heard the singing, she knew the bird was her lover's, and she bade all her maidens go in and drink wine in her room, and then the bird let the letter fall at her feet. It told her that her lover could wait no longer to hear word of her, for he had sent to her five times, and was near to dying of love.

The lady knew that her parents would not consent to her marrying and going away to Scotland, so she went to her father and begged a promise from him.

But first she sent the goshawk back to her lover bearing rings from her fingers, and a garland from her hair, and "the heart that's in my breast", and bade him meet her at the fourth church in Scotland. Then she gained her father's promise that if she should die in England he would have her buried in Scotland.

He gave his word, and she made the same request of her mother, her sister, and her seven brothers in turn. They all replied alike:

"Your asking is but small," they said,
"Weel granted it shall be."

Then the girl dropped down as if dead at her mother's feet, for she had already drunk a potent sleeping-draught. An old witch-wife who was sitting by the fire said, "Drop molten lead on her cheek, her chin and her lips, to try if she be really dead, for a lady will do much to win her lover." But the boiling lead made no difference: the lady lay, to all seeming, dead. Her brothers made her a bier of cedar-wood and gold, and her sisters wove her a shroud of satin and silk.

Meantime the goshawk had flown back to Scotland, and delivered the lady's tokens to his lord, who set forth at once with all his men to meet her.

Faithful to his promise, her father had come to the first church in Scotland, and there he caused the bells to be rung. At the second church he had the mass sung for her. At the third church he distributed gold for her sake; and at the fourth, they met her true love, who begged to see her face once more before she was buried. He tore the sheet from her white face, and at once she looked up at him, and smiled and spoke:

> "Give me a chive of your bread, my love,
> A bottle of your wine;
> For I have fasted for your love
> These long days nine."

> .   .   .   .

> "I came not here to fair Scotland
> To ly amang the dead;
> But I came here to fair Scotland
> To wear the gold so red."

F. J. Child, *The English and Scottish Popular Ballads*, II, p. 360.
TYPE 885A, MOTIFS: B.211.3 [*Speaking bird*]; B.455.4 [*Helpful hawk*]; D.1364.7 [*Sleeping potion: drink causes magic sleep*]; H.248.1 [*Sham dead person tested by drops of hot lead*].

The speech of the goshawk may hardly have been considered supernatural when the ballad was first made. This might be called a naturalized version of "The Earl of Mar's Daughter". The ballad "Willie Lyke-Wake" (Child) tells the same story without any supernatural element.

THE GIANT OF GRABBIST: I

We 'aven't got many Giants about our Zummerzet, I 'ear, but we 'ave one down to Dunster. Ah! Come up from Cornwall, 'e did, and 'e didn't like staying in Devon, 'cos 'is cousins there were a bit rough like. 'E come up from Exmoor, nice peaceful friendly place it is. But the folk on Exmoor, they didn't like size of 'im; bit scared they was. But then they found out that there wasn't no sheepstealers round about, cattle and sheep was thriving, and 'e didn't 'arm no one. They got quite fond of 'im.

And then farmers' wives they began to put their heads together. "Whatever did the poor girt veller veed on?"

Well, I think they was all quite ready to go and cook a dinner for 'im, but they found they needn't. You see word come up from Yarnton as 'e were fond o' fish,—'e did take and wade out down channel, right out to sea, and all the fishing-boats 'ad to do was to follow 'en. Oh! they come out o' Minehead 'arbour, loaded, they did, all the fishing-boats, right up Bristol way, to Portishead, and 'e'd go and 'e'd wade out there, and water'd come up to 'is armpits, and 'e'd scoop up girt shoals o' fish, and 'twas a wonderful time for the fishing-boats.

Well now, one time, old 'Lijah Crowcombe and 'is crew from the "Dorcas Jane", they'd managed to catch up. Oh! she were a leaky old craft were the "Dorcas Jane", and they was loaded right up, and 'er were a-wallowing in the waves when a storm comes up. Well, all craft ran for it, and they thought they were going down to bottom, when through the storm, and all the wind and the mist, the giant comes a-striding, and 'e picks up "Dorcas Jane", and afore they could say "Thank'ee", 'e puts 'er down quiet and safe-like, in Watchett 'arbour. Then off and away 'e go, back to Dunster.

Well, Dunster folk got quite fond o' 'im arter that, and they'd wait to wave to 'en when 'en came back from the sea. 'E come up along by the river, and 'e'd sit on the 'ill, with 'is feet on either side o' the castle, and wash the mud off 'is legs in the river Laune. Then off and away 'e'd go, on up the 'ill, and folks used to look out of their windows, to wave to 'en, and 'e'd wave back, and there was all the week's washing— dried!

THE GIANT OF GRABBIST: II
THE GIANT AND HAWKRIDGE CHURCH

Well now, the giant, 'e were very 'appy to Exmoor, and then the Old Gentleman, 'e decided 'e'd better come back. 'E didn't like seeing they little thatched churches going up all over the way. So when the folk of 'Awkridge thought they'd build theirselves a church, eight hundred feet up 'tis, the old man didn't like it, and then 'e found giant were 'elping. Ah! so Old Nicky, 'e tried to trip giant up. Giant were coming across by Spire Cross, wi' a load o' girt stones, and 'e tripped, and they went all abroad. Well, giant didn't say nothing, 'e didn't lose 'is temper, as old Nicky 'oped 'e would, and cause a storm. No, 'e just patiently bent, and 'e pick 'em up, one arter another, and 'e put 'em up on 'Awkridge for church. And then 'e came to a girt broken one, and 'e tossed 'en aside into the very wood where the Old Boy were a-sitting, chuckling, and that made 'en go off in a hurry. And 'e picks up the rest of the stones, as weren't no good for church, and 'e laid 'en across the stream, the river Barle it is, and there 'e made Tarr steps.

THE GIANT OF GRABBIST: III
THE WHITSTONES

Well, the giant 'e made up 'is mind as there wasn't room for 'e and old Nicky up on moor, and old Nicky, 'e just about made up 'is mind the same. Now you see, the giant, 'e liked St. Dubricius and all they little churches, so 'e and old Nicky, they got together, Porlock way, and they said they'd have a competition like. They'd each throw a big stone from Bossington Beacon over to Porlock Common, that be four miles, and 'ooever lost 'ud 'ave to leave the place for good and all.

Well, old Nick 'ad first throw and 'is stone, 'e flew out over the four mile, and 'e landed up on Porlock Common. And then, just afore giant were a-going to throw 'is, old Nick, 'e trip 'im up, and giant's stone, 'e fell down about three feet away from where old Nick's was; but 'e didn't go away. No, 'e just trip up old Nick 'isself, and 'e sat on 'en; right down on 'en 'e sat. There's some folks say 'e just smoked a pipe, quiet-like, and old Nick 'e just squirmed round underneath, but no! When giant had finished 'is pipe, then 'e pick up old Nick by 'is tail, and 'e say, "That wasn't a fair throw. We'll throw from Quantock later on. Meantime, you go and cool your head." And 'e toss old Nick up in the air, and 'e throw 'im right out down Channel, out over Porlock Bay, and then 'e smiled to 'isself, and 'e come away over the moor, quite 'appy like, till 'e got to Cottishead Moor, and there 'e found a poor little sucker, as 'ad got 'isself a-zinking in the zogs there, an' 'is little brown mother was a-crying for 'elp pitiful. Well, giant picked the silly little thing out, and 'e rub 'im down very gentle, with 'is girt finger, and 'e put 'en down by 'is little brown mother, and away 'e went.

THE GIANT OF GRABBIST: IV
THE STONES OF BATTLEGORE

Our old giant and old Nick, they did meet arter a while, on the Quantock Hills, up by West Quantock 'twas, and they was to throw their stones, and this time the giant was ready for old Nicky, and afore 'e could do anything, giant 'ad picked up 'is stone, and throwed right over to Battle-gore, six miles away. "Your turn now," 'e say.

Old Nicky were dancing wi' rage, and I think 'e were so cross about 'en, that 'is stone fell down, and the giant's was the furthest off. "Now," says the giant, "'tis your promise to go away from round here, and never come back no more. But as no one don't trust you, I'll make sure." And 'e pick up old Nicky by 'is tail, and 'e wade out down the Severn Channel, till 'e were right out to the sea, 'twere up to 'is armpits. And then 'e give 'im a good swing, three times round 'is 'ead, and let go. Well, I reckon the Old 'un landed somewhere about the West Indies; anyway, 'e get a good long swim back.

'E's back now o' course, but 'e don't shew 'isself in Zummerzet, 'case the giant be about.

I *The Giant of Grabbist and the Dorcas Jane*
Recorded from Ruth L. Tongue, 28 September 1963, as she recalled childhood memories of the tradition in Somerset, 1908–25. Tellers of the tradition were a farmer near Dunster, an Exmoor blacksmith, and a friend from Watchet.
TYPE 701 (variant). MOTIFS: F.531.3.9 [*Giants sit on mountains to wash their feet in a stream*]; F.531.3.1 [*Giant wades the ocean*]; N.812 [*Giant as helper*].
II *Hawkridge Church*
Recorded as above. Heard from an old hunt servant at Exford, from a farm labourer at Wilmersham, and from a thatcher at Porlock.
TYPE ML.5020, MOTIFS: A.977.1 [*Giant responsible for certain stones*].
III and IV *The Whitstones* and *The Stones of Battlegore*
Recorded 1963, heard from the following: John Ash, carter, at East Lucott, 1941; Mr Keal, a farmer, on East Lucott Farm, 1941; Mrs Stenner, cottager, Porlock area, 1944; Walter Badcock, coach driver, Minehead, 1952; Miss Brown of Bessington, 1959.
MOTIFS: F.531.3.2 [*Giant throws a great rock*]; A.977.2 [*Devil throws stones*].
A "sucker" is a young foal, and "zogs" is bogland.
¶ The motif of the friendly giant is not uncommon in English folklore. See, for instance, "Jack the Tinkeard".

THE GIANT WITH SEVEN HEADS [summary]

There was a little boy called Jack, and he went out one day and he met a little bird. And the bird said to him, "Don't go into that wood, or you'll meet the Giant with the Seven Heads." And Jack said, "I'm only looking for rabbits, I don't want a giant with seven heads." And he went a little farther, and met a snake. And the snake said to him, "Don't go into that wood, or you'll meet the Giant with the Seven Heads." And Jack said, "I'm only looking for rabbits, I don't want a giant with seven heads." So he went on further, and he met an owl, and the owl said, "Will you do something for me?" And Jack said, "What is it?" And the owl said, "Take this sword, and go and kill the Giant with Seven Heads." And Jack said, "I'm only looking for rabbits, I don't want a giant with seven heads, but I'll do it if you like." So he took the sword, and went on, and came over the hill, and a great horse passed, sixty feet high, and then it came back with a seven-headed giant riding it. And something called, "Jack! Jack!", and it was the little bird that had spoken to him first. And it called, "Jack! Jack! Take my wing." And Jack fetched its wing. Then it said, "Draw your sword!" So Jack drew the sword, and at once turned into a bird, and he flew up and cut off one of the giant's heads, and flew away before the giant could catch him. And so he went on until he had cut off all the giant's heads. And as the last head fell off, the Giant vanished, and Jack's long-lost brother stood in his place. And his brother thanked him, and Jack said, "Go off and tell them at home, because I've still got to catch my rabbits."

School of Scottish Studies, Hamish Henderson, from Jimmy McPhee (14), heard from his grannie.

MOTIFS: B.143.1 [*Bird gives warning*]; B.521 [*Animal warns of fatal danger*]; B.500 [*Magic power from animals*]; F.531.1.2.2 [*Many-headed giant*]; D.532 [*Transformation by putting on feather of helpful animal*]; D.711 [*Disenchantment by decapitation*].

¶ The theme of disenchantment brings this tale nearer to "The Laidly Worm" or "The Ugly Brother", than to the usual giant-killing type. It is one of our many native stories which is in a type of its own, and cannot be forced into any of the Aarne–Thompson types without doing violence to it.

THE GIANT-KILLER [Shetland]

A little boy able to drive the kine was very hungry. But his mother said there was no meal in the house. He bid her shake all the "bogis" and pocks and see if she could get any. And she did so and got as much as baked him a little "bruni". She set it on the hearth-stone against a peat to fire. He kept turning it, and at last as he set it down it rolled on its edge and rolled over the floor, and out the door, and on and on till it came to a little hole in a knoll into which it fell. The boy observed this and saw some smoke coming up the hole, so he began to dig down till he came.... Here was a great big blind "gay-kerl" (or kerl-wife) sitting sifting meal. So he took off his "breeks" and jacket, and tied about the foot of them and packed them full of meal and went home to his mother with it. Then he came back again with the sack for more. But at last the "gay-kerl" began to miss her meal and she said, "If only I kyent wha is stealin my meal!" At last as she moved her hand through the sieve she caught him by the little finger. She said, "Here's da teef it's teen my meal!" After this the giant came in and said:

"Fi fum fi fen
I fin da eir

266

o a eartli man
An bi hi whik
Ir bi hi did
A'll he his hid
Wi may supir brid."

But she said, "Yah, what fins du da eir o bit a been at a kra cam an slipped in da lum ita da fire?" She asked the boy, if he had caught her stealing his meal what would he have done to her. He said he would have bound her to the stoop of the handmill and fed her till she was so fat that she could neither see nor hear, and then he would have boiled and eaten her. She said, "As du wid a dun ta me, se'ill I du ta dee." So she bound him to the stoop of the mill, and fed him up till he was very fat. One day he said that he was beginning to lose his sight and hearing. So she hung up a cauldron of water over the fire, and at last asked the boy to go and listen if it were boiling. He said "Na, he was deaf, she would better listen herself." She went and laid her ear to the cauldron and he came up behind her and shoved her into it. When the giant came home he laid her up in a plate for the giant to eat. And the giant ate her all up till he came to the rump-bone, and worried upon it, and died. So the boy robbed the house of meal and silver plate and all that was in it, and he and his mother had no lack after that.

Shetland Folk-Book, III, p. 7. (Told by U. J. and other persons, also by K. S.)
TYPE 1121. MOTIFS: D.1313.1.2 [*Magic rolling cake indicates road*]; G.610 [*Theft from ogre*]; G.84 [*Fee-fi-fo-fum*]; G.82 [*Cannibal fattens victim*]; G.526 [*Ogre deceived by feigned ignorance of hero*]; G.512.3.2.1 [*Ogre's wife burned in her own oven*].

THE GIPSY WOMAN

See "Tom Tit Tot".

THE GIRL WHO FETCHED WATER
IN A RIDDLE

One day a little girl took a riddle to a well to fetch some water, but the water ran out of the riddle as fast as she poured it in. Two little robinets who were sitting on a hedge close by watched her as they twittered their songs. The birds made such a noise that the girl thought they were laughing at her, so she said, "Silly robins, how can I carry water in a riddle?"

The robinets said:

> "Stuff your riddle with moss,
> And daub it with clay,
> And carry your water
> Right away."

But the little girl said, "I shan't, you ugly birds," and dipped her riddle into the well again. The water ran out of the riddle again, but the third time the little girl did as the robinets had told her, when the riddle held the water, and the robinets were pleased.

S. O. Addy, *Household Tales and Popular Remains*, p. 40, from Calver, Derbyshire. TYPE 1180 (shortened version of 440). MOTIFS: H.1023.2.0.1 [*Carrying water in sieve: sieve filled with moss*]; B.122.1 [*Bird as adviser*].

See "The Prince Paddock".

¶ The legend is quoted by Reginald Scot:
"Leonardo Vairus saith that there was a praier extant, whereby might be carried in a sieve, water, or other liquor; I think it was Clam claie; which a crow taught a maid, that was promised a cake of a great quantitie, as might be kneded of as much floure as she could wet with the water that she brought in a sieve, and by that meanes she clam'd it with claie, and brought in so much water, as whereby she had a great cake, and so beguiled the sisters, etc. And this tale I heard among my grandam's maides."

THE GIRL WHO WENT THROUGH FIRE, WATER, AND THE GOLDEN GATE

A certain man and his wife had an only child and she was a girl. This girl was beloved by her father, but hated by her mother. When the girl was about eight years old her father died, and then the mother thought she would revenge herself upon the girl. So she made her do all the hard work in the house, and gave her many cruel tasks.

One day the mother sent the child to fetch something that lay beyond three fields that were bewitched. When the child drew near to the first field she saw that it was covered with fire, and she stood still at the edge of the field and dare not cross over it. As she stood there trembling with fear and weeping, a beautiful fairy appeared to her and said, "Fear not, for I will help thee."

Now the fairy carried a wand in her hand, which she waved across the field of fire, so that it ceased to burn, and the child went over. But after she had gone a little further on her way she came to a field which was covered with water, and could not get across. Then the beautiful fairy came near to her again as she wept, and waved her wand over the water, which rolled back on either side, so that she walked straight through the midst. So she went on her way again until she came to a house with a golden gate, which she could not open or get through. Then, as before, the fairy came with her wand and opened the gate.

And when she had opened the gate, she said to the child, "Wilt thou leave thy cruel mother and come and live with me?" And the child answered, "Yea, I will live with you, for you are so good and beautiful." So she left her cruel mother, and went to live with the good fairy in the house with the golden gate.

S. O. Addy, *Household Tales*, p. 28.

TYPE 510 (distant variant). MOTIFS: S.31 [*Cruel stepmother*]; N.815 [*Fairy as helper*]. ¶ This story is a poor and uneventful one. Possibly an improvised tale told by a nurse or parent and recounted to Addy. It bears no sign of having been passed from mouth to mouth.

THE GLASS BALL [summary]

There was once a woman who gave to each of her daughters a beautiful glass ball. The girls loved their balls, but one day while they were playing with them, one tossed her ball over the wall into the next garden. This garden belonged to a fox, an unsociable creature, who would never talk to his neighbours.

The girl was very much afraid of the fox, but she went to his door and knocked, and the fox came to the door, and said she should have her ball back if she would serve as his housekeeper for one year.

Unwillingly she agreed, but the fox made her very comfortable and happy until one day he said to her, "I am going away, and until I come back, there are five things you must not do. You must not wash up the dishes, sweep the floor, dust the chairs, look into the cupboard, nor look under my bed."

The girl promised, but when the fox had gone, she began to wonder why he had given her these strange orders. Soon she washed up all the dishes, to see what would happen, and at once a great bag of copper fell down in front of her. Then she swept the floor, and down fell a great bag of silver. So then she dusted the chairs, and down came a bag full of gold. She looked in the cupboard, and there was her glass ball! At last she went upstairs, and under the fox's bed lay the fox! Terrified, she ran downstairs, and out of the house, until she came to a lane. At the top of the lane she met a horse, and said to it,

"Horse of mine, horse of mine,
If you meet a man of mine,
Don't say that I've passed by."

And the horse said, "I will not."

Farther on she met first a cow, then a mule, then a dog, and a cat, and an owl, and to each of them she said the same thing, and they gave her the same reply.

The fox was following close behind and he said to the horse,

> "Horse of mine, horse of mine,
> Hast thou met a maid of mine?"

And the horse said, "She's just passed by."

The cow, the mule, the dog, the cat, and the owl all gave the same answer.

"Which way did she go?" said the fox to the owl.

"You must go over that gate, and across the field, and behind the wood you will find her," replied the owl.

So the fox ran off, but neither he nor the girl, nor the glass ball have ever been heard of since.

S. O. Addy, *Household Tales*, p. 18.

TYPE 480 (variant). MOTIFS: N.777 [*Pursuit of dropped ball leads to adventures*]; G.211.2.3 [*Witch in form of fox*]; G.204 [*Girl in service of witch*]; C.836 [*Tabu: disobedience*].

¶ The tale begins like "The Golden Ball" or "The Maid Freed from the Gallows", but continues with a version of "The Old Witch", in which the girl asks one creature after another to hide her, in this case unavailingly. It is not clear in this story whether the fox caught the girl or not; presumably he did.

THE GLASS HOUSE

There was a little girl selling oranges, and she went to a lady's house, which was made of glass. It had glass doors, and everything was glass. The girl asked her if she would purchase of her oranges, and the lady said she would have them all if her mother would let her come and be her little servant. So her mother let her go. One day she was cleaning the glass window, when it broke. Then she broke the floor, and when her mistress went to change her dress, the little girl ran outside to the gooseberry tree, and she said:

> "Gooseberry tree, gooseberry tree, hide me,
> For fear my mistress should find me,
> For if she does, she'll break my bones,
> And bury me under the marble stones."

And the gooseberry tree said, "Go to the butcher's." And when she got to the butcher's, she said:

"Butcher, butcher, hide me,
For fear my mistress should find me,
For if she does, she'll break my bones,
And bury me under the marble stones."

But the butcher said, "Go to the baker," and when she got there, she said:

"Baker, baker, hide me,
For fear my mistress should find me,
For if she does, she'll break my bones,
And bury me under the marble stones."

And the baker said, "Get into this bread box." And she got in, and he nailed it up. While she was at the baker's her mistress had been to the gooseberry tree, and it told her it had sent the little girl to the butcher.

When her mistress got to the butcher's, he said he had sent her to the baker's. So she went to the baker's, and he told her to go away; but she said she would let his house be searched, and she commenced. But when she came to the box that was nailed she shivered, and she made him undo the nails, and out came the girl. So her mistress took her with her, and as they were crossing a river the girl's mistress was leaning over a bridge, when the girl gave her a push, and she fell over and was drowned. And the little girl went singing merrily till she got to the glass house, and kept it as her own.

Norton Collection, II, p. 24. Told by Sarah Ellen Potter, aged 14, daughter of Mr George Potter of Castleton, Derbyshire, 1901. S. O. Addy, *Derbyshire Folk-Lore*, pp. 358–9. *Memorials of Old Derbyshire*, 1907.
TYPE 480 (half of the tale only), MOTIFS: F.771.1.6.2 [*Glass house*]; G.276 [*Escape from witch*].
¶ See "The Old Witch" and "The Glass Ball".

THE GLASS MOUNTAIN

A very long time back, I don't know how long, there was a woman who lived in a lone cottage with her three daughters. Well, one evening when it was getting on to dusk, a man knocked at the door, and asked if he could not spend the night there, as he had come a long way, and no other shelter was near at hand. The woman did not much like taking a stranger in, but hers was the only house for miles round, so she could not very well turn him away; and the end of it was she let him lie down by the fire. Then, when morning came, nothing would do for him but he must have the youngest of the three daughters for his wife; and the lass, she liked his looks well enough, so it was settled that way. They were married, and he took her off home with him. A fine, big place she found his house was, with everything in it anybody could want, so she thought she should do well enough there. But there was just one thing that was out of the way queer. When the grey of night-time began to come on, the man said to her. "Now you have got to choose which way it is to be: I must take the shape of a bull either by day or by night, one or the other; how will you have it?"

"You shall be a bull by day, and a man by night," the girl answered, and so it always was. At sunrise he turned into a bull, then at sundown he was a man again.

Well, use is everything, so after a while his wife got to think as much of him as if he had been like other folks. However, when a year had gone by, and she was likely to have a bairn, she began to think long of seeing her mother and sisters again, and asked her husband to let her go home to them for her confinement. He did not like that: he was quite against it, for fear she should let out what he was. "If you ever opened your mouth to any one about what you know, ill-luck would come of it," he said.

But still she hankered after her mother, and begged so hard that, being as she was, he could not deny her, and she got her own way.

Well, that time, everything went as right as it could be. The child was a boy, and fine and proud she was when her husband came to see it. The only trouble she had was that her mother and sisters were as curious as curious to find out why he never came to see her by daylight; and they had no end to their questions. So at last, when she was strong again, she was glad to go away home with him.

Still, the year after, the same thing happened again. She took such a longing to be nursed by her mother when the next bairn was to be born, that, willing or not, her husband had to let her have her liking. "But mind," he said, "we shall have the blackest of trouble if you ever tell what you know of me." Then she promised by all that was good to keep a quiet tongue about him: and she held to her word. Whenever her mother and sisters began to wonder and to ask, she put them off with one thing or another, so that when she took her second boy home with her she left them no wiser than they were before.

Well, the next year, another child was coming, and then she had just the same tale to her husband: she must go back to her mother, she could not bide away from her.

"If you will, why you will," said the man, "but remember what will come of it if you speak;" and then, though it went sorely against him, he let her and the children go.

This time, do as she would, her mother and sisters gave her no peace; they were fairly bursting with curiousness to know the far-end of her husband's comings and goings; and at last, on the day her third boy was born, they plagued her so much with their inquisitiveness that she could not hold out, and just told them the truth of it. Well, when evening drew on, she thought her husband would be coming to see the child, but the sunset went by, and the dusk went by, and the night went by, without a sight or sound of him. Then, after that, days and days slipped past, but still he stayed away.

When she was up and about again, she grew that sick of waiting and waiting, that she took her bairns with her, and set off to seek him. . . (Here the story is defective. I believe the wife returned to her husband's house, and finding it desolate, wandered out into the world in search of him, meeting with adventures analogous to those which befell the heroine of the Leitrim legend. My memory takes up the tale at the point where she is endeavouring to release her husband from the spell which prevents him recognizing her.)

So she sat down outside his door, combing her hair, and sang:

> "Bare bull of Orange, return to me,
> For three fine babes I have borne to thee,
> And climbed a glass hill for thee,
> Bare bull of Orange, return to me."

But his stepmother had given him a sleeping-drink, so he never heard her. Then on the second night she came to his door again, and sat combing her hair, and sang:

> "Bare bull of Orange, return to me,
> For three fine babes I have borne to thee,
> And climbed a glass hill for thee,
> Bare bull of Orange, return to me."

And this time he turned in his bed, and groaned, but his stepmother's sleeping-drink hindered him knowing that he heard his wife's voice. . . Then, on the third night, it was her last chance, and she sat outside the threshold of his door, and combed her hair and sang:

> "Bare bull of Orange, return to me,
> For three fine babes I have borne to thee,
> And climbed a glass hill for thee,
> Bare bull of Orange, return to me."

And he started up, and opened his chamber door; and so the stepmother's spells were all broken. He had his shape again, like other men, and they lived with their three children in peace and quietness ever after.

Norton Collection, I, pp. 276–7, from *Folk-Lore*, IV (1893), pp. 322–5. Related to Mabel Peacock when a child, by a servant from Brigg, Lincs., where there was an Irish colony.

Part of this has been forgotten. It must have been the same as "The Glass Mountains".

TYPE 425, MOTIFS: B.640.1 [*Marriage to a beast by day and a man by night*]; C.421 (*Tabu: revealing secret of supernatural husband*); C.932 [*Loss of husband for breaking tabu*]; H.1385.4 [*Quest for vanished husband*]; H.1114 [*Task: climbing glass mountain*]; D.2003.1 [*Husband magically forgets wife*]; D.2006.1 [*Forgotten wife reawakens husband's memory*]; D.791.2.2 [*Disenchantment can be done by wife*].

See also "The Black Bull of Norroway", "The Brown Bull of Ringlewood", "The Glass Mountains", "The Red Bull of Norroway", "The Three Feathers".

¶ American versions given in the *JAFL* are "The Louse Skin" and "Whiteberry Whittington".

THE GLASS MOUNTAINS

Long ago there was a young gentleman, a beautiful young man, he got married to a young lady. He was enchanted. He said to her, "Which would you rather I would be, a man at night and a bull in the daytime, or a bull at night and a man in the daytime?" She said, "I would rather have you a man at night and a bull in the day."

When they were one year married there was a young son born for them, and he told her, if anything would happen the child, not to cry one tear. So a big black dog came down the chimney and took the child out of her arms, and brought it with him. She never shed a tear.

The next year there was another boy born for them. Her husband told her, if anything would happen the second child, not to shed a tear. The black dog came a second time, and brought the other child with him. She never shed a tear.

The third year there was a daughter born for them. The husband told her, "If anything happens to this child, if you shed one tear, you will never see me again."

The black dog came down the chimney and took the daughter with him out of her mother's arms. The mother shed one tear, and her husband never returned. She was grieved and heart-broken, and she said she would go in search of her husband.

The first day she travelled a long journey, and she came to a little house. There was only an old man and woman and a little boy in the house. She asked lodging for the night, so they gave her lodging. In the morning, when she was going away, the little boy gave her a comb. He told her to mind it, that any person who combed their hair with it would be the nicest person in the world.

The next day, late in the evening, she came to another little house. There was an old man and woman and a little boy in it. She asked lodging for the night. She got it. The next morning, when she was going away, the little boy gave her a scissors, and he said, "Mind this, the worst clothes you will cut with this will become the nicest in the world."

The next day, late in the evening, she came to another little house, at the foot of the Glass Mountains. There was an old man and woman and a pretty little girl. She was blind of one eye. She asked lodging for the night. The old man said he would make a pair of glass slippers for her, if she would stop seven years with him, and that she could climb the Glass Mountains. The old man told her that her husband was living at the back of the Glass Mountains, and that he was married to another lady, and that all his enchantments were gone at the end of the seven years.

When she was going away the little girl gave her an egg, and told her when she would break it there would come four horses and a carriage out of it. So she climbed the Glass Mountains. There was a beautiful castle at the back of them. She walked about the avenue, and the lady came out and asked her what she wanted. She said she was hungry. She brought her in and gave her breakfast.

She took out the comb, and said that any person that would comb their hair with that would be the nicest person in the world, and if she let her sleep one night with her husband, she would give her the comb. So she said she would.

So night came on, and when her husband went to bed she gave him a drink and put sleeping-drops on it, so she let her to bed with him. She said:

"Three babes I bore for thee,
Three basin-full of tears
I shed for thee.
Seven long years I spent
Climbing up the glass mountains,
And my bonny bull of oranges,
Will you turn to me?"

She continued saying this the whole night, but he was so fast asleep he never found her.

She had to rise early before he awoke, and the mistress hid her until the gentleman went away shooting. She took out the scissors, and told her anything she would cut with that would be the nicest thing in the world, and she would give it to her if she would let her sleep another night with her husband. She said she would. So she gave him a drink this next night, and put sleeping-drops on it, so she let her sleep with her husband the second night. She said:

"Three babes I bore for thee,
Three basin-full of tears
I shed for thee.

18-2

> Seven long years I spent
> Climbing up the glass mountains,
> And my bonny bull of oranges,
> Will you turn to me?"

He was so fast asleep that he never found her. She had to rise early before he awoke. The mistress hid her. The gentleman arose and went away shooting. There was another young gentleman that slept in the next bedroom to them. He said to the gentleman next day, "There is a ghost in your bedroom, did you not hear it? I have heard it say for the last two nights:

> 'Three babes I bore for thee,
> Three basin-full of tears
> I shed for thee.
> Seven long years I spent
> Climbing up the glass mountains,
> And my bonny bull of oranges,
> Will you turn to me?'

"I never slept a wink for the last two nights but listening to it."

The gentleman said, "My wife gave me a drink for the last two nights, it made me sick."

The other gentleman said to him, "Do not take that drink to-night, but try and stop awake until you see would you find it."

The woman took out the egg, and broke it, and there came a coach and four horses out of it. She said she would give it to her if she would let her sleep the third night with her husband. She said she would. When her husband went to bed she brought him a draught with sleeping-drops on it. He said he would not drink it until she would bring him a cut of bread. She went for the bread, and he threw the drink in the grate, and he let on he was fast asleep. She let the woman go to bed with him. She said again:

> "Three babes I bore for thee,
> Three basin-full of tears
> I shed for thee.
> Seven long years I spent
> Climbing up the glass mountains,
> And my bonny bull of oranges,
> Will you turn to me?"

The gentleman did not speak for a long time; at last he turned to her and asked her was she his first wife, and she said, "Yes." He told her that they were her three children that were in the three little houses; and that it was the one tear that she dropped that blinded the little girl's eye. He told her when she would rise in the morning, and take breakfast, to go away to the foot of the Glass Mountains, and that he would be there as soon as her, and so he was. They two crossed the Glass Mountains, and brought their three children home to their own castle, and lived happy ever afterwards.

Norton Collection, I, p. 280 (*Folk-Lore*, IV, 1893, pp. 190–4).

TYPE 425 A. MOTIFS: B.640.1 [*Marriage to beast by day, man by night*]; C.32 [*Tabu: offending supernatural husband*]; R.10.3 [*Children abducted*]; C.482 [*Tabu: weeping*]; C.932 [*Loss of husband by breaking tabu*]; H.1385.4 [*Quest for lost husband*]; D.791.1.1 [*Disenchantment after seven years*]; H.1114 [*Climbing glass mountain*]; D.2006.1.4 [*Sale of bed*].

❡ Unusual features in this version are the children of the heroine, who give her the necessary magic gifts, and the blinding of her little daughter by the one tear she shed. Presumably the black dog who carried off the children was her husband in another form.

THE GOBBORN SEER

Once there was a man, Gobborn Seer, and he had a son called Jack.

One day he sent him out to sell a sheep-skin, and Gobborn said, "You must bring me back the skin and the value of it as well."

So Jack started, but he could not find any who would leave him the skin and give him its price too. So he came home discouraged.

But Gobborn Seer said, "Never mind, you must take another turn at it tomorrow."

So he tried again, and nobody wished to buy the skin on those terms.

When he came home his father said, "You must go and try your luck to-morrow," and the third day it seemed as if it would be the same thing over again. And he had half a mind not to go back at all, his father would be so vexed. As he came to a bridge, like the Creek Road out yonder, he leaned on the parapet thinking of his trouble, and that perhaps it would be foolish to run away from home, but he could not tell which to do; when he saw a girl washing her clothes on the bank below. She looked up and said, "If it may be no offence asking, what is it you feel so badly about?"

"My father has given me this skin, and I am to fetch it back and the price of it beside."

"Is that all? Give it here, and it's easy done."

So the girl washed the skin in the stream, took the wool from it, and paid him the value of it, and gave him the skin to carry back.

His father was well pleased, and said to Jack, "That was a witty woman; she would make you a good wife. Do you think you could tell her again?"

Jack thought he could, so his father told him to go by-and-by to the bridge, and see if she was there, and if so bid her come home to take tea with them.

And sure enough Jack spied her and told her how his old father had a wish to meet her, and would she be pleased to drink tea with them.

The girl thanked him kindly, and said she could come the next day; she was too busy at the moment.

"All the better," said Jack, "I'll have time to make ready."

So when she came, Gobborn Seer could see she was a witty woman, and he asked her if she would marry his Jack. She said, "Yes," and they were married.

Not long after, Jack's father told him he must come with him and build the finest castle that ever was seen, for a king who wished to outdo all others by his wonderful castle.

And as they went to lay the foundation-stone, Gobborn Seer said to Jack, "Can't you shorten the way for me?"

But Jack looked ahead and there was a long road before them, and he said, "I don't see, father, how I could break a bit off."

"You're no good to me then, and had best be off home."

So poor Jack turned back, and when he came in, his wife said, "Why, how's this you've come alone?" and he told her what his father had said, and his answer.

"You stupid," said his witty wife, "if you had told a tale you would have shortened the road! Now listen till I tell you a story, and then catch up with Gobborn Seer and begin it at once. He will like hearing it, and by the time you are done you will have reached the foundation-stone."

So Jack sweated and overtook his father. Gobborn Seer said never a word, but Jack began his story, and the road was shortened as his wife had said.

When they came to the end of their journey, they started building of this castle which was to outshine all others. Now the wife had advised them to be intimate with the servants, and so they did as she said, and it was "Good morning" and "Good day to you" as they passed in and out.

Now, at the end of a twelvemonth, Gobborn, the wise man, had built such a castle thousands were gathered to admire it.

And the king said: "The castle is done. I shall return to-morrow and pay you all."

"I have just a ceiling to finish in an upper lobby," said Gobborn, "and then it wants nothing."

But after the king was gone off the housekeeper sent for Gobborn and Jack, and told them that she had watched for a chance to warn them, for the king was so afraid they should carry their art away and build some other king as fine a castle, he meant to take their lives on the morrow.

Gobborn told Jack to keep a good heart, and they would come off all right.

When the king had come back, Gobborn told him he had been unable to complete the job for lack of a tool left at home, and he should like to send Jack after it.

"No, no," said the king, "cannot one of the men do the errand?"

"No, they could not make themselves understood," said the Seer, "but Jack could do the errand."

"You and your son stop here. But how will it do if I send my own son?"

"That will do."

So Gobborn sent by him a message to Jack's wife, "Give him *Crooked and Straight!*"

Now there was a little hole in the wall rather high up, and Jack's wife tried to reach up into a chest there after "crooked and straight", but at last she asked the king's son to help her, because his arms were longest.

But when he was leaning over the chest she caught him by the two heels, and threw him into the chest, and fastened it down. So there he was, both "crooked and straight!"

Then he begged for pen and ink, which she brought him, but he was not allowed out, and holes were bored that he might breathe.

When his letter came, telling his father he was to be let free when Gobborn and Jack were safe home, the king saw he must settle for his building, and let them come away.

As they left, Gobborn told him: Now that Jack was done with this work, he should soon build a castle for his witty wife far superior to the king's, which he did, and they lived there happily ever after.

Jacobs, *More English Fairy Tales*, p. 54.
TYPE 875D (variant). MOTIFS: H.586.3 [*Shortening the way*]; H.588 [*Enigmatic counsels of father*].
¶ Collected by Mrs Gomme from an old woman at Deptford. "Gobborn Seer" comes from the Irish "Goban Saor", a travelling carpenter, a godlike character somewhat in the tradition of Wayland Smith. The tale is to be found in Ireland. "The Peasant's Wise Daughter", to which this tale bears some resemblance, occurs in Kennedy's *Fireside Stories*. A wise wife, who compensates for her husband's lack of intelligence, is to be found in "A Pottle of Brains".

GOBLIN COMBE

There was a parcel of children, and they was a-picking primroses, see, and one poor little dear her wandered away on her lone self, right down into Goblin Combe. She were only a little trot, see, and didn't know no better. Well, when she do find she's a-lost she cries, and the tears do run down her dear little face, and dap on her pinafore like summer rain, and she do throw her little self a-down in her grief, and the primroses, they knocks against a rock. Then the rock opens, and there's the fairises, all come to comfort her tears. They do give her a gold ball, and they lead the dear little soul safe home—on account she was carrying primroses, see.

Well, 'twas the wonder of the village, and the conjuror, he got the notion he'd get his fistes on more than one gold ball when next the fairises opened the hill. So he do pick a bunch of primroses, and he go on up Goblin Combe, and he was glad enough to get to the rock, after all he see and hear on the way up. Well, 'twasn't the right day, nor the right number of primroses, and he wasn't no dear little soul—*so they took him!*

Primroses, culver-keys, and forget-me-nots, are all magic spring worts, but you have to have the right number in the bunch.

Collected by Ruth L. Tongue, who heard the account told in chorus by two old ladies from Clevedon, Somerset, in 1945. Published in *Folktales of England*.
TYPE 503 (variant). MOTIFS: F.211.2 [*Fairyland entrance under a stone*]; J.2415 [*Foolish imitation of a lucky man*].
¶ The latter motif is prominent in type 503, *The Gifts of the Little People*, widely reported from northern Europe, with scattered examples from the New World, and as far east as Japan. See nos. 36, 37 in *Folktales of Japan*.
Primroses and cowslips are both fairy flowers in English country tradition.
See "The Miser on the Gump" (B, Fairies).

THE GOLDEN BALL

There were two lasses, daughters of one mother, and as they came from the fair, they saw a right bonny young man stand at the house-door before them. They never saw such a bonny man before. He had gold on his cap, gold on his finger, gold on his neck, a red-gold watch-chain—eh! but he had brass. He had a golden ball in each hand. He gave a ball to each lass, and she was to keep it, and if she lost it, she was to be hanged. One of the lasses, 'twas the youngest, lost her ball. I'll tell thee how. She was by a park-paling, and she was tossing her ball, and it went up, and up, and up, till it went fair over the paling; and when she climbed up to look, the ball ran along the green grass, and it went right forward to the door of the house, and the ball went in and she saw it no more.

So she was taken away to be hanged by the neck till she was dead because she'd lost her ball.

But she had a sweetheart, and he said he would go and get the ball. So he went to the park-gate, but 'twas shut; so he climbed the hedge, and when he got to the top of the hedge, an old woman rose up out of the dyke before him, and said, if he wanted to get the ball, he must sleep three nights in the house. He said he would.

Then he went up into the house, and looked for the ball, but could not find it. Night came on, and he heard bogles move in the courtyard; so he looked out of the window, and the yard was full of them.

Presently he heard steps coming upstairs. He hid behind the door, and was as still as a mouse. Then in came a big giant five times as tall as he, and the giant looked round but did not see the lad, so he went to the window and bowed to look out; and as he bowed on his elbows to see the bogles in the yard, the lad stepped behind him, and with one blow of his sword he cut him in twain, so that the top part of him fell in the yard, and the bottom part stood looking out of the window.

There was a great cry from the bogles when they saw half the giant come tumbling down to them, and they called out, "There comes half our master, give us the other half."

So the lad said, "It's no use of thee, thou pair of legs, standing alone at the window, as thou hast no eye to see with, so go join thy brother"; and he cast the lower part of the giant after the top part. Now when the bogles had gotten all the giant they were quiet.

Next night the lad was at the house again, and now a second giant came in at the door, and as he came in the lad cut him in twain, but the legs walked on to the chimney, and went up them. "Go, get thee after thy legs," said the lad to the head, and he cast the head up the chimney too.

The third night the lad got into bed, and he heard the bogles striving under the bed, and they had the ball there, and they were casting it to and fro.

Now one of them has his leg thrust out from under bed, so the lad brings his sword down and cuts it off. Then another thrusts his arm out at the other side of the bed, and the lad cuts that off. So at last he had maimed them all, and they all went crying and wailing off, and forgot the ball, but he took it from under the bed, and went to seek his true love.

Now the lass was taken to York to be hanged; she was brought out on the scaffold, and the hangman said, "Now, lass, thou must hang by the neck till thou be'st dead." But she cried out:

> "Stop, stop, I think I see my mother coming!
> Oh, mother, hast brought my golden ball
> And come to set me free?"

> "I've neither brought thy golden ball
> Nor come to set thee free,
> But I have come to see thee hung
> Upon this gallows-tree."

Then the hangman said, "Now, lass, say thy prayers, for thou must die."

"Stop, stop, I think I see my father coming!
Oh, father, hast brought my golden ball
And come to set me free?"

"I've neither brought thy golden ball
Nor come to set thee free.
But I have come to see thee hung
Upon this gallows-tree."

Then the hangman said, "Hast thee done thy prayers? Now, lass, put thy head into the noose."

But she answered, "Stop, stop, I think I see my brother coming." And again she sang, and then she thought she saw her sister coming, then her uncle, then her aunt, then her cousin; but after this the hangman said, "I will stop no longer, thou'rt making game of me. Thou must be hung at once."

But now she saw her sweetheart coming through the crowd, and he held over his head in the air her own golden ball; so she said:

"Stop, stop, I see my sweetheart coming!
Sweetheart, hast brought my golden ball,
And come to set me free?"

"Aye, I have brought thy golden ball,
And come to set thee free,
I have not come to see thee hung
Upon this gallows-tree."

And he took her home, and they lived happy ever after.

Jacobs, *More English Fairy Tales*, p. 12. Contributed by Baring-Gould to the first edition of Henderson's *Folk-Lore of the Northern Counties*.

TYPE 326A*. MOTIFS: C.920 [*Death for breaking tabu*]; N.777 [*Dropped ball leads to adventures when recovery attempted*]; H.1411 [*Fear test: staying in haunted house*]; F.771.4.1 [*Castle inhabited by ogres*]; R.161.4 [*Lover rescues his lady from the gallows*].
¶ This appears to be a mixture of type 326A, a haunted house disenchanted by a man sleeping in it for a certain time, and the folk-song "A Maid Freed from the Gallows". The notion connecting the two has been often examined, for instance by M. Damant in his notes on "The Three Golden Balls", *Folklore*, VI, pp. 305–8, but the last word has probably been said by Tristram E. Coffin in "The Golden Ball and the Hangman's Tree", *Folklore International*, U.S.A. (1967), pp. 23–8. He established the unity of the theme.

THE GOLDEN CUP

There was once a lady who had one little daughter, and this daughter had a beautiful golden cup. Now one day the lady was going out to visit her friends, and her little daughter asked if she might go too. Her mother said, "No, dear, I cannot take you now, but you can have your golden cup to play with until I come back."

When the mother had gone the little girl said to the maid, "Fetch me my golden cup out of the cupboard."

The maid said, "I can't fetch it now, I am too busy."

But the little girl kept asking for the cup again and again, until at last the maid grew angry, and said, "If you ask for it again I'll cut your head off."

But the little girl asked for the cup once more, and thereupon the maid took her into the cellar, got the hatchet, and cut her head off. Then she got a pickaxe and a spade, and dug a hole, and buried the little girl under one of the stone flags in the cellar.

When the mother came back in the evening, she said, "Where's baby?"

The maid said, "I have let her go out for a walk."

"Then go and seek her," said the mother.

The maid went out, and when she came back she said, "I have looked for her everywhere and cannot find her."

Then the mother was deeply grieved, and she sat up all that night, and all the next night. On the third night as she sat alone and wide awake she heard the voice of her daughter outside the door saying, "Can I have my golden cup?"

The mother opened the door, and when her daughter had repeated the question three times she saw her spirit, but the spirit vanished at once, and she never saw it more.

S. O. Addy, *Household Tales*, p. 42, from Eckington in Derbyshire.
TYPE 720 (variant). MOTIFS: S.133 [*Murder by beheading*]; E.225 [*Ghost of murdered child*].

¶ This is a very distant variant of a far-flung story, "The Juniper Tree". The murderess here is a servant, not the mother, and the child's spirit does not take a bird form as in the full version.

See "The Cruel Stepmother and her little Daughter", "Lemon, Apple and Orange", "Little Rosy", "The Milk-White Doo", "The Murderous Mother", "My Mama did kill me", "Orange and Lemon", "The Rose Tree", "The Satin Frock", "The Story of Orange".

THE GOODMAN OF WASTNESS AND THE SELKIE

The goodman of Wastness was well-to-do, had his farm well-stocked, and was a good-looking and well-favoured man. And though many braw lasses in the island had set their caps at him, he was not to be caught. So the young lasses began to treat him with contempt, regarding him as an old young man who was deliberately committing the unpardonable sin of celibacy. He did not trouble his head much about the lasses, and when urged by his friends to take a wife, he said, "Women were like many another thing in this weary world, only sent for a trial to man; and I have trials enouch without being tried by a wife. If that ould fool Adam had not been bewitched by his wife, he might have been a happy man in the yard of Edin to this day." The old wife of Longer, who heard him make this speech, said to him, "Take doo heed de sell, doo'll may be de sell bewitched some day." "Ay," quoth he, "that will be when doo walks dry shod frae the Alters o' Seenie to dae Boar of Papa."

Well, it happened one day that the goodman of Wastness was down on the ebb [that portion of the shore left dry at low water] when he saw at a little distance a number of selkie folk on a flat rock. Some were lying sunning themselves, while others jumped and played about in great glee. They were all naked, and had skins as white as his own. The rock on which they sported had deep water on its seaward side, and on its shore side a shallow pool.

The goodman of Wastness crept unseen till he got to the edge of the shallow pool; he then rose and dashed through the pool to the rock on its other side. The alarmed selkie folk seized their seal skins, and, in mad haste, jumped into the sea. Quick as they were, the goodman was also quick, and he seized one of the skins belonging to an unfortunate damsel, who in terror of flight neglected to clutch it as she sprang into the water.

The selkie folk swam out a little distance, then turning, set up their heads and gazed at the goodman. He noticed that one of them had not the appearance of seals like the rest. He then took the captured skin under his arm, and made for home, but before he got out of the ebb, he heard a most doleful sound of weeping and lamentation behind him. He turned to see a fair woman following him. It was that one of the selkie folk whose seal skin he had taken. She was a pitiful sight; sobbing in bitter grief, holding out both hands in eager supplication, while the big tears followed each other down her fair face. And ever and anon she cried out, "O bonnie man! if there's onie mercy i' thee human breast, gae back me skin! I cinno', cinno', cinno', live i' the sea without it. I cinno', cinno', cinno', bide among me ain folk without me ain seal skin. Oh, pity a peur distressed, forlorn lass, gin doo wad ever hope for mercy theesel'!" The goodman was not too soft-hearted, yet he could not help pitying her in her doleful plight. And with his pity came the softer passion of love. His heart that never loved women before was conquered by the sea-nymph's beauty. So, after a good deal of higgling and plenty of love-making, he wrung from the sea-lass a reluctant consent to live with him as his wife. She chose this as the least of two evils. Without the skin she could not live in the sea, and he absolutely refused to give up the skin.

So the sea-lass went with the goodman and stayed with him for many days, being a thrifty, frugal, and kindly goodwife.

She bore her goodman seven children, four boys and three lasses, and there were not bonnier lasses or statelier boys in all the isle. And though the goodwife of Wastness appeared happy, and was sometimes merry, yet there seemed at times to be a weight on her heart; and many a long, longing look did she fix on the sea. She taught her bairns many a strange song, that nobody on earth ever heard before. Albeit she was a thing of the sea, yet the goodman led a happy life with her.

Now it chanced, one fine day, that the goodman of Wastness and his three eldest sons were off in his boat to the fishing. Then the goodwife sent three of the other children to the ebb to gather limpits and wilks. The youngest lass had to stay at home, for she had a beelan foot. The goodwife then began, under the pretence of house-cleaning, a determined search for her long-lost skin. She searched up and she searched down; she searched but and she searched ben; she searched out and she searched in, but never a skin could she find, while the sun wore to the west. The youngest lass sat in a stool with her sore foot on a cringlo. She says to her mother, "Mam, what are doo leukan for?" "O bairn, deu no tell," said her mother, "but I'm leukan for a bonnie skin tae mak a rivlin that wad ceur thee sare fit." Says the lass, "Maybe I ken whar hid is. Ae day, whin ye war a' oot, an' ded tought i war sleepan i' the bed, he teuk a bonnie skin doon; he gloured at it a peerie minute, dan folded hid and led hid up under dae aisins abeun dae bed." [Under the aisins—space left by slope of roof over wall-head when not beam-filled.]

When her mother heard this she rushed to the place, and pulled out her long-concealed skin. "Fareweel, peerie buddo!" [a term of endearment], said she to the child, and ran out. She rushed to the shore, flung on her skin, and plunged into the sea with a wild cry of joy. A male of the selkie folk there met and greeted her with every token of delight. The goodman was rowing home, and saw them both from his boat. His lost wife uncovered her face, and thus she cried to him: "Goodman o'

Wastness, fareweel tae thee! I liked dee weel, doo war geud tae me; bit I lo'e better me man o' the sea!"

And that was the last he ever saw or heard of his bonnie wife. Often did he wander on the sea-shore, hoping to meet his lost love, but never more saw he her fair face.

G. F. Black, *County Folk-Lore*, III, p. 173 (Orkney).
TYPE 400. MOTIFS: D.327.2 [*Transformation of seal to person*]; K.1335 [*Wooing by stealing clothes (skin) of bathing girl*]; D.721.2 [*Disenchantment by hiding skin*]; D.361.1.1 [*Swan maiden finds hidden wings and departs*].
¶ The Swan Maiden theme is generally applied to seals or mermaids in these islands. The parallel theme of the fairy wife is common in Wales. See "Wild Edric".

THE GREEN LADY: I

Once upon a time there was an old man who had two daughters. Now one of these girls was a steady, decent girl, and the other was a stuck-up, proud, conceited piece; but the father liked her best, and she had the most to eat, and the best clothes to wear.

One day the nice girl said to her father: "Father, give me a cake and bottle of beer, and let me go and seek my fortune." So the father gave her a cake and a bottle of beer, and she went out to seek her fortune. After she had walked a weary while through the wood she sat down by a tree to rest herself and eat her cake and drink her beer. While she was eating, a little old man came by, and he said: "Little girl, little girl, what are you doing under my tree?" She said: "I am going to seek my fortune, sir; I am very tired and hungry, and I am eating my dinner." The old man said: "Little girl, little girl, give me some dinner too." She said: "I have only some cake and a bottle of beer; if you like to have some of that, you may." The old man said he would; so he sat down, and they ate the cake and drank the beer all up. Then the little girl was going on further, and the old man said: "I will tell you where to seek your fortune. Go on further and further into the wood, until you come to a little old cottage, where the green lady lives. Knock at the door, and when she opens it, tell her you've come to seek service. She will take you in; mind you be a good girl, and do all she tells you to do, and you'll come to no harm." So the little girl thanked him kindly and went on her way. Presently she came to the little cottage in the wood, and she knocked at the door. Then the door was opened by a pretty green lady, who said: "Little girl, little girl, what do you want?" "I've come to seek service, ma'am," said the little girl. "What can you do?" said the green lady. "I can bake, and I can brew, and about the house can all things do," said the little girl. "Then come in," said the green lady;

and she took her into the kitchen. "Now", said she, "you must be a very good girl; sweep the house well; make the dust fly; and mind you don't look through the keyhole, or harm will befall you." The little girl swept the house well and made the dust fly. Then the green lady said: "Now go to the well, and bring in a pail of nice clean water to cook the supper in. If the water isn't clear, change it and change it till it is." Then the little girl took a pail and went to the well. The first pail she drew, the water was so muddy and dirty she threw it away. The next pailful she drew, the water was a little clearer, but there was a silver fish in it. The fish said: "Little girl, little girl, wash me and comb me and lay me down softly." So she washed it and combed it and laid it down softly. Then she drew another pailful. The water was a little clearer, but there was a gold fish in it. The fish said: "Little girl, little girl, wash me and comb me and lay me down softly." So she washed it and combed it and laid it down softly. Then she drew another pailful. This was clean water, but there was still another fish who said the same thing as the others had done; so she washed this one too, combed it and laid it down softly. Then she drew another pailful, and this was quite clear and fresh. Then the three fish raised their heads and said:

> "They who eat the fairies' food
> In the churchyard soon shall dwell.
> Drink the water of this well,
> And all things for thee shall be good.
> Be but honest, bold and true,
> So shall good fortune come to you."

Then the little girl hasted to the house, swept up the kitchen, and made the dust fly quickly; for she thought she would surely be scolded for being away so long, and she was hungry too. The green lady then showed her how to cook the supper and take it into the parlour, and told her she could take some bread and milk for herself afterwards. But the little girl said she would rather have a drink of water and some of her own cake; she had found some crumbs in her pocket, you must know. Then the green lady went into the parlour, and the little girl sat down by the fire. Then she was thinking about her place and what the fish had said, and she wondered why the green lady had told her not to look through the keyhole. She thought there could not be any harm in doing this, and she looked through the keyhole, when what should she see but the green lady dancing with a bogey! She was so surprised that she called out: "Oh! what can I see, a green lady dancing with a bogey!" The green lady rushed out of the room and said: "What can you see?" The little girl replied: "Nothing can I see, nothing can I spy, nothing can I see till the days high die." [probably *day I die*.] Then the green lady went into the parlour again to have her supper, and the little girl again looked through the keyhole. Again she sang, "Oh! what can I see, a green lady dancing with a bogey!" The green lady rushed out: "Little girl, little girl, what can you see?" The girl said: "Nothing can I see, nothing can I spy, nothing can I see till the days high die!" This happened a third time, and then the green lady said: "Now you shall see no more," and she blinded the little girl's eyes. "But," said the green lady, "because you have been a good girl and made the dust fly, I will give you your wages and you shall go home." So she gave her a bag of money and a bundle of clothes, and sent her away. So the little girl stumbled along the path in the dark, and presently she stumbled against the well. Now there was a fine young man sitting on the brink of the well; and he told her he had been sent by the fish of the well to see her home, and would carry her bag of money and her bundle for her. He told her, too, before starting on their journey to bathe her eyes in the well. This she did; and she found her eyes come back to her, and she could see as well as ever. So the young man and the little girl went along together until they arrived at her father's cottage; and when the bag was opened there was all sorts of money in it; and when the bundle was opened there was all sorts of fine clothes in it. And the little girl married the young man, and they lived happy ever after.

Now, when the other girl saw all the things her sister had got, she came to her father and said: "Father, give me a cake and a bottle of beer, and let me go and seek my fortune." Her father gave her a cake and a bottle of beer, and the same things happened to her as to her sister. But when the old man asked her for some dinner she said: "I haven't enough for myself, so I can't give you any;" and when she was at the green lady's house she didn't make the dust fly, and the green lady was cross with her; and when she went to the well and the fish got into her pails of water, she said the fishes were wet, sloppy things, and she wasn't going to mess her hands and clean frock with them, and she threw them back roughly into the well; and she said she wasn't going to drink nasty cold water for her supper when she could have nice bread and milk; and when the green lady took out her eyes for looking through the keyhole she didn't get a bag of money and a bundle of clothes for her wages, because she hadn't made the dust fly, and she had no one to help her and take her home. So she wandered about all night and all day, and she died; and no one knows where she was buried or what became of her.

Norton Collection, II, p. 17. *Folk-Lore*, VII (1896), pp. 411–14. Contributed by A. B. Gomme: "Told to me in childhood by Mary Ann Smith, nursemaid, a Hertfordshire woman, from what village or town I do not know. There should be another rhyme said when the girl is to bathe her eyes at the well, but I have no remembrance of it. The previous one said by the fish at the well is not complete; there were, I think, two or three more lines. Neither do I think the story is quite correct or in its original form; but this is as I learnt it, as nearly as I can remember."

TYPE 480. MOTIFS: Q.2 [*Kind and unkind*]; N.825.2 [*Old man helper*]; B.175 [*Magic fish*]; H.1192 [*Task: combing hair of fairies*]; C.300 [*Looking tabu*]; C.242 [*Tabu: eating food of witch*]; C.943 [*Loss of sight for breaking tabu*]; Q.111 [*Riches as reward*]; D.1505.5 [*Magic water restores sight*]; Q.327 [*Discourtesy punished*]; Q.341 [*Curiosity punished*].

¶ This *cante-fable* version of "Kind and Unkind" is, unfortunately, imperfectly remembered, for it is one of special interest, with the sinister green lady dancing with the devil. In tone it is more like "The Maiden Fair and the Fountain Fairy" than the other versions of 480.

See also "The Wal o' the Warld's End", "The Old Witch", "The Man with a Long Nose", etc.

THE GREEN LADY: II

Once upon a time there was a poor old man who had three daughters, and the eldest said: "Father, give me a cake and a bottle of water that I may go to seek my fortune."

Her father gave her a cake and bottle of water; and when she had gone a little way she met a little old man who asked her where she was going. She replied: "To seek service." "Oh," said he, "give me your cake and bottle of water, and go and knock at the house with the green door, and there you'll find your fortune." So she knocked at the door and a lady opened it, and asked her what she wanted. She told her, and the lady asked her what she could do. She made a dob [curtsey] and said: "I can bake and I can brew, and I can make an Irish stew." So the lady said she would take her, but she must never look up the chimney or into the clock. The next morning the lady's daughter rode downstairs on a black cat and asked her to cut some bread and butter. The girl said she would as soon as she had finished washing the hearth. Whereupon the young lady ran up in a rage, and her mother came down, cut off the girl's head, stuck it up the chimney, and put her body in the clock.

The second daughter then started to seek her fortune, and met with precisely the same adventures.

The third daughter followed in her sisters' footsteps until the young lady asked for bread and butter, when she jumped up and cut it for her immediately, whereupon they were extremely pleased. In the afternoon they went for a ride on the black cats, leaving the maid alone in the house. She immediately looked up the chimney, and in the clock, and discovered her sisters' heads and bodies. She took them in her arms and ran away with them as fast as ever she could, calling on the gooseberry bushes to cover her flight. When the lady and her daughter returned they were very angry at the loss of the maid and the bodies, so they took choppers in their hands, and, still riding the black cats, went into the garden. They asked all the bushes which way the girl had gone, but they would not answer, so they chopped them down. When they came to the gooseberry bushes, the first one said: "This way, that way, and I don't know which way." But the other said: "She went straight on across the river."

So they rode on into the river and were drowned.

Norton Collection, II, p. 19. *Folk-Lore*, VII (1896), pp. 414–15, contributed by W. B. Gerish: "Told by an old Norfolk woman, 95 years of age, who had heard the tale told 'score o' times', in her youth, but had never seen it in print. She died in 1895, aged 96. To the best of my belief, the story was called 'The Green Lady'."
TYPE 480. MOTIFS: G.204 [*Girl in service of witch*]; C.337 [*Tabu: looking up chimney*]; Q.325 [*Disobedience punished*]; L.50 [*Victorious youngest daughter*]; W.31 [*Obedience*]; G.241.1.4.1 [*Witch rides on a black cat*]; G.278 [*Death of witch*].
¶ This story is probably imperfect: the two sisters were probably originally restored to life.

THE GREEN MAN OF KNOWLEDGE [summary]

An old widow had a son, Jack, who was a fool, and did nothing all day long but sit by the fire. He had a Highland collie dog, the only thing he minded and watched. He would sit and play cards with his dog all day, even if the dog could not play back.

When Jack came to the age of twenty-one, he rose from the fireside, and said to his mother, "Mother, I'm going away to seek my fortune." His mother begged him to stay, for he had never been outside the garden gate, but Jack turned his back on her and his home and his dog, and walked out through the gate into a strange world indeed.

He came to a crossroads where there was a signpost saying "To the Land of Enchantment". He followed this road, and soon he grew very hungry, for he was a big man, and had quite outgrown the clothes he had worn for all the time he had been sitting by the fire. Presently he saw a horse-trough overgrown with moss by the side of the road, and as he bent down to drink, a robin perched on the side of the water said to him: "Hullo, Jack."

Jack was astonished at hearing a bird speak, but the robin told him that in the Land of Enchantment all birds and animals could speak, and when Jack asked how it knew his name, the robin said that they had been waiting for him for twenty-one years.

Jack told the robin how hungry he was, and the robin led him to a thatched cottage, where an old woman, a hundred years old, sat rocking herself in her chair. She bade him come in and get his supper.

There was a table laid with porridge and milk, and butter and scones, and a beautiful young girl waited on him. After he had eaten the girl took him upstairs and showed him a great feather bed, on which Jack soon fell asleep.

During the night he awoke, and was surprised to find himself lying on a sheepskin and three peats. Being accustomed to lying rough, this did not trouble him; he fell asleep again, and in the morning he was back in the feather bed.

He got up quickly, and downstairs he found breakfast waiting, and the young girl told him when he had eaten to go into the garden, where her grandmother would give him some advice. Jack said, "Advice never did any harm," so he went into the garden, and spoke cheerfully to the old woman, who bade him not to speak first to anyone he met on the road that day, but to wait for them to speak to him. Jack promised, and wished them goodbye, and set out again, but the girl ran after him, and gave him some food for the journey.

After walking a long way Jack heard the bells of a village church ringing, away in a hollow, and looking down he saw the village below him. Before going down to it, he sat to eat his bundle of food. Wrapped up in a corner of it was a gold piece, which he put in his pocket. When he came to the village he went into an inn, where he had a great drink of home-brewed ale and ate some scones, for Jack was always hungry.

In a corner three men were playing cards, in silence. One of them, a man of about fifty with a cunning clever face, was dressed all in green from head to foot.

Jack asked if he might join in the game. They asked if he had any money. He said, "A little." They said, "Can you play? We don't play with men that can't."

"I've practised a bittie in my day," said Jack, so they let him join the game.

The green man played well, but Jack was too strong for him. The other two dropped out after a time, but Jack and the green man played till the early morning.

At last the green man said, "You're too good for me. Goodbye, Jack."

"Who are you?" said Jack.

"The Green Man of Knowledge."

"Where do you live?"

"East of the moon, and west of the stars."

"That's a queer direction." But the Green Man was gone.

After that nothing would please Jack but to pursue the Green Man, and find out where he lived. He had won a great deal of gold at his card-playing, but he gave nearly all of it to the innkeeper to look after until he came back, keeping only a few gold coins for his journey. The innkeeper warned him that it would mean disaster if he followed the Green Man, but Jack replied, "A body has only once to die—why worry?"

So he went on until he came to another thatched cottage. He knocked at the door and a voice said, "Come in, Jack." He went in, and found all the same as before, but an even older woman, and an even lovelier girl. They fed him as before, and put him to bed, but before he went there, he noticed that the old woman was occupied with a round piece of knitting. When he came down in the morning the knitting was lying on the floor.

The old woman told him that he could never find the Green Man of Knowledge by himself, but that they were there to help him. She told him to sit down cross-legged and cross-armed on the piece of knitting, and not to look behind him, whatever happened. "Say, Away with you," she told him, "and when you arrive, whirl it three times round, and say, Home with you." Jack obeyed her exactly, and the knitting bore him through hail, fire, brimstone and water, but he was strong-minded and never looked back. When the knitting had flown away home, Jack heard the sound of a blacksmith tinkering on an anvil, and he entered the house. An even older woman than the other two was rocking herself by the fire. She was the smith's wife, and she told Jack to go to the smithy and he would find that the smith had something for him. The smith told Jack that he was now near the Green Man, but the way was hedged about with snares. First he would have to cross a river, but if he stepped on the bridge it would turn to a spider's web, and let him fall into the water, which would turn into boiling lava and kill him. But there was one way of escape. The Green Man had three daughters, who came down to bathe at ten o'clock every morning. As soon as they entered the water they became three swans. Two were black, but the youngest daughter was white. Jack must catch her by taking away her clothes, and hiding them. If he left so much as a hairpin he would have no power over her. Then the smith gave him a horseshoe, bidding him sit on it, and not look behind, and to return it in the same way as the knitting. The horseshoe carried Jack safely to the river, though, as before, the journey was terrible. He hid behind the bridge, and saw the three lovely maidens come down to bathe. They undressed, and Jack caught up every bit of the youngest daughter's clothing, and hid it. The elder ones came out, but the youngest called from the water, "Are you there, Jack? Please give me my clothes, Jack. Are you a gentleman?"

"No," he replied, "I'm no gentleman, I'm just Jack the fool."

"What have I to do, Jack?"

At last, protesting, she carried him across the river. He knocked at the door of the Green Man's house and the Green Man, astonished and shocked at seeing him, asked, "How did you get here, Jack?" Jack put him off with a tale and the Green Man took him into the house, but inside he at once pushed him into a small room with a trapdoor, where there was only a dry crust and some water, but in the night the youngest daughter came to him secretly with food and promised to help him escape from her wicked father. Next morning when the Green Man came, Jack pretended that he had never passed a more comfortable night. The Green Man was surprised, and now he proposed to set Jack three easy tasks. The first was to go down into a dry well, and fetch up his wife's engagement ring. Jack prepared to go at once, but was told to wait till the next day. Pretending to show him a picture of his wife, the Green Man pushed Jack into another cavity for the night. Again the youngest daughter came to his help and she promised to make a ladder of herself the next day, so that Jack could climb down into the well, and to clear the mud from the bottom so that he could find the ring. If he missed a step it would break a bone in her body, so Jack promised to be careful. Even with all care he slipped a step at the bottom, and feared he had broken the girl's neck, but he went on, found the ring and climbed out. The Green Man asked to see the ring, and who was helping him, but Jack gave no answer, and was again shut up in a wretched closet for the night. The daughter came and told him that he had broken her finger, but she had worn gloves so that her father should not notice. The next task, she told him, would be to build a castle in sixty minutes. In the morning Jack again pretended to the Green Man that he had slept in the greatest comfort. He was taken to the hill where the castle was to stand, and while he was looking out in despair the youngest daughter built it behind him. But she left a great hole in the middle, and when Jack cried out in alarm at it, she told him to say to the Green Man that he had left it for him to fill up. When Jack did so, the Green Man said, "Jack, who's helping you?" Jack answered, "I never had any friend but my old collie dog." So the Green Man said, "Well done, Jack," and proceeded to set him the third task. This was to clear out all the ants from a wood in half an hour. If he accomplished this he was to have as much money as he wanted, one of the Green Man's daughters for his wife, and his freedom.

The youngest daughter performed this task also, and the Green Man gave Jack a real feast and four great bags of gold, too much to count, and led him to the stables to choose a horse to carry him. Jack replied as usual, "Well, well," and on the way to the stables, he heard the girl's voice telling him to choose only the old mule. Against his own judgement and the urging of the Green Man, Jack did so, and the mule, who was really the youngest daughter herself, ran away with him faster than the wind. The Green Man followed, but she bade Jack take a drop of water from her left ear and throw it behind him, asking for lakes and seas and rivers behind, and a clear road in front.

This delayed the Green Man for a time, but he began to catch them up again, so the mule told Jack to find a spark of stone in her left ear and throw it behind him, wishing for mountains, hills, and dales behind him and a clear road in front. Yet again, after a time, the Green Man was catching up with them, but the little mule told Jack to throw behind him a spark of fire; and fire, hell and pits sprang up behind them and destroyed the Green Man and all his people. But in punishment for this, the girl was compelled to leave Jack for a year, after which she promised she would return to him. In the meantime he must let no one kiss him, or else he would forget all about her.

Jack went on to his home, and refused to let even his mother kiss him, but he could not stop his old dog from jumping up and licking him for joy at his return. So he forgot his girl, and within a year he was promised to a miller's daughter. On the night of the wedding, while he was busy in his room, a poor ragged girl came to the back door and asked for work. Jack willingly took her on to help for a few days, and the girl worked hard. When the guests were all assembled for the wedding, and were waiting for the preacher to arrive, she offered to entertain them with her wooden cock and hen, which she said could talk. Jack came to watch as well, and while they were pecking their corn, the hen said to the cock, "Do you remember me, Jack?"

"No," said the cock, and went on pecking.

"Do you remember the Green Man of Knowledge?"

"No, I don't remember him."

"Jack, do you remember me, the woman you love?"

"No, I'm sorry, but I don't know you."

"Jack, do you remember when I killed my own people for you?"

The cock looked up at that and said, "Yes, I do remember you."

And then Jack said, "It's you, lassie, is't?"

So Jack's wedding was cancelled, and he married the Green Man's daughter, and they lived happily ever after.

Hamish Henderson, *Scottish Studies*, II, part I, pp. 47 ff.

TYPE 313. MOTIFS: L.131 [*Hearth abode of unpromising hero*]; H.1220 [*Quest voluntarily undertaken*]; B.451 [*Helpful birds*]; H.1235 [*Succession of helpers on quest*]; K.1335 [*Wooing by stealing clothes of bathing maiden*]; G.465 [*Ogre sets impossible tasks*]; H.1132 [*Recovering lost object*]; E.33 [*Resuscitation with missing member—broken bone*]; H.1133 [*Task: building castle*]; H.1129 [*Tedious task*]; H.335.0.1 [*Bride helps suitor perform tasks*]; D.672 [*Obstacle flight*]; D.2004.2.1 [*Dog's licking produces forgetfulness*]; D.2006.1.3 [*Forgotten bride awakens lover's memory by conversation of birds*].

"The Green Man of Knowledge", collected in 1954 by Dr Hamish Henderson from Geordie Stewart, a travelling tinker, is published in full by the collector with a valuable analysis of the tale as known in these islands, and an examination of the features it has in common with the medieval poem "Sir Gawayne and the Green Knight".

Bolte and Polivka, II, pp. 516 ff., deal fully with the story, which is of world-wide distribution. Christiansen examines it in "A Gaelic Fairy-Tale in Norway", *Béaloideas*, I, 107 ff.

¶ The earliest known version is the tale of Jason and Medea; but Indian, African, Turkish, French, Scandinavian, Spanish, German, Austrian, Hungarian, and American-Indian versions are known, to give only a few. The American version, "Lady Featherflight", assumed to be of English origin, was given at the Transactions of the Second International Folk-Lore Congress, 1891.

"The Battle of the Birds" is the best-known version. There are many in Ireland, of which "The Wren and the Mouse" was published in *Béaloideas*, III (1931).

See also "Nicht Nought Nothing", "Green Sleeves", "Clever Pat", "Daughter Greengown".

THE GREEN MIST

[summary. Full tale appears in *The Folktales of England*]

In the old days, the Car-Folk had many strange ways and words to keep danger from them, and to bring good luck. In the churches the priests would sing their services, but the old people set more store by the old ways that the priests knew nothing about.

In the winter the bogles and such had nothing but evil to do, but in the spring the earth had to be wakened and many strange words were spoken that the people did not understand themselves: they would turn a mould in each field, and every morning at first dawn they would stand in the doorway with salt and bread in their hands waiting for the Green Mist to creep up which meant that spring had come. There was one family that had done all that had to be done year after year, and yet for all that, one winter heavy sorrow came on them, for the daughter, who had been the prettiest lass in the village, grew so pining and sickly, that at last she could not stand upon her feet. But she thought if she could greet the spring again she would live. Day after day they carried her out to watch, but the wintry weather held on, and at length she said to her mother: "If the Green Mist doesna come to-morrow, I can stay no longer. The earth is calling me and the seeds are bursting that will cover me, but if I could only live as long as one of those cowslips that grow by the door each spring, I swear I'd be content." The mother hushed her, for she did not know who might hear; the air was full of listeners in those days. But the next day the Green Mist came, and the girl sat in the sun, and crumbled the bread in her thin fingers, and laughed with joy; and as the spring went on she grew stronger and prettier every day that the sun shone, though a cold day could make her white and shivery as ever, and when the cowslips flowered she grew so strange and beautiful that they almost feared her. But she would never let her mother pluck a cowslip. But one day a lad came to the cottage, and he plucked a cowslip and played with it as they chatted. She did not see what he had done till he said goodbye, and she saw the cowslip lying on the earth.

"Did thee pull that cowslip?" she said, and her hand went to her head.

"Aye," he said, and stooped and gave it to her, thinking what a pretty lass she was.

She took it from him and stood looking round the garden, and then she gave a cry and ran into the house. They found her lying on her bed with the cowslip in her hand, and all day long she faded, and next morning her mother found her lying dead and withered like the withered flower in her hand.

The bogles had heard her wish and granted to her to live as long as the cowslips, and fade with the first that was plucked.

Mrs Balfour, "Legends of the Cars", *Folk-Lore*, II. Told by an old man from Lindsey. TYPE 1187. MOTIFS: E.764 [*Life bound up with external event*]; E.765.3.4 [*Girl lives until her cowslip is pulled*]; E.711.2.2 [*Soul in flower*].

¶ Baughman equates the "Devil in Little Dunkeld Manse" with this, but the situation is rather different.

GREEN SLEEVES [summary]

A King of Scotland had a son who was devoted to gambling and excelled at the game of skittles, so that no one dared compete with him in that game. A strange old man suddenly appeared and challenged him to play, on condition that the winner might ask of the loser whatever he wished, and the loser must comply on pain of death. The old man won, and charged the prince to tell him his name and place of abode before that day twelve months.

The prince took to his bed in despair, but was at last persuaded by his father, first to tell him the cause of his distress, and then to go and seek the answers to the old man's questions. After a long day's travel an old man, sitting outside his cottage, told him the rogue was named Green Sleeves. He was 200 years old, and sent the Prince 200 miles on to his brother, 400 years older, with the aid of magic slippers and a ball, to guide him. The slippers and ball would return of themselves on being kicked.

800 miles on, the third brother, 1000 years older, sent him to the river Ugie to intercept the three daughters of Green Sleeves, who would come to bathe, disguised as swans. He stole the swan-skin of the youngest, which had one blue wing, and so induced her to tell him the way to Green Sleeves' castle. Being unwillingly admitted by Green Sleeves, the Prince found endless difficulties—a bed of broken glass fragments, fish-skins and mouldy bread to eat—and three impossible tasks were imposed on him by Green Sleeves, but Blue Wing secretly helped him

through all, with the aid of a magic box containing thousands of fairies. The tasks were, first, to build a castle 1000 miles in length, breadth and height, including a stone from every quarry in the world, and covered with feathers of every kind of bird. The next task was to sow, reap and replace in the cask from which it came, a quantity of lint seed, as before in the space of a single day. Third and last was to clear a stable where 200 horses had stood for 200 years, and recover from it a golden needle lost by Green Sleeves' grandmother 1000 years before.

Green Sleeves now offered the Prince one of his daughters in marriage. They would have murdered him, but Blue Wing, by a trick, again saved him and they fled. Magic cakes hung on their bed delayed the pursuit, but finally Green Sleeves in seven-leagued boots followed them. Magic obstacles, a forest, a great rock, and a rushing river, enabled the Prince, directed by Blue Wing, to procure an egg from a certain bird's nest on top of a high hill. With this egg, aimed at a special point of his breast, Green Sleeves was slain, and the Prince rode home to procure a fitting escort for his bride before making her known to his parents. Blue Wing warned him against being kissed, but a lap-dog sprang up and licked him, and he forgot her.

Blue Wing hid in a tree above a pool, and two servants of a neighbouring goldsmith, mistaking her reflection for their own, refused, through pride in their supposed beauty, to serve him any more. Blue Wing took their place, and served the goldsmith, until two of his customers, a Prince's groom first, and then the Duke of Marlborough himself, fell in love with her. She tricked them both, by magic, having promised to sleep with each of them for one night, and then kept them spell-bound to some menial task, and so made her way, as the Duke's partner to a ball at court. Here, when the dancing was over, and tales were told and songs sung, Blue Wing produced a golden cock and hen, which talked, and reminded the Prince of all that had happened.

The new bride to whom he had been promised was dismissed, and Blue Wing and the Prince were married, with all honour and joy, and lived to see their large family grow up to take their place in due time.

Buchan, *Ancient Scottish Tales*, pp. 170–7.

TYPE 313. MOTIFS: N. 2.0.1 [*Play for unnamed stakes*]: H. 1219.1 [*Quest assigned as payment for gambling loss*]: D. 1313.1 [*Magic ball indicates road*]: D. 1520.10 [*Magic transportation by shoes*]: D. 361.1 [*Swan maiden*]: D. 721 [*Disenchantment by removing skin*]: H. 1010 [*Impossible tasks*]: H. 1102 [*Cleaning Augean stables*]: D. 672 [*Obstacle flight*]: D. 1521.1 [*Seven-league boots*]: D. 2004.2.1 [*Dog's licking produces forgetfulness*]: D. 2006.1.1 [*Forgotten fiancée reawakens husband's memory by detaining lovers by magic*]: H. 151. 1 [*Attention drawn by magic objects: recognition follows*].

See "Nicht Nought Nothing", "Daughter Greengown", "The Leaves that Hung but Never Grew", "The Green Man of Knowledge", "The Three Feathers".

THE GREY CASTLE

Once upon a time, and it wasn't in your time nor my time but it was in jolly good days, Jack left home. In his home he's left his poor old mother ahind on an owld box. And he was retermined to see life, 'cos he's never seen life afore.

He tramps along a dreary muddy road for miles and miles, and at long last he took a seat and reconsidered hisself, and he shook his head. "Why did I, poor foolish boy, leave my home? What is mine own mother doing now 'ithout me? I wonder."

He shook his head again, but he plucked up courage, brushed his coat and his cap, and started on tramp once more again. "Now, Jack, dere's only yourself you got to talk to," says he, as he sighs his way along the dreary road. He begins to feel tired again, so he rests his weary foot. De night is dark, and bright stars above him, but he could not speak to de stars.

All at oncet dere stood a bright light in front of him, so he glared at it a-one-side, and with his brain and his heart wondered and plondered what was going to be at de end. "Well, Jack old boy, cheer up, and now you must take a sleep."

At long last de morn is comed and de birds begin deir bright singing, what lightened his heart a great deal. And the sun was shining so beautiful he could see de rocks and meadows clearly, and a large grey castle on a hill in front of him. "Jack, my lad, you do not know what's afore you: dat castle may be your fortune."

Jack sighed again, tired and dreary, hungry and dirsty, he gazed a-one-side at a grey owld farm-house. He ventured to open de gate and knocked at de farm door, and asked de owld woman for a drink. De owld farmer-woman asked him quite snubbily as she handed him de tea: "What is a young man like you doing about de country: have you no work?" "No, dere isn't no work for Poor Jack," says he to dat owld farmer-woman. "Why?" she asks. "Well," says Jack, "it's like a good few of you farmers, you's a bit juberstitious of a man's stealing summat. But bein' as you's made such a brag and a boast 'bout it, we'll begin with you, missus. Is dere any work for poor Jack from you?" "Well, my man, only haarrd work."

Jack laughed as she stood wid her coarse apron at de door. "Give me de chancet, missus, to see what I could do." "Well!" says she, quite sneery, "what *can* you do?" "Excuse me," says Jack, quite on de laughing side, pulling his cap off so p'litely, and brushing back his black hair, "I'll give you an offer of work now, this instant minute. I'll chop dat big tree for you, Missus, into logs for your oven, for a little bite to eat."

"Well," says the woman, "here's my chopper." Jack smiles to hisself and mutters, "She's a hard piece of brick is dat farmer-woman."

He worked away, did Jack and, feeling very dreary, hungry and dirsty, brought de wood to de door. "Jack," says she (quite de thing now, you sees), "you've done more work nor any one of my men has done. Seat yourself down at dat table dis instant minute," she says, "and eat and drink of de best." "Now," thinks Jack to hisself, "it's only de start of a dream for you, my boy, it's only de first lesson. But somehow dese hard-hearted manly women comes soft-hearted at de end."

A'ter he'd done his food, he sits hisself down by de fireside and has a little smoke and plonders very deeply about his poor owld mother. And he starts to make amend very smartly, and asks de missus could he have a wash. "Ev course," says she quite cheerful, "it'll afresh you, Jack." And out he goes wid de bucket and soap (in a farm-house, you sees), and de farmer-woman hurries a'ter him, and relivers him de towel. "Thank you kindly," says Jack, "you bin just like a mother to me, but not ezackly like my poor owld mammie: she used to cling to me and pray for me more nor anybody in de world."

Well, de owld woman fetches him a suit now, b'longing to one of her sons, and begs him to stay de night. But all he says is: "How far is de next village from here, mum?" "You don't mean to say you will walk twenty miles to-night, Jack? I want you to stay wid me and I'll give you good money, and good food. Do you know owt about ploughing?" "No," he said quite stern to de owld woman, "de best ploughing as I ever done, mum, is ploughing de hard road. So I'll stay no longer nor to-night, and mind you call me up six o'clock in de mornin'."

De next morning is comed. He hears de gentle creak up de stairs, and up he jumps on de cheerful side. "Well, Jack," he says to hisself, "you do look a smart, brisk lad now. And you'll soon make away for your dear hard road." He enjoys his breakfast with de missus, and tells her straight he must leave dis same morning. (He still has dat grey castle on his mind—he would do oncet he'd seen it.) "Poor foolish Jack," says she with a jeery laugh, "I s'pose you's thinking of dat castle what you told me of. Dere's nowt dere for you, my boy, nowt whatsumdever! De very idea of you's going dere! poor foolish lad."

"Well," says Jack, "I'm retermined to see life, and life I *will* see."

So off he goes, carrying a little food wid him. He shuts de gate ahind him merrily, and starts a-laughing. "Thank God," he says, "I'm on de hard road again." He starts a bit of hard walking, as he didn't think nothing of dat twenty miles. So he walked and he walked till he see'd de castle grinning at him. He sits hisself down and has a little smoke and he smiles to hisself. "I'll soon make dat castle speak for itself too," says he, "it's bin on my brain long enough," he says.

Now he sees de lodge of dat castle, but he sees no light in dat lodge. But when he goes to de front door, he sees a bright light inside. So he smartens hisself and makes a 'tempt to knock at dat hard knocker. Now who comes out to him dere but an owld grey lady. She opens de door and gives him a little smile. "Whatever do you want here, my boy?" says she. "What a diff'rent voice she has," thinks Jack, "towards dat hard brick." And he laughs. "I wants to know, mother," he says, "who lives up at dat owld grey castle." "You come in, my boy, and I'll 'tempt to 'splain to you. But you's very late: it's turned seven!" (It's in the night, you see, in dem country places.)

"Are you looking for work?" asked the old lady. "Well, I been here dese thirty years," she says, "and I've seen no men like you walking about de land." (Poor hopes for Jack!) "But dere's no harm in you's going up. Dere's only an owld gentleman dere," she says, "and he's hard o' hearing." (God help poor Jack!) "Ah!" says Jack, "Never enter, never will." (He was cheering hisself up.) "When dere's a will, dere's a way. And I'm going up, mother," he says. "Good night, my boy, take care of you's self: you's got two mile yet to go up to dat castle."

Jack goes along through two big iron gates, and makes his way up to de castle. (Thank God!) He goes over owld humpy, owld bumpy, owld stones, of course, but he doesn't care nowt for dese humpy bumpy stones. He comed to de door of dat castle,—dirty big lumps of lead on dat door but a beautiful big knocker. He knocked on dat door.

Suddenly de door opened, but he seen no one dere. He could not understand it. Dat door closened again. He knocked again. Suddenly de door opened again. But still he seen no one dere.

So Jack stepped in den, cheekily. And what stood afore him? (Don't frighten!!) A little hairy owld man! "What can I do for you, my strange man?" he says. "I want work, Sir." "Ha! ha! ha!" says he, "*work* you want, is it? Come dis way, I'll show you WORK. Did anyone send you up here?" "No," says Jack, quite cheerful. "I must say you're a brave young man. Dere hasn't been anyone up here for thirty years. Well," he said, "I'll see about getting some WORK for you. When did you have something to eat last, my boy?" "Oh, I don't feel hungry, thank you," says Jack. "Well, I do," says de owld hairy man. "Come dis way," he say, "you have not seen de Master yet."

Jack begins to shiver. Jack begins to stare. And who should sit down at the great dinner table but a big Giant! Jack stared and stared. "Well, my brave man," he says, "come to look here for work, have you? Ha! Ha! I'll give you WORK, if WORK it is you want!" Jack begins to miss de little hairy man.

"Sit down here," he says. (Dat's de Giant.) Jack begins to look around

and shivers. He sees a 'normous plate afore him. "You've to eat all dat!"
(Poor Jack! he must have a big belly too.) "Remember you haven't seen
your master *yet*." "How many masters must I see?" thinks poor Jack to
hisself. "You'll want a place to sleep in, won't you?" "Yes," says Jack.
"Come here and I'll show you,"—and dere stands his dear little hairy
man again. Jack steps into the room and sees a 'normous big bed: "Too
big for me," he thinks to hisself. And who drops in dere but a bigger
Giant nor what he'd seen afore, what would have been the mainstay
of two Giants. "You're not sleeping with me?" says Jack, and he begins
to shiver again. "No, my man, dat is your bed to you's self." "Well,
I'll be very glad of a rest," says Jack. And he pulls his shoes off, does
Jack, and he puts his head down on de pillow (thank God he did), and
he snores and snores till morning. (You wouldn't hardly know was it
morning dere, it was always so dark—dat's why it's called de grey
castle, you see!)

A ten-pound knock comed to de door and shook de bed from under
him. "Come down for your breakfast, my man, come down!" Poor
Jack goes down for his breakfast (certainly he would do, wouldn't you
too?). And he sees de two Giants and the little s'rimp, de hairy man.
"Jack," says de Giant, "I want you to do some very hard work to-day.
You'll have to go into de green room to-day. Dere stands a table before
you, my boy, and you'll have to sleep dere for three nights, my boy, and
unpick every single bit of rag dat's in dat great big rug."

"I'll try my best, sir," says poor Jack, shivering again. The Giant went
away and slammed the door on him.

Dere only stood two candles for his work. (God help him! He must
have had good eyes too.) So he picked up de rug and started working.
At last he begin to tremble: he partly knew dere was *somebody* about.
And de 'normous big Giant with his glistening eyes came in. "Well,
Jack, have you found anything? Have you seen anything?" "What
d'you want me to see or find?" says Jack. "Is dere anything in dis dark
room to find or to see?" he says. "Seek not for inflamation," said de
big Giant, "but get on wid your work!" De door goes slam, wid a fast
lock. (Poor Jack!)

Jack begins to work again, and suddenly he looks towards a big long
chest what stood in de darkest corner. And he hears a whisper: "Pull it
from de middle, Jack, and your three days' task will soon be finished.
But do not say dat you heard anything."

De Giant comes in (dat Giant is a Devil, you know!) shining de room
up wid his glittering eyes: "You're doing your work wonnerful, Jack,
but I'm not quite satisfied. You must have seen someone to help you do
dat rug." "I don't know what you's talking about," says Jack. The
Giant goes out de same old way wid a slam of de door.

It suddenly struck Jack about de owld chest, what stood in de corner. He stepped up to it and was 'tempted to undo de lock. (Go ahead, Jack!) De word was spoken: "You can't undo dat lock. Look on de shelf, Jack, and look pretty sharp, and you'll find de key of de chest." Jack looks sharp, and finds de key.

He unlocks de chest, and suddenly de lid opens and he staggers back. He sees inside de glitter of a beautiful green dress, and a figure wid a pale face: a lovely lady. Den she up and spoke to Jack afore she lays down again. "Jack," she says, "I have been locked in dis chest for de last thirty years." Jack is staggered. "Are you a ghost?" he asks. "No," says she, "I'm human like what you are, dere's still a bit of life in me. I'm in my wedding dress," she says. "You are my brave man, Jack," she says, "and dose two Giants are 'chanted, and dat little hairy man is my father. And now, Jack, I've told you my secret. So don't hesitate, Jack; close de chest, fasten de lock, and say nothing." By this time de whole rug is unpicked.

At last bum! bum! bum! de Giant is coming. "Come in!" cries Jack. "My word, you have worked dat cloth beautiful, Jack. You must have found something, or seen someone. Dere's only one more thing, Jack," he says, "you've got to do for me: to go to dat pond outside de castle and find two diamond rings." "Well," says Jack, very disheartened, "it's impossible, Sir, to find two diamond rings." The Giant glared at him quite furiously.

Poor Jack goes out to dis dirty black pond, and he plondered to hisself could he find dese two diamond rings. At long last he sees a beautiful white swan, and Jack thinks to have a chat with dis swan. Suddenly it made up to him. And Jack got more frightened of de swan nor what he got of de Giants. "Poor Jack," says she, "Just follow me and I'll show you where are dose diamond rings." Jack followed de swan up to de pond. "Don't get disheartened, Jack, I've got dose diamond rings for you." And de swan lifted up her bill, and dere were de rings she'd picked up from de bottom of de pond. "And now, Jack, go back to dat Giant, and tell him you've seen no one, and give dose two rings into his own hands."

Back goes Jack, quite cheerful, steps into de green room, goes up to de chest de first thing, and opens de lid, and speaks gently to de lovely green lady. He shows her de diamond rings. "Jack," says she, "my good lad, give dem to dat Brute, and do not return here again to me. You will find me somewhere else."

Jack goes bravely from her, and steps up to de big Giant. "Here you are, you Brute!" he says. "What! what! what!" says de Giant, "dose same two diamond rings what caused a lot of bloodshed? Well," he says to Jack (quite de thing now, you sees), "you've fulfilled your work, you've beat me, Jack. And you've won de grey castle. You'll be 'poor'

Jack no longer! I must leave you for a minute. Go into de green room, Jack, and you shall have your reward."

Poor Jack goes into de other room quite happy, and proud. And a nice gentleman met him at de door. He was looking for de little hairy owld man, but he couldn't see him—only dis very nice gentleman to keep poor Jack company.

Suddenly he seed de castle all of a light-shine, what he'd never seed afore. De gentleman dances him into another great big room, and he could see de table laid out with chickens and ducks and all sorts of good things, and he was plondering where were de guests. And suddenly two beautiful young gentlemen appear, shining like de rising sun. He was looking for de two Giants, and lo and behold!—dese two young gentlemen.

Jack was quite excited and quite exhausted. Den who comes in a'ter, but a lovely lady in a pale green dress and a green veil. She comes up to Jack and says, "Jack, my boy, you have brokened our 'chantment." With dat, she throws back her green veil, and stands afore him—de handsomest young lady in all de land.

Den dey all gathered together—de father, de two brothers, and Jack and de lady—'ithout one enemy in de world. And Jack married de lovely lady. And so dey lived happy for ever more after.

Dora E. Yates, *Gypsy Folk-Tales*, pp. 161–7.
TYPE 400 (variant of 326). MOTIFS: N.711.2 [*Hero finds maiden in enchanted castle*]; D.753 [*Disenchantment by accomplishment of tasks*]; H.335.0.1 [*Bride helps suitor perform his tasks*]; B.469.2 [*Helpful swan*]. (Possibly D.361.1, *Swan maiden.*)
¶ This is a short and rather divergent version of type 400, without the loss of the wife and subsequent search for her, which is the norm. Some versions of 326 are not unlike this tale. See, for instance, "Ashypelt".
See also "The Princess of the Blue Mountains".

HABETROT

There was once a Selkirkshire lassie who was so idle that her mother could never teach her to spin. She was a merry, pretty lass, but her delight was to scramble about in the woods and hills and sit by the burns; and though her mother begged and scolded, she could never get her to sit long enough at her wheel to do any good there. At last her mother lost patience, and she took seven heads of lint and gave them to the lassie.

"See here, ye idle cuttie," she said. "Ye'll spin these se'en heids into yarn in three days, or I'll gie ye a skelping ye'll no forget."

The lassie knew her mother meant what she said, and she sat down to work. Her soft little hands were blistered with the harsh lint, and her lips were quite sore with licking the thread; but for two days she worked hard and had finished just half a head. She cried herself to sleep that night, for she knew she could never finish the rest of her task in one day; so the next morning she gave it up, and went out into the sunshine and clear air. She wandered up and she wandered down until she came to a little knoll with a stream running past it, and by the stream, sitting on a self-bored stone, was an old woman spinning. She looked up as the lassie came near, and her looks were friendly enough, but her lips were so long and thick that the lassie had never seen the like. The lassie smiled at her and came up.

"Gude day to ye, gudewife," she said, "ye're a grand spinner, but what way are ye sae lang-lippit?"

"Spinning' the thread, ma hinnie," said the old woman kindly.

"I sud be daein' that tae," said the lassie, "But it's to nae purpose, a canna dae't in the time."

"Fetch me yir lint, ma hinnie, and I'll spin it for ye," said the old wife. The lassie ran away to fetch it, and brought it gladly back.

"Whaur'll I get it again?" she said. "And what sall I ca' ye, gudewife?"

But the old wifie said nothing, but flitted away among the birches faster than you could expect. The lassie wandered up and down the knoll singing to herself; but at last she got sleepy and sat down on the knoll to sleep. When she wakened the sun had set, and the clear moon was shining down on to her. She had lain down with her head resting on a self-bored stone; and as she was just wondering where she would get her lint again she heard a voice from under her head saying: "Little kens the wee lassie on the brae-head that ma name's Habetrot."

She put her eye to the bore in the stone and saw right through into the knoll beneath her. It was like a deep cavern, full of spinners, and her friend Habetrot was walking up and down amongst them, watching their work. There was not one amongst them whose lips were not long and thick like hers. One was sitting a little apart, reeling the yarn, and she was the ugliest of them all, for she had long, thick lips and grey, starting eyes, and a big hooked nose. Habetrot came up to her.

"Mak' haste noo, Scantlie Meg," she said. "That's ma wee lassie's yarn, and I maun hae it ready to gie her as she gaes into her mither's door."

The lassie was glad to hear that, for she knew now where she was to wait for the yarn. So she set out for home, and on the doorstep Habetrot was waiting for her. The lassie thanked her gratefully, and asked what she could do for her in return.

"Nocht ava," said the kind fairy, "but dinna tell yir minnie wha spinned the yarn."

It was late now, and the lassie slipped quietly into the house, for her mother was abed. On the table lay seven black puddings which she had made while her daughter was wandering. The lassie had had nothing to eat all day and she was hungry; so she blew up the fire again, and fried the puddings and ate them, one after the other, until she had eaten all seven. Then she went to bed and slept with an easy heart.

Early next morning the gudewife came down. There on the table were seven beautiful smooth skeins of yarn, but there was no trace of the black puddings except a little burning of the frying pan. At the sight the gudewife was nearly out of her head with vexation and delight; and she ran out of the house exclaiming:

> "My daughter's spun se'en, se'en, se'en,
> My daughter's eaten se'en, se'en, se'en,
> And all before daylicht!"

The laird was riding by early to the hunt, and he heard her crying out like a mad thing.

"What is it ye're saying, gudewife?" he said.

"My daughter's spun se'en, se'en, se'en, My daughter's eaten se'en, se'en, se'en," said the gudewife again. "And if ye dinna believe me, Laird, come ben and see for yirsel."

The laird came in, and there were seven smooth skeins, and there was the pretty lass, all rosy and fresh from sleep; and he was so taken with her that he asked her to marry him. She was ready enough; but when the wedding was over, and the bridegroom began to talk of the fine yarn she would spin him, her heart failed her, for she could not bear to disappoint him. So she turned it over this way and that in her mind, and at last she went to the self-bored stone, and called on Habetrot by name to come and advise her.

"Bring yir man here, at the full moon, ma hinnie," said Habetrot, "and I'se warrant ye he'll no ask ye tae spin again."

So when the moon was full the lassie brought the laird to the self-bored stone, and leaning their ears to it, they heard Habetrot singing. At the end of the song she got up, and opening a door in the roots of a tree, she called them both in. They went up and down among the rows of spinners, and each one looked uglier than the last.

"They're an unco sicht," said the laird at last in a low voice. "Hoo is it they're sae lang-lippit, gudewife?"

"Wi' spinnin', Laird, wi' spinnin'," said Habetrot. "The bonniest mooth in the warld gets a sair twist to it wi' pu'in oot the thread."

"Then we'll hae nae mair spinnin' for ye, ma dearie," said the laird. "Dae ye hear? Ye maun let the wheel bide."

"Juist as ye say, gudeman," said the lass, with her heart dancing within her.

So from that day the lassie rode up and down the country with her husband and hunted and played with him; and very happy they were. And all the lint on the place was sent to Habetrot to spin.

From Henderson, *Folk-Lore of the Northern Counties*, p. 258. Retold by K. M. Briggs, *The Personnel of Fairyland*, p. 101.

TYPE 501. MOTIFS: H.914 [*Tasks assigned because of mother's foolish boasting*]; H.1092 [*Task: spinning impossible amount*]; D.2183 [*Magic spinning performed by supernatural helpers*]; J.51 [*Sight of deformed witches causes man to release wife from spinning duty*].

Habetrot is the fairy, or goddess, of spinning.

A similar story is told of Whuppity Stoorie, the wicked fairy of another tale.

HABIE'S WHISTLE [summary]

There were once an old man and woman who had one son and they were very poor. At last the old man said to the boy, "We've nothing for you here, you'd best go out into the world, and look for a job." He walked until he was tired and hungry and he met a wee man. The wee man gave him a magic table-cover, and when he sat down at it he could have anything he liked to eat. So he got on grandly and he went a long way, until he met another man who looked hungry and weary, and he asked him what kind of country it was ahead. "It's a desolate sort of country," said the man. "There's no one, and there's nothing to eat." "Well, sit down, and have something to eat, if you're hungry," said Jack, and they sat down at the table and had a grand feast. When they had eaten, the man began to boast himself that he had something even finer than the table. "Do you see this little whistle?" he said. "See what happens when I blow on it." He blew, and at once there was a great army of men marching along, and they bowed to him and said: "What are your orders?" and when he whistled again, they disappeared.

Jack thought it would be a fine thing to have an army like that at his command, so he offered the stranger to change with him, and the stranger was willing. So he took the table and Jack took the whistle and they went their different ways. So after Jack had walked on a long while he began to get hungry and to wish that he hadn't parted with his table. So he blew the whistle, and at once the army appeared, and said: "What are your orders?" "Go back that way," said Jack, "and you'll find a fellow carrying a table that belongs to me. Bring it back, as quick as you can." So they went and fetched back the table, and when he had it, he blew his whistle, and they all disappeared. So then Jack had both the table and the whistle, and he took them back to his father and mother, and they had all they wanted for the rest of their days.

School of Scottish Studies, H. Henderson, from Bella Higgins.

TYPE 569. MOTIFS: D.1472.1.7 [*Magic table produces food*]; D.1475.3 [*Magic soldier-producing pipe*]; D.831 [*Hero exchanges magic object for another, and by means of the second secures the first one again*].

¶ This tale has a wide distribution. There are 44 Irish versions given in *Béaloideas* and Baughman cites two English American ones. It is Grimm, no. 54. See "The Magic Knapsack".

THE HAND [summary]

Small shop attached to house near great heath infested by robbers. Only one house on the heath, inhabited by old man whom robbers spared, though they spared no one else. One of the robbers went down to rob the shop one winter evening.

Younger girl heard the shop bell, went in, saw shop door on the chain, and a hand groping. Terrified, took the bread knife and cut off the hand.* Hid it and afterwards buried it in the garden. At first she told no one, but afterwards confessed it to her family, who were proud of her. The robber got his arm bound up, went to London, and got a false hand. They were all determined to be avenged. The robber came courting the girl, took her for a walk, and carried her off. They decided to strip her naked, bind her to a tree, and stick her full of nails. They bound her to the tree, left a small boy to guard her, and went off to get nails. She persuaded the boy to loose her. They hid from the robbers, finally escaped to the old man's house. He let them hide upstairs, if they did not peep out. The robbers came to the house, the old man denied all knowledge of fugitives, the robbers were going, when one of them saw the girl peeping out. They turned back and said they'd break down the door if the old man wouldn't let them in. The old man picked up a cigar-box and opened it. A regiment of soldiers marched out, who cut down the robbers. The girl went home, and when she was old enough the boy married her.

Collected by T. W. Thompson from Gus Gray, at Cleethorpes, 7 October 1914.
TYPE 956A (variant). MOTIF: K.912.0.2 [*Robbers' hands off as they enter house*].
¶ This story belongs usually either to Novelle or Legends, but the sudden intrusion of the supernatural element places it among the Fairy Tales.
   See "The Clever Maid and the Robber" (A. IV).

THE HARES' PARLIAMENT

Mary and Pat lived in a nice wee house. Mary one day bought a looking-glass. When she was admiring herself in the glass, she noticed that her ears were growing long and furry and that she was getting wee-er and wee-er and when she looked down at herself she saw she was a hare. She ran out of the house and started skipping about. She felt herself drawn in a certain direction and skipped along. In the meantime, Pat came into the house, and began to look for Mary. Soon he spied the looking-glass. He too began to look at himself and the same thing

* See "Tom, Dick and Harry" in the Legends (B. Local).

happened to him. Out he ran and he also felt drawn in a certain direction. Soon he overtook Mary and they skipped along together. They noticed that there seemed to be a great many hares all going the same way as they were. At last they arrived at a big field at Clonallon which was filled with hares all dancing round. Mary and Pat danced round too. A great big hare called them all to order and began to speak. They could understand the hares' talk quite well and it was a sort of Parliament of hares. Before long, the boss hare said, "I can smell strangers, there are some here that should not be here at all." Mary and Pat felt sort of uneasy at this and when all the other hares turned and looked at them, they turned round and ran away but all the other hares ran after them. But Mary and Pat had a good start and got away safely and reached home. Mary went to the looking-glass to see what she looked like as a hare and when she looked into the glass she saw that she was turning back into a woman, and Pat into a man again.

Ulster Folk-Life, 1959, N. Cooper, told by Mrs Mulholland, Warrenpoint, from Mr Mulholland, Restrevor.

MOTIFS: D.851.1. [*Magic object purchased*]; D.579 [*Transformation by looking in mirror*]; D.117.2 [*Transformation: man to hare*].

¶ This seems rather a fragment of a story than a whole one, though the motifs composing it are perfectly traditional. It is possible that the hares were disguised witches, and that it was a witch mirror which Mary had accidentally acquired.

THE HAUNTED CASTLE

A young soldier, a gentleman's son, he was bold and fearless, and was often in trouble by his wild pranks. The Colonel and his officers knew he was clever and would be a credit to his ranks if they could get him steadied down, but he was always out for some exploits. There was a big dark dungeon with a heap of straw where any of the soldiers were put when they had done something wrong. One day there was a lot of soldiers in this dungeon, including this young man, the door was flung open and an officer entered. And a boot was flung at him, and the officer was badly hurt. The other officers came to his assistance, and to know who threw the boot; none of them would answer. The officer said if he did not get an answer in five minutes the whole lot of them would be punished. The young soldier stepped out and said he would not let his mates be punished for his work, and he owned up that it was him that threw the boot. So he was taken to headquarters where he was courtmartialled, and his punishment was that he would carry his full kit on his back and travel to the headquarters of their Colonel for his punishment, which they said would be very severe; and he was not to get any meat for his journey, which would be two days' travel. If he could beg any meat on the road he would be free to take it, otherwise he could go hungry. So he set out on the road. The sun was hot, and about midday he began to get hungry, and thought of asking at the first house he came to for some meat; but when he came to the house he did not like to beg, and he had no money. So he had to pass it, but the next house he would ask some meat. But when the next house came, he could not ask—that was one thing he did not like to do. The day was wearing on, and in the evening he was coming to a village, so he thought, "Surely I will get something here!" But ask or beg he could not, and had to pass it also. At last he came to some large gates, and a big board, and on it was written, "Meat and Lodgings Free." Here was the place he was looking for, and he rang the bell at the gate, and a woman came, and he pointed to the board on the gate, and asked if this was all right. "Perfectly right," said the woman, "but I must warn you that the Castle is haunted, and anyone that goes there and stops all night gets such a fright that they go wrong in the mind, and sometimes it kills them."

"Oh, I'm not afraid of ghosts. If I get food and a bed for the night I will be all right."

"Very well," said the woman, "but you have been warned, and you know the castle is haunted every night." So the young soldier passed on to the castle. He knocked on the door, and a young lady came to the door, and he asked her if food and lodgings were free here. "Yes," said the young lady, "but I hope you have been warned of the danger of staying here all night, as this castle is haunted."

"Oh, I don't mind your ghosts as long as I get a feed and a bed."

"All right," said the lady, "you know I and the maids don't stop here at night. You will be by yourself in the Castle, and the castle doors will be locked."

So the young lady got the soldier some dinner. A good dinner was set before him, and after he had got his dinner a large fire was put on, and she brought him some supper to take before he went to bed, and a roasted partridge, and told him to heat it up on the fire before eating it. And she brought him a lot of books to read. Then her and the maids locked up the castle and went away.

He sat near the fire and had a look at the books till near bedtime; then he got the frying-pan, and got his partridge into it, and was just busy frying it, when a white hand appeared and seized his partridge. "Hie! fry for yersell, ye Bastard," said the soldier.

And just then a white lady appeared before him.

"You are the first person who has had the courage to speak, and if you follow me, I will let you see why I cannot rest and disturb this castle. I was murdered by the young gentleman who I was to marry."

The soldier followed her, carrying the light, to a room. Then she pointed to some boards of the floor, and said, "If you lift those boards, you will find my body there. And now, when you know all, I can now rest in peace."

So she disappeared, and he went back to his supper, and then to bed, and had a good night's sleep. In the morning, when the lady and her maids arrived, the lady was surprised to see him in such good spirits, and asked him if he saw the ghost.

"Yes," he said, and told the lady what had happened. They got a carpenter to lift the boards in the room the lady ghost had pointed out, and her bones and part of her bridal dress was lying there. And the soldier told her that the ghost would no longer haunt the castle. The young lady was so pleased with this fearless soldier, she told him the only way she could repay him for freeing the castle of the ghost was herself. She was willing to marry him.

"Oh," said the soldier, "I can't do that, my lady, as I am on my way to the Colonel for punishment, and I must get on my way."

So he resumed his journey, and at last he reached the headquarters of the Colonel, and handed the Colonel the letter the officers had given him. He had also got a letter from the young lady at the Haunted Castle for him, as she said he was a friend. After reading the letters, the Colonel asked all about his journey, and what happened on his way. So he told him all.

"Well," said the Colonel, "your punishment is, you go back to the haunted Castle, and marry the young lady, who is my daughter, and I will be there presently, to see that the wedding is carried out, and I will also see to both of your welfare."

John Elliot MS., School of Scottish Studies. Yarrowford, Selkirk.
TYPE 326A*. MOTIFS: H.1411.1 [*Fear test: staying in haunted house*]; E.282 [*Ghosts haunt castle*]; E.231 [*Return from dead to reveal murder*]; E.441 [*Ghost laid by reburial*].
¶ This quite modern story contains all the essentials of 326A*, though in less grotesque form than usual. The punctuation has been modified.

See "The Golden Ball", "The Devil and the Hogshead", "A Wager Won". An Irish version is "The Headless Trunk".

THE HEDLEY KOW

There was once an old woman, who earned a poor living by going errands and suchlike, for the farmers' wives round about the village where she lived. It wasn't much she earned by it; but with a plate of meat at one house, and a cup of tea at another, she made shift to get on somehow, and always looked as cheerful as if she hadn't a want in the world.

Well, one summer evening as she was trotting away homewards she came upon a big black pot lying at the side of the road.

"Now *that*," said she, stopping to look at it, "would be just the very thing for me if I had anything to put into it! But who can have left it here?" and she looked round about, as if the person it belonged to must be not far off. But she could see no one.

"Maybe it'll have a hole in it," she said thoughtfully:

"Ay, that'll be how they've left it lying, hinny. But then it'd do fine to put a flower in for the window; I'm thinking I'll just take it home, anyways." And she bent her stiff old back, and lifted the lid to look inside.

"Mercy me!" she cried, and jumped back to the other side of the road, "*if it isn't brim full o' gold* PIECES!!"

For a while she could do nothing but walk and walk round her treasure, admiring the yellow gold, and wondering at her good luck, and saying to herself about every two minutes, "Well, I *do* be feeling rich and grand!" But presently she began to think how she could best take it home with her; and she couldn't see any other way than by fastening one end of her shawl to it, and so dragging it after her along the road.

"It'll certainly be soon dark," she said to herself, "and folk'll not see what I'm bringing home with me, and so I'll have all the night to myself to think what I'll do with it. I could buy a grand house and all, and live like the Queen herself, and not do a stroke of work all day, but just sit by the fire with a cup of tea; or maybe I'll give it to the priest to keep for me, and get a piece as I'm wanting; or maybe I'll just bury it in a hole at the garden foot, and put a bit on the chimney, between the chiney teapot and the spoons—for ornament like. Ah! I feel so grand, I don't know myself rightly."

And by this time, being already rather tired with dragging such a heavy weight after her, she stopped to rest for a minute, turning to make sure that her treasure was safe.

But when she looked at it, it wasn't a pot of gold at all, but a great lump of shining silver!

She stared at it, and rubbed her eyes, and stared at it again; but she couldn't make it look like anything but a great lump of silver. "I'd have sworn it was a pot of gold," she said at last, "but I reckon I must have been dreaming. Ay, now, that's a change for the better; it'll be far less trouble to look after, and none so easy stolen; yon gold pieces would have been a sight of bother to keep 'em safe. Ay, I'm well quit of them; and with my bonny lump I'm as rich as rich!"

And she set off homewards again, cheerfully planning all the grand things she was going to do with her money. It wasn't very long, however, before she got tired again and stopped once more to rest for a minute or two.

Again she turned to look at her treasure, and as soon as she set eyes on it she cried out in astonishment. "Oh, my!" said she, "now it's a lump of iron! Well, that beats all, and it's just real convenient! I can sell it as *easy* as *easy*, and get a lot o' penny pieces for it. Ay, hinny, an' it's much handier than a lot o' yer gold and silver as'd have kept me from sleeping o' nights thinking the neighbours were robbing me—an' it's a real good thing to have by you in a house, ye niver can tell what ye mightn't use it for, an' it'll sell,—ay, for a real lot. Rich? I'll be just *rolling*!"

And on she trotted again, chuckling to herself on her good luck, till presently she glanced over her shoulder, "just to make sure it was there still," as she said to herself.

"Eh my!" she cried as soon as she saw it, "if it hasn't gone and turned itself into a great stone this time! Now, how could it have known that I was just *terrible* wanting something to hold my door open with? Ay, if that isn't a good change! Hinny, it's a fine thing to have such good luck."

And, all in a hurry to see how the stone would look in its corner by her door, she trotted off down the hill, and stopped at the foot, beside her own little gate.

When she had unlatched it, she turned to unfasten her shawl from the stone, which this time seemed to lie unchanged and peaceably on the path beside her. There was still plenty of light, and she could see the stone quite plainly as she bent her stiff back over it, to untie the shawl end; when, all of a sudden, it seemed to give a jump and a squeal, and grew in a moment as big as a great horse; then it threw down four lanky legs, and shook out two long ears, flourished a tail, and went off kicking its feet into the air, and laughing like a naughty mocking boy.

The old woman stared after it, till it was fairly out of sight.

"WELL!" she said at last, "I *do* be the luckiest body hereabouts! Fancy me seeing the Hedley Kow all to myself, and making so free with it too! I can tell you, I *do* feel that GRAND—"

And she went into her cottage and sat down by the fire to think over her good luck.

Jacobs, *More English Fairy Tales*, p. 50.
TYPE 1415 (distant variant). In the typical version of this tale the wife thinks her husband's foolish exchanges are always for the better, and so wins him a wager. Here there is no husband, and the changes are performed by magic, but the result is equally happy.
MOTIFS: F.234.0.2 [*Fairy as shape-shifter*]; F.234.3 [*Fairy in form of object*]; J.346 [*Better be content with what you have*].
❡ Tricks of the kind played by the Hedley Kow are to be found in Part B, among the Bogy and Fairy Legends.

HOW JACK WENT TO SEEK HIS FORTUNE
[summary]

A boy named Jack set out to seek his fortune, and soon he met a cat.

"Where are you going, Jack?" said the cat.

"I am going to seek my fortune."

"May I go with you?"

"Yes," said Jack, "the more the merrier."

So on they went, jiggelty-jolt, jiggelty-jolt.

They went a little further and they met a dog, and after that a goat, then a bull, and then a rooster. Each of these held the same enquiry with Jack, and then joined his company. At nightfall they looked about for somewhere to stay, and when they reached a house, Jack told the others to wait, while he went up to it and looked through the window. Inside were some robbers, counting their money.

Jack went back to the others, and told them to keep quiet until he gave the word, and then all together to make as much noise as they could. So at the word the cat mewed, the dog barked, the goat bleated, the bull bellowed, and the rooster crowed, and the terrible noise they made frightened the robbers away.

Jack and the others went in, and in case the robbers should come back he put the cat in the rocking-chair, the dog under the table, the goat upstairs, and the bull in the cellar. The rooster flew up to the roof, and Jack went to bed.

When the robbers saw the house was again in darkness, they sent one of their number back to look to their money. But soon he returned to them in terror, and said, "I went to sit in the rocking-chair, and an old woman stuck her knitting-needles into me; and when I went to the table to look for the money, a shoe-maker underneath it stuck his awl into me. I went upstairs, and there was a man threshing, who knocked me down with his flail. In the cellar, a man chopping wood knocked me down with his axe, and worst of all, a little fellow up on the roof kept calling out, "Chuck him up to me-e! Chuck him up to me-e!""

Jacobs, *English Fairy Tales*, p. 24.

TYPE 130. MOTIFS: B.296 [*Animals go a-journeying*]; N.776 [*Light seen from lodging-place leads to adventure*]; K.335.1.4.1. [*Animals cry out; frighten robbers*]; K.1161 [*Animals hidden in various parts of the house attack owners and put them to flight*].

¶ This story has a wide distribution. This version only differs from the "Bremen Musicians" in having a man as leader of the band.

See also "The Bull, the Tup, the Cock and the Steg", and "Mr Korbes the Fox".

THE INCORRIBIGLE YOUTH [summary]

Farmer employed incorrigibly idle boy to watch sheep. Gave him sack to sleep in, meaning to catch him asleep and drown him. Persuaded youth to take his place and get his pay. Youth drowned. Farmer tried to roast him in oven. Another substitution. Tried to cut his feet off. Another substitution. (Details not remembered.)

T. W. Thompson. From Shony Gray, Grimsby, 8 November 1914.
TYPE 327C. MOTIF: K.842 [*Dupe persuaded to take prisoner's place in sack: killed*].

JACK AND HIS BARGAINS

Once upon a time, when there was kings an' queens in every county, an' that was neither in your time, nor my time, but 'twas in somebody's time, there lived a farmer oo 'ad seven cows an' a wery wild son. Now this son 'ad run 'is father into all kinds of debt, an' 'e couldn't pay 'is rent. So 'e sends Jack off to the fair with one of the cows, an' told 'im to get all the money 'e could for it.

On the road, Jack sees a man, oo axes 'im where 'e's goin'. "To the fair," ses 'e, "to sell my cow." "Ah," ses 'e, "don't take 'er to the fair, swap it with me for this wonderful stick," ses 'e. "It's the wonderfullest stick wot ever was, an' if you're ever in danger of your life, you say, 'Up stick an' at it,' an' it'll bate all your enemies senseless." So Jack swaps the cow for the stick.

'Ome 'e comes, an' there's the cloth spread on the table, an' all the vittles. "Well, my child," ses 'is father, "wot did you get for the cow?" Ses Jack, "I swapped it for this wonderful stick." "You young rascal," ses 'is father, an' 'e gets a stick to bate 'im. But Jack ses, "Up, Stick an' at 'im," an' the stick bates 'em up an' down, from one side of the room to the other, till they 'ad to cry for marcy.

So Jack calls 'im off, but 'e ses, "For God's sake, don't say no more about that stick, or I'll set 'im on again."

Well, time went on, an' they get poorer, an' the next fair cum round. An' the old man sends Jack off with the second cow. "Get the best you can," ses 'e. So, on the way, Jack sees the very selfsame man again. An' the man ses, "Swap the cow for this dear little bee, it's the wonderfullest singer as ever was, an' you'll draw people from all parts to listen to it." An' with that, the bee begins to sing the 'lightfullest songs as ever was sung. So Jack swaps 'is cow for this dear little bee, an' sets off 'ome. "Well," ses 'is father, "'ow much did the cow make?" "I swapped 'er for this dear little bee," ses Jack, an' with that the bee began to sing

314

the 'lightfullest songs as ever was 'eard, an' people from far an' near cum to 'ear it.

So when the next fair cums round, off Jack sets with the third cow, an' on the road 'e meets with this same man again. "Jack," ses 'e, "I've got the beautifullest fiddle as ever you see'd," ses 'e. "It'll play the 'lightfullest, beautifullest music as ever was 'eard, an' it'll draw people from far an' wide an' foreign parts to 'ear it." An' with that, the fiddle played the wonderfullest music of its own accord. "Swap the cow for the fiddle," ses 'e—an' so Jack swapped. When Jack goes 'ome, 'is father was in a terrible way, for 'e owed a matter o' two or three 'undred pounds.

Now, the King's daughter in them parts, 'ad never bin known to smile, an' the King said as anyone as could make 'is gal laugh three times should marry 'er. There was Lords an' Squires, an' Kings an' Princes an' wealthy men cum from all parts of the globe, but nary a one of 'em could make 'er smile. So up goes Jack in 'is ragged clothes, an' with "Up Stick an' at It", an' the Bee, an' the Fiddle. An' the Bee sings 'is dear beautiful songs, an' she smiles. An' then the Fiddle plays the 'lightfullest music as you ever 'eard, an' she smiles again; an' then the stick up's amongst 'em all, an' knocks 'em about all ways, an' she laughs outright. It would 'ave made the Devil laugh.

So Jack 'as to marry the King's daughter, an' they 'aves a big party, an' merrymaking, an' feasting. On the first night they goes to bed. Well, Jack just lies, an' doesn't turn this way nor that, but just as if 'e's made of stone—an' 'e was to 'ave a 'undred pounds for that—that was to pay for the first cow, you *dik*. In the morning she ses to the King, "What kind of a man is this, 'e never turned to me all night." "Oh," ses 'e, "p'raps 'e's strange, an' ain't got used with our ways of living." So the next night they goes to bed, an' Jack never turned to 'er—that was another 'undred pounds for the second cow—but *leste hinged adre* the *wodros*. So in the morning she ses, "Pa, what sort of a man is this? 'E *kelled* the *wodrus ĕĭklū*." "Oh," ses 'e, "p'raps 'e ain't 'customed with our livin' an' diet; but," 'e ses, "if 'e does it again, we'll throw 'im into the lions an' tigers to revour 'im." So they sends for the blacksmith to put a plate in the bed. The next night Jack does the same—an' that's a 'undred pound for the third cow. So in the morning they throws 'im into the wild beasties, but 'e takes 'is stick, an' ses, "Up, Stick, an' at It", an' the Stick bates the lions senseless, an' when she see'd what a proper man 'e was, she changed 'er mind, an' married 'im, an' they 'ad basketsfull of children.

An' if they ain't dead, they're livin' yet. An' there's my tale!

[The following note is appended: "The motive for abstention from cohabitation for the three nights is missing, but it may be suggested that, either the King conditionally offered Jack the one hundred pounds for each night, in order to bring disgrace upon him by trickery, and so avoid a *mésalliance*; or, that the man who owned the three wonders had instructed Jack as to his behaviour."]

Norton Collection, II, p. 122. From *Journal of the Gypsy Lore Society*, n.s. IV (1911), pp. 273–5.

TYPE 559. MOTIFS: D.837 [*Magic object acquired through foolish bargain*]; H.341 [*Suitor test: making princess laugh*]; D.1094 [*Magic cudgel*]; D.1233 [*Magic fiddle*]; H.1472 [*Test: sleeping by princess three nights without looking at her or disturbing her*].

JACK AND THE BEANSTALK: I

There was once upon a time a poor widow who had an only son named Jack, and a cow named Milky-white. And all they had to live on was the milk the cow gave every morning which they carried to the market and sold. But one morning Milky-white gave no milk, and they didn't know what to do.

"What shall we do, what shall we do?" said the widow, wringing her hands.

"Cheer up, mother, I'll go and get work somewhere," said Jack.

"We've tried that before, and nobody would take you," said his mother. "We must sell Milky-white, and with the money start shop, or something."

"All right, mother," says Jack, "it's market-day to-day, and I'll soon sell Milky-white, and then we'll see what we can do."

So he took the cow's halter in his hand, and off he started. He hadn't gone far when he met a funny-looking old man, who said to him: "Good morning, Jack."

"Good morning to you," said Jack, and wondered how he knew his name.

"Well, Jack, and where are you off to?" said the man.

"I'm going to market to sell our cow here."

"Oh, you look the proper sort of chap to sell cows," said the man. "I wonder if you know how many beans make five?"

"Two in each hand, and one in your mouth," says Jack, as sharp as a needle.

"Right you are," says the man, "and here they are, the very beans themselves," he went on, pulling out of his pocket a number of strange-looking beans. "As you are so sharp," says he, "I don't mind doing a swop with you—your cow for these beans."

"Go along," says Jack, "wouldn't you like it?"

"Ah! you don't know what these beans are," said the man, "if you plant them overnight, by morning they grow right up to the sky."

"Really?" says Jack, "you don't say so?"

"Yes, that is so, and if it doesn't turn out to be true, you can have your cow back."

"Right", says Jack, and hands him over Milky-white's halter and pockets the beans.

Back goes Jack home, and as he hadn't gone very far it wasn't dusk by the time he got to his door.

"Back already, Jack," said his mother. "I see you haven't got Milky-white, so you've sold her. How much did you get for her?"

"You'll never guess, mother," says Jack.

"No, you don't say so. Good boy! Five pounds, ten, fifteen, no, it can't be twenty."

"I told you you couldn't guess, what do you say to these beans; they're magical, plant them over-night and——"

"What!" says Jack's mother, "have you been such a fool, such a dolt, such an idiot, as to give away my Milky-white, the best milker in the parish, and prime beef to boot, for a set of paltry beans? Take that! Take that! And as for your precious beans, here they go out of the window. And now off with you to bed. Not a sup shall you drink, and not a bit shall you swallow this very night."

So Jack went upstairs to his little room in the attic, and sad and sorry he was to be sure, as much for his mother's sake, as for the loss of his supper.

At last he dropped off to sleep.

When he woke up, the room looked so funny. The sun was shining into part of it, and yet all the rest was quite dark and shady. So Jack jumped up and dressed himself, and went to the window. And what do you think he saw? Why, the beans his mother had thrown out of the window into the garden had sprung up into a big beanstalk which went up and up and up till it reached the sky. So the man spoke truth after all.

The beanstalk grew up quite close past Jack's window, so all he had to do was to open it and give a jump on to the beanstalk, which ran up just like a big ladder. So Jack climbed, and he climbed and he climbed and he climbed and he climbed and he climbed and he climbed till at last he reached the sky. And when he got there, he found a long broad road, going as straight as a dart. So he walked along and he walked along and he walked along till he came to a great big tall house, and on the doorstep there was a great big tall woman.

"Good morning, mum," says Jack, quite polite-like. "Could you be so kind as to give me some breakfast?" For he hadn't had anything to eat, you know, the night before, and was as hungry as a hunter.

"It's breakfast you want, is it?" says the great big tall woman. "It's breakfast you'll be if you don't move off from here. My man is an ogre, and there's nothing he likes better than boys broiled on toast. You'd better be moving on or he'll soon be coming."

"Oh, please, mum, do give me something to eat, mum. I've had nothing to eat since yesterday morning, really and truly, mum," says Jack. "I may as well be broiled as die of hunger."

Well, the ogre's wife was not half so bad after all. So she took Jack into the kitchen, and gave him a junk of bread and cheese, and a jug of milk. But Jack hadn't half finished these when thump! thump! thump! the whole house began to tremble with the noise of someone coming.

"Goodness, gracious me! It's my old man," said the ogre's wife. "What on earth shall I do? Come along quick, and jump in here." And she bundled Jack into the oven just as the ogre came in.

He was a big one, to be sure. At his belt he had three calves strung up by the heels, and he unhooked them and threw them down on the table, and said, "Here, wife, broil me a couple of these for breakfast. Ah! What's this I smell?

> "Fee-fi-fo-fum,
> I smell the blood of an Englishman,
> Be he alive, or be he dead
> I'll have his bones to grind my bread."

"Nonsense, dear," said his wife, "you're dreaming. Or perhaps you smell the scraps of that little boy you liked so much for yesterday's dinner. Here, you go and have a wash and tidy up, and by the time you come back your breakfast'll be ready for you."

So off the ogre went, and Jack was just going to jump out of the oven and run away when the woman told him not. "Wait till he's asleep," says she; "he always has a doze after breakfast."

Well, the ogre had his breakfast, and after that he goes to a big chest and takes out a couple of bags of gold, and down he sits and counts, till at last his head began to nod, and he began to snore till the whole house shook again.

Then Jack crept out on tiptoe from his oven, and as he was passing the ogre he took one of the bags of gold under his arm, and off he pelters till he came to the beanstalk, and then he threw down the bag of gold, which of course fell into his mother's garden, and then he climbed down and climbed down, till at last he got home and told his mother, and showed her the gold and said, "Well, mother, wasn't I right about the beans? They are really magical, you see."

So they lived on the bag of gold for some time, but at last they came to the end of it, and Jack made up his mind to try his luck once more up at the top of the beanstalk. So one fine morning he rose up early, and he climbed and he climbed and he climbed and he climbed and he climbed and he climbed, till at last he came out on to the road again and up to the great big tall house he had been to before. There, sure enough, was the great big tall woman a-standing on the doorstep.

"Good morning, mum," says Jack, as bold as brass. "Could you be so good as to give me something to eat?"

"Go away, my boy," said the big tall woman, "or else my man will eat you up for breakfast. But aren't you the youngster who came here once before? Do you know, that very day, my man missed one of his bags of gold."

"That's strange, mum," says Jack. "I daresay I could tell you something about that, but I'm so hungry I can't speak till I've had something to eat."

Well, the big tall woman was so curious that she took him in and gave him something to eat. But he had scarcely begun munching it as slowly as he could when thump! thump! thump! they heard the giant's footstep, and his wife hid Jack away in the oven.

All happened as it did before. In came the ogre as he did before, said "Fee-fi-fo-fum", and had his breakfast off three broiled oxen. Then he said, "Wife, bring me the hen that lays the golden eggs." So she brought it and the ogre said: "Lay," and it laid an egg all of gold. And then the ogre began to nod his head, and to snore till the house shook.

Then Jack crept out of the oven on tiptoe, and caught hold of the golden hen, and was off before you could say "Jack Robinson". But this time the hen gave a cackle which woke the ogre, and just as Jack got out of the house he heard him calling: "Wife, wife, what have you done with my golden hen?"

And the wife said: "Why, my dear?"

But that was all Jack heard, for he rushed off to the beanstalk, and climbed down like a house on fire. And when he got home he showed his mother the wonderful hen, and said "Lay" to it, and it laid a golden egg every time he said "Lay".

Well, Jack was not content, and it wasn't very long before he determined to have another try at his luck up there at the top of the beanstalk. So one fine morning he rose up early, and got on to the beanstalk, and he climbed, and he climbed and he climbed and he climbed, till he got to the top. But this time he knew better than to go straight to the ogre's house. And when he got near it he waited behind a bush till he saw the ogre's wife come out with a pail to get some water, and then he crept into the house and got into the copper. He hadn't been there very long when he heard thump! thump! thump! as before, and in came the ogre and his wife.

"Fee-fi-fo-fum, I smell the blood of an Englishman," cried the ogre. "I smell him, wife, I smell him."

"Do you, my dearie?" says the ogre's wife. "Then if it's that little rogue that stole your gold, and the hen that laid the golden eggs, he's sure to have got into the oven." And they both rushed to the oven. But Jack wasn't there, luckily, and the ogre's wife said: "There you are again, with your Fee-fi-fo-fum. Why, of course, it's the boy you caught last night, that I've just broiled for your breakfast. How forgetful I am, and how careless you are, not to know the difference between live and dead, after all these years."

So the ogre sat down to the breakfast, and ate it, but every now and then he would mutter: "Well, I could have sworn——", and he'd get up and search the larder, and the cupboards, and everything, only luckily, he didn't think of the copper. After breakfast was over, the ogre called out: "Wife, wife, bring me my golden harp." So she brought it, and put it on the table before him. Then he said: "Sing!" and the golden harp sang most beautifully. And it went on singing till the ogre fell asleep, and commenced to snore like thunder.

Then Jack lifted the copper-lid very quietly, and got down like a mouse and crept on hands and knees till he came to the table when up he crawled, caught hold of the golden harp and dashed with it towards the door. But the harp called out quite loud, "Master! Master!"; and the ogre woke up just in time to see Jack running off with his harp.

Jack ran as fast as he could, and the ogre came rushing after, and would soon have caught him only Jack had a start and dodged him a bit and knew where he was going. When he got to the beanstalk the ogre was not more than twenty yards away when suddenly he saw Jack disappear like, and when he came to the end of the road he saw Jack underneath, climbing down for dear life. Well, the ogre didn't like trusting himself to such a ladder, and he stood and waited, so Jack got another start. But just then the harp cried out: "Master! Master!" and the ogre swung himself down on the beanstalk, which shook with his weight. Down climbs Jack, and after him climbed the ogre. By this time Jack had climbed down and climbed down and climbed down till he was very nearly home. So he called out, "Mother! Mother! Bring me an axe, bring me an axe!" And his mother came rushing out with the axe in her hand, but when she came to the beanstalk she stood stock still with fright for there she saw the ogre with his legs just through the clouds.

But Jack jumped down, and got hold of the axe, and gave a chop at the beanstalk which cut it half in two. The ogre felt the beanstalk shake and quiver, so he stopped to see what was the matter. Then Jack gave another chop with the axe, and the beanstalk was cut in two and began to topple over. Then the ogre fell down and broke his crown and the beanstalk came toppling after.

Then Jack showed his mother his golden harp, and what with showing that and selling the golden eggs, Jack and his mother became very rich, and he married a great princess, and they lived happy ever after.

Norton Collection, I, p. 202, Jacobs I, pp. 59–67, as told him in Australia, *c.* 1860. TYPE 328. MOTIFS: D.837 [*Magic article acquired through foolish bargain*]; D.983.1 [*Magic bean*]; F.54.2 [*Plant grows to sky*]; G.532 [*Hero hidden, ogre smells human blood, deceived by wife*]; G.84 [*Fee, fi, fo, fum*]; G.610 [*Theft from ogre*]; B.103.2.1 [*Treasure-laying bird*]; D.1231 [*Magic harp*]; G.512 [*Ogre killed*].

¶ This is probably the original form, older than the early chapbook version with its moral fairy.

Cruikshank further moralized the story in his fairy book, by making the giant a drunkard, who was taken to Alfred's court and reformed. As in the chapbook story, he had stolen the magical objects and the castle from Jack's father.

JACK AND THE BEANSTALK: II [summary]

[The story is told in the usual way until Jack has climbed the Beanstalk.] He found himself in a strange desert country, and sat down to rest on a rock. A beautiful young woman approached, carrying a white wand, with a golden peacock at the top, and told him that she was a fairy, and that if he would carry out her commands exactly, she would help him. Jack gave his promise, and the fairy told him that his father, a rich and generous man, had been foully murdered by a giant, and Jack, then a baby of a few months old, had been imprisoned with his mother in a dungeon below the giant's castle. Later they were released but were sent almost penniless to a distant land, lest Jack's mother should tell the tale of her wrongs to any of the giant's neighbours.

The fairy herself had been the appointed guardian of Jack's father but, for an offence, she had been temporarily deprived of her powers under fairy law, and they had only been restored to her on the day when Jack was sent to sell his mother's cow.

It was she who had persuaded him to exchange the beans for the cow. The giant's wealth belonged to Jack by right, since it had been stolen by the giant from his father, and she would help him to recover it. But it was necessary that he should outwit the giant, whose love of gold would make him increasingly fierce as he discovered the theft of any part of it. Further, Jack must tell none of this to his mother until he had seen the fairy again.

This second meeting is not recorded in the story, but after the usual adventures, ending with the giant's fall from the beanstalk and his death, Jack begged his mother's forgiveness for all his past disobedience, and "became a pattern of affectionate behaviour and attention to his parent".

B. Chapbook version. Hartland, *English Fairy and Folk Tales*, p. 35.
TYPE 328. MOTIFS: F.347 [*Fairy adviser*]; F.312.2 [*Fairies control destinies of mortals*]. The other motifs the same as in previous version.

JACK AND THE BEANSTALK: C [summary]

Jack and his mother. Jack asked for a cake and a blessing, and went to look for work. Engaged to plough and told to make straight for an oak in middle of field. Ploughed it down and almost buried it. Dismissed. After a time, asked again for a cake and a blessing, and went to sell cow. Asked £15, but was content with 15 beans. Planted them, and they grew up to the sky.

One day Jack climbed up, and found a castle full of treasure. Took a golden crown, and gave it to his mother. Went again, and loaded himself with treasure. Followed by old woman who owned castle. He chopped down the beanstalk. She broke her neck, and Jack kept the treasure.

Thompson Notebooks. Eva Gray, 8 November 1914.
TYPE 328.

A preface of the servant taking the master's orders too literally. The usual story, except that it is an old woman, not a giant, from whom Jack steals.
ADDITIONAL MOTIFS: J.2465.12 [*Ploughing above the tree*]; J.229.3 [*Choice: a big piece of cake with my curse or a small piece with my blessing*]. This motif is much commoner in the Scottish than the English fairy tales.

JACK THE BUTTER-MILK

Jack was a boy who sold butter-milk. One day as he was going his rounds he met a witch who asked him for some of his butter-milk, and told him that if he refused to give it she would put him into a bag that she carried over her shoulders.

But Jack would not give the witch any of his butter-milk, so she put him into her bag, and walked off home with him.

But as she was going on her way she suddenly remembered that she had forgotten a pot of fat that she had bought in the town. Now Jack was too heavy to be carried back to the town, so the witch asked some men who were brushing the hedge by the roadside if they would take care of her bag until she came back.

The men promised to take care of the bag, but when the witch had gone Jack called out to them and said, "If you will take me out of this bag, and fill it full of thorns I will give you some of my butter-milk."

So the men took Jack out of the bag and filled it with thorns, and then Jack gave them some butter-milk, and ran home.

When the witch came back from the town she picked up her bag, threw it over her shoulder, and walked away. But she had not gone far before the thorns began to prick her back, and she said, "Jack, I think thou'st got some pins about thee, lad."

As soon as she had got home she emptied the bag upon a clean white sheet that she had ready. But when she found that there was nothing in the bag but thorns, she was very angry, and said, "I'll catch thee to-morrow, Jack, and I'll boil thee."

The next day she met Jack again, and asked him for some butter-milk, and told him that if he would not give it her she would put him in her bag again. But Jack said he would give her no butter-milk, so she put him into her bag, and again she bethought her that she had forgotten something for which she would have to go back to the town.

This time she left the bag with some men who were mending the road. Now as soon as the witch had gone, Jack called out to them and said, "If you will take me out and fill this bag full of stones, I will give you some of my butter-milk."

Then the men took Jack out of the bag, and he gave them the butter-milk.

When the witch came back she threw the bag over her shoulder as before, and when she heard the stones grinding and rattling she chuckled and said, "My word, Jack, thy bones do crack."

When she got home she emptied the bag on the white sheet again. But when she saw the stones she was very angry, and swore that she would boil Jack when she caught him.

The next day she went out as before, and met Jack again, and asked for some butter-milk. But Jack said "No," again, so she put him into her bag, and went straight home with him, and threw him out upon the white sheet.

When she had done this, she went out of the house and locked Jack in, intending to boil him when she came back. But whilst she was away Jack opened all the cupboards in the house and filled the bag with all the pots that he could find. After he had done this he escaped through the chimney, and got safe home.

When the witch came back she emptied the bag upon the sheet again, and broke all the pots she had in the house. After this she never caught Jack any more.

S. O. Addy, *Household Tales*, p. 7.

TYPE 327C. MOTIFS: G.441 [*Ogre carries victim in bag*]; K.526 [*Captor's bag filled with animals or objects, while captives escape*].

JACK AND THE GHOSTS [summary]

Once there was a lad called Jack, and as he was passing a churchyard at night he saw three ghosts fighting. He hurried past, but the ghosts came after him and brought him back to settle their dispute. They were well

pleased with the way he settled it and they gave him three presents—a
piece of dough and a needle and some cloth. They told him those would
be of great use to him, for they were magic. So Jack went on his way till
he came to a town and the first shop he came to was a baker's shop and
it was filled with ancient cakes, a hundred and fifty years old or so. He
went into the shop, but there was nothing fit to eat there and the baker
told him that the Queen had ordered him to bake her a cake, but he had
only a pound of flour in the place. "Leave it to me," said Jack, and he
went alone into the bakehouse, and said to the dough, "Do your work!"
And the dough set to, and baked itself into a most beautiful cake, and
and cakes and bread and pies until the shop was full. The baker was
delighted, and begged Jack to stay with him, but Jack wouldn't bide;
he went on to the next shop, and that was a tailor's, full of old, ragged
clothes. The tailor was in despair because the Queen had ordered him to
make her a most beautiful frock and he had nothing to make it of. So
Jack set the piece of cloth to work, and it made a most beautiful frock,
embroidered with gold, and the tailor took it to the Queen and begged
Jack to stay with him, but Jack wouldn't bide. The next shop he came to
was a shoemaker's, and the shoemaker had been ordered to make grand
shoes for the Queen. And here the needle set to and stitched and stitched
until it had made shoes for the Queen and the Princes and the whole
Court besides. Then the Queen sent out a notice that she wanted the
palace done up. And Jack presented himself with his needle and his cloth
and did up the palace so that there was nothing to equal it. And the Queen
gave him a great reward. But about this time pigs began to go missing
from the Royal pigsties, and for one reason or another they suspected
Jack. So they put a watch on him, and one night they caught him carrying
a pig in through the door instead of out. So they married him to the King's
Daughter, and they lived happily all their days.

School of Scottish Studies, H. Henderson, from Alex. Macdonald, Perthshire.
TYPE 585 (variant). MOTIFS: H.1430 [*Fearless traffic with ghosts*]; D.812.4 [*Magic
object received from ghost*]; D.1652.1 [*Inexhaustible food*]; D.1652.8 [*Inexhaustible
cloth*]; D.1181 [*Magic needle*].
¶ The type of this tale is difficult to determine. If we consider the Ghosts as Grateful
Dead it might be type 505. On the other hand, the magical objects which win a royal
bride bring it near to 585.

JACK AND THE GIANT [summary]

Jack, the son of a widow, went out to work, with a small cake and a blessing. Hired to a farmer. Sent with other men to cut wood; sat all day, and
at night dragged up two trees, and took them to farm. Farmer sent him
to put them back. Jack disgusted and went home. Exchanged cow for

beans. His mother threw them away. One rooted, and grew into an enormous beanstalk.

Jack climbed up it and stole magic club, tablecloth, and ass which dropped gold. Giant never caught him. Some men stole his magic goods, and put him in a sack to drown him. On the way they went into a pub to drink, man with flock of sheep passed by. Jack pretended he was being taken to marry the Princess. Changed places with man, and took his sheep. After the man was drowned, the murderers met Jack driving sheep, who said he had got them under the water, and there were plenty more. The men jumped in after them, and Jack got back the magic properties.

Thompson Notebooks, IX. From Taimi Boswell, Oswaldtwistle, 10 January 1915 (complete tale).
TYPES 328; 1535. ADDITIONAL MOTIFS: J.229.3 [*Choice: a big piece of cake with my curse, or a small piece with my blessing*]; F.621 [*Strong man: tree-puller*]; K.842 [*The trickster escapes from a sack by exchange with a shepherd*]; K.1051 [*Diving for sheep*].

JACK AND THE GIANT OF DALTON MILL

One day the Giant of Dalton captured a youth, on the adjoining wilds of Pilmoor, whom he led home, and kept secluded in the mill doing all the servile work, but always denied liberty or recreation. Jack was determined to have a holiday at the approaching Topcliffe fair. The fair day came—one of the hot days of July—and after a hearty meal, the giant lay down in the mill for his afternoon nap, still holding the knife with which he had been cutting his loaf of bone bread; but, as sleep overpowered him his fingers relaxed their hold of the weapon. Jack gently drew the knife from his grasp, and then firmly raising it with both hands, drove the blade into the single eye of the monster. He awoke with a fearful howl, but with presence of mind to close the mill door, and so prevent the escape of his assailant. Jack was fairly trapped, but his native ingenuity came to his aid. Being blinded, the giant could only grope for him. A large dog also lay asleep in the mill. To slay this, and hurriedly take off its skin, was the work but of a few minutes. This skin he then threw around himself; and running on all fours and barking like the dog, he passed between the giant's legs, got to the door, and unbarring it quickly escaped. Death claimed its victim, but the grave and the knife have survived to avouch the story to posterity.

Mrs Gutch, *County Folk-Lore*, II, *North Riding of Yorkshire*, p. 11; Parkinson, second series, pp. 235–6.
TYPE 1137 (Polyphemus story). MOTIFS: G.100 [*Giant ogre: Polyphemus*]; G.121.1.1 [*One-eyed giant*]; G.511 [*Ogre blinded*]; K.521.1 [*Escape by dressing in animal skin*].

The "noman" element does not occur in this, but is to be found in "Masell", "Mine Ainsel", "Maggie Moulach".

¶ The story is naturally very widespread. A modern Greek version is given in Dawkins, *More Greek Folk Tales* (1955), no. 4, "The Cyclops".

JACK AND THE GIANTS

How King Arthur's son, going to seek his Fortune, met with Jack, etc.

King Arthur's only son desired of his father to furnish him with a certain sum of money, that he might go and seek his fortune in the principality of Wales, where a beautiful Lady lived, whom he heard was possessed with seven evil spirits; but the King his father advised him utterly against it, yet he would not be persuaded of it; so that he granted what he requested, which was one horse loaded with money, and another for himself to ride on; thus he went forth without any attendants.

Now after several days travel, he came to a market-town in Wales, where he beheld a large concourse of people gathered together; the King's son demanded the reason of it, and was told that they arrested a corpse for many large sums of money, which the deceased owed when he died. The King's son replied, "It is a pity that creditors should be so cruel. Go bury the dead," said he, "and let his creditors come to my lodging and their debts shall be discharged." Accordingly they came, and in such great numbers that before night he had almost left himself moneyless.

Now Jack-the-Giant-Killer being there, and seeing the generosity of the King's son, he was taken with him, and desired to be his servant; it was agreed upon, and the next morning they set forward, when, riding out at the town-end, an old woman called after him, crying out, "He hath owed me twopence these five years; pray sir, pay me as well as the rest!" He put his hand into his pocket, and gave it her; it being the last he had left, the King's son turning to Jack, said, "I cannot tell how I will subsist in my intended journey." "For that," quoth Jack, "take you no thought nor care. Let me alone, I warrant you we will not want."

Now Jack, having a small spell in his pocket, which served at noon to give them a refreshment, when done, they had not one penny left betwixt them; the afternoon they spent in travel and familiar discourse, till the sun began to grow low, at which time the King's son said, "Jack, since we have no money, where can we think to lodge this night?" Jack replied, "Master, we'll do well enough, for I have an uncle lives within two little miles of this; he's a huge and monstrous giant with three heads: he'll fight five hundred men in armour, and make them to fly before him." "Alas," quoth the King's son, "what shall we do there? He'll certainly chop us both up at one mouthful! nay, we are scarce enough to fill one of his hollow teeth." "It is no matter for that," quoth Jack, "I myself will go before, and prepare the way for you: therefore tarry here, and wait my return."

He waits, and Jack rides full speed, when coming to the gates of the castle, he knocked with such a force, that he made all the neighbouring hills to resound. The giant with a voice like thunder, roared out, "Who's there?" He answered, "None but your poor cousin Jack." Quoth he, "What news with my poor cousin Jack?" He replied, "Dear uncle, heavy news, God wot." "Prithee, what heavy news can come to me? I am a giant with three heads, and besides thou knowest I can fight five hundred men in armour, and make them fly like chaff before the wind." "O! but", quoth Jack, "here's the King's son coming with a thousand men in armour to kill you, and so to destroy all that you have!" "Oh! cousin Jack, this is heavy news indeed: I have a large vault under the ground, where I will immediately hide myself, and thou shalt lock, bolt, and bar me in, and keep the keys till the King's son is gone."

Now Jack having secured the giant, he soon returned and fetched his master, they were both heartily merry with the wine, and other dainties which were in the house: so that night they rested in very pleasant lodgings, while the poor uncle, the giant, lay trembling in the vault underground.

Early in the morning, Jack furnished his master with a fresh supply of gold and silver, and then set him three miles forward on his journey, concluding he was then pretty well out of the smell of the giant, and then returned to let his uncle out of the hole, who asked Jack what he would give him in reward if his castle was not demolished. "Why," quoth Jack, "I desire nothing but the old coat and cap, together with this old rusty sword and slippers, which are at your bed-head." Quoth the giant, "Thou shalt have them, and pray keep them for my sake, for they are things of excellent use. The coat will keep you invisible, the cap will furnish you with knowledge, the sword cuts in sunder whatever you strike, and the shoes are of extraordinary swiftness; these may be serviceable to you, and therefore pray take them with all my heart." Jack takes them, thanking his uncle, and follows his master.

How Jack saved his Master's life, and drove the Spirits out of a Lady, etc.

Jack having overtaken his master, they soon after arrived at the Lady's house, who finding the King's son to be a suitor, she prepared a banquet for him, which being ended, she wiped his mouth with her handkerchief, saying, "You must shew me this one to-morrow morning, or else lose your head": and with that she put it into her own bosom.

The King's son went to bed very sorrowful, but Jack's cap of knowledge instructed him how to obtain it. In the middle of the night, she called on her familiar spirit to carry her to her friend Lucifer. Jack soon put on his coat of darkness with his shoes of swiftness, and was there as soon as her; by reason of his coat they could not see him. When she entered the place she gave the handkerchief to Old Lucifer, who laid it upon a shelf; from whence Jack took, and brought it to his master, who shewed it to the lady next day, and so saved his life.

The next night she saluted the King's son, telling him he must show her to-morrow morning the lips that she kissed last, this night, or else lose his head. "Ah," replied he, "if you kiss none but mine, I will": "'tis neither here nor there," said she, "if you do not death's your portion." At midnight she went as before, and was angry with Lucifer for letting the handkerchief go: "But now", said she, "I will be too hard for the King's son, for I will kiss thee, and he's to shew thy lips," which she did; Jack standing near him with his sword of sharpness, cut off the devil's head, and brought it under his invisible coat to his master, who was in bed, and laid it at the end of his bolster. In the morning, when the lady came up, he pulled it out by the horns, and shewed her the devil's lips which she kissed last.

Thus, having answered her twice, the enchantment broke, and the evil spirits left her; at which time she appeared in all her beauty, a beautiful and virtuous creature. They were married the next morning in great pomp and solemnity, and soon after they returned with a numerous company to the court of King Arthur, where they were received with the greatest joy, and loud acclamations by the whole court. Jack, for the many and great exploits he had done for the good of his country, was made one of the Knights of the Round Table.

Norton Collection, II, p. 66. *The History of Jack and the Giants* (Glasgow, 1807), pp. 8–12.

TYPE 507A.

This tale is a thinly disguised version of "The Grateful Dead", only lacking the link between Jack and the dead man; the ransomed dead man in "The Old Wives' Tale" was also called Jack. The tale is more explicit and widely distributed in Celtic areas; it is therefore interesting to come across this practically complete version in an English tale.

MOTIFS: Q.271.1 [*Debtor deprived of burial*]; E.341.1 [*Corpse is being held unburied, hero pays debt, and secures burial of corpse*]; D.833 [*Magic object acquired by tricking the giant*]; H.322.1 [*Suitor test: finding object hidden by princess*]; T.118 [*Girl enamoured of a monster*]; T.172.2.1 [*Grateful dead man kills princess's monster husband*]; D.763 [*Disenchantment by destroying enchanter*].

¶ See also "Four Eggs a Penny", "The Red Etin". Celtic versions are: "Jack the Master" and "Jack the Servant", Kennedy; "The Barra Widow's Son", Campbell, XXXII.

JACK THE GIANT-KILLER: I [summary]

In the reign of King Arthur, there lived near Land's End in Cornwall a wealthy farmer who had one son named Jack. He was so ready of wit that no one could worst him.

The Mount of Cornwall was kept at that time by a huge giant 18 feet high and 3 yards round. He lived in a cave in the middle of the Mount. His food was other men's cattle which he would seize from the mainland, and so he had devastated all Cornwall.

The magistrates proclaimed that the Giant's treasure should be given as a reward to anyone who killed the Giant. So Jack, on a dark winter's evening, dug a great pit outside the Giant's cave, covered it over with sticks and earth, and blew a loud blast on his horn. The giant rushed out in a rage, fell into the pit, and was killed by a great blow on his head from Jack's pickaxe.

Jack was rewarded with an embroidered belt with these words in gold letters:

> "Here's the right valiant Cornishman
> Who slew the Giant Cormelian."

Another giant, named Blunderbore, vowed vengeance for this; he lived in a wood on the road to Wales. He seized Jack, locked him into his castle, and fetched another giant to help him. Jack saw them coming, and throttled them by dropping a noose over their heads as they entered, sliding down the rope, and despatching them with his sword.

On his way to Wales, Jack begged a night's lodging at a large house, and found that it belonged to another giant, who pretended to welcome him, but in the night Jack heard him singing:

> "Though here you lodge with me this night,
> You shall not see the morning light;
> My club shall dash your brains outright."

Jack put a billet of wood in his bed, which the giant belaboured with his club, and startled the giant in the morning by saying that a rat had slightly disturbed his rest. He hid the hasty pudding which the giant gave him for breakfast in a bag inside his coat, then, saying he would show him a trick, he slit the bag, and when the pudding came out, the giant in imitation slit up his own belly, and so died.

In Wales, Jack met King Arthur's son, who was seeking to marry a beautiful lady, possessed with seven evil spirits. Admiring his generosity and justice, Jack took service with this prince, and as the prince had given away all his money, they asked for a night's lodging with a giant, who Jack said was his uncle.

He pretended to the giant that the prince had come with an army to destroy him, locked the giant into an inner room for "protection", and he and the prince took all they needed from the giant's stores. The giant also rewarded him by giving him a coat to make him invisible, a cap of knowledge, a sword to cut everything, and shoes of swiftness.

When they reached the home of the lady whom the prince was seeking, she set the prince two tasks. First to show him the handkerchief with which she wiped his mouth (which in the night she had given to Lucifer to keep) and this Jack recovered, being invisible, and returned to the prince, and secondly, to show her in the morning the lips she had kissed at night. She then kissed Lucifer himself, but Jack cut off Lucifer's head, and brought it to his master. The enchantment was thus broken, and the prince and the lady were married.

Later on Jack, having been furnished by King Arthur with a horse and all he needed, met a giant in a wood, dragging a lady and a knight by their hair. He cut off the giant's legs with his magic sword, and going in search of the giant's lair, he found it held by the brother of the slain giant, killed him also, and sent the two heads to the king. He set free a great number of captives whom the two giants had been saving for food.

On returning to the castle of the rescued knight and lady, he received a ring with the motto:

> "We are in sad distress, you see,
> Under a giant's fierce command,
> But gain our lives and liberty
> By valiant Jack's victorious hand."

A kinsman of the two slain giants next came to the castle to avenge their deaths, and smelling the invisible Jack, he cried out:

> "Fee, fi, fo, fum!
> I smell the blood of an Englishman!
> Be he alive or be he dead,
> I'll grind his bones to make me bread!"

But Jack had had the drawbridge sawn almost in two before the giant's arrival, and led the giant across it, so that it broke and the giant fell in. Jack threw a rope over his two heads, pulled him to shore with a team of horses, and cut off the heads.

Seeking further adventures, Jack was entertained one night by an old man who told him of another giant, Galligantus, who by magic had lured many knights and ladies into his castle, then turned them into different animals. The castle was guarded by two griffins which destroyed all comers. But Jack made himself invisible, and found upon the castle gate these words:

> "Whoever shall this trumpet blow,
> Shall soon the giant overthrow,
> And break the black enchantment straight;
> So all shall be in happy state."

Jack blew the trumpet, cut off the giant's head, the conjuror who had helped the giant flew up into the air, and the enchantment was broken. The head of Galligantus was sent to the King, Jack was married to a Duke's daughter, and the King gave them a great estate to live on.

E. S. Hartland, *English Fairy and Folk Tales*, p. 3.

TYPES 300, 328, 507A, 1115, 1088. MOTIFS: First incident: K.735 [*Captive in pitfall*]; G.512 [*Ogre killed*]; F.531.6.7 [*Giant's treasure*]; Q.111.6 [*Treasure as reward*].
Second incident: G.400 [*Person falls into ogre's power*]; F.511.0.2.2 [*Three-headed person*]; G.514.3 [*Ogre caught in a noose and killed*]; F.511.0.2.1 [*Two-headed person*].
Third incident: K.525.1 [*Substituted object kept in bed, while intended victim escapes*]; K.81.1 [*Food in bag. Hero cuts bag open*]; G.524 [*Giant deceived into killing himself*].
Fourth incident: for motifs see "Jack and the Giants".
Fifth incident: R.111.1.4 [*Rescue of maidens from giant*].
Sixth incident: G.84 [*Fee, fi, fo, fum*]; K.924 [*Giant falls through drawbridge*].
Seventh incident: D.6 [*Enchanted castle*]; G.111 [*Giant ogres possess castle*]; D.705.1 [*Castle disenchanted*].

JACK THE GIANT-KILLER: II

Once upon a time—a very good time it was—when pigs were swine and dogs ate lime, and monkeys chewed tobacco, when houses were thatched with pancakes, streets paved with plum puddings, and roasted pigs ran up and down the streets with knives and forks in their backs, crying, "Come and eat me!" That was a good time for travellers.

Then it was that I went off over hills, dales, and lofty mountains, far farther than I can tell you to-night, to-morrow night, or any other night in this new year. The cocks never crew, the winds never blew, and the devil never sounded his bugle-horn to this day yet.

Then I came to a giant castle; a lady came out of the door with a nose as long as my arm. She said to me, she says, "What do you want here? If you don't be off my door I'll take you up for a pinch of snuff." But Jack said, "Will you?" and he drew his sword and cut off her head. He went into the castle, and hunted all over the place. He found a bag of money, and two or three ladies hanging by the hair of their heads. He cut them down and divided the money between them, locked the doors and started off.

Then it was I went over hills, etc.

Then Jack came to another giant's castle, but there was a drop over the door. He slipped in as quickly as he could, but nevertheless the drop struck him on the side of the head and killed him. And the old giant came out and buried him. But in the night three little dogs, named Swift, Sure, and Venture, came and dug him up. One scratched him out of the ground, one breathed health into his nostrils, and brought him to life, while the other got him out of the grave. Then Jack put on his cloak of darkness, shoes of swiftness, and cap of knowledge. He went once more to the giant's door and knocked; when the giant came out, of course he could see nobody, Jack being invisible. He at once drew his sword, and struck the giant's head off. He plundered the house, taking all the money he could find, and went into all the rooms. He found four ladies hung up by their hair, and again dividing the money between them, turned them out and locked the door.

Then he went off again, over hills and dales, etc.

Then Jack came to another giant's castle. He knocked at the door, and an old lady came out; he told her he wanted a night's lodging. She said "My husband is sorely against Englishmen, and if he comes in he will smell the house all over to find one. But never mind, I'll put you in the oven." When the woman's back was turned, Jack got out of the oven and went upstairs into a bedroom. He put a lump of wood in the bed and hid underneath. By-and-bye the old giant came in. He said:

> "Fee, fi, fum,
> I smell the blood of an Englishman.
> Let him be alive, or let him be dead,
> I'll have his flesh to eat for my bread,
> And his blood to drink for my drink."

He then went down to supper, and after it he slept. On waking up he said to his wife, "Now I will find the man that's here." He went upstairs, club in hand, and hit the log in the bed three times. Every time Jack groaned under the bed, the giant said, "I think I've finished ye now." He went down again, talked to his wife for a bit, and went to bed.

At breakfast next morning, he was much astonished to see Jack, and said, "How d'ye feel this morning?" Jack said, "All right, only in the night a mouse gave me a slap with his tail!" Then they had breakfast, it was a hasty pudding. There was poison in Jack's, and instead of eating it, he put it in a little leather bag under his shirt. When they had breakfasted Jack said, "I can do something more than you." The giant said: "Can you?" "Yes", said Jack, and pulling a knife out of his pocket he slit the leather bag, and loosed all the pudding out on the ground. The giant, trying to follow Jack's example, pulled out a knife, and wounding himself, fell dead immediately. Then Jack found two or three ladies hanging up, cut them down, took a bag of money that was lying on the table, and then went out and locked the doors.

> "Be bow bend it,
> My tale's ended.
> If you don't like it,
> You may mend it."

Ella Mary Leather, *The Folk-Lore of Herefordshire* (1912), pp. 174–6, told by W. Colcombe at Weobley, 1909: Mr Colcombe (aged 80) learnt it from an old chapbook when a small boy.
TYPES 300, 1115, 1930. MOTIFS additional to the previous story: F.771.1.10 [*House made of cake*]; X.1208.1 [*Roast pigs run about with knives and forks stuck into them ready for eating*]; Z.10.3 [*Transition formula*]; D.1402.24.1 [*Giant kills people by sprinkling water on their heads*]; B.301.5 [*Faithful animals resuscitate master*]; Z.10.2 [*End formula*].

JACK AND THE KING'S DAUGHTER
[incomplete summary]

Jack was in search of work, and was employed as cowman by a certain King. The King had a daughter, and they were both concerned because one of the royal herd had lately been missing every night when the cows were brought from the pasture. Jack promised to be careful, and the first night when he brought the cows home, the King and Princess each counted them, and were pleased when they found the number was right.

The Princess was due to be devoured by a fiery dragon, but next day as Jack was minding his cows, an old man appeared to him, and promised to watch them if Jack would go to a stable near a pool, lead out the horse from the stable, and let it drink from the pool. Then he was to ride it to the rescue of the King's daughter. The horse drank the pool dry; Jack mounted it, and arrived just in time to fight the dragon. The clever horse first trampled the dragon with its hoofs, then discharged the whole pool of water, and drowned it.

The same old man helped Jack on two other occasions; on one of them he gave him a plum. The number of cows was never wrong after that, and Jack married the King's daughter.

Thompson Notebooks, B, summarized by Thompson, told by Matthew Wood, Bala, 28 August 1922.
TYPE 300. MOTIFS: P.412.1 [*Shepherd (cowherd), as hero*]; N.825 [*Old person as helper*]; B.11.10 [*Sacrifice of human being to dragon*]; B.11.11 [*Flight with dragon*]; B.184.1 [*Magic horse*].

JACK AND HIS GOLDEN SNUFF-BOX
[summary]

An old man and woman lived alone in a forest with their only son, Jack.

As Jack grew older he became a great reader, and longed to get away from the forest, and meet more people than just his parents; especially he longed to meet some pretty girls. One day when his father was away cutting wood in the forest, Jack told his mother that he had resolved to go away, for fear of going mad if he stayed longer at home. His mother sadly agreed, but she asked whether she should bake him a large cake with her curse, or a small one with her blessing. Jack chose to have a large cake, and as he went away with it, his mother stood on the house-top, and cursed him as he went.

Soon Jack met his father, and told him of his intention. His father also consented to his going, but when Jack had gone a little way along the road, his father called him back, and gave him a little golden snuff-box. He bade him not open it until he was near his death.

At nightfall Jack reached a house, where he begged a night's lodging. They treated him well, and the daughter of the house came into the kitchen where he was, and went and told her father that a young man was there. Her father came and asked Jack what he could do. Jack replied "Anything." So the gentleman told him that by eight in the morning he must provide a great lake in front of his mansion, with large men-of-war sailing on it. They were to fire a royal salute, and the last round must break the leg of his daughter's bed.

Jack now turned for help to his snuff-box, and when he opened it, three little red men hopped out, and asked what he wanted. Jack told them, and next morning all fell out as the master of the house had demanded. He was delighted with Jack, and said that if he could perform two more tasks, he should have his daughter in marriage. As before, Jack said his prayers, and resorted to the golden snuff-box. The first was to produce a great castle, standing on twelve golden pillars, and regiments of soldiers drilling in front of it, by eight o'clock in the morning. The second was to fell all the great trees in the park around the mansion. When these were done, there was a great hunting-party to celebrate Jack's wedding. But while they were all out, the valet chanced to find the golden snuff-box in Jack's pocket. He opened it, and the three little red men came out, and he bade them move the castle far across the seas.

When the hunting-party returned, and found no castle, there was great distress, and Jack was in disgrace. He was sent away, but was allowed a year to find the castle again.

334

In the course of his long travels, Jack at last came to the home of the king of all the mice, who promised to call upon all the mice in the world the next morning, to see if they could help. None of them had seen it, so the king sent Jack to his brother, the king of the frogs. One little mouse, at the gate of the castle, insisted on accompanying Jack, so Jack carried him in his pocket.

The frogs received him kindly, but Jack had no success with them either. So the king of the frogs sent him on to his other brother, the king of all the birds. As before, a little frog insisted on coming with him, so Jack tucked him into his other pocket. It was a much longer journey to the palace of the king of the birds, but each day Jack had been given a fresh horse, so they found the place at last, and in the morning, the king called all the birds together, and none had seen the fine castle on the golden pillars. Then they noticed that the eagle was missing. He came at last, from very far off, and in great haste, and said that he had just come from that very place where the castle was. The birds then killed a thief, to make food for the eagle, and taking what was left over, and carrying Jack on his back, the eagle flew off again, and brought him to the missing castle. But they had no notion how to find the snuff-box.

Then the little mouse in Jack's pocket said, "Let me down, and I will get it for you." It crept into the castle, found the box, and managed to bring it out.

As they flew over the sea, they began to quarrel about which of them had really got the box, and as they were passing it from hand to hand, and arguing, they dropped it into the sea. Then it was the frog's turn. For three days and nights he was under the water, and then came up only to breathe. But he dived again, and after another day and night, he brought the box up. Then they flew back to the castle of the king of the birds, and Jack sent the little red men to bring the castle of the golden pillars to him. They brought it, but only after waiting till all the occupants were away at a dance. The cook and one other maid alone were left behind, and they chose to go with the castle. So the little red men flew off just in time, as the whole party was on its way home.

On their nine days' flight they kept the Sunday holy, for one little man acted as priest, one as clerk, and the third as organist. But one of them caused a discord in the music, by sitting astride the organ pipe. The cook and the maid laughed at him so much that they nearly made the castle sink into the sea, by forgetting what they were really about.

At last they were back with Jack and the king, and the king was much pleased with them all, and with the castle. But Jack's year was nearly at an end, so he bade the little men take him from the birds to the king of the frogs first, and then of the mice, with no delay. At the third place Jack had to leave the castle behind, and make his way on his own horse, which became very wearisome and lonely, nor was he kindly welcomed on reaching home, since he had arrived without the castle. But he had his snuff-box, and soon sent the little men off to bring the castle back. He went with them to thank the king of the mice for minding the castle for him. They all returned, and Jack's wife came out to welcome him, and in her arms she carried their fine young son.

Jacobs, *English Fairy Tales*, p. 81; Dora E. Yates, *A Book of Gypsy Folk-Tales*, p. 173. TYPE 560. MOTIFS: J.229.3 [*Choice: a big piece of cake with my curse, or a small piece with my blessing*]; D.815.2 [*Magic object received from father*]; D.1131.1 [*Castle produced by magic*]; D.860 [*Loss of magic object*]; D.2136.2 [*Castle magically transported*]; B.455.3 [*Helpful eagle*]; D.882 [*Magic object stolen back*]; B.548 [*Animal retrieves lost object*]; D.882.2 [*Recovered object dropped into sea*].

¶ The hero makes the unusual choice of the large cake and his mother's curse. The return journey in the recovered castle is an unusually long one, and the way is enlivened by a merry gypsy woman.

JOCK AND HIS LULLS

There was a laddie, and they ca'd him Jock; and Jock said ae day to his mither: "Mither, I'm gaun awa' to seek my fortin." And his mither said: "Very weel, laddie; tak the riddle and the rine (riven) dish, and gang awa' to the wal, and fesh hame some water, and I'll mak ye a bannock." And if he fush hame muckle water, he was to get a muckle bannock; and if he fush hame little water, he was to get a little ane. Sae he took the riddle and the rine dish, and gaed awa' to the wal; and when he came to the wal, he saw a bonnie wee birdie sittin' on the wal brae, and when it saw Jock wi' the riddle and the rine dish, it said:

> "Stap it wi' fog, and clag it wi' clay,
> And that'll carry the water away."

And Jock said till't: "Ou ye nasty dirty cretur, div ye think I'm gaun to do as you bid me? Na, na!" And he wadna do what the birdie tell't him; sae a' the water ran oot o' the riddle, and he just fush hame a wee drappie i' the rine dish; and his mither bakit a little wee bannock for him, and that was aal he got, and he gaed awa' to seek his fortin.

Aweel, after he gaed awa' a while, the wee birdie cam to him, and said: "Gie's a piece, Jock, and I'll gie ye a feather oot o' my wings to mak a pair o' lulls to yersel." And Jock said, "Na, I'll no. It's a' your wyte I've sic a wee bannock, an' it's no eneuch to mysel'." Sae the wee birdie flew awa', and Jock gaed far and far and farer nor I can tell, or he cam to a king's hoose, and he gaed in and sought service. And they speer'd what he could do, and he said: "I can soop the hoose, and tak oot the ase, and wash the dishes, and keep kye." "Can ye keep hares?" "I dinna ken, but I'll try." Sae they tell't him if he could keep the hares, and fesh them a' hame at nicht, he would get the king's dochter; and if he didna fesh them hame, he would be hanged. Sae they set him oot i' the morning, wi' four-and-twenty hares, and a cripple ane. And he was awfu' hungry, because he had sic a wee bannock; sae he catched the cripple ane, and roasted it and ate it. And whan the other hares saw that, they a' ran awa'. Sae he cam hame at nicht withoot the hares, and the king was awfu' angry, and gared tak him and hang him.

Weel, his mother had another laddie, and they ca'ed him Jock tae, and Jock said to his mither: "Mither, I'm gaun awa' to seek my fortin." And his mither said: "Very weel, laddie; tak the riddle and the rine dish, and gang awa' to the wal, and fesh hame some water, and I'll mak ye a bannock." And if he fush hame muckle water, he was to get a muckle bannock; and if he fush hame little water, he was to get a little ane. Sae he took the riddle and the rine dish, and gaed awa' to the wal; and when he cam to the wal, he saw a bonnie wee birdie sittin' on the wal brae, and when it saw Jock wi' the riddle and the rine dish, it said:

> "Stap it wi' fog, and clag it wi' clay,
> And that'll carry the water away."

And Jock said: "Ay wull I, my bonnie birdie." Sae he stappit the riddle, and the rine dish wi' fog, and claggit them wi' clay, and fush hame a great lot o' water. And his mither bakit a great muckle bannock to him, and he gaed awa' to puss his fortin.

Weel, after he was on the road a bit, the wee birdie cam to him and said: "Gies a piece, Jock, and I'll gie ye a feather oot o' my wings to mak a pair o' lulls to yersel'." And Jock said: "Ay wull I, my bonnie birdie, for it was you that gared me get sic a muckle bannock." Sae he ga'e the wee birdie a piece, and syne the birdie said till him: "Pu' a feather oot o' my wing, and mak a pair o' lulls to yersel'." And Jock said: "Na, na, my bonnie birdie, I'll no pu' a feather oot o' yer wings, for it'll hurt ye." And the birdie said: "Hout na! just pu' a feather oot o' my wings, and mak a pair o' lulls to yersel'." Sae Jock pu'd a feather, and made a pair o' lulls to his sel', and gaed playin' along the road. Weel, he gaed far and far and farer nor I can tell, or he cam to a king's hoose, and he gaed in and sought service. And they speer'd what he could do, and he said, "I can soop the hoose, and tak oot the ase, and wash the dishes, and keep kye." "Can ye keep hares?" "I dinna ken, but I'll try." Sae they tell't him if he could keep the hares, and fesh them a' hame at nicht, he would get the king's dochter; and if he didna fesh them hame, he would be hanged. And they set him oot i' the mornin' wi' four-and-twenty hares and a cripple ane, and Jock played upon his lulls sae bonnie bonnie, that the hares a' danced round him and never ran awa', and he fush them a' hame at nicht. And the cripple ane couldna gang, sae he took it up in his arms and carried it. And the king was awfu' weel pleased, and gae him his dochter, and Jock was king after this king dicd; and ae day he opened a door i' the king's hoose, and there he saw his brither hingin' dead.—Sae ye see, bairns, &c.

R. Chambers, *Popular Rhymes of Scotland* (1870), p. 103, Fifeshire.

TYPE 570. MOTIFS: H.1023.2 [*Carrying water in a sieve*]; B.122.1 [*Bird as adviser*]; Q.2 [*Kind and unkind*]; H.1023.20.1 [*Carrying water in a sieve stopped with moss*]; L.13 [*Compassionate younger son*]; D.817 [*Magic object received from grateful person*]; H.1112 [*Task: herding rabbits*]; D.1441.1.2 [*Magic pipe calls animals together*]; H.335 [*Tasks assigned: bride as prize for accomplishment*].

❡ This tale has a wide distribution. The best-known example is the Scandinavian "Jesper who Herded the Hares".

JOCK AND THE MISER

Now this is the story of a very bad man who robbit everybody of their wealth. So he robbit a poor farmer of all his wealth and robbit his farm, and everybody he met he robbit, for he had a lot of money, and he had bought a palace, and he was turnt a misert,—he was payin' no money and he had a nice daughter, but he kep her in from the outside world,— never let her saw the outside world. So Jock and his mother—he robbit them of their farm and all their gold. He thought on a plan whit wey he could have his own back with the miser.

So wan night he thought noo that he wad dress his-sel' up as a tramp, and visit the palace. So he dressed his-sel' up as a tramp, and he went out and travelt a lot of miles to the palace, and when he cam to the palace he knocked at the back-door. He asked a piece (the door was opent by the old cook—he only kept one servant, who was an old cook).

So she felt sorry for the poor old tramp, and she tellt him that if the master had see him that he wad beheid him. But she's stolen in and give him some food. But bad luck—the master he'd seed him. He tell'd him that he wad get off, bit he was have to be a servant to him all his days and work for no pay.

So he workit on for a long time, but he got in touch wi' the daughter, and he won her good favours. So he asked her where the gold was kept, so she tellt him where her father kep the gold, so wan night—dark night—Jock he stole the gold, and put it in an old leather bag.

So he set on his journey now, and he travellt for a lot of miles till he cam til a horse what was lookin' over a dyke. So he passed the horse' and he travelled many more miles till he cam' til a cow. *It* was lookin' over a dyke. So he trampit on again for a lot of miles till he cam til an ass, and that was at four crossroads.

"Now", he says to the ass, "if ye see anyone lookin' for me," he says, 'put him the wrong road."

So the miser he misses the gold and he's after Jock. He comes to the horse. He says to the horse, "Did ye see an old man comin' on this road with an old wig-wag—an old leather bag—has stole all my gold and silver?"

"Yes," says the horse, "he's on the road."

So he tramps on many a mile till he comes to the cow. He says the same, he said, "Did ye see an old man comin' on this road with an old wig-wag—or an ol' leather bag—stole all my gold and silver?"

"Yes," she says, "he's on the road."

He tramps on again for many a mile till he cam' to the ass in the four crossroads. He says to the ass, he says, "Did ye see an old man comin' down this road with an ol' wig-wag or an ol' leather bag—stole all my gold and silver?"

"Yes," says the ass, "he's on this road."

But the ass put him the wrong road.

He travelt many a mile till he was weary, till he cam' til a forest. He lost hisself in the forest and the wolfs ate him up; and he [Jock] went back and got the young girl and the palace.

School of Scottish Studies, told by Robert Stewart, 27 Gaval St., Fetterangus, 1960.
TYPE 480 (variant).
¶ See "The Old Witch", etc.

JOCK AND HIS MOTHER [summary]

A poor woman had an only son named Jock. One day she told him that he was too lazy, and must go out and find some work to do. Jock was always quite obedient, so off he went, and on the first day he met a packman who, in return for Jock's carrying his pack all day, gave him a needle. On his way home Jock cut some bracken and hid the needle in the middle of it, so his mother told him he should have stuck it in his bonnet. Jock promised to remember next time, and the next day he met a man carrying plough socks [shares]. He carried them for him and was given one share for reward at the end of the day. He duly stuck it in his bonnet, and in stooping down to drink at a stream on his way home he lost both bonnet and share in the water. This time his mother said he ought to have tied it to a string and trailed it behind him.

So the next day Jock met a butcher, who made use of his services during the day, and gave him a leg of mutton at the end. Jock tied it to a string and dragged it behind him home, but his mother only said he should have carried it on his shoulder. Again Jock promised to remember, and next day, having worked for a horse-dealer, he was given a horse.

He tied its feet together, but could not carry it away on his back, so he left it by the road. So his mother said he should have jumped on its back and ridden home.

A gentleman living nearby had a daughter who was so melancholy that her father gave out that whoever could make her laugh should have her hand in marriage. The day after his mother's advice about the horse Jock was given a cow, and came riding home on the cow's back with the tail over his shoulder, and this made the girl burst out laughing. So Jock was married to the lady. The old priest who married them spent the night in their marriage chamber. While he was fast asleep, Jock woke up and felt a great desire for some of the honey they had had at their wedding-feast. His bride told him to get up and help himself out of the "honey-pig" in the press. Jock's hand stuck fast in the pig, so she told him to break it against the cheek-stone. But in the darkness Jock mistook the old priest's white wig for the stone, and hit it so hard with the honey-jar that the old man awoke crying out "Murder!" and Jock rushed from the room and hid among the beehives.

But that night thieves came to steal the hives, and in their haste they picked up Jock and the hives all together, and rolled them in a big plaid.

In crossing a burn one of them came upon Jock's lost bonnet and said, "I've found a bonnet." "Oh! That's mine!" cried Jock, and so alarmed the thieves that they tumbled him, bees, plaid and all into the burn, where Jock and the bees were all drowned together.

Chambers, *Popular Rhymes of Scotland*, p. 101.
TYPE 1696. MOTIFS: J.2461 [*What should I have done?*]; J.2461.1.1 [*Drags meat on a string*]; H.341 [*Suitor test: making the princess laugh*]; H.341.3 [*Making princess laugh by foolish action of hero*].

The catastrophes which follow the wedding are the unusual feature of this version.
¶ See also "Stupid's Mistaken Cries", "I'll be Wiser next Time", "Biddable Jock".

JOHN GLAICK, THE BRAVE TAILOR

John Glaick was a tailor by trade, but like a man of spirit he grew tired of his tailoring, and wished to follow some other path that would lead to honour and fame. This wish showed itself at first rather in dislike to work of all kinds than in any fixed line of action, and for a time he was fonder of basking idly in the sun than in plying the needle and scissors. One warm day as he was enjoying his ease, he was annoyed by the flies alighting on his bare ankles. He brought his hand down on them with force, and killed a goodly number of the plague. On counting the victims of his valour, he was overjoyed at his success; his heart rose to the doing of great deeds, and he gave vent to his feelings in the saying:

"Weel done! John Glaick,
Killt fifty flees at ae straik."

His resolution was now taken to cut out his path to fortune and honour. So he took down from its resting-place a rusty old sword that had belonged to some of his forbears, and set out in search of adventures. After travelling a long way, he came to a country that was much troubled by two giants, whom no one was bold enough to meet, and strong enough to overcome. He was soon told of the giants, and learned that the king of the country had offered a great reward and the hand of his daughter in marriage to the man who should rid his land of this scourge. John's heart rose to the deed, and he offered himself for the service.

The great haunt of the giants was a wood, and John set out with his old sword to perform his task. When he reached the wood, he laid himself down to think what course he would follow, for he knew how weak he was compared to those he had undertaken to kill. He had not waited long, when he saw them coming with a wagon to fetch wood for fuel. He hurriedly hid himself in the hollow of a tree, thinking only of his own safety. Feeling himself safe, he peeped out of his hiding-place, and watched the two at work. Thus watching he formed his plan of action. He picked up a pebble, threw it with force at one of them, and struck him a sharp blow on the head. The giant in his pain turned at once on his companion, and blamed him in strong words for hitting him. The other denied in anger that he had thrown the pebble. John now saw himself on the highway to gain his reward and the hand of the king's daughter. He kept still, and carefully watched for an opportunity of striking another blow. He soon found it, and right against the giant's head went another pebble. The injured giant fell on his companion in fury, and the two belaboured each other till they were utterly tired out. They sat down on a log to breathe, rest, and recover themselves. While

341

sitting, one of them said, "Well, all the king's army was not able to take us, but I fear an old woman with a rope's end would be too much for us now." "If that be so," said John Glaick, as he sprang, bold as a lion, from his hiding-place, "what do you say to John Glaick, wi' his aul roosty soord?" So saying, he fell upon them, cut off their heads, and returned in triumph. He received the king's daughter in marriage, and for a time lived in peace and happiness. He never told the mode he followed in his dealing with the giants.

Some time after a rebellion broke out among the subjects of his father-in-law. John, on the strength of his former valiant deed, was chosen to quell the rebellion. His heart sank within him, but he could not refuse, and so lose his great name. He was mounted on the fiercest horse that "ever saw sun or wind", and set out on his desperate task. He was not accustomed to ride on horseback, and he soon lost all control of his fiery steed. It galloped off at full speed, but fortunately in the direction of the rebel army. In its wild career it passed under the gallows that stood by the wayside. The gallows was somewhat old and frail, and down it fell on the horse's neck. Still no stop, but always forward at furious speed towards the rebels. On seeing this strange sight approaching towards them at such a speed they were seized with terror, and cried out to one another, "There comes John Glaick that killed the two giants with the gallows on his horse's neck to hang us all." They broke their ranks, fled in dismay, and never stopped till they reached their homes. Thus was John Glaick a second time victorious. Happily he was not put to a third test. In due time he came to the throne, and lived a long, happy, and good life as king.

Norton Collection, v, p. 153. *Folk-lore Journal*, VII (1889), pp. 163–5. Given to W. Gregor by W. Copland, schoolmaster at Tortorston, near Peterhead. He learned it forty-five years before from his father, who was nearly seventy years old, and lived in Strichen, North Aberdeenshire. It is not in the dialect of the district. Retold by Jacobs in *More English Fairy Tales*, p. 71.
TYPE 1640. MOTIFS: K.1951.1 [*Boastful fly-killer: seven at a blow*]; K.1082 [*Ogres duped into fighting each other*]; H.38.2.1 [*Tailor married to princess*]; K.1951.3 [*Sham warrior intimidates soldiers with his boasting*]; K.1951.2 [*Runaway cavalry-hero*].

JUBILEE JONAH

Jubilee Jonah were a kind good hard-working old chap as lived Goathurst way. His mother were so glad to have a boy she called him Jubilee but his Dad reckoned 'twas likely to prove unlucky and had 'en named Jonah too—just to even things out like.

Well, this here Jubilee Jonah had a grey dunk (his Dad called his dunk Salvation—very religious he was), so Jubilee Jonah done the same, only his being a Jenny ass he shortened it a bit to Sally.

Now one time they had a load to take in the flat cart all the way to Ash Priors. 'Twas a good load but Sally was strong and willing and load would pay well.

Now in those days they d'say the witches met down to Hestercombe. A real wicked lot they was—come from all over. There was one old man saw the Fiddington witch fly over Shervage wood on her broomstick. Passed right over his head high up she did on one of they wisht nights. There was two three to Tanton and Kingston St Mary and the bad old man down to Crowcombe, and they was all in a proper shiver-shake on account they hadn't been doing too well with their ill-wishings and they was terrified You Know Who 'ood come and fetch one of they away in his fire and brimstone. They hated Jubilee's Dad for being pious, and they thought Jubilee being reckoned a bit thick they might catch 'en out all of them being so clever and that would please You Know Who and take his mind off Hell fire.

So they set about it.

When Jubilee and Sally come up the steep bit to Broomfield, he were behind the cart pushing to help Sally on.

Out come this old witch. "One to push and one to pull—here's a pair of donkeys. Get in and ride too." Jubilee he never answered a word but Sally she let her have it instead and kicked her tother way round she did.

Then they went on.

"Yew shouldn't a done that, Sally," say Jubilee. "I got a criss cross on *my* back," say Sally. "I wouldn't like for to kick a woman," say Jubilee.

"I do, and I did if they'm like she," say Sally.

And on they went.

All down over Buncombe Hill they goes, Sally sitting back and Jubilee pulling back on cart's tail and a hard job 'twas.

Out come the old witch from Rose Cottage, near Frog Street.

"Two to pull", she say, "and two to hold, here's a pair of donkeys. Why don't 'ee both get in and ride downhill?"

Jubilee he never spoke but Sally she just let her have one as turned the old witch back avore.

"Yew shouldn't a done that, Sally," say Jubilee. "I got a criss cross on *my* back," say Sally. "I wouldn't like for to kick a woman," say Jubilee.

"I do, and I did, if they'm like she," say Sally.

And on they went.

Then they come on to Kingston St Mary—but the witches there wasn't risking trouble with a donkey remembering the criss cross on her back, and Jubilee Jonah he never said one word to a soul, so they let 'en go on droo.

So 'twas the rest of the way until they come by Sandhill and the bad old man from Crowcombe were there standing right in the path and afore Sally knowed what he would be about he'd looked her in the eyes and stopped her where she was.

"Such a gurt load, and such a little ass. Here's a pair of donkeys. Why don't 'ee carry load and cart and dunk and all?"

But Jubilee Jonah never looked him in the eye nor he didn't answer back. He just up and took a running kick and the bad old man from Crowcombe went tail over head droo the air, come down splish splash in Lawford Hill pond.

Then they went on and left their load to Ash Priors.

Coming home, Sally stopped by a bit of grass and Jubilee he had his bread and cheese. Then Sally says, "You kicked 'en proper." "There's a criss cross of hobnails to my two boots," say Jubilee Jonah. "He 'oodn't like the feel of they. Proper pair of donkeys us be."

"I got vower legs and a tail and a rough grey coat," says Sally.

"Well, I got a round frock and two legs with good hard boots. We'm both alike enough for any witch—Yes, we be a pair of donkeys sure enough—We can kick real serviceable."

So they went home happy.

Ruth L. Tongue, Somerset, Taunton Market, 1908.
MOTIFS: A.2221.1 [*Animals blessed for honouring Infant Jesus: cross on back of ass*]; G.242.1 [*Witch flies through air on broomstick*]; G.243 [*Witches' sabbath*]; G.275.1 [*Witch carried off by devil*]; G.273.1 [*Witch powerless against sign of cross*]; G.207 [*Male witch*]; G.221.4 [*Witch cannot be hurt if she looks attacker in face*].

KATE CRACKERNUTS

Once upon a time there was a King and a Queen, as in many lands have been. The king had a dochter, Kate, and the queen had one. The queen was jealous of the king's dochter being bonnier than her own, and cast about to spoil her beauty. So she took counsel of the henwife, who told her to send the lassie to her next morning fasting. The queen did so, but the lassie found means to get a piece before going out. When she came to the henwife's she asked for eggs, as she had been told to do; the henwife desired her to "lift the lid off that pot there" and see. The lassie did so, but naething happened. "Gae hame to your minnie, and tell her to keep the press door better steekit," said the henwife. The queen knew from this that the lassie had had something to eat, so watched the next morning, and sent her away fasting; but the princess saw some country folk picking peas by the roadside, and being very affable she spoke to them and took a handful of the peas, which she ate by the way.

In consequence, the answer at the henwife's house was the same as on the preceding day.

The third day the queen goes along with the girl to the henwife. Now, when the lid is lifted off the pot, off jumps the princess's ain bonny head, and on jumps a sheep's head.

The queen, now quite satisfied, returns home.

Her own daughter, however, took a fine linen cloth and wrapped it round her sister's head and took her by the hand and gaed out to seek their fortin. They gaed and they gaed far, and far'er than I can tell, till they cam to a king's castle. Kate chappit at the door and sought "a night's lodging for hersel' and a sick sister". This is granted on condition that Kate sits up all night to watch the King's sick son, which she is quite willing to do. She is also promised a "pock o' siller" "if a's right". Till midnight all goes well. As twelve o'clock rings, however, the sick prince rises, dresses himself, and slips downstairs, followed by Kate unnoticed. The prince went to the stable, saddled his horse, called his hound, jumped into the saddle, Kate leaping lightly up behind him. Away rode the prince and Kate through the greenwood, Kate, as they pass, plucking nuts from the trees and filling her apron with them. They rode on and on till they came to a green hill. The prince here drew bridle and spoke, "Open, open, green hill, an' let the young prince in with his horse and his hound," and, added Kate, "his lady him behind".

Immediately the green hill opened and they passed in. A magnificent hall is entered brightly lighted up, and many beautiful ladies surround the prince and lead him off to the dance, while Kate, unperceived, seats herself by the door. Here she sees a bairnie playing with a wand, and overhears one of the fairies say, "Three strokes o' that wand would mak' Kate's sick sister as bonnie as ever she was." So Kate rowed* nuts to the bairnie, and rowed nuts till the bairnie let fall the wand, and Kate took it up and put it in her apron.

Then the cock crew, and the prince made all haste to get on horseback, Kate jumping up behind, and home they rode, and Kate sat down by

* rowed = rolled.

the fire, and cracked her nuts, and ate them. When the morning came Kate said the prince had a good night, and she was willing to sit up another night, for which she was to get a "pock o' gowd". The second night passed as the first had done. The third night Kate consented to watch only if she should marry the sick prince. This time the bairnie was playing with a birdie; Kate heard one of the fairies say, "Three bites of that birdie would mak' the sick prince as weel as ever he was." Kate rowed nuts to the bairnie till the birdie was dropped, and Kate put it in her apron.

At cockcrow they set off again, but instead of cracking her nuts as she used to do, Kate plucked the feathers off, and cooked the birdie. Soon there arose a very savoury smell. "Oh!" said the sick prince, "I wish I had a bite o' that birdie." So Kate gave him a bit o' the birdie, and he rose up on his elbow. By-and-by he cried out again, "Oh, if I had anither bite o' that birdie!" So Kate gave him another bit, and he sat up on his bed. Then he said again, "Oh! if I had a third bite o' that birdie!" So Kate gave him a third bit, and he rose quite well, dressed himself, and sat down by the fire, and when "the folk came i' the mornin' they found Kate and the young prince cracking nuts th'gether". So the sick son married the weel sister, and the weel son married the sick sister, and they all lived happy and dee'd happy, and never drank out o' a dry cappy.

Norton Collection, II, p. 185. Collected by Mr D. J. Robinson of the Orkneys. Printed in *Longman's Magazine*, XIII; *Folk-Lore*, I, pp. 299–301.

TYPE: this is often arbitrarily included in type 711, to which it bears no real resemblance. The beginning is closely allied to the Flemish tale of Black Caroline and White Caroline.

MOTIFS: S.31 [*Cruel stepmother*]; P.284 [*Stepsister*]; D.1766.8 [*Magic results from fasting*]; D.683.2 [*Transformation by witch*]; F.302.3.4 [*Fairies entice men and then harm them*]; F.302.3.4.2 [*Fairies dance with youth till he goes insane*]; F.370 [*Visit to fairyland*]; F.211 [*Fairyland under hollow knoll*]; D.771.4 [*Disenchantment by using wand*]; D.764 [*Disenchantment by eating*].

¶ For the two attempts of the witch foiled by eating, see "De Little Fox". There is some resemblance to the second half of the story in "The Corpse Watchers" in Kennedy's *Legendary Fictions*, pp. 48–51.

THE KEY OF CRAIGACHOW
[shortened version]

There is said to be a cave under Craigachow where warriors and treasure are to be found if one can find the key to it. The fame spread so far that a man came all the way from Ireland to find it, and he went up to Craigachow, where there was a man digging divots to thatch the farm. And he asked if he knew where the key was. The man said: "I have no know-ledge of it. Ask the man carrying the divots. He's older than me." So he went to that man, and he said: "Ask the man loading them on the cart. He's older than me." But the man on the cart said: "Ask the man holding the ladder; he's older than me." But he said: "Ask the man on the roof; he's older than me". And the man on the roof sent him to the man in the house. In the house there was an old, old man rocking the cradle, and he piped up: "Ask him in the cradle; he's older than me." In the cradle was a wee, wee man, no bigger than a three weeks' bairn, and he said: "Ask him in by the fire." A snuff horn was hanging by the fire, and out of it peeped a wee, tiny man, and he said in a voice no bigger than a grass-hopper, "You'll find it in the great rush bush behind the house." He searched in the rush bush, and found the key, and unlocked the door and went in.

It was a great cave, and there were men sleeping all round it, and a table in the middle, and on the table were a horn and a cane. The Irishman picked up the horn and sounded it, and struck the men with the cane, and all the sleepers stirred. Then he blew again and struck them again, and they rose on their elbows, but with such a fearsome look that the Irishman was terrified, and set down the horn and fled, and the sleepers muttered, "It will be worse than ever." And the Irishman was so afraid that he dropped the key in a loch near, so it is not likely that any other man will open the cave of Craigachow.

The School of Scottish Studies, Hamish Henderson from Tom Wilson, Newtonmore. From his grandfather.
TYPES 726 and 766 (variant).
   The combination of these two types, "The Oldest on the Farm" and "The Seven Sleepers", is so unusual as to be almost unique.
MOTIFS: F.571.2 [*Sending to the older*]; D.1960.2 [*King asleep on mountain*]; E.502 [*The sleeping army*].
For 726, see also "Old Parr", "The Painswick Elders". For 766, see also "The Shepherd of Sewingshields".

THE KING OF THE BLACK ART
[condensed version]

There was once an old fisherman, and one day as he was fishing he drew out a long box, and inside was a baby boy. He took it home to his wife, and they brought it up as their own. When the boy was fourteen years old, a ship came to land, and on the bridge there was a man dressed as fine as a king, juggling with three poison-balls with spikes on them. The stranger came to shore, and seemed to take a great fancy to the boy;

he offered to take him away for a year and day, and to teach the boy his art. He wheedled so that the fisherman and his wife agreed, and the boy went away with the stranger. In a year and day the a ship was back, and the boy was back, tossing seven poison-balls. The old couple were so pleased that they allowed the stranger to take the boy for another year and a day, but he did not come back. So the old wife sent the fisherman to look for him. The fisherman travelled on and on, until in a wee hut in a wood he saw an old, old man, who asked him in for the night. The fisherman told the old man his story, and the old man said, "There's little doubt that the King of the Black Art has your son, and there is no more I can tell you; but maybe my eldest brother can help you. He lives a week's journey from here. Tell him I sent you." So the next morning the fisherman set out, and he journeyed for a week to the older brother's house. And if the first old man was old, this was three times older. But he asked the fisherman in, and gave him food and lodging, and told him what to do. He was to go on to the King of the Black Art's castle, and ring the bell and ask for his son. They would laugh at him, and the King would tell him to choose his son from among fourteen pigeons that he would throw up into the air, and he was to choose a little, weak, raggety-winged one, that flew lower than the rest. The fisherman did as he was told, and chose the raggety-winged pigeon. "Take him, and be damned to you!" said the King, and his son stood beside him. They went away together.

"I'd never have got free if you'd not come for me," said the boy. "The King of the Black Art and his two sons are at the head of all the wizards in the country. But I've learned something, and we'll get something back from them. Now, we're coming to a town where there is a market, and I'll change myself into a greyhound. All the lords and gentry will offer to buy me, but don't you sell me till the King of the Black Art comes. You can take five hundred pounds from him, but mind you, father, for your life, do not sell the collar and strap, but take it off me." So, in a moment, he'd turned himself into the finest greyhound dog that ever was seen, and the fisherman led him into the market. Knights and nobles were crowding round him to buy, but he would take no offers till the King of the Black Art and his two sons came into the place, and he would not let him have the dog under five hundred pounds. Then he took the strap from round the dog's neck, and tied a piece of string round it instead, and walked away. As soon as he was out of the town, there was his son beside him, for he had been the strap. They went on to another town, and the son turned himself into a grand stallion horse, but he warned his father not to sell the bridle with him, whatever he did. The knights and nobles came round him as before, for no such horse had ever been seen in those parts; but he would not sell him to anyone till the King of the Black Art and his two sons came, and he asked a thousand pounds from him. "He looks worth it," said the King of the Black Art, "and I'll give it if he is as good as his looks. But no man can buy a horse without trying it." The fisherman stood out for a while, but the King said, "Come to this wee house, and I'll show you the gold you'll get. But I must just ride him round the fair-ground." The glint of the gold was too much for the fisherman. He said, "Just ride him round the ground then," and the King leapt on the horse's back. The fisherman turned to look at the gold, and it turned to dung before his eyes, and when he looked back, the horse was gone.

The King of the Black Art rode the horse back to a stable where he was fastened up with other horses, and they were fed on salt beef, and not given a drop to drink till their tongues were swollen and coated. One day the King and his sons had gone hunting, and the boy spoke to the groom who brought their food, and begged to be given a drink. The groom was frightened, but the horse begged until he had compassion on it, and led it out to the stream. The horse begged him to loosen the bit so that he could drink, and when he did so it slipped its head out of the bridle, and slipped into the stream as a salmon. As he did so, all the bells of the castle rang, and the magicians dashed back from the hills, turned themselves into otters, and swam after the salmon. They came closer and closer, until they were almost on him, then he leapt into the air, and turned into a swallow. The otters turned into hawks, and pursued him. The swallow saw a lady sitting in a garden, flew to her, and turned into a ring on her finger. The hawks swept round her and flew away. Then the ring spoke. It said, "Lady, in a few minutes three labourers will come here, and offer to build up your dyke. When they have done it, they will ask for the ring from your finger for payment. But say to them that you would rather throw it into that bonfire, and throw it as you speak." The lady said she would do as he told her, and in a few minutes the three labourers arrived. They built up the walls as if by magic, and when she offered them money, they asked for the ring, but she threw it into the fire. The labourers turned themselves into three blacksmiths, and began to blow up the fire, but the ring hopped out on the other side into a pile of corn, and turned itself into a grain in the pile. The magicians turned into three cocks, and began to eat the corn, but the boy turned into a fox, and snapped off the three cocks' heads as quick as thought. So the King of the Black Art was defeated, and the boy rejoined his father, and they lived prosperously all their days by his magic art.

School of Scottish Studies, Hamish Henderson, from John Stewart.
TYPE 325. MOTIFS: D.1711.0.1 [*Magician's apprentice*]; S.212 [*Child sold to magician*]; H.1385.3.1 [*Quest for lost son*]; H.62.1 [*Recognition of person transformed to animal*]; D.612 [*Protean sale*]; K.252 [*Selling oneself and escaping*]; D.100

[*Transformation: man to animal*]; C.837 [*Tabu: selling bridle with horse*]; D.615.2 [*Transformation contest between master and pupil*]; D.610 [*Repeated transformation*]; D.641.1 [*Lover as bird visits mistress*]; L.142.2 [*Pupil surpasses magician*].

¶ This is a complete version of "The Magician and his Pupil", Grimm no. 68. It is widespread: Norwegian, Russian, French, Spanish, Greek, Highland and Irish versions are found, among others.

The English folk-song, "The Coal-Black Smith" (Baring-Gould), is an example of the contest.

See also "The Black King of Morocco".

THE KING OF THE CATS [summary]

Two drunken Irish tramps left their wives in a doss house, and went out on the tramp. Came to a large house, where they begged for a night's rest, and were allowed to spend the night in a haunted castle. Fire, food, etc. They went to bed. A great howling outside, and a company of cats, fashionably dressed, came in, with the King of the Cats at their head. They feasted off a magic tablecloth. Treated the tramps well. The King told them that the daughter of the king of the castle near them was ill. She had three kittens inside her, and could only be cured by three draughts from a magic well in the garden. In the morning they took the magic tablecloth, and Mick insisted on looking for the well. They found it, filled three bottles, and went, dressed up as quacks, to cure the Princess. At each draught, she cast up a kitten. They were richly rewarded. Mick sent Pat up to town with the treasure, telling him to give half to his wife, and went on by foot, using the magic cloth. Fed an old tramp, who offered to exchange cloth for a magic bottle filled with soldiers. Exchange made, but when Mick grew hungry he called out the soldiers, and told them to fetch the cloth. When he got to London, he found his wife living in poverty, while Pat was Lord Mayor. Visited the Mansion House. Pat would not own him, and sent soldiers against him. He called his soldiers out of the bottle, and they killed everyone in the Mansion House. Mick took over as Lord Mayor. One day Mick and his wife quarrelled, and the bottle was broken. Substitute bottle did not fit.

All the soldiers drowned, as Mick tried to revive the leader stuck in the top, by pouring beer over him. The beer trickled into the bottle, and that was the end of the soldiers.

Thompson Notebooks, IX, Oswaldtwistle, 10 January 1915.

TYPES 326 and 569. MOTIFS: H.1411.2 [*Fear test: staying in haunted house infested by cats*]; D.1472.1.8 [*Magic tablecloth*]; D.1421.5.3 [*Magic sack contains soldiers*]; D.881 [*Magic object recovered by using second magic object*]; D.866 [*Magic object destroyed*].

¶ Another story with the same title is to be found among the Legends. See also "Habie's Whistle".

THE KING OF ENGLAND
[condensed version]

There were once an old man and an old woman who lived on the side of a mountain, and they had two sons called William and Jack. They were very poor, and at last William thought it was time he pushed his fortunes. So he said to his mother, "Roast me a collop, and bake me a bannock, and I'll away to push my fortunes." And his mother said, "Will you take a wee bannock with my blessing, or a big bannock with my curse?" And he said, "I'll take the big bannock." So he got the big bannock and the curse. But before he went away, he said to his brother Jack, "I'll set up a token in the garden, so that you can see if all is right with me." So William set out, and he went on and on, further than I can tell you, or you can tell me. There was rest for the wee birds, but none for poor William. He was afraid of the wild beasts, so he went on through the night, and in the darkness he stumbled and fell down a precipice. And as he fell, he thought he saw a light in the cliff opposite, and he got up, and found a footpath, and got to a wee house where there was an old, old man sitting, roasting a sheep. He was a most fearsome-looking man, but he divided the sheep with William, and let him lie there the night. But he was so fearsome that William did not like to stay, and after the old man was asleep, he went on. He went on and on, till he saw a castle in the distance, and a lodge at its gate. An old woman let him in, and she said that they were so poor that they had only birds' feet to eat, but he could come in and share them. So he went in, and the old woman had two pretty daughters, and William had never seen a girl in his life, and was much taken by them. The old woman said the king of the castle was a Savage Man, and would set him dreadful tasks, but William would go on, and he knocked at the castle gate, and asked if the King had work for him. "Yes," said the king, "let him clear the nine-stalled stable." The servants told him that the horses were so savage that no man dared go near them, but William went. When he got to the stables, the doors were all filled up with dung, so he climbed on to the roof and let himself down through the skylight, and the whole place was full. So he got a spade and fork, and worked and worked, till he had the place all cleaned out. He fed the horses and watered them, and rubbed them down. "This is no way at all", he said, "to keep beautiful horses like these." And the horses liked him fine, and he had no trouble with them, but it took him three weeks to get the place clean. Then he cleaned himself up, and he began cleaning the harness, and it was all gold-mounted, but it had been so dirty, no one could see what it was. So he was sitting outside, cleaning the gold-mounted harness, when the Princess passed by, and there she saw the fairest man she had ever seen, and she went home, and took to her bed. And the king sent for all the doctors to see her, and among them was an old Scottish doctor, and he said, "I must see the Princess alone." And when he had talked to her, he said, "I know what is the matter with you; you are in love." "That must be it," said the Princess, and the doctor told the king, who came to ask the Princess about it, and she said: "I am in love with your groom of the nine-stalled stables." "Is he still alive?" said the king. "I thought he must have been dead long ago." The king went to see the groom, and when he saw him he said, "I don't blame my daughter. Had I been a woman, I should have done the same." They told William that the Princess was in love with him, and he must marry her to save her life. He was taken aback, but he went up to see her, and said he would marry her if it were to save her life. So the Princess got up, quite well again, and they had a grand wedding, and a great banquet, and after the banquet a dance. And William danced with all the ladies, and among them was one of the daughters of the old woman at the lodge. And as they were dancing, she put a thorn of sleep into him behind his ear, and he fell down like one dead. But the Princess wouldn't have him buried. She had him put in a lead coffin, and carried up to the topmost room of the castle, where she could look at him. One day, Jack went into the garden to look at his brother's token, and he found it all withered, so he knew he was in great peril. So he said to his mother: "Bake me a bannock, and roast me a collop, and I'll set out to seek my brother." And his mother said: "Will you have a wee bannock, with my blessing, or a big bannock with my curse?" So he said: "I'll have the wee bannock." And he set out after his brother.

He followed the same road as his brother, and went on further, etc. Like his brother, he fell down the precipice, and saw the light, and found the wee house. The old man said, "Where have you been all this while?" So Jack knew his brother had been before him. He said: "I went out and lost my way." The old man said: "Well, bide with me, and I'll teach you sword play." So Jack stayed a month with him, and learned all there was to know about sword play. Then he left the old man, and went on and on, until he came to the lodge. They were at dinner when he knocked at the door, and the girl who opened it screamed, "A ghost! a ghost! He's come back!" and they got up shrieking, and left the house. So Jack guessed they had had something to do with William's death. So he plundered the house, and finished the meal on the table, and took a purse with seven gold pieces in it. Then he went and knocked at the castle gate. When the butler opened it he took Jack for a ghost, and rushed back into the servants' hall, but the cook said: "I never hurt him, and, dead or alive, he'll never hurt me." So she took the Bible under her arm, and went to speak with Jack. And he told her who he was, and asked to see his brother's body.

The servants were sweir to take him, but he gave them the seven pieces of gold, and they took him up to the topmost room. He opened the coffin, and took his brother out, and he found the thorn of sleep behind his ear, and pulled it out. And at once William sat up, and rubbed his eyes. The Princess came into the room at this moment, and she ran up and kissed Jack, taking him for William. After her came the King, and he shook hands with Jack, and said he was glad to see him alive. For no one could tell one from the other.

The wedding rejoicings began again, and William and the Princess begged Jack to stay on with them in the castle. Jack was dissatisfied, for he wanted to push his fortunes himself, so that he would have something for his father and mother. But they said he must stay until the baby boy was born. At the end of nine months a baby boy was born, and the Princess said he must stay till she baked him seven oatmeal bannocks, and she mixed them with her own milk, and said he must give them to his enemy, and say, "Taste of my bread." His brother gave him a magic sword, and he set out. He walked and walked, further, etc., until at last he sat down on a green hill, and he looked down and saw an avenue of trees, and an old deserted road running between them. He went down and came to a gate, and he said, "I'll hold on this road." Then he heard a voice saying, "You'll hold on the road," and there was a little man with a sword in his hand, and a mill-wheel for a hat, who said, "I catch and kill everything that comes this way, man, bird, or beast. This is the Forbidden Land." "We'll see about that," said Jack, and they had the most deadly fight, and in the end Jack struck the sword out of the little man's hand. The little man said, "That's my sword you're fighting me with, or else you'd never have beaten me. However, now I am beaten, I am your servant. If you want me, you have only to say: 'Where are you, my little man, with the broad bonnet?'"

So Jack thanked him, and went on along the road, which led to an enchanted castle. Jack explored the castle, and in the topmost room he found a Princess. She said to him, "Take this topcoat, and these old shoes. They are the cloak of darkness, and the shoes of swiftness. Maybe, with their help, you can free me from my enchantment." They were terribly ragged and down-trodden, but Jack took them. After a while he saw an old man cutting rushes, and he thought he'd try if the cloak was a cloak of darkness, so he put it on. "Good morning to you," he said. "Where are you?" said the old man. "I'm here," said Jack, "in front of you." "I cannot see you," said the old man. Then Jack took off the coat, and he said, "Do you see me now?" "Aye, I see you now," said the old man. "What way did I not see you before?" "I was invisible before." "Well,

I've cut rushes here for two hundred years, and I've never seen the like of that before. But you had better take care, for the Black Knight comes here every seven years to try to catch the white-milk deer, his daughter, and it'll soon be the seven years." "Maybe I'll catch her first," said Jack. "If you did," said the old man, "you'd loose us all from the enchantment." So Jack put on the shoes of swiftness, and away he went to look for the white-milk deer. Soon he saw it in the distance. The deer made away, but if it ran fast, Jack ran faster, and he drove it till he got to a rocky precipice, and Jack thought he had it cornered, when the rock opened, and the deer fled inside with Jack after it. He followed along through rocky caves, till he found the deer lying panting. "Ah, I have you at last, my lady," said Jack. "Aye," she said, "you have me, and there's one thing for you to do. Do you see the well there? You must cut my head off my body, and fling them both down into that well." "But I don't want to hurt you, you pretty creature," said Jack. "There's no help for it. If you don't do that, I'll have to cut off your head." "I wouldn't wish you to do that," said Jack. So he cut off her head, and flung head and body down into the well. Then he thought to himself, "What a fool I was! The wee deer could never have taken my sword in its foot. What a fool I was to believe it! Why did I hurt the wee deer?"

But as he sat and grieved, he heard a voice behind him say: "Look up, Jack!" and there was a most lovely lady. "I am your white-milk deer," she said. "And now let us go home." The rock had closed upon them, but the Princess spoke the word, and it opened, and there was a road, and a grand carriage on it, and they got into it. But they had not gone far before they saw a horseman riding towards them, and the lady said, "This is the Black Knight, my father. He is the deadliest man on the face of the earth, and I fear he will kill you." The Black Knight rode up to them, drawing his sword. But just as he reached them, Jack said, "Taste of my bread," and held out a bannock to him. His face changed till he looked like another man, and he ate all the seven bannocks. Then he said, "Thank you, Jack, you've done for me what no other earthly man could have done, and you've freed my daughter from enchantment. There is just one thing more. I have a deadly serpent to fight, but that is for me to do." With that, the serpent came up, and he and the Black Knight fought till valleys were made into hills, and hills into valleys, but in the end the Black Knight won, and killed the serpent, and at that the many weary miles to the castle were shortened, and Jack's lady was none other than the one he had found in the enchanted room. So he married her, and fetched his father and mother to live with him, and they had great rejoicings.

School of Scottish Studies, Hamish Hamilton, from Andrew Stewart, Aberdeen.
TYPE 303. MOTIFS: J.229.3 [*Choice: a big piece of cake with my curse, or a small*

piece with my blessing]; E.761.3 [Life-token: flower fades]; H.1102 [Task: cleaning Augean stable]; L.161 [Lowly hero marries princess]; D.1182 [Magic pin]; D.1960 [Magic sleep]; G.551.4 [One brother rescues another].

D.765.1.2 [Disenchantment by removal of enchanting pin]; D.1081 [Magic sword]. (See D.1385.14 [Milk of two king's children protects Hero].) D.1361.12 [Magic cloak of invisibility]; D.1065.1 [Magic boots]; D.114.1.1.1 [Transformation: girl to deer]; D.711 [Disenchantment by decapitation]; D.764.1 [Disenchantment by drinking milk of queen].

¶ The two separate parts of this story are both good, and both contain points of some interest. In the first part, the unusual feature is the cleaning of the Augean stable without magic aid. The thorn of sleep is a common feature in Highland tales. In the second part a Celtic feature is the magic quality of the cakes mixed with a woman's milk.

THE KING OF ENGLAND AND HIS THREE SONS

Once upon a time there was an old king who had three sons; and the old king fell very sick one time and there was nothing at all could make him well but some golden apples from a far country. So the three brothers went on horseback to look for some of these apples. They set off together, and when they came to cross-roads they halted and refreshed themselves a bit; and then they agreed to meet on a certain time, and not one was to go home before the other. So Valentine took the right, and Oliver went straight on, and poor Jack took the left.

To make my long story short I shall follow poor Jack, and let the other two take their chance, for I don't think there was much good in them. Off poor Jack rides over hills, dales, valleys and mountains, through woolly woods and sheepwalks, where the old chap never sounded his bugle-horn, farther than I can tell you to-night or ever intend to tell you.

At last he came to an old house, near a great forest, and there was an old man sitting out by the door, and his look was enough to frighten you or anyone else; and the old man said to him:

"Good morning, my king's son."

"Good morning to you, old gentleman," was the young prince's answer; frightened out of his wits though he was, he didn't like to give in.

The old gentleman told him to dismount and to go in to have some refreshment, and to put his horse in the stable, such as it was. Jack soon felt much better after having something to eat, and began to ask the old gentleman how he knew he was a king's son.

"Oh dear!" said the old man. "I knew that you were a king's son, and I know what is your business better than what you do yourself.

So you will have to stay here to-night; and when you are in bed you mustn't be frightened whatever you may hear. There will come all manner of frogs and snakes, and some will try to get into your eyes and your mouth, but mind, don't stir the least bit or you will turn into one of those things yourself."

Poor Jack didn't know what to make of this, but, however, he ventured to go to bed. Just as he thought to have a bit of sleep, round and over and under him they came, but he never stirred an inch all night.

"Well, my young son, how are you this morning?"

"Oh, I am very well, thank you, but I didn't have much rest."

"Well, never mind that; you have got on very well so far, but you have a great deal to go through before you can have the golden apples to go to your father. You'd better come and have some breakfast before you start on your way to my other brother's house. You will have to leave your own horse here with me until you come back again, and tell me everything about how you got on."

After that out came a fresh horse for the young prince, and the old man gave him a ball of yarn, and he flung it between the horse's two ears.

Off he went as fast as the wind, which the wind behind could not catch the wind before, until he came to the second oldest brother's house. When he rode up to the door he had the same salute as from the first old man, but this one was even uglier than the first one. He had long grey hair, and his teeth were curling out of his mouth, and his finger- and toe-nails had not been cut for many thousand years. He put the horse into a much better stable, and called Jack in, and gave him plenty to eat and drink, and they had a bit of a chat before they went to bed.

"Well, my young son," said the old man, "I suppose you are one of the king's children come to look for the golden apples to bring him back to health."

"Yes, I am the youngest of the three brothers, and I should like to get them to go back with."

"Well, don't mind, my young son. Before you go to bed to-night I will send to my eldest brother, and will tell him what you want, and he won't have much trouble in sending you on to the place where you must get the apples. But mind not to stir to-night, no matter how you get bitten and stung, or else you will work great mischief to yourself."

The young man went to bed and bore all, as he did the first night, and got up the next morning well and hearty. After a good breakfast out comes a fresh horse, and a ball of yarn to throw between his ears. The old man told him to jump up quick, and said that he had made it all right with his eldest brother, not to delay for anything whatever. "For", said he, "you have a good deal to go through in a very short and quick time."

He flung the ball, and off he goes as quick as lightning, and comes to
the eldest brother's house. The old man receives him very kindly, and
told him he long wished to see him, and that he would go through his
work like a man and come back safe and sound. "To-night", said he,
"I will give you rest; there shall nothing come to disturb you, so that
you may not feel sleepy for to-morrow. And you must mind to get up
middling early, for you've got to go and come all in the same day; there
will be no place for you to rest within thousands of miles of that place;
and if there was, you would stand in great danger never to come from
there in your own form. Now, my young prince, mind what I tell you.
To-morrow, when you come in sight of a very large castle, which will
be surrounded with black water, the first thing you will do you will tie
your horse to a tree, and you will see three beautiful swans in sight, and
you will say, "Swan, swan, carry me over, in the name of the Griffin of
the Greenwood," and the swans will swim you over to the earth.
There will be three great entrances, the first guarded by four great
giants and drawn swords in their hands, the second by lions, the other by
fiery serpents and dragons. You will have to be there exactly at one
o'clock; and mind you leave there precisely at two, and not a moment
later. When the swans carry you over to the castle, you will pass all
these things, all fast asleep, but you must not notice any of them.

"When you go in, you will turn up to the right; you will see some grand
rooms, then you will go downstairs and through the cooking kitchen,
and through a door on your left you go into a garden, where you will
find the apples you want for your father to get well. After you fill your
wallet, you make all speed you possibly can, and call out for the swans
to carry you over the same as before. After you get on your horse, should
you hear anything shouting or making any noise after you, be sure not
to look back, as they will follow you for thousands of miles; but when the
time is up and you get near my place, it will be all over. Well now, my
young man, I have told you all you have to do to-morrow; and mind,
whatever you do, don't look about you when you see all those frightful
things asleep. Keep a good heart, and make haste from there, and come
back to me with all the speed you can. I should like to know how my two
brothers were when you left them, and what they said to you about me."

"Well, to tell you the truth, before I left London my father was sick,
and said I was to come here to look for the golden apples, for they were
the only things that would do him good; and when I came to your
youngest brother, he told me many things I had to do before I came here.
And I thought once that your youngest brother put me in the wrong
bed, when he put all those snakes to bite me all night long, till your
second brother told me, 'So it was to be,' and said, 'It is the same here,'
but said you had none in your beds."

"Well, let's go to bed. You need not fear. There are no snakes here."

The young man went to bed, and had a good night's rest, and got up next morning as fresh as newly caught trout. Breakfast being over, out comes the other horse, and, while saddling and fettling, the old man began to laugh, and told the young gentleman that if he saw a pretty young lady, not to stay with her too long, because she might waken, and then he would have to stay with her or to be turned into one of those unearthly monsters, like those he would have to pass by going into the castle.

"Ha! ha! ha! You make me laugh so that I can scarcely buckle the saddle straps. I think I shall make it all right, my uncle, if I see a young lady there, you may depend."

"Well, my boy, I shall see how you get on."

So he mounts his Arab steed, and off he goes like a shot out of a gun. At last he comes in sight of the castle. He ties his horse safe to a tree, and pulls out his watch. It was then a quarter to one, when he called out, "Swan, swan, carry me over, for the name of the old Griffin of the Greenwood." No sooner said than done.

A swan under each side, and one in front, took him over in a crack. He got on his legs, and walked quietly by all those giants, lions, fiery serpents, and all manner of other frightful things too numerous to mention, while they were fast asleep, and that only for the space of one hour, when into the castle he goes neck or nothing. Turning to the right, upstairs he runs, and enters into a very grand bedroom, and sees a beautiful Princess lying full stretch on a gold bedstead, fast asleep. He gazed on her beautiful form with admiration, and he takes her garter off, and buckles it on his own leg, and he buckles his on hers; he also takes her gold watch and pocket-handkerchief, and exchanges his for hers; after that he ventures to give her a kiss, when she very nearly opened her eyes.

Seeing the time short, off he runs downstairs, and passing through the kitchen to go into the garden for the apples, he could see the cook all fours on her back on the middle of the floor, with the knife in one hand and the fork in the other. He found the apples, and filled the wallet; and on passing through the kitchen the cook near wakened, but he was obliged to make all the speed he possibly could, as the time was nearly up. He called out for the swans, and they managed to take him over; but they found that he was a little heavier than before.

No sooner than he had mounted his horse he could hear a tremendous noise, the enchantment was broke, and they tried to follow him, but all to no purpose. He was not long before he came to the eldest brother's house; and glad enough he was to see it, for the sight and the noise of all those things that were after him nearly frightened him to death.

"Welcome, my boy; I am proud to see you. Dismount and put the horse in the stable, and come in and have some refreshments; I know you are hungry after all you have gone through in that castle. And tell me all you did, and all you saw there. Other kings' sons went by here to go to that castle, but they never came back alive, and you are the only one that ever broke the spell. And now you must come with me, with a sword in your hand, and must cut my head off, and must throw it in that well."

The young Prince dismounts, and puts his horse in the stable, and they go in to have some refreshments, for I can assure you he wanted some; and after telling everything that passed, which the old gentleman was very pleased to hear, they both went for a walk together, the young prince looking around, and seeing the place looking dreadful, as did the old man. He could scarcely walk from his toe-nails curling up like ram's horns that had not been cut for many hundred years, and big long hair. They come to a well, and the old man gives the Prince a sword, and tells him to cut his head off, and throw it in that well. The young man has to do it against his wish, but has to do it.

No sooner has he flung the head in the well, than up springs one of the finest young gentlemen you would wish to see; and instead of the old house and the frightful-looking place, it was changed into a beautiful hall and grounds. And they went back and enjoyed themselves well, and had a good laugh about the castle.

The young Prince leaves this young gentleman in all his glory, and he tells the young Prince before leaving that he will see him again before long. They have a jolly shake-hands, and off he goes to the next eldest brother; and, to make my long story short, he has to serve the other two brothers the same as the first.

Now the youngest brother began to ask him how things went on.

"Did you see my two brothers?"

"Yes."

"How did they look?"

"Oh! They looked very well. I liked them much. They told me many things what to do."

"Well, did you go to the castle?"

"Yes, my uncle."

"And will you tell me what you see in there? Did you see the young lady?"

"Yes, I saw her, and plenty of other frightful things."

"Did you hear any snake biting you in my oldest brother's bed?"

"No, there were none there; I slept well."

"You won't have to sleep in the same bed to-night. You will have to cut my head off in the morning."

The young Prince had a good night's rest, and changed all the appearance of the place, by cutting his friend's head off before he started in the morning. A jolly shake-hands, and the uncle tells him it's very probable he shall see him again soon when he is not aware of it. This one's mansion was very pretty, and the country around it beautiful, after his head was cut off. Off Jack goes, over hills, dales, valleys and mountains, and very near losing his apples again.

At last he arrives at the cross-roads, where he has to meet his brothers on the very day appointed. Coming up to the place, he sees no tracks of horses, and being very tired, he lays himself down to sleep, by tying the horse to his leg, and putting the apples under his head. Presently up come the other brothers, the same time to the minute, and found him fast asleep; and they would not waken him, but said one to another, "Let us see what sort of apples he has got under his head." So they took and tasted them, and found they were different to theirs. They took and changed his apples for theirs, and off to London as fast as they could, and left the poor fellow sleeping.

After a while he awoke, and seeing the tracks of other horses, he mounted and off with him, not thinking anything about the apples being changed. He had still a long way to go, and by the time he got near London, he could hear all the bells in the town ringing, but did not know what was the matter until he rode up to the palace, when he came to know that his father was recovered by his brothers' apples. When he got there, his two brothers were off to some sports for a while; and the king was glad to see his youngest son, and very anxious to taste his apples. But when he found out that they were not good, and thought that they were more for poisoning him, he sent immediately for the headsman to behead his youngest son, who was taken away there and then in a carriage. But instead of the headsman taking his head off, he took him to a forest not far from the town, because he had pity on him, and there left him to take his chance, when presently up comes a big hairy bear, limping upon three legs. The Prince, poor fellow, climbed up a tree, frightened of him, but the bear told him to come down, that it was no use of him to stop there. With hard persuasion poor Jack comes down, and the bear speaks to him and bids him, "Come here to me; I will not do you any harm. It's better for you to come with me and have some refreshments; I know that you are hungry all this time."

The poor young Prince says, "No, I am not hungry; but I was very frightened when I saw you coming to me first, as I had no place to run away from you."

The bear said, "I was also afraid of you when I saw that gentleman setting you down from the carriage. I thought you would have guns with you, and that you would not mind killing me if you saw me; but when I saw the gentleman going away with the carriage, and leaving you behind by yourself, I made bold to come to you, to see who you were, and now I know who you are very well. Are you not the King's youngest son? I have seen you and your brothers and lots of other gentlemen in this wood many times. Now before we go from here, I must tell you that I am in disguise; and I shall take you where we are stopping."

The young Prince tells him everything from first to last, how he started in search of the apples, and about the three old men, and about the castle, and how he was served at last by his father after he came home; and instead of the headsman taking his head off, he was kind enough to leave him his life, "and here I am now, under your protection".

The bear tells him, "Come on, my brother; there shall no harm come to you as long as you are with me."

So he takes him up to the tents; and when they see him coming, the girls begin to laugh and say, "Here is our Jubal coming with a young gentleman." When he advanced nearer the tents, they all knew that he was the young Prince that had passed by that way many times before; and when Jubal went to change himself, he called most of them together into one tent, and told them all about him, and to be kind to him. And so they were, for there was nothing that he desired but what he had, the same as if he was in the palace with his father and mother. Jubal, after he pulled off his hairy coat, was one of the finest young men amongst them, and he was the young Prince's closest companion. The young Prince was always very sociable and merry, only when he thought of the gold watch he had from the young Princess in the castle, and which he had lost he knew not where.

He passed off many happy days in the forest; but one day he and poor Jubal were strolling through the trees, when they came to the very spot where they first met, and, accidentally looking up, he could see his watch hanging in the tree which he had to climb when he first saw poor Jubal coming to him in the form of a bear; and he cries out, "Jubal, Jubal, I can see my watch up in that tree."

"Well, I am sure, how lucky!" exclaimed poor Jubal. "Shall I go and get it down?"

"No, I'd rather go myself," said the young Prince.

Now whilst all this was going on, the young Princess in that castle, seeing that one of the King of England's sons had been there by the changing of the watch and other things, got herself ready with a large army, and sailed off for England. She left her army a little out of the town, and she went with her guards straight up to the palace, to see the King, and also demanded to see his sons. They had a long conversation together about different things. At last she demands one of the sons to come before her; and the oldest comes, when she asks him, "Have you ever been at the castle of Melvales?" and he answers "Yes."

She throws down a pocket-handkerchief, and bids him to walk over it without stumbling. He goes to walk over it, and no sooner did he put his foot on it than he fell down and broke his leg. He was taken off immediately and made a prisoner of by her own guards. The other was called upon, and was asked the same questions, and had to go through the same performance, and he also was made a prisoner of. Now she says, "Have you not another son?", when the King begins to shiver and shake and knock his two knees together that he could scarcely stand upon his legs, and did not know what to say to her, he was so much frightened.

At last a thought came to him to send for his headsman, and inquire of him particularly, Did he behead his son, or was he alive?

"He is saved, O King."

"Then bring him here immediately, or else I shall be done for."

Two of the fastest horses they had were put in the carriage, to go and look for the poor Prince; and when they got to the very spot where they left him, it was the time when the Prince was up the tree, getting his watch down, and poor Jubal standing a distance off. They cried out to him, Had he seen another young man in this wood? Jubal, seeing such a nice carriage, thought something, and did not like to say No, and said Yes, and pointed up the tree; and they told him to come down immediately, there was a young lady in search of him with a young child.

"Ha! ha! ha! Jubal, did you ever hear such a thing in all your life, my brother?"

"Do you call him your brother?"

"Well, he has been better to me than my brothers."

"Well, for his kindness, he shall accompany you to the palace, and see how things turn out."

After they go to the palace, the Prince has a good wash, and appears before the Princess, when she asks him, Had he ever been at the castle of Melvales? With a smile upon his face, he gives a graceful bow. And says my Lady, "Walk over that handkerchief without stumbling." He walks over it many times, and dances upon it, and nothing happened to him. She said, with a proud and smiling air, "That is the young man," and out come the objects exchanged by both of them. Presently she orders a very large box to be brought in and to be opened, and out come some of the most costly uniforms that were ever worn on an Emperor's back; and when he dressed himself up, the King could scarcely look upon him from the dazzling of the gold and diamonds on his coat. He orders his two brothers to be in confinement for a period of time; and before the Princess asks him to go with her to her own country, she pays a visit to the bear's camp, and she makes some very handsome presents for their kindness to the young Prince. And she gives Jubal an invitation to go with them, which he accepts; wishes them a hearty farewell for a while, promising to see them all again in some little time.

They go back to the King and bid farewell, and tell him not to be so hasty another time to order people to be beheaded before having a proper cause for it. Off they go, all their army with them; but while the soldiers were striking their tents, the Prince bethought himself of his Welsh harp, and had it sent for immediately to take with him in a beautiful wooden case. They called to see each of those three brothers whom the Prince had to stay with when he was on his way to the castle of Melvales; and I can assure you, when they all got together, they had a very merry time of it. And there we will leave them.

Jacobs, *More English Fairy Tales*, p. 132.
TYPE 551. MOTIFS: H.1333.3.1.5 [*Quest for healing apple*]; H.1235 [*Succession o, helpers on quest*]; D.1526.2 [*Magic ball flight*]; B.184.1 [*Magic horse*]; D.961 [*Magic garden*]; T.475.2 [*Hero lies by princess in magic sleep, and begets child*]; H.81.1 [*Hero lies by sleeping girl, and leaves identification token with her*]; D.711 [*Disenchantment by decapitation*]; K.1932 [*Impostors claim reward gained by hero*]; K.512 [*Compassionate executioner*]; K.649.7.2 [*Helper dressed in bear's skin helps to escape*]; H.1381.2.1 [*Princess seeks unknown father of her child*]; D.1318.8 [*Magic cloth reveals guilt*]; L.10 [*Victorious younger son*].

KING HERLA

Herla was king of the Ancient Britons, and was challenged by another king, a pigmy no bigger than an ape, and of less than half human stature. He rode on a large goat; indeed, he himself might have been compared to Pan. He had a large head, glowing face, and a long red beard, while his breast was conspicuous for a spotted fawnskin which he wore on it. The lower part of his body was rough and hairy, and his legs ended in goats' hooves. He had a private interview with Herla, in which he spoke as follows: "I am lord over many kings and princes, over a vast and innumerable people. I am their willing messenger to you, although to you I am unknown. Yet I rejoice in the fame which has raised you above other kings, for you are of all men the best, and also closely connected with me both by position and blood. You are worthy of the honour of adorning your marriage with my presence as guest, for the King of France has given you his daughter, and indeed the embassy is arriving here to-day, although all the arrangements have been made without your knowledge. Let there be an everlasting treaty between us, because, first of all, I was present at your marriage, and because you will be at mine on the same day a year hence." After this speech he turned away, and moving faster even than a tiger, disappeared from his sight. The King, therefore, returned from that spot full of surprise, received the embassy, and assented to their proposals. When the marriage was celebrated, and the king was seated at the customary feast, suddenly, before the first course was served, the pigmy arrived, accompanied by so large a company of dwarfs like himself, that after they had filled all the seats at table, there were more dwarfs outside in tents which they had in a moment put up, than at the feast inside. Instantly there darted out from these tents servants with vessels made out of precious stones, all new and wondrously wrought. They filled the palace and the tents with furniture either made of gold or precious stones. Neither wine nor meat was served in any wooden or silver vessel. The servants were found wherever they were wanted, and served nothing out of the king's or anyone else's stores, but only from their own, which were of quality beyond anyone's thoughts. None of Herla's provisions were used, and his servants sat idle.

The pigmies won universal praise. Their raiment was gorgeous; for lamps they provided blazing gems; they were never far off when they were wanted, and never too close when not desired. Their king then thus addressed Herla: "Most excellent King, God be my witness that I am here in accordance with our agreement, at your marriage. If there is anything more that you desire, I will supply it gladly, on the condition that when I demand a return, you will not deny it." Hereupon, without waiting for an answer he returned to his tent and departed at about cock-crow with his attendants. After a year he suddenly came to Herla and demanded the observance of the treaty. Herla consented, and followed at the dwarf's bidding. They entered a cave in a very high cliff, and after some journeying through the dark, which appeared to be lighted, not by the sun or moon, but by numerous torches, they arrived at the dwarf's palace, a splendid mansion.

There the marriage was celebrated, and the obligations to the dwarf fittingly paid, after which Herla returned home loaded with gifts and offerings, horses, dogs, hawks, and all things pertaining to hunting and falconry. The pigmy guided them down the dark passage, and there gave them a (small) bloodhound (canem sanguinarium) small enough to be carried (portabilem), then, strictly forbidding any of the king's retinue to dismount until the dog leapt from his carrier, he bade them farewell, and returned home. Soon after, Herla reached the light of day, and having got back to his kingdom again, called an old shepherd and asked for news of his queen, using her name. The shepherd looked at him astonished, and said, "Lord, I scarcely understand your language, for I am a Saxon, and you a Briton. I have never heard the name of that queen, except in the case of one who they say was Herla's wife, queen of the earliest Britons. He is fabled to have disappeared with a dwarf at this cliff, and never to have been seen on earth again. The Saxons have now held this realm for two hundred years, having driven out the original inhabitants." The king was astonished, for he imagined that he had been away for three days only. Some of his companions descended from horseback before the dog was released, forgetful of the dwarf's commands, and were instantly crumbled to dust. The king then forbade any more of his companions to descend until the dog leapt down. The dog has not leapt down yet. One legend states that Herla for ever wanders on mad journeys with his train, without home or rest. Many people, as they tell us, often see his company. However, they say that at last, in the first year of our (present) King Henry (the second) it ceased to visit our country in pomp as before. On that occasion, many of the Welsh (*Wallenses*) saw it whelmed in the Wye, the Herefordshire river (*Waiam Herefordiae flumen*). From that hour, that weird roaming ceased, as though Herla had transferred his wandering (*Errores*, a pun containing the idea of error) to us, and had gained rest for himself. (A hit at contemporary politics.)

Folk-Lore of Herefordshire, E. M. Leather, p. 172. Derived from Walter Map's *De Nugis Curialium*.

TYPE 766 (variant). MOTIFS: F.377 [*Supernatural lapse of time in fairyland*]; F.379.1 [*Return from fairyland*]; F.378.1 [*Tabu: touching ground on return from fairyland*]; C.521 [*Tabu: dismounting from horse*]; C.927.2 [*Falling to ashes as punishment for breaking tabu*]; E.501.1.7.1 [*King Herla as wild huntsman*].

¶ The Irish tale of the Return of Ossian is one of the most poetic of many stories about the miraculous passage of time in fairyland. A widespread Japanese version is "Urashima Taro" (*Folktales of Japan*, no. 32). Hartland devoted three chapters to the subject in *The Science of Fairy Tales*. The Welsh story of Shon ap Shenkin is one of many Celtic versions.

See also "The Noontide Ghost", "The Stonemason of the Charltons".

THE KING OF THE HERRINGS: I

Somewhere very far away lived a quarryman. He was old, and his wife had never borne him any children. At last a son was born to them, and all the neighbours were amazed—the man and woman were so old to have a child.

The father died and the son took his place. And lo! an old man passes by, and the youth gazed upon him. Now the old man asks him: "Wilt thou come with me to seek our living?" "Yes," quoth Jack. "Then say that thou wishest me turned into an old nag."

"Done!" quoth Jack. "Get on my back; let us be off."

So off they set, the old nag and Jack along the road. Said the old nag to Jack: "If thou should'st chance to see or hear anyone in trouble on the way, go and find out what is the matter, and if thou canst do aught, do it."

And lo! and behold! here we are upon the road. And here we are taking the hill. And now the pair are well on their way. Quoth Jack to the nag: "I hear something." "Go and see what it is." Jack got down from the horse's back to see what was there. He saw a little herring that the tide had left stranded. Jack picked it up and put it back in the water. And lo! the fish swam right up to him. Quoth the fish to Jack: "Whatsoever I can do for thee, call upon me, the King of the Herrings, and I will do it."

Away they go over the hill. "Jack, touch nothing that thou seest, even though it be the finest thing thine eyes have ever beheld." And lo! the wind blew a feather into his mouth. Twice or thrice did he spit it out. Back came the feather again. He thought it a pretty feather, and put it in his pocket.

And now they come to an old castle. And they heard a great uproar within the castle. "Go and see what is the matter," said the old nag. Jack went up to the castle and knocked at the gate. No one came out to him. He opened the gate, and went in to see what was happening. He saw a giant lying on a bed, helpless. He could do nothing for himself: he was ill. There was no maid-servant to give him food. "What ails thee, friend?" "I have no serving-wench in this place. Go bring me food and a tankard of ale from below." The giant ate his bellyful, and bade Jack call upon him if ever he could do aught for him.

Now the pair are going downhill. Quoth the old nag: "What didst thou see on the mountain?" "I saw nothing but a little feather which the wind blew into my mouth." "Didst thou take the feather?" "Yes, I have it in my pocket." "This feather will bring us misfortune; but keep it, do not let it go."

And now the young man went to a grand mansion to look for work. The master of the house came out to see his craft with the quill. It was excellent: thou couldst not beat it.

Then he went in search of some place to sleep in. The master invited him to sleep in the house. "Nay," said Jack, "I will go to my old nag in the stable."

Everyone marvelled at his feats with this feather. One day the man-servant said to his master: "Call him hither, master, that I may get hold of his quill." The master called him. He came. The servant took away the quill, and put another on the table in its place.

"Master, I have it: the man who brought the feather here can bring the bird, too."

Said Jack to the old nag: "The master wants the bird." "Go, Jack, and ask him to give thee three days, and three purses of gold." They set off in search of the bird. "Jack, go up to the castle and walk in. Thou wilt see a company feasting at table. Touch nothing. In a corner thou wilt see a draggle-tailed bird in a cage. Go, take it, but tarry not."

Out he comes to the old nag carrying the bird. The pair returned, bringing the bird with them. Now the master and his servant talked it over as they looked at the bird. The servants said to the master: "The bird is pretty; the lady is prettier still." Quoth the servant to his master: "The man who brought the bird here can bring the lady too."

Jack went out to the old nag and told him that the master wanted the lady. "I warned thee about the feather, Jack. Go and ask him for three days and three purses of gold." Jack went back to ask the master. He got the money and the three days.

And away they go! They talk together on the road. Said the old nag to Jack: "Jack, do thou wish me turned into a ship upon the sea." As soon as the word was spoken there was the ship on the sea.

And here they are going aboard. The ship was laden with silk. Now they are sailing beneath the castle. "Jack, go up to the castle, and ask to see the lady. She whom thou wilt see coming out to thee is not the lady: ask to see the lady herself."

Jack went to the castle. He knocked at the gate, and lo! a lady appears. She was not the mistress; she was the housekeeper. He said to her, "I want to see the lady herself." The servant went in to tell her mistress. Anon the lady comes out. Jack told her there was a ship at anchor below the castle, and she stepped down to look at the silk. The lady came aboard, and one of the crew led her to the cabin where the silk was stored. Jack remained on deck. He weighed anchor, and the ship sailed away.

And now they are far out to sea. By this time the lady had finished her business and come on deck. When she saw that she had been trapped, she felt in her pocket, pulled out her keys, and flung them into the sea. The sea turned red as blood, and was troubled by a mighty storm.

Here they are back at the mansion. Jack led the lady inside. The master and the servant spoke a few words together. Quoth the servant to his master: "The man who brought the lady here can bring the castle too."

Jack went out to the old nag and told him. "Well, Jack, I warned thee about the feather, that it would bring us misfortune. Go back, Jack, and ask him for three days and three sacks of gold." Jack went back and got them.

When they were both well on their way, the old nag asked Jack: "What did the giant say to thee?" "He promised he would do anything for me." "Go to him and tell him what thou wantest."

So up Jack goes to the castle. He told the giant what he wanted, and the giant fell a-laughing at him. He sent him out to fetch his chain, but Jack could not lift a single link. Again the giant burst out laughing, and straightway strode out, picked up the chain, and slung it over his shoulder.

Now they both hasten down to the lady's castle. The giant fastened the chain to the castle, put it on his back, and carried it down to the lady's biding-place. There was a high wall round the lady's castle and the gate was locked. Quoth the lady to Jack: "I want my keys. I cannot open the gate."

Again Jack went out to consult the old nag. "Jack, I warned thee about the feather. Go back and ask for such and such things." He went back and got what he wanted.

So here they are again journeying along the road. "Jack, what did the little fish say to thee?" "'Whatsoever I can do for thee I will do: shouldst thou have need of me, thou must call upon the King of the Herrings.'"

Jack and the old nag made for the spot where he had found the fish, and hailed him. Lo! the fish swam up to him. Jack told him about the keys. "I will go in search of them, Jack!" He disappeared, and was gone a great while. He came back, but he had not found the keys. "Jack, I have not found them, I will try again." And again he was gone a great while. At last he reappeared, and he had found the keys, and he gave them to Jack. The herring swam away, and the old nag and Jack returned home.

Jack handed the keys to the lady. The lady asked Jack: "Which wouldst thou rather, Jack, that thy head or that thy master's head be cut off?" Jack stopped to think what answer he should make. Then he said to the lady: "Do not slay him, slay me." Quoth the lady: "Thou hast answered well, Jack, thou hast answered well. Hadst thou not spoken thus, thou wouldst have been slain. Now it is the master who will be slain."

Jack and the lady were married, and the master was slain. And the lady and Jack still live in the castle.

And now thou hast my tale!

Dora E. Yates, *Gypsy Folk-Tales*, p. 14; Also *Thompson Notebooks*, E.

TYPE 550. MOTIFS: N.825 [*Old person as helper*]; B.184.1 [*Magic horse*]; H.1241 [*Series of quests*]; H.919.1 [*Quests assigned at prompting of treacherous servants*]; H.1213 [*Quest for remarkable bird caused by finding one of its feathers*]; H.1381.3.1.1 [*Quest for bride for king*]; D.1123 [*Magic ship*]; K.1332 [*Abduction by taking aboard ship to inspect wares*]; N.812 [*Giant as helper*]; D.2136.2 [*Castle magically transported*]; H.1132.1.2 [*Recovering lost key from sea*]; B.548.2.2 [*Fish recovers key from sea*]; L.161 [*Lowly hero marries princess*].

¶ In the typical version of this story there are three brothers and a golden bird which steals the King's apples, which his three sons are set to guard, and the helper is a fox which the youngest son has befriended. Possibly in this version the unexplained old man is the ghost of the hero's father. Grimm no. 57 is an example of the standard version. In these islands it is to be found in Kennedy's *Fireside Stories*: "The Greek Princess and the Young Gardener".

The story is widespread through the world, but there is no other English version, except the shortened version, belonging to type 554A, to be found in the Thompson Notebooks. See summary below. Here the successive quests are omitted. The full version was published in the *Journal of the Gypsy Lore Society*, new series VIII (1914–15), pp. 211–13.

THE KING OF THE HERRINGS: II
[summary]

A boy throws a stranded herring back into the sea, and it promises to help him whenever it can. Years after, when the boy is a sailor, a lady loses her gold ring overboard, and says she would give anything to have it back. The boy offers to try, and she promises marriage. He calls the herring, and after three days' search it finds the ring. The lady now says she has dropped her keys. The herring fetches them up, and the lady and the boy are married.

Collected by T. W. Thompson.
TYPE 554A* or fragment of 550. MOTIFS: B.375.1 [*Fish returned to water: grateful*]; B.548.2.1 [*Fish recovers ring from sea*]; H.1132.1 [*Task: recovering lost object from sea*].

THE KING AND HIS THREE SONS
[summary]

A King promised his castle and lands to whichever of his three sons could shoot an arrow the farthest. Little Jack's flew right out of sight, so he won.

As Jack was walking out one day with his dog and gun he met a beautiful lady, who restored his arrow to him. They fell in love and were married; but she warned Jack that if he ever met her brother he must on no account ask him any questions.

Now Jack's father refused to keep his promise, and give him his castle; so Jack asked his wife if her brother would help him to get them. She blew a horn and a tiny man appeared who, when the angry King asked what *he* was doing here, immediately attacked and killed him.

So Jack and his wife left the little house by a rock where they had been living and settled in the castle.

Thompson Notebooks, B. Summarized from a version known to Matthew Wood, Bala, 28 August 1922.

TYPE 402 (variant). MOTIFS: H.921.1 [*Tasks set by king to his sons, to determine heir to kingdom*]; L.10 [*Victorious youngest son*]; C.30 [*Tabu: offending supernatural relative*]; C.410 [*Tabu: asking questions*]; K.231.2 [*Reward for accomplishment of task withheld*].

¶ This seems a half-forgotten version of the story of the three brothers and their contest for the heirship of the kingdom, perhaps something after the type of "The Three Feathers", type 402.

LADY ISABEL AND THE ELF-KNIGHT

Fair lady Isabel sits in her bower sewing,
Aye as the gowans grow gay
There she heard an elf-knight blawing his horn,
The first morning in May.

"If I had yon horn that I hear blawing,
And yon elf-night to sleep in my bosom."

This maiden had scarcely these words spoken,
Till in her window the elf-knight has luppen.

"It's a very strange matter, fair maiden," said he,
"I canna blaw my horn but ye call on me.

But will ye go to yon greenwood side?
If ye canna gang, I will cause you to ride."

He leapt on his horse, and she on another,
And they rode on to the greenwood together.

"Light down, light down, Lady Isabel," said he,
"We are come to the place where ye are to die."

"Hae mercy, hae mercy, kind sir, on me,
Till ance my dear father and mother I see."

"Seven king's-daughters here hae I slain,
And ye shall be the eight o them."

"O sit down a while, lay your head on my knee,
That we may hae some rest before that I die."

She stroaked him sae fast, the nearer he did creep,
Wi a sma charm she lulld him fast asleep.

Wi his ain sword-belt sae fast as she ban him,
Wi his ain dag-durk sae sair as she dang him.

"If seven king's-daughters here ye hae slain,
Lye ye here, a husband to them a'."

Child, *The English and Scottish Popular Ballads*, I, p. 55. From (*a*) Buchan's *Ballads of the North of Scotland*, I, p. 22*b*; (*b*) Motherwell's *MS*, p. 563.

MOTIFS: F.301.2.1 [*Elf-knight procures love-longing by blowing on horn*]; F.301.5 [*Elf-knight entices maiden away*]; F.389.4 [*Fairy killed by mortal*].
¶ See "May Colvin and False Sir John".

THE LAIDLEY WORM OF SPINDLESTON HEUGHS [summary]

The King had gone away from Bambrough Castle leaving Margaret, his only daughter, to care for it. Her brother the Child of Wynd was away also over the seas, and she was lonely, and longed for her father's return. At last he came, bringing with him a new wife whom Margaret made welcome, with all due courtesy. But one of the queen's attendant lords said,

"This princess of the North
Surpassed all of female kind,
In beauty and in worth."

This made the Queen, who was a witch, so jealous that she changed the princess into a hideous worm, which ravaged the countryside for seven miles all round with its venomous breath. Every day it drank the milk of seven cows. The cave in which it lay coiled up and the stone trough from which it drank are still to be seen in Spindleston Heughs, and the news of its devastations spread far and wide.

At last Margaret's brother the Child of Wynd heard of it and, fearing for his sister's safety, he returned home. The Queen saw his ship approaching with its silken sails all set, and she sent all her witch-wives to wreck it, but the ship was of rowan-wood and they had no power over it. Then she sent a shipload of armed men to board it, but they were repelled, and the ship came close to land. The Worm leapt up and down at the sight and nearly wrecked the ship each time it came close, but at last the Child beached it safely on Budle sand and waded ashore.

He laid his sword flat on the Worm's head, and swore to cut it off if it harmed him. But the Worm bade him lay aside his sword and give her three kisses, for she must be saved ere that day's sun set. He did as she bade him, and the Worm crawled away into its cave and came out again a naked lady. Her brother wrapped her in his mantle and together they went up to the castle, to be welcomed with great joy by the King their father. The wicked Queen was changed by Child Wynd into a hideous toad to crawl for ever about the sands of Spindleston.

Child, *The English and Scottish Popular Ballads*, I, pp. 311–13 (Kemp Owyne).
TYPE 402A* (variant). MOTIFS: G.205* [*Witch stepmother*]; D.192 [*Transformation to worm*]; D.791.2 [*Disenchantment by only one person*]; D.735.2 [*Three redeeming kisses*]; Q.581 [*Villain nemesis*]; G.211.6.1 [*Witch to toad*].

Motif D.732 [*Loathly lady. Man disenchants worm by embracing her*] has some bearing on this tale. See "The Marriage of Sir Gawayne".
¶ There is a paper by Coomaraswamy on "The Loathly Bride" in *Speculum* (1945), pp. 391 ff.

THE LAILY WORM [summary]

A boy and girl once had a wicked and cruel stepmother who, while their father was away, turned the boy into a "laily worm that lies at the fit o' the tree", and the girl into a "machrel of the sea". Every Saturday at noon the girl (perhaps for a short time restored to her proper form) came up out of the sea, and combed the laily worm's head with a silver comb and washed it in the sea.

As time passed the worm killed seven knights who came to find it, and after the last of them his own father came. Then the worm sang to him:

"Seven knights hae I slain,
　　Sin I lay at the fit of the tree.
　An ye were na my ain father,
　　The eight ane ye should be."

Then he sang to his father the whole story of his wife's wickedness, and he sent for her, and demanded to know where his son and his daughter Maisry were. She replied:

"Your son is at the King's court,
　　Serving for meat and fee.
　An your daughter's at our Queen's court—"

But he broke in, and told her she lied. Then she took a silver wand, and struck the worm three times, and he sprang up, no longer the little boy of seven on whom she had laid her spell, but a full-grown knight. Then she blew on a small shrill horn, and all the fish came up out of the sea to her, except the proud mackerel, who said,

"Ye shaipit me ance an unseemly shape,
　　An ye's never mare shape me."

So the knight her husband

"sent to the wood,
　For whins and for hawthorn,
And he has taen that gay lady,
　And there he did her burn."

Child, *The English and Scottish Popular Ballads*, no. 36, I, p. 315.
TYPE 450A (variant). MOTIFS: G.205 [*Witch stepmother*]; D.683.2 [*Transformation by witch*]; D.192 [*Transformation to worm*]; D.170 [*Transformation to fish*]; P.253.2

[*Sister faithful to transformed brother*]; D.794 [*Enchanted person attracts attention of rescuer*]; D.712.3 [*Disenchantment by striking*]; G.275.3 [*Witch burned*].
¶ See "Allison Gross".

THE LAMBTON WORM

A wild young fellow was the heir of Lambton, the fine estate and hall by the side of the swift-flowing Wear. Not a Mass would he hear in Brugeford Chapel of a Sunday, but a-fishing he would go. And if he did not haul in anything, his curses could be heard by the folk as they went by to Brugeford.

Well, one Sunday morning he was fishing as usual, and not a salmon had risen to him, his basket was bare of roach or dace. And the worse his luck, the worse grew his language, till the passers-by were horrified at his words as they went to listen to the Mass-priest.

At last young Lambton felt a mighty tug at his line. "At last," quoth he, "a bite worth having!" and he pulled and he pulled, till what should appear above the water but a head like an eft's, with nine holes on each side of its mouth. But still he pulled till he had got the thing to land, when it turned out to be a Worm of hideous shape. If he had cursed before, his curses were enough to raise the hair on your head.

"What ails thee, my son?" said a voice by his side, "and what hast thou caught, that thou shouldst stain the Lord's Day with such foul language?"

Looking round, young Lambton saw a strange old man standing by him.

"Why truly," he said, "I think I have caught the devil himself. Look you and see if you know him."

But the stranger shook his head, and said, "It bodes no good to thee or thine to bring such a monster to shore. Yet cast him not back into the Wear; thou hast caught him, and thou must keep him," and with that away he turned, and was seen no more.

The young heir of Lambton took up the gruesome thing, and, taking it off his hook cast it into a well close by, and ever since that day that well has gone by the name of the Worm Well.

For some time nothing more was seen or heard of the Worm, till one day it had outgrown the size of the well, and came forth full-grown. So it came forth from the well and betook itself to the Wear. And all day long it would lie coiled round a rock in the middle of the stream, while at night it came forth from the river and harried the countryside. It sucked the cow's milk, devoured the lambs, worried the cattle, and frightened all the women and girls of the district, and then it would

retire for the rest of the night to the hill, still called the Worm Hill, on
the north side of the Wear, about a mile and a half from Lambton Hall.

This terrible visitation brought young Lambton, of Lambton Hall,
to his senses. He took upon himself the vows of the Cross, and departed
for the Holy Land, in the hope that the scourge he had brought upon
his district would disappear. But the grisly Worm took no heed, except
that it crossed the river and came right up to Lambton Hall itself, where
the old lord lived on all alone, his only son having gone to the Holy
Land. What to do? The Worm was coming closer and closer to the
Hall; women were shrieking, men were gathering weapons, dogs were
barking and horses neighing with terror. At last the steward called out
to the dairy maids, "Bring all your milk hither," and when they did so,
and had brought all the milk that the nine kye of the byre had yielded,
he poured it all into the long stone trough in front of the Hall.

The Worm drew nearer and nearer, till at last it came up to the trough.
But when it sniffed the milk, it turned aside to the trough and swallowed
all the milk up, and then slowly turned round and crossed the river
Wear, and coiled its bulk three times round the Worm Hill for the night.

Henceforth the Worm would cross the river every day, and woe
betide the Hall if the trough contained the milk of less than nine kye.
The Worm would hiss, and would rave, and lash its tail round the trees
of the park, and in its fury it would uproot the stoutest oaks and the
loftiest firs. So it went on for seven years. Many tried to destroy the
Worm, but all had failed, and many a knight had lost his life in fighting
with the monster, which slowly crushed the life out of all that came near
it.

At last the Childe of Lambton came home to his father's Hall, after
seven long years spent in meditation and repentance on holy soil. Sad
and desolate he found his folk: the lands untilled, the farms deserted,
half the trees of the park uprooted, for none would stay to tend the nine
kye that the monster needed for his food each day.

The Childe sought his father, and begged his forgiveness for the curse
he had brought on the Hall.

"Thy sin is pardoned," said his father; "but go thou to the Wise
Woman of Brugeford and find if aught can free us from this monster."

To the Wise Woman went the Childe, and asked her advice.

"'Tis thy fault, O Childe, for which we suffer," she said; "be it thine
to release us."

"I would give my life," said the Childe.

"Mayhap thou wilt do so," said she. "But hear me, and mark me well.
Thou, and thou alone, canst kill the Worm. But, to this end, thou go to
the smithy and have thy armour studded with spear-heads. Then go to
the Worm's Rock in the Wear, and station thyself there. Then, when the

Worm comes to the Rock at dawn of day, try thy prowess on him, and God gi'e thee a good deliverance."

"And this I will do," said Childe Lambton.

"But one thing more," said the Wise Woman, going back to her cell, "If thou slay the Worm, swear that thou wilt put to death the first thing that meets thee as thou crossest again the threshold of Lambton Hall. Do this, and all will be well with thee and thine. Fulfil not thy vow, and none of the Lambtons, for generations three times three, shall die in his bed. Swear, and fail not."

The Childe swore as the Wise Woman bid, and went his way to the smithy. There he had his armour studded with spear-heads all over. Then he passed his vigils in Brugeford Chapel, and at dawn of day took his post on the Worm's Rock in the River Wear.

As dawn broke, the Worm uncoiled its snaky twine from around the hill, and came to its rock in the river. When it perceived the Childe waiting for it, it lashed the waters in its fury and wound its coils round the Childe, and then attempted to crush him to death. But the more it pressed, the deeper dug the spear-heads into its sides. Still it pressed and pressed, till all the water around was crimsoned with its blood. Then the Worm un-wound itself, and left the Childe free to use his sword. He raised it, brought it down, and cut the Worm in two. One half fell into the river, and was carried swiftly away. Once more the head and the remainder of the body encircled the Childe, but with less force, and the spear-heads did their work. At last the Worm uncoiled itself, snorted its last foam of blood and fire, and rolled dying into the river, and was never seen more.

The Childe of Lambton swam ashore, and, raising his bugle to his lips, sounded its note thrice. This was the signal to the Hall, where the servants and the old lord had shut themselves in to pray for the Childe's success. When the third sound of the bugle was heard, they were to release Boris, the Childe's favourite hound. But such was their joy at learning of the Childe's safety and the Worm's defeat, that they forgot orders, and when the Childe reached the threshold of the Hall his old father rushed out to meet him, and would have clasped him to his breast.

"The vow! the vow!" called out the Childe of Lambton, and blew still another blast upon his horn. This time the servants remembered, and released Boris, who came bounding to his young master. The Childe raised his shining sword, and severed the head of his faithful hound.

But the vow was broken, and for nine generations of men none of the Lambtons died in his bed. The last of the Lambtons died in his carriage as he was crossing Brugeford Bridge one hundred and thirty years ago.

J. Jacobs, *More English Fairy Tales*, p. 198; W. Henderson, *Folklore of the Northern Counties*; E. S. Hartland, *English Fairy and Folk Tales*, p. 78.

TYPE 300 (variant). MOTIFS: C.631 [*Tabu: breaking the sabbath*]; C.984 [*Disaster because of broken tabu*]; B.11.2.1.3 [*Dragon as modified fish*]; B.11.2.12 [*Dragon of enormous size*]; B.11.12.4.1 [*Dragon fed with great quantities of milk to keep him pacified*]; B.11.11 [*Fight with dragon*]; S.241 [*Jephthah's vow*]; C.987 [*Curse as punishment for breaking tabu*]; M.101 [*Punishment for broken oaths*].

¶ This is an imperfect version of the "Dragon-Slayer". For fuller versions, see "Assipattle and the Mester Stoorworm", "De Little Dull Calf" and "The Widow's Son and the King's Daughter". For the first part of the story see also "The Man who went Fishing on Sunday". The strong local flavour of the tale would also make it appropriate among local legends.

THE LEAVES THAT HUNG BUT NEVER GREW [summary]

A poor girl left her mother's house to look for work, and was taken in by the master of a great mansion. He said her task was to find the leaves that hung but never grew.

She set off in search of them and soon met a dwarf, who wished her "Good-day", and on returning to his home told his wife that he had seen a lovely young woman, who seemed to be in trouble.

Presently the girl knocked at the door of a small house. It was opened by a witch who promised to find her work, and took her in and gave her a good meal. A great black boar was chained up in one corner of the room, and the girl's task was only to look after the boar.

She dared not ask the witch about the leaves, and after a time she grew dissatisfied. She told this to the boar, and said her hands were becoming rough with work. The boar said, "Why did you come here?" and she told him, "To find the leaves that hung, but never grew."

Instantly the boar was changed into a young gentleman. He bade her go up to the witch's room and draw out a small wallet from under her pillow while she was sleeping; in it were the leaves. When she touched them she was to wish that the witch should not waken for a long time.

All this she did, and brought the leaves down, and shared them with the young man. They laid a spell on the poker, the broom, and the chair, and then made their escape. When the witch awoke she called the girl, and the poker answered, "I am raking out the fire." When she called again, the broom said, "I am sweeping the house." And at the third call, the chair said, "I am coming now." But when the witch discovered that the two had escaped, she was enraged, and sent her daughter to overtake them.

Just in time the two heard the witch's daughter coming, and the young man said, "Wish thyself a duck, and me a running stream, and when she tries to catch thee, dive beneath the water."

The trick succeeded, and the daughter went home and told the witch what she had seen. The witch guessed the truth, and sent her daughter back to get one feather from the duck's back. But she found neither duck nor stream. In the meantime, the two had gone on until they reached a crossroad, where their ways parted. The girl warned her lover not to let any of his family kiss him when he reached home, otherwise he would never be able to find her again. But in his joy at being back with them he forgot her words, and let them all kiss him. So he forgot the girl altogether, and she waited long for him and then went sadly home to her mother. After two days the lord of the mansion came to see whether she had found the leaves. She showed them to him and he was anxious to get them from her, for there was a great reward promised to whoever found them. To get rid of the girl he invited her to his castle, and lodged her in a room where there was a canopy with iron spikes, which was to descend on her head while she slept.

At midnight the stroke of the clock awoke the girl, and she saw the canopy coming down above her head. She thought of her leaves, drew one from her pocket, and at once the young man stood before her. He told her to wish the castle-dwellers all to stay asleep, and the two stole away.

He took her to his own home and asked her to marry him. She replied that she had been about to ask him the same thing. So they drove away to London and were married there, but afterwards they returned to his home in Wales.

They kept a mill beside the sea, and lived there happily ever afterwards.

D. E. Yates, *Gypsy Folk Tales*, p. 11.

TYPE 313C. MOTIFS: H.1210 [*Quest assigned*]; H.1333.2.3 [*Quest for extraordinary herb*]; D.955 [*Magic leaf*]; G.204 [*Girl in service of witch*]; D.114.3.2 [*Transformation: man to boar*]; D.789.6.1 [*Disenchantment by speaking proper words*]; D.1611 [*Magic object answers for fugitive*]; D.671 [*Transformation flight*]; D.2004.2 [*Kiss of forgetfulness*]; D.2006 [*Magic reawakening of memory*]; D.1364 [*Object causes magic sleep*].

❡ This is a diversified and shortened version of 313, with the task set to the heroine, not the hero.

For a more perfect example see "Nicht Nought Nothing".

THE LIDDLE DUNK FOAL or
WHY THE DONKEY IS SAFE

There was a liddle small dunk foal and he wanted to go look-see at life, so when his old mammy weren't a-looking he trit-trotted off on his wankly liddle legs.

First go off he met an old witch.

"I'll have 'ee!" say she, but when her touch 'n her got burned. "Drat!" says she, "Born on a Zunday, I'll be bound!"

"Like all dunks, my mammy d'say," say the liddle small dunk foal, and he went on along. Then he met Bogey.

"I'll have 'ee!" say Bogey, but when he grab 'n his fistesses fried. "Yow!" say Bogey, "Yew've a criss-cross on yewr back, keep away vrom me!"

"Like all dunks, my mammy d'say," say the liddle small dunk foal, and he went on along till he come to a gallitrap.

"Be off out of that!" say the Pixies. "Us can't ride 'ee, and now yur yew comes treading in our ring, and yew just seben days old!"

"So was all dunks once, so my mammy d'say," say the liddle small dunk foal.

Then they all says, "Be off whoame! Quick now!"

So he trit-trotted back to his mammy. And furst she kicked 'n fur gooin' stray and then she gived 'un his dinner.

Ruth L. Tongue, *Somerset Folklore*, pp. 55–6, 'gallitrap' fairy ring. From an Exmoor gipsy, 1936. MOTIFS: A.2221.1 [*Cross on the back of ass*]; G.303.16.3 [*Devil's power avoided by cross*]; Z.71.5 [*Formulistic number: seven*].
¶ See "Jubilee Jonah".

THE LITTLE BIRD

There was once a little girl who had a stepmother and the mother gave her a jug and sent her to fetch milk. And the wee girl said, "Can I take my skipping-rope?"

And the stepmother said: "You can take it, but if you break my jug, I'll kill you."

So she took the skipping-rope, and she skipped all the way there, and got the milk, and on the way she thought she'd take a little skip, and she broke the jug, and spilled the milk. And as she was standing crying a kind old lady said to her: "I've got a jug just the neighbour of that, and I'll give it you." So she fetched more milk, and carried it back to her mother. The mother looked at the jug, and said: "That's not my jug." "Oh, yes, it is," said the little girl. "Oh, no, it isn't," said the step-mother. "My jug had a red line on it, this has a blue. You've broken my jug!"

So she killed the wee girl, and baked her in a pie.

At dinner-time, the father came in. "Where's my wee lass?" he said.

"Oh, she's playing outside," said the woman. "Let her bide, and eat your dinner."

He began to eat, and he found a pinkie, with a wee ring on it. "This is my daughter's ring," he said. "You wicked woman, you've killed her, and I've a mind to kill you, but I will spare you."

Soon her brothers came in and heard what had happened, and they grieved sore.

And time went on till it was Christmas time; and on Christmas night a little bird came peeping to the window, and they sprinkled crumbs for it. Then it went up to the roof, and peeped down the chimney: "Brother, brother, look up, look up and see what I've got."

The brothers ran to look up, and the little bird dropped them down toys and sweets.

Then the bird peeped: "Father, Father, look up, look up, and see what I've got." The father looked up, and down dropped a suit of clothes and a letter.

The little bird peeped: "Mother, Mother, look up, look up, and see what I've got." The mother looked up, and a great stone fell on her head and killed her.

Then the husband opened the letter. It said: "Dear Father, my mother killed me, but now she is dead, I will come back to you on New Year's Eve."

So they buried the mother, and waited. On New Year's Eve, they heard a tap at the door, and when they opened it, a little bird flew in.

"Here I am, Father," it said.

"Can you not come back in your proper shape?" said the father.

"There was a ring on my stepmother's right pinkie," said the little bird; "and if you put it on to my pinkie, I'll come back into my proper shape."

So they dug up the stepmother, and took the ring off her pinkie, and put it on to the little bird's claw; and there she was, a little girl again; and she said: "My mother was not right bad. She had a devil in her, and that's out now, and she's gone to Heaven." So the four of them lived happily together.

H. Henderson, School of Scottish Studies, from Jimmy McPhee, aged 14, Caputh School, Perthshire.

TYPE 720. MOTIFS: S.31 [Cruel stepmother]; G.61 [Relative's flesh eaten unwittingly]; N.271 [Murder will out]; Q.211 [Murder punished]; Q.412 [Punishment: millstone dropped on guilty person]; E.610.1.1 [Reincarnation: boy to bird to boy].

Except for the gathering of the bones and the absence of the song, this is the complete "Juniper Tree" story, told in a village school. It is perhaps the commonest fairy-tale current in English tradition.

¶ It is widely distributed. "The Juniper Tree" (Grimm, no. 47) is the best known, but versions are found in France, Spain, Turkey, the West Indies, etc.

See also "Rosy", "The Rose Tree", "The Milk-White Doo", "Orange and Lemon", etc.

THE LITTLE BLACK BULL

See "The Seven Brothers", *Thompson Notebooks*. Fragmentary version of same story, heard from Gus Gray, Cleethorpes, 16 September 1914.

DE LITTLE BULL-CALF

Centers of yeahs ago, when all de most part of de country wur a wilderness place, deah wuz a little boy lived in a pooah bit of a poverty *ker*, an' dis boy's father guv him a deah little bull-calf. De boy used to tink de wurl' of dis bull-calf, an' his father gived him everything he wanted fur it.

Afterward dat his father died, an' his mother got married agin, an' dis wuz a werry wicious stepfather an' he couldn't abide dis little boy, an' at last he said, if de boy bring'd de bull-calf home agin, he wur a-goin' to kill it. Dis father should be a willint to dis deah little boy, shouldn't he, my Sampson?

He used to gon out tentin' his bull-calf every day wid barley-bread, an' arter dat, deah wus an old man comed to him, an' we have a deal of thought who dat wuz, *hoi*? An' he d'rected de little boy: "You an' youah bull-calf had better go away an' seek youah forchants."

So he wents an, an' wents an, as fur as I can tell you to-morrow night, an' he wents up to a farmhouse an' begged a crust of bread, an' when he comed back, he broked it in two, an' guv half an it to his little bull-calf.

An' he wents to another house, an' begs a bit of cheese crud, an' when he comed back, he wants to gin half an it to his bull-calf. "No!" de little bull-calf says, "I'm a-goin' acrost dis field into de wild wood wilderness country, where dere'll be tigers, lepers, wolfs, monkeys, an' a fiery dragin, an' I shall kill dem every one excep' de fiery dragin, an' he'll kill me." (De Lord could make any animal speak dose days. You know, trees could speak onst. Our blessed Lord he hid in de eldon bush, and it tell't an him, an' he says, "You shall always stink," an' so it always do; but de ivy let him hide into it, and he says: "It should be green both winter and summer.")

An' dis little boy did cry, you'ah shuah, and he says, "Oh! my little bull-calf, I hope he won't kill you." "Yes, he will," de little bull-calf says, "an' you climb up dat tree, an' den no one can come anigh you, but de monkeys, an' ef dey come de cheese crud will sef you. An' when I'm kilt de dragin will go away fur a bit, an' you come down dis tree, an' skin me, an' get my biggest gut out, an' blow it up, an' my gut will kill everything as you hit wid it, an' when dat fiery dragin come, you hit it wid my gut, an' den cuts its tongue out." (We know deah were fiery dragins dose days, like George an' his dragin in de Bible, but deah! it arn't de same wurl' now. De wurl' is tun'd ovah sence, like you tun'd it ovah wid a spade!)

In course he done as dis bull-calf tell't him, an' he climb't up de tree, an' de monkey climb't up de tree to him, an' he helt de cheese crud in his hand, an' he says, "I'll squeeze youah heart like dis flint-stone." An' de monkey cocked his eye, much to say, "Ef you can squeeze a flint-stone, an' mek de juice come outer it, you can squeeze me." An' he never spoked, for a monkey's cunning, but down he went. An' de little bull-calf wuz fightin' all dese wild things on de groun' an' de little boy wuz clappin' his hands up de tree an' sayin': "Go an, my little bull-calf! Well fit, my little bull-calf!" An' he mastered everything barrin' de fiery dragin, an' de fiery dragin kilt de little bull-calf.

An' he wents an, an' saw a young lady, a king's darter, staked down by de hair of her head. Dey wuz werry savage dat time of day, kings to deir darters, ef dey misbehavioured demselfs, an' she wuz put dere fur de fiery dragin to 'stry her.

An' he sat down wid her several hours, an' she says, "Now, my deah little boy, my time is come when I'm a-goin' to be worried, an' you'll better go." An' he says: "No," he says, "I can master it, an' I won't go." She begged an' prayed him as ever she could, to get him away but he wouldn't go.

An' he could heah it comin' far enough, roarin' an' doin', and' dis dragin come spitting fire, wid a tongue like a gret speart, an' you could heah it roarin' fur milts, an' dis place wheah de king's darter wur staked down, was his beat wheah he used to come. An' when it comed, de little boy hit dis gut about his face tell he wuz dead, but de fiery dragin bited his front finger offer him.

Den de little boy cut de dragin's tongue out, an' he says to de young lady: "I've done all dat I can, I mus' leave you." An' youah shuah she wuz sorry when he had to leave her, an' she tied a dimant ring into his hair, an' said good-bye to him.

Now den, bime bye, de old king comed up to de werry place where his darter was staked by de hair of her head, 'mentin' an' doin', an' especin' to see not a bit of his darter, but de prents of de place where she wuz. An' he wuz disprised, an' he said to his darter, "How come you seft?" "Why, deah wuz a little boy comed heah an' sef me, daddy." Den he untied her, an' took'd her home to de palast, for youah shuah he wor glad, when his temper comed to him agin.

Well, he put it into all the papers to want to know who seft his gal, an' ef de right man comed he wur to marry her, an' have hid kingdom an' all his destate. Well, deah wuz gentlemen comed fun all an' all parts of England, wid' deah front fingers cut aff an' all, an' all kinds of tongues, foreign tongues, an' beastes tongues, an' wile animals' tongues. Dey cut all sorts of tongues out, an' dey went about shootin' tings a purpose, but dey never could find a dragin to shoot. Deah wuz gentlemen comin' every other day wid tongues, an' diment rings, but when dey showed delr tongues, it warn't de right one, an' dey got turned off.

An' dis little ragged boy comed up a time or two, werry decolated like, an' she had an eye on him, an' she looked at dis boy, tell her father got werry angry, an' turn't dis boy out. "Daddy," she says, "I've got a knowledge to dat boy."

Yoy may say, deah wuz all kinds of kings' sons comin' up showin' deah parcels, an' arter a time or two dis boy comed up agin, dressed a bit better. An' de ole king says, "I see you've got an eye on dis boy, an' ef it is to be him, it has to be him." All de other *ryas* wuz fit to kill him, an' dey says, "Pooh! Pooh! tun dat boy out; it can't be him." But de ole king says, "Now, my boy, let's see what you got." Well, he showed de dimant ring, wid her name into it, an' de fiery dragin's tongue. *Dordi!* How dese gentlemen were mesmerized when he showed his 'thority, and de king tole him, "You shall have my destate, an' marry my darter."

An' he got married to dis heah gal, an' got all de ole king's destate, an' den de stepfather came an' wanted to own him, but de young king didn't know such a man.

Dora E. Yates, *A Book of Gypsy Folk-Tales*, p. 155.
TYPES 511A and 300. MOTIFS: S.32 [*Cruel stepfather*]; E.327 [*Dead father's friendly return*]; B.313.1 [*Helpful animal reincarnation of parent*]; K.62 [*Trickster squeezes cheese for stone*]; B.192 [*Magic animal killed*]; B.184.2.3.1 [*Magic bull to be flayed. The bull orders the hero to flay him and to use his skin for magic purposes*].

TYPE 300: D.1015.2 [*Magic gall-bladder of animal*]; B.11.10 [*Sacrifice of human being to dragon*]; B.11.2.11 [*Fire-breathing dragon*]; R.111.1.3 [*Rescue of princess from dragon*]; H.105.1 [*Dragon tongue proof*]; H.83 [*Rescue tokens*]; H.80 [*Identification by tokens*]; H.94 [*Identification by ring*]; L.161 [*Lowly hero marries princess*].
¶ See also "Ashpitel", "Rashin Coatie", "The Red Calf"; for type 300, "Assipattle and the Mester Stoor-Worm", "The Widow's Son and the King's Daughter".

DE LITTLE BULL-CALF, DE THREE GIANTS, AND DE FIERY DRAGON [summary]

Little boy Jack works for farmer, paid by gift of little bull-calf and advised what to do. Led by bull-calf into wood where bull-calf fights great bulls and is finally killed. Jack cuts off his pizzle and takes it with him. Takes work with farmer on edge of cabbage-field owned by three giants, warned not to let the cows stray into cabbage. Goes in, however, to eat pears and apples, and cows follow him.

First giant appears. He conquers him with the pizzle and obtains a coat of darkness. Second day, second giant, and Jack obtains belt of wisdom. Third day, sword of sharpness. A fiery dragon coming to destroy the princess. Jack goes in cloak of darkness to rescue her and cuts out dragon's tongue. Imposter cuts off head and claims princess. Next day Jack appears with the tongue and makes good his claim. Marries princess.

Thompson Notebooks, from Taimi Boswell, Oswaldtwistle, 11 January 1915.
TYPES 511A and 300.
Another version of "De Little Bull-Calf".
ADDITIONAL MOTIFS: D.812.11 [*Magic object received from giant*]; N.538.2 [*Treasure from defeated giant*]; D.1361.12 [*Cloak of invisibility*]; D.1300 [*Magic object gives supernatural wisdom*]; D.1400.1.4.1 [*Magic sword conquers enemy*].

THE LITTLE CINDER-GIRL

There was a small house, three daughters, and their mother. The two sisters thought themselves grand ladies, but as for the youngest, they used to hide her in the coal-hole so that no one would see her. They could not bear her, because she was so grimy. They were ashamed to see her about, and whenever anyone visited the house they would say to her: "Be off, little slut, and hide thyself."

The two sisters used to go to church. One Sunday after church, they came home, and began to talk about a prince whom they had seen there. The young girl overheard them.

Sunday came round again. The two sisters went to church while the young one stopped at home alone. And a little old woman came to the door a-begging. The young girl bade her enter, and made her some tea. After she had finished the old woman called the girl outside.

There was a white pebble near the door. Said the old woman: "Take that white pebble, and fling it against yonder rock. Thou wilt see a door there; open it and go in. Thou wilt see a chamber; thou wilt see apparel; thou wilt see a pair of golden slippers. Robe thyself, come out, and pass on to the next room. Thou wilt see a little horse, lead him outside, mount him, and ride to the church. Do not go far within, sit by the door, and let thy horse be tethered near it. Come out before the rest. The young prince will follow thee; he will try to catch thee and to find out who thou art. Hurry home, restore the clothes to the place thou didst take them from, return, and say naught."

For three weeks the young girl did as the old woman bade her. A grand lady entered the church, and there was nobody there who knew her. Everyone was gazing at her, and the prince fell ill with longing to know who she was. He kept his eyes fixed upon her, and he followed her to see whether he could find out. But she had gone too far for him to discover who she was.

The last week the old woman said to the young girl: "Mark what thou shalt do now. Do as I bid thee. Go to church, and this time thou must leave still earlier; the prince will follow thee. One slipper will drop from thy foot, and he will come after thee and find it."

Everything fell out as the old woman had said. The girl returned, put back all her finery, and dressed herself in her old clothes. The two sisters came home, and began to talk about the prince. And the young one was listening to them. She asked the two sisters whether she might go to church to see the prince.

"No, thou dirty little slut, go and hide thyself."

The prince wondered how he could discover the lady. At last he prepared a great banquet and sent a proclamation throughout the land, inviting the young ladies to attend. The damsels had no idea what the prince wanted.

The day arrived when the banquet was to be held. And here is the prince in the reception chamber! All the ladies came up to his chair. One lady sat down. The prince took the slipper and tried it on her foot. It did not fit. Out she went. Another lady approached: it did not fit. He tried them all, and there was not one there whom the shoe would fit. The two sisters were there, and the eldest, who was yearning for the prince, chopped a piece off her foot: she would have given her life to get him.

The prince asked: "Where are all the serving-maids?" One wench entered. Now the little cinder-girl comes in. The prince threw down the slipper. The young girl held out her foot. On went the slipper, and the prince recognized her. The eldest sister would have killed her if she had not been afraid.

Lo! then there were great preparations for the wedding. The wedding-day arrived. They left the church and returned home. There was a great company of lords and ladies feasting in the castle. At last all was over and the guests departed.

The pair lived together for a year, and the lady was with child. She was put to bed and bore a daughter. The eldest sister was sent for to come up to the castle and look after her. She brought a puppy up to the lady's room. She took away the babe and left the dog in bed beside her youngest sister. Then she took the child home and gave it to her mother. The prince saw the puppy and was horrified. But he said naught this time.

The lady was with child again. She was put to bed, and bore a son. The eldest sister was sent for to come up to the castle, and look after her sister. Again the eldest sister brought a puppy with her. She put it in the bed, and carried off the baby boy. She gave him to her mother. Then she returned to the castle to nurse her sister.

The prince came home. He went up to see his wife. The eldest sister was there. She lifted the blankets and drew forth the puppy. "Is it not a disgrace for a lady to give birth to a puppy?" The prince spoke no more. He summoned the serving-men: "Get ye down and make ready to burn her." His wife implored him to spare her once more. "If it should happen thus again I will take what comes." The prince relented: the lady was set free.

A year or two afterwards the lady was with child again. She was put to bed and bore another son. The eldest sister was sent for to come up to the castle. She brought a puppy to the castle, put it in the bed, carried off the child, and sent him to her mother.

The eldest sister was looking after the youngest. The prince came up to see his wife. The eldest sister lifted the blankets, drew forth the puppy, and showed it to the prince. "My God!" he exclaimed. "What a disgrace for a lady to give birth to a puppy!" The prince leapt to his feet in her bed-chamber. "Where are the men-servants?" They were summoned to drag her out of bed, and carry her down to be burnt.

Lo! The little old woman appears once more! The little old woman spoke to her. "Fear not. I am here. Thou shalt have thy children back again, all three."

The lady was to be burnt. She was carried out of doors. The prince came out of the castle. He paused to consider what he should do. His heart was too tender towards his wife to watch her burn. So he went away, and left her to be burnt by his men-servants.

"Nay," quoth the lady, "ye cannot burn me; my dear God is good and he will watch over me." She kept a stout heart because of what the old woman had said to her. "Let her go!" said the old woman. She was set free. "Thou shalt become a young sow in the midst of the forest." As soon as the word was spoken, the lady was transformed into a young sow.

The woman told the young sow: "Thou wilt be slain; the prince and his court will hunt thee to death. They will cut out thy liver and hang it beside the gate of the castle. Whoever takes it and repeats certain words will get whatever he desires. Fear not. Thou wilt be restored to life, and wilt regain thy husband and thy children."

She was in the forest for years, and then the prince's servants found her. They had seen her about for some days. They went home and told their master that there was a sow in the forest they had never seen before. "We will go and look for her. We will slay her to-morrow." The sow knew that the nobles and their train were after her. She hid herself.

Let us return to the children. Here are the three alone in the forest;

the two sisters had turned them adrift when their grandmother died. The sow found them. She spoke to the children. "They are hunting me," quoth the sow, "and mean to slay me." Saith the mother to her daughter, the eldest child, "When I am slain, go down to the castle, and beg a piece of my liver. Take the piece of liver and thou wilt get whatever thou desirest. I will return again to you. It was my sister who caused all this trouble."

They found the sow and slew her. The prince told them to bring her liver to the castle. They took her liver and it was hung beside the gate.

The girl went down to the river-side with her two little brothers. They sat down by the river. "Is not this a pleasant spot?" said the girl to her brother. "Would it were ours!" quoth the boy. "Well, I can get it. I am going down to the castle." "Do not stay long, sister." The girl went to the castle as the sow had bidden her; for the sow had told the girl if she desired anything she was to go down to the castle to get a piece of the liver, and her wish would be granted. She went and got the liver.

Back she came. "Now then, brother, come here. I will show thee something. Wouldst thou like a cottage here?" "I would indeed, sister." She told her brother what the sow had said. As soon as the word was spoken, there stood the cottage.

The three went to live in the cottage. They were there for years. One day a stranger called to light his pipe and stared at the three children. He knew not who they were. He went down to the castle and told the prince about the cottage and the three children. He told the prince that the three children were girt with golden belts. The prince offered the man a reward if he would bring the three belts to him. "I will go at once."

He set off, reached the cottage, and knocked at the door. Out came the sister. The stranger asked for a light for his pipe. "Come in," quoth the boy. "No," said the girl. "The man will do no harm, sister, let him enter."

The stranger came in and asked the younger boy to let him look at his belt. "Nay, brother, do not take off thy belt." "Sister, the man will do no harm." The man got the belt. He next asked the elder boy. "Nay," said the sister, "do not take off thy belt." He took it off and gave it to the stranger. He asked the girl for her belt. "No," replied the girl, "I will never take off my belt."

The man went down to the castle and gave the two belts to the prince. "I could not get the belt from the maiden. She would not part with it."

As soon as the two belts had been handed over, the two boys were turned into swans upon the river. The girl was left all alone now. Suddenly she remembered what the sow had told her. In the morning she went down to the castle, to get a piece of the liver, and returned home with it. "May my two brothers be restored to their former shapes!" As soon as the word was spoken she got her two brothers back again.

One day the sister was talking to the elder brother: "Oh, brother, if only our mother were with us! We must try and get our mother back" "Impossible," said the elder boy; "no, that is a thing that cannot be done." "Indeed," quoth the girl, "I will get her back again."

The girl went down to the river, taking the liver with her. "I want my mother back again." Immediately the word was spoken she recovered her mother. The girl fell down in amazement.

Together they went to the cottage and the mother kissed her two sons. "How didst thou bring me here?" she asked her daughter. "I will tell thee, mother. A young sow came to me after thou hadst been slain. She told me to go to the castle and get a piece of liver." "That is so," agreed her mother. "Canst thou bring thy father here?" "Yes," quoth the girl, "I will bring him here." "When?" asked the mother. The girl went outside. "Where art thou going?" asked her mother. "I will return. I am not going far."

The girl went to the river-side. "I wish my father to be restored to us." The word was spoken: there stood her father. He embraced his daughter, and hurried into the cottage. His wife was speechless with amazement. She recovered her senses. Said the prince to his wife: "Let us go home to the castle!"

"How didst thou contrive to bring me here?" asked her husband. "I will tell thee. Dost thou remember the liver which hung beside the castle gate?" "I do," said the prince. "After I had been slain, our daughter went to the castle to get a small piece of my liver, and when the word was spoken, lo! her wish was granted."

The prince, his wife, and children went down to the castle. They dwelt there for years, and the children grew up. Then the girl journeyed for a long time in foreign lands in order to see the world. She came home. Her father and mother were overjoyed to see her return. Both the parents died, and the children are living in the castle to this day.

Well! That was all the children had to suffer. There is no more to add. We have reached home with the help of God. And that is the end!

Dora E. Yates, *Gypsy Folk-Tales*, p. 25, no. 5.

TYPES 510 and 707. MOTIFS: S.12 [*Cruel mother*]; L.52 [*Abused youngest daughter*]; L.131 [*Hearth abode of unpromising heroine*]; N.825.3 [*Old woman helper*]; D.1050.1 [*Clothes produced by magic*]; N.711.4 [*Prince sees maiden at church and is enamoured*]; H.36.1 [*Identification by fitting of slipper*]; L.162 [*Lowly heroine marries prince*]; K.2212 [*Treacherous sister*]; K.2115 [*Animal birth slander*]; Q.414 [*Punishment: burning alive*]; N.825.3 [*Old woman helper*]; R.175 [*Rescue at the stake*]; D.114.3 [*Transformation: man (woman) to swine*]; D.1015.4 [*Magic liver of animal*]; H.151.1 [*Attention drawn by magic object*]; D.161.1 [*Transformation: man to swan*]; R.158 [*Sister rescues brothers*]; S.451 [*Outcast wife at last united with husband and children*].

¶ Type 510 has world-wide distribution. Studies made by M. R. Cox, *Cinderella*; A. B. Rooth, *The Cinderella Cycle*.
See "Ashpitel".

DE LITTLE FOX

In ole formel times, when dey used to be kings an' queens, deah wuz a king an' queen had on'y one darter. And dey stored dis darter like de eyes in dere head, an' dey hardly would let de wind blow on her. Dey lived in a 'menjus big park, an' one way of de park deah wuz a lodge-house, an' de oder en' deah wuz a great moat of water. Now dis queen died an' left dis darter, an' she wur a werry han'some gal—you're sure she mus' be, bein' a queen's darter!

In dis heah lodge-house deah wuz an ole woman lived, and in dem days deah wur witchcraft, an' de ole king used to sont fur her to go up to de palast to work, an' she consated herself an' him a bit. So one day dis heah ole gentleman wuz a-talking to dis ole woman, an' de darter gat a bit jealous, an' dis ole woman fun out dat de darter wuz angry, an' she didn't come anigh de house fur a long time.

Now de ole witch wuz larnin' de young lady to sew. So she sent fur her to come down to de lodge-house afore she hed her breakfast. An' de fust day she wents, she picked up a kernel of wheat as she wuz coming along, an' eat it. An' de witch said to her, "Have you hed your breakfast?" an' she says, "No!" "Have you hed nothing?" she says. "No," she says, "on'y a kernel of wheat." She wents two marnin's like dat, an' picked up a kernel of wheat every marnin', so dat de witch would have no powah over her—God's grain, you know, *rai*! But de third marnin' she on'y picked up a bit av orange peel, an' den dis ole *guẓberi' gorji'** witchered her, an' after dat she never sent fur her to come no more.

Now dis young lady gat to be big. An' de witch wuz glad. So she goned to de king, an' she says, "Your darter is dat way. Now, you know, she'll hev to be 'str'yed." "What! My beautiful han'some darter to be in de fambly way! Oh! no! no! no! et couldn't be!" "But it can be so, an' et is so!" said de ole witch.

Well, it wuz so, an' de ole king fun' it out, and was well-nigh crazy. An' when he fun' it out, for shuah dem days when any young woman had a misforchant, she used to be burnt, an' he ordered a man to go an' get an iron chair, an' a cartload o' faggots, an' she hed to be put into dis iron chair, an' dese faggots set of a light rount her, an' she burnt to death.

As dey had her in dis chair, and a-goin' to set it of a-light, dere wur an ole gentleman come up—dat was my ole dubel, to be shuah!—an' he says, "My noble leech,† don't burn her, nor don't hurt her, nor don't

---

* *goẓberi' gorji'* = witch   † leech = liege.

'str'y her, for dere's an ole wessel into de bottom of dat park; put her in dere an' let her go where God d'rect her to." So dey did do so, an' never think'd no more about her.

Durin' time dis young lady wuz confined of a little fox, and d'rectly as he wuz bornt he says; "My mammy, you must be werry weak an' low, bein' confined of me, an' nothin' to eat or drink, but I must go somewheres, an' get you somethin'!" "Oh! my deah little fox, don't leave me. Whatever shall I do wit'out you? I shall die broken-hearted." "I'm a-goin' to my grandfather, as I suspose", says de little fox. "My deah, you mustn't go, you'll be worried by de dogs." "Oh, no dogs won't hurt me, my mammy." Away he goned, trittin' an' trottin' till he got to his gran'fader's hall. When he got up to de gret boarden gates, dey wuz closed, an' dere wuz two or tree dogs tied down, an' when he goned in de dogs never looked at him.

One of de women comed outer de hall, an' who should it be but dis ole witch. He says, "Call youah dogs in, missis, an' don't let 'em bite me. I wants to see de noble leech belonging to dis hall." "What do you want to see him fur?" "I wants to see him for somethin' to eat an' drink fur my mammy, she's werry poorly." "An' who are youah mammy?" "Let him come out, he'll know." So de noble leech comed out an' he says: "What do you want, my little fox?" He put his hen' up to his head, such manners he had! "I wants somethin' to eat an' drink fur my mammy, she's werry poorly." So de noble leech tole de cook to fill a basket wid wine an' wittles. So de cook done so, and bring'd it to him. De noble leech says: "My little fox you can never carry it, I will sen' some one to carry it." But he says, "No, thank you, my noble leech," an' he chucked it on his little back, an' wents tritting an' trotting to his mammy.

When he got to his mammy, she says, "Oh, my deah little fox, I've bin crazy about you. I thought de dogs had eaten you." "No, my mammy, dey turn't deir heads de oder way." An' she took'd him an' kissed him an' rejoiced over him. "Now, my mammy, have somethin' to eat an' drink," says de little fox. "I got dem from my gran'father, as I suspose it is."

So he wents tree times. An' de second time he wents, de ole witch began smellin' a rat, an' she says to de servants, "Don't let dat little fox come heah no more; he'll get worried." But he says, "I wants to see de noble leech," says de little fox. "Youah werry plaguesome to de noble leech, my little fox." "Oh, no, I'm not," he says.

De las' time he comes, his moder dressed him in a beautiful robe of fine needlework. Now de noble leech comes up again to de little fox, an' he says, "Who is youah mammy, my little fox?" "You wouldn't know p'raps, ef I wuz to tell you." An' he says, "Who med you dat robe, my little fox?" "My mammy, to be shuah; who else should make

389

it?" An' de ole king wept an' cried bitterly, when he seed dis robe he had an, fur he think'd his deah child wur dead.

"Could I have a word wi' you, my noble leech?" says de little fox. "Could you call a party dis afternoon up at your hall?" He says, "What fur, my little fox?" "Well, ef you call a party, I'll tell you whose robe dat is, but you mus' let my mammy come as well." "No! no! my little fox, I couldn't have youah mammy to come." "Well, I shan't come, ef my mammy arn't to come." Well, de ole king agreed, an' de little fox tell'd him: "Now, deah mus' be tales to be telled, an' songs to be sing'd, an' dem as don't sing a song hez to tell a tale; an' after we hev dinner, let's go an' walk about in de garden; but you mus' 'quaint as many ladies an' gentlemen as you can to dis party, an' be shuah to bring de ole lady what live at de lodge."

Well, dis dinner was called, an' dey all had 'nuff to eat, an' after dat wur ovah, de noble leech stood up in de middit an' called for a song or tale.

Deah wuz all songs sing't an' tales tell't, tell it camed to dis young lady's tu'n. An' she says, "I can't sing a song, or tell a tale, but my little fox can." "*Pooydorda!*" says de ole witch, "tun out de little fox, he stinks!" But dey all called an de little fox, an' he stoods up an' says: "Once ont a time," he says, "deah wuz an ole-fashn't king an' queen lived togeder, an' dey only had one darter, an' dey stored dis darter like de eyes into deir head, an' dey 'ardly would let de wint blow an her." "*Pooydorda,*" says de ole witch, "tun out de little fox, it stinks." But deah wuz all de ladies an' gentlemen clappin' an' sayin', "Speak an, my little fox." "Well tole, my little fox!" "Werry good tale indeed!"

So de little fox speak'd an, and tell't dem all about de ole witch, an' how she wanted to 'stry de king's darter, an' he says: "Dis heah ole lady she fried my mammy an egg an' a sliced of bacon, an' ef she wur to eat it all, she'd be in de fambaley way wid some bad animal, but she only eat half on it, an' den she wor so wid me. An' dat's de ole witch deah!" he says, showin' de party wid his little paw.

An' den, after dis wuz done, an' dey all walked togeder in de garden, de little fox says: "Now, my mammy, I've done all de good I can for you, an' now I'm a-goin' to leave you," an' he strip't aff his little skin, an' he flewed away in de beautifulest white angel you ever seed in your life. An' de ole witch was burnt in de same chair dat wuz meant for de young lady.

Norton Collection, II, pp. 181–3. *Journal of the Gypsy Lore Society*, III, from Sampson's *Tales in a Tent*, pp. 204–7. Told in Liverpool by Wasti Grey.

TYPE 708. MOTIFS: G.200 [*Witch*]; D.1766.8.1 [*Fasting a part of magic ritual*]; T.511.7.2 [*Pregnancy from eating an egg*]; T.554 [*Woman gives birth to animal*]; L.112.1 [*Monster as hero*]; T.550.1 [*Monster child helps mother*]; S.431.1 [*Cast-off wife and child exposed in boat*]; D.1717.1 [*Magic power of monster child*].

In "Kate Crackernuts", the incident of the witch who can do no harm to the princess if she has eaten also occurs.

¶ See also "The Little Squirrel".

THE LITTLE RED HAIRY MAN

Once upon a time there was a lead miner in Derbyshire who had three sons, and he was very poor. One day the eldest son said he would go and seek his fortune, so he packed up his kit, and took something to eat with him and set off. After he had walked a long way he came to a wood, and being very tired he sat down upon a large stone by the wayside, and began to eat the bread and cheese that he had brought with him. Whilst he was eating he thought he heard a voice. So he looked about him and saw a little red man coming out of the wood covered with hair, and about the height of nine penn'orth of copper. He came close up to the eldest son, and asked for something to eat. But instead of giving him food the eldest son told him to be off, and kicked his foot out at the little man and hurt him, so that he went back limping into the wood.

Then the eldest son went on his way, and after a long time came home again as poor as he had left.

After the eldest son had returned, the second son said that he would go out and seek his fortune. When he came to the wood he sat down to rest and eat, and whilst he was eating the little red hairy man came out and begged for some food. But the second son went on eating until he had done, and threw the little man the crumbs and bits that were left. Then the little man told the second son to go and try his luck in a mine that he would find in the middle of the wood.

So the second son went to look for the mine, and when he had found it he said to himself, "Why, it's only an old worn-out mine, and I'm not going to waste my time over that." So he set off on his way, and after a long time came home again as poor as he had left.

Now by this time Jack, the youngest son, had grown up, and when the second son came home he said to his father, "I will go now and seek my fortune." So when he was ready he left home in the same way that his brothers had done. And when he came to the wood and saw the stone on the wayside, he sat down on it, and pulled out his bread and cheese and began to eat, and in a few minutes he heard somebody say, "Jack, Jack." So he looked about him and saw the same little red hairy man that his brothers had seen. The little man said he was hungry, and asked Jack to give him some of his bread and cheese, and Jack said he would and welcome. So he cut him a good lump and told him he could have more if he wanted. Then the little man came close up to Jack and told him that he only wanted to try him to see what sort he was.

"And now," said the little man, "I will help thee to get thy fortune, but thou must do as I tell thee."

So then he told Jack to go and find the old mine in the middle of the wood.

So Jack went, and when he got to the mine he found the little man had got there before him.

The opening of the mine was inside an old hut, and over the pit, in the middle of the floor, was a windlass. So the little man told Jack to get into the bucket, and began to let him down. So Jack went down, and down, and down, till at last he came to the bottom, when he got out and found himself in a beautiful country.

Whilst he was looking round about him the little man stood by him and gave him a sword and armour, and told him to go and set free a princess who was imprisoned in a copper castle in that country. And then the little man threw a small copper ball on the ground, and it rolled away, and Jack followed it until it came to a castle made of copper, and flew against the door. Then a giant came out of the castle, and Jack fought with him and killed him, and set the princess free, and she went back to her own home.

When Jack came back the little man told him that he must go to a silver castle and set another princess free. So the little man threw down a silver ball, and Jack followed it till it came to a splendid silver castle, and struck against the door so loudly that the giant who lived there came out to see what it was. And then Jack fought with him and killed him, and set the princess free.

Now some time after Jack had set free the princess in the silver castle, the little man said that he must now try to set another princess free who lived in a golden castle. So Jack said he would, and the little man threw down a golden ball, and it began to roll away, and Jack followed it until it came in sight of a magnificent gold castle, and then it went faster and faster until it struck the castle door, and made the giant who lived there come out to see what was the matter. Then Jack and the giant fought, and the giant nearly killed Jack, but at last Jack killed the giant and then went into the castle and found a beautiful lady there. Jack fell in love with her, and brought her to the little man, and he married them, and helped Jack to get as much gold from the gold castle as he wanted. And then he helped Jack and his wife up the mine, and they went to Jack's home.

Jack built a fine house for himself and another for his father and mother. But his two brothers were envious, and went off to the mine to see if they could not get some gold as well as Jack. And when they got into the hut they quarrelled as to who should go down first, and as they were struggling to get into the bucket the rope broke, and they both fell to the bottom of the pit. As they did not come back Jack and his father went to seek them. And when they got to the mine they saw that the sides of the pit had given way, and blocked it up. And the hut had fallen down, and the place was covered up for ever.

S. O. Addy, *Household Tales and Traditional Remains*, p. 50. (From Wensley, Derbyshire.)

TYPE 301A. MOTIFS: Q.2 [*Kind and unkind*]; L.13 [*Compassionate youngest son*]; N.825.2 [*Help from old man*]; F.92 [*Pit entrance to lower world*]; F.96 [*Rope to lower world*]; F.80 [*Journey to lower world*]; D.1313.1 [*Magic ball indicates road*]; F.771.1 [*Castle of unusual materials*]; R.11.1 [*Princess abducted by ogre*]; R.111.2.1 [*Princesses rescued from lower world*]; L.161 [*Lowly hero marries princess*]; Q.302 [*Envy punished*].

THE LITTLE REDMAN

Two brothers are reduced by the badness of the times to seek shelter in a hut built in the midst of a forest, where they subsist upon the juicy haunches of the King's deer. It appears that the same scarcity which drove the hunters to the woods affected also, in a similar way, the fairy denizens of the neighbouring wastes. One day, whilst the eldest brother remains behind to cook the meat, there enters a little Redman, with the modest request, "Plaze gie me a few broth." Up the ladder rushes the hunter to find the hatchet, intending to inflict summary vengeance upon the intruder; but in the meantime, the little Redman seizes the pot from the fire and makes off. The exasperated cook pursues, but soon loses the cunning fiend among the intricacies of the forest. After a similar adventure, befalling the other brother on the following day, it becomes the turn of the much-despised youngest to prepare the meal for the absent brethren. Profiting by the mishaps of his comrades, and well knowing that a caught Redman, like the Cluricaune, proved a treasure to his captor, he lies in wait for his visitor behind the door; and no sooner has the unsuspecting spirit entered, and given utterance to his usual phrase, "Plaze gie me a few broth," than he finds himself a prisoner. After many fruitless endeavours to escape, he conducts his captor to his residence—an old well, in a retired part of the forest; and there ransoms himself with such store of gold, that his vanquisher, to quote my narrator, "is made a mon on for life".

Norton Collection, I, p. 96. From Sternberg, pp. 196–7.

This story is put by Norton under type 301, but the resemblance is so slight as hardly to merit the ascription.

MOTIFS: F.233.3 [*Red fairy*]; F.391.2 [*Fairies borrow food from mortals*]; F.365.7 [*Fairies steal cooking*]; L.10 [*Victorious youngest son*]; F.387 [*Fairy captured*]; F.244.2 [*Fairy shows hiding-place of treasure in return for freedom*].

It is unusual for the fairy to remain in the power of the human who seizes it. A more usual turn is for the fairy to escape, as in "Clever Tom and the Leprechaun" (Keightley, pp. 373–5).

THE LITTLE SQUIRREL [summary]

Unchaste girls to be burnt. Washerwoman (witch) wants to marry King, and determines to destroy Princess. Tells her a young man wants to see her. Princess refuses to see him, twice. Washerwoman offers her food, she eats half an egg and half a slice of ham. Presently she becomes pregnant. Washerwoman denounces her to King. Princess understands nothing. Trial by council. Old man with white beard (the Lord) counsels delay. Princess to be put in boat on lake, left there without food. Gives birth to a squirrel. She understands nothing. Squirrel claims her as mother; it goes to palace to fetch food. People frightened. Princess loves squirrel. It goes again to palace, and demands investigation. Council, servants, washerwoman. Washerwoman tries to stop investigation, but squirrel declares the whole truth: An egg given by washerwoman; if the Princess had eaten whole egg a devil would have been born. Washerwoman burnt. Squirrel given golden kennel. Not long after, squirrel invites all to a party, strips off his skin, and flies away. Skin stuffed, and placed in golden kennel.

T. W. Thompson. Collected from Eva Gray at Grimsby, 31 October 1914.
TYPE 708. MOTIFS: Q.254 [*Girl punished for becoming pregnant*]; K.2293 [*Treacherous old woman*]; T.511.7.2 [*Pregnancy from eating an egg*]; S.322.1 [*Father casts daughter forth*]; T.554 [*Woman gives birth to an animal*]; T.550.1 [*Monster-child helps mother*]; G.275.3 [*Witch burned*].
Another version, "The Little Red Squirrel", was told by Taimi Boswell at Oswaldtwistle, 2 January 1915. This has the Cymbeline motif of a wager on a wife's chastity.
¶ See also "De Little Fox".

THE LITTLE WATERCRESS GIRL

There was once a little girl who had to sell watercresses for her living because she was very poor. One day she met an old witch who said to her, "If you will come and help me to keep my house I will sell your watercresses for you."

The little girl said, "I will try my best."

"But there is one thing you must promise me," said the witch, "and that is this: you must not look up the chimney."

The girl promised that she would not, and went to live at the witch's house. After she had been there a few days she wanted badly to look up the chimney, and she said to herself, "Surely there would be no harm in just having one peep."

So she peeped up the chimney, and saw a white bag there, and pulled it down. Then she opened it and found that it was full of money. Her eyes glistened at the sight of so much wealth, and she said, "I mean to keep this, for I am very poor."

So she carried the bag of money into an orchard close by where many fruit trees grew.

First of all she went up to the apple-tree, and said, "Apple-tree, apple-tree, hide me; and if anyone shall ask thee whether thou hast seen me, say 'I have not.'"

So the apple-tree promised to hide her. When the witch came back and found that her bag of money was gone she looked everywhere for the little watercress girl. She searched all through the house, and at last she went into the orchard.

First of all she went up to the gooseberry-bush, and said, "Gooseberry-bush, gooseberry-bush, hast thou seen a little girl with a white bag in her hand?"

But the gooseberry-bush said, "Nay." Then the witch went to every tree in the garden, asking each the same question, but all the trees said, "Nay."

At last she came to the apple-tree, which said, "Nay," like the other trees.

So the little girl was hidden by the apple-tree, and when the witch had gone to bed, she carried the bag of money home.

S. O. Addy, *Household Tales*, p. 11. From Nottinghamshire.

TYPE 480 (variant). MOTIFS: H.935 [*Witch assigns tasks*]; C.337 [*Tabu: looking up chimney*]; D.1658.1.5 [*Apple-tree grateful for being shaken*].

This is a fragmentary version of "The Old Witch", without the contrast between Kind and Unkind, nor any motive assigned for the apple-tree's benevolence.

¶ See also "The Glass Ball", "The Old Witch".

LOUSY JACK AND HIS ELEVEN BROTHERS
[summary]

An old woman had twelve sons. The youngest was lousy and despised by everyone. They all set out together to seek their fortunes, and went on till they came to a place where twelve roads met. Each took one, to re-meet after a year and a day. Jack went along the dirtiest road and came to a castle, with a golden phoenix over the door, which said, "If you venture into this castle, you will see things that make your blood run cold." Lousy Jack went in, and found it full of animals and people standing like statues. He explored all over it, and in a dark cellar he found a pile of thorns. He was so lousy that he enjoyed the scratching, and burrowed into the thorns till he touched the enchanted princess who was buried under them. It broke the enchantment and a light went on in the cellar, and the princess moved. Jack pulled the thorns off her, and when they went up from the cellar everyone was alive and working. Lousy Jack told the princess that he had found her accidentally, but she was ready to marry him. He said he must meet his brothers again. He told them, but not in detail, that he had freed the princess, and they threw him into a ditch so that they could claim the reward.

The eldest went and told the princess the story up to the breaking of the enchantment, but did not know that it was accidental. All the eleven were rejected. The princess made proclamation that she would wed her rescuer, and Jack, who had escaped out of the ditch, heard it, came, and made good his claim. He married the princess and was king; but he was lousy all his days.

Thompson Notebooks, from Taimi Boswell, Oswaldtwistle, 9 January 1915.
TYPE 326. MOTIFS: L.112.4 [*Dirty boy as hero*]; F.771.4.4 [*Castle where everyone is asleep*]; D.1960.4 [*Deathlike sleep*]; D.782 [*Disenchantment by physical contact*]; D.705.1 [*Castle disenchanted*]; K.1931.4 [*Impostors throw hero into pit*]; K.1932 [*Impostors claim reward earned by hero*]; L.10 [*Victorious youngest son*]; L.161 [*Lowly hero marries princess*].

THE MAGIC KNAPSACK [summary]

Poor Jack begged for food at a house where he was kindly taken in, and fed from a magic cloth. He snatched up the cloth and ran off. Next, he met an old soldier, who offered him for his cloth a knapsack, from which came out a regiment of soldiers each time he kicked it. Jack took the knapsack, kicked it, and made the soldiers take back the cloth from the old soldier.

He returned home, and found his parents in great trouble, for the king was about to have them turned out of their house. Jack kicked his knapsack, and ordered his soldiers to drive off the regiment sent by the king. The king, in anger, sent his whole army, but Jack's soldiers easily outnumbered them, and the king was forced to beg for mercy. Jack demanded his daughter in marriage, and with his soldiers soon conquered all the neighbouring shire-kings, and became king over the whole country.

Thompson Notebooks, F, written down by John Myers.
TYPE 569. See "Habie's Whistle".

THE MAIDEN FAIR AND THE FOUNTAIN FAIRY

Long, long ago a drover courted and married the miller of Cuthilldorie's only daughter. By the time the miller died, the drover had learned the trade and with his young wife set up as the miller of Cuthilldorie. He hadn't much silver to begin with, but an old Highland drover he knew lent him some.

By and by the young miller and his wife had a daughter, but on the very night she was born the fairies stole her away. The wee thing was carried far away from the house into the wood of Cuthilldorie, where she was found on the very lip of the Black Well. In the air was heard a lilting:

> "O we'll come back again, my honey, my hert,
>   We'll come back again, my ain kind dearie;
> And you will mind upon the time
>   When we met in the wood at the Well so wearie!"

The lassie grew up to be by far the bonniest lass in all the countryside. Everything went well at the mill.

One dark night there came a woodcock with a glowing tinder in its beak, and set fire to the mill. Everything was burnt and the miller was left without a thing in the world. To make matters worse, who should come next morning but the old drover who had lent them the silver, saying he had not been paid.

Now, there was a wee old man in the wood of Cuthilldorie beside the Black Well who would never stay in a house if he could help it. In the winter he went away, nobody knew where. He was an ugly bogle, not above two and a half feet high.

He had been seen only three times in the fifteen years since he came to the place, for he always flew up out of sight when anybody came near him. But if you had crept cannily through the wood after dark, you might have heard him playing with the water, and singing the same song:

> "O when will you come, my honey, my hert,
>   O when will you come, my ain kind dearie;
> For don't you mind upon the time
>   We met in the wood at the Well so wearie?"

Well, the night after the firing of the mill, the miller's daughter wandered into the wood alone, and wandered and wandered till she came to the Black Well. Then the wee bogle gripped her and jumped about singing:

"O come with me, my honey, my hert,
 O come you with me, my ain kind dearie;
 For don't you mind upon the time
  We met in the wood at the Well so wearie?"

With that he made her drink three double handfuls of the witched water, and away they flew on a flash of lightning. When the poor lass opened her eyes, she was in the middle of a palace, all gold and silver and diamonds, and full of fairies.

The King and Queen invited her to stay, and said she would be well looked after. But if she wanted to go home again, she must never tell anybody where she had been or what she had seen.

She said she wanted to go home, and promised to do as she was bidden.

Then the King said:

"The first stranger you meet, give him brose!"

"Give him bannocks!" said the Queen.

"Give him butter!" said the King.

"Give him a drink of the Black Well water!" they both said together.

Then they gave her twelve drops of liquid in a wee green bottle, three drops for the brose, three for the bannocks, three for the butter and three for the Black Well water.

She took the green bottle in her hand, and suddenly it was dark. She was flying through the air, and when she opened her eyes she was at her own doorstep. She slipped away to her bed, glad to be home again, and said nothing about where she had been or what she had seen.

Next morning, before the sun was up, there came a rap, rap, rap, three times at the door. The sleepy lass looked out and saw an old beggar-man, who began to sing:

"O open the door, my honey, my hert,
 O open the door, my ain kind dearie;
 For don't you mind upon the time
  We met in the wood at the Well so wearie?"

When she heard that, she said nothing, and opened the door. The old beggar came in, singing:

"O gie me my brose, my honey, my hert,
 O gie me my brose, my ain kind dearie;
 For don't you mind upon the time
  We met in the wood at the Well so wearie?"

The lassie made a bicker of brose for the beggar, not forgetting the three drops of the green bottle. As he was supping the brose he vanished, and there was the big Highland drover, who lent the silver to the miller, singing:

"O gie me my bannocks, my honey, my hert,
     O gie me my bannocks, my ain kind dearie;
   For don't you mind upon the time
     We met in the wood at the Well so wearie?"

She baked him some fresh bannocks, not forgetting the three drops from the wee green bottle. He had just finished eating the bannocks when he vanished, and there was the woodcock that fired the mill, singing:

"O gie me my butter, my honey, my hert,
     O gie me my butter, my ain kind dearie;
   For don't you mind upon the time
     We met in the wood at the Well so wearie?"

She gave him butter as fast as she could, not forgetting the three drops from the green bottle. He had only eaten a bite, when he flapped his wings and vanished, and there was the ugly wee bogle that gripped her at the Black Well, the night before, singing:

"O gie me my water, my honey, my hert,
     O gie me my water, my ain kind dearie;
   For don't you mind upon the time
     We met in the wood at the Well so wearie?"

She knew there were only three other drops in the green bottle and she was afraid. She ran as fast as she could to the Black Well, but who should be there before her but the wee ugly bogle himself, singing:

"O gie me my water, my honey, my hert,
     O gie me my water, my ain kind dearie;
   For don't you mind upon the time
     We met in the wood at the Well so wearie?"

She gave him the water, not forgetting the three drops from the green bottle. But he had scarcely drunk the witched water when he vanished, and there was a fine young Prince, who spoke to her as if he had known her all her days.

They sat down beside the Black Well.

"I was born the same night as you," he said, "and I was carried away by the fairies the same night as you were found on the lip of the Well. I was a bogle for so many years because the fairies were scared away. They made me play many tricks before they would let me go, and return to my father, the King of France, and make the bonniest lass in all the world my bride."

"Who is she?" said the maiden.

399

"The miller of Cuthilldorie's daughter," said the young Prince.

Then they went home and told their stories over again, and that very night they were married. A coach-and-four came for them, and the miller and his wife, and the Prince and the Princess, drove away singing:

> "O but we're happy, my honey, my heit,
> O but we're happy, my ain kind dearie;
> For don't you mind upon the time
> When we met in the wood at the Well so wearie?"

N. and W. Montgomerie, *The Well at the World's End*, pp. 23–8.

TYPE 440 (variant).

This is a highly elaborated version of "The Well of the World's End", retaining only the enchanted suitor in repulsive form and the recurrent rhyme, with its reference to a promise made at a well.

MOTIFS: F.321 [*Fairy steals child from cradle*]; F.321.3.1 [*Unbaptized child stolen by fairies found and rescued*]; F.234.2.2 [*Fairy in hideous form*]; F.234.1.15 [*Fairy in form of bird*]; F.320 [*Fairies carry people away to fairyland*]; D.813 [*Magic object received from fairy*]; D.1242.1 [*Magic water*]; C.675 [*Compulsion to give food to everyone met*]; D.731 [*Disenchantment by obedience and kindness*].

¶ See "The Well of the World's End".

MALLY WHUPPIE

Ance upon a time there was a man and a wife had too many children, and they could not get meat for them, so they took the three youngest and left them in a wood. They travelled and travelled and could see never a house. It began to be dark, and they were hungry. At last they saw a light and made for it; it turned out to be a house. They knocked at the door, and a woman came to it, who asked what they wanted. They said if she would let them in and gee them a piece. The woman said she could not do that, as her man was a giant, and he would fell them if he came home. They priggit that she would let them stop for a little while, and they would go away before he came. So she took them in, and set them doon afore the fire, and gave them milk and bread; but just as they had begun to eat a great knock came to the door, and a dreadful voice said:

> "Fee, fie, fo, fum,
> I smell the blood of some earthly one.

Who have you there, wife?" "Eh," said the wife, "it's three peer lassies caul' an hungry, an they will go away. Ye winna touch them, man." He said nothing, but eat up a great big supper, and ordered them to stay all night. Now he had three lassies of his own, and they were to sleep in the same bed with the three strangers.

The youngest of the three strange lassies was called Mally Whuppie, and she was very clever. She noticed that before they went to bed, the giant put straw rapes round her neck and her sisters', and round his ain lassies' necks he put gold chains. So Mally took care and did not fall asleep, but waited till she was sure every one was sleeping sound. Then she slippit out of the bed, and took the straw rapes off her own and her sisters' necks, and took the gold chains off the giant's lassies. She then put the straw rapes on the giant's lassies, and the gold on herself and her sisters, and lay down. And in the middle of the night up rose the giant, armed with a great club, and felt for the necks with the straw. It was dark. He took his own lassies out on the floor, and laid upon them until they were dead, and then lay down again, thinking he had managed fine. Mally thought it time she and her sisters were out of that, so she wakened them, and told them to be quiet, and they slippit out of the house. They all got out safe, and they ran and ran, and never stoppit until morning, when they saw a grand house before them. It turned out to be the king's house; so Mally went in, and told her story to the king. He said, "Well, Mally, you are a clever cutty, and you have managed well; but, if you would manage better, and go back, and steal the giant's sword that hangs on the back of his bed, I would give your eldest sister my eldest son to marry." Mally said she would try. So she went back, and managed to slip into the giant's house, and crept in below the bed. The giant came home, ate up a great supper, and went to bed. Mally waited until he was snoring, and she crept out, and raxed in ower the giant, and got doon the sword; but just as she got it oot ower the bed it gave a rattle, and up jumped the giant, and Mally oot at the door, and the sword with her; and she ran, and he ran, till they cam to the "Brig o' ae hair"; and she wan ower, but he cuddna, and he says, "Wae worth ye, Mally Whuppie! Lat ye never come again." And she says, "Twice yet, carle," quo she, "I'll come to Spain." So Mally took the sword to the king, and her sister was married to his son.

"Well," the king he says: "Ye've managed well, Mally; but if ye would manage better, and steal the purse that lies below the giant's pillow, I would marry your second sister to my second son." And Mally said she would try. So she set out for the giant's house, and slippit in, and hid again below the bed, and waited till the giant had eaten his supper, and was snoring sound asleep. She slippit out, and slippit her hand below the pillow, and got out the purse; but just as she was going out, the giant wakened, and after her; and she ran, and he ran, till they came to the "Brig o' ae hair", and she wan ower, but he cuddna, and he said, "Wae worth you, Mally Whuppie! Lat you never come again." "Ance yet, carle," quo she, "I'll come to Spain." So Mally took the purse to the king, and her second sister was married to the king's second son.

After that the king says to Mally, "Mally, you are a clever cutty, but if you would dee better yet, and steal the giant's ring that he wears on his finger, I will give you my youngest son to yoursel." Mally said she would try. So back she goes to the giant's house, and hides herself below the bed. The giant wizna lang ere he came hame, and, after he had eaten a great big supper, he went to his bed, and shortly was snoring loud. Mally crept out, and raxed in ower the bed, and got hold of the giant's hand, and she pirlt and pirlt until she got off the ring, but just as she got it off the giant got up, and grippit her by the hand, and he says, "Now I hae catcht you, Mally Whuppie, and, if I had deen as much ill to you as ye hae deen to me, what wad ye dee to me?"

Mally considered what plan she would fall upon to escape, and she says, "I would put you in a pyock, and I wad pit the cat inside wi' you, and the dog aside you, and a needle and thread and a shears, and I wad hang you up upon the wa', and I wad gang to the wood, and wile the thickest stick I could get, and I would come hame, and take you down, and lay upon you till you were dead."

"Well, Mally," says the giant, "I'll just do that to you."

So he gets a pyock, and puts Mally into it, and the cat and the dog beside her, and a needle and thread and shears, and hings her up upon the wa', and goes to the wood to choose a stick.

Mally she sings, "Oh, gin ye saw faht I see!"

"Oh," says the giant's wife, "faht divv ye see, Mally?"

But Mally said never a word but, "Oh, gin ye saw faht I see!" The giant's wife pleaded that Mally would take her up into the pyock till she would see what Mally saw. So Mally took the shears and cut a hole in the pyock, and took out the needle and thread with her, and jumpt down, and helpit the giant's wife up into the pyock, and sewed up the hole.

The giant's wife saw nothing, and began to ask to get down again; but Mally never minded, but hid herself at the back of the door. Home came the giant, and a great big tree in his hand, and he took down the pyock, and began to lay upon it. His wife cried, "It's me, man;" but the dog barkit, and the cat mewit, and he did not know his wife's voice. But Mally did not want her to be killed, so she came out from the back of the door, and the giant saw her, and he after her; and he ran, and she ran, till they came to the "Brig o' ae Hair", and she wan ower, but he cuddna, and he said, "Wae worth you, Mally Whuppie! Lat you never come again." "Never mair, carle," quo she, "will I come again to Spain."

So Mally took the ring to the king, and she was married to his youngest son, and she never saw the giant again.

Norton Collection, I, p. 182. Three folk-tales from Old Meldrum, Aberdeenshire, communicated to W. Gregor by Mr Moir. He had them from his mother, who wrote out "Mally Whuppie" (*Folk-Lore Journal*, II, pp. 68–71).

TYPES 327B; 328.

MOTIFS: (327B) S.321 [*Destitute parents abandon children*]; G.401 [*Children wander into ogre's house*]; G.530.1 [*Help from ogre's wife*]; G.84 [*Fee-fi-fo-fum*]; K.1611 [*Substituted caps (necklaces) cause ogre to kill his own children*].

(328) G.610 [*Theft from ogre*]; G.610.2 [*Stealing from ogre to help a friendly king*]; G.450 [*Falling into ogre's power*]; G.441 [*Ogre puts victim in bag*]; K.526 [*Captor's bag filled with animals while captive escapes*]; K.842 [*Dupe persuaded to take prisoner's place in a sack: killed*]; L.0 [*Victorious youngest child*]; L.162 [*Lowly heroine marries prince*].

Of all the Hop o' my Thumb stories this is the most amoral. De la Mare does his best for it by calling it "Mally Whuppie and the Double-Faced Giant", but no treachery on the giant's side can excuse the ingratitude to his wife.

An Irish version told by Kennedy in *Fireside Stories* is very close to "Mally Whuppie"; "Whittlegaire", another story from County Leitrim, published in *Folk-Lore*, IV (1893), is very similar, with an ogress instead of a giant and a boy instead of a girl.

❡ See also "The Enchanted Mountain", "Black Brottie" and the "Jack and the Beanstalk" tales.

THE MAN IN THE WILDERNESS

Tom, Dick, and Jack were going to the Fair. They came to a wood where there was a Bad 'Un, and no one could send him to the Red Sea. He asked travellers a question, and if they couldn't tell it they were never seen any more. So Tom says: "I'm the eldest. I'll go first."

So they waited. By and by Tom came back, and he said:

> "The Man in the Wilderness asked of me,
> 'How many blackberries grow in the sea?'
> I answered him bravely, as I thought good:
> 'As many red herrings as grow in the wood.'

And he had to let me go."

So Dick said: "Now it's my turn."

And they waited, and by and by Dick came back, and he said:

> "The Man in the Wilderness asked me why
> His hen could swim and his pig could fly.
> I answered him briskly, as I thought best:
> 'Because they were born in a cuckoo's nest.'

And he had to let me go."

Then it was little Jacky's turn. So they waited, and all of a sudden there was a great puff of smoke, and by and by little Jacky came back and said:

> "The Man in the Wilderness asked me to tell
> The sands in the sea, and I counted them well.

26-2

Says he with a grin: 'And not *one* more?'
I answered him bravely, 'You go and make sure!'
So he had to go, and the Bad 'Uns in the Red Sea will keep him."
Then Tom, Dick, and little Jacky went to the Fair quite safely.

From Ruth L. Tongue's great-grandmother, Lincolnshire, 1860.
TYPE 1178. MOTIF: H.543 [*Escape from devil by answering his riddles*].

This excellent tale, which has been handed down in one family for four generations, may well have originated with the great-grandmother. It seems more probable that the tale was built round the rhyme, rather than having originated it.

See "The Fause Knight on the Road".

THE MAN WHO DIDN'T BELIEVE IN GHOSTS AND 'CHANTMENTS [summary]

There was a poor man who didn't believe in ghosts or enchantments. A friend told him of an enchanted house near by, and they agreed to spend a night in it. The squire, who had built himself another house, welcomed their attempt. They went into a fine room, with a bare table, and when they wished for dinner, it floated into the room.

Table magically cleared when they had finished and pipes and tobacco appeared. The same with supper. An uproar upstairs. They went to see what caused it and met a man in football clothes who advised them to go to bed. Comfortable bed, but an uproar like that downstairs. They went down to see what it was, and saw a football match. Weak play. Unbeliever joined in and kicked ball through window. He and his companion thrown out and stunned. Went back to house and saw an evening party watching a play. They all vanished. The two men wished for supper, and began to look for it.

The first ghost came in in evening dress and told them where to get it, but he claimed every mouthful himself. At last the unbeliever got angry, and broke the plate on his head. This broke the enchantment. The ghosts resumed their proper forms, and the two men were rewarded.

Thompson Notebooks, IX. From Taimi Boswell, Oswaldtwistle, 10 January 1915.
TYPE 326. MOTIFS: Q.82 [*Reward for fearlessness*]; H.1411 [*Fear test: staying in haunted house*]; D.1472.1.5 [*Magic palace supplies food and drink*]; E.577 [*Dead persons play games*]; D.712.3 [*Disenchantment by striking*].

See also "The Tinker and the Cutler".

THE MAN WHO WENT FISHING ON SUNDAY

There was once a man they called Jack the Fool. Oh, he had all his wits about him and a good few more, but he just couldn't be happy unless he was up to some game to make the neighbours stare and cause a lot of talk and set him grinning. One Sunday when the Church bells began to ring, he came down the stairs in his work clothes.

"'Tis Sunday," said his old mother.

"I know that," says Jack the Fool with a grin.

"And the Church bells are rin'ing," said his old mother.

"I can hear 'em," says he with another grin.

"You'll be late for Church today," says his old mother.

"I'm not going," says he. "I'm going fishing!"

"Fishing on *Sunday*!" says his old mother, all taken aback at this dangerous folly of his. "You've had all the week to fish."

"Fish weren't biting," says he.

"'Tis a mortal sin," said she.

"Then I'll have the Devil's own luck," said he and he took his tackle and went out grinning from ear to ear. And she was that frightened she was in too much dread to say one word more in case the Church bells stopped ringing and then such words would be terribly dangerous, but she did call after him in warning,

> "You will go
> Down Below!"

Jack the Fool didn't listen, but went and sat on the bank of the Mere and sorted his tackle, and the Church bells went on ringing and all the neighbours passed by to Church.

"Fishing on Sunday!" they said in horror. "'Tis a mortal sin!"

"Then I'll have the Devil's own luck," says Jack the Fool, grinning all the more.

But at that they all backed away and cried—

> "You will go
> Down Below!"

And they hurried away to Church in case the bells stopped ringing.

"It's a bit warmish Down There," Jack the Fool shouted after them. "I'm happy as I am," and he launched his boat out on the Mere.

The sun shone and the Church bells rang, and Jack the Fool caught a fine fish. "I said my luck was in," he thought. "And so it is."

And it *was*. He fished and he fished and he quite forgot it was Sunday, or where he was, he just went on baiting his hook again and again, and soon his boat was loaded with fish and his grin grew so wide it almost met at the back. *Then* the Church bells stopped and the sun went in and *he caught Old Nick*! All ready and waiting for him, wet and shiny and scaly with smoke coming out of his nostrils.

"Oh, dear! Oh dear!" moaned Jack the Fool. "You can't come near. 'Tis a Sunday."

"The bells have stopped rin'ing," said Old Nick.

"But I'm a Christian soul," said Jack the Fool and his teeth chattered like pebbles in a bucket.

"And chose to go fishing instead of going to Church to pray," said Old Nick, and he put one wet hand on the boat side.

Well, at that Jack the Fool was so terrified he couldn't remember a single prayer; all he could say was, "Oh dear! Oh dear! I'm cold with fear."

"You won't be cold long," says Old Nick and *he tipped the boat right over.*

And they did go
Down Below!

So there *isn't any more to tell you.*

Ruth L. Tongue: "My third cousin, Matthias John told this to my cousins Patty and John and myself on the lawn of Mother's old Whitchurch home one summer afternoon in 1911. It was afterwards written down for me by my mother. The mere was either Ellesmere or a local mere near Whitchurch (in Shropshire). I have heard briefer versions of the story down Severn and Wye, but its locality is usually told as Severn, the boat is a coracle and the fool is spearing salmon. There is a faintly recalled Somerset version of this near Clevedon where they say the devil rose and drowned him in the tidal bore. In this version the devil was caught in his salmon net."

A Severn River tale or a Welsh Border tale.
MOTIFS: C.631 [*Tabu: breaking the sabbath*]; G.303.10.7 [*Devil gives luck with fishing*]; G.303.16.12 [*Ringing of church bell causes devil to lose his power*]; G.303.6.2.14 [*Devil appears to sabbath-breakers*].
⁋ For another tale of a Sunday fisherman who caught more than he reckoned for, see "The Lambton Worm".

THE MAN WHO WOULDN'T
GO OUT AT NIGHT [dialect modified]

There was a farmer, a great upstanding chap, and he wouldn't go out after dark, not for anything. It was not so bad in the Summer, but when All Hallows was come and gone things grew terribly awkward. There might be stock to feed and cows to milk and lambs to help into this world, but he wouldn't put a foot outside the door after sunset, not if you begged him on your bended knees. What was worse, his wife was expecting a child and she asked him flat out if he'd fetch the doctor if her pains came on her at night, and he had to admit that he wouldn't. She knew there must be something far amiss there, because he fairly doted on her. So she begged and prayed him to tell her what was the matter, and at last it came out.

It seemed when he was a foolish youngster that he had sold his soul to the Devil, old Bogey, he called him, for prosperity on the farm, and now the time had come to pay. Old Bogey was hanging round the farm to snap him up if he set foot over the threshold after dark. The door was well guarded with horseshoes and a piece of mountain ash, but once beyond them and the farmer was a lost soul.

Well the poor wife was hard set to it to know what to do, but she made up her mind she must save her husband, and the farm and stock beside. So she took an iron plough colter and she made it red-hot in the fire, and she rolled out a great piece of pastry and made a deep cross in it, and filled the cross with salt; then she put the red-hot colter into the pie, with the cross turned inside so that it didn't show. When it was done she sent her man into the bed-chamber, and she opened the farm door and stretched out her hand with the pie.

"Are you there, sir?" she said. "My man's just a-getting ready to come, and here's a warm bite for you whilst you're a-waiting."

Bogey took the pie and bit into it hard, and he pretty near broke every tooth in his head, and the cross and the salt were like poison to him. Just then the wife cried out from her chamber, "We're a-coming, sir, we're a coming."

"Who's we?" said Bogey, anxious all of a sudden.

"Why, I'm a-coming with my dear man," she said, "to cook for the both of you."

With that they say old Bogey let out a yell that sunk two ships off Lundy, and he took himself off to Taunton as fast as he could fly. And what I've seen of the Taunton folk, he stayed there for good and all.

Collected by Ruth L. Tongue. Recorded from her on 29 September 1963, as heard at Brampton Ralph Women's Institute in 1962. She knew other versions told between

1930 and 1940, by a blacksmith at Vellow, a cottage woman at Monkshields, and a farmer's wife at Elworthy. First published in *The Folktales of England*, 1965. Also in *Somerset Folklore*.

TYPE 330 (variant). MOTIFS: M.211 [*Man sells soul to the devil*]; K.212 [*Devil cheated by being frightened*].

The Irish tale of Finn McCoole (Patrick Kennedy, *Legendary Fictions of the Irish Celts*, London 1866, pp. 303–5) uses the same theme.

¶ See also "Dule upon Dun", "Will the Smith".

THE MAN WITH A LONG NOSE

There was once a man who had a very long, long nose, and everything he did, he did it with his long nose. He opened his door with his long nose, and he made his breakfast with his long nose. Everything he did, he did it with his long nose.

One morning as he was making his breakfast with his long nose, there was a knock at his door. He opened the door with his long nose. And there stood a maid. "What do you want," said he, "knocking at my door so early in the morning?" "I want a master," she said. "Well," said Long-Nosey, "I want a servant; you and I are well met. To-morrow, when you are making the breakfast, you must not look up the chimney, lest something falls down and kills you." "Oh, no", she said, "I shall not do that." Next morning, however, when she was making the breakfast, she looked up the chimney, and down came a bag full of money. She took it up, and went off, running along the road with it. She ran until she came to an old horse eating grass by the wayside. The horse was chained to a post thrust into the ground. When she was passing, the horse said, "Flit me,* pretty maid, and I'll not tell." "You! You ugly beast," she said. "Who would flit you?" Then she went on running again, till she came to the riverside, and hid herself among the bushes there.

In a little while, the man with the long nose came running, and breathing, and he said to the horse:

> "Did you see a maid running zigzag,
> And in her hand a long leather bag,
> With all the gold that e'er I won, since the time I
> was a boy yet?"

"She is before you! She is before you!" said the horse. "She is down at the side of the river." So he went there, and found her among the bushes, and having beaten her with a stick, he took his money home, and put it again in the chimney.

*flit me = move me.

Another day soon after, as he was making his breakfast with his long nose, he heard someone knocking at his door. So again he opened the door with his long nose, and there was a very pretty maid standing there. "What do you want?" said Long-Nosey. "Please, sir, I want a master." He liked the way she spoke, so he said: "Well, I want a servant; you and I are well met. You must not look up my chimney to-morrow, when you are making the breakfast, lest something falls down and kills you." She promised with a sweet smile that she would not look up the chimney.

But she did not keep her word. Next morning, when she was making the breakfast, she looked up the chimney, and down fell the bag full of money. She at once snatched it up, and ran along the road, till she came to the old horse.

The horse said, "Flit me, pretty maid, and I'll not tell." "Poor beast," she said. "I'll do that." So she removed the horse to another piece of grass, and then ran and hid herself in the weed.

Soon after, Long-Nosey came running and breathing, and running and breathing. When he came to the horse, he cried:

> "Did you see a maid running zigzag,
> And in her hand a long leather bag,
> With all the gold that e'er I won, since
> the time I was a boy yet?"

But the horse only shook his head, and went on eating his grass. Long-Nosey, thinking he had come the wrong way, went back again, but he never found his money.

If you have money, do not be too watchful of it, and never talk about it, "for riches certainly make themselves wings; they fly away as an eagle towards heaven".

Norton Collection, II, pp. 25–6. *Miscellanea of the Rymour Club*, II, pp. 200–1, contributed by "Toush".
TYPE 480 (an abbreviated version). The motif *Kind and unkind* rather abbreviated.
MOTIFS: F.543.1 [*Remarkably long nose*]; C.337 [*Tabu: looking up chimney*]; Q.2 [*Kind and unkind*]; B.350 [*Grateful animals*].
See also "The Old Witch".

THE MARRIAGE OF SIR GAWAIN [summary]

Some days after Christmas, King Arthur met in the forest at Tarn Wadling a baron armed with a club, who bade him either fight him on the spot, or ransom himself by returning on New Year's Day, and telling him what women most desired. Arthur questioned all whom he met for several days, in vain, and on his way back, he met a woman in scarlet, so hideous that he could hardly bear to look at her; but she promised to help him in return for his promise that Sir Gawain should wed her.

When Arthur gave the baron the answer she had whispered to him, the baron cried out that she was his sister, and that he would burn her if he could catch her.

Arthur returned to his court, and led his knights to find Gawain's promised bride.

They all cried out in horror at sight of her, except Gawain, who took her home, and when they were in bed together, she turned into a young and beautiful girl, but she asked him whether he would rather have her so by night or by day, since he could not have both. Gawain left the choice to her, and this broke a spell, and she became perpetually beautiful. She had been bewitched by a jealous stepmother, and condemned to wander in hideous shape on the moor, until she met a knight who would let her have all her will. And this was indeed the answer to the baron's question. What a woman wants most is her own will. Bewitched at the same time, he had been compelled to challenge all whom he met either to fight or to answer his hard riddle.

Child, *The English and Scottish Popular Ballads*, I, p. 288.
TYPE 402A* (variant). MOTIFS: H.541 [*Riddle propounded with penalty for failure*]; D.732 [*Loathly lady*]; D.1870 [*Magic hideousness*]; D.621.3 [*Ugly by day: fair by night*].
    The ballad is fragmentary; the story, as pieced together by Child, is the same as Chaucer's "Wife of Bath's Tale". A ballad on the same theme is "King Henry".
¶ See also "The Laidley Worm of Spindlestone Heughs".

MASELL

There was a brave young man who undertook to spend the night in a mill to which the fairies were known to come. His companions, whose dare he had accepted, threw a dead duck down the chimney to frighten him. But he plucked the duck, lit a fire, and began to roast it, turning it with a stick. Presently, a fairy, a little man, came up to him and said:
"What's your name?"
"Masell."
"But what's your name?"
"Masell."
And on and on he went, asking the same question and getting the same answer, until the young man grew tired of it, and hit the fairy with the hot, greasy stick.

The little fairy yelled with pain, and ran out, and the young man heard the other fairies crowding round him, and saying:
"Who did it, Sanroch?"

"Masell, Masell."

"Ach!" said the fairies, and away they went with him, leaving the young man to roast his duck in peace.

Miss Charlotte Macdonald, Morayshire.

TYPE 1137.

It is doubtful whether this story should not be put under local legends, under which will be found the closely connected "Me Aan Sell" and "Maggie Moloch", which are definitely attached to localities. See B, IX.

The roasting of the duck occurs in an American version of the story.

MOTIF: K.602 ["Noman": escape by assuming equivocal name: sometimes "Myself"].

THE MASTER AND HIS PUPIL

There was once a very learned man in the north country who knew all the languages under the sun, and who was acquainted with all the mysteries of creation. He had one big book bound in black calf and clasped with iron, and with iron corners, and chained to a table which was made fast to the floor; and when he read out of this book, he unlocked it with an iron key, and none but he read from it, for it contained all the secrets of the spiritual world. It told how many angels there were in heaven, and how they marched in their ranks, and sang in their quires, and what were their several functions, and what was the name of each great angel of might. And it told of the devils of hell, how many of them there were, and what were their several powers, and their labours, and their names, and how they might be summoned, and how tasks might be imposed on them, and how they might be chained to be as slaves to man.

Now the master had a pupil who was but a foolish lad, and he acted as servant to the great master, but never was he suffered to look into the black book, hardly to enter the private room.

One day the master was out, and then the lad, impelled by curiosity, hurried to the chamber where his master kept his wondrous apparatus for changing copper into gold, and lead into silver, and where was his mirror in which he could see all that was passing in the world, and where was the shell which when held to the ear whispered all the words that were being spoken by anyone the master desired to know about. The lad tried in vain with the crucibles to turn copper and lead into gold and silver,—he looked long and vainly into the mirror; smoke and clouds fleeted over it, but he saw nothing plain, and the shell to his ear produced only indistinct mutterings, like the breaking of distant seas on an unknown shore. "I can do nothing," he said, "as I know not the right words to utter, and they are locked up in yon book." He looked round, and see! the book was unfastened; the master had forgotten to lock it before he went out. The boy rushed to it, and unclosed the volume. It

411

was written with red and black ink, and much therein he could not understand; but he put his finger on a line, and spelled it through.

At once the room was darkened, and the house trembled; a clap of thunder rolled through the passages of the old mansion, and there stood before the horrified youth a horrible form, breathing fire, and with eyes like burning lamps. It was the Evil One, Beelzebub, whom he had called up to serve him.

"Set me a task!" said a voice like the roaring of an iron furnace.

The boy only trembled, and his hair stood up.

"Set me a task, or I shall strangle thee!"

But the lad could not speak. Then the evil spirit stepped towards him, and putting forth his hands touched his throat. The fingers burned his flesh. "Set me a task."

"Water yon flower," cried the boy in despair, pointing to a geranium which stood in a pot on the floor.

Instantly the spirit left the room, but in another instant he returned with a barrel on his back, and poured its contents over the flower; and and again and again he went and came, and poured more and more water, till the floor of the room was ankle-deep.

"Enough, enough!" gasped the lad; but the Evil One heeded him not; the lad knew not the words by which to dismiss him, and still he fetched water.

It rose to the boy's knees, and still more water was poured. It mounted to his waist, and Beelzebub ceased not bringing barrels full. It rose to his armpits, and he scrambled to the table-top. And now the water stood up to the window and washed against the glass, and swirled around his feet on the table. It still rose; it reached his breast. In vain he cried; the evil spirit would not be dismissed, and to this day he would have been pouring water, and would have drowned all Yorkshire, had not the master remembered on his journey that he had not locked his book, and had therefore returned, and at the moment when the water was bubbling about his pupil's chin, spoken the words which cast Beelzebub back into his fiery home.

Norton Collection, II, p. 148. Baring-Gould, appendix to Henderson, 16, pp. 343–4. Presumably Yorkshire.

TYPE 325*. MOTIFS: D.1711.0.1 [*Magician's apparatus*]; J.2411.4 [*Imitation of magician unsuccessful*].

¶ The story of "The Magician's Apprentice" is fairly widespread, and has been used several times as the plot of a puppet-play.

A story very similar to this is told of the schoolmaster at Linton, near Grassington, and may indeed be the same tale.

MAY COLLIN AND FALSE SIR JOHN [summary]

May Collin was pressed night and day by Sir John, a knight from the north, to marry him. He gave her no rest and at last she consented. The same day he mounted her before him on his horse and rode away with her, taking much gold from her parents' store. They rode till they came to a dreadful place of towering cliffs, with the sea far below, known as Bunion Bay. There Sir John alighted and bade May Colvin alight also,

> "For here I've drowned eight ladies fair,
> The ninth one you shall be."

But first he ordered her to take off her fine dress and shoes, for they were too good to waste. She bade him turn his back while she undressed,

> "For it never was comely for a man
> A naked woman to see."

When he turned she swiftly pushed him over the cliff into the sea and, paying no heed to his cries for help, she mounted his horse and rode back to her home.

Her parrot greeted her:

> "What have you done with false Sir John
> That went with you yestreen?"

She promised it a golden cage, and three meals a day instead of its one, if it would keep her secret. Her father came in to see why the parrot was making so much noise, and the parrot said:

> "The cat she came to my cage door,
> The thief I could not see,
> And I called to fair May Collin
> To take the cat from me."

Then May Collin told her parents all the truth, and they went with her to the place where Sir John's body had fallen, and there it still lay, though his diamond ring had been broken in two by the fall, and the waves were tossing all round.

They buried him under some green grass near by, that no one might find his body.

Child, *The English and Scottish Popular Ballads*, I, pp. 57–8.
MOTIFS: T.72.1 [*Maid eloping with false lover is forced by him to strip*]; K.1645 [*Woman ordered to strip makes lover turn his back; pushes him into water*]; B.211.3 [*Speaking bird*]; D.469.9 [*Helpful parrot*].
There are many versions of this ballad, and in some the knight is explicitly described

as an elf-knight. In another, "Oh, heard ye of a bloody knight" (Sharpe's *Ballad Book*, 1827), the knight forces May Collin to go with him by means of a charm.
¶ See "Lady Isabel and the Elf-Knight".

THE MILK-WHITE DOO [summary]

A man working in the fields caught a hare. While his wife was cooking it she tasted it so often that there was none left. So she called their son Johnnie to have his hair combed, and while combing it she killed him. She cooked him for their dinner, but while her husband was eating, he took up a foot.

"That's surely my Johnnie's foot," he said, but she denied it. Then he found a hand, and said, "That's surely my Johnnie's hand." After dinner little Katy their daughter took up her brother's bones, and buried them. They grew into a milk-white dove, which flew away and came to two women washing clothes. It sang:

> "Pew, pew,
> My minny me slew,
> My daddy me chew,
> My sister gathered my banes,
> And put them between two milk-white stanes;
> And I grew, and I grew,
> To a milk-white doo,
> And I took to my wings, and away I flew."

The women promised it all the clothes if it would sing again, which it did and then flew away with the clothes. In the same way it got a heap of silver from a man who was counting it, and a millstone from a miller. It flew home with all these, dropped small stones down the "lum", and when Katy came out to see what was the matter, the dove threw down the clothes to her, then the silver to its father, and lastly the millstone on to its mother's head, which killed her. So the husband and daughter lived happy ever after.

R. Chambers, *Popular Rhymes of Scotland*, p. 49.
TYPE 720.
    The regular type, a boy, as in "The Juniper Tree", though a girl is more usual in England.
MOTIFS: G.61 [*Relation's flesh eaten unwittingly*]; E.607.1 [*Bones of dead collected and buried. Return in another form*]; E.613.0.1 [*Reincarnation of murdered child as bird*]; Q.412 [*Millstone dropped on guilty person*].
¶ See also "The Rose Tree", "The Little Bird", "Rosy".

THE MISER AND THE FAIRIES
OF THE GUMP [condensed]

It was well known all over St. Just that the Little People held their revels
on the Gump when the moon was full. They hardly seemed to mind
human observation, and many of their human friends had visited them,
and received small but valuable presents. It was the rumour of these
presents which allured an old miser living in St. Just to pay the Gump a
visit. He set out by the clear light of the Harvest Moon, and as he toiled
up the Gump he heard music all around him. It was soft but compelling,
so that when it was merry he was forced to dance and caper, and when it
changed to a sadder note he wept. But where it came from puzzled him
until he had climbed to the top of the Gump, when he was certain that it
came from directly under his feet. Suddenly it grew much louder; the
hill beneath him opened with a blaze of light and an immense procession
of tiny people came out. They seemed to pay no attention to him, though
he crouched gaunt and black in the white moonlight; only a company
of Spriggans, who were the first to come out, surrounded him.

The Spriggans were the only ugly creatures of the multitude; after
them came a great number of fairy children in gauze and gold, who
scattered flowers as they went. And the great beauty of the flowers was
that they rooted themselves as they touched the earth, so that the hillside
was soon a mass of primroses and all sweet, low-growing flowers. Then
out came the little knights in green and gold, and their bevies of fairy
ladies, singing more beautifully than nightingales, and then the tiny,
beautiful King and Queen. They all moved up to the top of the Gump,
and settled themselves in their thousands at the banquet that appeared
there. It was a sight which no man that saw it could forget, though he
lived to be a hundred. Every furze bush around the hill glittered with
fairy lights; the whole ground was starred with tiny flowers, and the air
sweet with the scent of them. Each little figure of the thousands which
sat at the feast was perfect in form and feature. Only the Spriggans who
guarded the outer ring were grotesque and forbidding, even in their
tiny size.

But a man can see only what he is able to see; and the miser's whole
heart was set on the minute golden plates and cups on which the feast
was served; and on the golden thrones of the King and Queen. He threw
himself flat on the ground, and crawled on his belly like a snake round
the Gump to the back of the King's throne. All behind him was darkness,
all in front of him was light. With his eyes fixed greedily on the riches
before him, he never noticed that he was surrounded by his guard of
Spriggans.

He crawled inch by inch up to the throne, and the fairies ate and drank, laughed and sang as if no human eye saw them. Immediately behind the throne he stopped and raised himself with his hat in his hand, to catch the whole royal dais under it as a boy catches a butterfly. As he raised himself he suddenly saw that every eye of those thousands was fixed on him. But his greed was stronger than his fear, and he was darting down his hat when a single whistle rang out, and he found his arm caught as if by a thousand strings.

The lights flickered out. The miser rolled to the ground, and felt himself held to it tightly by the threads drawn over him. With a sound like the buzzing of a swarm of bees, the fairies were over him, pricking and pinching. He was in agony, but he could neither move nor cry out. The tallest of the Spriggans began a triumphant dance upon his nose. But the moon was paling. At last a cry arose among his tormentors, and was taken up by all of them: "Away, away! I smell the day!" And in a moment they all vanished. When the sun rose, the miser found himself lying on the dewy grass, covered with thousands of threads of gossamer. He broke them easily enough, and hobbled down the Gump, aching in every limb.

At first he told no one of what had happened to him; but as he grew older he told one or two cronies, and the story has served as a warning to the covetous ever since.

Hunt, *Popular Romances of the West of England*, p. 98, retold by K. M. Briggs, *The Personnel of Fairyland*, p. 66.

TYPE 503 III. MOTIFS: F.340 [*Gifts from fairies*]; F.211 [*Fairyland under hollow knoll*]; F.239.4.3 [*Fairy is tiny*]; F.262.3.6 [*Fairy music causes joy*]; F.456.1 [*Spriggans*]; F.350 [*Theft from fairies*]; F.361.2.3 [*Fairies bind man fast to ground after he has attempted to capture fairy prince and princess*].

See "The Fairy Cup", B, fairies.

MOLLY WHUPPIE

See "Mally Whuppie".

MOSSYCOAT

Dere was once a poor owld widda-woman as lived in a little cottage. She'd two daughters; de younger on 'em was about nineteen or twenty, and she was very beautiful. Her Mother was busy ivry day, a-spinning of a coat for her.

A hawker cam courting dis girl; cam reg'lar he did, and kept on a-bringing of her dis thing and dat. He was in love wid her, and badly wanted her to marry him. But she warn't in love wid him; it didn't fall out like dat; and she was in a puzzlement what she'd best do about him. So one day she ext her mother. "Let he come," her mother telt her, "and git what you can out'n him, while I finish dis coat, after when you won't have no need'n him, nor his presents neether. So tell him, girl, as you won't marry him, unless he gits you a dress o' white satin with sprigs o' gowld on it as big as a man's hand, and mind as you tells him it mus' fit exac'ly." Next time de hawker cam round and ext her to wed him, de girl telt him just dis, de wery same as her mother 'ed said. He took stock 'n her size and build, de hawker did; and inside of a week he was back wid de dress. It answered de describance alright, and when de girl went upstairs wid her mother and tried it on, it fit her exac'ly. "What should I do now, mother?" she ext.

"Tell him", her mother says, "as you won't marry him unless he gits you a dress med o' silk de colour o' all de birds o' de air; and as afore, it must fit you exac'ly." De girl telt de hawker dis, and in two or three days he was back at de cottage, wid dis coloured silk dress de girl 'ed exted for; and being as he knowed de size, from de 'tother 'un, in course it fit her exac'ly. "Now what should I do, mother?" she ext. "Tell him", her mother says, "as you won't marry him unless he gits you a pair o' silver slippers as fits you exac'ly." De girl telt de hawker so, and in a few days he called round wid 'em. Her feet was only about three inches long, but de slippers fit her exac'ly: dey was not too tight, neether was dey too loose. Agen de girl ext her mother what she should do now. "I can finish de coat to-night," her mother said, "so you can tell de hawker as you'll marry him tamorra, and he's to be here at 10 o'clock."

So de girl telt him dis. "Think-on, my dear," she says, "10 o'clock in de morning." "I'll be dere, my love," he says, "by God, I will."

Dat night her mother was at work on de coat till late, but she finished it alright. Green moss and gowld thread; dat's what it was med on; jus' dem two things. "Mossycoat," she called it, and give de name to her younger daughter, as she's med it for. It was a magic coat, she said, a Wishing Coat, she telt her daughter; when she'd got it on, she telt her, she'd only to wish to be somewhere and she'd be dere dat very instant, and de same if she wanted to change hersel' into summat else, like be a swan or a bee.

Next morning de mother was up by it was light. She called her younger daughter, and telt her she mus' now go into de world and seek her fortune; and a han'some fortune it was to be: she was a foreseer, de owld mother was, and know'd what was a-coming.

She give her daughter mossycoat to put on, and a gowld crown to tek wid her, and she telt her to tek as well de two dresses and de silver slippers she'd hed off 'n de hawker, but she was to go in de clo'es as she wore ivery day, her working clo'es, dat is. And now she's ready for to start, Mossycoat is. Her mother den tells her she is to wish hersel' a hundred miles away, and den walk on till she comes to a big hall; and dere she's to ex for a job.

"You won't hev far to walk, my blessed," she says—dat's de mother—"and dey'll be sure to find you work at dis big hall."

Mossycoat did as her mother telt her, and soon she foun' hersel' in front of a big gentleman's house. She knocked at de front door, and said as she was looking for work. Well, de long and de short of it was as de mistress hersel' come to see her; and she liked de look'n her, de lady did.

"What work can you do?" she ext.

"I can cook, your ladyship," said Mossycoat, "in fact I's in de way o' being a wery good cook, from what peoples 'es remarked."

"I can't give you a job as cook," de lady tells her, "being as I got one already; but I'd be willing for to imploy you to help de cook, if so be as you'd be satisfied wid dat."

"Thank you, ma'am," says Mossycoat, "I s'd be real glad'n de place."

So it was settled as she was to be under-cook. And after when de lady'd showed her up to her bedroom, she took her to de kitchen and interdoosed her to de t'other sarvants.

"Dis is Mossycoat," she tells 'em, "and I've ingaged her," she says, "to be under-cook."

She leaves 'em den, de mistress does; and Mossycoat, she goes up to her bedroom agen, to unpack her things, and hide away her gowld crown and silver slippers, and her silk and satin dresses.

It goes wi'out saying as de tother kitchen-girls was fair beside theirsel's wid jealousy; and it didn't mend matters as de new girl was a dam sight beautifuller nor what any o' dem was. Here was dis wagrant i' rags put above dem when all she was fit for at best was to be scullery girl. If anybody was to be under-cook, it stands to sense it sud 'ev been yan o' dem, as really knowed about things, not dis girl i' rags and tatters, picked up off'n de roads. But dey'd put her in her place, dey would. So dey goes on and on, like what women will, till Mossycoat comes down ready to start work. Den dey sets on her. "Who de devil did she think she was, setting hersel' above dem? She'd be under-cook, would she? No dam' fear dey relow of dat. What she'd 'ev to do, and all she was fit for, was to scour de pans, clean de knives, do de grates, and such-like; and all she'd git was dis." And down come de skimmer on top of her head, pop, pop, pop. "Dat's what you deserves," dey tell her, "and dat's what you can expect, my lady."

And dat's how it was wid Mossycoat. She was put to do all de dirtiest work, and soon she was up to de ears in grease, and her face as black as soot. And every now and agen, first one and then another o' de servants 'ld pop, pop, pop her a-top o' de head, wid de skimmer, till de poor girl's head was dat sore, she couldn't hardly bide it.

Well, it got on, and it got on, and still Mossycoat was at her pans, and knives, and grates; and still de sarvants was pop, pop, popping her on de head wid de skimmer. Now dere was a big dance coming on, as was to last three nights, wid hunting and other sports in de daytime. All de headmost people for miles round was to be dere; and de master, and mistress, and de young master,—dey'd niver had but one child—in course dey was a-going. It was all de talk among de sarvants, dis dance was. One was wishing she could be dere; another 'ld like to dance wid some'n de young lords; a third'ld like to see de ladies' dresses, and so dey went on, all excepting Mossycoat. If only dey'd de clo'es, dey'd be all right, dey thought, as dey considered deirselves as good as high-titled ladies any day. "And you, Mossycoat, you'd like to go, wouldn't you now?" dey says, and down comes de skimmer on her head, pop, pop, pop. Den dey laughs at her, which goes to show what a low class o' people dey was.

Now Mossycoat, as I've said afore, was wery handsome, and rags and dirt couldn't hide dat. De t'other sarvants might think as it did, but de young master'd hed his eyes on her, and de master and mistress, dey'd al'ays taken partic'lar notice of her, on account of her good looks. When the big dance was coming on dey thought as it'd be nice to ex her to go to it; so dey sent for her to see if she'd like to. "No thank you," she says, "I'd nivver think o' such a thing. I knows my place better an dat," she says. "Besides, I'd greasy all de one side'n de coach," she tells 'em, "and anybody's clo'es as I comed up agenst." Dey meks light on dat and presses her to go, de master and mistress does. It's wery kind on 'em, Mossycoat says, but she's not for going, she says. And she sticks to dat.

When she gets back into de kitchen, you may depend on it, de t'other sarvants wants to know why she'd bin sent for. Had she got notice, or what was it? So she telt 'em de master and mistress 'ed ext her would she like to go to the dance wid 'em. "What? You?" dey says. "It's unbeliev-able. If it hed been one o' we, now, dat'd be different. But you! Why, you'd nivver be relowed in, as you'd greasy all the gentlemen's clo'es, if dere was any as'ld dance wid a scullery-girl; and de ladies, dey'd be forced to howld dere noses w'en dey passed by you, to be sure dey would." No, dey couldn't believe, dey said, as de master and mistress had ivver ext *her* to go to de ball wid 'em. She must be lying, dey said, and down come de skimmer a-top of her head, pop, pop, pop.

Next night, de master and de mistress, and deir son, dis time, ext her to go to de dance. It was a grand affair de night before, dey said, and she sud er bin dere. It was going to be still grander to-night, dey said, and dey begged of her to come wid 'em, 'specially de young master. But no, she says, on account of her rags, and her grease, and dirt, she couldn't, and she wouldn't; and even de young master couldn't persuade her, though it warn't for de want o' trying. The t'other sarvants just didn't believe her, when she telt 'em about her being invited agen to de dance, and about de young master being wery pressing.

"Hark to her!" dey says. "What'll de upstart say next! And all dam lies," dey says. Den one'n 'em, wid a mouth like a pig-trough, and legs like a cart-horse, catches howld'n de skimmer, and down it comes, pop, pop, pop, on Mossycoat's head.

Dat night, Mossycoat decided as she'd go to de dance in right proper style, all on her own, and wi'out nobody knowing it. De first thing she does is to put all de t'other sarvants into a trance; she just touches each on 'em, unnoticed, as she moves about, and dey all falls asleep under a spell as soon as she does, and can't wake up again on deir own; de spell has to be broke by somebody wid de power, same as she has through her magic coat, or has got it some other way. Next Mossycoat has a real good wash; she'd niver bin reloved to afore, sin' she'd bin at de hall, as de t'other sarvants was retermined to mek and to keep her as greasy and dirty as dey could. Den she goes upstairs to her bedroom, throws off her working clo'es and shoes, and puts on her white satin dress wid de gowld sprigs, her silver slippers, and her gowld crown. In course, she had Mossycoat on underneath. So as soon as she was ready, she jus' wished hersel' at de dance, and dere she was, wery near as soon as de words was spoke. She did jus' feel hersel' rising up and flying through de elements, but only for a moment. Den she was in de ballroom.

De young master sees her standing der, and once he catched sight'n her he can't tek his eyes off her; he'd nivver sin anybody as han'some afore, or as beautifully dressed. "Who is she?" he exes his mother; but she doesn't know, she tells him.

"Can't you find out, mother?" he says, "can't you go and talk to her?" His mother sees as he'll nivver rest till she does, so she goes and inter-dooses hersel' to de young lady, and exes her who she is, where she comes from, and such as dat; but all she could git out'n her was as she come from a place where dey hit her on de head wid de skimmer. Den presently, de young master he goes over and interdooses hissel', but she doesn't tell him her name nor nothing; and when he exes her to hev a dance wid him, she says, no, she'd rather not. He stops aside of her though, and keeps exing her time and agen, and at de finish she says as she will, and links up wid him. Dey dances once, up and down de room; den she says she mus' go, dere and den. "Alright," he says—dere was nothing else he could say—"I'll come and see you off." But she jus' wished she was at home, and dere she was. No seeing her off for de young master, dere warn't; she jus' went from his side in de twinkle of an eye, leaving him standing dere gaping wid wonderment. Thinking she might be in de hall or de porch a-waiting of her carriage he goes to see, but dere's no sign on her anywheres inside or out, and nobody as he exted sin her go. He went back to de ballroom, but he can't think o' nothing or nobody but her, and all de time he's a-wanting to go home.

When Mossycoat gits back home, she meks sure as all de t'other sarvants is still in a trance. Den she goes up and changes into her working get-up, and after when she'd done dat, she comes down into de kitchen agen, and touches each'n de sarvants. Dat wakens 'em, as you might say: anyways, dey starts up, wondering whatever time o' day it is, and how long dey bin asleep.

Mossycoat tells 'em, and drops a hint as she may have to let de mistress know. Dey begs on her not to let on about 'em, and most'n 'em thinks to give her things if she won't. Owld things, dey was, but wid a bit o' wear in 'em still—a skirt, a pair o' shoes, stockings, stays, and what not. So Mossycoat promises as she won't tell on 'em. An' 'at night, dey don't hit her on de head wid de skimmer.

All nex' day de young master is unrestful. He can't settle his mind to nothing but de young lady as he'd fell in love wid last night at de wery first sight'n her. He was wondering all de time would she be dere agen to-night, and would she vanish de same as she done last night; and thinking how could he stop her, or catch up wid her if she was for doing dis a second time.

He must find out where she lives, he thinks, else how's he to go on after when de dance is over. He'd die, he tells his mother, if he can't git her for his wife; he's dat madly in love wid her. "Well," says his mother, "I thought as she was a nice modest girl; but she wouldn't say who or what she was, or where she came from, except it was a place where dey hit her on de head wid de skimmer."

"She's a bit of a myst'ry, I know," says de young master, "but dat don't signify as I want her any de less. I must hev her, mother," he says, "whoivver and whativver she is; and dat's de dear God's truth, mother, strike me dead if it ain't."

Women sarvants 'es long ears, and big mouths, and you may be sure as it wasn't long afore de young master, and dis wonderful han'some lady he'd fell in love wid, was all de talk in de kitchen.

"And fancy you, Mossycoat, thinking as he specially wanted *you* to go to de dance," dey says, and starts in on her proper, meking all manner o' nasty sarcastical remarks, and hitting her on de head wid de skimmer pop, pop, pop for lying to 'em (as dey said). It was de same agen later on, after when de master and mistress hed sent for her, and ext her once more to go to de dance wid 'em, and once more she'd defused. It was her last chance, dey said—dat was de sarvants—and a lot more besides, as ain't worth repeating. And down came de skimmer atop of her head, pop, pop, pop. Den she put de whole devil's breed 'n 'em into a trance like she done a night afore, and got hersel' ready to go to de dance, de only difference being as dis time she put her tother dress on, de one med o' silk de colour of all de birds o' de air.

She's in de ballroom now, Mossycoat is. De young master bin waiting and watching for her. As soon as he sees her, he exes his father to send for de fastest horse in his stable, and hev it kept standing ready saddled at de front door. Den he exes his mother to go over and talk to de young lady for a bit. She does dat, but can't larn no more about her, 'an she did the night afore.

Den de young master hears as his horse is ready at de door; so he goes over to de young lady, and exes her for a dance. She says jus' de same as de night afore, "No," at first, but "Yes," at the finish, and jus' as den, she says she mus' go after when dey've danced only once de length'n de room an' back.

But dis time, he keeps howld'n her till dey gits outside. Then she wishes hersel' at home, and is dere nearly as soon as she's spoken. De young master felt her rise into de air, but couldn't do nothing to stop her. But p'raps he did jus' touch her foot, as she dropped one slipper: I couldn't be sure as he did, it looks a bit like it, though. He picks de slipper up; but as for catching up wid her, it would be easier by far to catch up wid de wind on a blowy night. As soon as she gits home, Mossycoat changes back into her owld things; den she looses de tother sarvants from de spell she'd put on 'em. Dey've been asleep agen, dey thinks, and offers her one a shilling, another a half a crown, a third a week's wage, if she won't tell on 'em; and she promises as she won't.

De young master's in bed next day, a-dying for de love of de lady as lost one 'n her silver slippers de night afore. De doctors can't do him not de leastest good. So it was give out what his state was, and as it was only de lady able to wear de slipper as could save his life; and if she'd come forrad, he'd marry her. De slipper, as I said earlier on, was only but three inches long, or dereabouts. Ladies came from near and far, some wid big feet and some wid small, but none small enough to git it on, however much dey pinched and squeezed. Poorer people came as well, but it was jus' de same wid dem. And in course, all de sarvants tried, but dey was out'n altogither. De young master was a-dying. Was dere nobody else, his mother ext, nobody at all, rich or poor? "No," dey telt her, everybody tried, excepting it was Mossycoat.

"Tell her to come at once," says de mistress.

So dey fetched her.

"Try dis slipper on," she says—dat's de mistress.

Mossycoat slips her foot into it easy enough: it fits her exac'ly. De young master jumps out o' bed, and is jus' a-going to tek her in his arms. "Stop," she says, and runs off; but afore long, she's back agen in her satin dress wid gowld sprigs, her gowld crown, and both her silver slippers.

De young master is jus' a-going to tek her in his arms. "Stop," she says, and agen she runs off. Dis time she comes back in her silk dress de colour of all de birds o' de air. She don't stop him dis time, and as de saying used to be, he nearly eats her. After when dey's all settled down agen, and is talking quiet-like, dere's one or two things as de master and mistress and de young master'ld like to know. How did she git to de dance, and back agen, i' no time, they exed her. "Just wishing," she says; and she tells 'em all as I've telt you about the magic coat her mother 'ed med for her, and de powers as it give her if she cared to use 'em. "Yes, dat explained everything," dey says. Den dey bethinks deirselves of her saying as she came from where dey hit her on de head wid de skimmer. What did she mean by dat, dey wants to know. She meant just what she said, she telt 'em: it was al'ays coming down on her head, pop, pop, pop. Dey was right angry when dey heard dat, and de whole'n de kitchen sarvants was telt to go, and de dogs sent after 'em, to drive de varmints right away from de place.

As soon as dey could, Mossycoat an' de young master got married, and she'd a coach and six to ride in, ai, ten if she liked, for you may be sure as she'd everything as she fancied. Dey lived happy ever after, and had a basketful o' children. I was dere when the owld son come of age a-playing de fiddle. But dat was many years back, and I shouldn't wonder if de owld master and mistress isn't dead by now, though I've nivver heard tell as dey was.

Thompson, Notebooks, VII. Collected from Taimi Boswell, a gypsy, at Oswaldtwistle, Lancashire, 9 January 1915. Manuscript collection.
TYPE 510B. MOTIFS: D.1470.1 [*Magic wishing object*]; F.821.1.5 [*Dress of gold, silver, colour of sun, etc.*]; H.36.1 [*Slipper test*]; L.162 [*Lowly heroine marries prince*]; N.711.6 [*Prince sees heroine at ball, and is enamoured*]; R.221 [*Heroine's threefold flight from ball*].

In England this is well known as "The Story of Catskin"; see the rhymed version in J. O. Halliwell, *The Nursery Rhymes of England* (London, 1843), pp. 10–15. But there are important variations to note in the present text. In the first place, it is coloured by a travelling man's outlook. It is the technique of gypsies and tinkers to go to the front door and try to see the mistress of the house; they have a rooted distrust of servants and underlings. In many versions of the tale, it is the young master who ill-treats the heroine, and not the servants. The unnatural love of the father is left out of this tale, and Mossycoat is courted by a pedlar.

In many variants the magic powers are bestowed by the dead mother; Boswell's text is unusual in the mother being still alive, though she disappears out of the story as soon as the magic petticoat has been given. In one variant the heroine is dressed in a wooden gown which becomes covered with moss. Otherwise, "Mossycoat" is unique.

¶ Type 510B is practically world-wide in distribution. A Japanese variant was given in *Folktales of Japan*, and Baughman cites several American versions. See also "Cap o' Rushes" and "Catskin".

NICHT NOUGHT NOTHING

There once lived a king and a queen. They were long married, and had no bairns; but at last the queen had a bairn, when the king was away in far countries. The queen would not christen the bairn till the king came back, and she said: "We will just call him *Nicht Nought Nothing* until his father comes home."

But it was long before he came home, and the boy had grown a nice little laddie. At length the king was on his way back; but he had a big river to cross, and there was a spate, and he could not get over the water. But a giant came up to him and said, "If you will give me Nicht Nought Nothing, I will carry you over the water on my back." The king had never heard that his son was called Nicht Nought Nothing, and so he promised him. When the king got home again, he was very pleased to see his queen again, and his young son. She told him she had not given the child any name but Nicht Nought Nothing until he should come home himself. The poor king was in a terrible case. He said: "What have I done? I promised to give the giant who carried me over the river on his back Nicht Nought Nothing."

The king and the queen were sad and sorry, but they said: "When the giant comes, we will give him the hen-wife's bairn; he will never know the difference." The next day the giant came to claim the king's promise, and he sent for the hen-wife's bairn; and the giant went away with the bairn on his back.

He travelled till he came to a big stone, and there he sat down to rest. He said: "Hidge, Hodge, on my back, what time of day is it?" The poor little bairn said, "It is the time that my mother, the hen-wife, takes up the eggs for the queen's breakfast." The giant was very angry, and dashed the bairn on the stone and killed it. They tried the same with the gardener's son, but it did no better. Then the giant went back to the king's house, and said he would destroy them all if they did not give him Nicht Nought Nothing this time. They had to do it; and when they came to the big stone, the giant said, "What time o' day is it?" and Nicht

424

Nought Nothing said: "It is the time that my father, the King, will be sitting down to supper." The giant said: "I've got the right one now"; and took Nicht Nought Nothing to his own house, and brought him up till he was a man.

The giant had a bonny dochter, and she and the lad grew very fond of each other. The giant said one day to Nicht Nought Nothing, "I've work for you to-morrow. There is a stable seven miles long, and seven miles broad, and it has not been cleaned for seven years, and you must clean it to-morrow, or I'll have you for my supper." The giant's dochter went out next morning with the lad's breakfast, and found him in a terrible state, for aye as he cleaned out a bit, it aye fell in again. The giant's dochter said she would help him, and she cried a' the beasts o' the field, and a' the fowls o' the air, and in a minute they carried awa' everything that was in the stable, and made it a' clean before the giant came home. He said, "Shame for the wit that helped you; but I have a worse job for you to-morrow." Then he told Nicht Nought Nothing that there was a loch seven miles long, and seven miles deep, and seven miles broad, and he must drain it the next day, or else he would have him for his supper.

Nicht Nought Nothing began early next morning, and tried to lave the water with his pail, but the loch was never getting any less; and he did not ken what to do; but the giant's dochter called on all the fish in the sea to come and drink the water, and they soon drank it dry. When the giant saw the work done, he was in a rage, and said: "I've a worse job for you to-morrow; there's a tree, seven miles high, and no branch on it, till you get to the top, and there is a nest, and you must bring down the eggs without breaking one, or else I will have you for my supper." At first the giant's dochter did not know how to help Nicht Nought Nothing, but she cut off first her fingers, and then her toes, and made steps of them, and he clomb the tree, and got all the eggs safe, till he came to the bottom, and then one was broken. The giant's dochter advised him to run away, and she would follow him. So he travelled until he came to a king's palace, and the king and queen took him in, and were very kind to him. The giant's dochter left her father's house, and he pursued her, and was drowned. Then she came to the king's palace where Nicht Nought Nothing was. And she went up a tree to watch for him. The gardener's dochter, going down to draw water in the well, saw the shadow of the lady in the water, and thought it was herself, and said: "If I'm so bonny, if I'm so brave, do you send me to draw water?" The gardener's wife went, and said the same thing. Then the gardener went himself, and brought the lady from the tree, and had her in. And he told her that a stranger was to marry the king's dochter, and showed her the man, and it was Nicht Nought Nothing, asleep in a chair. And she saw him, and cried to him: "Waken, waken, and speak to me!" But he would not waken, and syne she cried:

"I cleared the stable, I laved the loch, and I clomb the tree,
And all for the love of thee,
And thou wilt not waken and speak to me."

The king and queen heard this, and came to the bonny young lady, and she said: "I canna get Nicht Nought Nothing to speak to me, for all that I can do."

Then were they greatly astonished, when she spoke of Nicht Nought Nothing, and asked where he was, and she said, "He sits there in the chair."

Then they ran to him and kissed him, and called him their own dear son, and he wakened, and told them all that the giant's dochter had done for him, and of all her kindness. Then they took her in their arms, and kissed her, and said she should be their dochter, for their son should marry her. And they lived happy all their days.

Andrew Lang, *Folk-Lore*, I, told by Miss Craig. From *Revue Celtique*, t. III.
TYPE 313.
¶ For motif numbers see "Daughter Greengown". See also "The Green Man of Knowledge", "The Leaves that Hung but never Grew", "The Black Dog of the Wild Forest".

THE NOONTIDE GHOST

'Tis a old ancient tale they do tell about farm [i.e. our farm]. There were a queer old chap kept a-hanging round village. Folk did see 'en to owl-light and night-time, some did zay he shined like a spunky—as you'd call a Jacky-my-lanthorn—but some volks'll tell 'ee anything. He come in noontime too, but all was afeard to speak to 'en for all his clothes was of a strange fashion.

Then one noon he come to view outside our varm door, and the granny couldn't abear his sorrow, she ups and speaks to 'en, as priest d'say she should. "In the name of the Lord, why troublest thou me?" she say, and a-called out, "Yew poor unhappy zoul, come tell I."

And the old grey ghost he zay, "Where be my mill then? And my son's cottage by the oak coppices? There be a gurt stone mill by river, and no cottage, and only one gurt aged old oak?" Then the granny she see the rights of it. "Be church still there?"

"They've a-got a new stone once since I went to market 'smorning, and I did promise Bet I 'oodn't stay late. Where be my dear old wife?"

The granny she see how 'twas, but she kept her peace and only say, "*WHO* did 'ee meet on the road?"

"A queer sort of chap, and we got to wagering games and old merriment, and he d'want me to stay longer, but I gain-sayed 'en, Bet 'ood be a-waiting. Where be my dear wife?"

And then, they d'say, there were a light, and a wind that smelled sweet as a primrose bank, and a voice like a throstle in song, said, "Come whoame now, my dear. Yew don't belong down there no more. Come on whoame." And the sad old ghost he give a bewtivul smile and he went clean away.

"Collected and sent to me by friends. This was taken down as the old man spoke, and sent on to me. He must have been a recognized teller of folk-tales, and possibly a singer too. The farm may have been near Porlock or Luccombe. The Exmoor forest demon would be from Dunkery where the Horner church-goers in 1902 would not go to Evensong in the winter at Luccombe, because he waited for them at Dunkery foot, by the ruined chapel, as a stag or a ram. The Reverend Mr Acland therefore held the service in the afternoon." Miss Acland, 10 December 1963

Ruth L. Tongue, told by a very old farmer in 1929, Horner, Luccombe, and Porlock area. TYPE 471 A. MOTIFS: F.377 [*Supernatural lapse of time in fairyland*]; F.379.1 [*Return from fairyland*]; F.401.1 [*Spirits dressed in antique clothes*]; E.545.19.1 [*The dead cannot speak unless spoken to*]; E.545.19.2 [*Proper way of addressing ghosts*]; E.754.2 [*Saved soul goes to heaven*].

See also "King Herla", "The Stonemason of the Charltons".

THE OLD HANDMILL [summary]

There were two brothers, one was rich and the other poor. The poor one used to go every now and then to his brother to get help from him. One day when he went, his brother gave him a ham. He was carrying it home when he met a little man, who advised him to go into the nearest house and offer it in exchange, but not to take anything but an old hand-mill behind the door.

So the poor brother did this. The people in the house were keen to get the ham, but they were not so ready to part with the old handmill. But they said to each other, "He'll not know how to use it, and we'll get it back." But the poor brother did know how to use it, for the little man had told him. He took it home, and he said to the mill: "Grind, mill, grind!"; and it ground out salt. Now salt was very scarce in those days and people came from far and wide to buy the salt, and captains came sailing over the sea to buy it, and many of them wanted to buy the mill, but the man would never sell it.

He was in a fine house now and his wife had a servant lassie, and one day when he was out a sea-captain came and tried to buy the handmill, and the servant lassie sold it. The captain took it on to his ship and set sail, and when he was out to sea he said: "Grind, mill, grind!" and the mill began to grind salt. But the captain did not know how to stop the mill, and it went on grinding and grinding till it sank the ship, and at the bottom of the sea it still goes on grinding.

So that's why the sea is salt.

School of Scottish Studies, H. Henderson, from Tom Wilson. Heard from his grandfather.

TYPE 565. MOTIFS: N.825.2 [*Old man helper*]; D.851 [*Magic object acquired by exchange*]; D.1601.21.1 [*Self-grinding salt-mill*]; A.1115.2 [*Why the sea is salt: magic salt-mill*].

¶ Grimm, no. 103. This tale is well distributed through the world, most European countries, China, Indonesia, etc.

A great number of manuscript examples are cited in *The Types of the Irish Folk-Tale*, and printed versions are cited in *Folk-Lore and Legends* (*Ireland*), and *Tales of Ireland*, McGallagher.

THE OLD SMITH [summary]

An old blacksmith lived on a hill with his wife and her mother. The only thing he knew how to make was ploughshares. One day a boy on horseback came into the smithy, and when the old man said he was not able to shoe his horse the youth asked his leave to do it himself. He cut off his horse's legs, threw them on the fire, and blew it hard with the bellows, then he hammered the legs on the anvil, took them out and put them back on the horse. He paid the smith a golden guinea and went away.

The smith thought he would try the same way to shoe his mother-in-law's old mare. But when he cut off her legs he did not know how to staunch the blood, and when he threw them on the fire they were soon burnt to cinders. So he threw the old mare's body away over the hedge.

Soon after, the youth appeared again, leading two old women. He asked the smith to make them young again, and when the smith confessed that he could not, borrowed his tools and, having bound the two women, he blew up a great fire, placed them upon it and blew up the fire as before. He took the two bodies from the fire, and hammered them hard on the anvil. When he set them down they had become young and beautiful. Again the boy paid the smith a golden guinea and went away.

The smith next tried to do the same for his wife and mother-in-law, who were always quarrelling and were a great distraction to him. But again he only succeeded in burning them both to ashes. In his despair he set out into the world, though it was the depth of winter, and he had not even a hat on his head. Presently the same boy caught up with him and offered to come with him. The old smith refused, saying that the boy was nothing to do with him. Nevertheless, the boy, walking barefoot, went with him, and told him that in a nearby castle the lord of it was lying sick. The smith said he could do nothing for him so the boy said, "Let us go there together, say that I am your servant."

When they reached the castle, and said that they had come to heal the great lord of it, the butler took them in and gave them plenty to eat and drink, and then took them up to the lord's bedchamber. The boy called for a knife, water, a pot and a spoon. He cut off the lord's head, and spat on his hands to staunch the blood. He boiled the head in the water, put it back in its place, and the lord was well. They were rewarded with a sack of gold, but when the boy asked for a pair of shoes as his share of the gold, the old smith said he had only enough for himself. So the little boy went away and left him.

Soon the smith was overtaken by two men who robbed him of his money, so he wandered on alone, and presently came to another castle. Here too, the lord of it was lying sick, and the old smith attempted to repeat the miracle done by the boy. But as before, he could not staunch the blood, and when he threw the head into the boiling water, it was almost boiled to rags. Someone knocked at the door, and the smith in terror said, "No one must come in here." "Not the barefoot boy?" was the reply. Then the smith opened the door, and the boy came straight up to the lord's body and staunched the blood. He stirred the pot with a golden spoon, and with great difficulty restored the head to its proper shape. He put it back on the lord's body, and the lord sat up, quite healed. He gave them two sacks of gold, and this time the smith was ready to give it all to the boy.

But the boy said, "I only want shoes." When he had his shoes they went on to a great lord's house, who had a wizard whom no one could beat. The lord said that anyone who could beat the wizard would be rewarded with three sacks of gold.

They were admitted to the house and given food; then they were shown an old house where was a huge pair of bellows. With it the wizard blew up half the sea. But the boy blew up a great fish that drank up all the sea-water. Next the wizard blew up from the fire a great rain of corn, and the boy blew up a cloud of birds that ate up all the corn. The wizard blew up a host of rabbits, and the boy blew up three greyhounds that ate up all the rabbits. So the wizard was defeated and they won the three sacks of gold. With the money the smith built a new smithy, some houses, a workshop and three inns.

One day while he was at work an old woman came and begged a night's lodging, in return for which she gave the smith three wishes. He wished first that the man who picked up his hammer should never be able to put it down again until he gave him leave; next that whoever sat in his chair, should not be able to get out of it until he set him free; and thirdly that whoever got into his pocket should not get out until he let him. The old woman then thanked him for his hospitality, and went away.

Not long afterwards the smith was getting short of money, and a man came to him and asked whether he was willing to sell himself. The smith agreed, in return for a sack of gold, and bargained for five years' freedom. At the end of the time the Evil One returned, and the smith handed him his hammer to finish a piece of work while he made ready to go with him. He went to an inn, and then to another to drink, but presently the Evil One came up to him, the hammer still in his hand. The smith pretended to think he had stolen it, but the Devil promised him another five years of life if he took the hammer off his hand. At the end of these years the devil appeared again, asked him pleasantly, as usual, how he was, and the smith invited him to sit down in his own chair while he was finishing a piece of work. Then again he went off to the inn to drink, and when the devil wished to follow him the chair was stuck to his back. The smith saw him come into the inn, and said, "What is that man doing with my chair?"

The devil again promised him an extra five years of life if he would release him from the chair. Again at the end of the time he arrived at the smithy, but this time the smith was already out at the inn drinking. He said to the devil, "I have called for ale. Turn yourself into a pound in my pocket, so that I can pay for it, and then I will come with you." The devil remained in the pocket all that day, and during the night, the smith heard him crying out under his head. He took the pocket to the smithy, and hammered it so hard on the anvil that the devil cried out for mercy, and promised to leave him alone for ever. So the smith let him go.

At last the smith died, and he went to the devil's door and knocked. The imp who came to the door told the devil that the smith was there. But the devil would not have him in for fear he should kill them all. He bade the imp light a wisp of straw, and light him up to heaven instead, and that is how the smith got into heaven.

Dora E. Yates, *Gypsy Folk-Tales*, p. 31.

TYPES 753 (variant); 330. MOTIFS: E.782.4 [*Horse's leg cut off and replaced*]; J.2411.2 [*Imitation of miraculous horse-shoeing unsuccessful*]; D.1886 [*Rejuvenation by burning*]; J.2401 [*Fatal imitation*]; E.12 [*Resuscitation by decapitation*]; J.2411.1 [*Imitation of magic rejuvenation*]; M.211 [*Man sells soul to devil*]; Q.115 [*Reward: any boon one asks*]; J.2071 [*Three foolish wishes*]; D.1413.6 [*Chair to which person sticks*]; D.2171 [*Magic adhesion*]; D.1413.1.9 [*Wallet from which one cannot escape*]; Q.565 [*Man admitted to neither heaven nor hell*]; K.2371.1 [*Heaven entered by a trick*].

This is a collection of what are practically three tales, connected by the hero being a smith and a dubious character.

¶ See also "The Tailor of Clitheroe", "Will the Smith", "The Blacksmith from Ireland".

OLD THOMPSON'S GHOST [summary]

On the 14th of July, 17—a burial had taken place in the churchyard of Kirby Malhamdale. Two people remained in the churchyard: the sexton, who was a boy of the village named Kitchen, and an old soldier, who was sitting on a nearby stone. Kitchen took in his hands a skull, and the soldier, watching him, told him it was that of a military man named Thompson who had died soon after the time of Queen Mary. He had done much harm to the place in his lifetime, and it was rumoured that he still revisited the scene of his childhood from time to time, and played some of his old tricks. Hearing this, the boy kicked the skull and it rolled away. "You dare not do that again," said the soldier. "Why not?" and the boy kicked the skull again. "Now," said the soldier, "take the skull in your hands, and say, 'Let the owner of this meet me at midnight, and invite me to a banquet, spread on yon green stone by his bony fingers.'" He added:

> "Come ghost, come devil,
> Come good, come evil,
> Or let old Thompson himself appear,
> For I will partake of his midnight cheer."

The boy laughed, and repeated the words. He went home, and that night went to bed at his usual hour of ten o'clock without having told anyone of his encounter. He was roused by a rattling at his door-latch, and a voice singing beneath his window. Looking out, he was amazed to see the old soldier standing below. But the soldier called on him to fulfil his engagement, and so strange and compelling a light was in his eyes that the boy, though now thoroughly afraid, promised to come down. He watched till the man had disappeared in the mist of the night, and then made his way to the vicar's house. He knocked loudly at the door, and the vicar, who was sitting up late in meditation, opened it. Seeing the boy's terror, and having made out something of his incoherent story, he promised to go with him to the graveyard. They arrived exactly as midnight was striking, but at first there was nothing unusual to be seen. But suddenly the boy pointed to the eastern end of the church, and the vicar now distinguished a tall shadowy figure gliding between the tombstones. It stopped before them, and the man now recognized the form described to him by the boy. "One, two," it said. "How is this? I have one more guest than I invited; but it matters not. All is ready. Follow me." It beckoned, and led them round under the east window of the church where, on an old green stone near to Thompson's grave, a banquet was indeed spread out. Gazing at the smoking meats, young Kitchen asked himself at what fire they had been cooked! The seats

431

set around were coffins, and their host sat down on one at the head of the strange table, and motioned to them to sit also. The vicar rose to ask a blessing, but the stranger interrupted him.

"The blessed faith of my forefathers was mine," he said. "I cannot listen to a Protestant grace." As he ceased, they heard from within the church the strains of a *De Profundis*, and could see a flame playing over the monuments of the Lamberts, and moving lights playing over the various hatchments. "A *De Profundis* is the most proper grace to be sung at the banquets of the dead," pronounced the host, and they sat down. Just then the vicar chanced to remark, "Why, where's the salt?" Immediately their host vanished, and of the rich banquet nothing remained but the mossy stone on which it had been spread.

[Tradition says that the word "salt" reminded the spirit of the Red Sea, which all ghosts dread, and for fear of being driven there, it had thought best to disappear before more could be said.]

Hone, *Table Book*, p. 516.
TYPE 470 (variant). MOTIFS: E.235.5 [*Return from dead to punish kicking of skull*]; E.238 [*Dinner with the dead; dead man invited to dinner*]; G.303.16.14.1 [*Priest chases devil away*]; G.272.16 [*Salt protects against witches*].

This *Don Juan* fragment is unusual in England. It is doubtful whether the Old Soldier is the devil or Old Thompson. He is reminiscent of The Old Soldier in Hans Andersen's "Red Shoes". In tales of the witches' sabbats the mere mention of salt was enough to cause all to disappear.

THE OLD WITCH

Once upon a time there were two girls who lived with their mother and father. Their father had no work, and the girls wanted to go away and seek their fortunes. Now one girl wanted to go to service, and her mother said she might if she could find a place. So she started for the town. Well, she went all about the town, but no one wanted a girl like her. So she went on farther into the country, and she came to a place where there was an oven where there was lots of bread baking. And the bread said, "Little girl, little girl, take us out, take us out. We have been baking seven years, and no one has come to take us out." So the girl took out the bread, laid it on the ground, and went on her way. Then she met a cow, and the cow said, "Little girl, little girl, milk me, milk me! Seven years have I been waiting, and no one has come to milk me." The girl milked the cow into the pails that stood by. As she was thirsty she drank some, and left the rest in the pails by the cow. Then she went on a little bit farther, and came to an apple-tree so loaded with fruit that its branches were breaking down, and the tree said, "Little girl, little girl, help me shake my fruit. My branches are breaking, it is so heavy." And the girl said, "Of course I will, you poor tree." So she shook the fruit all off, propped up the branches, and left the fruit on the ground under the tree. Then she went on again till she came to a house.

Now in this house there lived a witch, and this witch took girls into her house as servants. And when she heard that this girl had left her home to seek service, she said that she would try her, and give her good wages.

The witch told the girl what work she was to do. "You must keep the house clean and tidy, sweep the floor and the fireplace; but there is one thing you must never do. You must never look up the chimney, or something bad will befall you."

So the girl promised to do as she was told, but one morning as she was cleaning, and the witch was out, she forgot what the witch said, and looked up the chimney. When she did this a great bag of money fell down in her lap. This happened again and again. So the girl started to go off home.

When she had gone some way, she heard the witch coming after her. So she ran to the apple-tree and cried:

> "Apple-tree, apple-tree, hide me,
> So the old witch can't find me;
> If she does she'll pick my bones,
> And bury me under the marble stones."

So the apple-tree hid her. When the witch came up she said:

> "Tree of mine, tree of mine,
> Have you seen a girl
> With a willy-willy wag, and a long-tailed bag,
> Who's stole my money, all I had?"

And the apple-tree said, "No, mother, not for seven year."

When the witch had gone down another way, the girl went on again, and just as she got to the cow she heard the witch coming after her again, so she ran to the cow and cried:

> "Cow, cow, hide me,
> So the old witch can't find me;
> If she does she'll pick my bones,
> And bury me under the marble stones."

So the cow hid her.

When the old witch came up, she looked about and said to the cow:

> "Cow of mine, cow of mine,
> Have you seen a girl
> With a willy-willy wag, and a long-tailed bag,
> Who's stole my money, all I had?"

And the cow said, "No, mother, not for seven year."

When the witch had gone off another way, the little girl went on again, and when she was near the oven she heard the witch coming after her again, so she ran to the oven and cried:

> "Oven, oven, hide me,
> So the old witch can't find me;
> If she does she'll break my bones,
> And bury me under the marble stones."

And the oven said, "I've no room, ask the baker." And the baker hid her behind the oven.

When the witch came up, she looked here and there and everywhere, and then said to the baker:

> "Man of mine, man of mine,
> Have you seen a girl
> With a willy-willy wag, and a long-tailed bag,
> Who's stole my money, all I had?"

So the baker said, "Look in the oven." The old witch went to look, and the oven said, "Get in and look in the furthest corner." The witch did so, and when she was inside the oven shut her door, and the witch was kept there for a very long time.

The girl then went off and reached her home with her money-bags, married a rich man, and lived happy ever afterwards.

The other sister then thought she would go and do the same. And she went the same way. But when she reached the oven, and the bread said, "Little girl, little girl, take us out. Seven years have we been baking, and no one has come to take us out," the girl said, "No, I don't want to burn my fingers." So she went on till she met the cow, and the cow said, "Little girl, little girl, milk me, milk me, do. Seven years have I been waiting, and no one has come to milk me." But the girl said, "No, I can't milk you, I'm in a hurry," and went on faster. Then she came to the apple-tree, and the apple-tree asked her to help shake the fruit. But the girl said, "No, I can't; another day p'raps I may," and went on till she came to the witch's house.

Well, it happened to her just the same as to the other girl—she forgot what she was told, and one day when the witch was out, looked up the chimney, and down fell a bag of money. Well, she thought she would be off at once.

When she reached the apple-tree, she heard the witch coming after her, and she cried:

> "Apple-tree, apple-tree, hide me,
> So the old witch can't find me.

If she does she'll break my bones,
And bury me under the marble stones."

But the tree didn't answer, and she ran on further.
Presently the witch came up and said:

"Tree of mine, tree of mine,
Have you seen a girl
With a willy-willy wag, and a long-tailed bag,
Who's stole my money, all I had?"

The tree said, "Yes, mother, she's gone down that way."
So the old witch went after her and caught her, she took all the money
away from her, beat her, and sent her off home just as she was.

Jacobs, *More English Fairy Tales*, p. 94.
TYPE 480. MOTIFS: Q.2 [*Kind and unkind*]; D.1658.2.1 [*Grateful stove*]; B.394
[*Cow grateful for being milked*]; D.1658.1.5 [*Apple tree grateful for being shaken*];
G.204 [*Girl in service of witch*]; C.337 [*Tabu: looking up chimney*]; D.1658.3.4
[*Grateful objects help fugitive*]; G.276 [*Escape from witch*].

In an Irish version of this tale, given in MacManus's *Donegal Fairy Stories*, the long
black bag full of money has been stolen by the witch from the girl's mother.

The standard version of 480 is the Mother Holle story, where the good, willing girl
is magically rewarded, and the bad girl punished. This motif is to be found in "The
Princess of Colchester", but without the motif of service in the witch's house.
¶ See also "The Green Lady", "The Glass Ball", "The Man with a Long Nose".

THE OLD WOMAN AND THE FAIRY

There was once an old woman who lived in the ruins of a castle that stood
in the midst of a great forest. This old woman used to kidnap girls to
help her in many ways, and she taught them witchcraft. These girls
feared the old woman, but one of them—who was very conceited and
vain—said to the other girls that she could do anything that the old woman
might set her to do, no matter how hard it was. So the other girls told the
old woman what the vain girl had said.

"Oh, we'll see about that," said the old woman. So she called the vain
girl to her and said, "You must make twenty-one shirts to-day, and be
clammed if you can't finish them." Then the old woman went out.

The girl knew that she could not make so many shirts in one day,
so she sat crying in the house. But she had not been crying long before
she heard a noise in the room, and turning round, she saw a sweet-faced
lady, who said, "Why dost thou cry?"

"Because I have to make twenty-one shirts to-day," said the girl, "and
I know I can't get them done, and I shall be clammed if I can't."

"We will have them done," said the sweet-faced lady, "before the day is over." So she helped the girl, and the shirts were done before the old woman came back.

So the other girls told the old woman what the vain girl had done.

"No matter," said the old woman. "I'll set her a job to do that I know she can't get done." So she called the vain girl to her again, and said, "You must dress five feather-beds to-day,* and be clammed if you can't get them done."

As the girl sat crying the sweet-faced lady appeared to her again, and said, "Don't cry. I am a fairy, and will always be near thee." So the beds were dressed that day by the kind lady's help.

After this the old woman gave the girl harder and harder tasks every day, but she never failed to get them done. Then the old woman, and the other girls, asked her how she managed to get so much work done, but the sweet-faced lady told her not to make it known, because she was going to help her to get away from the castle to her own home. So the girl would not tell, and in the course of time the kind lady helped her to escape to her own home, where she was received as one from the dead.

S. O. Addy, *Household Tales*, p. 46. North Derbyshire.

TYPE 501 (variant). MOTIFS: G.204 [*Girl in service of witch*]; H.935 [*Witch assigns tasks*]; N.815 [*Fairy as a helper*]; H.973.1 [*Task performed by fairy*].

This is no more than a summary of a tale. "The Broken Pitcher" is in something of the same vein.

THE OLD WOMAN WHO LIVED IN A VINEGAR BOTTLE

Once upon a time there was an old woman who lived in a vinegar bottle. One day a fairy was passing that way, and she heard the old woman talking to herself.

"It is a shame, it is a shame, it is a shame," said the old woman. "I didn't ought to live in a vinegar bottle. I ought to live in a nice little cottage with a thatched roof, and roses growing all up the wall, that I ought."

So the fairy said, "Very well, when you go to bed to-night you turn round three times, and shut your eyes, and in the morning you'll see what you will see."

So the old woman went to bed, and turned round three times and shut her eyes, and in the morning there she was, in a pretty little cottage with a thatched roof, and roses growing up the walls. And she was very surprised, and very pleased, but she quite forgot to thank the fairy.

* The process consists in taking the feathers out of the beds, putting them into a sieve, and cleaning them with the fingers.

And the fairy went north, and she went south, and she went east, and she went west, all about the business she had to do. And presently she thought, "I'll go and see how that old woman is getting on. She must be very happy in her little cottage."

And as she got up to the front door, she heard the old woman talking to herself.

"It is a shame, it is a shame, it is a shame," said the old woman. "I didn't ought to live in a little cottage like this, all by myself. I ought to live in a nice little house in a row of houses, with lace curtains at the windows, and a brass knocker on the door, and people calling mussels and cockles outside, all merry and cheerful."

The fairy was rather surprised; but she said: "Very well. You go to bed to-night, and turn round three times, and shut your eyes, and in the morning you shall see what you shall see."

So the old woman went to bed, and turned round three times and shut her eyes, and in the morning there she was in a nice little house, in a row of little houses, with lace curtains at the windows, and a brass knocker on the door, and people calling mussels and cockles outside, all merry and cheerful. And she was very much surprised, and very much pleased. But she quite forgot to thank the fairy.

And the fairy went north, and she went south, and she went east, and she went west, all about the business she had to do; and after a time she thought to herself, "I'll go and see how that old woman is getting on. Surely she must be happy now."

And when she got to the little row of houses, she heard the old woman talking to herself. "It is a shame, it is a shame, it is a shame," said the old woman. "I didn't ought to live in a row of houses like this, with common people on each side of me. I ought to live in a great mansion in the country, with a big garden all round it, and servants to answer the bell."

And the fairy was very surprised, and rather annoyed, but she said: "Very well, go to bed and turn round three times and shut your eyes, and in the morning you will see what you will see."

And the old woman went to bed, and turned round three times, and shut her eyes, and in the morning there she was, in a great mansion in the country, surrounded by a fine garden, and servants to answer the bell. And she was very pleased and very surprised, and she learned how to speak genteelly, but she quite forgot to thank the fairy.

And the fairy went north, and she went south, and she went east, and she went west, all about the business she had to do; and after a time she thought to herself, "I'll go and see how that old woman is getting on. Surely she must be happy now."

But no sooner had she got near the old woman's drawing-room window than she heard the old woman talking to herself in a genteel voice.

"It certainly is a very great shame," said the old woman, "that I should be living alone here, where there is no society. I ought to be a duchess, driving in my own coach to wait on the Queen, with footmen running beside me."

The fairy was very much surprised, and very much disappointed, but she said: "Very well. Go to bed to-night, and turn round three times and shut your eyes; and in the morning you shall see what you shall see."

So the old woman went to bed, and turned round three times, and shut her eyes; and in the morning, there she was, a duchess with a coach of her own, to wait on the Queen, and footmen running beside her. And she was very much surprised, and very much pleased. BUT she quite forgot to thank the fairy.

And the fairy went north, and she went south, and she went east, and she went west, all about the business she had to do; and after a while she thought to herself: "I'd better go and see how that old woman is getting on. Surely she is happy, now she's a duchess."

But no sooner had she come to the window of the old woman's great town mansion, than she heard her saying in a more genteel tone than ever: "It is indeed a very great shame that I should be a mere Duchess, and have to curtsey to the Queen. Why can't I be a queen myself, and sit on a golden throne, with a golden crown on my head, and courtiers all around me."

The fairy was very much disappointed and very angry; but she said: "Very well. Go to bed and turn round three times, and shut your eyes, and in the morning you shall see what you shall see."

So the old woman went to bed, and turned round three times, and shut her eyes; and in the morning there she was in a royal palace, a queen in her own right, sitting on a golden throne, with a golden crown on her head, and her courtiers all around her. And she was highly delighted, and ordered them right and left. BUT she quite forgot to thank the fairy.

And the fairy went north, and she went south, and she went east, and she went west, all about the business she had to do; and after a while she thought to herself: "I'll go and see how that old woman is getting on. Surely she must be satisfied now!"

But as soon as she got near the Throne Room, she heard the old woman talking.

"It is a great shame, a very great shame," she said, "that I should be Queen of a paltry little country like this instead of ruling the whole round world. What I am really fitted for is to be *Pope*, to govern the minds of everyone on Earth."

"Very well," said the fairy. "Go to bed. Turn round three times, and shut your eyes, and in the morning you shall see what you shall see."

So the old woman went to bed, full of proud thoughts. She turned round three times and shut her eyes. And in the morning she was back in her vinegar bottle.

Camp-fire story, 1924.
TYPE 555 (variant). MOTIFS: C.773.1 [*Tabu: making unreasonable requests*]; D.1761. [*Magic results produced by wishing*]; L.420 [*Overweening ambition punished*]. ¶ The motif of the spared fish and the greedy wife is absent. A lively version of "The Fisherman and his Wife" was heard in Oxfordshire in 1965, but the source could not be traced, and it seems likely that it was derived directly from Grimm, no. 19. The story has a wide distribution. Forty-one Irish versions are given in *Béaloideas*, XIV, pp. 273 ff.

ONE TREE HILL

There were once three tall trees on a hill and on moonlight nights singing could be heard and three green ladies danced there. No one dared go near except the farmer and he only climbed the hill once a year on Midsummer Eve to lay a posy of late primroses on the root of each tree. The leaves rustled and the sun shone out, and he made quite sure he was safe indoors before sunset. It was a rich farm and he often said to his three sons, "My father always said our luck lies up there; when I'm dead don't forget to do as I did, and my father before me, and all our forbears through the years."

And they listened, but did not take much heed, except the youngest.

When the old man died the big farm was divided into three. The eldest brother took a huge slice, and the next brother he took another, and that left the youngest with a strip of poor rough ground at the foot of the hill; but he didn't say much but set to work about it and sang as he worked and was indoors before sunset.

One day his brothers came to see him. Their big farms were not doing very well and when they saw his rich little barley fields and the few loaded fruit trees, and his roots and herbs growing so green and smelling so sweet, and his three cows giving rich milk, they were angry and jealous.

"Who helps you in your work?" they asked. "They say down in the village there's singing and dancing at night. A hard-working farmer should be abed."

But the youngest never answered.

"Did we see you up the hill by the trees as we came? What were you about?"

"I was doing as Father told us years ago. 'Tis Midsummer Eve," he said quietly enough then. But they were too angry to even laugh at him.

"The hill is mine," cried the eldest. "Don't let me see you up there again. As for the trees, I need timber for my new great barn, so I'm cutting one down. And you two can help me." But the second brother found he had to go to market, and youngest never answered. The next day, Midsummer Day too, the eldest came with carts and men and axes, and called to his youngest brother, who was busy in the herb garden, but he only said, "Remember what day it is." But the eldest and his team went on up the hill to the three trees. When he laid his axe to the first tree it screamed like a woman, the horses ran away and the men after them but the eldest went on hacking. The wind howled and the two other trees lashed their branches in anger. Then the murdered tree fell down, down on top of him and killed him. Bye and bye his servants came and took the dead man and the dead tree away and then there were only two Green Ladies on moonlit nights.

The second brother came back from market and took both the farms for himself, and the youngest he still worked his little strip of land and took primroses up the hill on Midsummer Eve. But the big farms didn't prosper at all and one Midsummer Eve the second brother saw the youngest brother up by the two trees. He was afraid to go up there, so he yelled, "Come off my land and take your cows away breaking my hedges down. I'll build a stout timber fence round my hill and I'll cut down one of the trees to make it with." That night there was no dancing together, there was no music but the crying of many leaves, and the youngest brother was very sad. The next morning the second brother came with an axe and the two trees shuddered but he only made sure there was no wind to drop the tree his way. The tree screamed like a woman as it fell and the youngest brother watching from the lane below with his cows saw the last tree lift a great branch and bring it down on his brother's head and kill him.

People came and took the second dead tree and man away, and the youngest brother now had all three farms, but he still lived in his little farm near the hill and the lonely Green Lady. And sometimes she would dance alone to a sad little tune on moonlit nights, and he always left a bunch of late primroses at the roots of the one tree every Midsummer Eve and his farms prospered from that day.

There are many people nowadays who won't climb One Tree Hill, especially on Midsummer Eve, and one or two very old people remember being told when they were little children that it must never be fenced because it belonged to a Green Lady.

The hill and the tree are standing there alone.

It is a sad and dangerous place.

[*Collector's Note.* Told on a charabanc tour on a run to Grindleford and the Sheffield moors, by a Derbyshire couple, in 1935. The interest in this is the tree worship still retained, the fairy mound, and the incorporation of the Three Brothers motif. Primroses are magic plants, especially in late May and June.]

Ruth L. Tongue, from Baslow, Derbyshire.
MOTIFS: F.440.1 [*Green vegetation spirit*]; V.11.1 [*Sacrifice (gift) to tree*]; F.441.6.1
[*Wood-spirits responsible for sickness and failure*]; C.518 [*Cutting down tree tabu*];
L.13 [*Compassionate youngest son*]; C.43.2 [*Tabu: cutting certain trees, lest tree-spirits
be offended*]; L.0 [*Victorious youngest child*].

ORANGE AND LEMON

There were once a mother and a father who had two daughters, Orange
and Lemon. The mother liked Lemon best, and the father Orange. The
mother used to make Orange do all the dirty work, as soon as the father
had turned his back. One day, she sent her to fetch milk, and said,
"If you break the pitcher, I'll kill you." As Orange returned, she fell
down and broke the pitcher, and so when she came home, she hid herself
in the passage. When the mother came out, she saw the broken pitcher,
and the girl, and took her into the house, when the girl cried:
  "Oh, mother! Oh, mother! don't kill me!"
  The mother said, "Close the shutters in."
  "Oh, mother! Oh, mother! don't kill me!"
  "Light the candle."
  "Oh, mother! Oh, mother! don't kill me!"
  "Put the pan on."
  "Oh, mother! Oh, mother! don't kill me!"
  "Fetch the block we chop the wood on."
  "Oh, mother! Oh, mother! don't kill me!"
  "Bring the axe."
  "Oh, mother! Oh, mother! don't kill me!"
  "Put your head on the block."
  "Oh, mother! Oh, mother! don't kill me!"
But the mother chopped off her head, and cooked it for dinner. When
the father came home, he asked what there was for dinner.
  "Sheep's head," replied the mother.
  "Where's Orange?"
  "Not come from school yet."
  "I don't believe you," said the father. Then he went upstairs and found
fingers in a box, whereupon he was so overcome that he fainted. Orange's
spirit flew away to a jeweller's shop and said:

> "My mother chopped my head off,
> My father picked my bones,
> My little sister buried me,
> Beneath the cold marble stones."

They said: "If you say that again we will give you a gold watch." So she said it again, and they gave her a gold watch. Then she went off to a bootshop, and said:

> "My mother chopped my head off,
> My father picked my bones,
> My little sister buried me,
> Beneath the cold marble stones."

And they said: "If you say it again, we will give you a pair of boots." So she said it again, and they gave her a pair of boots. Then she went to the stonemason's and said:

> "My mother chopped my head off,
> My father picked my bones,
> My little sister buried me,
> Beneath the cold marble stones."

And they said, "If you say it again, we will give you a piece of marble as big as your head." So she said it again, and they gave her a piece of marble as big as her head.

She took the things, and flew home, and sat at the top of the chimney, and shouted down:

> "Father, father, come to me,
> And I will show thee what I've got for thee!"

So he came, and she gave him a gold watch.
Then she shouted down:

> "Sister! sister! come to me,
> And I will show thee what I've got for thee."

So she came, and she gave her a pair of boots.
Then she shouted down:

> "Mother! Mother! come to me,
> And I will show thee what I've got for thee."

The mother, who thought the others had got such nice things, put her head right up the chimney, when the big block of marble came down and killed her. Then Orange came down and lived with her father and Lemon happily ever after.

Norton Collection I, p. 196. *Folk-Tales of the Magyars*, pp. 418–20, notes, W. H. Jones.

TYPE 720. MOTIFS: see "The Little Bird".

This tale approximates closely to the main type, "The Juniper Tree" (Grimm, no. 47). It is one of the commonest of the surviving Märchen in England, and is widespread everywhere.

¶ See "Rosy", "The Rose-Tree", "The Satin Frock".

THE OWL WAS A BAKER'S DAUGHTER
[summary]

A fairy once went into a baker's shop, disguised as a poor, ragged old woman, and begged for a piece of dough. The baker's daughter gave her a tiny piece, and the old woman begged that she might be allowed to put it into the oven with the bread.

But when she took the bread out, the girl saw that the dough had swelled into the biggest loaf in the oven. So she would not give that to the old woman. At last, however, she gave her another piece, about half the size of the first, to go in with the second batch. But that swelled up even larger than the first one, and so the old woman couldn't have that either. But she begged for the very tiniest piece, and the girl gave her a bit hardly bigger than your thumb, and shoved it in with the third batch. And it came out bigger than the others. The stupid, greedy girl was frightened at last, and turned great round eyes on the old woman, who had thrown down her cloak, and was standing there tall and shining, "Why, who, who..." she stammered. "*Whoo—whoo* is all you shall ever say again," said the fairy. "The world has borne too long with your selfish, greedy ways." She struck her with her staff, and the girl turned to an owl, and flew hooting out into the night. "Lord, we know what we are, but know not what we may be."

Halliwell, O. *Nursery Rhymes*, p. 256, quoting from *The Gentleman's Magazine*, LXXIV, p. 1003. In this variant the visitor is a fairy, not Our Lord. This version comes from Herefordshire.
TYPE 751. MOTIFS: F.237 [*Fairies in disguise*]; F.393 [*Fairy visits among mortals*]; D.1652.1.2 [*Halved cake grows miraculously larger*]; Q.1.1 [*Inhospitality punished*].
¶ See also "The Greedy Peasant Woman", A.1.

THE PADDO

A poor widow was one day baking bannocks, and sent her dochter wi' a dish to the well to bring water. The dochter gaed, and better gaed, till she came to the well, but it was dry. Now, what to do she didna ken, for she couldna gang back to her mother without water; sae she sat down by the side o' the well and fell a-greeting. A Paddo then came loup-loup-louping out o' the well, and asked the lassie what she was greeting for; and she said she was greeting because there was nae water in the well. "But," says the Paddo, "an ye'll be my wife, I'll gie ye plenty o' water." And the lassie, no thinking that the poor beast could mean anything serious, said she wad be his wife, for the sake o' getting the water. So she got the water into her dish, and gaed away hame to her mother, and thought nae mair about the Paddo, till that night, when, just as she and her mother were about to go to their beds, something came to the door, and when they listened, they heard this sang:

> "O open the door, my hinnie, my heart,
> O open the door, my ain true love;
> Remember the promise that you and I made,
> Down i' the meadow where we twa met."

Says the mother to the dochter: "What noise is that at the door?" "Hout," says the dochter, "it's naething but a filthy Paddo." "Open the door", says the mother, "to the poor Paddo." So the lassie opened the door, and the Paddo came loup-loup-louping in and sat down by the ingle-side. Then he sings:

> "O gie me my supper, my hinnie, my heart,
> O gie me my supper, my ain true love;
> Remember the promise that you and I made,
> Down i' the meadow where we twa met."

"Hout," quo' the dochter. "Wad I gie a filthy Paddo his supper?" "O ay," said the mother, "e'en gie the poor Paddo his supper." So the Paddo got his supper; and after that he sings again:

> "O put me to bed, my hinnie, my heart,
> O put me to bed, my ain true love;
> Remember the promise that you and I made,
> Down i' the meadow where we twa met."

"Hout," quo' the dochter. "Wad I put a filthy Paddo to bed?" "O ay," says the mother, "put the poor Paddo to bed." And so she put the Paddo to his bed. (Here let us abridge a little.) Then the Paddo sang again:

> "Now fetch me an axe, my hinnie, my heart,
> Now fetch me an axe, my ain true love;
> Remember the promise that you and I made,
> Down i' the meadow where we twa met."

The lassie wasna lang o' fetching the axe; and then the Paddo sang:

> "Now chap aff my head, my hinnie, my heart,
> Now chap aff my head, my ain true love;
> Remember the promise that you and I made,
> Down i' the meadow where we twa met."

Well, the lassie chappit aff his head; and no sooner was that done, than he started up the bonniest young prince that ever was seen. And the twa lived happy a' the rest o' their days.

[The above is from the memory of Charles K. Sharpe, Esq., who heard it from his nurse, Jenny, at his father's house of Hoddam in Dumfrieshire, about the year 1784.]

R. Chambers, *Popular Rhymes of Scotland* (1870), p. 87.

TYPE 440. MOTIFS: B.211.7.1 [*Speaking frog*]; S.215.1 [*Girl promises herself to animal suitor*]; D.195 [*Transformation: man to frog*]; D.711 [*Disenchantment of animal by decapitation*]; L.162 [*Lowly heroine marries prince*].

The motif of drawing water in a sieve has been altered to drawing water from a dry well.

¶ See also "The Frog", "The Frog Prince", "The Girl who fetched Water in a Riddle", "The Well of the World's End".

For a naturalized version of this tale, with a man disguised as a frog, see "The Frog Lover", A. III.

RHYMES FROM "THE MAIDEN AND THE FROG"

"Stop with fog*
And daub with clay;
And that will carry
The water away."

"Open the door, my hinny, my heart,
Open the door, my own darling;
Remember the words you spoke to me,
In the meadow by the well-spring."

"Go wi' me to bed, my hinny, my heart,
Go wi' me to bed, my own darling;
Remember the words you spoke to me,
In the meadow by the well-spring."

(This rhyme is said twice.)

"Chop off my head, my hinny, my heart,
Chop off my head, my own darling;
Remember the words you spoke to me,
In the meadow by the well-spring."

* moss

TYPE 1180, Halliwell, *Nursery Rhymes and Tales*, p. 163.

PEERIFOOL [shortened version]

There was once a widowed Queen in Rousay, who was living in a small house with a kail-yard and a cow, and they found all their cabbages were being taken.

The eldest daughter said to the Queen she would put a blanket round her, and watch all night in the kail-yard. So after night fell, a very big giant came into the yard, and he began to cut the cabbages and put them into a creel.

The Princess said what was he doing with her mother's kail, and he said if she was not quiet, he would take her too. But she would not be quiet, so he flung her into the creel, and carried her away with the creel. When he got home he told her the work she had to do; she had to milk the cow, and take her up to the hills called Bloodfield, then she had to take wool, and wash, and tease, and comb, and card and spin it, and make it into cloth. When the giant had gone, she milked the cow, and drove her into the high hills, then she made a bowl of porridge for herself. As she was supping it, a crowd of peerie [little] yellow-headed folk came running in, asking for some.

She said:

> "Little for one, and less for two,
> And never a grain have I for you."

So they went away, and she set to on her wool, but she could do nothing with it. At night the giant came back, and he was very angry, and took a strip of skin off her, from the crown of her head to the sole of her foot, and threw her up over the rafters, among the hens, where she could neither move nor speak. And the same thing happened to the second daughter.

The third night the youngest Princess sat down to watch, and the giant carried her off as he had done her sisters, and set her the same tasks. She drove the cow up to the high hills, and she made herself a bowl of porridge, but when the peerie folk came in, she told them to get something to sup with.

Some got heather cows, and some got broken dishes, but they all got a share of her porridge. When they had gone, a peerie yellow-headed boy came in, and asked if she had any work for him. He could do anything with wool. She said she had plenty of work, but nothing to pay him with, but he said he would do it for nothing if she would tell him his name. So she got him the wool and he went out. When it was getting dark, an old woman came to the door and asked her for lodging. She dared not grant it, so the old woman went out to the high knowe, and lay under it for shelter. But it was hot, and she climbed up to the top for air. There was a crack at the top, and light coming out, and the old woman heard a voice saying: "Tease, teasers, tease; card, carders, card; spin, spinners, spin; for Peerie Fool, Peerie Fool, is my name." She looked in, and there she saw the peerie folk working and the peerie boy running round them. The old woman thought she had news worth a lodging, and went back to tell the Princess. When the peerie boy came back with the cloth, the Princess guessed one name, and then another, and at last she said: "Peerifool is your name." He threw down the wool, and ran off very angry. As the giant was coming home that night, he met a great number of peerie folk, with their tongues hanging out of their mouths, and their eyes hanging out in their cheeks. He asked them what was the matter, and they said it was pulling out the wool so fine. The giant said he had a bonnie goodwife at home, and if she had done her work this time, he would never make her work so again. When he came home, she had a great store of cloth, and he was very pleased with her. Next day when the giant went out, the Princess found her sisters, and she took them down from the rafters, and put the strips of skin back on them, and she hid the eldest in a big creel, and put some fine things in with her, and grass on top, and in the evening she asked the giant to carry it to her mother's to feed the cow. The giant would do anything for her now, so he carried it, and the next night he carried the second sister in the same way. The third day she told the giant that one more creel would do, and she would have it ready, but she might be out herself for a short while. So then she hid herself in the basket, with all the fine things she could find, and pulled grass over herself, and the giant carried her home. But the Queen and her two daughters had a great boiler of boiling water ready, and when he had set down the basket, they poured it over him from the upper window, and that was the end of the giant.

Orkneys, *County Folk-Lore*, III, pp. 222–6. D. J. Robertson, *Longman's Magazine*, XIV. TYPES 311 and 500. MOTIFS: G.400 [*Person falls into ogre's power*]; R.11.1 [*Princess abducted by monster*]; H.1092 [*Task: spinning an impossible amount in one night*]; Q.2 [*Kind and unkind*]; H.521 [*Test: guessing unknown propounder's name*]; N.475 [*Secret name overheard by eavesdropper*]; C.432.1 [*Guessing name of supernatural creature gives power over him*]; J.51 [*Sight of deformed witches causes man to release wife from spinning duty*]; R.157.1 [*Youngest sister rescues older*]; G.551.2 [*Rescue of sister from ogre by another sister*]; E.0 [*Resuscitation*]; G.501 [*Stupid ogre*]; G.561 [*Ogre tricked into carrying his prisoners home on his back*].

¶ "Fitcher's Bird" (Grimm no. 46), is the best–known version of this tale, but that contains no element of type 500. Type 311 is widespread throughout Europe.

For type 500 see also "Tom Tit Tot", "Duffy and the Devil", "Whuppity Stoorie".

PIPPETY PEW

See "The Milk-White Doo".

THE POOR WIDOW AND HER SON [summary]

A poor stonebreaker died and left his wife with five children, the youngest
a boy. She tried all ways to get food for them, and at last collected some
stones and boiled them in the pot, pretending they were potatoes. The
children were starving. Old man with white hair and red cloak comes
begging to door. (The duvel.) She lets him in to warm himself, and he tells
her to look in the pot. Plum puddings and potatoes. Stops them eating,
and tells them to look in cupboard. Full of bread. To look in brewhouse—
full of beer and gingerpop. Again he stops them and tells them to say grace.
Four little girls know it, little boy does not. Stranger lets them eat, but
says little boy will be turned into three things before he learns to say
grace. First, a milk-white deer in neighbouring lord's park. Lord's
daughter falls in love with the deer, and tries to capture it in vain. Next,
a goldfish in the stream. The lord's daughter loved that, but couldn't
catch it. Third, a parrot, which flew into the castle. That she loved too,
but could never catch it. Each day the old man came to ask if the boy
could yet say grace. As a parrot he learnt it at the lord's table. So the
old man turned him back into human shape, a handsome cavalry man
riding a fine horse. The lady loved him more than ever, and her father
consented to their marriage. He took his bride to the park, and showed
her his transformations. She had never loved but one man.

Collected by T. W. Thompson from Eva Gray at Grimsby, 2 December 1914.
TYPE 750*. MOTIFS: Q.1.1 [*Gods in disguise reward hospitality*]; D.114.1.1 [*Transformation: man to deer*]; D.171 [*Transformation: man to carp*]; D.157 [*Transformation:
man to parrot*]; D.700 [*Person disenchanted*].
   The "Duvel" here seems to have taken the place of Christ. It seems that this fairy
tale is nearer to an Exemplum. Varieties of the tale are to be found among Legends. It
is possible that the "duvel" may have been the ghost of the father.
   See "Christ and the Peas", "A Loaf of Bread", "The Traveller's Corn Sack".

THE PRINCESS OF THE BLUE MOUNTAINS

A poor widow who had but an only son, indulged him so much that he
grew lazy, and at length would no so much as obey her in anything, so
that she was forced to drive him through violence from her solitary
habitation.

Having now nowhere to fly for shelter when the merciless storms approached, he thought it better to take heart and pursue his fortune in a strange land. He began his journey early one morning in May, when trees were budded, and fields looked green, and continued till he reached the side of a rapid river, where he sat down; at times he rose to make a desperate plunge, but as oft his heart recoiled from the apparent danger he had to undergo. In this dilemma a lady on the opposite bank had observed all his motions, and knew his fear, made a sign to him to venture in, which he did, and safely reached the opposite shore. The lady now took him under her protection, gave him meat and comfortable clothes, and bade him be easy as to his future journey. She then requested of him to go into a beautiful garden, and pull, and bring unto her the fairest flower; but after having searched it all over, he returned, and said that she was the most beautiful flower in all the garden. On hearing this, she asked of him if he would accept of her for his wife, with which he most readily answered yes! She then said that if he knew but half of the dangers that he would have to encounter for her sake, he never would have made such a choice. However, says she, I will do the best to preserve you; at least I will give you such armour that, if rightly used, no one will be able to overcome you. Know then, adds she, that I am the Princess of the nine runners of the Blue Mountains, that was stolen away from my father's court by Grimaldin the demon; and with his legions you will have to fight before you can set me free. This night you will be attacked by three legions of his demons; but here are three black sticks and an unction. Each stick will beat off a legion of the demons, and the unction, if you chance to receive any hurt, as soon as applied, will make you whole again. Use these things well, for now I must leave you. She had no sooner fled from his presence, than the demons made their appearance, and asked his business there, which he answered not at all out of countenance, for he had great faith in the armour with which the lady had chosen to invest him. They then thinking to beat his brains out, lifted up their clubs, but the young man parried their blows so artfully that he got no hurt. He then fell to beating them with his black sticks, which had the desired effect of obtaining a complete victory, as the lady had foretold. Next morning the princess paid a visit to our young hero, and remarked that he was the first that had had the courage to withstand the sight of so many fierce cannibals, and hoped he would be able to encounter many more next night; and with that she gave him six other sticks, one for each legion, and an additional supply of the unction, in case he were wounded. The lady visited him as on the former occasion, in the morning after the engagement, and expressed her joy at seeing him well. She however told him, that that night he had twelve legions of demons to fight with the tyrant Grimaldin at their head. He replied that he found himself twelve times stronger than at first, and was nowise afraid to meet with them all. She then gave him as before a black stick for every legion, with more of the unction in case he should be by any means hurt, as Grimaldin was more cunning than any of the others which had come before him. She then took her departure, and he to prepare anew for the re-encounter with the demons.

They then began to assemble in battle array, when their captain asked him what was his business there. He told him he had come to rescue a princess from his horrid thraldom and slavery, and that he would do, or die in the manly attempt. "Then you shall die," said Grimaldin. "Not yet," Will said, "I have more good to perform first." Grimaldin then caused his demons to strike but Will having had the charmed sticks, beat them all off. Grimaldin now began to fume and rage, and with a bold stroke made at Will brought him to the ground, but he immediately applying the ointment, became as whole as ever, and rose more strengthened than before, and beat off Grimaldin also. Next morning, as she was wont to do, the lady appeared, and seeing him safe from harm, told him he had now no more dangers to fear, all were past and gone, provided he would abide by her counsel. She then gave him a book, wherein was written the lives of all the chiefs of her nation, and requested him to keep reading the same, and upon no account to take his eyes off it; for, if he did, it would cause him much sorrow. She also told him that, by due attention to the reading of that book, he would soon become one of her father's favourites, and be transported to the country where she was going, which was a great way off. He had no sooner begun to read than he heard many voices calling him all sorts of opprobrious and bad names, to attempt him to look off his book; but he withstood all their temptations. Unluckily, however, one person called out, "Who will buy apples?" which he hearing, and being exceedingly fond of that fruit, he chanced to gaze around him, and was immediately thrown with considerable violence, against an old woman's basket. For some time he knew not where he was, so much was he stunned by the suddenness of the shock. On recovering himself a little, he saw an old man resting on a seat in the shade of his cottage, to whom he applied for information of the kingdom of the nine runners of the Blue Mountains. The old man said that he did not know, but he would call an assembly of the fishes of the sea, and ask of them. He did so but none could answer him. He then told him that perhaps his brother could assist to find it, as he was five hundred years older than he, who himself was only two; but the place of his residence was four hundred miles further off; however, that could be easily overcome, as he would give him a pair of swift slippers, and a ball to roll before him, which would bring him safely and shortly to the place. He did as desired, and found himself at the second old man's door. He soon after made his appearance; Will then asked him as he had done his brother, but could not inform him without calling a council of the birds. Which he shortly after having done, they all appeared at his call unless one very old eagle; but none of them knew. At length the eagle arrived, who excused himself by saying that he had been long away, as he was engaged carrying a witch to a far distant place of the world. The eagle was then questioned as to his knowledge of this kingdom, who replied that he knew it well, and had orders to carry Will on his back to it, with a good supply of oxen and other provisions. They then mounted, and the eagle flew off. When they arrived at the kingdom, they alighted, and Will dismounted. He had not travelled long till he reached a house, hung around with black, where Will asked for lodgings, but was refused upon the account that the proprietor of the house was that day to suffer death, having been selected for that purpose by a giant, which had come from an unknown country, and had made their nation to pay a human victim to him daily as a sacrifice for his table, and that the king's daughter was offered in marriage to anyone who would deliver their country from this terrible cannibal. She had once been delivered from the oppression of Grimaldin by a Scottish chieftain, but had lost him on her return to her father, which she regretted mightily. Will, hearing these things, again dressed himself in armour, went out next morning, and after a hard struggle slew the giant. He was then recognized by the Princess, who told her father, who at once consented to their union, and at his death bestowed on him his kingdom.

Will then sent for his mother, and they lived all together, long and happy.

Norton Collection, I, p. 259. From Buchan, *Ancient Scottish Tales*, pp. 61–4.

TYPE 400. MOTIFS: L.100 [*Unpromising hero*]; N.711.2 [*Hero finds maiden in magic castle*]; D.758.1 [*Disenchantment by three nights under punishment*]; D.763.2 [*Disenchantment by defeating enchanter in combat*]; C.932 [*Loss of wife through breaking tabu*]; H.1385.3 [*Quest for vanished wife*]; H.1235 [*Succession of helpers*]; B.223 [*Kingdom of birds*]; B.455.3 [*Helpful eagle*]; G.512 [*Ogre killed*]; L.161 [*Lowly hero marries princess*].

"Wild Edric" and the other tales of the Fairy Wife, with their violation of tabu, have some motifs in common with this tale. It is widely dispersed. Grimm, nos. 92, 93, and 103, are examples.

See L. Hibberd, *Mediaeval Romance in England*, pp. 200 ff.

There are many Welsh versions of the Fairy Wife, e.g. "The Lady of Llyn y Fan Fach". A Highland version is "The Widow". "Sir Conal Galhun" is a Highland variant (Campbell). The tale turned up in America, and is recorded in *Tales of Cloud Walking Country*—"The Princess". There are many Finnish or Scandinavian versions, and quite a number in Greece, of which three are given in Dawkins' collections. It also appears in Turkey, India and China.

THE PRINCESS WITH THE
WHITE PETTICOAT

There was once a king who had an only daughter, but her mother the queen dying while she was young, the king married another queen who also had a daughter, but far less beautiful than the king's daughter. The new queen was grieved at this, but more particularly when all the princes paid their addresses to her, and no one seemed to heed her favourite daughter, who was morose and ugly. The queen then determined to dispose of her stepdaughter by some means or another, that her own daughter might get married to one of the sovereign princes who had been making love to the other. She then proposed to marry the king's daughter to an old doited king, a near relation of her own, that she might no longer be a barrier in the way of her own daughter's good fortune. However, all her wiles and stratagems availed her nothing; nor would she listen to the voice of the old king, who used very fair and flattering words, in order to gain her over to his embraces. When fair means would not do, the queen was to try foul, and for that purpose, one day sent her to a neighbouring wood to take the air, and to refresh herself, as she pretended to have a great care for her; but her real intention was that the old king with a few of his accomplices might find and carry her off when unsuspected, and when she was out of the reach of assistance from her father. The princess having gone to the wood as desired, was amusing herself with pulling some of the little variegated flowers that sprang up in her path through the wood, when a bird fluttered over her head, and in the following words warned her of her danger:

"Flee, flee,
E'er you married be."

This timely notice caused her immediately to leave the place, and to wander where she knew not whither. However, in the midst of her aberrations night came on, and with it despair; for she had now lost her way, and was many miles from her father's palace. She then sat down and cried, till, on looking wistfully around for some kind and friendly shelter, she observed at a little distance a glimmering light, which partially shone through a thicket of brambles, and raised in her for the first time a ray of hope. She then directed her footsteps to where the light shone, and in a short time found herself in a snug little cottage, without any inmates. As she approached the fire to warm herself, she heard the noise of horses, and the voice of men to come near, which again put her to some uneasiness. She then thought of secreting herself in some convenient place in the house, as she was loath to venture out, and expose herself a second time to the inclemency of the weather, and the risk of being devoured by wild beasts, so found a place, but not sufficiently secure, as there shortly after arrived a company of gentlemen in the habits and dress of huntsmen; although in reality, young princes. After they had caroused and eaten and drunken heartily, one of them started up as if he had heard or seen something unknown to the rest, and declared there was some person in the house besides themselves. Some of them rose up in opposition to this, and said that it could not be; but to their amazement and surprise, out came the princess from her lurking hole, ready to die for fear, as some of them offered rudeness to her. One of the young Neros, however, stood up in her defence, for she told them she was but a poor wanderer, and designed no harm, but his strength failed him, as he had to contend with a good many, who seized her by a golden girdle she had round her body; but as it broke, she escaped, and carried with her the other half. Having again been put to her wits' end, she at length arrived at a king's palace, and asked for lodgings, which being obtained, she next inquired if she could get a place as a servant in that family, when she was answered that she might. On their requiring to know her name, she said that it was Jenny White-Petticoat, and that she was willing to assist in doing anything of which she was capable. She was then put into the kitchen to assist the cook, but rose from post to post till she became one of the maids of honour to the young princess. The prince had made love to several of the ladies at court, but none had gained his heart but Jenny, who, he was sorry, was so far below his degree in birth and parentage, not knowing her history. He communicated his feelings to his sister, and wished her advice and assistance in making the selection among the ladies, for a wife to him. She then proposed to him to try some experiment which she had in view, and which would infallibly put him upon a sure plan of knowing the best woman. She feigned sick, and sent for one of the ladies to come and visit her, which was no sooner done than she said in secret that she was with child to her footman. The lady, by way of consolation, answered, that she also had one to her footman, but now passed for a virgin as pure as any one, and bade her not despair, for she would soon recover from that, and no one would know. She sent for another lady, who told her she herself had had two children, one to the footman, and another to the groom, but was now as pure a maiden as ever. A third lady was sent for, and told the same story as the former, when she answered that having but one child was but a trifle, for she had had three; one to the footman, one to the groom, and another to the butler, and still passed for a virgin as well as any at the court. At length she sent for Jenny White-Petticoat, alias the princess, to whom also she told the same story as she had done to all the former ladies, but was answered in quite a different manner, by saying that she was a disgrace to royalty, and therefore ought to be burned; and that she would assist at her execution, for it was not fit for her to live the life of a princess. "Hold, hold," says the princess, "I am innocent; it is all a trick to discover who of the ladies of the court have been chaste, and who have not, in their early years; and I have been successful. You, I find, have been faithful, and to you alone shall my brother, the prince, pay his addresses, if agreeable to you." Jenny gave him permission to become her suitor, and afterwards informed him that she was the wanderer whom he had defended some time ago, in the hunting lodge, when attacked by the rest of his companions; and as a proof of what she asserted, she produced the other half of the broken golden girdle, which she had preserved as a memorial of the danger she had been in. They were afterwards married, when she made known her whole history, which rejoiced the prince greatly. She afterwards let her father know she was happily married, and to whom; which he received with exceeding great joy, and afterwards paid them a visit. They lived long and happy.

Norton Collection, II, p. 259. From Buchan, *Ancient Scottish Tales*, pp. 48–50. TYPES 510 (variant), 886 (variant). MOTIFS: S.31 [*Cruel stepmother*]; L.55 [*Step-daughter heroine*]; B.143.1 [*Bird gives warning*]; T.311.1 [*Flight of maiden to escape marriage*]; H.400 [*Chastity test*].

Type 976A, "Which was the Noblest Act?", has some relationship to this story, in the test question by which the unchaste maidens betray themselves.

¶ For 510 see "Catskin", "Cap o' Rushes", etc.

THE PROPHECY

There was once a rich man, and he had brass; that he had. One day he was riding out of t' town, and he saw an old witch, and her child had fallen intut mire, and she axed rich man to lug him out, but he wouldn't do nowt o' t' sort. Eh! she were angry!

She said to him, "Tha must have a son, and he shall dee afore he be turned twenty-one."

Well, he had a son, and he was flayed lest what she said should come true.

So he built a tower all round, and there was no door, no but a window high up. And he put bairn in there. And he put an old man in tower to fend for bairn, and he sent him food and clothes, and all he wanted by a rope up intut chamber. Well, when t'lad was one-and-twenty, ont' very day, it was cold, and t'lad was right starved, so he said tu told man, that he'd fain have a fire, and they let down rope and they pulled up a bundle of wood. T'lad hugged bundle, and cast it in t' fire, and as he cast it, a snake came out from t'bundle in which it had been hidden, and it bit t'lad, and he died.

She wor a bad un, wor that witch!

Norton Collection, III, p. 12; Yorkshire, Baring-Gould; Appendix to Henderson, p. 336. TYPE 934. MOTIF: M.370.1 [*Prophecy of death fulfilled*].
¶ Numerous Irish versions of this tale are found. Otherwise it seems commonest in Eastern Europe, Finland, Lithuania, Russia, Roumania, and Hungary.

RASHIE-COAT [summary]

Rashie-Coat was a king's daughter whose father desired her to marry a man whom she did not love. She went to seek advice from the henwife, who told her to say she would not marry him unless they gave her a coat of beaten gold.

They gave her this, but still she did not want to marry the man, and this time the henwife told her to ask for a coat made of feathers of all the birds of the air. Even this was given to her, for the king sent a man with a great heap of corn, who cried out, "Each bird take up a pea, and put down a feather." Even now the girl went back again to the henwife, who said, "Say you will not take him unless they give you a coat of rushes and a pair of slippers."

They gave her these, and the henwife said she could not help her any more.

So the girl left her home, and went and sought service in a king's house. And she became a kitchen-maid. On Sunday she was left at home to cook the dinner, but a fairy came in, and told her to put on her coat of beaten gold, and go to church with the rest, and said she would cook the dinner. So the girl went, and the fairy said,

> "Ae peat gar anither peat burn,
> Ae spit gar anither spit turn,
> Ae pat gar anither pat play,
> Let Rashie-coat gang to the kirk the day."

In church the king's son fell in love with Rashie-coat, but she slipped away so quickly at the end that he could not tell where she had gone.

Next Sunday the same thing happened, but the fairy told Rashie-coat to put on her coat of feathers, and this time the king's son followed her out, but he could not see which way she went. The next Sunday the fairy told her to put on her coat of rushes and the slippers, and again the king's son slipped out of church after, and that time he managed to catch hold of her. But she slipped from his grasp and ran off, leaving one of her slippers behind in her haste. The prince took it up, and proclaimed that the lady who could wear it should be his wife. Many tried the slipper on in vain, and the old henwife made her daughter cut her foot and so squeeze it in to the slipper. So the prince took her up on his horse and was riding away, when a bird sitting on a tree sang out as they passed,

> "Nippit fit and clippit fit
> Ahint the king's son rides;
> But bonny fit and pretty fit
> Ahint the cauldron hides."

And when he heard this the prince flung off the henwife's daughter, and found Rashie-Coat hiding behind the cauldron, crying for her lost slipper.

The slipper fitted her exactly, and they were married, and lived happily ever after.

Chambers, *Popular Rhymes of Scotland*, p. 66.
TYPE 510.
¶ See "Cap o' Rushes", "Mossycoat", "Catskin".

RASHIN COATIE

There was a king and a queen, as mony ane's been few have we seen and as few may we see, and the queen she deeit, and left a bonnie little lassie; and she had naething tae gie the wee lassie but a little red calfy, and she tellt the lassie whatever she wanted the calfy would gie her.

The king married again, an ill-natured wife, wi' three ugly dochters o' her ain. They didna like the little lassie, because she was bonnie; they took awa' a' her braw claes that her ain mither had geen her, and put a rashen coatie on her, and gart her sit in the kitchen neuk, an' a'body ca'd her Rashin Coatie. She didna get anything to eat but what the rest left, but she didna care, for she went to her red calfie, and it gave her everything she asked for. She got good meat from the calfy, but her ill stepmother gart the calfie be killed, because it was good to Rashin Coatie. She was very sorry for the calfie, and sat down and grat. The dead calfy said to her:

> "Tak me up, bane by bane,
> And pit me aneath yon grey stane,

and whatever you want, come and seek it frae me, and I will give you it."

Yuletide came, and the rest put on their braw claes, and was gaen awa' to the kirk. Rashin Coatie said, "Oh, I would like to gang to the kirk too!" but the others said, "What would you do at the kirk, you nasty thing? You must bide at hame and make the dinner." When they were gone to the kirk, Rashin Coatie did na ken how to make the dinner, but she went up to the grey stone, and she told the calf that she could not make the dinner, and she wanted to win to the kirk. The calfie gave her braw claes, and bade her gang into the house and say:

"Every peat gar ither burn,
Every spit gar ither turn,
Every pot gar ither play,
Till I come frae the kirk this guid Yule day."

Rashin Coatie put on the braw claes that the calfy gave her, and went awa' to the kirk, and she was the grandest and the brawest lady there. There was a young prince in the kirk, and he fell in love with her. She cam' awa' before the blessing, and she was home before the rest, and had off her braw claes, and had on her rashin coatie, and the calfy had covered the table, and the dinner was ready and everything in good order when the rest cam' hame. The three sisters said to Rashin Coatie, "Oh, lassie, if you had only seen the braw lady that was in the kirk to-day, that the young prince fell in love with!" She said: "Oh, I wish ye would let me gang with you to the kirk to-morrow!" for they used to gang three days after ither to the kirk. They said: "What should the like o' you do at the kirk, nasty thing? The kitchen work is good enough for you."

The next day they went away and left her, but she went back to her calfy, and he bade her repeat the same words as before, and he gave her braver claes, and she went back to the kirk, and a' the world was looking at her, and wondering where sic a grand lady came from; and as for the young prince, he fell more in love with her than ever, and bade somebody watch where she went back to. But she was back afore anybody saw her, and had off her braw claes, and on her rashin coatie, and the calfy had the table covered, and everything ready for the dinner.

The next day the calfy dressed her in brawer claes than ever, and she went back to the kirk. The young prince was there, and he put a guard at the door to keep her, but she jumped over their heads, and lost one of her beautiful satin slippers. She got hame before the rest, and had on the rashin coatie, and the calfy had all things ready. The young prince put out a proclamation that he would marry whoever the satin slipper would fit. All the ladies of the land went to try on the slipper, and with the rest the three sisters, but none would it fit, for they had ugly broad feet. The henwife took in her daughter, and cut off her heels and her toes, and the slipper was forced on her, and the prince was to marry her, for he must keep his promise. As he rode along to the kirk with her behind him, a bird began to sing, and ever it sang:

"Minched fit and pinched fit
Beside the King she rides,
But braw fit, and bonny fit,
In the kitchen neuk she hides."

The prince said, "What is that the bird sings?"

And the henwife said: "Nasty lying thing! Never mind what it says;" but the bird sang ever the same words. The prince said: "Oh, there must be someone that the slipper has not been tried on." But they said, "There is none but a poor thing that sits in the kitchen neuk, and wears a rashin coatie." But the prince was determined to try it on Rashin Coatie, and she ran awa' to the grey stone, where the red calfy dressed her yet brawer than ever, and she went to the prince, and the slipper jumped out of his pocket and on to her foot, and the prince married her, and they lived happily all their days.

Folk-Lore, I (Andrew Lang); told by Miss Margeret Craig, Elgin.
TYPE 510. MOTIFS: S.31 [*Cruel stepmother*]; L.55 [*Stepdaughter heroine*]; B.313.1 [*Helpful animal reincarnation of parent*]; B.335 [*Helpful animal killed*]; D.842.3 [*Magic object from grave of helpful animal*]; N.711.4 [*Prince sees maiden at church and is enamoured*]; H.36.1 [*Slipper test*]; K.1911.3.3.1 [*False bride's mutilated foot*]; B.143.1 [*Bird gives warning*].

This version contains the primitive element of the reincarnation of the dead mother in animal form.

"Rashie-Coat" is much the same story, but with a beginning like "Catskin" or "Mossycoat".

See also "Cap o' Rushes", "Catskin", "Mossycoat", "Ashpitel" and "The Red Calf", which is another version of "Rashin Coatie".

THE RED BULL OF NORROWAY

Once upon a time there lived a king who had three daughters; the two eldest were proud and ugly, but the youngest was the gentlest and most beautiful creature ever seen, and the pride not only of her father and mother, but of all in the land. As it fell out, the three princesses were talking one night of whom they would marry. "I will have no one lower than a king," said the eldest princess. The second would take a prince, or a great duke even. "Pho, pho," said the youngest, laughing, "you are both so proud; now I would be content with 'The Red Bull o' Norroway'." Well, they thought no more of the matter till the next morning, when as they sat at breakfast, they heard the most dreadful bellowing at the door, and what should it be but the Red Bull come for his bride! You may be sure they were all terribly frightened at this, for the Red Bull was one of the most horrible creatures ever seen in the world. And the king and queen did not know how to save their daughter. At last they determined to send him off with the old henwife. So they put her on his back, and away he went with her till he came to a great black forest, when, throwing her down, he returned roaring, louder and more frightfully than ever; they then sent, one by one, all the servants, then the two eldest princesses;

458

but not one of them met with any better treatment than the old henwife, and at last they were forced to send their youngest and favourite child.

On travelled the lady and the bull through many dreadful forests and lonely wastes, till they came at last to a noble castle, where a large company was assembled. The lord of the castle pressed them to stay, though much he wondered at the lovely princess and her strange companion. When they went in among the company, the princess espied a pin sticking in the bull's hide, which she pulled out, and to the surprise of all, there appeared, not a frightful wild beast, but one of the most beautiful princes ever beheld. You may believe how delighted the princess was to see him fall at her feet and thank her for breaking his cruel enchantment. There were great rejoicings in the castle at this; but alas! at that moment he suddenly disappeared, and though every place was sought, he was nowhere to be found. The princess, however, determined to seek through all the world for him, and many weary ways she went, but nothing could she hear of her lover. Travelling once through a dark wood, she lost her way, and as night was coming on, she thought she must now certainly die of cold and hunger; but seeing a light through the trees, she went on till she came to a little hut where an old woman lived, who took her in, and gave her both food and shelter. In the morning, the old wifie gave her three nuts, that she was not to break till her heart was like to break, "and owre again like to break"; so shewing her the way, she bade God speed her, and the princess once more set out on her wearisome journey.

She had not gone far till a company of lords and ladies rode past her, all talking merrily of the fine doings they expected at the Duke o' Norroway's wedding. Then she came up to a number of people carrying all sorts of fine things, and they, too, were going to the duke's wedding. At last she came to a castle, where nothing was to be seen but cooks and bakers, some running one way and some another, and all so busy, they did not know what to do first. Whilst she was looking at all this, she heard a noise of hunters behind her, and some one cried out: "Make way for the Duke o' Norroway," and who should ride past but the prince and a beautiful lady! You may be sure her heart was now "like to break, and owre again like to break" at this sad sight; so she broke one of the nuts, and out came a *wee wifie carding*. The princess then went into the castle, and asked to see the lady, who no sooner saw the wee wifie so hard at work, that she offered the princess anything in her castle for it. "I will give it to you," said she, "only on condition that you put off for one day your marriage with the Duke o' Norroway, and that I may go into his room alone to-night." So anxious was the lady for the nut, that she consented. And when dark night was come, and the duke fast asleep, the princess was put alone into his chamber. Sitting down by his bedside, she began singing:

"Far hae I sought ye, near am I brought to ye;
Dear Duke o' Norroway, will ye no turn and speak to me?"

Though she sang this over and over again, the duke never wakened, and in the morning the princess had to leave him without his knowing that she had ever been there. She then broke the second nut, and out came a *wee wifie spinning*, which so delighted the lady that she readily agreed to put off her marriage another day for it; but the princess came to no better speed the second night than the first; and, almost in despair, she broke the last nut, which contained a *wee wifie reeling*; and, on the same condition as before, the lady got possession of it. When the duke was dressing in the morning, his man asked him what the strange singing and moaning that had been heard in his room for two nights meant. "I heard nothing," said the duke, "it could only have been your fancy."

"Take no sleeping-draught to-night, and be sure to lay aside your pillow of heaviness," said the man, "and you also will hear what for two nights has kept me awake." The duke did so, and the princess coming in, sat down sighing at his bedside, thinking this the last time she might ever see him. The duke started up when he heard the voice of his dearly loved princess; and with many endearing expressions of surprise and joy, explained to her that he had long been in the power of an enchantress, whose spells over him were now happily ended by their once again meeting. The princess, happy to be the instrument of his second deliverance, consented to marry him; and the enchantress, who fled that country, afraid of the duke's anger, has never since been heard of. All was again hurry and preparation in the castle; and the marriage which now took place at once ended the adventures of the Red Bull o' Norroway, and the wanderings of the king's daughter.

Norton Collection, I, p. 270. From Chambers, *Popular Rhymes*, pp. 99–101.
TYPE 425, MOTIFS: S.215.1 [*Girl promises herself to animal suitor*]; S.252 [*Vain attempts to save promised child*]; D.700 [*Person disenchanted*]; H.1385.4 [*Quest for vanished husband*]; H.1233.1.1 [*Old woman helps on quest*]; N.681.1 [*Wife finds lost husband about to marry another*]; D.2006.1.4 [*Forgotten fiancée buys place in husband's bed and reawakens his memory*].
¶ See also "The Black Bull of Norroway", "The Small-Tooth Dog".

THE RED CALF

Ance a long time ago, there was a gentleman had two lassies. The oldest was ugly and ill-natured, but the youngest was a bonnie lassie and good; but the ugly one was the favourite with her father and mother. So they ill-used the youngest in every way, and they sent her into the woods to herd cattle, and all the food she got was a little porridge and whey.

Well, amongst the cattle was a red calf, and one day it said to the lassie, "Gee that porridge and whey to the doggie, and come wi' me."

So the lassie followed the calf through the wood, and they came to a bonnie hoosie, where there was a nice dinner ready for them, and after they had feasted on everything nice, they went back to the herding.

Every day the calf took the lassie away, and feasted her on dainties, and every day she grew bonnier. This disappointed the father and mother and the ugly sister. They expected that the rough usage she was getting would take away her beauty; and they watched and watched until they saw the calf take the lassie away to the feast. So they resolved to kill the calf; and not only that, but the lassie was to be compelled to kill him with an axe. Her ugly sister was to hold his head, and the lassie who loved him had to give the blow and kill him. She could do nothing but greet, but the calf told her not to greet, but to do as he bade her; and his plan was that instead of coming down on his head she was to come down on the lassie's head who was holding him, and then she was to jump on his back, and they would run off. Well, the day came for the calf to be killed, and everything was ready—the ugly lassie holding his head, and the bonnie lassie armed with the axe. So she raised the axe, and came down on the ugly sister's head, and in the confusion that took place she got on the calf's back, and they ran away, and they ran and better nor ran till they came to a meadow where grew a great lot of rashes; and, as the lassie had not on many clothes, they pu'ed rashes and made a coatie for her, and they set off again, and travelled, and travelled, till they came to the King's house. They went in and asked if they wanted a servant. The mistress said she wanted a kitchen lassie, and she would take Rashin-coatie. So Rashin-coatie said she would stop if they keepit the calf too. They were willing to do that. So the lassie and the calf stoppit in the King's house, and everybody was well pleased with her; and when Yule came they said she was to stop at home and make the dinner, while all the rest went to the kirk. After they were away the calf asked if she would like to go. She said she would, but she had no clothes, and she could not leave the dinner.

The calf said he would give her clothes, and make the dinner too. He went out, and came back with a grand dress all silk and satin, and such a nice pair of slippers. The lassie put on the dress, and before she left she said:

> "Ilka peat gar anither burn,
> An' ilka spit gar anither turn,
> An' ilka pot gar anither play,
> Till I come frae the kirk on gude Yule day."

So she went to the kirk, and nobody kent it was Rashin-coatie. They wondered who the bonnie lady could be; and, as soon as the young prince saw her, he fell in love with her, and resolved he would find out who she was, before she got home; but Rashin-coatie left before the rest, so that she might get home in time to take off her dress, and look after the dinner.

When the prince saw her leaving, he made for the door to stop her; but she jumped past him, and in the hurry lost one of her shoes. The prince kept the shoe, and Rashin-coatie got home all right, and the folk said the dinner was very nice.

Now the prince was resolved to find out who the bonnie lady was, and he sent a servant through all the land with the shoe. Every lady was to try it on, and the prince promised to marry the one it would fit. The servant went to a great many houses, but could not find a lady that the shoe would go on, it was so little and neat. At last he came to a henwife's house, and her daughter had little feet. At first the shoe would not go on, but she paret her feet and clippit her toes, until the shoe went on. Now the prince was very angry. He knew it was not the lady he wanted; but because he had promised to marry whoever the shoe fitted, he had to keep his promise.

The marriage day came, and, as they were all riding to the kirk, a little bird flew through the air, and it sang:—

"Clippit feet an' paret taes is on the saidle set;
But bonnie feet an' braw feet is in the kitchen neuk."

"What's that ye say?" said the prince. "Oh," says the henwife, "would ye mind what a feel bird says?" But the prince said, "Sing that again, bonnie birdie." So the bird sings:—

"Clippit feet an' paret taes is on the saidle set;
But bonnie feet an' braw feet sits in the kitchen neuk."

The prince turned his horse and rode home, and went straight to his father's kitchen, and there sat Rashin-coatie. He kent her at once, she was so bonnie; and when she tried on the shoe it fitted her, and so the prince married Rashin-coatie, and they lived happy and built a house for the red calf, who had been so kind to her.

Norton Collection, II, p. 73.

"Three folk-tales from Old Meldrum," Aberdeenshire. Communicated to W. Gregor by Mr. Moir. He had them from his mother, who wrote out "The Red Calf". *F.L.J.* II, 188, pp. 72–4.

TYPE 510. MOTIFS as in "Rashin Coatie", from which it only differs in the escape of the Red Calf and the murder of the ugly sister.

THE RED ETIN

There were ance twa widows that lived ilk ane on a small bit o' ground, which they rented from a farmer. Ane of them had twa sons, and the other had ane; and by and by it was time for the wife that had twa sons to send them away to spouss their fortune. So she told her eldest son ae day to take a can and bring her water from the well, that she might make a cake for him; and however much or however little water he might bring, the cake would be great or sma' accordingly; and that cake was to be a' that she could give him when he went on his travels.

The lad gaed away wi' the can to the well, and filled it wi' water, and then came hame again; but the can being broken, the maist part o' the water had run out before he got back. So his cake was very sma'; yet sma' as it was, his mother asked if he was willing to take the half of it with her blessing, telling him that if he chose rather to have the hale, he would only get it wi' her curse. The young man, thinking he might hae to travel a far way, and not knowing when or how he might get other provisions, said he would like to hae the hale cake, come of his mother's malison what like; so she gave him the hale cake, and her malison alang wi't. Then he took his brither aside, and gave him a knife to keep till he should come back, desiring him to look at it every morning, and as lang as it continued to be clear, then he might be sure that the owner of it was well; but if it grew dim and rusty, then for certain some ill had befallen him.

So the young man set out to spouss his fortune. And he gaed a' that day, and a' the next day; and on the third day, in the afternoon, he came up to where a shepherd was sitting with a flock o' sheep. And he gaed up to the shepherd, and asked him wha the sheep belanged to; and the man answered:

"The Red Etin of Ireland
Ance lived in Bellygan,
And stole King Malcolm's daughter,
The King of fair Scotland.
He beats her, he binds her,
He lays her on a band;
And every day he dings her
With a bright silver wand,
Like Julian the Roman,
He's one that fears no man.
It's said there's ane predestinate
To be his mortal foe;
But that man is yet unborn,
And lang may it be so."

The young man then went on his journey; and he had not gone far, when he espied an old man with white locks herding a flock of swine; and he gaed up to him and asked whose swine these were, when the man answered:

"The Red Etin of Ireland,
Ance lived in Bellygan,
And stole King Malcolm's daughter,
The King of fair Scotland.
He beats her, he binds her,
He lays her on a band;
And every day he dings her
With a bright silver wand.
Like Julian the Roman,
He's one that fears no man.
It's said there's ane predestinate
To be his mortal foe;
But that man is yet unborn,
And lang may it be so."

The the young man gaed on a bit farther, and came to another very old man herding goats; and when he asked whose goats they were, the answer was:

"The Red Etin of Ireland
Ance lived in Bellygan,
And stole King Malcolm's daughter,
The King of fair Scotland.
He beats her, he binds her,
He lays her on a band;
And every day he dings her
With a bright silver wand.
Like Julian the Roman,
He's one that fears no man.
It's said there's ane predestinate
To be his mortal foe;
But that man is yet unborn,
And lang may it be so."

This old man also told him to beware o' the next beasts that he should meet, for they were of a very different kind from any he had yet seen.

So the young man went on, and by and by he saw a multitude of very dreadfu' beasts, ilk ane o' them wi' twa heads, and on every head four horns. And he was sore frightened, and ran away from them as fast as he could; and glad was he when he came to a castle that stood on a hillock, wi' the door standing wide to the wa'. And he gaed into the castle for shelter, and there he saw an auld wife sitting beside the kitchen fire. He asked the wife if he might stay there for the night, as he was tired wi' a lang journey; and the wife said he might, but it was not a good place for him to be in, as it belanged to the Red Etin, who was a very terrible beast, wi' three heads, that spared no living man he could get hold of. The young man would have gone away, but he was afraid of the beasts on the outside of the castle; so he beseeched the old woman to conceal him as well as she could, and not tell the Etin that he was there. He thought, if he could put over the night, he might get away in the morning, without meeting wi' the beasts, and so escape. But he had not been long in his hidy-hole, before the awful Etin came in; and nae sooner was he in, than he was heard crying:

"Snouk but and snouk ben,
I find the smell of an earthly man;
Be he living, or be he dead,
His heart this night shall kitchen my bread."

The monster soon found the poor young man, and pulled him from his hole. And when he had got him out, he told him that, if he could answer him three questions, his life should be spared. The first was, Whether Ireland or Scotland was first inhabited? The second was, Whether man was made for woman, or woman for man? The third was, Whether men or brutes were made first? The lad not being able to answer one of these questions, the Red Etin took a mell and knocked him on the head, and turned him into a pillar of stone.

On the morning after this happened, the younger brither took out the knife to look at it, and he was grieved to find it a' brown wi' rust. He told his mother that the time was now come for him to go away upon his travels also; so she requested him to take the can to the well for water, that she might bake a cake for him. The can being broken, he brought hame as little water as the other had done, and the cake was as little. She asked whether he would have the hale cake wi' her malison, or the half wi' her blessing; and, like his brither, he thought it best to have the hale cake, come o' the malison what might. So he gaed away; and he came to the shepherd that sat wi' his flock o' sheep, and asked him whose these sheep were. The man answered:

"The Red Etin of Ireland
Ance lived in Bellygan,
And stole King Malcolm's daughter,
The King of fair Scotland.
He beats her, he binds her,
He lays her on a band;
And every day he dings her
With a bright silver wand.

Like Julian the Roman,
He's one that fears no man.
It's said there's ane predestinate
To be his mortal foe;
But that man is yet unborn,
And lang may it be so."

The young man then went on his journey; and he had not gone far, when he espied an old man with white locks herding a flock of swine; and he gaed up to him and asked whose swine these were, when the man answered:

"The Red Etin of Ireland
Ance lived in Bellygan,
And stole King Malcolm's daughter,
The King of fair Scotland.
He beats her, he binds her,
He lays her on a band;
And every day he dings her
With a bright silver wand.
Like Julian the Roman,
He's one that fears no man.
It's said there's ane predestinate
To be his mortal foe;
But that man is yet unborn,
And lang may it be so."

Then the young man gaed on a bit farther, and came to another very old man herding goats; and when he asked whose goats they were, the answer was:

"The Red Etin of Ireland
Ance lived in Bellygan,
And stole King Malcolm's daughter,
The King of fair Scotland.
He beats her, he binds her,
He lays her on a band;
And every day he dings her
With a bright silver wand.
Like Julian the Roman,
He's one that fears no man.
It's said there's ane predestinate
To be his mortal foe;
But that man is yet unknown,
And lang may it be so."

This old man also told him to beware of the next beasts that he should meet, for they were of a very different kind from any he had yet seen.

So the young man went on, and by and by he saw a multitude of very dreadfu' beasts, ilk ane o' them wi' twa heads, and on every head four horns. And he was sore frightened, and ran away from them as fast as he could; and glad was he when he came to a castle that stood on a hillock, wi' the door standing wide to the wa'. And he gaed into the castle for shelter, and there he saw an auld wife sitting beside the kitchen fire. He asked the wife if he might stay there for the night, as he was tired wi' a lang journey; and the wife said he might, but it was not a good place for him to be in, as it belanged to the Red Etin, who was a very terrible beast, wi' three heads, that spared no living man he could get hold of. The young man would have gone away, but he was afraid of the beasts on the outside of the castle; so he beseeched the old woman to conceal him as well as she could, and not tell the Etin that he was there. He thought, if he could put over the night, he might get away in the morning, without meeting wi' the beasts, and so escape. But he had not been long in his hidy-hole, before the awful Etin came in; and nae sooner was he in, than he was heard crying:

> "Snouk but and snouk ben,
> I find the smell of an earthly man;
> Be he living, or be he dead,
> His heart this night shall kitchen my bread."

The monster soon found the poor young man, and pulled him from his hole. And when he had got him out, he told him that, if he could answer him three questions, his life should be spared. The first was, Whether Ireland or Scotland was first inhabited? The second was, Whether man was made for woman, or woman for man? The third was, Whether men or brutes were made first? The lad not being able to answer one of these questions, the Red Etin took a mell and knocked him on the head, and turned him into a pillar of stone.

The other widow and her son heard of all that had happened frae a fairy, and the young man determined that he would also go upon his travels, and see if he could do anything to relieve his twa friends. So his mother gave him a can to go to the well and bring home water, that she might bake him a cake for his journey. And he gaed, and as he was bringing hame the water, a raven owre abune his head cried to him to look, and he would see that the water was running out. And he was a young man of sense, and seeing the water running out, he took some clay and patched up the holes, so that he brought home enough of water to bake a large cake. When his mother put it to him to take the half cake wi' her blessing, he took it in preference to having the hale wi' her malison; and yet the half was bigger than what the other lads had got a'thegither.

So he gaed away on his journey; and after he had travelled a far way, he met wi' an auld woman, that asked him if he would give her a bit of his bannock. And he said he would gladly do that, and so he gave her a piece of the bannock; and for that she gied him a magical wand, that she said might yet be of service to him, if he took care to use it rightly. Then the auld woman, wha was a fairy, told him a great deal that would happen to him, and what he ought to do in a' circumstances; and after that she vanished in an instant out o' his sight. He gaed on a great way farther, and then he came up to the old man herding the sheep; and when he asked whose sheep these were, the answer was:

> "The Red Etin of Ireland
> Ance lived in Bellygan,
> And stole King Malcolm's daughter,
> The King of fair Scotland.
> He beats her, he binds her,
> He lays her on a band;
> And every day he dings her
> With a bright silver wand.
> Like Julian the Roman,
> He's one that fears no man.
>
> But now I fear his end is near,
> And destiny at hand;
> And you're to be, I plainly see,
> The heir of all his land."

The young man then went on his journey; and he had not gone far, when he espied an old man with white locks herding a flock of swine; and he gaed up to him and asked whose swine these were, when the man answered:

> "The Red Etin of Ireland
> Ance lived in Bellygan,
> And stole King Malcolm's daughter,
> The King of fair Scotland.
> He beats her, he binds her,
> He lays her on a band;
> And every day he dings her
> With a bright silver wand.
> Like Julian the Roman,
> He's one that fears no man.
>
> But now I fear his end is near,
> And destiny at hand;
> And you're to be, I plainly see,
> The heir of all his land."

Then the young man gaed on a bit farther, and came to another very old man herding goats; and when he asked whose goats they were, the answer was:

> "The Red Etin of Ireland
> Ance lived in Bellygan,
> And stole King Malcolm's daughter,
> The King of fair Scotland.
> He beats her, he binds her,
> He lays her on a band;
> And every day he dings her
> With a bright silver wand.
> Like Julian the Roman,
> He's one that fears no man.
>
> But now I fear his end is near,
> And destiny at hand;
> And you're to be, I plainly see,
> The heir of all his land."

This old man also told him to beware o' the next beasts that he should meet, for they were of a very different kind from any he had yet seen.

When he came to the place where the monstrous beasts were standing, he did not stop nor run away, but went boldly through amongst them. One came up roaring with open mouth to devour him, when he struck it with his wand, and laid it in an instant dead at his feet. He soon came to the Etin's castle, where he knocked and was admitted. The auld woman that sat by the fire warned him of the terrible Etin, and what had been the fate of the twa brithers; but he was not to be daunted. The monster soon came in, saying:

> "Snouk but and snouk ben,
> I find the smell of an earthly man;
> Be he living or be he dead,
> His heart shall be kitchen to my bread."

He quickly espied the young man, and bade him come forth on the floor. And then he put the three questions to him; but the young man had been told everything by the good fairy, so he was able to answer all the questions. When the Etin found this, he knew that his power was gone. The young man then took up an axe and hewed aff the monster's three heads. He next asked the old woman to shew him where the king's daughter lay; and the old woman took him up stairs, and opened a great many doors, and out of every door came a beautiful lady who had been imprisoned there by the Etin; and ane o' the ladies was the king's daughter. She also took him down into a low room, and there stood two stone pillars that he had only to touch wi' his wand, when his twa friends and neighbours started into life. And the hale o' the prisoners were overjoyed at their deliverance, which they all acknowledged to be owing to the prudent young man. Next day they a' set out for the king's court, and a gallant company they made. And the king married his daughter to the young man that had delivered her, and gave a noble's daughter to ilk ane o' the other young men; and so they a' lived happily a' the rest o' their days.*

Chambers, *Popular Rhymes of Scotland*, p. 89.

TYPE 303 (variant). MOTIFS: H.1023.2.1.1 [*Carrying water in a sieve filled with moss*]; J.229.3 [*Choice: a big piece of cake with my curse, or a small piece with my blessing*]; G.84 [*Fee-fi-fo-fum*]; D.231 [*Transformation: man to stone*]; B.122.1 [*Bird as adviser*]; H.1023.2.1 [*Carrying water in a leaky vessel*]; D.813 [*Magic object received from fairy*]; R.111.1.1 [*Rescue of princess from ogre*]; G.551.4 [*One brother rescues another from ogre*]; L.161 [*Lowly hero marries princess*].

This tale deviates considerably from type 303, "The Blood Brothers".

The introduction of the third successful hero, who is a neighbour, not a brother, looks as if there was a confusion of two tales here. The *cante fable* form shows the antiquity of the tale, which was mentioned in *The Complaynt of Scotland* in 1584.

There is a theological form about the riddles which marks them as belonging to that period. Jacobs, in his retelling of the tale, substitutes earlier ones. "Etin" was used in England for "giant", in the sixteenth century, but survived in Scotland for longer.

The typical form of type 303 is in Grimm, no. 60, also 85. Kurt Ranke ("*Die Zwei Brüder*", FFC, CXIV) lists some 770 versions.

¶ See also "Child Rowland" and "The Dräglin Hogney".

THE RED LION OF THE FOREST
[condensed]

There was once a widow with three sons, and they went off one by one to seek their fortunes. The two eldest never returned, so the youngest set out the way they had gone. He had not gone far before he heard a great noise, and saw a lion, a hawk, and a wolf disputing over the carcase of a ram. They called to him to settle the dispute, and he divided the carcase so fairly between them that they were very grateful to him. The hawk gave him a feather, and the lion and wolf a tuft of hair, and these gave him their strength and powers, so that he could even take their forms if he wished it. He thanked them and went on until he came to a Palace. He walked round it, and saw a most beautiful Princess sitting at an upper window. He took out the hawk's feather, and wished himself a hawk, and flew up into the room, and turned back into a man. The Princess screamed, and all the guards ran up into the room, but before they came the man had turned into a hawk and flown away. Again he flew up, and again the

* The above story is from Mr Buchan's curious manuscript collection.

Princess screamed, and the King and all the guard hurried into the room, and again found no one. The King was angry at this, and said to the Princess: "If you scream again without cause, I will have you killed." So when the hawk flew up again, and turned into a man, the Princess did not give the alarm, and listened to what he had to say. He courted her so well that she grew fond of him. And she told him how the Champion was courting her. So he said: "To-morrow I will change into a little bird. Carry me down on your hand, and say: 'Look what a bonny wee bird I have.' And I will dirty your hand. Then throw me down." She promised to do as he said, and next morning she carried the wee bird down to dinner with the King, and said: "Look what a bonnie wee bird I have!" And the wee bird dirtied her hand, and the King said, "Throw it down, the dirty thing!" So she threw it down, and it turned into a handsome young man, who fought the Champion, and killed him. So he married the Princess, and they lived very happily together.

Now there was a river running past the King's Palace, and there were seven swans on the river, and every so often—after one year, one day, and seven hours—if you fed them you turned into a swan too. The Princess had been so happy that she forgot the time, and went down and fed the swans, and she turned into one, and sailed away down the river with them. So her husband went down to the river to find her. He went on till he came to a great rock with a cave in it, and in the cave was a man who had never seen a man before. But the Prince made friends with him, and gave him some nuts he had gathered on the way, and the man told him what he must do. He spent the night there, and then went on. He had not gone far when he heard a great roaring, and a lion came towards him. He took out his hair, and turned into a lion, and after a great fight he killed the lion and went on. And then a wolf attacked him, and he fought it in wolf's form, and killed it too. And then a hawk flew at him, and he turned into a hawk, and fought and killed it. Then he came to a little house, and the swans were in it, and an old witch woman, and he heard her say: "I had seven swans, and now I have eight." And he broke through the window to come at her, and when she saw him, she touched the eight swans, and turned them into stone; but before she could touch him, he cut off her head. Then he took the wand, and touched the eighth swan with the other end of it, and she turned back into his own Princess. He said: "Shall I turn back the other seven swans?" And she said: "They were bad; you had best leave them as they are." So they left them, and went home to the Palace, and lived happy there.

School of Scottish Studies: H. Henderson, from Sandy McPhee, Perthshire. Heard from his father.
TYPE 554. MOTIFS: L.10 [*Victorious youngest son*]; B.392 [*Hero divides spoil for animals*]; B.350 [*Grateful animals*]; D.532 [*Transformation by putting on feathers, etc.*];

B.528.2 [*Animals help hero win princess*]; C.752 [*Tabu: doing things after a certain time*]; C.962.2 [*Transformation to bird for breaking tabu*]; H.1385.3 [*Quest for vanished wife*]; D.231 [*Transformation: man to stone*]; D.700 [*Person disenchanted*].
¶ See also "The King of the Herrings".

THE ROSE TREE [summary]

Once a good man had a daughter by his first wife, and a son by his second. The stepmother hated the daughter, who was very beautiful, with golden hair, cherry-red lips, and milk-white skin. One day she sent the girl to buy a pound of candles, but on her way home, she put down the candles to climb a stile, and a dog ran up and carried them off. She returned to the shop, but the same thing happened again, and even a third time. Then, having no money left, the child returned to her stepmother. Pretending not to be angry, the stepmother began to comb the girl's hair. The hair hung right over her knees and down to the ground, so she said she could not comb it over her knees with an ordinary comb, and sent her to fetch first, a billet of wood, and then an axe. With these she cut off the girl's head.

She cut out her heart and liver, and stewed them for her husband's supper.

But he complained of the strange taste, and the little brother refused to eat at all. He grieved for his sister, and buried her body in a box under a rose tree. When the tree flowered, a white bird sat and sang among its branches:

"My wicked mother slew me,
My dear father ate me,
My little brother whom I love
Sits below, and I sing above
Stick, stock, stone dead."

Then the bird flew away to a cobbler's shop, and then to a watchmaker's, and last to a place where three millers were picking a millstone. Each of them begged the bird to sing its beautiful song again, and in payment the cobbler gave the bird a pair of little red shoes, the watchmaker gave a gold watch and chain, and the millers hung the millstone round its neck. The bird flew off to its home with the shoes in one claw, and the watch and chain in the other.

It rattled the millstone against the eaves of the house, and the stepmother said, "It thunders." The little boy ran out to see, and the bird dropped the shoes at his feet. It rattled again, and the father ran out, and the bird dropped the watch and chain at his feet. Then it rattled again, and the stepmother, saying, "Perhaps the thunder has a present for me too," ran out to see, when the bird dropped the millstone on her head, and she fell down dead.

Jacobs, *English Fairy Tales*, p. 15.
In the Lincolnshire version (Gutch and Peacock, p. 325, cf. Baring-Gould, *N.Q.*, VIII, p. 82) the rhyme given to the little brother is as follows:

> "My mother killed me,
> My father picked my bones,
> And my little brother buried me
> Under the cold marble stones."

TYPE 720.

This is a full version of type 720, with the burying of the bones by the brother, the rewards and punishment, but no disenchantment of the dead child. It is possible that the dog that carried away the candles was the stepmother in a witch-form.

¶ See also "Rosy", "The Milk-White Doo", "The Satin Frock".

ROSY

Rosy were a little maid as had a stepmother and her were so wicked and good-for-nothing as twopennorth of God-help-us stuck on a stick. Rosy hadn' no love for she.

One day her took 'n sended Rosy for to get some 'at out of gurt chest up over in tallat. And the lid valled down on Rosy and killed 'n.

There her was with her head cutted off by this lid, and this wicked toad took'n and cooked'n and made she into pies vor her vather and her two liddle sisters. And they took'n and they went and eat'n and like'n too, and thic wicked toad her buried all they bones.

But Rosy her 'comed again' like a ghostie bird all a-trembley and a-whivery and singeth:

> "My Mammy her killed I 'n put I in pies;
> My vather did eat I 'n 'er said I were nice;
> My two liddle zisters they zucked my bones,
> And buried I under they marly stones,
> They marly stones, they marly stones,
> And buried I under they marly stones."

And when her vather heard'n, he took a cold shiver, and he run, and the liddle zisters run too—and no one wouldn' neighbour with the wicked toad—zo her died lonesome.

Ruth L. Tongue, oral collection. Corfe; Clatworthy. Recorded from Ruth L. Tongue, 29 September 1963, as she heard it from a Blackdown shepherd in Somerset in 1903. The tune was learned from Brendon Hills children, who sang it to a kind of singing game in Taunton in 1907.

TYPE 720. MOTIFS: E.613.0.1 [*Reincarnation of murdered child as bird*]; G.61 [*Relative's flesh eaten unwittingly*]; N.271 [*Murder will out*]; S.31 [*Cruel stepmother*].

Type 720 is well-known in the Grimm version, no. 47, "The Juniper Tree", and is found throughout Europe.

¶ See also "The Rose Tree", "The Satin Frock", "Orange and Lemon".

The School of Scottish Studies, Edinburgh, has two texts collected by Hamish Henderson, "Orangie and Applie", from Aberdeen, and a version of special interest from Perthshire, told by fourteen-year-old Jimmy McPhee. Here the murdered girl is brought back to her true form when her mother's grave is dug up and the ring turned on her finger. For fuller notes see *Folktales of England*, p. 27.

ST. GEORGE FOR MERRY ENGLAND
[summary]

St. George was the son of the Earl of Coventry, the High Steward of England. When he was still a baby his mother died, and he was stolen from his nurses by Kalyb, a wicked enchantress, who stole and devoured newborn children. She would have done the same to George, but he was strangely marked, with a dragon on his breast, a red cross on his right hand, and a golden garter round his left leg.

Because of these signs Kalyb spared him, and every day grew fonder of him, until her only desire was to keep him by her for ever. But George's heart was set on deeds of chivalry, and he begged her to let him go. She took him down into a dungeon, and showed him the six Champions of Christendom enchanted there. "And you shall be the seventh, and greatest of them all, if you will stay with me," she said.

Then she showed him all her stables, where seven beautiful horses stood. The swiftest and strongest of them all was called Bayard, and she offered him to George if he would stay with her, but he would not. Then she took him into the armoury, with weapons of all kinds, and showed him armour that nothing would pierce and the great sword, Ascalon, which should be his if he would stay with her, but he would not.

And at last, desperate for love of him, she offered him her magic wand which gave her all her power. He took it and touched the rock in front of him and it opened, and showed him all the bodies of infants that she had destroyed. He was very angry at the sight, and by the power of the wand he made her enter into the rock and closed it on her, so that she was imprisoned there and all her enchantments were at an end. So he freed the Six Champions of Christendom, and they rode out together into the world. Presently they came to a place where seven roads met, so each champion took a road and they parted.

St. George's road led him to the sea, and he took ship and sailed to Egypt. The whole land of Egypt was full of misery and desolation, and

St. George learnt from a hermit with whom he rested that a poisonous dragon was ravaging the land, who could only be kept quiet by having a maiden sacrificed to him every day. All the maidens in the land had been devoured, except the King's daughter, Sabra, and she was to go to the dragon that day.

At this St. George set out, and met the Princess's train and turned them back, and went himself to meet the dragon in their stead. It was a deadly fight, and St. George would have been slain but that the dragon knocked him under the shade of a flowering orange, with a scent so sweet that no poisonous beast could penetrate there. He rested and refreshed himself with its fruit and at length he killed the dragon and cut off its head. The King of Egypt had promised his daughter's hand to whoever could save her from the dragon, so he sent a chariot for George, and the betrothal began merrily. But Almindor, the Black King of Morocco, had long courted Sabra, and he told the King of Egypt that George would make her into a Christian as, indeed, he meant to do. So King Ptolemy of Egypt pretended that a further trial of George's prowess was needed, and sent him down with a letter to the King of Persia. The letter entreated the King to put the bearer to death, and when at length he arrived at the King of Persia's court he was entrapped into a dreadful dungeon, where he was chained up and hungry lions were loosed on him to tear him to pieces. But he wrenched out the ring that held him to the wall, and throttled the lions.

After that no one dared attack him, but he was left closely confined, until he used the staple which he had wrenched out of the wall to break his way out, and took a horse and rode away from Persia. On his way he killed a giant and rescued a lady, but he left her heir to the giant's castle and pressed on to find his own Princess Sabra. Before he reached her he passed into the domain of a wizard, Ormadine, who held St. David enchanted, but whose power would be broken when a champion from the North pulled a magic sword out of a stone. The sword almost leaped into his hand, and Ormadine's power was over. St. George was only just in time; after his seven years' absence Princess Sabra had been forced to marry Almindor of Morocco. She preserved her virginity by a magic golden chain.

St. George put on ragged clothes and went among the beggars who received alms from the Princess. As he knelt he showed her the betrothal ring she had given him, and they stole away together. In Greece they found all the Six Champions assembled, and they were in the midst of tourneys and rejoicings when a hundred heralds came from every part of the Paynim world, to challenge Christendom to battle. Then every Champion went back to his own country and gathered an army, and the battle was raised with the Paynim world, and the Kings of Persia and

Egypt and Morocco were all conquered, and George was chosen to reign over all three countries.

He and Sabra reigned there, but when they had established peace and prosperity, they left the countries to regents, and went back to Coventry, where they lived in all happiness, and had three stalwart sons.

From the chapbook, *The Seven Champions of Christendom*.

This story was also retold by Flora Annie Steel in Arthur Rackham's *Book of English Fairy Tales*.

TYPE 300. MOTIFS: G.346 [*Devastating monster lays waste to land*]; B.11.10 [*Sacrifice of human being to dragon*]; T.68.1 [*Princess offered to rescuer*]; N.681 [*Lover arrives home just as mistress is about to marry another*]; K.1816.0.3.1 [*Hero in menial disguise at heroine's wedding*]; H.80 [*Identification by tokens*].

These are some of the ordinary motifs common in Type 300. Many others are introduced into the story, which wanders on through the exploits of the other six champions, who are, however, subordinated to St. George. Amongst these motifs are: R.10.4 [*Witch abducts hero*]; D.2078.1 [*Witch imprisoned in boulder*]; D.1359.3.3 [*Magic fruit exhilarating*]; K.978 [*Uriah letter*].

Use is made throughout the chapbook of many of the Arthurian motifs. The mummers' play, *St. George and the Turkish Knight*, either borrows from this version of the tale or has inspired it. The ballad of Hind Horn (Child, I, p. 187) has in common with this story the magic diamond ring given by the Princess as a token and the return of the hero disguised as a beggar in time to rescue the Princess from a hated wedding.

For the legend as it was at one time received see Part B under "Saints", [XI].

THE SATIN FROCK

There was once a little girl called Mary, who had a satin frock, and her mother told her that if she got a dirty mark on it she would kill her. One day as Mary was going a walk, some cows that were passing by splashed her frock with mud. Then Mary went and sat on a doorstep and began to cry. The woman in the house, hearing her cry came out, and Mary told her that she dare not go home because she had got her frock dirty, and that her mother had threatened to kill her if she got it dirty. So the woman took her in, and washed the mud from her frock, and then dried it. She then sent the little girl on her way, telling her to mind and not get it dirty again, and then her mother would not kill her. So Mary went on her way, but lower down the road a horse that was running by splashed her frock again. When she got home her mother took her in the cellar and cut her head off, and hung it on the wall.

When her father came home he said: "Where is our Mary?" Her mother told him she had gone to her grandmother's to stay all night. When bed-time came, he said: "I will fetch the sticks up," but his wife said: "No, I will;" but he said: "No, I will fetch them up:" and she said; "No, I will;" but he would not let her fetch them. When he had got down in the cellar he saw the head hung up, so when he had come out of the cellar, he asked his wife what it was. She told him that it was a sheep's head that she was going to make some broth of for to-morrow's dinner. When he came home to dinner next day, he said: "This broth is nice, but it does taste like our Mary." When his wife heard this, she was very frightened; but when her husband found out what had been done, he took her in the cellar and killed her.

Norton Collection, II. From *Folk-Lore*, VIII (1897), pp. 394–5.
TYPE 720.
¶ This is a prosaic and naturalistic version of type 720. For other versions see "Little Rosy", "The Milk-White Doo", etc.

THE SEVEN BROTHERS [summary]

Seven brothers fond of going to dances, but anxious to have a sister. Decided to go away. Mother expecting child, promises to put a wind spinning mill on the roof if it is a girl, a plough if it is a boy. Boys go to their grandmother, a witch, who puts a mark on their heads so that they can see the sign, however far off they are. A beautiful daughter born, the Mother so pleased that she forgets the sign. The girl grows up, when she goes to dances hears about her brothers, and decides to seek them. Grandmother gives her magic apple to guide her. She rolls it, and it leads very far to resting-place in magic house. On again next day to another magic house. The third day reaches wood in which her brothers are living. Tidies house, and hides. Brothers angry, except youngest, Johnny, who guesses who it is. After several days younger brother catches her and they settle down. Brothers hope their employer will marry her. Warn her against he-witch in cottage near. One day the fire goes out, and she goes to borrow fire from witch. He makes condition that he may suck her finger. Bites it, and she becomes ugly. Brothers annoyed, and warn her to have no traffic with pedlar, who will be witch. Pedlar comes and persuades her to buy seven combs for her brothers. When they comb themselves they turn into bullocks. They ask her to drive them home. She sets out (now beautiful again), and on the way meets gentleman who persuades her to marry him. Bullocks to be kept in luxury. Child born. Husband goes to a meet. Cook persuades other servants to silence, and throws girl into dry well. She is saved by a cross-piece on which she sits. Cook gets into bed with baby. When husband returns, asks him to shoot the small bull-calf. Husband surprised, but goes. Bullocks stampede to well. Husband hears true wife calling. Rescues her, throws cook downstairs and kills her. They drive the bullocks home, where the grandmother disenchants them. [Tale hastily concluded.]

Collected by T. W. Thompson, from Eva Gray at Grimsby, 31 October 1914.

TYPE 451 (variant). MOTIFS: Z.71.5.1 [*Seven brothers and one sister*]; T.595 [*Sign hung out informing brothers whether mother had boy or girl*]; N.344.1 [*Wrong sign leads to boys' leaving home*]; D.1313.6 [*Magic apple indicates road, rolls ahead*]; N.831.1 [*Mysterious housekeeper*]; D.133.2 [*Transformation: man to bull*]; K.1911 [*The false bride*]; B.335.2 [*Life of helpful animal demanded as cure for feigned sickness*].

The only normal version of 451 is found among the Irish folk tales, e.g. "The Twelve Wild Geese", Kennedy, *Old Fireside Tales of Wexford*.

THE SEVEN MYSTERIES OF THE LUCK

An old woman and two sons and an Irishman had a farm which could not keep them as the land was poor, so they had ate up nearly all except some arrowroot. And Tom says: "Give me some arrowroot, and I'll go and seek my fortune. It's easier to scheme a fortune than work for one." So the old mother give Tom the piece of root, and off he goes sucking at this root.

He walks and walks for about three days, and he comes to a man sitting on a tree-stump, and holding a horse. And he says to Tom, "I'm hungry," and asks for a bit of arrowroot that Tom was still sucking at. So Tom says, "This arrowroot you can help your strength up with for ever, and if you'll swap me for the horse, we'll do a deal." So they swaps, but Tom did not give him all the root; he slyly broke him a piece off in the bend of his arm, at the elbow.

And this horse he got was a notive [noted] horse, which when you turned her head to the sun, and said, "Lion, *hind* sovereigns," it did so, about a bushel.

So Tom takes the horse, and goes back to an inn, where they had before refused him a drink, as he had had no money. But before he goes there he had tried the horse, and said, "Lion, *hind* sovereigns," and it did a lot; but Tom thinks: "Well, I'll not want to carry these, as I can get plenty more," so he shoves them in a bush. So on he goes to the inn, and asks for a meal and bed, and that the horse should be well looked after, as it was a valuable mystery horse. And he showed the people how it *hind* sovereigns, and treated all the people there to all they could eat and drink, before he went to bed. So the woman who kept the inn said to her husband, "We must have that horse," and they stole it, and put another in its place.

So Tom gets up in the morning, and pays his bill, with what was left from the night before, and gets home, and tells his mother all about the mystery horse. And his mother was so pleased she calls his brother and the Irishman to see the fortune they were going to get. And out in the yard they leads the horse, and Tom says, "Lion, *hind* suvereigns," but nothing came, so he gave it a hiding, but 'twas no good. So Tom said, "Never mind, mother, it will do to plough the garden. But it's a mystery he won't do it now."

So Bill says, "Mother, give me a bit of root, and I'll go and seek my fortune; it's no use all of us stopping here and starving." So he gets a bit of root, and he walks and walks, till long and by last, he comes to where Tom had met the man with the horse. And here he sees a man with a table on his head, and the man says, "What yous ating?" And Bill says, "It's a piece of arrowroot, and you can go for ever nibbling at it." So the man says, "I'm hungry and tired, and I'll swap you for this table." "Well, what's the table good for?" says Bill. So the man says: "I'll show you. All you have to do when you are hungry, is to sit down and say, 'Table spread,' and all manner of good food will come, and drink." So Bill thinks: "Our fortune's come now. I'll have it and go home, and we'll keep a refreshment house, and the table will find all the food." So they swaps, and arter a bit, the table being a bit heavy, he puts it down, and sits down to it, and says, "Table, spread," and all manners of food and drink came on, and he had what he wanted. So he went on, and he met two men who were hungry, and Bill says: "Wait a bit and I'll get you a feed," and they had a good feed and plenty of drink. And the three goes, and they came to an inn where they could get drink, but no food. So Bill says, "Never mind, I've a table here will get us all we want." And this inn was where Tom was robbed of his horse, and the woman there stole his table, and put another like it in its place.

Bill takes it home and says: "Mother, we've our fortunes made now." And they was all hungry, and Bill says, "Come on, and have just what yous has a mind to." And he puts the table down, and they all sits round, and Bill shouts out, "Table, spread," but nothing came, and nothing could they get. And Bill says: "Well, it's a mystery; but never mind, Mother, it'll do to put a few cups and saucers on."

Well, now they didn't know hardly what to do, as the farm would not keep the lot of them, so they talks it over, and the Irishman at last says: "Well, give me the last bit of root, and I'll try my best." And the old woman says, "Well, I don't think it's much use, as British is more keen nor Irish; but anyhow, have it and go." And the Irishman's boots had got bad with digging the land, so the old woman says, "Take my old boots, as they are better than yours." And the Irishman puts the boots under his arm, and sets off, nibbling at his bit of arrowroot.

And after three days he comes to where Tom met the horse, and Bill the table, and there was a man sitting there with a pair of clogs on, and he says to the Irishman, "What yous ating?" Irish says, "It's a bit of root, which, so long as you sucks at, you can walk for ever on." And the man says, "Swap me the root for the clogs." "Well, what's the clogs good for?" says the Irishman.

"Well," says the man, "these clogs will dance, or kick, or walk, just as you ask them, and you won't need to use your legs at all; the clogs will do the lot." So he swaps, and puts the clogs on, and says, "Clogs, dance," and the clogs danced, and then he says, "Clogs, kick," and they kicked till he could hardly stand on his feet; and then he remembered to say, "Clogs, walk," and they walked up hill and down.

And long and by last he comes to an inn, the same inn where Tom and Bill had been robbed. And he shows the people there what the clogs could do, and the woman wanted to steal the clogs, so she persuaded the Irishman to stay the night. Well, he stayed there, and in the night she stole the clogs, and put them under her bed. And later on, her husband came home, and she started telling him about the mysterious clogs, and she happened to say, "Clogs, kick," and the clogs up and kicked her and her husband, till they shouted for help.

And the Irishman had thought there was something wrong, and he says, "Give me a horse and a table what you stole, and I'll stop them kicking." And he got them, and he stopped the clogs.

Off he goes home with clogs, horse, and table, and tells them how it had all happened. And then Tom says, "That's my horse;" and Bill says, "That's my table;" and the Irishman says, "Clogs, kick," and the clogs kicked Bill and Tom till they said they would let the Irishman have the lot. But later on the Irishman, being good-hearted, gave up the lot to the old woman. And Tom he had also found the first pile of suvereigns that Lion had done, and brought them. And the old woman said: "Well, it's a fair mystery how you come to do it so well."

Arter a while Bill and the Irishman goes to seek further fortunes together, and they comes to a seaport town, and walks down the docks. And they says as whoever first sees a sign asking for a man was to have the first chance for it. And walking all the dock wall they sees a sign on a ship, and Bill sees it first, and trying to get on the ship he falls in the water. And he calls out to the Irishman, "Send us a line." The Irishman says, "It will be a mystery if you wants a line where you are going," and Bill drowns.

Norton Collection, II, p. 139.

Journal of the Gypsy Lore Society, n.s. VIII (1914–15), pp. 224–7. Told to Mr A. James by Jonathan Ayres, near Cardiff, 1915. In T. W. Thompson's *English Gypsy Folk-Tales*.
On another occasion, Ayres ended up this story as follows:
"Old Buzzie Lock trod on a piece of tin,
It bended,
An' my story's ended."

TYPE 563. MOTIFS: B.103.1 [*Treasure-dropping animal*]; D.1472.1.7 [*Magic table produces food and drink*]; D.1401 [*Magic object cudgels person*]; J.2355.1 [*Fool loses magic objects by talking about them*]; D.861.1 [*Magic object stolen at inn*]; D.881.2 [*Recovery of magic objects by use of magic cudgel*].

Here, as in "The Red Etin", the third brother is represented by someone outside the family. The irrelevant ending is characteristic of the gypsy tale, into which odd features are often introduced.

¶ See also "The Ass, the Table and the Stick".

SILKEN JANET or MUCKETTY MEG

> Blue eye beauty,
> Brown eye bonny,
> Grey eye grumpy,
> Green eye greedy,
> Black eye pick the pie,
> Lie in bed and tell a lie.

There was a pretty lass they called Jane, but she was proud and greedy and very poor. She thought her looks made a lady of her, and she wouldn't lift a finger to sweep or dust or clean herself, or help on the farm, or mind the sheep.

She said they were dirty, and when they answered her, "Dirty beast," she didn't like it.

She wouldn't milk the cows, she said they were mucky, and when they answered her "Mucky Minny," she didn't like that either.

As for the pigs, she said they smelled, and when they answered, "Stinking slut," she liked it no better.

One day she stole some silk from a Ladies' Bower on the Fairy Knowe and made herself a fine gown over her old rags, but she didn't wash; then she went to walk on the Fairy Knowe, and when they saw her on *their* land, in all her dirt and stolen finery, they had a mind to punish her. So all the beasts began to call out at her:

> "Silken Janet she wears a fine gown,
> She stole it, she stole it from Down a Down,
> She never paid a penny,
> Because she hadn't any."

They made such a racket that people heard, and they caught Silken Janet, and were going to take away her fine dress, but it was so dirty they said she should be hanged in it. Then she cried out to the beasts to help her, but they all answered:

> "Nobody likes a grimy lass,
> Nobody wants a stinking slut,
> Nobody needs a dirty beast,
> Go away and roll in the muck."

Well, she couldn't anyway, even if she wanted to.

Then she cried out to the lads, "Will you not help a pretty lass?" But they answered her:

"Nobody likes a grimy lass,
Nobody likes a stinking slut,
Nobody wants a dirty beast,
Go away and roll in the muck."

And she couldn't anyway, and the hangman got the rope round her neck—and then she saw a fine gentleman in green, and called out to him, "Will you not save a pretty lass?"

And he said, "Leave it to me, but you must pay me your two blue eyes."

"What will I see with?" she begged.

"Green ones," said he, and took away her blue ones, and left her with green.

Well, she cried, but the rope was still there. "I'll give you my fine golden gown," she said.

"It's stolen! I'll not touch it. I want real gold," he said.

"I have none," she cried.

"There's all your pretty gold hair under the dirt. I'll take that."

And he cut it all off.

"Now go and wash it in the river."

And she got out of the rope and the crowd, and ran down to the river so fast she fell right in.

When she climbed out, she had lost the tresses of hair, so she sat and cried. But nobody came to hang her, and when she looked down, the golden gown had been washed off her, and her rags were clean as a gowan.

Then the pig came by. "Good morning, clean lass," said he.

Then a sheep came by. "Pretty clean curly locks," said she.

Then a cow came by with a pail on her horns. "I'll let you milk me, my clean pretty lass," she said. "There's a crowd looking for a dirty golden slut that was to be hanged, and I don't want them to have my milk."

So she set to milking, and did it quite well. And when the crowd came by, she kept her face hid against the cow. But the gentleman in green took her by the hair and looked at her. "This is a clean lass," he said. "She's got a lint white linen gown, and curly lint white locks. She's got *green eyes*!" They were so disappointed they threw her in the river again.

When she climbed out this time, she couldn't see any crowd, or any gallows, or any gentleman in green. She was all in her washed rags, and her long golden hair hung down to dry about her, and she was on the Fairy Knowe.

"I best be out of here," she said, and ran for home. She ran till her dry rags fluttered in the wind, and her golden hair streamed out around her and she met a young farmer.

"Good morning, blue eyes," he said. "I'm looking for a clean pretty wife to work all her days. Will you marry me?"

"That I will gladly," said Silken Janet.

Ruth L. Tongue, "A North-Country Tale, told by an old Lancashire lady, 1939".

Note 1. The teller of this tale was an evacuee from the city. Her grandparents were Cumberland and Westmorland on her mother's side, and Durham and Northumberland on her father's, but she herself was born in Lancashire, and married a Lancastrian.

Note 2. A North Country W. I. member said her mother used to chant to a grubby child: "Go away and roll in the muck like Mucketty Meg."

MOTIFS: F.350 [*Theft from fairies*]; Q.212 [*Theft punished*]; Q.322 [*Dirtiness punished*]; M.242 [*Bargains and promises between mortals and supernatural beings*]; R.161.4 [*Lover rescues his lady from the gallows*]; B.210 [*Speaking animals*].

This *cante-fable* is on something the same lines as "The Maid freed from the Gallows".

There are several points of interest in the story. The Ladies' Bower on the Fairy Knowe is worth note as pointing back to the Bower made for the fairies in the medieval play by Adam de la Halle, *Le Jeu d'Adan*.

❡ See "The Golden Ball".

SILLY JACK AND THE WEE ROBIN or SILLY JACK AND HIS WISE BROTHER
[summary]

Two sons—a bannock and a collop—curse or blessing. Jack, the despised younger son, chooses the blessing, and is advised by his mother to take the first turn left to the castle. He was sitting down to eat and drink, when his brother "comes up, a poor thing, with blistered feet". He goes on to the castle. The King gives him a silver sixpence, and tells him to give it to the guard. The guard takes up Jack's message, and the King (who turns out to be a duke) tells him to bring Jack up.

Given tasks to do in the garden. A maid comes to talk to him, and tells him how to do them. Warns him to go. He sits down by a spring to take a little more of his bannock and a robin comes up, and asks for some crumbs, which he gives.

The robin tells him to take a feather from her tail. Then she shows him the way to the North Gate, where he finds his brother in worse case than before. He returns to ask for more tasks from the King. There is an obscure reference to the Beheading Game. He is set to drain a pool and get a lost ring from it. He does so by means of the feather. He is given whins to cut. The robin visits him again and asks for more crumbs, and gives him another feather, by means of which he cuts the whins. The third task is to move a great rock. The robin appears again and gets the last of his bannock, gives him another feather, and tells him to go to sleep. The rock is moved while he sleeps. The last task is performed, but the Duke/King says Jack must be imprisoned for three nights and days.

The robin visits him and gives him a feather. He gives this into the hand of his guard, who is frozen by it, and so successively to all he meets except one, who refuses the feather. The Duke invites him to a banquet but Jack hands him the feather, and he too is frozen. The maid comes in and asks Jack to pull a feather from her tail. He recognizes her as the robin. They are married.

School of Scottish Studies, Hamish Henderson, from Davie Stewart. Heard from his grandmother. This story was a good deal confused in the telling; at times the identity of the two brothers was very indeterminate. It had some very vivid moments, however, when the narrator was well started. There was quite a dramatic attempt to give a laird's accent to the king—a curious inward stifled ha-ha-ing voice. The incidents with the robin were lively and playful.

The characteristic motifs of type 313 are recognizable in this tale, though somewhat jumbled.

¶ See "Nicht Nought Nothing", "Green Sleeves", "Daughter Greengown".

SILVERTOES AND TIMBERTOES

Timbertoes was a tree and Silvertoes was a tree.

Timbertoes was a mighty oak and Silvertoes was a graceful young birch, and *he* grew on the edge of the forest and *she* grew by the Mere. One day the Wind came by and stopped to chat with Timbertoes. "I gave you a wild night last night, old friend," he said. "I hope you stood up to it."

"I think I lost a small top bough, but that's the first in 50 years," said Timbertoes. "It was injured as a twig and was always weakly."

"*I* only lost a few leaves," interrupted Silvertoes quite rudely, "but I can still dance a beautiful dance. I am not old and ugly and heavy!"

The Wind looked down at her. "Do you know you are growing across the Path?"

"What Path?" said Silvertoes saucily—but one doesn't speak to the Wind like that, so she went on, "We-ell, it doesn't go anywhere."

"Doesn't it?" said the Wind gravely, then he added more kindly, "If I were you I'd grow the other way."

"I couldn't see myself in the water," objected Silvertoes.

The Wind gave a gentle sigh and all her little green leaves twinkled. "You might *just* be in time," he said. "You are a pretty young thing—but even I don't care very much for witches' brooms."

And he went away.

One day there came a Swineherd with all his pigs and *he* kicked Silvertoes hard, "Growing across the Path you are. Move over now!"

"I can't see myself in the water if I do," said Silvertoes.

"Handsome is as handsome does," said the Swineherd and he kicked Silvertoes again, but he took off his cap to Timbertoes and all the pigs looked up from their acorns and grunted their thanks. When they went away, the Swineherd tried to heave Silvertoes over a bit, but she wasn't going to budge, so he stopped at last. "You are a pretty young thing," he admitted, "but I don't like witches' brooms."

A few mornings later there came a wild pony, and the next morning a stag, and the next morning a fox and they all kicked or butted or scrabbled at Silvertoes and they all said the same thing about witches' brooms. So Silvertoes complained to Timbertoes.

"You are young enough still to have just time enough to grow your branches away from the Path," said Timbertoes; but Silvertoes shook with temper.

"You silly old tree!" she cried, "I couldn't see myself in the water, and *I'm* quite sure the Path leads nowhere. If anyone else says witches' brooms to me I'll tell them about that ugly bush hidden in *your* branches."

"They all know it's there," said Timbertoes solemnly. "It has been growing there for 500 years."

But Silvertoes didn't even listen; all she said was, "Then it's high time you got rid of it." And she went on admiring her leaves in the water.

One afternoon all the birds came and roosted in Timbertoes and were very polite to him, but Robin Redbreast and his wife Jenny Wren were sorry for Silvertoes and tried to help her.

"There's still just enough time to move over a little tiny bit," they begged. "Just off the Path. You can do it, if you try."

"I shan't try," said Silvertoes. "The Path doesn't go *anywhere*."

And the very next evening a band of holy men came along the Path and Silvertoes was right across their way. They sent for a wood-cutter with a sharp axe and though Silvertoes shivered and sighed he cut her right down and made a big fire of her, saying, "I don't like witches' brooms."

By the light of its flames the holy men sang, and then they took a golden sickle and cut off the silver bough that Timbertoes guarded and bore it away.

"Now I shall be lonely for another 100 years," thought Timbertoes and he looked at the glowing red ashes. "No witches ever dared bother me. She was a pretty young thing and very pleasant to look on."

And he gave a sigh.

A Welsh Border tale from Wem, near Whitchurch, 1909. Ruth L. Tongue.
This is a traditional tale inasmuch as it has been handed down in one family from

the eighteenth century to the twentieth, but it is clearly the invention of one teller, and was early crystallized, though written down for the first time in 1913.

The introduction of the Druids and the mistletoe seems a literary fancy.

Ruth Tongue's account is: "One of Mother's old cousins, Miss Patty Jones, was told it as a little girl in 1840 by her grandmother, who was born in 1771. She always told it in precisely the same way, and so did Cousin Patty, although it had a very mid-Victorian 'literary' phraseology—I did however meet with this in the early 1900s among older people. Written out by my mother, 1913."

THE SINGING BRIDE [summary]

There was a King who took great delight in singing, and he sent out his three sons to find wives, and the son who could bring back the most beautiful singer should have the kingdom. They set out together, and when they came to a place where four roads met, they tossed up as to which each should take.

The youngest son's was by a lonely untrodden track. Before they started, they stuck their three knives into the post, so that they could see who was back first. The youngest went along by the lonely path for long enough, until he came to a croft, and they were busy at the hay. He asked the old man working there where the road led to, and he said it led up to the mountains where there was no one, and invited him to stay at the croft, and help with the hay harvest. The Prince said he would stay for three days, and he worked very hard, and settled in well, and when the three days were up, he stayed on a while longer. One day while he was having his dinner, he heard a most lovely singing from the next room. He asked who it was, but the old lady wouldn't say. He listened and listened in delight, for he loved singing as well as his father did, till the old man said, "You can marry her if you like, but you mustn't see her." "How can I do that?" said the Prince. "You must marry her through the keyhole." At first the Prince wouldn't hear of it, but the singing went on till he was half out of his wits with the beauty of it, and at last he consented. They fetched a priest, and he pushed his ring through the keyhole, and married his bride without seeing her or touching her. Then he wanted to take his bride back to his father, for the time was nearly up.

"Better wait," they said. "No," said the Prince, "I'd better go on, or I'll not be in time." "I'll fetch you the bride then," said the old man, and he went out of the room, and came back with a pewter plate, and on the plate was a reeking curd. The Prince was ready to faint. "Is this the bride you've given me?" he said. "You've not dealt fairly with me." "Maybe we've dealt better than you know," said the old man. "Take her home with you." "Wrap it up then," said the Prince. "Put it into all the bags you have in the house, so that I'll not smell the reek of it." So they put it into all the bags they had in the house, and the Prince set out with the bag on his shoulders.

When he got to the cross-roads, he saw that his knife was the only one left, so he knew that his brothers were before him, and he hurried after them. But the nearer he got to the Palace, the worse he felt about the insult he would put upon them all. So when he got to the garden, he left the bag behind a bush, and went on to the Palace, where the contest was already on. And most beautiful singing it was, but suddenly in a pause they heard a voice far more beautiful, singing such as they had never heard, coming from the next room.

The Prince knew the voice, and tried to stop the King, but the King hurried into the next room, and there was a most beautiful girl, singing like an angel. So the youngest brother won the kingdom.

School of Scottish Studies, H. Henderson, from Bella Higgins, Aberdeenshire. Told by her grandmother, Mary McPhee.
TYPE 402 (variant). MOTIFS: H.1210.1 [*Quest assigned by father*]; H.1381.3.1[*Quest for bride*]; T.110 [*Unusual marriage*]; H.1242 [*Youngest brother succeeds on quest*]; D.732 [*Loathly lady*]; D.700 [*Person disenchanted*].
This is a short version of the tale, with only one quest instead of three. An unusual feature is the effort to make the enchanted bride as revolting as possible.
¶ See also "Jack and the Puddock", "The Three Feathers".

THE SMALL-TOOTH DOG

Once upon a time there was a merchant who travelled about the world a great deal. On one of his journeys thieves attacked him, and they would have taken both his life and his money if a large dog had not come to his rescue and driven the thieves away.

When the dog had driven the thieves away he took the merchant to his house, which was a very handsome one, and he dressed his wounds and nursed him till he was well.

As soon as he was able to travel the merchant began his journey home, but before starting he told the dog how grateful he was for his kindness, and asked him what reward he could offer in return and he said he would not refuse to give the most precious thing he had.

And so the merchant said to the dog: "Will you accept a fish I have that can speak twelve languages?"

"No," said the dog, "I will not."

"Or a goose that lays golden eggs?"

"No," said the dog, "I will not."

"Or a mirror in which you can see what anybody is thinking about?"

"No," said the dog, "I will not."

"Then what will you have?" said the merchant.

"I will have none of such presents," said the dog; "but let me fetch your daughter, and bring her to my house."

When the merchant heard this he was grieved, but what he had promised had to be done, so he said to the dog, "You can come and fetch my daughter after I have been home for a week."

So at the end of the week, the dog came to the merchant's house to fetch his daughter, but when he got there he stayed outside the door, and would not go in.

But the merchant's daughter did as her father told her, and came out of the house dressed for a journey and ready to go with the dog.

When the dog saw her he looked pleased, and said:

"Jump on my back, and I will take you away to my house."

So she mounted on the dog's back, and away they went at a great pace, until they reached the dog's house, which was many miles off.

But after she had been a month at the dog's house she began to mope and cry.

"What are you crying for?" said the dog.

"Because I want to go back to my father," she said.

The dog said: "If you will promise me that you will not stay there more than three days I will take you there. But first of all," said he, "what do you call me?"

"A great, foul, small-tooth dog," said she.

"Then," said he, "I will not let you go."

But she cried so pitifully that he promised again to take her home.

"But before we start," he said, "tell me what you call me."

"Oh," she said, "your name is 'Sweet-as-a-honey-comb'."

"Jump on my back," said he, "and I'll take you home."

So he trotted away with her on his back for forty miles, when they came to a stile.

"And what do you call me?" said he, before they got over the stile. Thinking she was safe on her way, the girl said, "A great, foul, small-tooth dog."

But when she said this, he did not jump over the stile, but turned right round again at once, and galloped back to his own house with the girl on his back.

Another week went by, and again the girl wept so bitterly that the dog promised to take her to her father's house.

So the girl got on the dog's back again, and they reached the first stile, as before, and then the dog stopped and said:

"And what do you call me?"

"Sweet-as-a-honey-comb," she replied.

So the dog leaped over the stile, and they went on for twenty miles until they came to another stile.

"And what do you call me?" said the dog with a wag of his tail.

She was thinking more of her father and her own house than of the dog, so she answered, "A great, foul, small-tooth dog."

Then the dog was in a great rage, and he turned right round about, and galloped back to his own house as before.

After she had cried for another week, the dog promised again to take her back to her father's house. So she mounted upon his back once more, and when they got to the first stile, the dog said: "And what do you call me?"

"Sweet-as-a-honey-comb," she said.

So the dog jumped over the stile, and away they went—for now the girl made up her mind to say the most loving things she could think of—until they reached her father's house.

When they got to the door of the merchant's house, the dog said, "And what do you call me?"

Just at that moment the girl forgot the loving things she meant to say, and began: "A great——", but the dog began to turn, and she got fast hold of the door latch, and was going to say "foul," when she saw how grieved the dog looked and remembered how good and patient he had been with her, so she said,

"Sweeter-than-a-honey-comb."

When she had said this she thought the dog would have been content and have galloped away, but instead of that he suddenly stood upon his hind-legs, and with his fore-legs he pulled off his dog's head and tossed it high in the air. His hairy coat dropped off, and there stood the handsomest young man in the world, with the finest and smallest teeth you ever saw.

Of course they were married, and lived together happily.

S. O. Addy, *Household Tales*, p. 1. Derbyshire.
TYPE 425C. MOTIFS: B.620.1 [*Daughter promised to animal suitor*]; C.32 [*Offending supernatural husband*]; Q.41 [*Politeness rewarded*].

⁋ This is c of Type 425, best known in its French form *La Belle et la Bête*, but also occurring in Grimm (no. 88). It is widely reported throughout Europe, Lithuania leading with thirty versions. Baughman cites examples from five American states.

Forms nearer to 425 A are "The Black Bull of Norroway", "The Red Bull of Norroway", "The Three Feathers", "The Glass Mountains".

THE SMITH AND HIS DAME

God that died on a tree yield His grace unto them that will hearken unto me, and I shall tell of a marvel.

In Egypt there dwelt a smith, who prospered long and well, and had land and fee and husbandmen at his bidding. This smith was a cunning artificer, and could, by my troth, work in any metal; and he was wont to boast that, save himself, there was none that followed that same craft worth a straw.

Now Our Blessed Lord was wrath with this smith by reason of his pride and vain-glory, and thought how He might compass his chastisement. And so it happened on a day, that, as he stood at his forge working, Our Lord came unto him secretly, and said unto him: "Lo, I have a thing for thee to do; and if thou canst do it, thou shalt be well paid, i' faith."

"Say on," replied the smith, as one that wist not who spake thus unto him, "for I am a master of all this cunning; and whatever thou shalt be pleased to command, it shall be done to point."

Then said Our Blessed Lord to him: "Canst thou make a yard of steel to lead a blind man, so that he may never fall? If so thou canst this accomplish, then I will salute thee a master of thy calling."

Then the smith fell into a study, and presently answered the stranger thus: "Sir, I trow thou art mad, or something worse to talk of such things. If a man be blind, he must have a fellow who can see to lead him in the way. For if two blind men walk together, they commonly both fall into the ditch; and how should a blind man with a blind rod, be the steel never so hard, find his way? Nay, it is false."

"Well," said Our Blessed Lord unto the smith, "I can make such a rod, or I can restore an old man to his youth, as he was before."

"I have an old quean here with me," the smith said, "she is my wife's mother, and it is forty years or more since she set foot to ground. By my faith, if thou couldst make her young again, then right glad were I."

Our Lord said: "Where is she? Let me see her, and I shall shew thee a feat beyond thy reach."

The smith hastened to fetch his dame, where she lay a-bed.

"Mother," quoth he, "art thou asleep? I have come for thee, that thou mayest be made young again." And he pulled her out of the place where she lay, and carried her on his shoulders back to the stranger, and her cries and struggles heeded not.

Our Lord said unto him: "Verily, smith, it shall be done unto her as I say. Take her now, and put her on thy forge, and make her fast, that she fall not therefrom, and with thy bellows blow thy best."

He blew as he was commanded by the stranger, till the fire roared, and the old wife was as red as a hot coal; yet pain suffered she none.

The smith said: "Now it is all over. She will never eat meat more. I have blown till I sweat."

"Let me alone," quoth the stranger. "Thou shalt behold anon a full fair woman in place of thy old beldame."

He blessed her, and said unto her, "Dame, awake." And he bade the smith to strike her with his hammer, and straightway she arose, and was comely and young to the sight.

Our Lord said to the smith: "She is whole once more. We have made her young again with hammer and bellows. There is none in Egypt that may surpass her. Behold, one that was an old crone is now as though she were thirty years of her age. Now acknowledge me for thy master."

"Sir," then quoth the smith, "I dare well say that, an' a man were dead, thou mightest make him live again by thy excellent craft and mastership. Now, what shall I pay thee, ere thou goest, to teach me this art?"

Our Lord rejoined: "What thou seekest is in vain: thou canst never compass these things. And I prythee do not essay them, lest thou shouldest be deceived. But leave thy boasting; for whatsoever thou knowest, there is ever much to learn. My name is Jesus, and I now depart from thee to go into another country."

And Our Lord was lost to view.

When Our Lord was no longer manifest to the smith, the smith went and called his wife Joan, desiring her to come to him; who cried out, and asked him if he wist not well that she was in no case to come, as he bad her, for she was lame, and might not walk, and she was waxing in years, so that her sight failed her, and her bones ached. She feared to fall at every step she took.

The smith was forgetful of the admonition which Our Lord had given him, and thought that he might do with her even as Christ Jesus had done with the old wife his mother; and so he sent unto her: "Come forth, and at a stroke I will make thee young as thou wast before. Look! thy own mother, that could neither walk nor see, is as merry as a bird, and her complexion is like a rose."

Then when the woman came, and saw her mother, how she was young and lusty, she said unto her, "Art thou my mother indeed?"

"Yea," quoth she, "*benedicite*!"

"Who made thee whole, then, mother?" she asked.

"Even one", she answered, "that came this way. Men call his name Jesus."

"Verily he has worked a wonder by thee; for even yesterday thou wast but a feeble trot."

"Wife," said the smith, "had I a right hot fire, I could make thee as thy mother is." And he fetched a quarter of coals, and took his bellows, and blew till there was a white heat.

"Lo," cried the smith, "there is none in all this country can do this save I." And he laid hold of his wife to place her on the forge.

"What art thou doing, thief, with me?" she cried. "Knowest thou not that I am thy own wife?"

"I go to burn thee, as I did thy sweet mother," quoth the smith.

"Traitor, if thou burnest me, thou shalt hang on a tree," she shouted. "Curses upon thee! Did we not keep thee, when thou hadst nought? And goest thou about to burn me?"

"Fear not," said the smith, "thou shalt with the fire and the hammer be made as when I saw thee first. Come." And he took her by the middle, to fasten her on the forge. But she struggled and kicked and sware, and when he had her at last well on the furnace, she caught him by the hair, and smote him in the eye, and called loudly for help.

He waxed wrath hereat, and cast her clean into the flames, and once she rose, and twice, essaying to rend him with her nails. But he heaped on the coals, and then the water, and set to work with his bellows, and blew as hard as he could. "Ha! Ha!" he cried, "I shall make thee young again yet, I see well."

Then when she lay still, he raised her up, and hammered at her with all his might, till both her legs dropped from her.

"What is this?" he said aghast. "Wilt thou not be young, wife? What! thou art not dead? Come, speak a word. Say *Bo*!"

But she uttered no word, and anon an arm fell into the flame; and the smith threw down his hammer, and ran into the street like one distracted, shouting for Jesus to come to him.

Then incontinently appeared Our Lord unto the smith, and said unto him, "Man, what hast thou done?"

"I sought to do as thou hadst done by my dame before, and make my wife young by burning her in the furnace, and beating her with the hammer."

"Did I not shrewdly advise thee, man," quoth Jesus, "not to venture herein? Thou hast burned thy wife, and slain her."

"Ah! good Lord," answered the smith, "I cry for mercy. I disobeyed you, Lord."

"Thou repentest thy sin," said Jesus, "and as thou prayest, so it shall be done."

And He blessed her, and bad her arise: and she arose straightway, and seemed as bright as a blossom, and a thousandfold fairer than she was before.

She sank on her knees, and prayed to God on high, and the smith fetched his mother: and all those three knelt together, and held up their joined hands, to give praise and glory to Heaven.

Our Lord then said to the smith: "See that thou never do this thing more, for it is a craft which thou canst not learn. But I grant unto thee this boon, that over all thy fellows in the mystery which thou professest thou shalt have lordship, and that none, save he seek thy counsel and aid, may prosper."

These words He delivered to the smith, and again He enjoined him in no wise, to his life's end, to intermeddle with such things as belonged not to man: and so He departed into other lands, to do like acts of grace and mercy.

Let us all give thanks that there is such a Lord, and pray that He may bring us to His bliss!

So endeth the tale of the smith, which that burned his dame, and made her whole again by the help of Christ Jesus.

W. Carew Hazlitt, *Tales and Legends of National Origin*, p. 28.
TYPE 735.
¶ See "The Old Smith".

THE SMITH AND THE DEVIL [summary]

In the days when Our Lord and St Peter were walking about the earth, they came to a smithy and read over the door: "Here dwells the master over all masters."

The smith had made a bargain with the Devil to belong to him at the end of seven years, if in the meantime he might be the master over all the other smiths. Our Lord then performed many wonders to prove that He was master over the smith himself, and finally granted the smith three wishes. The smith first wished that anyone who climbed into his pear-tree should have to stay there until he gave him leave to get down, second that whoever sat in his easy-chair should have to stay there till he asked him to get up, and third, that whoever got into his steel purse should remain there until he asked him to get out. St Peter rebuked him for not having first wished for God's grace and goodwill, but the smith replied that that would be too high a wish for him.

The next time the Devil visited him the smith kept him fast until he agreed to lengthen his time of grace, and so it went on until at last the smith hammered the Devil so tightly into his steel purse that the Devil begged for mercy, and promised to come no more.

But later on, the smith, fearing that he had no chance of going to Heaven, decided to make it up with the Devil, for fear that after his death he might find no place to rest. So he tried to get into Hell, but the Devil roared out that all the nine locks of Hell were to be locked against him, "for the smith would turn Hell topsy-turvy".

So the smith made his way to Heaven, where St Peter was just opening the gates a very little way to let in a poor little half-starved tailor. The smith threw his sledge-hammer to hold the gate open, "and if he didn't get in then, when the gates were ajar, I don't know what has become of him".

C. S. Burne and G. F. Jackson, *Shropshire Folk-Lore* (Trubner & Co., Ludgate Hill, 1883), p. 36.

TYPE 330A. MOTIFS: M.211 [*Man sells soul to devil*]; K.1811 [*Gods (saints) in disguise visit mortals*]; J.2071 [*Three foolish wishes*]; D.1413.1 [*Tree from which one cannot descend*]; D.1413.6 [*Chair to which person sticks*]; D.1413.9.1 [*Wallet from which one cannot escape*]; K.213 [*Devil pounded in knapsack till he releases man*]; Q.565 [*Man admitted to neither Heaven nor Hell*]; K.2371.1.3 [*Heaven entered by a trick*].

¶ See also "Dule upon Dun", "The Man who wouldn't go out at Night", "St Dunstan and the Devil", B, XI, "The Old Smith."

SNOW-WHITE [summary]

Child born according to mother's wish, with skin as white as snow, and cheeks as red as blood. Speaking mirror. Stepmother orders groom to take child into forest and kill her, bringing back heart. Groom spares child, kills young boar, and brings its heart back. Queen eats heart. Snow-White wanders through wood, and is found fainting by three robbers, who carry her to their cave. She cleans and cooks for them. Warned not to go out or open door of cave. Queen hears of Snow-White's whereabouts. Sends huntsman to search. He finds her but cannot capture her. Queen attempts murder, disguised as pedlar-woman. Means to strangle Snow-White with necklet. Robbers open the door, and take her basket. Attempt as countrywoman with poisoned flowers and apples. Bunch of flowers left at door of cave and burnt by robbers. Poisoned apples thrown in glade, and picked up by Snow-White. Apparent death.

Glass coffin in which she lies for seven years. Prince falls in love with her. Persuades robbers to let him take coffin. Fall of one of the bearers. Coffin lid slips off, apple falls out of Snow-White's mouth. She recovers, and marries Prince. Wicked Queen roasted in a brick-kiln.

Collected by T. W. Thompson from Traienti Lovell, wife of Ephraim Heron, at Blackburn, 13 September 1914.

TYPE 709. MOTIFS: Z.65.1 [*Red as blood, white as snow*]; D.1323.1 [*Magic clairvoyant mirror*]; K.512.2 [*Compassionate executioner: substituted heart*]; S.111.4 [*Murder with poisoned apple*]; F.852.1 [*Glass coffin*]; N.711 [*King accidentally finds maiden and marries her*]; E.21.1 [*Resuscitation by removal of poisoned apple*].

This is the nearest version to Grimm, no. 53, in English, though there are many in

Ireland. In a number of versions, as in this, the helpers are robbers instead of dwarfs. It seems probable, therefore, that this is not just a retelling of a chapbook version of Grimm. A variation is that Snow-White never admits the stepmother into the cave but is betrayed by a poisoned apple left in a flowery glade, where she goes under the care of one of the robbers to pick nosegays.

SORROW AND LOVE [summary]

Farmer has three lovely daughters. Going to fair. Asks each one what she would like. First two ask for fine clothing, youngest for a pennyworth of sorrow and love.

Farmer tries everywhere, but can't buy it. On the way home, handsome young man on fiery horse overtakes him, and learns his trouble. Says he knows where to get sorrow and love, and will get it for the girl, but must see her first. Girl falls deeply in love with him. Appoints to meet her at the crossroads at eight o'clock exactly. Because she is a second late he pulls off her glove, bites the tip off her finger, and tells her if she can find him again he will marry her. His name is Squire King Caley. Rides off and girl follows. She at length reaches his castle, crosses frozen moat, and asks to be servant. Woman there means to marry Squire. Takes her on to do rough work. Jealous of her beauty, and makes her black her face and hide her hair. Still jealous, dismisses her. Girl goes away weeping. Meets an old woman who will give her a magic gift if she can weep a bowl full of tears. Does so without difficulty, and is given a pear which makes wonderful music when cut. Girl barters pear for leave to stay on. The one who washes blood off shirt to wed Squire. Girl performs this. False bride claims credit. Squire says bride has a tip off her finger. False bride cuts off hers. Squire not deceived. Says bride must be able to wear glove. False bride fails. True bride succeeds. Squire says: "You have had your sorrow; now you shall have love."

Collected by T. W. Thompson from Gus Gray at Cleethorpes, 26 September 1914.
TYPES 425 [variant]; 938A [variant]. MOTIFS: L.211 [Modest request: present from journey]; J.214 [Choice: suffering in youth or old age]; H.1385.4 [Quest for vanished husband]; Q.482.1 [Princess serves as menial]; H.1233.1.1 [Old woman helps on quest]; D.821 [Magic object received from old woman]; D.2006.1.4 [Forgotten fiancée buys place in husband's bed]; H.373 [Bride test]; K.1911.3.3.1 [False bride mutilates herself to pass test: is detected].
¶ King Caley is the name of the villain in another gypsy tale, "The Cellar of Blood", a variant of Mr Fox. Other, more usual forms of 425 are "The Black Bull of Norroway", "The Small-Tooth Dog", etc.

THE SPRING OF THE SIXPENCE

There were a poor farmer and his family as was overlooked by an old witch down the lane. Night times, she'd go out as a hare, see, or she'd send her gurt black cat, and mischief was bound to follow. Hens 'oodn't lay, cows went dry, or butter 'oodn't come, so how could farm prosper? 'Twas a good varm tew, mind. Well, the little boy he try to help and he went off to ask the Pixies. He shouldn't have adone it, but they had a liking vor 'en. No matter how bad things was he never vorgot to sweep hearth for their welcome, and put out a pail of spring water, even if there wadn't a crop of cream in the house. So the Pixies they give'n a bag of gold, and he remembered his manners, and thanked 'en proper. But when he came away back, he think, "'Tis fairy gold, and 'twill all aturn to withered leaf. 'Twas very kind of 'they', but 'twould only make my poor mother sorrow more. Perhaps I'd ought to asked 'en if They 'oodn't mind tew much if I dipped their gold in running water afore I tooked 'en whoame." So he go on down to the Spring, see, and sure enough, the bag of gold melts away—but the Spring, she (liked) him tew. So she change it to a silver sixpence. He remembered his manners this time tew, then he put the sixpence in his pocket, and he went on along whoame.

When Varmer see the sixpence, he say, "I've a better use for he than to spend it." And he load his gun with 'en, and he shot the old witch. She never come around no more, and varm grew rich as rich. But the little boy, he saw to it they Pixies had a dish of cream every night, and he spoke his thanks to the Spring when he fetched the water.

Ruth L. Tongue: Told by Clara, an old farm servant. "My correspondent and scribe was the eldest daughter of the farm, and Clara chattered on very fast, and when asked what she had said, would sulk, and stop altogether. The gaps were filled by the small brothers who practically knew the tale by heart."

Somerset, Blackdown Hills. 1930.
MOTIFS: Q.41 [*Politeness rewarded*]; F.342.1 [*Fairy gold*]; D.927 [*Magic spring*] D.1385.4 [*Silver bullet protects against witches*].

It is doubtful whether this tale should be classed as a legend or a fairy tale. The emphasis placed on the moral tilts the balance towards fairy tale.
¶ See "Fairy Merchandise", B. IV.

THE STEPNEY LADY

You may give Three Stars or Eusebia's compliments, which you please, to Mr. Malcolm, and acquaint him I should have answered his obliging reply to my query (concerning the lady buried at Stepney) sooner; but I had been hunting the ballad stalls for the old song without success; though all the old women are well acquainted with it, my memory is not good enough to give any stanzas of it as a specimen, so the story shall be at Mr. M.'s service in humble prose.

A gentleman, benighted in travelling, is sheltered in a cottage, where the good wife is in labour; he draws the horoscope of the infant, and finds it destined to be his future bride; this his pride revolting against, he pretends compassion to the circumstances of the parents, who are easily induced to part with one child from a numerous brood to a rich man, who promises to provide so much better for it than they can: he carries it off with an intention to destroy it, but, not being hardened enough to imbrue his hands in its blood, he leaves it in some lonely forest to, at least, as certain destruction; here some shepherd or cottager finds it, takes it home to his wife, who nurses it with great tenderness, as has been ever usual in these stories, from the time of Romulus and Remus. She grows up in all the bloom of beauty. Again her future spouse is drawn by his stars to this spot; stricken with her beauty, but hearing her history, from her supposed father, is again enraged, and meditates her death; covering his design with pretended love, gets her a second time into his hands; again melted by her tears and petitions, throws his ring into a river they was near, vowing to destroy her if ever she appeared before him without that ring. After several adventures, she gets into service as a cook in a family. Here, gutting a large fish, to her great astonishment she finds this ring, which she carefully keeps; and, not long after, he comes; threatens, but on seeing the ring, finds it in vain to resist destiny; and, her planet having now the full ascendancy, they form a very happy conjunction. I do not know, Mr. Urban, whether you will find this old woman's tale worth inserting. I have endeavoured to relate it as concisely as I could.

Yours, etc. EUSEBIA.

Norton Collection, III, p. 12 A. *Gentleman's Magazine*, 1794, pt. I, pp. 128–9; reprinted in *The Gentleman's Magazine Library*...ed. G. L. Gomme, *English Traditional Lore* (1885), p. 122.

TYPE 930A.

¶ See "The Fish and the Ring".

Possibly the ballad referred to is "The Yorkshire Knight, or The Fortunate Farmer's Daughter", preserved by Ingledew in *Ballads and Songs of Yorkshire* (London, 1860), pp. 193–202.

THE STONEMASON OF THE CHARLTONS

There was a Church being built, and the work went well. The chief stonemason was called Old Jacob. He was a very godly man, and his hands was guided. Now this didn't please Old Harry [i.e. the Devil] at all. He tried all ways to stop Church being finished, and in the end he decided to carry off the stonemason, Old Jacob.

So he gets two black impets and he change 'en to look so like his liddle grandarters as two peas in a pod. They come crying and a-calling Old Jacob from his holy labour, and he put down his hammer and chisel and went outdoor to comfort their grief.

But, avore he tooked both feet off holy ground, he were stopped short and didn't move no furder. They two impets run back to Old Harry, who wasn't best pleased. "We got 'en with his one foot on earth, but we couldn' go a step nearer the holy ground," say they impets. And what do 'ee think had a-saved Old Jacob? There was a fine smiling Saint-chap standing and a-listening to summat, so Old Jacob he listens too, and 'twas a colley-bird up in a tree singing to praise God so sweet and tuneable as any angel.

The Saint he stand and listen, and Old Jacob he stand and listen in great delight.

Then he remember his holy work and his grandchildren. He can't see nothing of they, nor he can't a-find his hammer and chisel. Then he do discover the church be a-finished long since, and folks a-praying in it. There was a lovely shaft of sun fell to his feet. "There be your heavenly ladder, Old Jacob. 'Tis been a-waiting yew three hundred years. Off with 'ee to Paradise. Climb on up." So Old Jacob he climbed and he climbed while the folk marvelled. And then the Saint and the ladder and Old Jacob vanished right away, and the colley-bird stopped singing.

Ruth L. Tongue: "This was told to me at a tea-party in the Midlands by an East Somerset farmer's family who were visiting a military camp, in 1917. Most of it was told by an old lady of over 70 who was a notable tale-teller in her locality, and is probably a repeated monkish traditional tale from the Glastonbury area. There is a carving of Old Harry in Charlton Mackrell church."

TYPE 471A. MOTIFS: D.2011.1 [*Years seem moments while man listens to song of bird*]; G.303.3.1.16 [*Devil appears as a child*]; E.754.2 [*Saved soul goes to heaven*].

This is a lively retelling of the tale of "Felix the Monk" from *The Golden Legend*. Retold by Longfellow in *The Golden Legend* (p. 467).

The other side of the theme, the miraculous passage of time in fairyland, is the subject of many Celtic legends, of which "The Return of Ossian" is the most famous. ¶ See also "The Noontide Ghost".

STRONG JACK

The' was wonst an owld woman whad had only but one son, an' his name was Jack. An' she kept him in bed till he was twenty-one years of age. Whatsumever, about a month afoare, she sent for the tailor, an' had him measured for a suit o' clothes. On the day when he is twenty-one his owld mother calls Jack early, an' tells him he is to get up, which he does. He finds a new suit o' clothes put ready for him, so he dresses hisself, and a'ter when he has dressed he has a good look at hisself in the glass. He looks fine, he thinks. Of course he'd never had a suit o' clothes on in his life afoare. Then he goes downstairs, an' has his breakfast wid his owld mother. An' when he thinks of hisself sat up to the table wid his mother he can't help but laugh: it seems so funny to him what has never bene out'n bed afoare.

Now a'ter when they'd finished breakfast his owld mother says to him: "Jack," she says, "I wants you now to go to the farm over there, an' bring me some straw for the pig to lie on. The farmer," she says, "has gi'ed me leave to get some."

"Right," says Jack. "I'll go, mother. But, mother," he axes, "what rope shall I take?" "Oh! I got only but one rope," she tells him. "Well, where is it?" he axes. "Hanging up in the kitchen," she says. So Jack goes an' gets the rope—a t'emendous big thick rope it was, as thick as my arm—an' then off he sets to the farm.

Whatever to you, on the road he meets wid the farmer hisself. "Hello! my lad," says the farmer, "Where may you be come from?" "Out'n bed," Jack tells him. "My mother," he says, "has kept me in bed for twenty-one years, an' I'm only just now got up. An' being as she has done so much for me," he says, "I want to be a help to her now, so I was just a-going," he says, "to fatch her that straw for the pig, what you gi'ed her the promise on." "Very good, my lad," says the farmer, "you can go an' get as much as ever you can carry."

Jack thanks him, an' bids him good morning, an' goes on now till he comes to the stackyard. He takes the rope, an' he throws it round the whole'n one stack—an' it wa'n't the littlest neither—an' he lifts, an' he pulls, till he gets the stack fair an' square on to his back. Then he goes off home wid it, an' when he gets it there, he sets it down in the front garden. "There, mother," he says, "that'll last you a long while, I'll lay it will." An' a'ter when he has done this he goes off into the back garden to dig her up a few 'tatoes.

So whatever to you, the farmer soon comes to the owld woman's cottage to see what's gotten his stack, an' there he finds it in front'n the house in the front garden. "Morning, missus," he says. "Is that son o' yours at home?" "Yes," she tells him, "he's in the back garden, digging up a few 'tatoes for the dinner." "I'll just go an' have a word wid him," says the farmer. "Well aye," she says, "do." So the farmer goes through into the back garden. "Hello! young fellow," he says. "What the hang-ment do you mean by taking the whole'n one o' my stacks?" "Well," says Jack, "you said as I was to have as much straw as ever I could carry, didn't you? That's all I've ta'en, master. An' besides," he says, "it'll be a good thing for my poor owld mother, for it'll last her a long time." "I da' say it will," says the farmer; "but never mind, we'll say no moare about it."

Now the farmer gets a-gate talking wid Jack, an' a'ter a bit he axes him what work he can do. "Oh, annythink," says Jack, "as I knows how to." "An' you wants work, Jack," he axes. "Yes," says Jack, an' he was very pleased at the thoughts of getting a job. "I'd be glad of anny work," he says, "for now I wants to keep my owld mother, being as she has kept me for twenty-one years." "Do you think you could manage to carry water?" the farmer axes him. "Yes," says Jack, "I could do that first class." "Very well, then, my lad," says the farmer, "come to my house to-morrow morning early: it's washing-day." "Right you are," says Jack, "I'll be there."

Next morning, when Jack goes, the farmer gi'es him two buckets an' tells him to go across the field—a very big field it was—to the well, an' fatch enough water to fill the boiler for washing. Away Jack goes, an' he fatches two bucketfuls, an' pours 'em into the boiler, an' then he fatches two moare, an' two moare agen; an' he goes on this way, aye for three or four hours, an' yet he can't see the boiler getting not the leastest little bit fuller. "Dang it," he says, "I will fill it." So whatever should he do now, but the' is a big barrel—a t'emendous big cask—stood close by to the boiler; well, he gets this, an' puts it onto his back an' then off he goes to the well agen wid this big barrel on his back, an' the two buckets in his hands. He fills this barrel an' the two buckets, an' brings the three 'n they, an' empties the lot into the boiler. He does this two or three times moare, an' then the farmer comes to see how he's getting on. "Stop, Jack," he says. "That'll do. You've fatched too much."

Whatsumever to you, as Jack was going home that night from the farmer's who should he meet wid but a sowldier. "Hello! my fine fellow," the sowldier calls out to him, "are you looking for work?" "Yes," Jack tells him. "My mother," he says, "has kept me in bed for twenty-one years, an' now I wants to earn a bit o' money to keep her." "Well, what can you do?" the sowldier axes him. "Oh! annythink," says Jack, "as I knows how to." "Will you 'list?" says the sowldier. "Yes," says Jack. So Jack 'lists, an' they puts him in a cavalry rigiment.

Now it wa'n't above a month a'ter Jack had 'listed but what a big war breaks out, an' of course he is sent to the front. Soon he's right in the thick 'n it. He shoots down scoares an' scoares 'n the enemy till his ammonition is all used up, an' then he lays about him wid the butt end'n his rifle, an' kills scoares an' scoares moare that way. At last poor Jack's horse was shot down from under him. But that wa'n't the end—oh! no. What does he do but catch howld'n his horse by the tail, an' walk right into the middle'n the enemy, swinging it round an' round his head, an' i' that way he wiped out 'most all the lot'n the tother side.

Now a'ter when the war is over, an' Jack comes back home agen, the King gi'es him his own da'ghter for winning the battle for him. So Jack gets married to her an' they goes to live in a grand palace, an' they lives happy together ever a'ter.

Norton Collection, II, p. 166. *Journal of the Gypsy Lore Society*, n.s. VIII (1914–15), pp. 213–16. Collected from Noah Lock, camping in Anglesey, 1914, by T. W. Thompson.

TYPE 650A.

⁋ See "Tom Hickathrift" and "The Twenty-One-Year-Old Giant".

TAM LIN [summary]

All girls who wore the gold of maidenhood were warned against going to Carterhaugh, for it was haunted by Tam Lin, who would take a forfeit from them, their rings or their mantles or their maidenhood itself. But the wood had been given to Fair Janet by her father, so she went there to pluck flowers, in spite of danger. Tam Lin's horse was standing by the well, and as soon as she had pulled a rose he started up and caught her. She answered him boldly, and he let her go back to her father's court; but it was soon plain that she was with child. An old lord reproached her with it, and she went back to Carterhaugh and plucked a double rose to summon Tam Lin. He started forth in anger, but she asked him what he was and if she could win him for a husband. He told her he had been a mortal man, but had fallen from his horse and been caught by the Fairy Queen. He liked it well enough in Fairyland, but the fairies had to pay a teind to Hell every seven years, and he feared he would go next. Then he told her how she might win him away from the fairies that very night, for it was Hallow E'en, and at midnight the fairies would ride past Miles Cross. She must let pass a black horse and then a brown, and then would come a milk-white steed, and he would be riding it with one hand gloved and one hand bare, with his bonnet cocked up and his hair combed down. She must pull him off his horse and hold him fast whatever the fairies might do, and at last they would turn him into a red-hot sword, which she must cast into the well, and then he would be freed.

All this came true. When the white steed passed, Janet ran to it and pulled its rider down. The Fairy Queen turned Tam Lin into an esk and an adder, then to a bear, a lion, a red-hot gad of iron, and last into a burning sword. This Janet flung into the well, and Tam Lin came out, a naked knight. She threw her green mantle over him and made him her own. The Fairy Queen cried out angrily from a bush of broom that she had lost the fairest knight of her company, and that if she had known what was brewing she would have taken out his living eyes and given him eyes of wood.

F. J. Child, *The English and Scottish Popular Ballads*, I, p. 340.
TYPE 425 (variant). MOTIFS: F.320 [*Fairies carry people away to fairyland*]; C.515 [*Tabu: plucking flowers*]; F.301.1.1.2 [*Girl summons fairy lover by plucking flowers*]; D.610 [*Repeated transformation*]; D.757 [*Disenchantment by holding enchanted person during successive transformations*].

This ballad is a compendium of Scottish fairy beliefs. The carrying away of anyone who is unconscious of fairy ground, the transformations of mortals to fairies when they are kidnapped, the teind to Hell, the disenchantment through various transformations, finally confirmed by the putting on of a mortal garment, are all worth noting. Scott gives the same tale a literary form in "Alice Brand".

TATTERCOATS

In a great Palace by the sea there once dwelt a very rich old lord, who had neither wife nor children living, only one little granddaughter, whose face he had never seen in all her life. He hated her bitterly, because at her birth his favourite daughter died; and when the old nurse brought him the baby, he swore that it might live or die as it liked, but he would never look on its face as long as it lived.

So he turned his back, and sat by his window looking out over the sea, and weeping great tears for his lost daughter, till his white hair and beard grew down over his shoulders and twined round his chair and crept into the chinks of the floor and his tears, dropping on to the window-ledge, wore a channel through the stone, and ran away in a little river to the great sea. And, meanwhile, his granddaughter grew up with no one to care for her, or clothe her; only the nurse, when no one was by, would sometimes give her a dish of scraps from the kitchen, or a torn petticoat from the rag-bag; while the other servants of the Palace would drive her from the house with blows and mocking words, calling her "Tatter-coats", and pointing at her bare feet and shoulders, till she ran away crying, to hide among the bushes.

And so she grew up, with little to eat or to wear, spending her days in the fields and lanes, with only the gooseherd for her companion, who would play to her so merrily on his little pipe, when she was hungry or cold, or tired, that she forgot all her troubles, and fell to dancing, with his flock of noisy geese for partners.

But, one day, people told each other that the King was travelling through the land, and in the town near by was to give a great ball, to all the lords and ladies of the country, when the Prince, his only son, was to choose a wife.

One of the royal invitations was brought to the Palace by the sea, and the servants carried it up to the old lord who still sat by his window, wrapped in his long white hair and weeping into the little river that was fed by his tears.

But when he heard the King's command, he dried his eyes and bade them bring shears to cut him loose, for his hair had bound him a fast prisoner and he could not move. And then he sent them for rich clothes, and jewels, which he put on; and he ordered them to saddle the white horse, with gold and silk, that he might ride to meet the King.

Meanwhile Tattercoats had heard of the great doings in the town, and she sat by the kitchen-door weeping because she could not go to see them. And when the old nurse heard her crying she went to the Lord of the Palace, and begged him to take his granddaughter with him to the King's ball.

But he only frowned and told her to be silent, while the servants laughed and said, "Tattercoats is happy in her rags, playing with the gooseherd, let her be—it is all she is fit for."

A second, and then a third time, the old nurse begged him to let the girl go with him, but she was answered only by black looks and fierce words, till she was driven from the room by the jeering servants, with blows and mocking words.

Weeping over her ill-success, the old nurse went to look for Tattercoats; but the girl had been turned from the door by the cook, and had run away to tell her friend, the gooseherd, how unhappy she was because she could not go to the King's ball.

But when the gooseherd had listened to her story, he bade her cheer up, and proposed that they should go together into the town to see the King, and all the fine things; and when she looked sorrowfully down at her rags and bare feet, he played a note or two upon his pipe, so gay and merry, that she forgot all about her tears and her troubles, and before she well knew, the herdboy had taken her by the hand, and she, and he, and the geese before them, were dancing down the road towards the town.

Before they had gone very far, a handsome young man, splendidly dressed, rode up, and stopped to ask the way to the castle where the King was staying; and when he found that they too were going thither, he got off his horse and walked beside them along the road.

The herdboy pulled out his pipe and played a low sweet tune, and the stranger looked again and again at Tattercoat's lovely face till he fell deeply in love with her, and begged her to marry him.

But she only laughed, and shook her golden head.

"You would be finely put to shame if you had a goose-girl for your wife!" said she; "go and ask one of the great ladies you will see to-night, at the King's ball, and do not flout poor Tattercoats."

But the more she refused him the sweeter the pipe played, and the deeper the young man fell in love; till at last he begged her, as a proof of his sincerity, to come that night at twelve to the King's ball, just as she was, with the herdboy and his geese, and in her torn petticoat and bare feet, and he would dance with her before the King and the lords and ladies, and present her to them all, as his dear and honoured bride.

So when night came, and the hall in the castle was full of light and music, and the lords and ladies were dancing before the King, just as the clock struck twelve, Tattercoats and the herdboy, followed by his flock of noisy geese, entered at the great doors, and walked straight up the ball-room, while on either side the ladies whispered, the lords laughed, and the King seated at the far end stared in amazement.

But as they came in front of the throne, Tattercoat's lover rose from beside the King, and came to meet her. Taking her by the hand, he kissed her thrice before them all, and turned to the King.

"Father!" he said, for it was the Prince himself, "I have made my choice, and here is my bride, the loveliest girl in all the land, and the sweetest as well!"

Before he had finished speaking, the herdboy put his pipe to his lips and played a few low notes, that sounded like a bird singing far off in the woods; and as he played, Tattercoats' rags were changed to shining robes sewn with glittering jewels, a golden crown lay upon her golden hair, and the flock of geese behind her became a crowd of dainty pages, bearing her long train.

And as the King rose to greet her as his daughter, the trumpets sounded loudly in honour of the new Princess, and the people outside in the street said to each other:

"Ah! now the Prince has chosen for his wife the loveliest girl in all the land!"

But the gooseherd was never seen again, and no one knew what became of him; while the old lord went home once more to his Palace by the sea, for he could not stay at Court, when he had sworn never to look on his granddaughter's face.

So there he still sits by his window, if you could only see him, as you some day may, weeping more bitterly than ever, as he looks out over the sea.

Jacobs, *More English Fairy Tales*, p. 61; Mrs Balfour, *Legends of the Cars*; Norton Supplementary Collection, no. XXXVIII.

TYPE 510 [distant variant]. MOTIFS: S.42 [*Cruel grandfather*]; L.111.4 [*Orphan heroine*]; N.810.5 [*Supernatural person disguised as servant as helper*]; D.1355.1.2 [*Magic love-producing pipe*]; D.364 [*Transformation: goose to person*]; L.162 [*Lowly heroine marries prince*].

This tale is loosely linked to the Cinderella story by the motifs of the ill-used heroine, the supernatural helper, the transformation at the royal ball, and the marriage of the heroine to the prince.

It is one of the best examples of those English fairy tales which differ materially from the general European pattern. "Kate Crackernuts" is another example, and others are to be found in some of the tales collected by Ruth Tongue, and in the Nursery Tale of "The Three Bears".

¶ For distant parallels see "Rashie Coat", "Catskin", etc.

THAT'S ENOUGH TO GO ON WITH

There was a little boy and a little girl, and they lived in a poor little hut, and they never had enough to eat, but their granny taught them good manners, and people liked them for it, and sometimes they'd give them a bite here and there—old cabbage leaves, a little scrumpy, or turnip for the pot, even a few bones for soup, or stale crusts the hens left over, and they always said: "No more, please. That's enough to go on with, thank you kindly," when they got it, so they did fairly well.

Now there was a fat rich farmer who lived close by, with fine orchards, and corn ricks, and a herd of cows, but he sold every cabbage leaf, and he counted all his turnips, he never had any meat (it cost money) and there weren't any crusts left over either—so he grew richer and richer, and fatter and fatter. When the little boy and the little girl took their little goat to grass, they had to go along a lane near his fields, and his dog chased them away. And he came and threw stones at their old granny picking up twigs in her own little plot, and said she was a witch and stole his cows' milk, and that was a terrible lie. Their little goat did give just one sup of milk among them. So the little boy and girl and the goat had to go farther away to find grass the farmer couldn't call his, and one day the poor hungry little goat broke its tether and ran away into the Little Men's Wood, where the grass grew thick. The little boy and the little girl ran after the goat, for they knew no one ever went there and they were very frightened, but they remembered their good manners and they called out, "Please forgive our hungry goat—may we come into your wood and catch her? Thank you kindly," and on they went. But the little goat wasn't eating grass, she was eating strawberries as fast as she could. The wood was red with them. The little boy and the little girl looked and

505

looked and then they said, "We are very hungry, and so is our granny at home. May we pick a handful?"

And the mischievous little men called out: "Pick all you want." For the strawberries were magic ones and you had to go on eating and eating unless you gave thanks. But the granny had taught them well, and they only picked a double handful to take home to her and ate far less than the goat, then they said, "No more, please—that's enough to go on with, and thank you kindly," and the goat was able to stop gobbling and go with them safe out of the wood.

They never went short of rich milk after that, and ripe strawberries grew in their bit of garden all the year round, so they never went hungry either. Now one day the fat farmer spied their strawberries all red in the snow and he up and oped their gate and in he came.

"Where did you steal the strawberries I grow to sell?" he shouted and *that* was a terrible lie.

But they told him they must have come from the Little Men's Wood.

"That wood is mine too!" he yelled, and *that* was a worse lie still, for the Little Men heard him.

Then he picked every strawberry in the garden, and began to eat them, while the children watched quietly. They knew when he went another crop would ripen again for their supper time—but the farmer, he raved for more.

"They grow in the Little Men's Wood," said they, and off he rushed as fast as he could to get there. There were hundreds of berries growing in the snow and he ate, and he ate, and he couldn't stop to say "Please", and he ate, and he ate, and he didn't ask leave, and he ate, and he ate, and he didn't know how to say "That's enough" or "Thank you kindly", so he ate and he ate all day, and all night, and all the week thro', and when Sunday came *he burst with a bang*.

Ruth L. Tongue. Somerset, 1917. "From the mother of a schoolfellow who had died. It was sent to me in a letter. They lived in the Charltons area and this tale was told by their gardener's wife, who had been their nanny. Rosie had always loved it and laughed at it and quoted it."

TYPE 503 (variant). MOTIFS: F.216 [*Fairies live in forest*]; Q.2 [*Kind and unkind*]; D.981 [*Magic fruit*]; L.200 [*Modesty brings reward*]; Q.277 [*Covetousness punished*]; Q.327 [*Discourtesy punished*].

¶ See "Goblin Coombe", "Spring of the Sixpence".

THE THREE BROTHERS AND THE THREE TASKS or SILLY JACK AND THE LORD'S DAUGHTER [dialect modified]

There was once a poor old woman who had three sons, James and John and Jack. James and John had a good opinion of themselves, but they thought Jack soft, because he bided about the house helping his Mother. They were very poor, and one day James said to his Mother, "Bake me a a bannock and roast me a collop, and I'll away into the world to push my fortune." "Whether will you have a big bannock with my curse, or a wee bannock with my blessing?" said his Mother. "Bake me the biggest bannock you can get, and it will be little enough," said James. He was greedy. So his Mother baked him a bannock with all the meal in the house, and she roasted all the meat in the house for his collop, but when he went, she stood at the door and said, "Curse ye, curse ye wherever ye go." James set off and he wandered far. There was rest for the wee birds, but there was none for poor Jack.* And at last he sat down by a clear spring at the side of the road to eat his bannock and collop. And as he was eating, a wee hairy man came up and said: "Will you give me the crumbs that fall from your mouth?" "Get oot o' my road!" said James, and he finished it all himself, and went to drink of the spring. But it was full of puddicks' spewings, and he couldn't touch it. There was rest for the wee birds, but there was none for poor Jack.* So he went on thirsty and weary, until he came to a Castle, and he knocked at the door, and asked for a job. "Yes, you'll get a job," said the Lord. "There are three tasks to do, and if you fail in them you lose your head, and if you do them, you shall marry my daughter." Well, James thought he'd try it, so he was taken in, and given the best of attention that night. And his first task was to kill a three-headed giant.

So in the morning they gave him a horse and a sword, and everything he needed, and he set out. Soon there were three roars, and the trees shook, and up came the giant crying:

> "Vee, vi, vum,
> I feel the smell of an Englishman.
> Let him be dead, or let him be alive,
> I'll crunge his bones for meal."

James was frightened, but he thought he'd do his best, so he made for the giant, and the giant killed him with one blow, and went off. And the Lord had James's head cut off, and stuck on the Castle gate. A year and a

* This a short version of "a run."

day went by, and they had no news of James at the cottage. So John said he'd go, and he asked his Mother to bake him a bannock and roast him a collop, and he was as greedy as his brother, and everything happened to him as it had happened to James. And a year and a day went by with no news of John. Then Jack said: "Mother, I'm doing no good here, for I can get no work, and I'm just eating up your food. You'd be better without me. Bake me a bannock and roast me a collop, and I'll away after my brothers and push my fortune, and whatever I get you shall share." His Mother didn't want to part with him, for he was all the comfort she had, but at length she said: "Very well, whether will you have a wee bannock with my blessing, or a big bannock with my curse?" "Oh, Mother," said Jack, "do you think I'd take a big bannock, and leave the house bare, and you with nothing to eat. Bake me a wee, wee bannock, but mind and bless me, Mother." So she baked him a wee bannock, and when he went away, she stood at the door and said: "Bless ye, bless ye, wherever you go."

Jack went on and on till he was thirsty and hungry, and he thought he'd eat his bannock and collop by the side of a clear well. And he was just started when a wee hairy man came up, and said; "Give us a crumb, Jack, out of your mouth." "You look very hungry," said Jack. "Come and sit down, and have a piece with me." And he gave the wee man half of what he had. "Thank you, Jack," said the wee man. "Let's have a drink." They leaned down to the well to drink, and it was full of the purest wine, and Jack got great refreshment.

"Here, Jack," said the wee man, "here's a sword for you. You'll find it of great use to you, for it's a wishing sword. You just touch it and wish, and you'll have what you want." Jack did not believe him, but he thanked him, and buckled on the sword, and went on his way. There was rest for the wee birds, but there was none for poor Jack.* He went on and on, and got hungry and weary, and at last he said, "I wish there was a good table spread for me here, so that I could get a good meal." And as he spoke, he touched the sword, without meaning to, and there was a table before him. He ate and drank all he wanted, and said to himself: "The wee man was right then; it was a magic sword." So he wished for a horse to ride on, and rode on to the Lord's Castle, where he rang, and asked for a job. The Lord said he had three tasks for him, and if he did them he should have the Lord's daughter, and three bushels of gold, but if he failed he would lose his head. He must kill the three-headed giant, and fetch back the Lady, who was guarded by a fiery dragon, and a two-headed snake. So Jack got the best of attention that night, and in the morning he set out with his horse and his magic sword. And presently he heard three roars, and all the trees shook, and the Giant came up, crying:

"Vee, vi, vum,
I feel the smell of an Englishman.
Let him be dead, or let him be alive,
I'll crunge his bones for meal."

"Please, sword, protect me," said Jack, and the sword leaped out of its scabbard, and cut off the giant's three heads, and Jack put them into a sack, and carried them back to the Lord, who was very pleased with him, and made him a great feast. The next day he set out to the mountain pass, which was guarded by a fiery dragon. No man could get near it, but he asked the sword to help him, and it flew through the air, and fought with the fiery dragon, and killed it, and Jack carried back the head to the Lord, who was even more delighted, and made Jack a grander feast. The next day he set out to the Castle where the Lord's daughter was imprisoned, which was guarded by a two-headed snake. Again the sword jumped out of its scabbard, and fought the serpent, and cut off its two heads. Jack went into the Castle, and found the Lord's daughter enchanted there, but he broke the enchantment and took her home, and Jack married her, and had the three bushels of gold and the Castle, and he sent for his mother to live with them.

School of Scottish Studies, Jeannie Robertson. Told her by her grandfather.
TYPE 577 (variant). MOTIFS: H.335 [*Tasks assigned to suitors: bride as prize*]; H.901.1 [*Heads placed on stakes for failure in performance of tasks*]; J.229.3 [*Choice: a big piece of cake with my curse, or a small piece with my blessing*]; Q.2 [*Kind and unkind*].
 Suitor tasks: G.550 [*Suitor task: Rescue from ogre*]; H.335.3.1 [*Suitor task: To kill dragon*]; H.335.3.4 [*Suitor task: To kill snake guarding princess's chamber*]; L.13 [*Compasionate youngest son*]; D.822 [*Magic object received from old man*]; D.1470.1 [*Magic wishing object*]; D.1581 [*Tasks performed by use of magic object*]; H.1242 [*Youngest brother alone succeeds on quest*]; L.161 [*Lowly hero marries princess*].

THE THREE DOGS [summary]

There was an old woman had a son, Jack the Water-Carrier they called him, and he was too idle to do a bit of work. The old woman had three cows, and one day she said to her son: "I's getting very old, Jack, and I'm not able to look after the cows. Do you take one of them and sell it at the market."

"All right," said Jack.

"Well," said the old woman, "take Daisy, and try to get twelve golden sovereigns for her."

So Jack set off with Daisy, and on the way he met a butcher.

"That's a nice cow," said the butcher, "What do you want for her?"

"I want twelve golden sovereigns," said Jack.

"Oh, I couldn't give you that," said the butcher, "but I'll give you this greyhound dog. It's the fleetest in the world for chasing rabbits and hares, and it will take you right to them."

Jack took a great fancy to the greyhound, and in the end he changed it for the cow.

His mother wasn't well pleased, and she soon sent Jack to sell the second cow; but the butcher met him, and he bartered the cow for another dog, and he did the same thing with the third cow; so now Jack had three dogs, Swift, Able and Noble, and they were certainly fine hunters. Noble knew where the game was, Able could break down any wall or dig up any burrow, and Swift could run anything down. Jack and his mother never wanted for game, but the King began to get very angry at their poaching, and he sent down his torturer, who stuck a sharp bone into Jack's bed, which wounded him when he lay on it.

Jack was ill for some time, and when he recovered his dogs had gone. So he set out to look for them.

He went on and on till he came to a little cottage, with an old woman in it, who knew his name and his errand. She said that the three dogs had passed, very wearied, and one of them had spewed up his heart and liver and lungs behind a bush at the cottage door. She told Jack to wrap them in a cloth and take them with him. Then she gave him a pair of shoes that would go fifty miles to a stride, and told him to go on to her elder sister. She fed him, and let him sleep there for the night, and next morning he went on to the older sister, who told him that the second dog had spewed up his heart and liver and lungs, and he must take them and go on to the third sister, who was the oldest of them all. This old woman told him that the dogs were there, but under a spell, and she told him how to disenchant them. He must pick up the heart, liver and lungs of the third dog, and must hide behind the wall of a little cemetery. The witch would fly by, and the three dogs would be with her. He must get in the first word, and then she would be forced to disenchant the dogs. He hid under the wall until he heard the howling of dogs, and saw a ball of fire go over him. Then he cried out: "Hey, hey! Where are you going?"

She stopped at that, shivering, and he said, "I want my dogs."

She came to him, and the dogs with her, nothing but skin and bone and she handed him an old axe. The first dog looked up at him, and said: "Jack, you must cut off our heads, one by one."

Jack was very unwilling to do that, but they told him he must, and he chopped off Swift's head. At once Swift turned into Jack's long-lost brother, for Jack had had three brothers that had disappeared.

So Jack cut off Able's head, and Noble's, and there were his three brothers who had been enchanted. So all four went back to their mother, and she was very happy to see them.

School of Scottish Studies, collected by Hamish Henderson from Andrew Stewart.

This tale belongs to no recognized type, and is perhaps a little broken down, as there is no mention, until their disenchantment, of the three lost brothers; but a good many motifs are incorporated in it.

N.421 [*Lucky bargain*]; B.312.2 [*Helpful animals obtained by exchange*]; H.2135 [*Succession of helpers on quest*]; D.1521.1 [*Seven-league boots*]; B.182.1.1.2 [*Magic dog transformed person*]; D.711 [*Disenchantment by decapitation*].

THREE FEATHERS

Once upon a time there was a girl who was married to a husband that she never saw. And the way this was that he was only at home at night, and would never have any light in the house. So the girl thought that was funny, and all her friends told her there must be something wrong with her husband, some great deformity that made him want not to be seen.

Well, one night when he came home she suddenly lit a candle and saw him. He was handsome enough to make all the women of the world fall in love with him. But scarcely had she seen him when he began to change into a bird, and then he said: "Now you have seen me, you shall see me no more, unless you are willing to serve seven years and a day for me, so that I may become a man once more." Then he told her to take three feathers from under his side, and whatever she wished through them would come to pass. Then he left her at a great house to be laundry-maid for seven years and a day.

And the girl used to take the feathers and say: "By the virtue of my three feathers may the copper be lit, and the clothes washed, and mangled, and folded, and put away to the missus's satisfaction."

And then she had no more care about it. The feathers did the rest, and the lady set great store by her for a better laundress she had never had. Well, one day, the butler, who had a notion to have the pretty laundry-maid for his wife, said to her, he should have spoken before but he did not want to vex her. "Why should it when I am but a fellow-servant?" the girl said. And then he felt free to go on, and explain he had £70 laid by with the master, and how would she like him for a husband.

And the girl told him to fetch the money, and he asked his master for it, and brought it to her. But as they were going upstairs, she cried, "O John, I must go back, sure I've left my shutters undone, and they'll be slashing and banging all night."

The butler said, "Never you trouble, I'll put them right," and he ran back, while she took her feathers, and said: "By virtue of my three feathers may the shutters slash and bang till morning, and John not be able to fasten them nor yet to get his fingers free from them!"

And so it was. Try as he might, the butler could not leave hold, nor yet keep the shutters from blowing open as he closed them. And he *was* angry, but could not help himself, and he did not care to tell of it and get the laugh on him, so no one knew.

Then after a bit the coachman began to notice her, and she found he had some £40 with the master, and he said she might have it if she would take him with it.

So after the laundry-maid had his money in her apron as they went merrily along, she stopt, exclaiming: "My clothes are left outside, I must run back and bring them in." "Stop for me while I go; it is a cold frost night," said William. "You'd be catching your death." So the girl waited long enough to take her feathers out and say, "By virtue of my three feathers may the clothes slash and blow about 'till morning, and may William not be able to take his hand from them nor yet to gather them up." And then she went away to bed and to sleep.

The coachman did not want to be every one's jest, and he said nothing.

So after a bit, the footman comes to her and said he: "I have been with my master for years and have saved up a good bit, and you have been three years here, and must have saved up as well. Let us put it together, and make us a home or else stay on at service as pleases you."

Well, she got him to bring the savings to her as the others had, and then she pretended she was faint, and said to him: "James, I feel so queer, run down cellar for me, that's a dear, and fetch me up a drop of brandy." Now no sooner had he started than she said: "By virtue of my three feathers, may there be slashing and spilling, and James not be able to pour the brandy straight nor yet to take his hand from it until morning!"

And so it was. Try as he might, James could not get his glass filled, and there was slashing and spilling, and right on it all, down came the master to know what it meant!

So James told him he could not make it out, but he could not get the drop of brandy the laundry-maid had asked for, and his hand would shake and spill everything, and yet come away he could not.

This got him in for a regular scrape, and the master when he got back to his wife said, "What has come over the men, they were all right until that laundry-maid of yours came. Something is up now though. They have all drawn out their pay, and yet they don't leave, and what can it be anyway?

But his wife said she could not hear of the laundry-maid being blamed, for she was the best servant she had and worth all the rest put together.

So it went on until one day as the girl stood in the hall door, the coachman happened to say to the footman: "Do you know how that girl served me, James?" And then William told about the clothes. The butler put in, "That was nothing to what she served me," and he told of the shutters clapping all night. So then the master came through the hall, and the girl said: "By virtue of my three feathers may there be slashing and striving between master and men, and may all get splashed in the pond."

And so it was, the men fell to disputing which had suffered the most by her, and when the master came up all would be heard at once and none listened to him, and it came to blows all round, and the first they knew they had shoved one another into the pond.

So when the girl thought they had had enough she took the spell off, and the master asked her what had begun the row, for he had not heard in the confusion.

And the girl said, "They were ready to fall on any one; they'd have beat me if you had not come by."

So it blew over for that time, and through her feathers she made the best laundress ever known. But to make a long story short, when the seven years and a day were up, the bird-husband, who had known her doings all along, came after her, restored to his own shape again. And he told her mistress he had come to take her from being a servant, and that she should have servants under her. But he did not tell of the feathers.

And then he bade her give the men back their savings.

"That was a rare game you had with them," said he, "but now you are going where there is plenty, so leave them each their own." So she did; and they drove off to their castle, where they lived happy ever after.

Jacobs, *More English Fairy Tales*, pp. 34–8. Collected by Mrs Gomme from some hop-pickers near Deptford.

THE THREE FEATHERS or
JACK AND THE PUDDOCK I [summary]

There was once a King and he had three sons, and their names were Tom and James and Jack. Jack was despised by the others as soft and feeble.

After a time the King fell ill, and he wanted to decide which of his sons was to succeed him. So they were all to go out for a year and a day to find the most beautiful ring. But first the good advisers took them to the top of the castle, and gave them each a feather, and they were to go the way their feather blew. Tom's feather went to the North, and James's to the South, and Jack's feather whirled round, and dropped right down at the back of the castle. The two brothers laughed at him. "Poor Jack," they said. "It's plain you're just going to stop about here all your days, picking up scraps in the kitchen." And they mounted their grand horses and rode away. Jack was so disheartened that for eleven months he never even looked for his feather, but at last he thought he'd go and look for it, and there he found it all amongst the nettles, sticking through an iron ring on a flagstone. He pulled up the stone, and there was a winding staircase and he went down it, and at the bottom he heard something saying, and it was a green frog, "You've been an awful long time looking for us, Jack," it said. "You've not left us much time to get the ring." "I never knew you were here," said Jack. "You might have looked," said the frog. However, it took Jack into some fine little rooms, and there they had a feast, and the frogs danced and sang, and Jack was so happy with them that he stayed a whole month. The day after the month the chief frog said to Jack, "Your brothers are back, and it is time you were back too. Here is your ring." And he gave Jack the finest ring in the world. When Jack got back his brothers were there already, and showing their rings to the King and his good advisers. They were certainly very beautiful rings, but when the good advisers saw Jack's ring they said that it was worth the others put together.

The two elder brothers were angry at this, and said that it was not fair, when they had ridden far and wide, and Jack had idled round the Castle all the year. So to satisfy them, the King set them another test. They were to follow their feathers again, and bring back the most beautiful bride they could find to match the ring. This time Tom's went South, and James's went West, but Jack's swirled round again, and fell in the Castle yard.

This time Jack was thoroughly disheartened, for he thought: "The frogs might pick up an old ring in the foundations of the castle, but where would they find a lovely Princess and what would she have to say to me if they did?" So he waited till only a fortnight and a day was left to him, and then he went down to look for his feather. The green frog was sitting waiting for him on top of the stone. "Jack, Jack," it said, "You've been an awful long time coming to us. You haven't left us long to work in. But come along down." So Jack went down, and they had a great feast, and a little wee frog jumped on his knee, and Jack kept stroking it and slapping it, and saying, "Poor wee froggie, pretty wee froggie," and it looked up in his face with its bright eyes. When the fortnight was up, the old frog said, "Well, we've got your bride for you, and here she is." Jack was fair taken about. "What, me marry a wee green froggie!" he said. "They'll all call me daft." "I promise you, you'll not be the worse for it," said the old frog. "Will you trust us?" "Well, you've been very kind to me," said Jack, "so I'll do it." So a frog minister came, and they were wedded.

Then the old frog said, "Go up to the castle, and your bride will come to you." So Jack came up the stairs, and there in the courtyard was a gold coach, and the footman signed to him to get in, and soldiers came marching up, and there was the loveliest lady with them, and Jack said, "Are you my wee froggie?" And she said, "I am, and these are my subjects that were all enchanted, and you have freed them." So they went to Jack's father, and when he saw the lovely lady he jumped clean out of bed with joy. Tom and James had brought bonnie brides, but no one had any doubt who was the loveliest.

School of Scottish Studies, H. Henderson, from Andrew Stewart. This tale was amplified by Andrew Stewart in 1956, and makes an interesting illustration of the variations which the same storyteller can make if he has a congenial audience.

Told him by his father. A song, but he had forgotten it.

Another version told by Jean Thomson, with the Wife Quest (married through the keyhole as in "The Singing Bride").

THE THREE FEATHERS or JACK AND THE PUDDOCK II [summary]

There was once a King, and he began to be old and ill, and the doctors told his eldest son that he had not long to live. The eldest told the two others.

He thought he would be King, but the King's good advisers said that the three brothers would have to push their fortune. They were to see which of them could get the most beautiful tablecloth. Each prince was given an eagle's feather. They were to climb the tower of the castle, and let their feathers fly, and each was to follow his feather. The youngest son, Jack, was idle and slovenly, and everyone despised him. They loosed their feathers. One went North, and one went West, but Jack's feather fluttered down amongst the nettles at the foot of the tower. The two brothers rode away, and Jack went back to the kitchen where he scraped the pots. The brothers had a year and a day for their quest.

A day before the end of the year, Jack thought he'd look for his feather. He went about among the nettles, and he heard a sound of sobbing—a little green frog was sitting crying by his feather on a big flagstone. "We thought you were never coming, Jack," she said. "There's not much time to find the table-cover. Lift the flagstone." Jack heaved it up, and found steps going down. The frog plopped down in front of him, and he found himself in a fine dwelling all lit with electric light. There were frogs going about it, and they gave him a good meal, and the little frog sat on his knee, and looked up at him with golden eyes, while he stroked it. At length they brought a brown-paper parcel, and told him it was the best table-cover in the land, and he was to give it to the King to open. He went up and met the two brothers coming riding in with their covers.

Both were very fine, but when the King opened Jack's it was embroidered with diamonds and rubies, and there was nothing to touch it in the land. The brothers said he had stolen it, and begged the King to set another test; so this time they were given a year and a day to find the most beautiful ring. Jack went earlier this time, and the days passed very pleasantly, so that he was just in time to meet the two brothers. They each had a beautiful ring, but Jack's had a diamond in it that would have bought the whole kingdom. Still the brothers begged for another chance, and suggested that they should each bring back a bride, and the one most fit to wear the ring should be Queen. Jack was very dismayed at this, for where could he find a Princess among the frogs? There were only two hours left when he went, and his little frog was weeping bitterly. The oldest of the frogs begged Jack to trust them, and consent to marry the little frog, Susan, and he would not repent it. They sent him to the kitchen to have his tea, and presently they called him out into the courtyard, and there a beautiful coach was standing, with a Princess in it so beautiful that Jack was ashamed of himself and his squalid clothes. But the old frog, who was now a King, told him to turn round three times, and at once he was as handsome and richly dressed as any King in the world. His father and brothers hardly knew him, but when at length they recognized him, and saw his bride, the brothers were so ashamed that they locked their own brides into the lavatory until they could take them home.

Jack was made King, and he was so kind to the poor that everyone loved him, and he is reigning still.

School of Scottish Studies, Hamish Henderson. Narrator, Andrew Stewart, Glasgow, 1956. TYPE 402. MOTIFS: H.1210.1 [*Quest assigned by father*]; H.1242 [*Youngest brother alone succeeds on quest*]; H.1319.4 [*Quest for the most beautiful ring*]; H.1301.1 [*Quest for the most beautiful bride*]; B.313 [*Helpful animal an enchanted person*]; B.493.1 [*Helpful frog*]; D.700 [*Person disenchanted*]; D.742 [*Disenchantment by promise to marry*].

¶ This tale is fairly widespread through Europe, but rare in England. "Jack and the Fox" is a version, with the Cat Bride, given in *JAFL*, XXXVIII, p. 345. It is from North Carolina.

THREE-FOR-A-POT

There was once a lad called Jack who lived with his Mother in a wee house, and the King's castle was at the far side of the glen. One day Jack went out to cut sticks for his Mother, and he began to cut down a withered thorn. When he began to cut the thorn, he heard a roaring inside: "Let me out! Let me out! I'm Three-for-a-Pot in here." So he cut the thorn very carefully, and Three-for-a-Pot hopped out. It looked like a great three-legged pot, but it spoke. "Thank you, Jack," it said. "You've freed me. I can see you're very poor, so I'll show you how to get some money." "Thank you," said Jack, "I could do with that." So Three-for-a-Pot hopped along beside him to his Mother's house, and told him to take two blankets, and put them into it. Jack did that, and Three-for-a-Pot flew away through the air, and landed in the King's Palace, where the King was counting out some money, and looked for a safe place to put it. And he saw a great iron pot beside him, with two blankets in it, so he put the money in the pot, and wrapped it in the blankets. But at once the pot rose in the air, and sailed out of the Palace, and the King had no notion where it had gone. But the pot carried it back to Jack and his Mother. And then the pot fetched them sheep, and all they wanted. And when they were well set up, it turned into a man, who lived with them, and married, and settled down.

School of Scottish Studies, H. Henderson, from A. Macdonald.
TYPE 502 [variant], MOTIFS: D.252 [*Transformation: man to pot*]; D.841 [*Magic object accidentally found*]; D.1470 [*Magic object as provider*]; D.700 [*Person disenchanted*].
    This rather naïve tale seems to fit into no special category.

THREE GOLD HEADS

Long before Arthur and the Knights of the Round Table, there reigned, in the eastern part of this land, a King, who kept his court at Colchester. He was witty, strong, and valiant; by which means he subdued his enemies abroad, and planted peace among his subjects at home.

Nevertheless, in the midst of all his earthly glory, his queen died, leaving behind her an only daughter, about fifteen years of age, under the care of her royal husband. This lady, for her courtly carriage, beauty, and affability, was the wonder of all that knew her; but, as covetousness is the root of all evil, so it happened here.

The King hearing of a Lady, who had likewise an only daughter, for the sake of her riches, had a mind to marry her; tho' she was old, ugly, hook-nos'd and hump-back'd, yet all could not deter him from marrying her. The daughter of the said piece of deformity was a yellow dowdy, full of envy and ill-nature, and in short, was much of the same mould as her mother. This signified nothing, for in a few weeks, the King, attended by the nobility and gentry, brought the said piece of deformity to his palace, where the marriage-rites were performed. Long they had not been in the court, before they set the King against his own beautiful daughter, which was done by false reports and accusations. The young princess having lost her father's love, grew weary of the court, and on a certain day meeting with her father in the garden, she desired him, with tears in her eyes, to give her a small subsistence, and she would go and seek her fortune, to which the King consented, and ordered her mother-in-law to make up a small sum according to her discretion. To her she went, who gave her a canvas bag of brown bread, a hard cheese, with a bottle of beer; though this was but a very pitiful dowry for a King's daughter. She took it, returned thanks, and so proceeded, passing through groves, woods and valleys, till at length she saw an old man sitting on a stone, at the mouth of a cave, who said, Good-morrow, fair maiden, whither away so fast? Aged father, says she, I am going to seek my fortune. What hast thou in thy bag and bottle? In my bag I have got bread and cheese, and in my bottle good small beer; will you please to partake of either? Yes, said he, with all my heart. - - - With that the lady pulled out her provision, and bid him eat and welcome. He did, and gave her many thanks, telling her there was a thick thorny hedge before her, which will appear to you impassible, but take this wand in your hand, strike three times, and say, Pray, hedge, let me come through, and it will open immediately: then a little further, you will find a well, sit down on the brink of it, and there will come up three golden heads who will speak, and what they require, that do. Then, promising she would, she took her leave of him. - - Coming to the hedge, and following the old man's directions, the hedge divided, and gave her a passage; then coming to the well, she had no sooner sitten down, but a golden head came up with a singing note, Wash me, comb me, lay me down softly; Yes, said the young lady: then putting forth her hand, with a silver comb performed the office, placing it upon a primrose bank. Then came up a second and a third, saying as the former, which she complied with; and then pulling out her provision, ate her dinner. Then, said the heads one to another, What shall we do for this lady, who hath used us so very kindly? The first said, I will cause such addition to her beauty, as shall charm the most powerful prince in the world. The second said, I will endow her with such perfume, both in body and breath, as shall far exceed the sweetest flowers. The third said, My gift shall be none of the least, for as she is a king's daughter, I'll make her so fortunate, that she shall become queen to the greatest Prince that reigns.—This done, at their request she let them down into the well again, and so proceeded on her journey.—She had not travelled long, before she saw a king hunting in the park with his nobles; she would have shunned him, but the king having a sight of her, made towards her, and between her beauty and perfumed breath, was so powerfully smitten that he was not able to subdue his passion, but proceeded on his courtship, where, after some compliments and kind embraces, he gained her love. And bringing her to his palace, he caused her to be clothed in the most magnificent manner.

This being ended, and the king finding that she was the King of Colchester's daughter, ordered some chariots to be got ready, that he might pay him a visit. The chariot, in which the king and queen rode, was beautified with rich ornamental gems of gold. The King her father was at first astonished, that his daughter had been so fortunate as she was, till the young King made him sensible of all that had happened. Great was the joy at court among the nobility, except the queen and her club-footed daughter, who were ready to burst with malice, and envied her happiness;

and the greater was their madness, because she was now above them all.—Great rejoicings, with feasting and dancing, continued many days. Then at length, with the dowry her father gave her, she returned home.

[Her hump-backed sister-in-law,] perceiving that her sister was so happy in seeking her fortune, would needs do the same; so disclosing her mind to her mother, all preparations were made; not only rich apparel, but sweet-meats, sugar, almonds, etc. in great quantities, and a large bottle of Malaga sack.

Thus furnished, she went the same road, as her sister, and coming near the cave, there sat the old man, who said, Young woman, whither so fast?—What is that to you, said she.—Then, said he, what have you in your bag and bottle? She answered, Good things, which you shall not be troubled with. Won't you give me some? said he. No, not a bit, not a drop, unless it would choak you. The old man frowned, saying, Evil fortune attend thee.—Going on, she came to the hedge, through which she espied a gap, where she thought to pass, but going in the hedge closed, and the thorns ran into her flesh, so that with great difficulty she got out. Being now in a bloody condition, she looks for water to wash herself, and looking round she saw a well, and sitting down, one of the heads came up to her saying, Wash me, comb me, lay me down softly. But she bang'd it with her bottle, saying, Hang you, take this for your washing. So the second and third heads came up, and met with no better welcome than the first, whereupon the heads consulted amongst themselves, what evils to plague her with for such usage. The first said, Let her be struck with leprosy in her face. The second said, Let an additional stink be added to her breath. The third bestowed on her a husband, though but a poor country-cobler. This done, she goes on till she came to a market-town, and it being market-day the people smelled a stink, and seeing such a mangy face, all fled; but a poor cobler, who, not long before, had mended the shoes of an old hermit, who, having no money, gave him a box of ointment for the cure of the leprosy, and a bottle of spirits for a stinking breath. Now the cobler, having a mind to do an act of charity, was minded to try an experiment; so going up to her, asked her, who she was?—I am, said she, the King of Colchester's daughter-in-law.—Well, said the cobler, if I restored you to your natural complexion, and make a sound cure both in face and breath, will you in reward, take me for a husband?—Yes, friend, replied she, with all my heart.—With this, the cobler applied the remedies, and they worked the effect in a few weeks, which being done they were married. After some few days spent in town, they set forward for the court at Colchester. At length, coming there, and the queen understanding she had married nothing but a poor cobler, fell into distraction, and in wrath hanged herself. The death of the queen pleased the King much, who was glad he had got rid of her so soon. Having buried her, he gave the cobler one hundred pounds, on condition that he and his lady would quit the court. The cobler received it, and promised he would. Then, setting up his trade in a remote part of the kingdom, they lived many years, he mending shoes, and she spinning thread.

Norton Collection, II, pp. 2–4. *History of the Four Kings* (Glasgow, 1789).
TYPE 480. MOTIFS: S.31 [*Cruel stepmother*]; L.55 [*Stepdaughter heroine*]; Q.41 [*Politeness rewarded*]; Q.42.1.1.1 [*Reward for giving last loaf*]; N.825.2 [*Old man helper*]; Q.2 [*Kind and unkind*]; H.1192 [*Task: combing hair of fairies*]; D.1860 [*Magic beautification*]; D.1870 [*Magic hideousness*].
¶ *The Three Heads in the Well* is a motif which occurs both in English and Celtic folk-tales.

The Three Heads, with an accompanying rhyme, are found in Peele's *The Old Wives' Tale*. In a Scandinavian version, "Whitetoes and the Bushy Bridge", the heads are loathsome, not golden. See also "The Wal at the Warld's End".

THE THREE-LEGGED HARE [summary]

Twin brothers so much alike that their mother cut off the top of Jack's little finger to show the difference. Jack decided to leave home, telling Tom that if their water turned to blood he would know that something had happened to him.

Jack found work and did well, and married his master's daughter. Each day a three-legged hare came up to him when he was working in the fields and, against his master's warning, he decided to shoot it. He chased it on horseback, but it led him on until nightfall. They came to a lighted cottage, and an old woman let Jack in when he asked for a night's shelter. She was a witch, and by day was the three-legged hare. She made him tie up his dogs with two of her hairs. Then she gave him supper, but when he began to poke the fire she sprang on him and they wrestled fiercely.

Jack called his dogs to help him, but they could not move, and the witch felled him with her stick, and he became a black cat. She turned his dogs to stone and his horse into a dun cow.

At home Tom saw that the water had turned red. He set out to rescue his brother. He went to Jack's home and pretended to sleep with his wife, but put a six-foot sword between them in the bed. Everyone took him for Jack, and in the morning, at work in the field, he set off after the three-legged hare. Arriving at the hut, he pretended to tie up his dogs with her hairs, but threw them into the fire. So when the witch sprang on him, the dogs rescued him, and in terror she confessed the truth.

She gave him a magic fan, and told him to stand on a square slab in the middle of the field and wave the fan, and he would find his brother. He did so, and all the cattle in the field turned into lords and ladies and the black cat into Jack, the dogs came back to life, and the witch was burnt to death.

On the way home Tom teased Jack about sleeping with his wife, and Jack hit him with the witch's magic staff and turned him to stone. But when he got home his wife asked him why he had put the sword between them in the bed, and Jack saw the truth. He went back and disenchanted Tom, and Tom married Jack's wife's sister.

Thompson Notebooks, F. Written out by John Myers, of Low Furness.
TYPE 303. MOTIFS: F.577.2 [*Brothers identical in appearance*]; E.761 [*Life token*]; L.161 [*Lowly hero marries princess*]; G.263 [*Witch injures, enchants or transforms*]; G.551.4 [*One brother rescues another*]; K.1311.1 [*Husband's twin brother mistaken by wife for her husband*]; T.351 [*The sword of chastity*]; D.700 [*Disenchantment*]; N.342.3 [*Jealous and over-hasty man kills his rescuing twin brother*]; D.1663.1 [*Wands of life and death*].
¶ There is a world-wide distribution of this tale (Grimm, nos. 60 and 85). Ranke lists 770 versions in *Die Zwei Brüder*. It is well represented in this country. See "The Dräglin Hogney", "The King of England", "The Red Etin", etc.

THE THREE SONS [summary]

A poor man led his sons to three road-ends and told each of them to follow one, and to return after three years, when he had learnt a trade.

Jack followed an old Roman road, covered in grass, and presently met a man whom he asked for work. The man sent him to a hut at the bottom of the lane, and told him to say that the captain had sent him. Jack found there a gang of robbers, and promised to stay with them for five years. He became the cleverest thief of them all; but at the end of three years, remembering his promise to his father, he asked leave to go home. They would not hear of it, but in the end said he might go if he would first sleep three nights in a certain cave. The first night ghosts and skeletons appeared to scare him, but the second night he took his gun and fired at them, and killed some; they were members of the gang who had come to frighten him. The third night the captain ordered his men to rush on Jack, but he fled from them far into the cave, finally digging his way out, and joined his father and brothers at the lane's end.

The eldest, Tom, had become the cleverest joiner in the world, the second the cleverest shot, and Jack the cleverest thief. To test them, the old man made Jack steal an egg from under a sitting bird without moving it. Will had to shoot the egg into halves without spilling the yolk, and Tom to join it up again.

Then their father took them to the shore, and showed them a lonely island, where a Princess was chained up, and bells were set round it which roused a great eagle when they rang. Tom built a boat, and Jack got past the bells without touching them, and rescued the Princess. But he touched one bell on the way back, and the eagle swooped and would have seized them, but Will shot it through the tiny red spot which was its only vulnerable part. The eagle fell flat into the boat and smashed it, but Jack held up the Princess in the water, while Tom mended it, so they were saved, and Jack married the Princess.

Thompson Notebooks, F. Written down by John Myers.

TYPE 653. MOTIFS: F.660.1 [*Brothers acquire extraordinary skill: return home and are tested*]; K.305.1 [*Thieving content: first steals eggs from under bird*]; F.661.4 [*Skilful marksman shoots eggs*]; F.662.1 [*Skilful tailor sews up broken eggs*]; T.68.1 [*Princess offered as prize to rescuer*]; R.166 [*Brothers having extraordinary skill rescue princess*]; F.662.2 [*Skilful tailor sews together scattered planks in capsized boat*].

¶ In this version of the tale there is no contest, but the Princess is given to the third son.

This is a well-distributed tale (Grimm no. 129). Many examples have been recorded in Ireland, of which eighty-three were published in *Béaloidéas*, II, pp. 191 ff. A literary version occurs in *Pentamerone* and studies of it have been made by Anderson, Bassett and Cosquin.

THE THREE WISHES

A little man came to a wee house on a wet day and asked for supper, and they gave him a bowl of soup and some bread, and when he went he gave them a little round thing, and it would give him three wishes. So the next morning the man said, "Soup again! I wish I had a pudding for a change!" And there was a pudding. "Oh, you fool!" said his wife, "One wish gone! I wish the pudding was on your head!" And it was. "That's two wishes gone!" said the man. The wife said, "You ought to have wished for a bar of gold or anything." "I wish the pudding was off my head," said the man. And that was the three wishes gone.

School of Scottish Studies, from Robert Stewart (aged 11), Fetterangus.

TYPE 750A. MOTIFS: Q.1.1 [*Gods (saints) in disguise reward hospitality*]; D.1761.0.2 [*Limited number of wishes granted*]; J.2071 [*Three foolish wishes*].

¶ This is only half the type, the reward of hospitality foolishly wasted. See also "The Woodman and the Hatchet".

TIB AND THE OLD WITCH

A Tinker in our town had but one daughter, whose name was Tib, and because her father would not let her marry a miller's man named Jobson nothing would serve her but she must go and seek her fortune; so over hills and mountains, through groves and lonesome woods she passed, till at length she met with an old woman, who said unto Tib, Where are you going? To seek service, says Tib. Will you live with me? replied the old woman; my family is small, myself, my cat, and my dog. Tib answered, With all my heart. So home they went to her cottage, which stood by the side of a grove on the bank of a pleasant river. She no sooner entered in at the door, than she beheld the shelves furnished with abundance of earthen ware and glasses. She had not lived long with her, before Tib had committed a fault, for which the old woman was resolved to break every bone in her skin. To that end she put her into a sack, and having tied the mouth of the same she went to the grove to cut a stick; but while she was gone, Tib, with a penknife opened the sack and got out; and put the dog and cat into it, filling it up with pans, pipkins, etc., then dragged it to the door, that the old woman might not come in to miss them, who on her return, thinking that Tib had rowled thither began to lay on like a fury; when the dog howled, the cat mewed, and the pipkins cracked; while the old woman cries out, Ah! howl if you will, and be pox'd; for before you come out of this sack, I'll thrash your bones to chaff.—Now Tib stood at a distance, laughing to see how busy she was in destroying her own furniture, then fled for it, and never after returned.

Norton Collection, I, p. 200. From *The Four Kings* (1823), pp. 20–2.
TYPE 327 [variant]. MOTIFS: G.204 [*Girl in service of witch*]; K.526 [*Captor's bag filled with animals or objects while captives escape*].
¶ See "Jack the Buttermilk", "Fairy Gip and Witch One-Eye".

TITTY TOD

Two farmers had a dispute as to the qualifications of their wives. Not being able to agree, a bet was laid with reference to the spinning of a certain quantity of flax. It so happened that one of the wives could not spin; and whilst she sat wringing her hands in an agony of shame and despair at the thought of her husband and neighbours becoming acquainted with her inability to perform an operation then deemed so indispensable in housewifery, a very little old woman entered the house, to whom after some entreaty, she related the cause of her sorrow. The old woman promised to spin the flax, on condition that she should retain the thread, if, when she should return with it, the good-wife was not able to guess her name at three guesses. This was agreed to; and the old woman departed with the flax. The cowherd boy on the farm, hearing a noise issuing from a green knoll, peeped in at a hole—and saw a number of little females, sitting spinning flax; whilst, all the time, a withered old woman danced about, and sang, "Little does the good-wife o' the Ha' ken that my name is Titty Tod." The boy, on his return home, told what he had witnessed; and thus enabled the good-wife to baffle the old woman—who, of course, was a fairy.

Norton Collection, II, p. 37. Told in the South of Scotland, "L.R." in *Athenaeum*, 2 January 1847, p. 18.

TYPE 500.

¶ See "Tom Tit Tot", "Habetrot", "Whuppity Stoorie", etc.

It is noticeable that there seems a resemblance in the names of many of these spinning spirits: Tom Tit Tot, Tryten a Tratyn, Trit-a-Trot and Habetrot all echo each other. This fairy was much less malignant than the impet Tom Tit Tot, but less benevolent than Habetrot.

TOM AND THE GIANT BLUNDERBUSS
[summary]

Tom lived west of Hayle, probably in Lelant. He could eat as much as three men and do the work of six, but he was lazy, and only once in a while did he have an industrious fit. Then, indeed, he delighted in his great strength, for he would roll the largest rocks from the fields for "grounders", or foundation stones for walls or bridges. He measured 4 feet from shoulder to shoulder, and was square-built and straight down from shoulder to loins.

His mother begged him to do something for his living, and at last Tom undertook to drive a brewer's van, in the hope of getting plenty of strong drink. He went to live in Market-Jew where the brewery was, and there one day he saw ten men trying to lift a fallen tree on to a dray. Tom lifted it single-handed without stopping his oxen or looking behind him.

On the road to St Ives was a giant's dwelling, blocking the way with great rocks, at a place still called "The Giant's Hedges". It had a gate on the Market-Jew side, and another on the side nearest St Ives. The road, therefore, had to go all round the outside of this estate, but when Tom had done this once, and was returning from St Ives, encouraged by three or four gallons of strong beer which he had drunk, he decided to open the gates and drive straight on. After a mile or so he came to an inner wall round the giant's castle, and a deep ditch outside it. So again he drove his oxen, Neat and Comely, through the gates, but a little cur barking at them roused the giant, who came out in a rage and, uprooting a young elm-tree for a cudgel, challenged Tom to fight. Without unyoking his oxen, Tom turned his cart upside-down and removed one wheel for a shield and the axle-tree. They fought, and before long Tom drove the axle-tree right through the giant's body, making a great hole, which he tried in vain to plug with clods of turf, for Tom had no malice, and loved fair play. The giant too, captivated by Tom's valour, before he died made him heir to his castle and all his wealth. The castle was guarded by two great dogs, Catchem and Tearem, but by calling them by their names Tom could pass them safely.

Tom, when he could do no more for the giant, for the plug of turf kept slipping from his wound, left him dead and returned to his master, telling him that his rich uncle had died and left him all his estates, so that he must leave at once to bury him.

He would take no wages for his day's work except free beer with his supper; then he returned to the giant's castle, and found the last of the giant's many wives, all the rest having died mysteriously, though the giant had told Tom that he had had nothing to do with their deaths. They soon decided to be married, gave the carcass of a sheep to Catchem and Tearem by way of celebration, and went off to the caves of the castle to discover the giant's treasure.

Hunt, *Popular Romances*, p. 55.
TYPE 650 (variant). MOTIFS: F.610 [*Remarkably strong man*]; F.624 [*Mighty lifter*]; F.628.2.3 [*Strong man kills giant*].
¶ See continuation, "Tom the Giant and Jack the Tinkeard". See also "Tom Hickathrift".

TOM THE GIANT AND THE TINKEARD WITH THE WIZARD PENGERSWICK

(Tom the Giant had killed an older giant in fair fight, and had taken up his abode in the giant's castle, and married Jane, the last of his many wives. A clever tinkeard came to the castle, and in time he and Tom became friends.

The tinker taught Tom all his skill at singlestick, and the use of metals, and he showed Jane how to make her little son, young Tom, a coat of bull's hide, fitted to his shape, such as the tinkeard himself wore. Tom at last quarrelled with the tinkeard for being too friendly with Jane, but they settled it in a great wrestling match, in which Tom was judged the better man.)

When Tom had fairly thrown the tinkeard in the wrestling match, which, it must be remembered, was seen by the miners of Tregender, at which Tom was much pleased, although he did not express his pleasure, it was settled that Tom was the best man. This was sealed over a barrel of strong ale, and a game of quoits was proposed, while Jane was taking up the dinner. Tom had often wished, but never more so than now, that the green sloping banks against the inside of the castle walls had not been there, that he might have a fair fling of the quoits from end to end of the court. Tom's third throw in this game was a very strong one, and the quoit cut a great piece of turf from the banks, laying bare many graylooking stones, small rounded balls, and black sandy stuff.

"Look here you, Jack," says Tom, "whatever could possess the old fools of giants to heap up such a lot of black and gray mining-stones against the wall? Wherever could they have found them all?"

Jack carefully looked at the stuff thus laid bare, clapped his hands together, and shouted—

"By the gods, it's all the richest tin!"

Now Tom, poor easy-going soul, "didn't knaw tin", so he could scarcely believe Jack, though Jack had told him that he came from a tin country.

"Why, Tom," says Jack, "thee art a made man. If these banks are all tin, there is enough here to buy all the land, and all the houses, from sea to sea."

"What do I care for the tin; haven't I all a man can desire? My lands are all stocked with sheep and horned cattle. We shall never lack the best beef and mutton, and we want no better than our honest homespun."

Jane now made her appearance, announcing that dinner was ready. She was surprised at seeing so much tin, but she didn't say anything. She thought maybe she would get a new gown out of it, and go down to St. Ives Fair. Notwithstanding that Tom and Jane professed to treat lightly the discovery of the tin, it was clear they thought deeply about it, and their thoughts spoiled their appetites. It was evidently an accession of wealth which they could not understand.

Tom said he didn't know how to dress tin, it was of little use to him. Jack offered to dress it for the market on shares. Tom told him he might take as much as he had a mind to for what he cared. After dinner, the giant tried to sleep, but could not get a snore for the soul of him. Therefore, he walked out into the court, to get some fresh air, as he said, but in reality to look at the tin. Jane saw how restless Tom was, so she unhung his bows and arrows, and told him he must away to the hills to get some kids and hares.

"I shan't trouble myself with the bows and arrows," says Tom; "all I want are the slings Jack and I have in our pockets. Stones are plenty enough, hit or miss, no matter; and we needn't be at the trouble to gather up the stones again."

Off went Tom and Jack, followed by young Tom and Jane, to the Towednack and Zennor hills. They soon knocked down as many kids, hares, and rabbits as they desired;—they caught some colts, placed the children on two of them and the game on the others, and home they went. On their return, whilst waiting for supper, Jack wandered around the castle, and was struck by seeing a window which he had not before observed. Jack was resolved to discover the room to which this window belonged, so he very carefully noticed its position, and then threw his hammer in through it, that he might be certain of the spot when he found the tool inside of the castle. The next day, after dinner, when Tom was having his snooze, Jack took Jane with him, and they commenced a search for the hammer near the spot where Jack supposed the window should be, but they saw no signs of one in any part of the walls. They discovered however, a strangely fashioned, worm-eaten oak hanging press. They carefully examined this, but found nothing. At last Jack, striking the back of it with his fist, was convinced from the sound, that the wall behind it was hollow. He and Jane went steadily to work, and with some exertion they moved the press aside, and disclosed a stone door. They opened this, and there was Jack's hammer lying amidst a pile of bones, evidently the relics of some of old Blunderbuss's wives, whom he had imprisoned in the wall, and who had perished there. Jane was in a great fright, and blessed her good fortune that she had escaped a similar end. Jack, however, soon consoled her by showing her the splendid dresses which were here, and the gold chains, rings, and bracelets, with diamonds and other jewels, which were scattered around. It was agreed that Tom for the present should be kept in ignorance of all this. Tom awoke, his head full of the tin. He consulted with Jack and Jane. They duly agreed to keep their secret, and resolved that they would set to work the very next day to prepare some of the tin stuff for sale. Tom as yet scarcely believed in his wealth, which was magnified as much as possible by Jack, to bewilder him. However, several sacks of tin were duly dressed, and Tom and Jack started with them for Market-Jew, Tom whispering to Jack before he left the castle, that they would bring home a cask of the brewer's best ale with 'em. "It is a lot better than what Jane brews with her old-fashioned yerbes: but don't 'e tell her so."

The brewer of Market-Jew was also mayor, and, as it appears, tin-smelter, or tin merchant. To him, therefore, Tom went with his black tin, and received not only his cask of beer, but such an amount of golden coin—all of it being a foreign coinage—as convinced him that Jack had not deceived him. This brewer is reputed to have been an exceedingly honest and kind-hearted man, beloved by all. It was his practice, when any of the townspeople came before him, begging him to settle their disputes,—even when they "limbed" one another,—to shut them up in the brewery-yard, give them as much beer as they could drink, and keep them there until they became good friends. Owing to this practice he seldom had enough beer to sell, and was frequently troubled to pay for his barley. This brewer, who was reputed to be "the best mayor that ever was since the creation of gray cats," gave rise, from the above practice of his, to the proverb still in daily use, "Standing, like the mayor of Market-Jew, in his own light."

The mayor was always fat and jolly. He was an especial favourite, too, with the Lord of Pengerswick, who is believed to have helped him out of many troubles. He had bought his tin of Tom and Jack, such a bargain, that he resolved to have some sport, so a barrel of beer was broached in the yard, and the crier was sent round the town to call all hands to a "courant" (merrymaking). They came, you may be certain, in crowds.

There was wrestling, hurling,—the length of the Green from Market-Jew to Chyandour, and back again,—throwing quoits, and slinging. Some amused themselves in pure wantonness by slinging stones over the Mount; so that the old giant, who lived there, was afraid to show above ground, lest his only eye should get knocked out. The games were kept up right merrily until dusk; when in rode the Lord of Pengerswick on his enchanted mare, with a colt by her side. The brewer introduced Tom and Jack, and soon they became the best of friends. Tom invited Pengerswick to his castle, and they resolved to go home at once and make a night of it. Pengerswick gave Tom the colt, and, by some magic power, as soon as he mounted this beautiful animal, he found himself at home, and the lord, the brewer, and Jack with him. How this was brought about Tom could never tell, but Jack appeared to be in the secret. Tom was amazed and delighted to find Jane dressed like a queen, in silks and diamonds, and the children arrayed in a manner well becoming the dignity of their mother.

Jane, as soon as Tom and Jack had left her, had proceeded to the room in the wall, and with much care removed the jewels, gold, and dresses, caring little, as she afterwards said, for the dead bones, although they rattled as she shook them out of the robes. In a little time she had all the dresses in the main court of the castle, and having well beaten and brushed them, she selected the finest,—those she now wore—and put the rest aside for other grand occasions.

The condescension of the great Lord of Pengerswick was something wonderful. He kissed Jane till Tom was almost jealous, and the great lord romped about the court of the castle with the children. Tom was, on the whole, however, delighted with the attention paid to his wife by a real lord, but our clear-headed Jack saw through it all, and took measures accordingly.

Pengerswick tried hard to learn the secret of the stores of tin, but he was foiled by the tinkeard on every tack. You may well suppose how desirous he was of getting Jack out of the way, and eventually he began to try his spells on him. The power of his necromancy was such, that all in the castle were fixed in sleep as rigid as stones, save Jack. All that the enchanter could do produced no effect on him. He sat quietly looking on, occasionally humming some old troll, and now and then whistling to show his unconcern. At last Pengerswick became enraged, and he drew from his breast a dagger and slyly struck at Jack. The dagger, which was of the finest Eastern steel, was bent like a piece of soft iron against Jack's black hide.

"Art thou the devil?" exclaimed Pengerswick.

"As he's a friend of yours," says Jack, "you should know his countenance."

"Devil or no devil," roared Pengerswick, "you cannot resist this," and he held before Jack a curiously shaped piece of polished steel.

Jack only smiled, and quietly unfastening his cow's hide, he opened it. The cross, like a star of fire, was reflected in a mirror under Jack's coat, and it fell from Pengerswick's grasp. Jack seized it, and turning it full upon the enchanter, the proud lord sank trembling to the ground, piteously imploring Jack to spare his life and let him go free. Jack bade the prostrate lord rise from the ground. He kicked him out of the castle, and sent the vicious mare after him. Thus he saved Tom and his family from the power of this great enchanter. In a little time the sleep which had fallen upon them passed away, and they awoke, as though from the effects of a drunken frolic. The brewer hurried home, and Tom and Jack set to work to dress their tin. Tom and Jane's relations and friends flocked around them, but Jack said, "Summer flies are only seen in the sunshine," and he shortly after this put their friendship to the test, by conveying to them the idea that Tom had spent all his wealth. These new friends dropped off when they thought they could get no more, and Tom and Jane were thoroughly disgusted with their summer friends and selfish relations. The tinkeard established himself firmly as an inmate of the castle. No more was said about the right of the public to make a king's highway through the castle grounds. He aided Tom in hedging in the waste lands, and very carefully secured the gates against all intruders. In fact, he also quite altered his politics.

Jack had a desire to go home to Dartmoor to see his mother, who had sent to tell him that the old giant Dart was near death. He started at once, on foot. Tom wished him to have Pengerswick's colt, but Jack preferred his legs. . . . He reached home. The old giant was at his last gasp. Jack made him give everything to his mother before he breathed his last. When he died, Jack carefully buried him. He then settled all matters for his mother, and returned to the West Country again.

Hunt, *Popular Romances*, p. 66.
MOTIFS: F.531.6.8.3.3 [*Giants wrestle with each other*]; F.531.6.7 [*Giant's treasure*]; F.531.6.8.5 [*Giants' social relations*].
¶ See "Tom and the Giant Blunderbuss".

TOM HICKATHRIFT [summary]

Tom was the son of Thomas Hickathrift, a poor day-labourer in the Isle of Ely, before the days of William the Conqueror, but the father died while the son was still young, and he seemed unable to learn his lessons at school, and was idle and lazy at home. His mother loved him and waited on him, and Tom grew and grew, till at ten years old he was 8 feet high and ate as much as four or five ordinary men. One day his mother needed some straw, and begged Tom to fetch it from a kindly farmer who had promised her as much as she wanted. Tom refused to go unless she first borrowed him a cart rope. With this he went to the farm, loaded up a ton of straw, and went off with it over his shoulder. After that everyone wanted Tom to work for them and he became more industrious. One day a woodman asked his help in bringing home a tree. Tom picked up the tree, and laid it in the cart, while four other men who had been unable to drag the tree between them, stood by wondering at his strength. As a reward, Tom asked for "a stick for my mother's fire", picked up a still larger tree, and went off with that. He now became famous at all kinds of sport, till at last no one dared to challenge him. Once he intervened at a football game, and kicked the ball so far that it was lost. The other players were very angry, but Tom picked up a great spar and scattered them all. On the way home he was waylaid by four robbers. He killed two and grievously wounded the others, and went home with £200 of their spoils. But at last Tom met his match in a tinker who challenged him to fight, and beat him. Tom took the tinker home and tended his wounds, and they became fast friends. Then Tom went to work for a brewer who wanted his beer taken every day to Wisbech. The brewer gave him a new suit of clothes and plenty to eat and drink, so Tom was content. But it was a weary journey to Wisbech, 20 miles by the road, because a great giant kept part of the marshland through which there lay a much shorter road. Tom resolved to defy the giant, so one day he flung open his gates and drove his cart and horses through them. The giant rushed out at him and threatened to hang his head on a nearby tree, where many other heads were already hanging. He ran into his cave to fetch his club, and Tom, being unarmed, took the axle-tree and one wheel from his cart for shield and buckler. There was a great fight, and at last the giant begged for a rest and a drink. But Tom said, "My mother did not teach me such wit; who'd be a fool then?" At last the giant yielded, and begged Tom to take him as his servant. But Tom laid blows upon him till he was dead, then went into the cave, where he found a great store of gold and silver. The next day he and his master and other townsfolk of Lynn came to the cave, and Tom was adjudged the owner of the cave. The land the giant had kept by force was made common to a number of poor people, and part of it was given to Tom to farm and support his mother, Jane Hickathrift, and himself. He built a great house in place of the cave and made a deer park and kept men and maids and lived happily to the end of his days.

Jacobs, *More English Fairy Tales*, p. 42.
TYPE 650 (variant). MOTIFS: F.611.2.3 [*Strong hero's long nursing*]; F.611.3.1 [*Strong hero practises uprooting trees*]; F.613.2 [*Strong man's labour contract: all the grain he can carry*]; G.613 [*Giant robber with club*]; F.628.2.3 [*Strong man kills giant*].

Motif F.613.2 occurs in a tradition of William of Lindholme. "On one occasion William of Lindholme went to borrow some straw of a neighbour. The latter told him to take as much as he could carry on his back. No sooner said than done. The borrower stuck the agricultural fork he had in his hand into a stack, and walked off with it entirely" (M. Peacock, *Folk-Lore of Lincolnshire*, p. 171).

See also "Strong Jack", "Tom and the Giant", "The Twenty-One-Year-Old Giant".

THE HISTORY OF TOM THUMB [summary]

In the days of King Arthur the magician Merlin, disguised as a beggar, once stopped at the cottage of a poor ploughman, and asked for some refreshment. The man and his wife gave him a hearty welcome, and brought him a bowl of milk, and some coarse brown bread. Merlin was so much pleased with their kindness, that he wished to help them. For, in spite of their air of frugal comfort and neatness, he could see that they were unhappy. The poor wife told him that this was because they had no children, and added, "If only I had a son no bigger than my husband's thumb, I should be perfectly happy."

Merlin was pleased with this fancy, and granted her wish. In due time a boy was born to them, who never grew any bigger than a man's thumb.

The queen of the fairies heard of him, and came to see him. She admired him, and kissed him, and named him Tom Thumb. At her bidding the fairies dressed him in a hat made of an oak-leaf, a shirt of spiders' web, jacket of thistle-down, and trousers of feathers. His stockings were of apple-rind, tied with one of his mother's eyelashes, and his shoes of mouse-skin, with the hair inside.

As Tom grew older, he became full of trickery. He would creep into the bags of the other boys, and steal the cherry stones that they used for their games.

But at last one of the boys caught him at this, and to punish him, he drew the cord at the neck of the bag tight, and shook it up and down, so hard that poor Tom was nearly bruised to death. In his pain he roared out that he would never play such a trick again.

Another day he climbed up on to the edge of the bowl when his mother was making a pudding, and fell into the batter, and was tied up in the pudding-cloth, but as soon as he felt the boiling water, he kicked and struggled so much that his mother thought the pudding was bewitched, and threw it out of the window. It was picked up by a tinker, who put it into his pack, but Tom cried out so loud that the tinker flung away the pudding in terror. It broke into bits, and Tom crawled out and walked home. His mother was overjoyed; she washed the batter off, kissed him, and put him to bed to recover.

One day she was in the field milking, and had tied Tom to a thistle, in case the wind blew him away. A cow saw his oak-leaf hat, and swallowed the thistle, the hat, and Tom at one mouthful. But the roaring Tom made in her throat so startled her that she let him fall, and his mother caught him in her apron.

Tom's father made him a whip of barley-straw to drive cattle with, but Tom fell into a furrow, and a raven picked him up in its beak, and carried him to the top of a giant's castle, where it dropped him. The giant, whose name was Grumbo, picked him up and swallowed him like a pill. Tom kicked and struggled inside him, so the giant threw him up again and he fell into the sea that washed the castle walls. Here he was swallowed by a large fish, which was caught soon afterwards, and served up to King Arthur at dinner. Tom jumped out onto the table, and the king was so delighted with such a tiny man that he made Tom his dwarf, and he used to amuse all the knights of the Round Table. Often the king took Tom with him in his pocket when he went hunting. One day, hearing that Tom's parents were poor, he took him into his treasury, and told him to carry to them as much as he could. Tom put a silver threepenny piece into a water-bubble purse, and struggled home, a forty-eight hours' journey with it on his back.

His mother received him with joy, and put him to bed in a walnut-shell before the fire to recover from his weariness. He fell ill, for she feasted him for three days on a hazel-nut which should have lasted him a month.

At last, however, he was fit to return to court, and, as the ground was slippery with rain, Tom's mother tied him to a little parasol which she made of cambric paper, and blew him off into the air, and he arrived safely, to delight the king and his courtiers again with his skill and pranks.

He worked so hard that he again fell ill, but the queen of the fairies heard of it, and came in a chariot drawn by winged mice, and carried Tom off to fairyland, where he stayed till he was fully recovered. He returned to the court floating on a current of air, and arrived just as the cook was carrying a bowl of frumenty across the yard, so Tom fell into the bowl, and the cook's face was splashed with the hot food. He was so angry that he went to the King, and complained that Tom had done it for a mischievous trick. The King condemned Tom to be beheaded for high treason, but Tom jumped for safety into the nearest cavity, which happened to be the mouth of a miller who stood gaping at him. The miller, not knowing what he had swallowed, went home, and when Tom heard the noise of the mill at work, he knew he was clear of the court, and began to kick and jump about in the miller's inside, and to sing and shout, so that the miller thought he was bewitched, and so did the doctors who were summoned to his aid.

But when the miller happened to yawn widely, Tom jumped right out of his mouth, and landed on the table. The miller in a rage threw him into the river, where a salmon gobbled him up, and in time Tom Thumb found himself taken back again to court, and imprisoned in a mousetrap until the king had time to attend to him. After a week the king sent for him, pardoned him and restored him to favour, and even made him a knight. He was given a new suit of clothes, a shirt of butterfly wings, and boots of chicken hide, a needle for a sword, and a mouse to ride, which made him a sight to divert all the court. Once a large cat swallowed the mouse and Tom together, but Tom fought so bravely inside the cat that it let them both fall from its mouth, and a nobleman caught him in his hat.

After this the Fairy Queen again carried Tom to fairyland, where he stayed so long that King Arthur and all his friends had died by the time he returned, and King Thunstone was on the throne. Tom's appearance caused great surprise at court, but the king received him with delight, gave him a palace to live in, a span high with a door an inch wide, and a coach drawn by six small mice. This made the Queen jealous, and she accused Tom to the king of having treated her with disrespect. Fearing the King's anger, Tom escaped, first into a snail-shell, and then on the back of a large butterfly which flew with him into the air, but afterwards came back to the court, where Tom fell off into a watering-can. Again he was imprisoned in a mousetrap, and again forgiven (a cat having released him from the trap). But he perished at last in a fierce battle with a spider, which poisoned him with its breath, though Tom fought bravely for a long time. The whole court went into mourning, and erected a marble monument to Tom's memory, with an epitaph recounting his deeds and and their grief.

Hartland, *English Fairy and Folk Tales*, p. 272.

TYPE 700. MOTIFS: F.535.1.1 [*Adventures of thumbling*]; Q.1 [*Hospitality rewarded*]; T.553 [*A child the size of a thumb wished for and born*]; F.911.3.1 [*Midget swallowed by a cow*]; F.535.1 [*Person the size of a thumb*]; F.535.1.1.1 [*Thumbling drives waggon by sitting in horse's ear*]; F.535.1.1.10.2 [*Thumbling hides in snailshell*]; F.535.1.1.12 [*Thumbling carries needle as sword*]; F.535.1.1.14 [*Thumbling carried on hat-brim*]; B.557 [*Unusual animal as riding-horse*].

¶ This is an old chapbook version of an international tale-type. The adoption by the Fairy Queen, and the service in King Arthur's court are out of the general line of the tale, and are probably due to the author of the chapbook, though Thumbelina in Hans Andersen's story also went to live with the fairies.

Charlotte Yonge embroidered the story in "Sir Thomas Thumb", but her production bears little resemblance to a folktale.

For the pudding incident, see "Dathera Dad", B, Legends, Fairies.

TOM TIDDLER'S GROUND

Tom Tiddler were a-scaring they blackly-tops and he come on a lump
of gold out in middle of field. He look all around, and weren't nobody
about to tell 'twas theirs, so Tom he say, "Findo, Keeps. But 'tis likely
fairy gold!" So he hid 'en in the hole by their thorn-tree. Then he go on
a bit, and he find a lump of silver, and he done the same again. Then he go
on with his labour, and he found a liddle bag of pennies. "That's my
size," says Tom, so he keeps 'un, and by and by he buys a farm. Nobody
questions about a heap of pennies saved up over the years. Farm did well
till someone overlooked 'un, and cows begun pining, so Tom he up and
off to the Fairy Thorn.

"What's come of yew?" say the Fairies. "Have 'ee a bit of luck to
spare?" say Tom. "I did return thy gold and silver." "Ask all as you go,"
say the Fairies, "someone have come and a-stole it again." So Tom goes
off, and he sees a pyatt, so he crosses his feet and spit, and then say
mannerly, "Please, have 'ee see the Fairies' gold?"

> "Gold? Gold?
> Oh, no! Oh, no!
> I never steal gold,
> So off you go," say the Pyatt.

So next he come on a Toad, and he crook his fingers at her—he thinks,
"'Tis old Sal on her goings" (mischief in disguise), but he say mannerly,
"Please, have 'ee seed the Fairies' Gold?"
And old Sal croaks,

> "Gold? Gold?
> Oh, no! Oh, no!
> I never steal gold,
> So off you go!"

So next he come on Mr. Fox, and he'm pretty certain by now 'tis Old
Wizard Black, but he'd a-got salt in his pocket, so he say, "Please, Mr.
Fox, have 'ee seed Fairies' Gold?" And Mr. Fox snarled to him, "NO!
Be Off!" and then Tom Tiddler knowed the thief. Well, he told the
huntsmen, and hounds chased 'un right over Tom Tiddler's ground, and
the Fairy Thorn catched in his coat, and held 'en for hounds to kill—and
that ended Mr. Fox.

Then they go look under Fairy Thorn, and there was a gurt heap of
withered leaf. Now Wizard Black died sudden, so that ended the gold
and silver.

And Tom Tiddler's farm went well, and bird boys sing about 'en to this day.

And that ends my tale.

Ruth L. Tongue: Somerset, Mendips, "Found 1964, in my early collecting papers. forgotten". The Mendip Bird Boys used to call:

> 'Shua O, shua O, shoo, shoo!
> Shua oh! shua oh! shoo shoo shoo, all ye birds.
> Out of my master's ground, into Tom Tiddler's ground.
> Shoo all ye birds, hilly-ho!'"

MOTIFS: F.348.4 [*Gifts of gold and silver not to be accepted from fairies*]; F.359 [*Theft from fairies*]; F.361.2 [*Fairy takes revenge for theft*]; A.2542.1.1 [*Magpie is unlucky*]; G.211.6.1 [*Witch in form of toad*]; G.211.2.3 [*Witch in form of fox*]; G.275.12 [*Witch in form of animal is killed as a result of injury to the animal*].

This story is probably not so old as the rhyme which it explains. Such tales are invented and perpetuated in the nursery.

¶ See "The Man in the Wilderness".

TOM TIT TOT

Well, once upon a time there were a woman, and she baked five pies. And when they come out of the oven they was that overbaked, the crust were too hard to eat. So she says to her darter:

"Maw'r," says she, "put you them there pies on the shelf an' leave 'em there a little, an' they'll come agin." She meant, you know, the crust 'ud get soft.

But the gal she says to herself, "Well, if they'll come agin, I'll ate 'em now." And she set to work and ate 'em all, first and last.

Well, come supper time, the woman she said: "Goo you, and git one o' them there pies. I dare say they've come agin now."

The gal she went an' she looked, and there warn't nothin' there but the dishes. So back she come, and says she, "Noo, they ain't come agin."

"Not none on 'em?" says the mother.

"Not none on 'em," says she.

"Well, come agin or not come agin," says the woman, "I'll ha' one for supper."

"But you can't, if they ain't come," says the gal.

"But I can," says she, "Goo you an' bring the best of 'em."

"Best or worst," says the gal, "I've ate 'em all, an' you can't ha' one till that's come agin."

Well, the woman she were wholly bate, an' she took her spinnin' to the door to spin, and as she spun she sang:

> "My darter ha' ate five, five pies to-day.
> My darter ha' ate five, five pies to-day."

The King he were a' comin' down the street an' he hard her sing, but what she sang he couldn't hare, so he stopped and said:

"What were that you was a singin' of, Maw'r?"

The woman, she were ashamed to let him hare what her darter had been a doin', so she sang, 'stids o' that:

"My darter ha' spun five, five skeins to-day,
My darter ha' spun five, five skeins to-day."

"S'ars o' mine!" said the king, "I never heerd tell of anyone as could do that."

Then he said: "Look you here, I want a wife and I'll marry your darter. But look you here," says he, "'leven months out o' the year she shall have all the vittles she likes to eat, and all the gownds she likes to git, and all the cump'ny she likes to hev; but the last month o' the year she'll ha' to spin five skeins ev'ry day, an' if she doon't, I shall kill her."

"All right," says the woman, for she thowt what a grand marriage that was. And as for them five skeins, when te come tew, there'd be plenty o' ways o' gettin' out of it, an' likeliest, he'd ha' forgot about it.

Well, so they was married. An' for 'leven months the gal had all the vittles she liked to ate, and all the gownds she liked to git, an' all the cump'ny she liked to hev.

But when the time was gettin' oover, she began to think about them there skeins an' to wonder if he had 'em in mind. But not one word did he say about 'em, and she whoolly thowt he'd forgot 'em.

Howsivir, the last day o' the last month, he takes her to a room she'd nivir set eyes on afore. There worn't nothin' in it but a spinnin' wheel and a stool. An' says he, "Now, me dear, hare yow'll be shut in to-morrow with some vittles and some flax, and if you hain't spun five skeins by the night, yar hid'll goo off."

An' awa' he went about his business. Well, she were that frightened. She'd allus been such a gatless mawther, that she didn't so much as know how to spin, an' what were she to dew to-morrer, with no one to come nigh her to help her. She sat down on a stool in the kitchen, an' lork! how she did cry!

Howsiver, all on a sudden she hard a sort of a knockin' low down ont he door. She upped and oped it, an' what should she see but a small little black thing with a long tail. That looked up at her right kewrious, an' that said:

"What are yew a cryin' for?"

"Wha's that to yew?" says she.

"Nivir yew mind," that said. "But tell me what you're a cryin' for?"

"That 'oon't dew me noo good if I dew," says she.

"You doon't know that," that said, an' twirled that's tail round.

"Well," says she, "that oon't dew no harm, if that doon't dew no good," and she upped and told about the pies an' the skeins an' everything.

"This is what I'll do," says the little black thing. "I'll come to yar winder iv'ry mornin' an' take the flax an' bring it spun at night."

"What's your pay?" says she.

That looked out o' the corners o' that's eyes, an' that said:

"I'll give you three guesses every night to guess my name, an' if you hain't guessed it afore the month's up, yew shall be mine."

Well, she thowt she'd be sure to guess that's name afore the month was up.

"All right," says she, "I agree."

"All right," that says, an' lork! how that twirled that's tail.

Well, the next day, har husband he took her inter the room, an' there was the flax an' the day's vittles.

"Now there's the flax," says he, "an' if that ain't spun up this night off goo yar head." An' then he went out an' locked the door.

He'd hardly goon, when there was a knockin' agin the winder. She upped and she oped it, and there sure enough was the little oo'd thing a settin' on the ledge.

"Where's the flax?" says he.

"Here te be," says she. And she gonned it to him.

Well, come the evenin', a knockin' come agin to the winder. She upped and she oped it, and there sure enough was the little oo'd thing with five skeins of flax on his arm.

"Here te be," says he, an' he gonned it to her.

"Now what's my name," says he.

"What, is that Bill?" says she.

"Noo, that ain't," says he. An' he twirled his tail.

"Well, is that Ned?" says she.

"Noo, that ain't," says he. An' he twirled his tail.

"Well, is that Mark?" says she.

"Noo, that ain't," says he. An' he twirled harder, an' awa' he flew.

Well, when har husband he come in, there was the five skeins riddy for him.

"I see I shorn't hev for to kill you to-night, me dare," says he. "Yew'll hev yar vittles and yar flax in the mornin'," says he, an' awa' he goes.

Well, ivery day the flax an' the vittles, they was brought, an' ivery day that there little black impet used for to come mornin's an' evenin's. An' all the day the mawther she set a tryin' fur to think of names to say to it when te come at night. But she niver hot on the right one. An' as that got to-warts the ind o' the month, the impet that began for to look soo maliceful, an' that twirled that's tail faster an' faster each time she gave a guess.

At last te came to the last day but one.

The impet that come at night along o' the five skeins; an' that said:

"What, hain't yew got my name yet?"

"Is that Nicodemus?" says she.

"Noo, t'ain't," that says.

"Is that Sammle?" says she.

"Noo t'ain't," that says.

"A-well, is that Methusalem?" says she.

"Noo, t'ain't that norther," he says.

Then that looks at her with that's eyes like a cool o' fire, an' that says,

"Woman, there's only tomorrer night, an' then yar'll be mine!" An' awa' te flew.

Well, she felt that horrud. Howsomediver, she hard the King a comin' along the passage. In he came, an' when he see the five skeins, he says, says he:

"Well, my dare," says he, "I don't see but what you'll ha' your skeins ready tomorrer night as well, an' as I reckon I shorn't ha' to kill you, I'll ha' supper in here tonight." So they brought supper, an' another stool for him, and down the tew they sat.

Well, he hadn't eat but a mouthful or so, when he stops an' begins to laugh.

"What is it?" says she.

"A-why," he says, "I was out a-huntin' to-day, an' I got awa' to a place in the wood I'd never seen afore. An' there was an old chalk pit. An' I heerd a sort of a hummin' kind o'. So I got off my hobby, an' I went right quiet to the pit, an' I looked down. Well, what should there be but the funniest little black thing yew iver set eyes on. An' what was that dewin' on, but that had a little spinnin' wheel, an' that were spinnin' wonnerful fast, an' a twirlin' that's tail. An' as that span, that sang:

> "Nimmy nimmy not,
> My name's Tom Tit Tot."

Well, when the mawther heerd this, she fared as if she could ha' jumped outer her skin for joy, but she di'n't say a word.

Next day, that there little thing looked soo maliceful when he come for the flax. An' when night came, she heerd that a knockin' agin the winder panes. She oped the winder, an' that come right in on the ledge. That were grinnin' from are to are, an' Oo! that's tail were twirlin' round so fast.

"What's my name?" that says, as that gonned her the skeins.

"Is that Solomon?" she says, pretendin' to be afeard.

"Noo, t'ain't," that says, an' that come fudder into the room.

"Well, is that Zebedee?" says she agin.

"Noo t'ain't," says the impet. An' then that laughed, an' twirled that's tail, till yew cou'n't hardly see it.

"Take time, woman," that says; "next guess an' you're mine." An' that stretched out that's black hands at her.

Well, she backed a step or two, and she looked at it, an' then she laughed out, an' says she, a-pointin' of her finger at it,

> "Nimmy nimmy not,
> Yar name's Tom Tit Tot."

Well, when that hard her, that shruck awful, an' awa' that flew into the dark, an' she niver saw it noo more.

E. S. Hartland, *County Folk-Lore*, I, p. 43 (Suffolk section). (Told by an old servant to the writer when a child.) A.W.T., 'Suffolk Notes and Queries', *Ipswich Journal*, 15 January 1878.

Reprinted by Edward Clodd from *The Ipswich Journal*, 'Notes and Queries', edited by F. Hindes Groome, from a lady who had heard it from an old Suffolk nurse.

TYPE 500. MOTIFS: H.1092 [*Tasks: spinning impossible amount in one night*]; H.521 [*Test: guessing unknown propounder's name*]; N.475 [*Secret name overheard by eavesdropper*].

¶ Edward Clodd elaborated the article, "The Philosophy of Rumpelstiltskin" (*The Folk-Lore Journal*, 1889), into a book, *Tom Tit Tot, an Essay on Savage Philosophy in Folk-Tale* (1898), in which he examines the primitive name-tabus. "Rumpelstiltskin" (Grimm, no. 55), is the best known version of this widespread tale. It is most frequent in Ireland, Germany, Denmark and Finland.

See also "Duffy and the Devil", "Whuppity Stoorie", "Titty Tod".

This version is in the Suffolk dialect. "Maw'r" or "Mawther" means "daughter", or "girl"; "gatless", "heedless" or "careless".

The question of what happened at the end of the next eleven months is neatly answered in the appended sequel.

THE GIPSY WOMAN [sequel to "Tom Tit Tot"]

Well, the hool o' that yare, the mawther she'd the best o' livin' an' the best o' cump'ny, till the 'leventh month was nare oover.

An' then, her husban' says to her, says he: "Well, me dare, to-day, that's the end o' the month, an' to-morrer yow'll ha' to begin an' spin yare five skeins ivvery day."

She hadn't nivver given a thawt but what he'd clane forgotten about it; an' now, what to dew she did not know. She knew she couldn't reckon noo moor on Tom Tit Tot, an' she couldn't spin a mite herself: an' now har hid 'ud have to come off!

Well, pore Toad, she set herself down agin on a stule in the backhouse, an' she cried as if har heart 'ud break.

All at onst, she hared someone a knockin' at the door. Soo she upped an' onsnecked it, an' there stood a gipsy woman, as brown's a berry.

"A why, what's this to-dew hare?" sez she, "What a'ir yew a-cryin' for like that?"

"Git awa', yow golderin' mawther," says she. "Doon't yew come where yew ain't no good."

"Tell me yar trouble, an' maybe I *shorl* be some good," says the woman.

Well, she looked soo onderstandin' that the gal she upped an' toold her.

"Wha's that all?" sez she. "I ha' holped folks out o' wuss than this, an' I'll help you out o' this."

"Ah! but what de yew arst for dewin' of it?" sez the gal, for she thowt how she'd nare gonned herself awa' to that snaisty little black impet.

"I doon't ask nothun' but the best suit o' clothes yow ha' got," the gipsy said.

"Yow shall hev 'em, an' welcome," says the gal, an' she runned an' ooped the hutch where har best gownd an' things was, an' giv' 'em to the woman, an' a brooch o' gay goold. For she thowt to herself, "If she's a chate an' can't help me, an' may hid is cut off, that woon't make noo matters if I *hev* giv' awa' my best gownd."

The woman, she looked rarely plazed when she see the gownd: an' sez she: "Now then, yow'll ha' to ask all the fooks yew know to a stammin' grand partery, an' I'll come tew't."

Well, the mawther, she went to har husban' an' says she: "My dare, bein' that 'tis the larst night afoor I spin, I shud like to hev a partery."

"All right, me dare," sez he.

Soo the fooks wuz all arst, an' they come in their best cloothes; silk an' sattuns, an' all mander o' fine things.

Well, they all had a grand supper o' the best o' vittles, an' they liked theirselves rarely well. But the gipsy woman she niccer come nigh, an' the gal her heart was in her mouth.

One o' the lords as was right tired o' dancin', said that it wornt far from bull's noon, and te wus time te goo.

"Noo, noo, dew yew sta' a little longer," says the gal. "Le's hev a game o' blind man's buff fust." Soo they begun to play.

Just then the door that flew oopen, an' in come the gipsy woman. She'd woished herself, an' coomed her hair, an' whelmed a gay an' gah hankercher round har hid, an' put on the grand gownd, till she looked like a Queen come in.

"S'ars o' mine, whu's that?" says the King.

"Oo, that's a frind o' mine," saz the gal. An' she looked to see what the gipsy 'ud do.

"What, are yew a playin' blind man's buff?" sez she. "I'll jine in along on ye."

An' soo she did. But in her pocket what wuz there but a little gotch of cold cart-grease; an' as she run she dipped har hand in this hare grease, an' smudged it on the fooks as she run by.

That warn't long afore somebody hollered out. "Oo lork, there's some rare nasty stuff on my gownd."

"Why, soo there is on mine," sez another, "that must ha' come off o' yow."

"Noo, that that di'n't. Yow ha' put it onto me." An' then nigh ivvery-body began to holler an' quarrel with ache other, ache one a thinkin' that the tother had goon an' smirched 'em.

Well, the King he come forrerd an' he heerd what was the matter. The ladies was a cryin', an' the gentlemen was a shoutun', an' all their fine things was daubed oover.

"Why, wha's this?" he sah, for there was a great mark on his cootsleeve. He smelt of it an' then he turned up his noose, an' says he: "That's cart-grease."

"Noo, that ain't," sez the gipsy woman. "That's off my hand. Tha's spindle grease."

"Why, wha's spindle grease?" sez he.

"Well," says she, "I ha' bin a great spinner i' my time, an' I span an' span an' span five skeins a day. An' becos I span se much the spindle grease that worked inter my hands, and now woish 'em as often as I may, I naster every thing I touch. An' if yer wife spins like I, she'll ha' spindle grease like I."

Well, the King he looked at his coot sleeve, an' he rubbed it an' snuffed at it an' then he said: "Look yew hare, me dare, an' listen what I sa' to yew. If ivver I see ye with a spindle agin in yar hands, yar hid'll goo off." Soo she hadn't never to spin noo more.

An' tha's all.

Norton Collection, II, p. 42. *East Anglian*, VII (1897–8), sec. iii. Probably 1897. From Miss L. A. Fison and Mrs Walter Thomas, her sister, from their nurse. Also in *Merry Suffolk* (1899), pp. 102–3, where the spelling of the dialect is somewhat different. In the *Merry Suffolk* version "Tom Tit Tot" ends with the traditional sentence: "Lork! How she did clap her hands for joy. 'I'll warrant my master'll ha' forgot all about spinning next year,' says she."

If it stands by itself, this should be allotted to type 501, not to type 500.

THE TWENTY-ONE-YEAR-OLD GIANT

[summary]

An old woman kept her son Jack in bed until he was twenty-one. Then dressed in a new suit he came down and she sent him to the near-by farm to get straw. He took an enormous rope, and explained to the farmer, who gave him leave to take all the straw he could carry. With the rope Jack heaved a whole stack onto his back and carried it home. Next day the farmer came to ask why he had taken so much, and finding that he had carried it himself, offered him work as a water-carrier.

Jack given two buckets to fill from the well for the farmer's boiler for washing-day. After several hours it seemed no fuller, so he loaded a huge cask on his back, and filled it as well as the buckets once or twice, then the farmer said he had fetched more than enough.

On his way home Jack was persuaded to enlist, to earn money to help his mother. Soon sent to war with a cavalry regiment; shot a great many of the enemy, and when no ammunition was left he killed more with the butt-end of his rifle. When his horse was shot under him he swung it round and round his head, and so wiped out almost the whole of the survivors. As a reward, the king gave Jack his daughter in marriage.

Thompson Notebooks, E. Picked up by Noah Lock, from his cousin Vernon Taylor. TYPE 650 (variant). MOTIF F.611.2.3 [*Strong hero's long nursing*]; F.613.2 [*Strong man's labour contract: all the grain he can carry*]; F.614.10 [*Strong hero fights whole army alone*].
¶ See "Tom Hickathrift", "Strong Jack".

THE TWO HUMPS [summary]

There were two hump-backed men lived each at one end of a glen. One was called "Humph at the Heid o' the Glen", and the other was called "Humph at the Fit o' the Glen". They were friends, and every Sunday they took time to visit each other. One Sunday Humph at the Fit o' the Glen was on his way to visit Humph at the Heid o' the Glen, and as he passed a wee plantation he heard a sound of singing, "Saturday, Sunday, Saturday, Sunday", again. He thought he could put a bit to that, so he sang very sweetly, "Saturday, Sunday, Monday, Tue-uesday".

There was a sound of clapping. They were three fairies that lived in the glen, and one said to the other, "Brother, what will you give him for that lovely bit he's added to the song?" "I'll take away his humph from his, and what will you give him?" "I'll give him health and happiness all his days. And what will you give him?" he said to the third. "I'll give him that he'll never know want."

Well, as the Humph went up the glen, he got lighter and lighter and straighter and straighter, until they didn't know him for the same man when he knocked at his friend's door. But he told his friend all that had happened to him, and his friend could hardly wait till the next Sunday.

On the Sunday he went hurrying down the glen, and at the plantation he heard the singing: "Saturday, Sunday, Monday, Tues-uesday." And without any time or tune he rattled out, "Saturday, Sunday, Monday, Tuesday, Wednesday, Thursday, Friday, Saturday!" But there was no clapping. Then one fairy said to another. "What shall we do to him for spoiling our lovely song?" "If he has a humph on his back, he shall have one a thousand times bigger."

"He shall be so ugly no man shall want to look at him."

"He shall be in pain and suffering till the day he dies."

As he spoke a great weight came on him—a hump as big as a mountain.

He crawled back to the head of the glen, but he couldn't get in at his door. He had to lie outside for the rest of his life, and when he died it took twenty-four coffins to hold him.

School of Scottish Studies, Hamish Henderson, from Bella Higgins. From her mother's grandmother.

TYPE 503. MOTIFS: F.261 [*Fairies dance*]; F.331.3 [*Mortal wins fairies' gratitude by joining their song and completing it by adding the names of days of the week*]; F.344.1 [*Fairies remove hunchback's hump*]; F.341.1 [*Fairies give three gifts*]; N.471 [*Foolish attempt of second man to overhear secrets; he is punished*].

¶ This is a particularly ruthless version of a widespread type (Grimm, no. 182). It is treated by Greverus in *Die Geschenke des kleinen Volkes*, *Fabula*, I, pp. 263 ff. Good examples are to be found in both Ireland and Wales. See also "The Two Tailors", "Goblin Coombe", "That's Enough to go on with".

TWO MOONS IN MAY

My grandfather used to tell us there was a dear old couple lived over near Pitminster, Old Sammy and Old Nanny, and they had a little farm with an acre of hay, and an acre of corn, and a bit of a garden. They kept a cow, and a pig in a stye and two-three hens and a dunk to carry the panniers to Taunton Market. They hadn't much to sell—a few eggs, a bit of butter, green stuff from the garden, and berries and some little sweet apples like Quarendens—but they were famous knitters, and people always bought their stockings, so they just about got by.

You never know what the weather is at this year—there was another just the same in grandfather's time.

On May Day Old Sammy says, "There's a full moon tonight."

"That's bad," says Old Nanny, "I must be very careful when I look up—'tisn't a very lucky time when They're about." But she knew better than to name any names.

Then Old Sammy says, "And there's a full moon on the 31st too."

"That's worse," says Old Nanny. "Two moons in May, no corn, no hay. But we'll get by somehow."

Well, the weather was shocking all through hay-time. They had to hang it out on the fences to dry the little that hadn't gone black, and the corn stood in all the rain till it sprouted, but somehow they got by. There were no plums, and the raspberries they went mouldy, and the sow only reared five piglets instead of twelve. The stockings just about kept them, and then they hadn't any money to buy more wool. Rent Day was coming, and they sold their Sunday Blacks, and still it rained. Then they knew they'd have to sell the old dunk, and the cow and her calf, to cover the rent, and a few shillings to last all winter. My grandfather said Old Nanny was sitting by their bit of fire and sobbing, "I'll have no dish of milk to set out o' nights," for they kept to the old ways. "It's the first time, all our married lives." Old Sammy went all the way to the spring for some clear water for her instead. "They'll know and not blame us," he thought. Then out in the road he saw three bags lying. One was blue, and very full, and chinked, and the next was red and smaller and half-full, and the last was a pretty little green thing, all flat and empty. Old Sammy calls Old Nanny, but she's too updry about losing the cow, so then he remembered his new pair of stockings, and there were still a few apples, so he takes them to market instead. Old Nanny she stopped crying, and milked the cow and brushed the dunk, because after to-morrow's Rent Day, none of them would be there, and she hid the three bags safe away in the thatch roof till someone should come and claim them. When Old Sammy came home, he said, "I had Bellman cry they dree lost bags of market money. There was plenty claimed 'em, but nobody rightly, so I came on home." Then along came Old Sal Slack, the black witch. "They bags is mine."

"What's the words on 'em?" asks Old Nanny.

"Harum Scarum," says Sal.

"Out you go," they said, and showed her off.

And then a poacher he came and claimed the bags, but he said the words on them were "Oliver's dark," so he had to be off too.

And then as the old folks were sitting by the few bits of fire ever so sadly, there came a stranger in green. "I want my bags," said he and smiled at them. My Grandfather said they felt better at once but they asked him what words were on the bags. "None at all," said he, and they knew he was the right one. "But I'll leave them with you to-night, because you put out cream last night too, and went without, and I'll be along to see Lawyer about rent in the morning."

Next morning there was the stranger in green outside the gate, smiling at them.

"Now you take the old dunk right away from here to graze. He might spoil things for me. Give me the three bags, and don't come back till the sun is over the elm-tree top."

So they did that—somehow, when he smiled again, they went and left him with the cow and the three bags.

The stranger in green went and sat outside on the bench, and he put the three bags out in a row beside him.

Then the Lawyer rode up on a ewe-necked, rat-tailed pony old nag. "I've come for my rent, and the farm too," he said, but the stranger in green points to the fat blue bag that clinked. "There 'tis," he said. "Just count it." The lawyer counts the gold and there's another ten pieces at the bottom he somehow forgot to count. "That's just about right," he says, all in a hurry—but he had to give the stranger in green a full receipt for the year's rent and the farm before he got away. Then Parson came along on a fine hunting cob. "Remember my tithes," he said, and he took the red bag—but he had to sign a receipt too, and when the sun was over the elm-tree top, the stranger in green was ready to go too. "Here's the little green bag," he said, "No one claims it. And don't forget the cream to-night," and off he went somewhere. It seemed as if he just disappeared and the sun came out and the weather cleared up. "We'll get by now," said Old Nanny, "but there's nothing to eat at all but the cream! We might sell the little green bag—'tis empty, and 'tis pretty." But when they felt it, there was a bit of money in the lining. They hoped it might be a sixpence, but it was a whole golden guinea.

They had something to eat that night and a good fire and when they went to put the bag safely away, there was another guinea in it. The bag was never empty after that.

My Grandfather used to say the Lawyer found the red bag full of yellow moss next morning, and when Parson remembered service time, Sexton saw his coat-tails were on fire when he went into God's House, and so they pulled out the blue bag all charred and black.

But Old Sammy and Old Nanny, they got by very well after that.

Ruth L. Tongue, Somerset.
The general theme of this story is common enough, but it does not fall into any recognizable tale-type.
MOTIFS F.332.0.1 [*Fairy grateful to mortal for daily food*]; F.236.1.6 [*Fairy in green clothes*]; F.341.1 [*Fairies give three gifts*]; F.342.1 [*Fairy gold*]; F.348.0.1 [*Fairy gift disappears, or turns to something worthless when tabu is broken*]; D.1451 [*Inexhaustible purse*].

TWOPENNY PRISS

There was a handsome girl whose mother kept telling her that if she wanted to get on in the world she must mind her manners.

The silly creature tossed her head. She was not going to bother about that. But when she found no one would have her she changed her mind enough to marry a higgler who had a blackthorn handy to teach her how to speak civilly to customers.

But he never cured her and she went and had a daughter just as uncivil.

In the end the higgler was glad enough to die of a fever and be well rid of them both.

So then she married a well-to-do farmer and a fine life she and her girl led him too—but she *was* going up in the world, though their manners were not keeping step.

They had frills and finery but they screamed and gabbled like geese.

The farmer at last grew sad and tired and ashamed, and he decided on a move, but as he spent a lot of time with his men, he asked their advice.

"I'm thinking of taking Bullet Farm," he said.

"'Tis a good farm, master," they agreed.

"So I hear," said the farmer.

"But it has a queer name indoors," said they.

"We won't be living indoors."

"The Miss and Missus will."

"That's what I mean."

So to Bullet Farm they all went, and since the farmer worked outside, and his wife and her daughter lazed about inside, things might have gone better, but there was one room where the door opened all by itself and it was kept nailed up, and nothing would suit Miss and Missus but to have it unnailed, and to have it for their own grand parlour like his Lordship's lady at the great Hall.

One day Miss was at her needlework when the door creaked and swung open a little.

"Come in, whoever you are, and be dratted," she yelled out, and in IT came.

When she looked up, because of the cold mist, she gave such a scream that the hens all ran squeaking to roost on the barn rafters for safety, but IT just tossed her right through the open window head down into the new turned potato beds.

When they dug her out she started running, and she didn't stop till she met a gipsy, and he looking at her furbelows thought he was on to a good thing, and got her to run away to London with him.

He kept a blackthorn stick handy too.

Well, her mother went pining and whining and driving everybody crazy with her temper till she decided to go and sit in the parlour.

The door creaked and swung open a little. "Drat you, fool! Come on in and hurry up about it." And in IT came.

Well, she gave a yell that frightened the pig into a fit, and she ran with IT after her. She ran right upstairs to the attics screaming like a gleenie, but IT caught up with her, and tossed her out of the attic window and she broke her neck.

Well, they gave her a decent funeral, but it wasn't long till Farmer got back his old kindly ways, and the menfolk whistled about their work, and Twopenny Priss sang as she cooked and scrubbed and polished and swept.

Twopenny Priss had been the farm maid for ten years. She came from the Parish Overseers when she was just large enough to fetch and carry and be useful, and in time she got to do all the work, but Missus had never paid her more than twopence a year, and that wasn't going to buy her a husband.

She was homely and wholesome, with a kind face you could warm your heart at, and a tongue as kind as her face, and she thought it a sad thing the parlour should be unswept and dusty.

The farm men warned her.

"There's something bad there—an unquiet spirit," they said.

"The poor lonely thing," said Twopenny Priss, "and not a Christian soul to help it."

"Remember what happened to Miss and Missus."

"I'll take my Bible and say my prayers, for me and IT," says Priss. And in she went with her Bible and her broom and by and by the door creaked and swung open slowly.

"Come in and welcome, in God's name," called Twopenny Priss, and in IT came.

The mist was bitter cold, but Twopenny Priss took her little Bible out of her apron pocket and spoke out bravely: "In the name of the Lord, why troublest thou me?"

Then the mist went, and there stood the ghost of the old miser that had owned the farm years back, and died all alone, and nobody knew what he had done with his money. The ghost beckoned and said, "Come," and Priss followed.

Then he stood by the great hearth-stone and pointed down. "So your gold is there, is it?" said Priss. "You poor unhappy soul, it weighs too heavy for you to get away, and you can't take it with you, can you?" Then the ghost said, "Lift!" and Twopenny Priss slid the stone away. Underneath was a small black chest, and some bags of money. Then the ghost cried out in a glad voice, "Free at last!" and went away for ever.

Twopenny Priss ran to fetch her master, and when he saw all the wealth, he said, "Here's a fine dowry for you, Priss." But Priss said sadly, "I'm too homely for a husband. Who'd want to marry me?" "Bless your kind loving heart," said the farmer, "I would, and I will to-morrow." And he did.

Ruth L. Tongue. Worcestershire. Mrs Edwin Tongue, 1940, from her grandmother: heard in Worcestershire about 1878.

TYPE 326A.* MOTIFS: E.281.3 [*Ghost haunts particular room in house*]; E.200 [*Malevo-*

lent return from dead]; Q.327 [Discourtesy punished]; Q.2 [Kind and unkind]; E.545.19.2 [Proper means of addressing ghosts]; E.410 [Dead unable to rest in peace]; E.371 [Return from dead to reveal hidden treasure].

¶ The Cinderella motif is implicit in this tale, though the heroine is a servant-girl, not a daughter.

THE TWO SWANS

The' was wonst a young lady what was very much in love, an' on re-count'n this her father an' mother they both turned agen her, an' her father said as if ever she should speak wid the young gentleman agen, he should have 'em 'headed, the both'n they. Now this young lady's parents, they lived in a very big house, nearby to the side'n a lake, an' on this lake the' was two swans. It was a very nice place for a bit o' sweethearting, down by this lake—all trees, an' walks, an' bits o' paths—an' it was here the young lady an' gentleman was in the habit o' meeting wid one another.

Now a'ter what the young lady's father had said—an' he meant it, mind—they had to be very careful they wasn't seen, for they still went on meeting wid one another just the same as afoare. Whatever to you, all went well for a goodish while, till one day they was catched proper, an' by the owld gentleman, the young lady's father, hisself. Now as soon as he seen they was f'un' out, the young gentleman he takes to his heels, an' runs for his life, till he comes to a t'emendous big river, what he jumps into, an' swims across to the tother side—a very fine swimmer he was. An' as for the young lady, she ups an' follows him as hard as ever she can, but when she comes to the river she doesn't know however to get across, for it was a very broad river, an' running that strong. Whatsumever, she bethinks herself'n the two swans on the lake, an' she calls to the one'n they to come, an' it comes, an' she gets on to its back, an' it swims wid her across. An' now as they're both'n they together agen, an' safe from getting catched, the first thing the two sweethearts does is to go an' get married.

So whatever to you, being as she was now safely married, the young lady was all for their going back home agen, but the young gentleman he didn't seem to see no sense in this; he didn't want to be 'headed. It wa'n't no good though, as the young lady had made up her mind to it. "Do you go then," he says, "an' I'll come a bit later on, for I'm certain sure," he says, "as if I was to go wid you now your father'd be in sich a temper, he'd 'head the both'n we." But she wouldn't hear'n this, not at no price. "What is the good'n getting married then?" she axes. "No, we must both go," she says, "for it would be better to be 'headed together 'an 'at we should ever be parted." In the end, of course, she has her way.

So they goes back to the river, an' calls for the two swans. An' they gets on to the two swans' backs, an' the swans carries them across to the tother side, an' as the two sweethearts goes walking along the river bank arm in arm, same as they would do for sure, the two swans goes wid 'em, one on each side. Well, whatever to you, they goes on an' they goes on till they gets back to the lake agen, the two swans walking by their sides, all the whole way. An' now they gets on to the two swans' back agen, one on to each, an' the swans swims out wid them, right into the middle'n the lake, an' then they stops. An' the two sweethearts sleeps there that night on the two swans' backs among the feathers.

Next morning they gets up right early, an' goes up to the house. Nobody's about yet, so they creeps round till they finds a window open, an' they climbs in by this, an' gets to bed together in one'n the bedrooms. They might ha' been there p'r'aps five or six hours, afoare one'n the sarvants comes into the room to sweep, an' finds 'em there. She goes at wonst, this sarvant does, an' tells the mistress.

Now whatever to you, the mother'n this young lady, she doesn't want for her daughter to be 'headed, nor yet the young gentleman neither, for she sees as her child has set her heart on him. So she goes to her husband, and she tells him as she has just heeard as the young people is safe, an' as she knows where they've got to. "Well, where?" he axes. "Oh! that," she says, "I won't tell you, not unless you'll first gi'e me the promise not to do 'em anny harm." "I shan't promise no sich thing," he says; "I'll 'head the both'n they. Now, where are they? Tell me, woman, and be quick about it." "No, I shan't," she says, "not till you've promised. Give 'em a good recommanding," she says, "but don't restroy them." He gets terrible angry, the owld gentleman does, but it's no use, she won't tell him; so at last he takes the oath that he'll spare their lives. Now, being as he's gi'en the promise, she tells him. "You'll find 'em in bed together," she says, "in sich-an'-sich a bedroom, an' what you got to do is to make the young gentleman marry her at wonst—aye, at wonst." "By God," he says, "I will that, but they deserves to be 'headed, the both'n they."

He goes straight to this bedroom now, where his da'ghter an' the young gentleman is, an' he knocks at the door. They calls him to come in. There they are in bed together, an' he could ha' f'un' it in his heart to kill 'em stone dead on the spot. "You knows what you got to expect?" he axes. "Yes," they answers, an' they didn't seem to care, not a bit. An' wid them being so brave-like, an' not caring, his heart goes out for they, an' he promises as he won't do them not the leastest bit o' harm if the young gentleman'll only do but one thing. "I'll do annythink," the young gentleman answers up, "even if it should cost me my life." "Well, then," he says, "I wants you to go an' get married to my da'ghter at wonst." "That's anpossible," says the young gentleman. "What!!" he says, "you refuse to do it? Then I shall 'head the both'n you." "Well, I'm very sorry," says the young gentleman, "but I can't do it. We're married already, you see." "Married already! How do you make that out?" he axes. "When were you married, an' where were you married, I should like to know." "Oh! we were married yesterday," the young gentleman tells him, "over into sich-an'-sich a place," mentioning its name. "That's nothink, only but a pack o' lies," he says, "for you couldn't never get there, not on recount'n the big river the' is to cross." "Oh, I swimmied over," says the young gentleman. "Well, maybe you did," he says—he didn't believe him of course—"or maybe you didn't, but my da'ghter, however should she get across?" "Go an' ax the swans, daddy," she tells him. "Do you think to make a fool'n me, girl," he says. "How should they know, poor dumb creatures like them?" "Well, go an' ax 'em," she says, "an' then you'll find out."

He's terrible angry agen, the owld gentleman is, an' he thinks they're making a fool'n him. Whatsumever, he goes in the end, and the swans tells him how the young gentleman swimmed across the river, an' how they carried his sweetheart over to him, an' how they fetched the both'n they back, an' how the two sweethearts slept that night, on their backs in the middle'n the lake.

Now a'ter when he'd heeard this, an' when he knowed by it the young people hadn't been telling him no lies, he began to think as he'd been very hard on they. So he gi'ed his da'ghter an' his new son-in-law a big house close by to his own, an' there they lived happy ever a'ter. An' for annythink as I know, they're living there still.

Norton Collection, VI, p. v. From *Journal of the Gypsy Folk-Lore Society*, n.s. VIII (1914–15), part 3, p. 20q. Also in *Thompson Notebooks*, E, and *English Gypsy Folk-Tales*, collected by T. W. Thompson, pp. 208–11. From Noah Lock in Anglesey.
MOTIFS: T.97 [*Father opposed to daughter's marriage*]; B.469.2 [*Helpful swans*]; B.211.3 [*Speaking bird*].

THE UGLY BROTHER [summary]

There was once a man who was very ugly. He had one eye in front of his head, and one at the back, and he lived all alone, and went hunting for his living. He did not know he had a brother. One day he went out hunting, and he got to a strange part of the country, and saw a big notice up, "No Trespassers". But he went on, and he came to a kind of golden bar, with drinks, and food of all sorts; but there was no one to be seen. He went in, and helped himself to a drink, and he heard a terrible roar, and hid under the table. And in came a man just like him.

He was very ugly, with one eye at the front of his head, and one at the back, but when the huntsman saw him he was not frightened at all, because he knew he must be his own brother, and he came out from under the table, and the ugly brother was pleased to see him, and they sat down to a meal together. The next day the man went out to see what he could see about the place, and he heard a great noise, and saw two white ghosts fighting against six black ghosts. And he joined in on the white ghosts' side, and kicked the six black ghosts. The next day it was eight white against one black, and this time he took the black one's part. Then the next day he saw eight white fighting against one black, and the last time there was one white against eight black. He killed all eight. Then the last ghost said to him: "There's a tree there, and up it you'll find a skep, and in the skep a swarm of bees, and in the middle of the swarm a well, and if you bathe in the water of the well, you'll be the better of it." So he climbed the tree and went into the skep, and pushed his way into the swarm of bees, and bathed in the well. And when he came out, he was the bonniest man in all Scotland. And he went back to his brother's house. When his ugly brother saw him, he snatched up his sword. But the man said: "Don't you know me? I'm your brother."

"I don't care whether you are my brother or not," said the ugly brother. "You were like me, but now you're bonny." "I'll tell you how I got bonny, and you can get bonny too." So the ugly brother climbed the tree, and bathed in the well, and he came out just like his brother, and they were the two bonniest men in all Scotland.

School of Scottish Studies, Hamish Henderson, from Alexander Macdonald.
MOTIFS: L.112.1 [*Monster as hero*]; D.52.2 [*Ugly man becomes handsome*]; E.467 [*Revenants fight each other*]; E.461 [*Fight of revenants with living person*]; D.1866.1 [*Beautification by bathing*].
¶ This tale differs entirely from the ordinary one of the monster disenchanted (types 709, 711, etc.) because there is no love interest. The fighting in the castle brings it nearer to type 326 (the fearless youth), but the ugly twins are an entirely original feature. The account of the fighting seems to be confused.

THE WAL AT THE WARLD'S END

There was a king and a queen, and the king had a dochter, and the queen had a dochter. And the king's dochter was bonnie and guid-natured, and a'body liket her; and the queen's dochter was ugly and ill-natured, and naebody liket her. And the queen didna like the king's dochter, and she wanted her awa'. Sae she sent her to the wal at the warld's end, to get a bottle o' water, thinking she would never come back. Weel, she took her bottle, and she gaed and gaed or [ere] she cam to a pownie that was tethered, and the pownie said to her:

"Flit me, flit me, my bonnie May,
    For I haena been flitted this seven year and a day."

And the king's dochter said: "Ay will I, my bonnie pownie, I'll flit ye." Sae the pownie ga'e her a ride owre the muir o' hecklepins.

Weel, she gaed far and far and farer nor I can tell, or she cam to the wal at the warld's end; and when she cam to the wal, it was awfu' deep, and she couldna get her bottle dippit. And as she was lookin' doon, thinkin' hoo to do, there lookit up to her three scaud men's heads, and they said to her:

> "Wash me, wash me, my bonnie May,
> And dry me wi' yer clean linen apron."

And she said: "Ay will I; I'll wash ye." Sae she washed the three scaud men's heads, and dried them wi' her clean linen apron; and syne they took and dippit her bottle for her.

And the scaud men's heads said the tane to the tither:

> "Weird, brother, weird, what'll ye weird?"

And the first ane said: "I weird that if she was bonnie afore, she'll be ten times bonnier." And the second ane said: "I weird that ilka time she speaks, there'll a diamond and a ruby and a pearl drap oot o' her mouth." And the third ane said: "I weird that ilka time she kaims her head, she'll get a peck o' gould and a peck o' siller oot o' it."

Weel, she cam hame to the king's coort again, and if she was bonnie afore, she was ten times bonnier; and ilka time she opened her lips to speak, there was a diamond and a ruby and a pearl drappit oot o' her mouth; and ilka time she kaimed her head, she gat a peck o' gould and a peck o' silver oot o' it. And the queen was that vext, she didna ken what to do, but she thocht she wad send her ain dochter to see if she could fa' in wi' the same luck. Sae she ga'e her a bottle, and tell't her to gang awa' to the wal at the warld's end, and get a bottle o' water.

Weel, the queen's dochter gaed and gaed or she cam to the pownie, an' the pownie said:

> "Flit me, flit me, my bonnie May,
> For I haena been flitted this seven year and a day."

And the queen's dochter said: "Ou, ye nasty beast, do ye think I'll flit ye? Do ye ken wha ye're speakin' till? I'm a queen's dochter." Sae she wouldna flit the pownie, and the pownie wadna gie her a ride owre the muir o' hecklepins. And she had to gang on her bare feet, and the hecklepins cuttit a' her feet, and she could hardly gang ava.

Weel, she gaed far and far and farer nor I can tell, or she cam to the wal at the warld's end. And the wal was deep, and she couldna get her bottle dippit; and as she was lookin' doon, thinkin' hoo to do, there lookit up to her three scaud men's heads, and they said till her:

> "Wash me, wash me, my bonnie May,
> And dry me wi' yer clean linen apron."

And she said: "Ou, ye nasty dirty beasts, div ye think I'm gaunie wash ye? Div ye ken wha ye're speakin' till? I'm a queen's dochter." Sae she wadna wash them, and they wadna dip her bottle for her.

And the scaud men's heads said the tane to the tither:

"Weird, brother, weird, what'll ye weird?"

And the first ane said: "I weird that if she was ugly afore, she'll be ten times uglier." And the second ane said: "I weird that ilka time she speaks, there'll be a puddock and a taid loup oot o' her mouth." And the third ane said: "And I weird that ilka time she kaims her head, she'll get a peck o' lice and a peck o' flechs oot o' it." Sae she gaed awa' hame again, and if she was ugly afore, she was ten times uglier; and ilka time she opened her lips to speak, there was a puddock and a taid loupit oot o' her mouth; and ilka time she kaimed her head, she gat a peck o' lice and a peck o' flechs oot o' it. Sae they had to send her awa' fra the king's coort. And there was a bonnie young prince cam and married the king's dochter; and the queen's dochter had to put up wi' an auld cobbler, and he lickit her ilka day wi' a leather strap. *Sae ye see, bairns, &c.*

R. Chambers, *Popular Rhymes of Scotland*, p. 105. Fifeshire.
TYPE 480. MOTIFS: S.31 [*Cruel stepmother*]; L.55 [*Step-daughter heroine*]; H.934.3 [*Tasks assigned by stepmother*]; B.350 [*Grateful animals*]; H.1192 [*Task: combing hair of fairies*]; D.1454.2 [*Treasure falls from mouth*]; D.1860 [*Magic beautification*]; Q.111 [*Riches as reward*]; Q.2 [*Kind and unkind*]; M.431.2 [*Curse: toads from mouth*]; D.1870 [*Magic hideousness*]. This tale is mentioned in *The Complaynt of Scotland*, 1548.
¶ See also "Three Gold Heads".

WANTED A HUSBAND [summary]

[Told in the first person.] A young gypsy heard a town crier announcing that some grand lady wanted a husband. Description like himself. Warned that the lady had already had seven husbands, but thought he'd try his luck. He suited her, and they were married. In the middle of the first night he missed her from the bed, but she was back in the morning. The second night the same; the third night he followed her. She went to a graveyard and dug into a loose grave. He followed, and saw her eating. "Hello, my dear, what are you eating on?" "Corpse, you bugger, corpse!"

Thompson Notebooks, VI. From Reuben Gray, Old Radford, Notts, 22 December 1914.
TYPE 363 (variant). MOTIFS: T.172.0.1 [*All husbands have perished on bridal night*]; E.251.3.1 [*Vampires eat corpses*].
¶ There is a vague connection here with "The Grateful Dead" (type no. 507A), but the supernatural element has been suppressed. The bride has no supernatural husband.

THE WATCHERS BY THE WELL
[The Hare and the Harbourer, part II]

There was a harbourer that had a comfortable cottage all to himself, and he wanted a wife to share it.

To be sure it stood in a haunted wood, and a fast river ran in front of it, in which Nicky-Nicky-Nye lurked, so it wasn't any surprise no one visited him except White Mary, who was a mile away all on her own too— but she was a "healer", and a wise woman, and old at that, so she did pretty well: but though he was sensible and courageous, and knew exactly what to do and had the proper kind of help, he dreamed of yellow curls and blue eyes.

So off he goes to find them, and he stops to tell White Mary his intentions.

My dear soul! She knew all about it—looks at him with her piercing eyes, and says never a word but, "Even the wisest don't always think when they're well off."

The harbourer says something about pretty as a May-day dawn, and White Mary says, "Tell me that when she's ten years wed,"—but she couldn't daunt him, and she saw it. "Bring your yellow curls and blue eyes to see me," she says. "Then maybe she hasn't an empty head, and can do with a bit of luck. Anyways *you'll* be in need of it. Where's the spannel then? Left it behind to guard your wits as well as your cottage?"

But even that didn't daunt him, though he never liked anyone to speak of his spayed bitch, that very very few but the "gifted" ever see, but everyone whispered about, and White Mary felt very sorry she'd vexed him. Still, she knew she had to warn him, and goes on, "'Tis in my mind *they*'ve put this folly into yours. Oh, yes to be sure,—the cottage will be safe with the spannel around, and you'll come back a wiser man than before, and so you'll be as safe as ever you was—but what about an empty head even if it's got yellow curls like a daffodil and big blue eyes?"

But he was vexed at her, so she let him go on his way, hoping she hadn't spoken out in vain.

Well, to be sure, her words went with him, so she hadn't.

Bye and bye he come down a hill and below, washing linen in the river, he saw the prettiest maid he had ever seen except in dreams. He called out in delight to a farmer working at rebuilding a stone wall—"Tell me, who is that lovely lass with the blue eyes and the yellow curls?"

"Oh, is she about, then?" says the farmer. "What mischief is she at now?"

"She's washing linen in the river."

"And a-listening and watching with those big innocent eyes she has!"

"Lovely eyes," says the harbourer, but the farmer scowls and bangs a stone into place. "What's her name, and has she a mother?"

"She has so," says the farmer, and very grim he was. "And she's known as 'Lizzie's Luck', and there's not a man in the countryside would marry her."

"I would," said the harbourer.

"Wait while I tell you what you'll get with a lass that thinks her looks give her the right to give herself all the airs of a born countess, and ruin those about her. Her mother had a nice farm but it wasn't good enough for her, so she sold it unbeknown while her mother was working in the fields and now they live in an old cowshed. Her mother had ten good cows but they weren't good enough for a girl with her curls and blue eyes. She sold them too—but I was there to buy them, and all the pigs and poultry—I was by then."

"And now you'd wish to get the mother too?"

"I would so," shouted the farmer, "and give the poor woman comfort and happiness. She'd marry me in a winking if that useless hussy were gone—but who'd rid us of her?"

"I would," said the harbourer, "and turn her into a good wife in two or three years, for even you must admit she's wonderful pretty."

Then the farmer had a good look at him. "Ah, I've heard of you," he says—"Live up country not far from White Mary where no one else would. Not but what you are helped," he went carefully—"A proper nice-looking man like you might be the finish of her whimsies."

"Then I'll wed her," says the harbourer, "for you must admit she's wonderful pretty."

"Handsome is as handsome does," growled the farmer. "Look at her now, idling and sidling closer, to listen to talk that shouldn't concern her, and letting all her mother's washing float away down stream for her poor mother to run all down two fields, and wade in and rescue."

"Not this time," said the harbourer, and he went to where she was standing smiling sideways at him, and she was wonderful pretty too.

"Your mother's washing is in the water," he says. "I'll help you get it out."

And he picks her up, which she very well liked, and tosses her right into the deepest pool among the washing.

"Now you needn't mind getting wet," he says. "And wash a lot of whimsies away too. You won't need them where you're going. I'm taking you to be my wife—we'll see your mother and the priest first," and off he takes her, with the farmer all a-grin following after.

And when the harbourer saw her tired worried mother, he wouldn't stay for a minute longer—that mother had been wonderful pretty once, and now with the little hussy safely married to him and out of mischief, he'd leave it to the farmer to bring the smiles to her face again.

So off to Church the four of 'em went, and three of them glad to go—as to the fourth, she hadn't had time to change her mind or her wet frock—and he was a real man, and his hair was raven black, and his eyes blue and a bit frightening, and she'd never get another chance like this. So they left the priest, and the other happy pair, and after her husband kissed her, she was happy too—and she *was* wonderfully pretty.

He found her easy to kiss, and she had to own she was enjoying herself, but being the contrary little fool she was, she starts to get uppish. The harbourer just takes a careful look along his ash stick, and puts it down once more, and she looks at her drying frock, and remembered getting in the washing, and takes another think.

It nearly lasted a mile, but a great farm dog rushes out at her, barking. She yells to her husband to use the stick, quick, but he just stands quiet, and speaks quiet to the dog, and it goes away friendly and quiet.

Well, she doesn't think much of that. "You didn't even hit it," she grumbles.

"Your new father gave the stick to me," says he, "but he didn't mean it to be used on dogs."

She didn't like the sound of that. "I'm going back home!" she says with a stamp.

"And where's that?" says he.

"To my mother, so I will!"

"Oh no, you won't," says he. "You can't. She's living in Farmer's home now—and he won't give you a welcome."

She liked the sound of that still less. "I want to go and get all my clothes," she stamped.

"Your mother give you the one you've got on—all the rest were hers. Now she'll be glad to get her own back."

So there she was—one eye on her husband and one on the farmer's wedding present, and only one draggled gown to her name, so she went into a howling rantum-tantrum outside White Mary's house.

Then someone tossed a nosegay from the door, and a voice said, "Noisy temper, no brains. Best pick your Luck quick."

What does the fool do but spit, and trample her nosegay to bits in the road.

White Mary just closes the door, as her husband takes the stick to her once, and if she yelled afore, 'twas nothing to this time.

"He's learning," says White Mary, "and she'll have to learn the hard way now."

They were nearly home when he stops, and looks at her dragging and snivelling and sulking behind him. "We're nearly home," he says, "and if you'd behaved on the way, you'd know by now what's to be done, where you're going, and to keep a civil quiet tongue, and *whatever* you may see *don't alter anything anywhere.* There's a good lass."

Well, she liked his kiss, but she wasn't going to do what he told her—she was the bride. But somehow she didn't come out with it till they were over the bridge safe into the garden. Then she ran down to the river, because he'd drawn her away, and says, to show him, "I'll do my washing here."

But he picks her up, and takes her right to the edge, and says, "You can, if you want Nicky-Nicky-Nye to help you, since you have let him see you."

And when she sees Nicky's two green eyes watching her deep down below the foam, she gives a yell, and hangs on to her dear husband, and a big white and gold spannel comes running out of the cottage to help her, but she kicks out at it and yells, "Be off, you dirty beast." And all in a second it wasn't there any more.

That scared her, and when she looked at her husband's grim white face, it scared her still more. "You've thrown away your luck,—but you shan't ruin *mine.* You've clamoured about all you've seen, and lost a good friend for me, and you've shown yourself and your fear to Nicky-Nicky-Nye. We'll try a dose of Farmer's ashplant, before you make any more mischief."

And she learned almost as fast as Farmer hoped, and behaved herself for a bit.

At the end of the week, she caught a glimpse of the spannel run to her husband as he went into the wood. "It's me it should be taking care of," she whimpered. "Left all alone in the cottage for a whole day." So she went into the garden and all round it were queer stones, under the hedges, and she thought they were so ugly she threw three of them right away into the wood before she remembered she mustn't alter anything, and she was afraid—but she daren't seek for them or run away over the bridge with Nicky-Nicky-Nye watching underneath it, and she did hope her husband wouldn't know.

But that night, as they sat in the firelight with his three great hounds asleep at their feet, there came shrill laughter and dancing in the garden, and the three great hounds whimpered in terror, and their hair stood up, but something rose from behind her husband, and he opened the door for it.

Then the jeers turned to shrieks, and there was a growl and a bark, and a silence again. Then something she couldn't see padded back into the room again, and the harbourer barred the door once more.

Then he reached for the ashplant. "What did you meddle with?" he said, and she just said, "Only three stones." She was beginning to learn about keeping silence, so he let her off lightly—*she* didn't think so, for she blubbered, "I can put three more back."

"That won't help us now," said he. "Never go out to the garden unless it is bright sunlight.—You'll be guarded if you really mean to be sensible." And she did try, with one eye on the wedding present, and after a while she caught one or two glimpses of the spannel bitch leaning against her husband's knee, and she didn't like it any better. "Ugly old bitch," she said to herself, until she remembered the horrid laughter, and was glad she hadn't spoken out loud. However, she did mind while her husband was about, but there came a day when he had to be away till next morning, and she cried bitterly. "I'd ask White Mary to bide with you," said the harbourer. "But you stamped on her Luck, and threw away her magic stones. You can't expect her to come. If you shutter all windows, and stay downstairs to-night by a good fire, somebody will guard you, if you don't speak at all." And he kissed her, and went away over the bridge.

Well, the sun was shining, and she thought she'd fill the water pail from their Wishing Well, but there was only a steady trickle of sweet water, and she got tired of waiting. "I'll make a nice deep pool for the pail for me to dip in," she says, and she pulled up the stone round it, and trampled the mossy basin, and then she looked up at a growl, and there's the yellow and white spannel and she heaves a stone at her, and hit her. "Good job too, you ugly, spying beast," she yells, and drags the injured spannel into the woodshed, and slams the bolt on her, and then, not till then, mind, does she remember what she wasn't to do.

Well, she'd altered the Wishing Well, and couldn't do much about that, but she still thought her looks might save her, if her husband saw her curls decked in the seven red ribbons hanging on the ash-tree above the Wishing Well.

So she took them, and very pretty she looked too, but she didn't feel very happy as it drew on to dusk, and then she daren't go out and loose the bolt from the shed—she'd left it too late.

She made a good fire, but the thin jeering laughter outside broke out suddenly, and there were no dogs—ugly or not—to bark and drive them away. And then there came a rapping and a scraping like great hands along the shutters, and she yelled, and ran upstairs, and of course the window was open, and a great twiggy hand came groping for her, and she just stands and screams. Then someone outside spoke, and the jeering laughter stopped at once, and that horrible branchy hand paused, and then someone outside unbolted the shed door, and the spannel dashed out barking and worrying something, and she fell in a faint.

At last she came to, and heard the voice—a good voice, "Unbar the door and let us in, or they'll come back."

And she did, and in walked White Mary, with the spannel limping on three legs. White Mary barred the door, and went and sat by the fire all night, and never said a word.

Nor did the bride—She was learning fast, and forgetting her curls, but when it was cock-crow White Mary looked at her and her red ribbons. "Too late to mend matters by taking any more Luck," she said. "You'll learn before you ruin him, I hope. Now take a look what came out of the wood through the gap you made in my magic stones." She daren't look at the queer footmarks. "And now, look what was set free to wander and get back its red ribbons." And she saw there was no ash-tree above the Wishing Well, but there was a great branch below the window all gnawed with dog's teeth.

"Here's a year's work for us both to make all safe again, and no meddlers," says White Mary to the spannel. "She's learning fast, but here comes her husband to make her learn even faster."

Over the bridge he came all in a hurry to be early, but when he saw the ash-bough, and the state of the Wishing Well, and the red ribbons in his wife's curls, and the limping spannel, he didn't ask a single question, but set about her with the ashplant till she run crying to White Mary.

"She'll do now," says White Mary. "And when she can think about others, she'll make you a nice little wife."

And she went away, but later she came again, and the spannel stayed around, and wasn't she glad the times she could see it, and bye and bye it was most times, after the baby came. Then White Mary stood godmother, after she'd filled the gaps in the stones into the wood, and rebuilt the Wishing Well, with mosses and herbs, and the sweet water was gushing out in its old slender spout, and there was a little ash-tree nodding above it with seven red ribbons.

Yes, the harbourer was a happy man, with a good loving wife, and since the baby didn't give her time to play with her curls, she played with his, and his dad's black ones, and looked prettier than ever.

But Nicky-Nicky-Nye was still a-watch, for all White Mary could do, and one day the baby went crawling away down the garden path straight to the river. His mother saw and ran, and so did the spannel, but before they could grab the baby, a scaly wet arm whipped up out of the water's very edge, and pulled him in. There were two tremendous splashes.

She went in after the baby, deep, deep water and all, and grabs it, and the spannel gets a good jawful of a wet scaly arm, and hangs on.

Then White Mary comes running over the bridge, and the harbourer comes rushing out of the wood, and they catch hold too, and pull her and her baby safe into the garden again, but the spannel, she doesn't let go.

Then Nicky-Nicky-Nye yells and wails—but the spannel doesn't let go. So he takes himself off, a hundred mile down the river and never comes back, and the spannel has a long swim safe home.

When she comes in, there's Her a-cuddling of the baby she saved, and Him a-kissing of her pretty curls, and White Mary smiling—and they all see the white and gold spannel come and sit right alongside the wife's knee.

White Mary smiles at her. "You'll do now," she said.

Miss Tongue comments: "Like so many Welsh Border tales, it carries a wealth of old traditions in it; particularly those of a spayed bitch, and a white and red-gold spaniel; white with red ears being the colour of 'Herla's Hounds', the fairy hounds, and spaniels being a very ancient breed."

Ruth L. Tongue, from a Mendip parson, who heard it from a New Forest gypsy. Welsh Borders: Shropshire to Monmouthshire.

TYPE 903A*. MOTIFS: T.254 [*The disobedient wife*]; T.256.3 [*Quarrelsome wife rebuked by a good whipping*]; N.828 [*Wise woman as helper*]; C.523.1 [*Tabu: digging up certain stones*]; E.439.6 [*Ghosts cannot come near spayed bitch*]; D.1380.16 [*Magic dog protects*]; F.420.5.2.1.5 [*Water-spirit drags children into river*]; F.420.1.4.2 [*Water-spirits have body covered with fish-scales*]; V.1.7.1.2 [*Ash as sacred tree*]; D.1385.2.5 [*Ash protects against spells and enchantments*]; D.926 [*Magic well*].

¶ This tale, though it is basically that of the taming of a wilful wife, is chiefly interesting for the magical beliefs it illustrates.

According to Aubrey (*Remaines of Gentilism*, p. 53), a spayed bitch was a protection against ghosts and spirits. The same is said in Thoms' *Anecdotes and Traditions* (1839), p. 100. Ruth L. Tongue says that she has only heard the full story once, but has heard fragments of it all her life.

See "The Hare and the Harbourer" (B, XIII).

THE WATERS OF LIFE

Now this is a story of a gentleman who was a very good gentleman, good to everybody, but he was dying. He sent for the doctor, and the doctor said there was nothing that could cure him in the world—they must find the Waters of Life.

So the doctor told him that the Waters of Life was many—aboot hunders of miles away, so they wad have to get somebody to find the Waters of Life before he could be cured. So he sent for his eldest son and told him that he'd to find the Waters of Life.

So he set on his journey, and eftir travellin' monie a mile he came to where there was a rabbit who had been hurtit. So he kickit the rabbit out of his road, and walkit on. He walked on a lot of miles till he lost his-sel' in a deep forest—was never heard of again.

So time went on for a while and he sent for the second son, and he told him that he must find the Waters of Life to save his father. So he set on his journey. After he'd travelled many a mile he came to the rabbit that was lyin' hurtit, and he also kickit the rabbit out of his road.

So it cam' to the youngest son. He says, "Oh," he says, "son, try and find me the Waters of Life." So he set on his journey. So he travellt many a mile till he came to the rabbit. He liftit the poor rabbit up, tried to doctor it, and laid it down gently at the roadside. After he'd travellt a lot of miles, he was gettin' tired. When he lookit round he saw the rabbit at his back. So he says, "Jack," he says, "you're very tired," he says. "What are you lookin' for?"

"Oh," he says, "I'm lookin' for the Waters of Life to save my father."

"Well," he says, "jump on my back. I'll take ye to the Waters of Life."

"Oh," Jack says, "I couldn't jump on a little rabbit's back."

"Oh, yes," he says, "jump on my back, and I'll take ye to the Waters of Life."

So he jumped on the rabbit's back, and after he was on, they travellt a lot of miles, till they cam' to the Waters of Life. So eftir he got his flask full of water he returned on the return journey—the rabbit took him til a palace, where he got food, where there was a young princess who fell in love with him.

So he returnt and he saved his father's life, and goed back and got his princess.

School of Scottish Studies. Told by Robert Stewart, Fetterangus.

TYPE 551. MOTIFS: H.1321.2 [*Quest for healing water*]; Q.2 [*Kind and unkind*]; L.13 [*Compassionate younger son*]; B.313 [*Helpful animal*]; H.1242 [*Youngest brother alone succeeds on quest*].

This is a short, probably half-forgotten version of a well-known folk-tale. In this country, the gypsy tale "The King of England and his Three Sons" is the only full version.

WATER IN A SIEVE

A young woman was on a journey. Night came down, and she lost her way. After wandering a little, she came to a place which seemed likely to give her shelter for the night. She entered and composed herself to such rest as she could draw out of her resting-place. By-and-by a little dog came, and lay down by her side.

Shortly after Kelpie made his appearance, and said to her, "Mack bed, bonnie lass, a'll lie wi' you the nicht." She was at a loss what to say or do, to keep Kelpie away. The doggie came to her help, and told her to say she had no blankets to make a bed. She said, "I have nithing t' mack a bed wi'." Kelpie disappeared, but returned after a little, and threw into the the place, where the woman and the dog were, a quantity of bedding, and repeated his former words: "Mack bed, bonnie lass, for a'll lie wi' you the nicht." What was now to be done? The doggie again came to the rescue. "Tell him y're thirsty, an bid him fess a drink in sieve an rivven dish," said the cunning animal. She did so, and Kelpie set off to fetch the water. He soon came back with the complaint: "They winna haud in." "Then stop them wi' fog." Away went Kelpie to gather fog, and to stop up the meshes of the riddle and the crack in "te rivven dish". Hard did Kelpie toil, but still the water escaped. By the time he came back, day had dawned, and the maiden was free.

Norton Collection, III, p. 97. N. Scotland. *Folk-Lore Journal*, I (1883), p. 294, W. Gregor.

TYPE 1180. MOTIFS: F.420.6.1.1 [*Water man woos mortal girl*]; F.420.3.4.2 [*Water spirit must be in water before dawn*]; F.420.1.3.3 [*Water spirit as horse*]; H.1023.2 [*Task: carrying water in a sieve*]; B.421 [*Helpful dog*].

¶ In 'A Cycle of Stories current in Radnorshire' (*Folk-Lore*, XLIII, p. 425), by W. I. Watkins, Davies foils the Devil by telling him to draw water in a sieve.

For other instances of this task see "The Well of the World's End", "The Girl who Fetched Water in a Riddle."

THE WEE DUCK [summary]

There was an old woman who had been left by her husband, and she was travelling the road with her grandson, and there was no one to help her. She called at a house, and the woman there gave her a drink of tea, and told her that if she went on she would come to a castle, and the king there was looking for a wife, and any wife would do, young or old. And the old woman said she would marry anyone who would look after her grandson. So on they went to the castle and knocked at the door, and the King took them in, and married the old woman, but he hated the grandson, and determined to destroy him. So he said to him that he must do three tasks, or else he was to be killed. The first was to fetch up his first wife's ring out of a deep pond into which it had fallen. Jack didn't know how he was to do this, and he wandered into the garden thinking, and he saw a little lame duck hobbling along, and he gave it some bread he was eating. To his surprise, the duck spoke to him, and asked what was worrying him. Jack told it about the ring, and it dived down into the pond and fetched it up. But the second task was worse, for Jack was to stay the night in a tower of the castle that was haunted with dead men. However, the duck gave Jack a little key, and told him to unlock one of the bars of the window, so that he could slip through, and watch what went on from outside. Just before twelve, Jack slipped out, and watched when the King came in with some of his men, and searched for Jack to kill him. When they'd gone, Jack slipped back, and in the morning claimed that he had performed the task. So next night the King told him to sleep above the Queen's bed. As he was lying there, the King's men came in, and put out his eyes, and tied him to a piece of wood, which they launched on the river. Jack floated down, but the duck followed him and untied his hands. Then it guided him to a well, and told him to bathe his eyes. His sight came back again, and he determined to kill the King. The duck told him he must do it in the presence of the Queen. So he hid about the castle till the King and Queen were together, then he stuck a knife into the King and he died. The duck took a key from the sole of his shoe, and opened a little cupboard. He knocked down a crystal bottle that was in it, and wetted himself with the liquid, and turned into a man who had been enchanted by the Queen. Jack killed the Queen, and he and his old Grannie lived together in the castle. [There is some confusion here, because the Grannie should have been the Queen.]

School of Scottish Studies, Hamish Henderson. Told by Walter Johnson.
MOTIFS: S.32 [*Cruel stepfather*]; H.901 [*Tasks imposed on pain of death*]; H.931 [*Tasks assigned to get rid of hero*]; B.571 [*Animals perform tasks for man*]; H.1132.1.1.1 [*Task: recovering ring from water*]; B.391 [*Animal grateful for food*]; B.469.4 [*Helpful duck*]; D.161.3 [*Transformation: man to duck*]; D.766 [*Disenchantment by liquid*]; D.1242 [*Magic fluid*].

This is evidently a broken-down story. It employs a number of familiar motifs, but no type can be allotted to it.

THE WEE HEN

The School of Scottish Studies. Hamish Henderson, from Bella Higgins. Version of "The Two Brothers" (Grimm). A very long story, remembered by Bella Higgins in outline only.

THE WELL OF THE WORLD'S END [summary]

A girl once had a stepmother who hated her so much that she was made to do all the hard work of the house, and at last the stepmother determined to get rid of her altogether. She gave her a sieve and bade her fill it with water at the well of the World's End. The girl had no notion where to go until an old woman gave her directions.

When at last she reached the well and could not fill her sieve she sat down and wept, till a frog on the edge of the well told her to

> "Stop it with moss, and daub it with clay,
> And then it will carry the water away."

In return for this help the girl had to promise to do whatever the frog told her for one night. Her stepmother was angry when she returned with the water, but she said nothing.

That night the frog rapped at their door, and sang:

> "Open the door, my hinny, my heart,
> Open the door, my own darling;
> Remember the words that you and I spoke,
> Down in the meadow at the World's End Well."

The stepmother insisted that the girl let the frog in, and, still in the same form, it demanded first,

> "Lift me to your knee, my hinny, my heart,
> Give me some supper, my hinny, my heart,"

then,   "Go with me to bed———"

and lastly,   "Chop off my head———"

Very unwillingly the girl performed her part, but at last when she cut off the frog's head a handsome young Prince appeared, and told her that she had freed him from an enchantment. To her stepmother's dismay, he took her away to his Palace, where they were married and lived happily.

Jacobs, *English Fairy Tales*, p. 215.
TYPE 440. MOTIFS: H.1023.2 [*Task: carrying water in a sieve*]; B.211.7.1 [*Speaking frog*]; D.711 [*Disenchantment by decapitation*]; L.162 [*Lowly heroine marries prince*].
¶ See also "The Paddo", "The Frog Prince", "The Maiden and the Frog", "The Girl who Fetched Water in a Riddle".

THE WERE-WOLF [fragment] AND THE PIED PIPER

This is a man that workit in a big forest, and he met in with a very pretty young lady one day—oh, she was a lovely woman, and he married her. But after he was married she began to take wanderings every night at twelve o'clock—she always rose from his side, and wandered. So next day there was terrible deeds was done round the place of killin' little children, but they could never get who was killin' them.

So this went on for a long time, and they could never get who was killin' this little babies; they were always tooken at a certain time at night and was killed.

So still this woman always took to the wanderin'—she was a very beautiful woman [*electrical fault on tape*] and he wasna very good to the poor folk—he was very greedy, he wadnae put out money.

But one day the town got swarmt full of rats, and the people was pestered wi' rats. Their very food was gettin' eaten—their water was gettin' spoiled—children in the cradle was gettin' bitten by rats. So they went and put their complaint to the Mayor, but he couldnae get rid of them (?) nother.

So one day there were a beautiful gentleman turnt up to the Mayor's house, and he said he would make a pact—if he would pay him he would clear the town of the rats.

So they made the pact that he would clear the town of the rats. So he took out his pipe and started to play, and the music drew all the rats from the houses to follow the piper.

So he took them til a hillside, and when he took them to this hillside the hill opent, and in went all the rats, and he cam back out again, and the hill closed, so he cam back for his money.

Oh, bit the Mayor, he refused to give him money. He was that greedy he backit out of his bargain.

"Oh, weel," says the gentleman, he says, "I'll have my own back."

So he took his pipe again,—he started to play, and instead of rats that followed it was all the children. He marched them to the hillside and the hill opent, and in went the children—they were never no more seen, and he turnt and cam' back.

"I've cleart the town of all the children."

School of Scottish Studies, told by Lucy Stewart and Robert Stewart.

MOTIF D.1427.1 [*Magic pipe compels one to follow*].

The story-teller seems to have forgotten his story half-way through, and ended up with another.

¶ The motif of the pipe is used in a pamphlet quoted by Harland and Wilkinson, *Lancashire Legends*, pp. 152–3. Otherwise the tale is only known in Britain in the rather doubtful version of "The Pied Piper of Franchville". B, Legends, IX.

THE WHITE-MILK DEER [dialect modified]

There was once a poor old widow who had one son. Jack was little and simple, but at length his Mother told him he must learn what was right, so he set out and learned. Then he told his Mother it was not fit for him to stay and live on her, but he must go out into the world and push his fortune. So she gave him her blessing, and he set out. He went on and on, further than I could tell you, or you could tell me, till he sat down by the road, weak and weary, and fell asleep. And it seemed to him that he dreamed, and in his dream an old woman with a high hat and a red cloak, and a cat on her shoulder came to him, and said, "I will help you if you do what I tell you." But he knew her for a witch, and said, "Hold away, you old witch. The Good Man will help me, not you." And he awoke, still hungry and weary. And he went to wash himself in a burn. And there was a wee fall, and there was a little wee fairy dancing up and down in it, and it said: "Thank you, Jack; you've freed me from an ill spell by your resistance to the witch. What can I do for you?"

And Jack said: "If it was not a dream, and I've really freed you, you might give me a good meal." "I'll do that," said the fairy, and at once a cloth was spread with such a lot of good things on it that Jack had more than he could eat. "Now," said the fairy, "I know where you're going. You're going to seek your fortune. And you'll come to a great castle, but the King's a bad man, and he'll set you hard tasks, and be wishful to kill you. But you'll get help, and if you follow good counsel, you'll win through." So Jack thanked the fairy, and went on and on, further than I could tell you, or you could tell me, until he came to a great castle, and he knocked at the lodge. An old woman let him in, and said it was too late to see the King that night, but he should sleep in the lodge. So she asked him his story, and he told her all about how poor his Mother was, and how he set out to seek his fortunes, and they became friends. In the morning Jack went to the King, and offered his services.

The King said, "You're a poor weak fellow to serve me, and if you fail three times in any task I set you, you'll have to lose your head." "Weak or strong," said Jack, "I can only do my best." "Well," said the King, "you shall go hunting for me, and shoot me a white-milk deer." Jack was a good shot, and he took a gun, and hounds and a hawk, and went out to the hunting. He shot hares and birds, until he saw a white-milk deer, and he took a good aim straight at it, but the bullet never touched it. The King was terribly angry at him, and the same thing happened next day, and when he missed again, the King said, "To-morrow night I will have your head," and Jack went greeting to the lodge.

The old woman said, "What ails ye, Jack?" "Oh, Grannie," he said, "If I don't hit the white-milk deer to-morrow, they'll have my head." "Take this silver sixpence," said the old woman, "and use it for a bullet." So Jack put the silver into his cartridge, and next day he wounded the deer. "You've got me, Jack," she said, "and to-morrow I'll come to meet you, and shall bring me home." So Jack went back and told the King. "You've wounded her," said the King, "but you've not brought her home." And next day he gave Jack a draught which sent him sound asleep. Lords and Princess and nobles came, but Jack slept through it all. And the next day the same thing happened.

Then the old woman said to him: "To-morrow's your last chance. Take one of the hares you've killed, and skin it, and carry it over your shoulder, and you'll not sleep." Jack did as she said, and the milk-white deer came to him in the form of a Princess, and they were married, and I was at the wedding, and got a good welcome.

School of Scottish Studies, H. Henderson, from Willie Johnson, 1956.
TYPE 313 (variant). MOTIFS: L.114 [*Unpromising hero*]; K.66 [*Dream contests*]; G.270 [*Witch overcome*]; F.330 [*Grateful fairies*]; H.901 [*Tasks imposed on pain of death*]; H.971.1 [*Tasks performed with help of old woman*]; D.712.7 [*Disenchantment*

by shooting]; G.271.4.8 [*Breaking spell by shooting bewitched object*]; D.1385.4 [*Silver bullet protects against ghosts, giants and witches*]; D.1972 [*Lover's magic sleep at rendez-vous*]; D.1978 [*Waking from magic sleep*].

This tale only fits very loosely into the categories of Type 313. The wizard king who imposes tasks and the daughter in animal form to be disenchanted are the main connections. For some unexplained reason the story is called "The White-Milk Deer" instead of "The Milk-White Deer."

¶ For the true type of this tale see "Nicht Nought Nothing".

WHUPPITY STOORIE: I [summary]

The goodman of Kittlerumpit went to a fair one day and never came back. Some thought he had enlisted, but others said the press-gang had caught him.

His wife was left with a small son to bring up, and very little else except her sow. The sow was nearly due to farrow, and the woman hoped greatly for a good litter of piglets. But one morning, when she went to feed her, the sow was lying on her back, dying; and the poor woman was so distressed, that she sat down on a stone and cried more sorely than ever before, even for the loss of her husband.

Behind her house was a great fir-wood, and when she looked up from her weeping and was drying her eyes, she saw coming up the brae an old woman, "amaist like a leddy", dressed in green, with a white apron, a black velvet hood, a steeple-crowned beaver hat, and a long walking-staff, as tall as herself. The goodwife curtsied to this old woman, and began to tell her sad tale, but the old woman abruptly cut her short, and said she knew the sow was ill, and she had come to cure it. "What will ye gie me gin I cure her?" she asked. "Ony thing your leddyship's madam likes," replied the goodwife.

The green woman entered the sty, gazed long at the pig, and began to mutter to herself words that sounded like

"Pitter, patter,
Haly water."

She took from her pouch a small bottle, and rubbed the sow's snout and cheeks and the tip of its tail with some kind of oil. "Get up, beast," she said, and at once the sow jumped up with a grunt, and walked over to the trough for her breakfast.

The goodwife joyfully asked the fairy woman what she could do for her in return, but the fairy again cut short her protestations and said she only demanded, and *would* have, the baby boy. Now the goodwife's distress was greater than ever, but the fairy's only response was to tell her that she was bound by fairy law not to take the child till the third day from that time, and not then, if the goodwife could in the meantime tell her her name.

For the whole of the first day the woman could do nothing but hug her son and weep, but on the second day she wandered out into the pine-wood, and presently she came to a hollow, an old quarry with a spring at the bottom of it, and there she heard the hum of a spinning-wheel, and heard a voice singing. She crouched down among the gorse and saw the green fairy spinning away and singing:

> "Little kens our good dame at hame
> That Whuppity Stoorie is my name."

Now the goodwife returned home and resolved to have a jest with the fairy. So she sat down on the knocking-stone, and hid the baby behind it and pretended to be in the depths of grief. Very soon the green fairy came up, and demanded her reward. The goodwife begged and prayed her to take the sow instead, but the fairy replied that she had not come for swine's flesh. Then she begged her to take herself, but the fairy scornfully answered, "Who would meddle with the likes of thee?" This so angered the goodwife that, with a mocking curtsey she replied, "I might have had the wit to know that the likes of me is not fit to tie the worst shoe-string of the high and mighty princess Whuppity Stoorie." The fairy leapt high up in the air, as though blown up by gunpowder, and rushed screaming down the brae as though witches had been after her.

Chambers, *Popular Rhymes of Scotland*, p. 72.
TYPE 500 (variant). MOTIFS: H.521 [*Task: guessing unknown propounder's name*]; N.475 [*Secret name overheard by eavesdropper*]; C.432.1 [*Guessing name of supernatural creature gives power over it*].
    This tale varies from "Tom Tit Tot", etc., in having no spinning test.
¶ See "Tom Tit Tot", "Duffy and the Devil", "Titty Tod".

WHUPPITY STOORIE: II [summary]

There was once a gentleman who had a fine house, fine furniture, looking glasses and curtains, and he married a young lady who had been very delicately brought up. The lady had never learnt to spin, and her husband was very angry when he discovered this. One day before starting on a journey, he told her that in his absence she must not only learn to spin, but must have spun a hundred hanks of thread before his return.

Greatly distressed, the lady wandered away into the country, and at last she sat down on a flat stone on a hillside, and cried. But soon she heard faint music coming from under the stone, so she lifted the stone, and saw a cave beneath it, in which were sitting six little ladies in green, each spinning at a wheel, and singing:

> "Little kens my dame at hame
> That Whuppity Stoorie is my name."

The lady walked into the cave, and they welcomed her kindly, and asked her to sit down. She noticed that their mouths were all twisted to one side, but did not venture to ask the reason. They, however, asked why she was so sad, and she told them. "Oh, is that all?" said they, speaking out of their cheeks. "Yes, and isn't it a very good *all* too?" she answered. Then they told her that if she would only ask them all to dinner on the day of her husband's return, they would very easily put an end to her trouble.

So when the goodman came home he found the house in such a bustle of preparations for dinner, that he had no chance to ask his wife about her spinning. Then the six little ladies arrived in a coach and six, still wearing their green gowns. The goodman politely lighted them upstairs with a pair of wax candles, and all went so well that during dinner he ventured to ask them how it happened that they all had their mouths twisted in the same way.

They replied, "Oh, it's with our constant *spin-spin-spinning*." "Then," cried the gentleman, "Tom, John, and Dick, go and burn every rock and reel and spinning wheel in the house, for I'll not have my wife to spoil her bonny face with *spin-spin-spinning*." And so the two of them lived happily together for the rest of their days.

Chambers, *Popular Rhymes of Scotland*, p. 76.
TYPE 501 (variant). MOTIFS: H.1092 [*Task: spinning impossible amount*]; G.201.1 [*Hags deformed from much spinning*]; M.233 [*Deformed witches invited to wedding-party in exchange for help*]; J.51 [*Sight of deformed witches causes man to release his wife from spinning duty*].

In this version of the tale the six spinning fairies do not fulfil the task for the wife; their deformity persuades the husband to abandon it. The name of the fairies, though overheard, has sunk into insignificance.
¶ See also "Habetrot".

THE WIDOW'S SON AND
THE KING'S DAUGHTER

There was a widow woman who had only one son whom she indulged in every habit of laziness, never putting him to do any kind of work for fear of offending him. At length her finances became exhausted, and she was under the necessity of asking some meal on credit; but having applied to a neighbour, she was refused, with the sarcastic remark that she should put her son to work for her, and then she would not be under obligations to anyone. Having returned empty-handed, and want staring them in the face, for the first time, she now told her son he must do something for a living to himself, as she could support him now no longer. He took the hint, and next morning arose by break of day, packed up his little ward-robe, tied it on his back, and in this manner took his departure.

After having travelled the greater part of a long summer day, he stopt at a house near a wood, where he asked lodgings for the night, as he was faint for want of meat, and weary with travel. His request was granted, and some meat set before him, of which he ate greedily. The goodman of the house said that he should be working, and not going about idle. The young man replied that he would most cheerfully, if any one would employ him. The farmer then sent him to the field to herd cattle, but strictly enjoined him not to go near a certain field where a giant lived, for if he did, he would undoubtedly be devoured, and the cattle sacrificed to the hungry maw of the greedy giant. He had not long herded the cattle, when, espying the tempting fruit that hung upon some trees in the forbid-den garden of the giant's, he longed to taste it, and rather than not satisfy his longing appetite, he would run the risk of his life. Jack then went up into one of the finest trees, and began to pluck and eat of the choicest of the fruit, when an old woman chanced to pass, and did ask of him some of the fruit, which was readily granted to her; when she in return gave him three black rods, with a sword, that whomsoever he chanced to strike with the sword, they would immediately drop down dead. Shortly after the disappearance of the old woman, out came one of the giants, for there were three of them, and demanded of him his authority for destroying of the fruit; and at the same time said, if that he did not come down from the tree immediately, he would eat him up alive. This did not daunt the spirit of Jack, who had great faith in the magical sword; so on the giant tearing the tree up by the roots in order to throw Jack down, he was struck with the sword and laid senseless at the feet of his young master. On the morrow, Jack went again to the fruit field, and behold, another giant came running up to him in great fury, who also demanded his business in that place; but Jack killed him also. The third day, Jack went to pluck of the fruit, when the third giant made his ap-pearance, and requested to know to whom the cattle belonged, as he must have some of them to supper; but Jack who by this time had concealed himself in the hollow of a tree, cried from thence,—Ask my leave first. On hearing this the giant turned round with an angry countenance, and says, O, you pigmy, is it you have killed my two brothers? I shall be revenged of you before long. Jack, however, killed him as he had done the two former giants, then went to their castle, which was not far off, but kept by a blackamoor. This blackamoor Jack soon made deliver up the keys of all the treasures in the castle, and to be at all times at his command. He now left this part of the country, and returned home, where he found the people weeping. Having asked the cause, he was told that a dragon had come and imposed upon them a serious task, which was a young lady as a sacrifice to him every day, and to-morrow the princess was to become a victim to his rage unless any one should step forward in her defence, and rid the country of this monster. Jack having heard the terms, immediately ordered his man to saddle and bring to him one of the best of his horses, with the white armour. Having all things in readiness, he went to the princess, whom he found bound to a stake, and told her the cause of his coming, that it was in her defence; and, that if she would marry him, he would save her life, or die in the attempt. To this she consented, and he laid his head on her knee, and was lulled asleep. During the time he lay asleep, she wove in his hair a ringlet, with white stones, very precious, and beautiful to behold. She had no sooner accomplished the charm in his hair than she saw the dragon coming to devour her, when she awoke him out of his pleasant slumber. On approaching the princess, Jack drew his sword, and stood between her and the danger to which she was exposed. He made several brave and well-aimed thrusts at the dragon, but, owing to the fire which it vomited up he never prevailed, nor could the dragon succeed in destroying the lady, but was obliged to flee to save its life, for it was becoming much exhausted. Next day the dragon returned, and so did Jack, clothed in red armour, but neither was more successful than on the preceding day, for the dragon still kept Jack at bay by vomiting fire, which was likely to burn him up. However, Jack again beat it off and caused it to take wing and fly away. On the third day Jack chose a camel, and caused it to swallow a great quantity of water, and therewith went a third time to fight. The dragon again appeared in quest of the princess, but Jack being now his match, having caused the camel to lay in a plentiful supply of water, he dared him to the fight. The dragon, as on the two former occasions, began to spout fire upon Jack, but the camel in return spouted water, so as to quench the dragon's fire, so that in a little time it became worsted, when Jack laid so well about him as to deprive it of life. Having now overcome the monster in single combat, he cut off its head, and carried it along with him. The princess now became his betrothed wife, when he again went away in search of new adventures, till at the end of nine months the princess bore an heir, but she nor her father knew to whom, for Jack had not made himself known unto her nor her father previous to his going away. The old king was now much vexed at his daughter not knowing the father of her child, and upbraided her unmercifully, as being a prostitute, and a disgrace to the royal name. This made her one day go with her father to ask counsel of a fairy, who told them that the father of the child, and none else, would be able to take the lemon from the child which it then held in its hand. On their return from the abode of the fairy, the king caused a meeting of all the lords, squires, bishops, lairds, farmers, and afterwards their servants to take place at the king's palace, on a certain day, which was then named, and try to take the lemon from the child's hand; but it baffled the power and skill of the whole multitude then assembled. At length, Jack made his appearance, and had no sooner touched the child's hand, than the lemon left. The king then, surprised, commanded that both should be put into a bottomless boat, and be sent to a distant island. They had not been long in the boat when a lady appeared, and told him that she was the fairy who had given him the sword that killed the giants, and defended the princess from the fury of the dragon; and that she would still be their friend; and as a proof of this she touched the boat, when it became whole, and their clothes that were ragged became very fine. They then returned to the harbour, dressed in all the splendour of royalty, in which they appeared at court. Great honours were paid to them, and a rich feast prepared for their entertainment, of which they partook most readily. After dinner, the best wine was set before them, and they invited to drink freely, but in a short space, the king missed his gold cup, which only made its appearance at table on particular occasions. Jack had pocketed it, for the purpose of observing the king's countenance on the discovery. The king wondered much where it could be found, when Jack says, he thought that kings wondered continually, for he was the same when his daughter was likely to be devoured by the dragon. He then threw down the cup, and with it the dragon's head, saying, in me behold the cause of all your wonder, for it was I who stole your cup, and it was I who saved your daughter from becoming a victim to the fury of the monstrous dragon. And as a further proof of his statement, added the princess, behold in his hair the identical ringlet which I wove with white stones the first day he attacked the dragon. The king then caused them to be publicly married, attended with rejoicing and feasting, which lasted many days. Jack afterwards sent for his mother, and treated her with great kindness, while he inherited the crown on the old king's death.

Norton Collection, I, p. 79. From Buchan, *Ancient Scottish Tales*, pp. 55–8.
TYPE 300. MOTIFS: L.114 [*Hero of unpromising habits*]; P.412.1 [*Shepherd as hero*]; D.813 [*Magic object received from fairy*]; D.1254 [*Magic stick*]; D.1081 [*Magic sword*]; K.912 [*Giants' heads cut off one by one*]; B.11.2.11 [*Fire-breathing dragon*]; D.1975 [*Dragon-fighter's magic sleep*]; B.11.11 [*Fight with dragon*]; H.105 [*Parts of slain animal as token of slaying*]; C.422.1 [*Tabu: revealing dragon-fighter's identity*]; H.481.1 [*Infant indicates his unknown father by handing him an apple* (lemon)]; Q.466 [*Embarkation in leaky vessel as punishment*]; N.815 [*Fairy as helper*]; H.83 [*Rescue tokens*]; L.161 [*Lowly hero marries princess*].
¶ See also "De Little Bull-Calf", "Assipattle".

THE WIDOW'S SON AND AN OLD MAN

There was a poor widow who had a number of children, and to whom she could not get sufficient meat nor clothes. One night in order to still their clamorous tongues, and to get them quietly to bed, she put into the pot a stone, making them believe at the time it was meat, and before they were awakened it would be ready. A little after there came in a stranger who asked lodgings, but as there was no meat in the house to give him, she told him that he could not lodge there that night, as she had nothing for supper. On seeing the pot on the fire, he asked of her what it contained, when she told him. He then replied that it was a leg of excellent mutton, which he would show her, and taking it out of the pot, convinced her of its reality. He next requested her to go to the other end of the house where she would find in a chest plenty of bread and other provisions. She found the bread as he had said, and awakened her children to partake of the same. After having eaten heartily, the eldest boy begged the stranger next to tell them some amusing little tale, with which he readily complied. The tale being told as requested, he asked payment from the boy, who said he had nothing to give. The stranger then took him with him to a river side, where he threw him in, and turned him into a fish, and bade him tell at the end of seven days what he could give; but when the time limit was expired, he asked the boy the same question as he had done before, and received the same answer. He then turned him into a serpent, which twisted itself around a large tree, and at the end of seven days, asked the former question, and received the former answer. Next he turned him into a magpie, and at the end of seven days asked the former question, but now received a different answer. The magpie prayed heaven to bless him for so good a story. The stranger then replied, If you had said this at first, you would have saved yourself and me both unnecessary trouble. Go now to yon old castle which is enchanted, and kept by a giant, not far off; the guards in it will all be fast asleep. After having gone through many rooms, you will find the King of Scotland's daughter sleeping on a marble table. Touch the talisman above her head, and she will awake and teach you what is best to be done for her recovery, and those in the other apartments in the castle. Saying this, he left him. The young man went, and found everything as the stranger had told; so that, when the princess awoke, she asked him how he had got through the guards, which he answered, with many other questions. She then told him that the giant's life lay in an egg, which if destroyed, he would immediately die. She also told him that it was kept by an old woman, who, if he could dispose of her in any manner of way, he would find the egg, which he could easily break, and when broken they would be safe. She then directed him to the abode of the old witch, which he found, and bidding her good-morrow said, You are not well, I see. No, says she, but if you would take me to the air I would be better. He then took her upon his back, and threw her into a large fire, when she went out of the chimney with a noise resembling thunder. He next found the egg, which he destroyed also, when the giant fell with a tremendous crash a lifeless corpse on the ground before the castle. Then all the prisoners who slept awoke, and testified their joy, and gave him thanks for their deliverance. Each went their own way, and he went home with Malcolm's daughter, and received her in marriage from the old King, as a testimony of his gratitude for her deliverance. The King also conferred on him some of the courtly honours, and it is said to be from him that the whole dukes of Buccleuch have descended. They were afterwards blessed with a numerous and happy family.

Norton Collection, I, p. 98. From Buchan, *Ancient Scottish Tales*, pp. 53–4.
TYPE 302. MOTIFS: Q.1.1 [*Gods in disguise receive hospitality*]; D.170 [*Transformation: man to fish*]; D.191 [*Transformation: man to snake*]; D.151.9 [*Transformation: man to magpie*]; D.700 [*Person disenchanted*]; R.11.1 [*Princess abducted by ogre*]; E.710 [*External soul*]; E.711.1 [*Soul in egg*]; K.956 [*Murder by destroying external soul*]; R.111.1 [*Princess rescued from captor*]; L.161 [*Lowly hero marries princess*].
¶ The beginning of this tale is the same as "The Poor Widow and her Son" (q.v.). The motif of the poor woman boiling stones as soup, to pacify her famished children, is common in English folk-tradition, though not to be found in the Thompson Motif-Index. The mention of the Princess as King Malcolm's daughter links this tale with "Red Etin."

WILD EDRIC

TYPE 400 (variant). See Part B, Legends, v.

WILL THE SMITH

Once upon a time there came to a blacksmith's shop late one night, a traveller whose horse had cast a shoe, and he wanted the blacksmith to put it on for him. So Will (that was the man's name) was very ready, and he soon had it on again all right. Now the traveller was no other than the Apostle St. Peter himself, going about to preach the Gospel; and before he went away he told the blacksmith to wish a wish, whatever he chose, and it should be granted him. "I wish," says Will, "that I might live my life over again." So it was granted him, and he lived his life over again, and spent it in drinking and gambling and all manner of wild pranks. At last his time came, and he was forced to set out for the other world, thinking of course, to find a place in Hell made ready for him; but when he came to the gates, the Devil would not let him in. No, he said, by this time Will had learnt so much wickedness that he would be more than a match for him, and he dared not let him in. So away went the smith to Heaven, to see if St. Peter, who had been a good friend to him before, would find him a place there; but St. Peter would not, it wasn't very likely he would! and Will was forced to go back to the Old Lad again, and beg and pray for a place in Hell. But the Devil would not be persuaded even then. Will had spent two lifetimes in learning wickedness, and now he knew too much to be welcome anywhere. All that the Devil would do for him, was to give him a lighted coal from Hell-fire, to keep himself warm, and that is how he comes to be called Will-o'-the-Wisp. So he goes wandering up and down the moors and mosses with his light, wherever he can find a bit of boggy ground, that he can 'tice folks to lose their way in and bring them to a bad end, for he is not a bit less wicked and deceitful now than he was when he was a blacksmith.

Burne and Jackson, *Shropshire Folk-Lore*, p. 34.
TYPE 330 (variant). MOTIFS: K.1811 [*Saints in disguise visit mortals*]; Q.115 [*Any boon that may be asked*]; Q.565 [*Man admitted to neither Heaven nor Hell*]; A.2817 [*Origin of Will-o'-the-wisp*].
¶ The outwitting of the Devil is omitted from this tale, which is more like the song "The Old Man who in Sussex did dwell". For the most perfect version of the tale, see "Dule upon Dun".

THE WONDERFUL WOOD

In old times was a cruel king who liked to ride hunting young maidens, and after he caught them (and had his wicked way with them) he killed them with his sharp blade. All the fathers and mothers sent their daughters away to safety if they could, but there was one little maid in a lonely cottage who couldn't go. Her granny was too poor to send her, so she kept her hid and earned their bread by spinning. Now there was a wonderful wood near the cottage and nobody dare go into it, not even the wicked king because of the great oak tree that grew there. One market day the granny was ill, so the little maid she had to take along the hanks of wool or they'd starve.

She cried and her granny cried too and kissed her and blessed her and told her to go on her tiptoes all the way, and not to go through the wonderful wood though it was the quickest way. The little maid minded and off she went all on her tiptoes carrying the bundle of wool. She hadn't got far when she caught sight of the cruel king riding along in the distance. She didn't run or make any stir but all on her tiptoes she walked into the wonderful wood.

> She walked thro' the wood where the oaken tree stood,
> And she curtsied did she to the oaken tree,

And he let her go down to the town, the town,
From the wood, the wonderful wood.

So that was all right, wasn't it? But the cruel king had seen her go and that wasn't all right, was it? He spurred his horse and he took out his sharp blade and rode after her.

He rode through the wood where the oaken tree stood,
And he cursed did he at the oaken tree,
And he took his sharp blade for to murder the maid,
But a bough it fell quick and it broked his neck,
In the wood, the wonderful wood.

So that was all right, wasn't it? But his men came looking for him. They could see him through the trees. The wicked crew were bent on revenge and they galloped into the wood to cut the oak tree down.

O they rode in the wood where the oaken tree stood,
To cut down the tree, the oaken tree,
Then the tree gave a groan and summoned his own,
For the trees closed about and they never got out
Of the wood, the wonderful wood.

So that was all right, wasn't it?

The tale of the tree that stood all, Warwickshire, 1916. A local folk tale told by Miss Lily Kingston Streetly, near Sutton Coldfield Park, Warwickshire.
MOTIFS: T.320 [*Escape from undesired lover*]; R.312 [*Forest as refuge*]; D.941 [*Magic forest*]; C.612 [*Forbidden forest*]; D.950.2 [*Magic oak-tree*]; V.1.7 [*Worship of trees*]; C.51.2.2 [*Tabu: cutting sacred trees or groves*].
¶ The flight from the lecherous king is commoner in such saints' legends as that of St. Winifred, and in the Greek myths, than in fairy tales. The King in Addy's tale "The Fairy and the Ring" is of something this kind. Ruth L. Tongue has collected several stories that illustrate tree beliefs; see "One Tree Hill" and "The Tree's Revenge". B, Legends, Supernatural.

THE WOODMAN AND THE HATCHET

One day a woodman was told by his master to cut down some trees that stood near a very deep river. The woodman, however, had lost his hatchet, so he went and borrowed one from a neighbour. And so he walked along the river side until he came to the trees which his master had told him to cut down. So he began to chop at the first tree, but before he had struck many blows the head of the hatchet flew off and fell into the deep water, so that the poor woodman could not get it out again. The woodman was very troubled about this, because the hatchet was not his own, and as he stood fretting about his loss by the river side a little fairy man appeared on the top of the water, and walked up to him, and asked him what he was fretting about. The woodman said, "I've lost my neighbour's hatchet-head in this water, and I can't get it out."

The fairy said, "Where did it fall in?" and the woodman showed him the place.

"Give me the shaft," said the fairy.

So the woodman gave him the shaft, and he threw it into the water in the place where the head had fallen in.

"Keep your eyes fixed on the spot where the shaft fell in," said the fairy, "and the hatchet will rise up out of the water with the head on, just as it was when you borrowed it."

So the woodman did as he was told and kept his eyes fixed on the spot, when shortly he heard a rumbling noise in the water, and after the rumbling had ceased the hatchet appeared in the very place where the fairy had thrown the shaft in. Then the woodman took the hatchet out of the water, but on looking up to thank the little fairy he found that he had gone.

S. O. Addy, *Household Tales*, p. 34, from Sheffield.
MOTIF: N.815 [*Fairy as helper*].

It is uncertain whether this little anecdote should rank as a folk-tale or a legend. Its brevity and lack of plot make it more like a legend, but there is no evidence that it was ever believed.

YALLERY BROWN [summary]

There was once a lad called Tom Tiver, who worked on Hall Farm. As he was walking home one fine July night, he heard the most piteous whimpering and wailing, as it might be a lost child. He looked around, but he could see nought. Then presently he heard the sobbing again, and words all mixed up with it. "Ooh, the stone, the great big stone! Ooh, the stone on top!" He looked about, and there was a great flat stone, the Strangers' table they called it, half buried in weeds and clotted grass. And the voice came from under it, but fainter now. Tom was gey feared, but the whimpering was so piteous that he had no heart to leave it, so he heaved up the stone, and there beneath it lay a tiddy thing, no bigger than a year-old baby, with long cotted hair and beard twisted round its body. The hair and beard were gold, and as soft as thistledown, but its face was brown as the earth, and just a heap of wrinkles with two bright black eyne in the midst. It stared up at Tom mazed like, for a minute, and then it piped up: "Tom, thou'rt a good lad."

Tom touched his hat, and he thought to himself, "Lord, for sure 'tis a bogle."

"No," says the tiddy thing, as quick as quick, "I'm no bogle, but ye'd best not ask me what I be. Anyway, thou'st done me a better turn than thou knowest, and I be a good friend of thine."

Tom's knee-bones struck together when he found the uncanny thing knew his secret thought, but he said as civil as he could: "Might I be axing to know your honour's name?"

"H'm," says the thing, "thou mayst call me Yallery Brown, for 'tis my nature. And now, what can I do for ye? Art wanting a wife, or gold, or help with thy work? I'll give thee any of the three."

"I've no use for a wife," said Tom, "nor yet for gold, but I can't abide work, and if thou'll give me a helping hand, I'll thank ye for it."

"None o' that now!" says the thing. "I'll help and welcome, but I want no thanks, and mind, if I hear a thanks from you, you'll see no more of me. But if thou need'st help, just say, 'Yallery Brown, come from the mools, for I wants 'ee,' and I'll be there." With that, he picked a dandelion clock, and blew it into Tom's eyes, and was gone.

In the morning, Tom thought it was no more than a dream, but when he went down to work, there it was, all done. And so it went on day by day, and however much Tom was set to do, Yallery Brown did it in a twinkling. At first Tom thought he was in clover, but soon things didn't look so bright, for though Tom's work was done, the other lads' was all undone, and soon they began to see Yallery Brown flitting about at night, and they blamed it all on poor Tom. Sometimes Tom thought he'd work for himself, and not be beholden to the tiddy thing, but he couldn't— true as death he couldn't. The spade wouldn't stay in his hand, the plough ran away from him, and the hoe kept out of his grip. At last it got so bad, that his master gave Tom the sack, for none of the rest could work along with him, and Tom trudged away in a fine passion, to think how Yallery Brown had dealt with him. "I've done with him from this day on," he said, and he called out loud. "Yallery Brown, come out of the mools. I want thee." No sooner had he spoken than his leg was tweaked from behind, and there was the tiddy thing, with his shining yellow hair, and his brown puckered face, and his wicked black eyes. "Look here, master," says Tom. "I'll thank 'ee to leave me alone. I want none of thy help, see!" The uncanny thing burst out into a screeching laugh, and it piped out: "Thou'st thanked me, Tom. I warned thee not, thou big fool, but tha's thanked me."

"I don't want to have no more to do with thee," says Tom. "Pretty sort of help thou's given me, and I don't want it no more."

"And you won't get it," says Yallery Brown. "I've worked for thee, like I said, but now I'll work against thee." And it began to twirl and spin round him, singing:

"Work as thou will,
Thou'lt never do well:

Work as thou may'st,
Thou'lt never gain grist;
For harm and mischance, and Yallery Brown
Thou'st let out thyself from under the stone."

And as it sang it spun round and round, and its hair and beard floated all about it, till it looked like a great dandelion puff, and so it vanished away, and Tom never saw it again, but he felt him, he felt him working against him all the days of his life, for he worked here, and he worked there, but nothing that he set his hand to ever prospered, and always he seemed to hear in his head Yallery Brown's song:

"Work as thou will,
Thou'lt never do well:
Work as thou may'st,
Thou'lt never gain grist;
For harm and mischance, and Yallery Brown
Thou'st let out thyself from under the stone."

Mrs Balfour, *Tales of the Cars*, retold in Jacob's *More English Fairy Tales*.
TYPE 331 (variant). MOTIFS: R.181 [*Demon enclosed in bottle (under stone) released*]; R.188 [*Rescued person horrifies rescuers*]; F.403.2.2.4 [*Spirit in bottle as helper*]; F.348.5.2 [*Mortal not to thank fairy for gifts*]; C.46 [*Tabu: offending fairy*]; F.360.0.1 [*Malevolent beings in other world*].

In this form of the tale, the released spirit is not returned to its place of captivity, and its rescuer becomes its victim.

See "The Fairy Follower", B, Legends, Fairies. For a completer type of 331 see "Laying a Ghost", B, Legends, Ghosts.

YOUNG BEKIE [summary]

Young Bekie was a knight from Scotland, who served the King of France, but before a year of his service was up he fell in love with the King's only daughter, Burd Isbel, and for this he was thrown into prison. There the rats and mice gnawed his yellow hair, and he fell into a sorry plight, until Burd Isbel herself came to his rescue:

"She's gien him a shaver for his beard,
A comber till his hair,
Five hunder pounds in his pocket,
To spen, an nae to spair."

She also gave him a noble horse and a hound, and they made a vow that in three years he should return and make her his bride.

Young Bekie went home, but a year afterwards he was forced into marriage with a Duke's daughter, on pain of losing all his lands if he did not. He grieved sorely for Burd Isbel, but could get no message to her. But as she was asleep a "Belly Blin" came to the foot of her bed, and warned her to take ship quickly, and seek out Young Bekie. She went down to the shore, and the Belly Blin himself rowed her across the sea. They came to Young Bekie's gate (she had brought two of her mother's Marys with her dressed all in green, and herself in scarlet) and heard the music playing for the wedding-feast. She sent up a message by the old porter, who had served the house for thirty-three years, but said he had never seen three such ladies before. Then Young Bekie knew who they must be, and he came down and welcomed them, sent his bride home with rich gifts in compensation, and brought Burd Isbel to his house in her place.

Child, *The English and Scottish Popular Ballads*, I, pp. 454–83 ("Young Beichan, C"). TYPE 313 (variant). MOTIFS: R.41.3 [*Captivity in dungeon*]; R.162 [*Rescue by captor's daughter*]; D.2003 [*Forgotten fiancée*]; N.815 [*Fairy as helper*].

¶ This fairy ballad is one of those which appear to be founded on the tradition of Gilbert à Becket's love story:

"Becket was the son of a London citizen, who had followed Edgar Atheling on his crusading expedition, and was made prisoner in Syria; he obtained his liberty through the affection of a Syrian lady, an emir's daughter, who followed her lover after his departure, and succeeded in finding him in London, although she knew but two European words, 'London' and 'Gilbert'—the place of abode, and the Christian name of her lover. The pagan maiden was baptized by the favourite Norman name of Matilda, and from that romantic union sprang Thomas à Becket" (Agnes Strickland, *The Queens of England*, I, p. 184).

The Billy Blind is a helpful domestic spirit of the Scottish Borders who is occasionally mentioned in ballads.

Other ballads on the same theme, but without the supernatural helper, are "Young Beichan" and "Lord Bateman".